Lecture Notes in Artificial Intelligence 13208

Subseries of Lecture Notes in Computer Science

Series Editors

Randy Goebel
University of Alberta, Edmonton, Canada

Wolfgang Wahlster
DFKI, Berlin, Germany

Zhi-Hua Zhou
Nanjing University, Nanjing, China

Founding Editor

Jörg Siekmann
DFKI and Saarland University, Saarbrücken, Germany

More information about this subseries at https://link.springer.com/bookseries/1244

Vládia Pinheiro · Pablo Gamallo ·
Raquel Amaro · Carolina Scarton ·
Fernando Batista · Diego Silva · Catarina Magro ·
Hugo Pinto (Eds.)

Computational Processing of the Portuguese Language

15th International Conference, PROPOR 2022
Fortaleza, Brazil, March 21–23, 2022
Proceedings

Springer

Editors
Vládia Pinheiro ⓘ
Universidade de Fortaleza
Fortaleza, Brazil

Raquel Amaro ⓘ
Universidade Nova de Lisboa
Lisbon, Portugal

Fernando Batista ⓘ
INESC-ID
Lisbon, Portugal

Catarina Magro ⓘ
University of Lisbon
Lisbon, Portugal

Pablo Gamallo ⓘ
CiTIUS - Universidade de Santiago de
Compostela
Santiago de Compostela, Spain

Carolina Scarton ⓘ
University of Sheffield
Sheffield, UK

Diego Silva ⓘ
Federal University of São Carlos
São Carlos, Brazil

Hugo Pinto
Sentimonitor
Porto Alegre, Brazil

ISSN 0302-9743   ISSN 1611-3349 (electronic)
Lecture Notes in Artificial Intelligence
ISBN 978-3-030-98304-8   ISBN 978-3-030-98305-5 (eBook)
https://doi.org/10.1007/978-3-030-98305-5

LNCS Sublibrary: SL7 – Artificial Intelligence

This Springer imprint is published by the registered company Springer Nature Switzerland AG
The registered company address is: Gewerbestrasse 11, 6330 Cham, Switzerland

Preface

This volume presents the 15th edition of the International Conference on the Computational Processing of Portuguese (PROPOR 2022), held at the University of Fortaleza, in Fortaleza, Ceará, in Brazil, during March 21–23, 2022. Given the situation of the COVID-19 pandemic, PROPOR 2022 was moved to fully online.

Coming into its 30th year of existence, PROPOR continues to be the main scientific meeting in the fields of language and speech technologies for Portuguese and on the basic and applied research issues related to this language. The meeting is a very rich forum for researchers dedicated to the computational processing of Portuguese, promoting the exchange of experiences in the development of methodologies, language resources, tools, applications, and innovative projects. In this edition, a new track division was proposed with a new Linguistics and Resources track and an Industry track, alongside the General track. A total of 88 submissions were received for the main event, of which 33 were to the General track, 29 to the Linguistics and Resources track, and 6 to the Industry track, involving 152 different authors from many countries worldwide, such as Portugal, Brazil, Spain, Norway, France, and Germany.

This volume presents 36 full and 4 short papers, selected from the 88 submissions, which reflects an acceptance rate of 51% for full papers and 45% overall. Each paper was reviewed by 3 reviewers from a total of 59 academic institutions and companies. Full papers are organized thematically and show research and developments in resources and evaluation, natural language processing tasks, natural language processing applications, speech processing and applications, and lexical semantics. In this edition, reflecting the current trends in the field, the topics with the largest number of submissions and acceptance were related to resources and evaluation and natural language tasks and applications. Following the PROPOR tradition of welcoming and introducing new members to the community, there is also a section for the best dissertation and thesis, selected from the 6 candidates presented this year.

For PROPOR 2022, the selected team of invited speakers represents the worldwide importance of the field, not only in academia but also in very well-established companies. They were as follows:

- Maria José Bocorny Finatto, Full Professor at the Federal University of Rio Grande do Sul, Brazil
- Rada Mihalcea, Professor at the University of Michigan, USA
- Sebastião Miranda, Head of Development at Priberam, Portugal.

In parallel, PROPOR 2022 hosted 3 workshops on the following topics: automatic speech recognition for spontaneous and prepared speech and speech emotion recognition in Portuguese; universal dependencies; and digital humanities and natural language processing. The proceedings of the workshops are not included in this volume as the organizers of each workshop arranged them separately. The event also included a session for systems demonstration and a tutorial, focusing on parallel corpora building and lemmatization criteria and annotation systems.

Our sincere thanks go to every person and institution involved in the complex organization of this event, especially to the members of the Program Committee of the main event, the dissertations contest and the associated workshops chairs, the invited speakers, and the general organization staff. We are also grateful to the agencies and organizations that supported and promoted the event.

January 2022

Vládia Pinheiro
Pablo Gamallo
Raquel Amaro
Carolina Scarton
Fernando Batista
Diego Silva
Catarina Magro
Hugo Pinto

Organization

General Chairs

Vládia Pinheiro   University of Fortaleza, Brazil
Pablo Gamallo   University of Santiago de Compostela, Spain

Program Chairs

Raquel Amaro   NOVA University Lisbon, Portugal
Carolina Scarton   University of Sheffield, UK

Editorial Chairs

Fernando Batista   INESC-ID and Iscte, Portugal
Diego Silva   Federal University of São Carlos, Brazil

Demo Chairs

Wellington Franco   Federal University of Ceará, Brazil
Juliano Norberto Sales   University of Passau, Germany
Luís Trigo   University of Porto, Portugal

Best MSc/MA and PhD Dissertation Award Chairs

Daniela Claro   Federal University of Bahia, Brazil
Idalete Dias   University of Minho, Portugal

Workshops and Tutorials Chairs

Larissa de Freitas   Federal University of Pelotas, Brazil
Marcos Garcia   University of Santiago de Compostela, Spain

Track Chair Linguistics and Resources

Catarina Magro   University of Lisbon, Portugal

Track Chair Industry

Hugo Pinto   Sentimonitor, Brazil

Local Organization Committee

Vládia Pinheiro   University of Fortaleza, Brazil
Wellington Franco   Federal University of Ceará, Brazil

Steering Committee

Helena Caseli   Federal University of São Carlos, Brazil
Amália Mendes   University of Lisbon, Portugal
Vládia Pinheiro   University of Fortaleza, Brazil
Paulo Quaresma   University of Évora, Portugal
Evandro Seron Ruiz   University of São Paulo, Brazil

Program Committee

Alberto Abad   INESC-ID and Instituto Superior Técnico,
                                      Universidade de Lisboa, Portugal
André Adami   University of Caxias do Sul, Brazil
José João Almeida   University of Minho, Portugal
Sandra Aluísio   University of São Paulo, Brazil
Evelin Amorim   University of Porto, Portugal
João Balsa   University of Lisbon, Portugal
Cláudia Barros   Federal Institute of São Paulo, Brazil
Fernando Batista   INESC-ID and Iscte, Portugal
Daniel Beck   University of Melbourne, Australia
Luciana Benotti   National University of Córdoba, Argentina
Antonio Bonafonte   Amazon, Spain
António Branco   University of Lisbon, Portugal
Vera Cabarrão   Unbabel and INESC-ID, Portugal
Pável Calado   INESC-ID and Instituto Superior Técnico,
                                      Universidade de Lisboa, Portugal
Arnaldo Candido Junior   Federal University of Technology - Paraná, Brazil
Paula Cardoso   Federal University of Lavras, Brazil
Helena Caseli   Federal University of São Carlos, Brazil
Sheila Castilho   Dublin City University, Ireland
Berthold Crysmann   CNRS and University of Paris, France
Ariani Di Felippo   Federal University of São Carlos, Brazil
Gaël Dias   University of Caen Normandy, France
Brett Drury   INESC-TEC, Portugal

Aline Paes	Fluminense Federal University, Brazil
Gustavo Paetzold	Federal University of Technology – Paraná, Brazil
Adriana Pagano	Federal University of Minas Gerais, Brazil
Valeria de Paiva	Topos Institute, USA
Ivandré Paraboni	University of São Paulo, Brazil
Thiago Pardo	University of São Paulo, Brazil
Fernando Perdigão	University of Coimbra, Portugal
Martín Pereira-Fariña	University of Santiago de Compostela, Spain
José Ramom Pichel	imaxin software and University of Santiago de Compostela, Spain
Prakash Poudyal	Kathmandu University, Nepal
Carlos A. Prolo	Federal University of Rio Grande do Norte, Brazil
Paulo Quaresma	University of Évora, Portugal
Violeta Quental	Pontifical Catholic University of Rio de Janeiro, Brazil
Alexandre Rademaker	IBM Research and FGV/EMAp, Brazil
Carlos Ramisch	Aix-Marseille University, France
Amanda Rassi	Somos Educação, Brazil
Livy Real	IBM, Brazil
Natália Resende	Federal University of Santa Catarina, Brazil
Ricardo Ribeiro	INESC-ID and Iscte, Portugal
Vitor Rocio	Universidade Aberta and INESC-TEC, Portugal
Irene Rodrigues	University of Évora, Portugal
Ricardo Rodrigues	CISUC and Polytechnic Institute of Coimbra, Portugal
José Saias	University of Évora, Portugal
Diana Santos	Linguateca and University of Oslo, Norway
Eloize Rossi M. Seno	Federal Institute of São Paulo, Brazil
Christopher Shulby	Defined.ai, USA
Augusto Soares da Silva	Catholic University of Portugal, Portugal
João Silva	University of Lisbon, Portugal
Mário J. Silva	INESC-ID and Instituto Superior Técnico, Universidade de Lisboa, Portugal
Nádia Silva	University of São Paulo, Brazil
Rubén Solera Ureña	INESC-ID, Portugal
António Teixeira	University of Aveiro, Portugal
Isabel Trancoso	INESC-ID and Instituto Superior Técnico, Universidade de Lisboa, Portugal
Marcos Treviso	Instituto Superior Técnico, University of Lisbon, Portugal
Oto Vale	Federal University of São Carlos, Brazil
Renata Vieira	CIDEHUS and University of Évora, Portugal

Aline Villavicencio   University of Sheffield, UK
Derek F. Wong   University of Macau, Macau
Marcos Zampieri   Rochester Institute of Technology, USA

Additional Reviewers

Danielle Caled   INESC-ID and Universidade de Lisboa, Portugal
Iria de Dios Flores   University of Santiago de Compostela, Spain
John Ortega   University of Santiago de Compostela, Spain
Herbert Pinto   Open University, Portugal
Mário Rodrigues   University of Aveiro, Portugal

Sponsor

americanas sa

Contents

Natural Language Processing Tasks

Natural Language Processing Applications

Speech Processing and Applications

Lexical Semantics

Short Papers

Best MsC/MA and PhD Dissertation

Resources and Evaluation

UlyssesNER-Br: A Corpus of Brazilian Legislative Documents for Named Entity Recognition

Hidelberg O. Albuquerque[1,2]([⊠]) [iD], Rosimeire Costa[3] [iD], Gabriel Silvestre[4] [iD],
Ellen Souza[1,4] [iD], Nádia F. F. da Silva[3,4] [iD], Douglas Vitório[1,2] [iD],
Gyovana Moriyama[4] [iD], Lucas Martins[4] [iD], Luiza Soezima[4] [iD],
Augusto Nunes[4] [iD], Felipe Siqueira[4] [iD], João P. Tarrega[4] [iD], Joao V. Beinotti[4] [iD],
Marcio Dias[3] [iD], Matheus Silva[3] [iD], Miguel Gardini[4] [iD], Vinicius Silva[4] [iD],
André C. P. L. F. de Carvalho[4] [iD], and Adriano L. I. Oliveira[2] [iD]

[1] MiningBR Research Group, Federal Rural University of Pernambuco, Recife, Brazil
{hidelberg.albuquerque,ellen.ramos}@ufrpe.br
[2] Centro de Informática, Federal University of Pernambuco, Recife, Brazil
{alio,damsv}@cin.ufpe.br
[3] Institute of Informatics, Federal University of Goiás, Goiás, Brazil
nadia.felix@ufg.br
[4] Institute of Mathematics and Computer Sciences, University of São Paulo,
São Paulo, Brazil
{gdalforno7,gymori,lucasfmartins16,lbrsoezima,augustonunes,
felipe.siqueira,joao.tarrega,joaobeinotti,miguelgardini,
vinicius.adolfo.silva}@usp.br, andre@icmc.usp.br

Abstract. The amount of legislative documents produced within the past decade has risen dramatically, making it difficult for law practitioners to consult and update legislation. Named Entity Recognition (NER) systems have the untapped potential to extract information from legal documents, which can improve information retrieval and decision-making processes. We introduce the UlyssesNER-Br, a corpus of Brazilian Legislative Documents for NER with quality baselines. The presented corpus consists of bills and legislative consultations from Brazilian Chamber of Deputies. We implemented Conditional Random Field (CRF) and Hidden Markov Model (HMM) models, and the promising F1-score of 80.8% in the analysis by categories and 81.04% in the analysis by types, was achieved with the CRF model. The entities with the best average F1-score results were "FUNDlei" and "DATA", and the ones with the worst results were "EVENTO" and "PESSOAgrupoind". The corpus was also evaluated using a BiLSTM-CRF and Glove architectures provided by the pioneering state-of-the-art paper, achieving F1-score of 76.89% in the analysis by categories and 59.67% in the analysis by types.

Keywords: Annotation schema · Named Entity Recognition · Legal information retrieval

V. Pinheiro et al. (Eds.): PROPOR 2022, LNAI 13208, pp. 3–14, 2022.
https://doi.org/10.1007/978-3-030-98305-5_1

1 Introduction

The legal domain, which includes a large variety of legal texts, such as legislation, case law, and scholarly works [14], has been facing multiple challenges in the era of digitisation. Document collections are rapidly growing and their analysis can only be tackled with the help of assisting technologies [9]. Named Entity Recognition (NER) aims to identify mentions of rigid designators from text belonging to predefined semantic types [15]. Identifying references to entities in text was recognized as one of the important sub-tasks of Information Extraction (IE) [15]. However, NER not only acts as a standalone tool for IE, but also plays an essential role in a variety of Natural Language Processing (NLP) applications such as text understanding, information retrieval, and others [10].

NER is focused upon the identification of semantic categories such as person, location and organization but, in domain-specific applications, other typologies have been developed that correspond to *task*, *language*, or *domain* specific needs. With regard to the legal domain, the lack of freely available corpora has been a barrier for researches in the field area [9]. Legal documents are unique and differ greatly from newspaper texts [9]. Even in the legal domain, there are sub-areas with specific named entities such as the Legislative one with references to entities related to the law making process.

The Brazilian Chamber of Deputies has processed more than 144 thousand bills [5]. Each bill needs to be formalized as an initial legislative document *draft* and an optional justification document, which are submitted for discussion and voting. For a typical bill, a large number of documents is produced. This content is massive, and keeps increasing. Besides, the unstructured nature of these documents makes their organization, access, and retrieval a challenging task [5].

In this paper, we describe a corpus, the "UlyssesNER-Br", developed for NER in legislative documents from the Brazilian Chamber of Deputies, containing eighteen types of entities structured in seven semantic classes or categories. The research is conducted in the context of the *Ulysses* project, an institutional set of artificial intelligence initiatives with the purpose of increasing transparency, improving the Chamber's relationship with citizens, and supporting the legislative activity with complex analysis [2].

The remainder of this paper is structured as follows: Sect. 2 briefly presents the major related studies. Section 3 describes, in details, the process behind the annotation of the dataset, including the different semantic classes annotated. Sec. 4 describes the UlyssesNER-Br characteristics, followed by an evaluation. Section 5 brings the conclusion and highlights future works.

2 Related Work

The use of NER techniques for the legal domain has been explored in different languages and domains [3,4,9,16,17,19]. However, corpora are scarce for the legal domain in Portuguese. This section highlights some initiatives with relevant contributions to this domain and language.

Luz de Araujo, et al. [13] presented the "LeNER-Br", a dataset with 70 legal documents from Brazilian judicial courts and laws, using entities already defined in other corpora and adding new entities to extract legal knowledge: "Legislacao" for laws, and "Jurisprudencia" for legal decisions resulting from legal processes. Using the BiLSTM-CRF and Glove architectures, it was reached F1-score of 88.82% for legal cases and 97.04% for legislation.

Alles [1] developed the "DOU-Corpus" for NER from 470 documents made in the Official Gazette of the Union (Diário Oficial da União - DOU), an official bulletin of the Brazilian federal government. New entities were used for the domain, such as "Cargo" (professional occupation), "Lei" (law), "Numero" (cash used in the texts), "Processo" (processes), and "Valor-monetario" (financial values). Using the OpenNLP tool, the results were evaluated both quantitatively and qualitatively. The precision, coverage and F-score of the model were respectively 95.3%, 60.7%, and 44.5%.

Castro [6] developed a NER model for the Portuguese language in the domain of Labor Justice in Brazil. The author initially proposed to improve the accuracy of NER models for the Portuguese language, using architectures and word representations based on Deep Neural Networks. 1,305 documents were used, in which the annotations of the entities were executed in a semi-supervised way, using classical entities and creating the entities for the legal context: "Funcao" (role), "Fundamento" (legal provisions), "Tribunal" and "Vara" (characteristics of Brazilian legal organizations), in addition to "Valor_Acordo", "Valor_Causa", "Valor_Condenacao" and "Valor_Custas" (for different types of values in labor lawsuits). The BiLSTM-CRF network obtained results above 80% accuracy.

Luz de Araujo, et al. [12] introduces "VICTOR", a dataset was built from documents of the Brazilian Supreme Court, comprising more than 692 thousand documents, manually annotated by a team of specialists. In addition to the dataset itself, the authors present as contributions the classification of data into two distinct types of tasks: classification of the type of document, doing a distinction was made between the types of legal documents, and classification of the theme of the process, identifying and assigning one or more repercussion themes to each extraordinary appeal of the processes. The dataset was made available in three versions: the first containing data for the theme assignment task, the second containing only documents labeled for both tasks, and the last one, a subsample of the second version. Using the networks CNN and Bi-LSTM and CRF post-processing technique, the experiments show that the sequential nature of processes can be leveraged to improve document type classification.

3   Method

3.1   Semantic Classes

UlyssesNER-Br has seven semantic classes or categories. Based on HAREM [18], we defined five typical categories: *person, location, organization, event* and *date*. In addition, we defined two specific semantic classes for the legislative domain: *law foundation* and *law product*. The *law foundation* category makes reference to

Table 1. UlyssesNER-Br: categories and types.

Category	Type	Description	Example
DATA (Date)	—	Date	01 de janeiro de 2020
EVENTO (Event)	—	Event	Eleições de 2018
FUNDAMENTO (Law foundation)	FUNDlei	Legal norm	Lei no 8.666, de 21 de junho de 1993
	FUNDapelido	Legal norm nickname	Estatuto da Pessoa com Deficiência
	FUNDprojetodelei	Bill	PEC 187/2016
	FUNDsolicitacaotrabalho	Legislative consultation	Solicitação de Trabalho n° 3543/2019
LOCAL (Location)	LOCALconcreto	Concrete place	Niterói-RJ
	LOCALvirtual	Virtual place	Jornal de Notícias
ORGANIZAÇÃO (Organization)	ORGpartido	Political party	PSB
	ORGgovernamental	Governmental organization	Câmara do Deputados
	ORGnãogovernamental	Non-governmental organization	Conselho Reg. de Medicina (CRM)
PESSOA (Person)	PESSOAindividual	Individual	Jorge Sampaio
	PESSOAgrupoind	Group of individuals	Família Setúbal
	PESSOAcargo	Occupation	Deputado
	PESSOAgrupocargo	Group of occupations	Parlamentares
PRODUTO DE LEI (Law product)	PRODUTOsistema	System product	Sistema Único de Saúde (SUS)
	PRODUTOprograma	Program product	Programa Minha Casa, Minha Vida
	PRODUTOoutros	Others products	Fundo partidário

entities related to laws, resolutions, decrees, as well as to domain-specific entities such as bills, which are law proposals being discussed by the parliament, and legislative consultations, also known as job requests made by the parliamentarians. The *law product* entity refers to systems, programs, and other products created from legislation. Therefore, some categories have also types as shown in Table 1.

3.2   Annotation Process

The UlyssesNER-Br corpus notes were performed by 3 groups of annotators, in which each group was composed of 2 undergraduate students who were responsible for the annotation while a graduate student performed the curatorship. Disagreements were discussed at regular intervals and the final document was agreed upon by everyone on the team.

The annotation process took place in 3 phases. In the first phase, training was carried out, in which 5 legislative consultations and 4 bills were annotated by all teams. In the second phase, the documents were transferred daily to the teams, in which a daily monitoring of the Cohen's kappa agreement measure was carried out, and frequent meetings were held with the curators and annotators. At the end of this phase, 50 bills and 295 legislative consultations were annotated.

In the third phase, the meetings were held only when requested by the annotators or curators, and the Cohen's kappa was calculated only at the end of the phase. 100 bills and 500 legislative consultations were annotated in this phase.

It's worth mentioning that a bill is associated to one of the 22 knowledge areas from the legislative consultancy. Thus, we randomly selected almost the same numbers of bills per area in order to cover all areas and expand the vocabulary.

The annotation was performed using the INCEpTION [7][1] tool, that provides an environment for various types of annotation tasks in written text, such as Co-reference Resolution, Part-of-speech tagging, among others. The Fig. 1 shows two examples of the entities annotation process. At the end of the annotation process, the teams achieved the averages in Cohen's kappa: 91%, 94% and 88% for Team 01, Team 02 and Team 03 respectively.

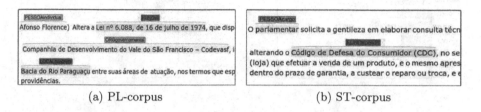

(a) PL-corpus   (b) ST-corpus

Fig. 1. Entity annotation process using INCEpTION

4   The UlyssesNER-Br Corpus

In this section, we present the UlyssesNER-Br corpus regarding its structural statistical properties, along with a performance evaluation of the most common models for the NER tasks. Two types of legislative documents were used to build this corpus: bills (*projetos de lei - PL*), public documents available on the Chamber's portal on the Web[2], and legislative consultations (*solicitações de trabalho - ST*), internal documents provided by the staff of the Chamber of Deputies. For the sake of simplicity, the "UlyssesNer-Br_PL-corpus" will be referred as *PL-corpus* and the "UlyssesNer-Br_ST-corpus" as *ST-corpus*. Moreover, all statistical results are based on a confidence level of 95% and the terms "category" and "entity" will be used interchangeably.

4.1   PL-corpus

Starting with the PL-corpus, it has $9,526$ sentences. From this total, $6,249$ sentences (66%) have just one token, e.g., $x = (\text{".""})$ or $x = (\text{",""})$, due to the documents structure. The estimation of the average number of sentences per document led to 63.50 whose confidence interval is given by $(46.15, 80.86)$. The corpus has $138,741$ tokens, whereas $11,833$ are unique. The estimation of the number of tokens per sentence was performed as well but, in this case, we removed the sentences with only one token as they can be classified as *outliers*. The mean

---

[1] https://inception-project.github.io/.
[2] https://www.camara.leg.br/buscaProposicoesWeb/.

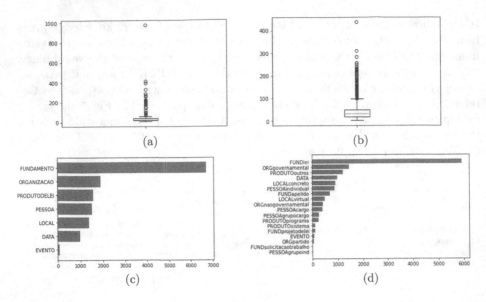

Fig. 2. PL-corpus: distribution of (a) the sentences per document and (b) tokens per sentence on the corpus. Entities by frequency of: (c) categories and (d) types.

was estimated to 40.43 and its confidence interval was (39.23, 41.46). Sentences with more than 100 tokens were considered *outliers*, as well.

Figure 2(a) and (b) illustrate the documents and sentences length. Figure 2(c) and (d) shows the number of times each category and type appear on the PL-corpus. The representation by categories helps out by equalizing most of the rare entities. On the other hand, the distribution of types allows us to visualize their corpus frequency, from the most frequent ("FUNDlei", "ORGgovernamenal" and "PRODUTOoutros") to the least frequent ("ORGpartido", "EVENTO" and "FUNDprojetodelei").

4.2   ST-corpus

In the case of the ST-corpus, it has 790 sentences, since each of its documents are roughly composed by a single sentence. There are 77, 441 tokens, whereas 11, 053 are unique. The average number of tokens per document was 98.03 and its confidence interval was (91.75, 104.30). Figure 3(a) shows the distribution of the size of each document with respect to the number of tokens. The *outliers* shown in the figure are similar to PL-corpus, but in this case the sentences have many tokens without semantic meaning, such as sequences of commas and periods. Moreover, Fig. 3(b) and (c) show the likelihood of appearance of the categories and types on ST-corpus: in the analysis by categories, the only difference between PL-corpus and ST-corpus is the exchange of entities "LOCAL" and "PESSOA" in the odds of appearance. In the analysis by types, the probability of appearance in ST-corpus is quite similar to that in PL-corpus. The difference depends more

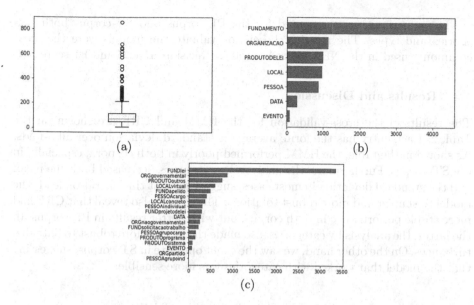

Fig. 3. ST-corpus: (a) distribution of the size of each document by the number of tokens. Entities by frequency: (a) of categories and (b) of types

on "DATA" type entities which are very common in PL-corpus, but end up being rarer in ST-corpus. On the other hand, "LOCALvirtual" rarely appeared in the first one and is one of the most common in ST-corpus.

4.3   Evaluation

Two common approaches for the NER tasks were selected for the evaluation: a generative approach represented by the Hidden Markov Model (HMM) [11]; and a discriminative approach, represented by the Conditional Random Fields (CRF) [8]. The latter used a set of 91 features and its implementation is supported by the *sklearn-crfsuite* API[3], a thin wrapper around CRFsuite for training. The experiment was done as follows:

1. We divided the sentences in each corpus into training and testing sets, 75% for training (equivalent to 7,144 sentences for PL-corpus and 592 for ST-corpus) and 25% for testing (equivalent to 2,382 sentences for PL-corpus and 198 for ST-corpus);
2. The next step was to apply a 5-fold cross-validation to the training set in order to extract statistics to analyse the impact of aggregation on the models performances;
3. Finally, we re-trained both models on the entire training set and evaluated them on the testing set to check which entities were the hardest ones to learn.

---

[3] https://sklearn-crfsuite.readthedocs.io/.

The experiment was repeated for the PL-corpus and ST-corpus both categories and types. The metrics chosen to evaluate the models were the most commonly used in the NER task: Accuracy, Precision, Recall and F1-score.

4.4 Results and Discussion

The results of the cross-validation for the HMM and CRF are shown on the Table 2. Each entry has the form: average ± standard deviation over all 5-folds. As shown in the table, the HMM performed poorly in both corpora, especially in the ST-corpus. Furthermore, the analysis by categories decreased both the mean and the standard deviation in most cases, suggesting that this operation leads the model to simpler and more robust solutions. The results also reveal that CRF had more stable performance in both corpus, but with better results in PL-corpus. In the latter, the analysis by categories also made the model more robust to data disturbances. On the other hand, we saw the exact opposite in ST-corpus, suggesting that the model that worked with categories was more sensible.

Table 2. Overall results in cross-validation.

Corpus	Model	Classes	Accuracy	Precision	Recall	F1-score
PL-corpus	HMM	Categories	93.07 ± 0.78	60.45 ± 2.18	30.82 ± 1.81	40.74 ± 1.83
		Types	93.08 ± 0.85	65.22 ± 3.12	33.98 ± 4.19	44.56 ± 4.29
	CRF	Categories	97.27 ± 0.77	83.42 ± 0.91	70.40 ± 1.54	76.28 ± 1.12
		Types	97.13 ± 1.05	83.47 ± 2.33	70.36 ± 3.82	76.30 ± 3.16
ST-corpus	HMM	Categories	90.32 ± 1.04	56.38 ± 6.16	9.45 ± 0.78	16.12 ± 1.33
		Types	90.71 ± 1.23	60.40 ± 8.52	10.90 ± 2.83	18.36 ± 4.41
	CRF	Categories	96.19 ± 0.67	76.26 ± 4.01	51.37 ± 4.46	61.32 ± 4.45
		Types	95.98 ± 0.55	78.03 ± 2.86	50.60 ± 3.79	61.26 ± 3.19

Despite differences in modeling categories and types, when comparing the mean of each metric for both approaches and both models, we could conclude that there is no statistical difference between them, i.e., there is no difference between modeling associated entities into categories or singularized into types. Even so, the former can force models to learn a much simpler and robust solution.

Moving on to the test suite, the HMM had difficulty in differentiating entities by category and by type in both corpora, even though the working results were in the ST-corpus. The types with the best performance were "DATA" and "PESSOAcargo". Although the types in the "FUNDAMENTO" category appeared quite frequently in both corpora, the model failed to distinguish them from the others. This can be explained by the fact that these entities must have a rich variety of patterns and, since the model is based on counting word pairs, it could not learn that such patterns are in the same class.

The CRF outperformed the HMM in all tasks, suggesting that discriminative models may be more likely to succeed in the UlyssesNER-Br. As shown in

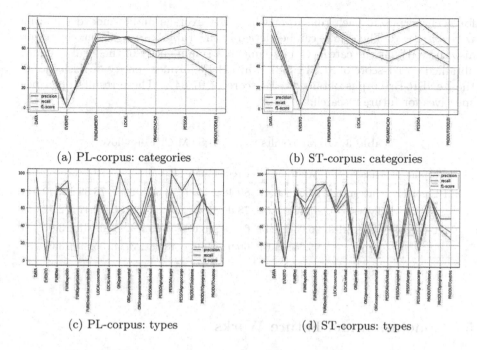

(a) PL-corpus: categories   (b) ST-corpus: categories

(c) PL-corpus: types   (d) ST-corpus: types

Fig. 4. CRF results: chances of success by categories and types

Fig. 4(a) and (b), the categories "DATA", "FUNDAMENTO", "LOCAL" and "PESSOA" were the ones that the model was easier to point out. The absence of examples of the "EVENTO" entity led the model to completely ignore it. The entities "ORGANIZACAO" and "PRODUTODELEI" demonstrated an average performance. In PL-corpus, the entities by categories was recall of 76.19% and the F1-score of 80.89%. In ST-corpus, we had a recall of 53.77% and a F1-score of 62.61%.

In the analysis by types, the most difficult entities for CRF in this corpus was "LOCALvirtual" in PL-corpus, due to the small number of observations and semantic textual complexity, while "EVENTO", "FUNDsolicitaçãotrabalho" and "PESSOAgrupoind" were ignored due to the scarcity or total absence of these entities. In ST-corpus, we could see a behavior very similar, with the exception that the presence of the entity "FUNDsolicitaçãotrabalho", obtaining a high score. We also emphasize the scarcity of the "EVENTO and "ORGpartido" types, which generated bad results, in addition to the inexistence of the "PESSOAgrupoind" entity. The Fig. 4(c) and (d) demonstrate these results.

To establish a link between this work and the state of the art, the BiLSTM-CRF + Glove learning model provided by Luz de Araujo, et al. [13][4] was applied in the UlyssesNER-Br corpus, with no changes to the original parameters. Therefore, five runs were performed, randomly modifying the training and test data

---

[4] https://github.com/peluz/lener-br.

for each corpus in each run, from which the average and standard deviation were extracted. The results can be viewed in the Table 3. In addition, the results also showed that the category "Fundamento" (main entity of the legal domain), obtained an F1-score of 81.83 ± 5.87, while the equivalent entity "Legislacao" in the LeNER-Br corpus obtained a F1-score of 97.04%. These results open perspectives for future research.

Table 3. Overall results using BiLSTM-CRF + Glove

Corpus	Classes	Accuracy	Precision	Recall	F1-score
PL-corpus	Categories	97.66 ± 0.47	80.48 ± 2.69	73.63 ± 2.65	76.89 ± 2.49
	Types	97.12 ± 0.52	78.05 ± 3.1	67.64 ± 2.18	72.47 ± 2.52
ST-corpus	Categories	96.06 ± 1.14	68.19 ± 3.6	53.13 ± 4.55	59.67 ± 3.97
	Types	95.64 ± 1.07	66.9 ± 3.08	48.08 ± 3.74	55.89 ± 3.07

5   Conclusion and Future Works

This work presented UlyssesNER-Br, a corpus of Brazilian Legislative Documents for Named Entity Recognition. UlyssesNER-Br was created from texts of bills and legislative consultations from the Brazilian Chamber of Deputies. The texts were annotated and curated manually by 3 work teams in 3 phases, and contain named entities that represent organizations, people, law products, location, fundamentals of law, events and dates. The Hidden Markov Model (HMM) and the Conditional Random Fields (CRF) machine learning models were used to evaluate the corpus. The results showed that the CRF model has a greater chance of success in NER tasks, with an average F1-score score of 80.8% in the analysis by categories and 81.04% in the analysis by types. To establish a link with the state of the art, we also evaluated the corpus using a BiLSTM-CRF and Glove architectures provided by the referential work of this domain in Portuguese, achieving F1-score of 76.89% and 59.67% in the analysis by categories and types, which demonstrates perspectives for future investigations, looking for a better refinement of the corpus through other learning models. In addition, there is an expansion of the corpus in progress, adding documents to generate two other corpora, one based on responses to public surveys and the other based on speech analysis in order to increase the number of entities as we have few examples. The access link to these corpus is available in the project repository.[5]

Acknowledgements. This research is carried out in the context of the Ulysses Project, of the Brazilian Chamber of Deputies. Ellen Souza and Nadia Félix are supported by FAPESP , agreement between USP and the Brazilian Chamber of Deputies.

---

[5] https://github.com/Convenio-Camara-dos-Deputados/ulyssesner-br-propor.

André C. P. L. F. de Carvalho and Adriano L. I. Oliveira are supported by CNPq. To the Brazilian Chamber of Deputies and to research funding agencies, to which we express our gratitude for supporting the research.

References

1. Alles, V.J.: Construção de um corpus para extrair entidades nomeadas do Diário Oficial da União utilizando aprendizado supervisionado. Master's thesis, Departamento de Engenharia Elétrica, Universidade de Brasília, Brasília, DF (2018)
2. Almeida, P.G.R.: Uma jornada para um Parlamento inteligente: Câmara dos Deputados do Brasil. Red Información, Edición N° 24 (2021)
3. Angelidis, I., Chalkidis, I., Koubarakis, M.: Named entity recognition, linking and generation for Greek legislation. In: Proceedings of 31st International Conference on Legal Knowledge and Information Systems, JURIX 2018 (2018)
4. Badji, I.: Legal entity extraction with NER systems. Master's thesis, Escuela Técnica Superior de Ingenieros Informáticos, Universidad Politécnica de Madrid (2018)
5. Brandt M.B.: Modelagem da informação legislativa: arquitetura da informação para o processo legislativo brasileiro. Faculdade de Filosofia e Ciências da Universidade Estadual Paulista (UNESP) (2020)
6. Castro, P.V.Q.: Aprendizagem profunda para reconhecimento de entidades nomeadas em domínio jurídico. Masters thesis, Programa de Pós-graduação em Ciência da Computação, Universidade Federal de Goiás (2019)
7. Klie, J.C., Bugert, M., Boullosa, B., Eckart de Castilho, R., Gurevych, I.: The INCEpTION platform: machine-assisted and knowledge-oriented interactive annotation. In: Proceedings of the 27th International Conference on Computational Linguistics: System Demonstrations, COLING 2018 (2018)
8. Lafferty, J.; McCallum, A., Pereira, F.: Conditional random fields: probabilistic models for segmenting and labeling sequence data. In: Proceedings of the 18th International Conference on Machine Learning (2001)
9. Leitner, E.; Rehm, G.; Moreno-Schneider, J.: A dataset of German legal documents for named entity recognition. In: LREC 2020–12th International Conference on Language Resources and Evaluation, Conference Proceedings (2020)
10. Li, J.; Sun, A.; Han, J.; Li, C.: A survey on deep learning for named entity recognition. In: IEEE Transactions on Knowledge and Data Engineering (2020)
11. Loper, E., Bird, S.: NLTK: The Natural Language Toolkit (2002)
12. Luz de Araujo, P.H., Campos, T.E., Braz, F.A., Silva, N.C.: VICTOR: a dataset for Brazilian legal documents classification. In: Proceedings of the 12th Conference on Language Resources and Evaluation (LREC 2020), Marseille (2020)
13. Luz de Araujo, P.H., de Campos, T.E., de Oliveira, R.R.R., Stauffer, M., Couto, S., Bermejo, P.: LeNER-Br: A Dataset for Named Entity Recognition in Brazilian Legal Text. In: Villavicencio, A., et al. (eds.) PROPOR 2018. LNCS (LNAI), vol. 11122, pp. 313–323. Springer, Cham (2018). https://doi.org/10.1007/978-3-319-99722-3_32
14. Maxwell, K.T., Schafer, B.: Concept and context in legal information retrieval. Front. Artif. Intell. Appl. **189**, 63–72 (2008)
15. Nadeau, D., Sekine, S.: A survey of named entity recognition and classification. Lingvisticae Investigationes **30**(1), 3–26 (2007)

16. Pirovani, J. P. C.: CRF+LG: uma abordagem híbrida para o reconhecimento de entidades nomeadas em português. PhD thesis, Universidade Federal do Espírito Santo (2019)
17. Quaresma, P., Gonçalves, T.: Using linguistic information and machine learning techniques to identify entities from juridical documents. In: Francesconi, E., Montemagni, S., Peters, W., Tiscornia, D. (eds.) Semantic Processing of Legal Texts. LNCS (LNAI), vol. 6036, pp. 44–59. Springer, Heidelberg (2010). https://doi.org/ 10.1007/978-3-642-12837-0_3
18. Santos, D., Cardoso, N.: A golden resource for named entity recognition in Portuguese. In: Vieira, R., Quaresma, P., Nunes, M.G.V., Mamede, N.J., Oliveira, C., Dias, M.C. (eds.) PROPOR 2006. LNCS (LNAI), vol. 3960, pp. 69–79. Springer, Heidelberg (2006). https://doi.org/10.1007/11751984_8
19. Váradi, T., et al.: The MARCELL legislative corpus. In: Proceedings of the 12th Language Resources and Evaluation Conference. European Language Resources Association (2020)

A Test Suite for the Evaluation of Portuguese-English Machine Translation

Mariana Avelino[1][(✉)] , Vivien Macketanz[2] , Eleftherios Avramidis[2] ,
and Sebastian Möller[1,2]

[1] Technische Universität Berlin, Berlin, Germany
m.amaralgarciaavelino@campus.tu-berlin.de
[2] German Research Center for Artificial Intelligence (DFKI), Berlin, Germany
{vivien.macketanz,eleftherios.avramidis,sebastian.moeller}@dfki.de

Abstract. This paper describes the development of the first test suite for the language direction Portuguese-English. Designed for fine-grained linguistic analysis, the test suite comprises 330 test sentences for 66 linguistic phenomena and 14 linguistic categories. Eight different MT systems were compared using quantitative and qualitative methods via the test suite: DeepL, Google Sheets, Google Translator, Microsoft Translator, Reverso, Systran, Yandex and an internally built NMT system trained over 30 h on 2,5M sentences. It was found that ambiguity, named entity & terminology and verb valency are the categories where MT systems struggle most. Negation, pronouns, subordination, verb tense/aspect/mood and false friends are the categories where MT systems perform best.

Keywords: Machine translation · Evaluation · Portuguese · Test suite

1 Introduction

In an increasingly interconnected world, bridging gaps in communication is ever more important. The value of machine translation (MT) is therefore hard to overstate, and hand-in-hand with a great demand for MT is a demand for tools that can evaluate MT output. After all, only through evaluation can weakness in MT systems be identified and addressed.

This study traces the development of a new test suite for the fine-grained linguistic analysis of the language pair Portuguese-English. Eight different translation systems were evaluated using the new test suite: DeepL, Google Sheets, Google Translate, Microsoft Translator, Reverso, Systran and Yandex, along with an in-house NMT system. Key contributions include:

– The first MT test suite for evaluating Portuguese-English translations on a fine-grained level via 66 phenomena organized in 14 categories.[1]

---

[1] The test suite has been made publicly available to aid further research: https://github.com/mariana200196/testsuite-pt-br_en.

© Springer Nature Switzerland AG 2022
V. Pinheiro et al. (Eds.): PROPOR 2022, LNAI 13208, pp. 15–25, 2022.
https://doi.org/10.1007/978-3-030-98305-5_2

- The corroboration of previous research that ambiguity is one of the most challenging linguistic categories for MT systems to resolve.
- The identification of categories where MT systems perform very well on average (negation, pronouns, subordination, verb tense/aspect/mood and false friends) and very poorly on average (ambiguity, named entity & terminology and verb valency).
- The finding that Reverso significantly outperforms other state-of-the-art MT systems in the translation of multi-word expressions, which include idioms, collocation and verbal multi-word expressions.

The paper is structured as follows: Sect. 2 summarizes related work in the field of MT evaluation. Section 3 describes this paper's methodological approach, including the experimental setup. Section 4 details the findings. Finally, Sect. 5 concludes the paper and provides an outlook for future research.

2   Related Work

There is general consensus in the scientific community that the most accurate way to evaluate the quality of MT output is via professional human translators. Unfortunately, this method is not scalable. There is thus a need for more automated evaluation processes which are fast and cost-effective. Over the years, various automatic MT evaluation methodologies have been proposed. Currently, the most widely used method is the BLEU score, as it is quick, language-independent and correlates highly with human evaluation [19]. Unfortunately, this method has known limitations [9,21]. As Barreiro and Ranchhod [5] explain, while a BLEU score might be useful to those who only need black-box answers to questions such as 'does the system work better today than yesterday?' or 'which MT system performs better?', it cannot provide a transparent diagnosis. In an effort to address these limitations, the use of test suites has been proposed.

A test suite investigates several linguistic phenomena and uses non-generic, manually-devised sentences as test sets. It measures quantitative performance and diagnoses qualitative shortcomings in translation. Test suites thereby deliver fine-grained evaluations of translation quality which help researchers form hypotheses as to why certain errors happen (systematically) and come up with strategies for improving the systems [7]. In recent years, various test suites have been created. Most of these focus on particular phenomena (e.g., [6,8,11,20]) with only very few performing a systematic evaluation of multiple phenomena simultaneously. Macketanz et al. [17,18] and Avramidis et al. [3,4] perform a systematic evaluation of more than one hundred phenomena for German-English translation, a practice which we also follow for our chosen language pair. Test suites also differ in the way the MT outputs are evaluated. Some test suites rely on manual labour to check the translations (e.g., [12]) while others provide fixed reference translations. Macketanz et al. [16] propose a semi-automatic evaluation powered by regular expressions and limited human annotation, a method which we adopt for our language pair, too.

3   Method

3.1   Creation of the Test Suite

There are four steps to creating a semi-automatic test suite for a new language direction: (1) producing a paradigm, (2) writing regular expressions, (3) fetching translations and (4) resolving warnings.

Given a chosen language pair, categories and subcategories (referred to as "phenomena" in this paper) should be determined for investigation, for example verb tense (category) and simple past (phenomenon). Then, sentences should be devised to test for the phenomena and an annotator should write rules to control the correctness of machine translations. These rules can be subdivided into "positive regular expressions" and "negative regular expressions". Once the test sentences and regular expressions have been created, the test sentences should be given as input to the MT system(s) and the output fetched. After that, the translations should be fed into the test suite. If the MT output matches a positive regular expression, the translation should be considered correct. If the MT output matches a negative regular expression, the translation should be considered incorrect. If a MT output does not match either a positive or negative regular expression, or if these contradict to each other, the automatic evaluation should produce a "warning" to be manually resolved by the annotator.

For each phenomenon, category and system being tested, the test suite should output an accuracy score:

$$\text{accuracy} = \frac{\text{correct\_translations}}{\text{sum\_of\_test\_items}} \tag{1}$$

To reveal the best system, a one-tailed t-test is performed. All the systems which are not significantly worse than the best system should be grouped together with it in a "first class".

3.2   Limitations of the Method

The accuracy calculation described above is a very intuitive way to assess MT quality. There are, however, some general limitations to keep in mind. For instance, systems that excel at handling a few specific phenomena will be at a disadvantage compared to well-rounded systems, even if the well-rounded systems don't excel at any one phenomenon. Also, a very high score for a phenomenon does not necessarily mean that the MT for that phenomenon has been cracked. Perhaps the difficulty of the test sentences simply needs to be raised to offer a better suited "challenge set" [12].

Referring specifically to our test suite, there are two additional limitations to consider. Firstly, the low number of test sentences per phenomenon can be misleading. As there are only five test sentences per phenomenon, relative differences in accuracy between systems loom larger than absolute differences. For example, if system A translates 3/5 sentences correctly for phenomenon P and system B translates 4/5 sentences correctly for phenomenon P, B's accuracy score for P will be a whole 20% higher (80%) than A's (60%) even though the difference is only one sentence. Secondly, the unequal number of phenomena per category creates bias. Systems which perform well in categories that encompass many phenomena are likely to have their performance scores inflated. For example, systems which translate verbs well are likely to get a higher overall score than those systems which struggle to translate verbs correctly, even if the latter systems perform better at many more categories than the former.

3.3   Experimental Setup

The Portuguese-English test suite described in this paper was created by a Brazilian-born native speaker of Portuguese and English. The test sentences are therefore written in Brazilian Portuguese. The test suite comprises 14 categories, 66 phenomena and 5 test sentences per phenomenon. The categories and phenomena were partly inspired by the categories and phenomena present in existing test suites [4], partly by personal observations of common MT errors and partly by previous research [5,10].

Table 1. Corpora used for training our NMT system.

Corpus	# sentences	Set
Europarl [14]	2,0M	Training
Global Voices [22]	92,0k	Training
backtranslations	25,9k	Training
Books [22]	1,4k	Training
TED-2013 [22]	0,2M	Validation
Tatoeba [22]	0,2M	Validation

Eight different translation systems were evaluated using the test suite: DeepL (deepL), Google Translate (googl), Microsoft Translator (MS), Reverso (revers), Systran (systr), Yandex (yandx), Google Sheets (gglSh)[2] and a NMT system developed internally (own). The first six systems are commercial systems which came highly recommended in blogs for Portuguese speakers seeking translation services. Given that they are commercial systems, they can be thought of as state-of-the-art. Our own system was developed using the Marian NMT framework[3] [13]. Training was conducted over approximately 30 h and 2,5M sentences (Table 1). Corpora with sentences from spoken language or newspaper language were preferred to keep the vocabulary of the training set as similar as possible to that of the test set. For the same reason, Brazilian Portuguese corpora were chosen over European Portuguese where possible.

---

[2] Google Sheets, a spreadsheet program with a cell-wise translation function, was chosen to offer an opportunity for comparison against Google Translate.

[3] https://github.com/marian-nmt/marian-examples/tree/master/training-basics-sentencepiece.

4 Findings

4.1 Overall Performance of MT Systems

The average accuracies of each system are shown in Table 2. Micro-average refers to Eq. 1. Category macro-average calculates the mean in such a way that categories are weighted equally and phenomenon macro-average weights the phenomena equally. Google, Reverso and DeepL are the best performing systems for all three accuracy scores with no significant difference in performance. According to the category macro-average and phenomenon macro-average, Microsoft Translator and Systran are also first-class.

Yandex was the worst performing system, doing worse on average than our system. The poor performance of our system can likely be attributed to insufficient training data. With regards to Yandex, one might speculate that poor performance is partly due to the system interpreting all Portuguese inputs as European Portuguese by default. Brazilian and European Portuguese, though very similar, differ at times in terms of spelling and grammar, so a machine trained to expect European Portuguese might struggle when confronted with Brazilian Portuguese. In fact, several Brazilian researches have commented on how training a system on European Portuguese corpora to then translate Brazilian test sentences reduces the BLEU scores of the output [1,10,15]. Unlike Yandex, the other commercial systems can distinguish between European and Brazilian Portuguese or default to Brazilian Portuguese.

4.2 BLEU vs. Test Suite Scores

Different studies [4,11,12] are divided as to whether system ranking according to BLEU scores correlates with system ranking according to test suite scores. To examine this, reference sentences for the test items were created and a BLEU score was calculated for each system.

The BLEU ranking shuffles the order of the top performing systems (Google, Reverso, DeepL, SYSTRAN, and Microsoft Translator), but not the order of the worst performing ones (Google Sheets, own, and Yandex). Worth noting is that the score gap between the top performing and worst performing systems is far less pronounced in BLEU (only 2 points difference between Microsoft Translator and Google Sheets). After reading all the translated output from the different systems, it becomes evident that the 17 point gap between Microsoft Translator and Google Sheets produced by the test suite is more representative of reality. The BLEU score makes it seem as though the difference in MT quality between Reverso and Microsoft is comparable to the quality difference between Microsoft and Google Sheets when it is not. Microsoft MT quality is far closer to that of Reverso than Google Sheets is to that of Microsoft Translator.

4.3 Categories

The test suite revealed that the best performing category was negation, where all systems scored 100%. Other categories with an average accuracy of 80% or

Table 2. Test suite accuracy (%) per category for 8 Portuguese to English MT systems.

category	#	googl	rever	deepL	MS	systr	gglSh	own	yandx	avg
ambiguity	11	54.5	72.7	72.7	63.6	54.5	45.5	↓27.3	54.5	55.7
coord. & ellipsis	18	**100.0**	**100.0**	**88.9**	77.8	**88.9**	38.9	61.1	44.4	75.0
false friends	5	80.0	80.0	80.0	80.0	80.0	80.0	100.0	60.0	80.0
function word	13	76.9	76.9	76.9	76.9	76.9	46.2	30.8	38.5	62.5
ldd & interrogative	50	**82.0**	**74.0**	**70.0**	**70.0**	**72.0**	48.0	44.0	56.0	64.5
mwe	19	57.9	↑**84.2**	68.4	**63.2**	**63.2**	**68.4**	47.4	**63.2**	64.5
ne & terminology	20	**75.0**	**50.0**	**65.0**	**60.0**	**65.0**	**55.0**	↓30.0	**50.0**	56.3
negation	5	100.0	100.0	100.0	100.0	100.0	100.0	100.0	100.0	100.0
non-verbal agreement	5	**80.0**	**100.0**	**80.0**	**80.0**	40.0	40.0	**60.0**	0.0	60.0
pronouns	13	**100.0**	**100.0**	**100.0**	**100.0**	**100.0**	61.5	76.9	38.5	84.6
punctuation	10	80.0	60.0	50.0	70.0	70.0	60.0	60.0	70.0	65.0
subordination	39	**92.3**	**92.3**	**92.3**	**89.7**	**89.7**	74.4	74.4	66.7	84.0
v. tense/aspect/mood	113	**92.0**	**92.0**	**92.9**	90.3	**91.2**	73.5	69.0	60.2	82.6
verb valency	10	80.0	60.0	80.0	60.0	50.0	60.0	30.0	40.0	57.5
categ. macro-average	331	**82.2**	81.6	**79.8**	**77.3**	74.4	60.8	57.9	53.0	70.9
phen. macro-average	331	**85.1**	**83.7**	**82.5**	79.7	**80.5**	62.4	57.7	55.8	73.4
micro-average	331	**85.5**	**84.0**	**83.1**	80.4	**80.7**	63.1	58.6	56.5	74.0
BLEU	331	54.3	49.5	54.8	47.2	51.5	45.1	38.0	27.7	46.0

Boldface indicates the best accuracies in every category (row) based on a one-tailed t-test. Accuracies two standard deviations higher and lower than the average per category are indicated respectively by ↑ and ↓. Test sentences which produced warnings are excluded from the accuracy calculations.

more were pronouns (84,6%), subordination (84,0%), verb tense/aspect/mood (82,6%) and false friends (80%).

The worst performing category was ambiguity with an average score of 55,7%. Studies into MT quality for English-Portuguese [5,10] likewise found that translation errors relating to ambiguous words were among the most common. Other categories where the systems performed poorly (below 60%) were named entity & terminology (56,3%) and verb valency (57,5%).

In Table 2 the systems which performed more than two standard deviations above the mean and those which performed more than two standard deviations below the mean are indicated with upward-facing or downward-facing arrows, respectively. Reverso performed extremely well at translating multi-word expressions (MWE) in comparison to other systems. This category encompasses phenomena such as idioms. Our system performed quite poorly in the categories ambiguity and named entity & terminology. Its poor performance handling ambiguity likely correlates with previous findings that NMT systems require a far higher amount of training data to learn how to translate ambiguous words correctly relative to other phenomena [2,10]. On a related note, our system probably lacked sufficient exposure to location names, proper names etc. in the training data, and so failed to correctly translate many named entities.

Table 3. Test suite accuracy (%) of the 10 worst performing phenomena.

Phenomenon	#	googl	rever	deepL	MS	systr	gglSh	own	yandx	avg
direct object omissions & polar questions	5	0.0	0.0	0.0	0.0	0.0	0.0	0.0	0.0	0.0
idiom	4	0.0	↑75.0	25.0	0.0	25.0	25.0	0.0	0.0	18.8
indicativo pretér. imperf	5	40.0	40.0	40.0	40.0	0.0	20.0	0.0	20.0	25.0
proper name	5	60.0	20.0	40.0	20.0	40.0	0.0	20.0	20.0	27.5
quotation marks	5	60.0	20.0	0.0	40.0	40.0	20.0	40.0	40.0	32.5
mediopassive voice	5	60.0	40.0	60.0	40.0	40.0	40.0	0.0	0.0	35.0
focus particle	5	40.0	40.0	40.0	40.0	40.0	60.0	20.0	40.0	40.0
domain specific	5	40.0	40.0	40.0	40.0	40.0	60.0	↓0.0	60.0	40.0
null object	3	100.0	100.0	66.7	66.7	100.0	0.0	0.0	33.3	58.3
collocation	5	20.0	60.0	40.0	40.0	20.0	60.0	40.0	60.0	42.5

4.4 Phenomena

Table 3 shows the ten most incorrectly translated phenomena (the full table can be found in the project github). A comparison reveals that some of the phenomena with the most translation errors on average (e.g., proper name, mediopassive voice) indeed belong to some of the worst performing categories, but not all. For example, the phenomenon direct object omission & polar question (which did not have a single sentence translated correctly) belongs to the category coordination & ellipsis, which is not among the categories with the most translation errors. Furthermore, indicativo pretérito imperfeito is also in the bottom 10 phenomena, yet it belongs to one of the best performing categories: verb tense/aspect/mood. Were the test suite less fine-grained, some problematic phenomena would have remained hidden within well-performing categories.

Reverso is the only system that performed two standard deviations better than the mean, doing so for idioms. Idioms belong to the category MWE, where Reverso also achieved an accuracy two standard deviations above average. The 3 worst performing MT systems overall (Google Sheets, own and Yandex) had accuracies two standard deviations below the mean for multiple phenomena.

4.5 Qualitative Analysis

By allowing the inspection of test sentences and their translations, test suites additionally help researchers understand where MT systems are struggling and why. Here we examine 4 phenomena to develop assumptions about their errors.

Mediopassive Voice. Mediopassive voice asserts that a person or thing both performs and is affected by the action represented. A Portuguese example is presented in Table 4. The incorrect, literal translation of "Vendem-se casas" was not an isolated incident. An examination of all test sentences revealed that the systems tended to translate mediopassive voice word-for-word. This inevitably produced wrong outputs, because mediopassive sentences in Portuguese must generally be converted into passive or active voice to preserve their meaning in English. This complexity is compounded by the rarity of mediopassive voice, making it a challenging phenomenon indeed for MT systems.

Table 4. Examples of phenomena with failing and (if existing) passing MT outputs.

Mediopassive Voice	
Vendem-se casas.	
Houses are for sale.	*reference translation*
Houses sell.	fail
This house is for sale.	pass
Direct Object Omission & Polar Question	
Ele estuda todos os dias? Estuda.	
Does he study everyday? Yes./ He does./ Yes, he does.	*reference translation*
Does he study everyday? Studies.	fail
Idiom	
Está chovendo a cântaros.	
It's raining cats and dogs./ It's raining heavily.	*reference translation*
It's raining vases.	fail
It's raining cats and dogs.	pass
False Friends	
Onde você pôs a agenda da vice-diretora?	
Where did you put the deputy director's planner?	*reference translation*
Where have you put the deputy director's agenda?	fail

Direct Object Omission and Polar Question. In Portuguese, when replying to a 'yes' or 'no' question (polar question), it is uncommon to answer with 'yes' or 'no'. Instead, the verb from the question is used as a one-word reply and any direct/indirect object is omitted. The example test sentence in Table 4 has a very straightforward translation, yet all systems failed completely. A common output resulted from literally translating "Estuda" into "Studies". After inspecting the incorrect translations, one might hypothesize that the systems' widespread failure is due to their insensitivity to inter-sentence context.[4]

Idiom. An idiom is a group of words established by usage that have a meaning not deducible from those of the individual words. They present a challenge to human translators and machines alike because the figurative nature of idioms usually demands interpretation and explanation during translation. An analysis of the MT outputs revealed that systems often successfully translated Portuguese idioms which had an equivalent English idiom (see Table 4). In contrast, idioms which did not have an English equivalent were consistently mistranslated.

False Friends. A false friend is a set of words that in different languages look or sound similar, but differ in meaning. There is the expectation that machines should not mistranslate false friends because they "learn" only what words in one language map to in the other language. Machines should therefore be impervious to the cues that mislead humans, namely how a word sounds and looks. While mistranslations are rare, Table 4 reveals that they can still happen in exceptional

---

[4] During the paper review process, the test sentences for direct object omissions & polar question were re-translated and DeepL translated all of them correctly.

cases when a word is both a false friend (e.g. "agenda" is a word in Portuguese and English) and lexically ambiguous ("agenda" in Portuguese can mean either "planner" (a journal) or "agenda" (someone's underlying plan).[5] The test suite has found MT systems to be more robust against false friends than lexical ambiguity, so it is likely that what was classified as a false friend error is in fact a consequence of lexical ambiguity, but we cannot be certain.

5 Conclusion

As part of this research, the first test suite for the language direction Portuguese-English was developed. It is designed for fine-grained linguistic analysis and comprises 330 test sentences for 66 phenomena and 14 categories. Via the test suite, the translation quality of eight MT systems was evaluated quantitatively and qualitatively (DeepL, Google Sheets, Google Translator, Microsoft Translator, Reverso, Systran, Yandex and our own system). It was found that ambiguity remains one of the most challenging linguistic categories for MT systems. Alongside ambiguity, named entity & terminology and verb valency are the categories where MT systems fail the most on average. On a phenomenon-level, direct object omissions & polar questions is where all systems struggled the most. Positive findings were that negation, pronouns, subordination, verb tense/aspect/mood and false friends are the categories where MT systems perform the best on average. It was also observed that Reverso performs exceptionally well in the translation of multi-word expressions, in particular idioms. In order to aid future research, this test suite has been made publicly available.

We see three main areas for improvement: (1) increasing the number of test sentences per phenomena to allow for more statistically sound and reliable observations, (2) developing a complementary English-Portuguese test suite and (3) enriching the test suite with harder test sentences, as well as new phenomena.

Acknowledgments. The work was accomplished as a semester project, co-ordinated by Neslihan Iskender, part of the MSc program of Media Informatics (TU Berlin). The supervision was funded by the projects TextQ (German Research Foundation; DFG) and SocialWear (German Ministry of Research and Education; BMBF).

References

1. Aires, J., Lopes, G., Gomes, L.: English-Portuguese biomedical translation task using a genuine phrase-based statistical machine translation approach. In: Proceedings of the First Conference on Machine Translation: Volume 2, Shared Task Papers, pp. 456–462. Association for Computational Linguistics, Berlin, Germany, August 2016. https://doi.org/10.18653/v1/W16-2335

---

[5] The lexical ambiguity of "agenda" was overlooked when the test sentence was created; test sentences should only test one phenomenon at a time. More philosophically-minded readers might therefore want to debate whether the incorrect translation boils down to a human or machine error.

2. Avramidis, E., Macketanz, V., Lommel, A., Uszkoreit, H.: Fine-grained evaluation of quality estimation for machine translation based on a linguistically motivated test suite. In: Proceedings of the AMTA 2018 Workshop on Translation Quality Estimation and Automatic Post-Editing, pp. 243–248. Association for Machine Translation in the Americas, Boston, March 2018. https://www.aclweb.org/anthology/W18-2107

3. Avramidis, E., Macketanz, V., Strohriegel, U., Burchardt, A., Möller, S.: Fine-grained linguistic evaluation for state-of-the-art machine translation. In: Proceedings of the Fifth Conference on Machine Translation, pp. 346–356. Association for Computational Linguistics, November 2020. https://aclanthology.org/2020.wmt-1.38

4. Avramidis, E., Macketanz, V., Strohriegel, U., Uszkoreit, H.: Linguistic evaluation of German-English machine translation using a test suite. In: Proceedings of the Fourth Conference on Machine Translation (Volume 2: Shared Task Papers, Day 1), pp. 445–454. Association for Computational Linguistics, Florence, August 2019. https://doi.org/10.18653/v1/W19-5351

5. Barreiro, A., Renchhod, E.: Machine translation challenges for portuguese. Lingvisticæ Investigationes **28**, 3–18 (2005). https://doi.org/10.1075/li.28.1.03bar

6. Bojar, O., Mírovský, J., Rysová, K., Rysová, M.: EvalD reference-less discourse evaluation for WMT18. In: Proceedings of the Third Conference on Machine Translation: Shared Task Papers. pp. 541–545. Association for Computational Linguistics, Brussels, October 2018. https://doi.org/10.18653/v1/W18-6432

7. Burchardt, A., Macketanz, V., Dehdari, J., Heigold, G., Peter, J.T., Williams, P.: A linguistic evaluation of rule-based, phrase-based, and neural MT engines. Prague Bull. Math. Linguist. **108**, 159–170 (2017). https://doi.org/10.1515/pralin-2017-0017

8. Burlot, F., et al.: The WMT'18 morpheval test suites for English-Czech, English-German, English-Finnish and Turkish-English. In: Proceedings of the Third Conference on Machine Translation: Shared Task Papers. pp. 546–560. Association for Computational Linguistics, Brussels, October 2018. https://doi.org/10.18653/v1/W18-6433

9. Callison-Burch, C., Osborne, M., Koehn, P.: Re-evaluating the role of BLEU in machine translation research. In: Proceedings of the 11th Conference of the European Chapter of the Association for Computational Linguistics, pp. 249–256, Trento, Italy, April 2006. https://doi.org/10.1145/1083784.1083789

10. Caseli, H., Inácio, M.: NMT and PBSMT error analyses in English to Brazilian Portuguese automatic translations. In: Proceedings of the 12th Language Resources and Evaluation Conference, pp. 3623–3629. European Language Resources Association, Marseille, May 2020. https://aclanthology.org/2020.lrec-1.446

11. Guillou, L., Hardmeier, C., Lapshinova-Koltunski, E., Loáiciga, S.: A pronoun test suite evaluation of the English-German MT systems at WMT 2018. In: Proceedings of the Third Conference on Machine Translation: Shared Task Papers, pp. 570–577. Association for Computational Linguistics, Brussels, October 2018. https://doi.org/10.18653/v1/W18-6435

12. Isabelle, P., Cherry, C., Foster, G.: A challenge set approach to evaluating machine translation. In: Proceedings of the 2017 Conference on Empirical Methods in Natural Language Processing, pp. 2486–2496. Association for Computational Linguistics, Copenhagen, September 2017. https://doi.org/10.18653/v1/D17-1263

13. Junczys-Dowmunt, M., et al.: Marian: fast neural machine translation in C++, pp. 116–121, July 2018. https://doi.org/10.18653/v1/P18-4020

14. Koehn, P.: Europarl: a parallel corpus for statistical machine translation. In: Proceedings of the tenth Machine Translation Summit, vol. 5, pp. 79–86, Phuket, Thailand (2005). http://mt-archive.info/MTS-2005-Koehn.pdf
15. Lopes, A., Nogueira, R., Lotufo, R., Pedrini, H.: Lite training strategies for Portuguese-English and English-Portuguese translation. In: Proceedings of the Fifth Conference on Machine Translation, pp. 833–840. Association for Computational Linguistics (2020), https://aclanthology.org/2020.wmt-1.90
16. Macketanz, V., Ai, R., Burchardt, A., Uszkoreit, H.: TQ-AutoTest - an automated test suite for (machine) translation quality. In: Proceedings of the Eleventh International Conference on Language Resources and Evaluation (LREC 2018). European Language Resources Association (ELRA), Miyazaki, May 2018. https://aclanthology.org/L18-1142
17. Macketanz, V., Avramidis, E., Burchardt, A., Uszkoreit, H.: Fine-grained evaluation of German-English machine translation based on a test suite. In: Proceedings of the Third Conference on Machine Translation: Shared Task Papers, pp. 578–587. Association for Computational Linguistics, Brussels, October 2018. https://doi.org/10.18653/v1/W18-6436, https://aclanthology.org/W18-6436
18. Macketanz, V., Avramidis, E., Manakhimova, S., Möller, S.: Linguistic evaluation for the 2021 state-of-the-art machine translation systems for German to English and English to German. In: Proceedings of the Sixth Conference on Machine Translation, pp. 1059–1073. Association for Computational Linguistics, November 2021. https://aclanthology.org/2021.wmt-1.115
19. Papineni, K., Roukos, S., Ward, T., Zhu, W.J.: BLEU: a method for automatic evaluation of machine translation. In: Proceedings of the 40th Annual Meeting on Association for Computational Linguistics, pp. 311–318. Association for Computational Linguistics, USA (2002). https://doi.org/10.3115/1073083.1073135
20. Rios, A., Müller, M., Sennrich, R.: The word sense disambiguation test suite at WMT18. In: Proceedings of the Third Conference on Machine Translation: Shared Task Papers, pp. 588–596. Association for Computational Linguistics, Brussels, October 2018. https://doi.org/10.18653/v1/W18-6437
21. Smith, A., Hardmeier, C., Tiedemann, J.: Climbing Mont BLEU: the strange world of reachable high-BLEU translations. In: Proceedings of the 19th Annual Conference of the European Association for Machine Translation, pp. 269–281 (2016), https://aclanthology.org/W16-3414
22. Tiedemann, J.: Parallel data, tools and interfaces in OPUS. In: Proceedings of the Eighth International Conference on Language Resources and Evaluation (LREC 2012), pp. 2214–2218. European Language Resources Association (ELRA), Istanbul, May 2012. http://www.lrec-conf.org/proceedings/lrec2012/pdf/463_Paper.pdf

MINT - Mainstream and Independent News Text Corpus

Danielle Caled(✉) ⓘ, Paula Carvalho ⓘ, and Mário J. Silva ⓘ

INESC-ID, Instituto Superior Técnico, Universidade de Lisboa, Lisbon, Portugal
{dcaled,pcc,mjs}@inesc-id.pt

Abstract. Most misinformation corpora are composed of explicitly *real* and *fake* news content. This results from the idea that misinformation can be approached as a binary classification problem. However, such approach oversimplifies the diversity of properties usually associated with credibility of different textual genres and types. To address this problem, we created MINT, a comprehensive annotated corpus of online articles collected from mainstream and independent Portuguese media sources, over a full year period. The collected articles include: *hard news, opinion* articles, *soft news, satirical news,* and *conspiracy* theories. This paper describes the main linguistic properties underlying each category, and provides some insights based on the analysis of an annotation initiative performed by online readers. The results show that (i) conspiracy theories and opinion articles present similar levels of subjectivity, and make use of fallacious arguments; (ii) irony and sarcasm are not only prevalent in satirical news, but also in conspiracy and opinion articles; and (iii) hard news differ from soft news by resorting to more sources of information, and presenting a higher degree of objectivity.

Keywords: Corpus · Misinformation · Opinion · Satire · Conspiracy

1 Introduction

Misinformation detection has been increasingly addressed by the Natural Language Processing (NLP) community concerned with methods for identifying false or misleading information, generically known as *fake news.*

Fake news detection has been focusing predominantly on distinguishing real from fake content [15], approaching misinformation detection as a dichotomous problem. As most resources conceived within the scope of misinformation studies comprise only these two categories, they fail to consider the diversity of existing textual genres and types, including soft news and fictional news stories, mainly created for entertaining purposes. In turn, most misinformation corpora consider only the most extreme cases in the credibility spectrum (e.g., hard news collected from mainstream newspapers *vs.* news previously labeled as fake by fact-checking agencies), making the automatic classification task deceptively simple and misaligned with reality. However, credibility should be regarded as a complex construct, presenting several dimensions in a continuum.

© Springer Nature Switzerland AG 2022
V. Pinheiro et al. (Eds.): PROPOR 2022, LNAI 13208, pp. 26–36, 2022.
https://doi.org/10.1007/978-3-030-98305-5_3

This paper presents the MINT (Mainstream and Independent News Text) corpus, which was specifically developed to address the gaps on misinformation corpora, especially for Portuguese. MINT is composed of more than 20 thousand articles collected from 33 Portuguese mainstream and independent media over a whole year, covering different styles, subjects, and serving different communication purposes.

The collected articles were classified into five categories, namely *hard news*, *opinion*, *soft news*, *satire*, and *conspiracy*. Although far from exhaustive, this list includes content presenting different properties that must be taken into account in misinformation studies. For example, hard news stories are supposed to involve a neutral and objective reporting, while opinions are characterized by their inherent subjectivity, which is a relevant feature for distinguishing reliable from unreliable news [8,26]. On the other hand, soft news usually approaches light topics, including sensational, disruptive and entertainment-oriented news, which generally resort to *clickbait* strategies to attract the readers' attention [17]. Some of these characteristics may also be found in non-credible news articles, namely in satirical news, created for humorous purposes, and conspiracy theories, fabricated to deceive the reader [4].

We discuss the main linguistic properties of each collection and present the preliminary results of an evaluation on crowdsourced annotations by online news readers of Portuguese media. Those annotations, addressing aspects previously associated with news credibility [2], can foster a better understanding of the main differences among the articles published by the media sources, allowing the development of computational models to correctly approach misinformation detection.

2   Related Work

Binary classification of misinformation has several conceptual problems, including the establishment of a proper definition of real (or credible) news. For example, some authors associate credibility with a greater degree of factuality and a lesser degree of sentiment in the text [1,5,24]; others highlight a variety of aspects, including adherence to journalistic practices/editorial norms, impartial reporting, and the inclusion of statistical data, credible sources, quotes, and attributions in text [12,21]. However, non-adherence to these standards should not be used by itself as a proxy for text credibility. Accordingly, opinion pieces are expected to be subjective, and to present an emotionally charged tone [2,6,12]. A more paradigmatic example involves satire, which, despite being fictional, mimics the tone, style, and appearance of factual news, leading some authors to label this type of content as fake [19]. Other efforts, in turn, argue that satire does not intend to deceive readers and, therefore, should be considered as an independent class when classifying misinformation [9,18].

To address the unrepresented news categories in misinformation classification, Molina et al. organized a taxonomy differentiating *real news* from a variety of controversial news, namely *hoaxes, polarized content, satire, misreporting, opinion, persuasive information*, and *citizen journalism* [12]. MINT's categories *hard news, opinion, satire*, and *conspiracy* correspond to Molina et al.'s *real news, opinion, satire*, and *hoaxes*, respectively. In our study, we have extended the MINT collection with a new nuance of real news, the *soft news* category, representing "light" or "spicy" stories with a "low level of substantive informational value" [11].

Despite the variety of corpora supporting misinformation classification, few linguistic resources are available for Portuguese (e.g., [13,14]). The Fake.Br corpus, a pioneering initiative in Portuguese, includes news articles, labeled as *true* or *false* [13], collected from three major news agencies, and four fake news sources, respectively. However, Fake.Br is strongly biased regarding text length, typos, and sentiment [23], which makes the analysis simplistic and the classification less challenging. Moura et al. developed another news articles collection focused on Portuguese [14]. In this corpus, also a collection of binary classified resources, all the real articles in this collection were scraped from a single source. This hinders the reliability of this collection for misinformation classification due to the lack of diversity of representative credible sources. MINT, on the other hand, containing texts from 33 different mainstream and independent media channels, offers a higher spectrum of news categories and information sources.

The corpora most similar to MINT are the ones comprising news articles from different topics. The NELA-GT series includes articles in English that were harvested from different mainstream, hyperpartisan, and conspiracy sources [16]. FacebookHoax comprises information extracted from Italian Facebook pages, scientific news, and conspiracy websites [25]. Like MINT, both NELA-GT and FacebookHoax assign a credibility label based on the source-level reliability. Hardalov et al. also assembled a collection consisting of credible, fictitious, and funny news written in Bulgarian, resorting to similar strategies for building a corpus in an under-resourced language [7]. This work is related to ours since it contains news collected from mainstream, satirical and fictional sources, covering different topics, such as politics and lifestyle.

3   Corpus Organization

The MINT corpus consists of two different, but complementary, resources: *MINT-articles*, and *MINT-annotations*. MINT-articles, the main resource, corresponds to the entire collection of news articles extracted from mainstream and independent channels (Sect. 3.1). MINT-annotations is a supplementary resource, containing the manual annotations for a subset of the MINT-articles collection (Sect. 3.2). With the insights gained from the corpus annotations, we can therefore understand the specific and shared characteristics of the categories included in the corpus.

3.1   MINT-articles

The MINT corpus includes 20,278 articles, published by the Portuguese mainstream and independent media, from June 1st, 2020 to May 31st, 2021.

The copyright of the articles in MINT is held by their authors. To process the articles, we developed a Python script to download the news articles' content. We extracted their metadata to JSON files containing the article's unique identifier, MINT category, source, URL, publish date, headline, author(s), description, tags, and the URLs of the top image and videos in the article's page.

All MINT articles were assigned to a category through the heuristic rules defined bellow. Table 1 presents examples of article headlines from each MINT category.

Hard News (6000 documents): News collected from the *politics, society, business, technology, culture,* and *sports* sections from nine mainstream news websites. Since this content is published by reputable news sources, verified by the Portuguese regulatory authority for social communication (ERC[1]), they were blindly labeled as hard news.

Opinion (6000 documents): Articles collected from the *opinion* section of 10 mainstream and independent newspapers and magazines. In general, the collected articles approach controversial and contemporary topics related to events with great notoriety in the mainstream media.

Soft News (6000 documents): News extracted from *celebrity, fashion, beauty, family,* and *lifestyle* sections of six magazines, tabloids, and newspaper supplements.

Satire (1029 documents): Articles extracted from two well-known websites, self-declared as fictional, humorous, and/or satirical in their editorial guidelines. They parody the tone and format of traditional news stories, by exploring the use of rhetorical devices, such as irony and sarcasm.

Conspiracy (1249 documents): For identifying conspiracy stories, we explored websites that had previously published at least five articles supporting conspiracy theories, particularly about the origin, scale, prevention, diagnosis, and treatment of the COVID-19 pandemic. We resorted to the COVID-19 theme as it is recurring issue, addressed both by the mainstream and independent media during the MINT collection period. Thus, we investigated the five conspiracy topics regarding the COVID-19 pandemic previously described by Shahsavari et al. [20], and manually inspected a set of candidate websites; only six websites met the selection criteria. The topics covered by these sources are diverse, ranging from *politics, economics, conflicts, health issues,* to *technology.*

3.2   MINT-annotations

To understand the readers' ability to distinguish the news articles' categories, we conducted a human assessment study focused on information content indicators

---

[1] https://www.erc.pt/pt/listagem-registos-na-erc.

Table 1. Illustrative examples of headlines included in MINT.

Alias	Category	Examples
H-N	Hard News	*O que já se sabe sobre a origem da Covid-19?* (What is already known about the origin of Covid-19?)
OPI	Opinion	*Os políticos no palco da pandemia* (Politicians on the pandemic stage)
S-N	Soft News	*Príncipe Harry surpreende ao aparecer na televisão britânica* (Prince Harry makes surprise appearance on British TV)
SAT	Satire	*Reabertura de cabeleireiros e barbeiros: Já é mais fácil conseguir a vacina do que um corte* (Reopening of hairdressers and barbers: It is easier to get the vaccine than a haircut)
CON	Conspiracy	*Máscaras faciais representam riscos graves para a saúde* (Face masks pose serious health risks)

[26]. These indicators are commonly used as proxies for assessing news articles credibility, addressing semantic and discourse dimensions, such as the headline accuracy, the presence of reasoning errors, and sentiment intensity [3].

The survey was publicized in different news outlets, inviting Portuguese online readers to assess a news article randomly selected from MINT-articles. Together, these annotations compose the MINT-annotations collection. These include 750 judgments on 335 different news articles, distributed, by category, as follows: 71 hard news, 63 opinion pieces, 66 soft news, 69 satires, and 65 conspiracy articles. Each assessment was carried out by a different reader . The annotators answered two types of questions:

i) Dichotomous questions. Yes/No questions aimed at assessing the presence or absence in text of specific properties listed below:
- Sources of information: Does the article cite information sources?
- Subjectivity: Does the author express his/her own opinion in the article?
- Irony and sarcasm: Does the author resort to irony/sarcasm in the article?
- Personal attack: Does the article attack, directly or indirectly, individuals or organizations?
- Appeal to fear: Does the author resort to fear as a persuasion strategy?

ii) Five-point Likert scale questions. Questions assessing the overall article credibility, and other dimensions on the news headline (i.e., the degree of headlines' accuracy, *clickbaitiness*, sentiment intensity, irony/sarcasm) and news body content (i.e., reliability of the sources of information mentioned in text, linguistic accuracy, sentiment intensity, and sensationalism).

The information provided by online readers can be used to estimate the degree of similarity and divergence among the various categories of articles included in the MINT corpus, and understand which features are perceived as the most relevant by readers for assessing news credibility [2].

Table 2. Style and complexity characterization of MINT ($\#s$, $\#w$, w/s are the number of sentences, number of words, number of words per sentence, resp.).

	Headline					Body Text				
	H-N	OPI	S-N	SAT	CON	H-N	OPI	S-N	SAT	CON
Avg $\#s$	1.12	1.08	1.12	1.01	1.03	13.72	28.31	15.61	5.29	55.49
Avg $\#w$	11.76	7.17	12.1	14.58	10.36	414.75	672.24	297.13	115.42	1372.34
Avg w/s	10.94	6.76	11.28	14.48	10.14	32.63	25.53	20.92	27.09	26.05

4 Corpus Characterization

In this section, we present statistics derived from a set of metrics often used in computational linguistics to characterize the MINT news texts (Sect. 4.1). We also go through some insights obtained from the crowdsourced annotations (Sect. 4.2).

4.1 Linguistic Characterization

Table 2 presents quantitative metrics related to style and text complexity, which estimate the average number of sentences ($\#s$) and words ($\#w$) comprised in the headline and body text. We have also calculated the average number of words per sentence (w/s), which may help distinguishing elementary from complex sentences. We notice that headlines from opinion articles tend to be shorter, while satire headlines are longer, when compared to the headlines belonging to the remaining categories. Despite the wide diversity on the body length of articles in each category, the obtained statistics show that satirical news stories are usually short, comprising a restricted number of simple sentences. This may indicate that the story introduced in the headline is not deeply developed in the body text. In contrast, the most extensive articles are from the conspiracy category, on average, up to three times longer than the articles reporting hard news. This apparently contradicts the previous studies focused on Portuguese, which state that false articles are usually shorter than credible articles [13,14]. When comparing hard with soft news, we can observe that the former tends to be longer and use more complex linguistic structures.

Table 3 provides a set of metrics that have been explored in the research on news credibility [27,28]. To generate those statistics, we performed part-of-speech (POS) tagging using the Python package spacy[2] (version 2.2.5), relying on pt_core_news_sm model, trained on the Universal Dependencies and WikiNER corpus. Also, we estimated the sentiment information using SentiLex [22]. With regard to sentiment, we only present the information on the headline since this information did not seem relevant in the characterization of the news body.

The results indicate that adjectives are less used in sentences from shorter news texts, namely those belonging to soft news and satire categories, while

---

[2] https://spacy.io/.

Table 3. Linguistic characterization of MINT corpus.

Average metrics	H-N	OPI	S-N	SAT	CON
Ratio of sentences containing adjectives	0.75	0.70	0.52	0.56	0.71
Ratio of sentences containing adverbs	0.70	0.70	0.63	0.75	0.66
Ratio of sentences containing conjunctions	0.66	0.63	0.57	0.57	0.60
Ratio of sentences containing numerals	0.44	0.20	0.22	0.18	0.26
Ratio of indefinite pronoun per sentence	0.50	0.59	0.44	0.53	0.50
Ratio of personal pronoun per sentence	0.24	0.35	0.38	0.34	0.35
Lexical expressivity [27]	0.32	0.40	0.32	0.34	0.38
Ratio of modifiers (adapted from [27]; norm. by #content words)	0.23	0.27	0.23	0.24	0.26
Pausality [27]	4.87	3.58	3.45	3.56	3.55
Redundancy (adapted from [28]; #function words norm. by #w)	0.31	0.33	0.30	0.32	0.32
Modality* (adapted from [28]; norm. by #s)	0.11	0.13	0.07	0.13	0.12
Ratio of headlines containing sentiment terms	0.46	0.40	0.51	0.43	0.51

*Modality was estimated through the most frequent modal verbs in Portuguese (i.e., *poder*, *dever*, *ter de*, *precisar*), indicating (im)possibility, contingency, or necessity.

adverbs are chiefly frequent in satirical news. Globally, these modifiers are mostly used in texts where a higher degree of subjectivity is expected, namely in opinion articles and conspiracy theories. Conversely, the hard news, which should be objective and neutral by principle, use comparatively fewer personal pronouns (only found in quotations or citations included in the news body), and more numerals, which is critical for attesting the text credibility [10]. Conjunctions and punctuation marks (pausality) are also more recurrent in hard news, corroborating the perception of textual cohesion and the idea that authors opt for more complex linguistic constructions. Additionally, sentiment terms are more frequent in headlines from soft news and conspiracies, which are often sensationalist, and employ an emotionally charged tone. On the other hand, soft news use comparatively fewer modal verbs and indefinite pronouns, which support the idea that they adopt a direct and focused narrative. Finally, the data shown in Table 3 also suggests that opinion and conspiracy articles are quite similar, with the exception of a slightly more pronounced use of indefinite pronouns in opinion articles.

Table 4 presents the top-10 most frequent content words in the headlines of each news category in MINT. In general, topics related to the COVID-19 pandemic permeated all categories, either directly or indirectly. Accordingly, the most frequent content words include *covid-19* or *covid*, or related terms, such as *casos* (*cases*), *pandemia* (*pandemic*), and *vacina* (*vaccine*), explicitly referring to the new coronavirus. In addition, it is interesting to stress the prominence

Table 4. 10 most frequent content words in the headlines of each category.

H-N	covid-19, portugal, governo, diz, casos, vai, novo, contra, anos, ser
OPI	portugal, pandemia, futuro, ser, novo, país, covid-19, europa, governo, política
S-N	amor, big, brother, cristina, covid-19, filha, ferreira, filho, revela, anos
SAT	vai, portugueses, marcelo, ser, portugal, costa, novo, governo, vão, pessoas
CON	covid-19, contra, pandemia, vacina, eua, covid, parte, portugal, vacinas, grande

of the terms *novo* (*new*) and *ano* (*year*) in almost all the categories, which are probably linked to the emergence of the *new* virus and its impact in the *year* considered in our corpus. Another characteristic shared by almost all categories is the use of terms related to the national geopolitical context, such as *governo* (*government*), *país* (*country*), portugueses (*Portuguese*), and *Portugal*. Interestingly, the satirical articles focus mainly on the political actors involved in the national agenda, such as the Portuguese President (*Marcelo* [Rebelo de Sousa]), and the Prime Minister of Portugal ([António] *Costa*). On the contrary, the soft news focus chiefly on popular reality shows (*Big Brother*), entertainers (*Cristina Ferreira*), and personal relationships through terms like *filha* (*daughter*), and *filho* (*son*). Moreover, this type of content explores sentiment and emotions, e.g., *amor* (*love*) and makes use of predicates such as *revelar* (*reveal*), which are usually found in clickbait titles. On opposite, the most frequent verb in hard news is the declarative form of the verb *dizer* (*say*), which is probably used to introduce citations in text. With regard to conspiracies, with the exception of the use of the qualitative adjective *grande* (*big*), and the reference to United States (*EUA*), an important player in the global affairs, the most frequent terms are quite similar to the ones found in the hard news. This aspect is not surprising, since conspiracy approaches track news topics, and try to mimic real news.

4.2   Insights from Crowdsourced Annotations

Figure 1 summarizes the answers to the dichotomous questions under the perspective of online news readers. The result reinforces the similarity between the opinion and conspiracy articles, also observed in Table 3. The incidence of subjective information, a feature usually observed in opinion articles, also appears as a strong characteristic of conspiracies. Moreover, both categories present a high level of irony and/or sarcasm, and often use fallacies, in particular, personal attacks (i.e., the author attacks a specific individual or organization rather than attacking the substance of the argument itself). On the other hand, hard news usually follows the journalistic standards and practices, including accuracy (materialized, for instance, by the use of reliable sources of information), objectivity, and impartiality. Those characteristics are also observed in soft news, although to a lesser extent. As expected, users are capable of easily identifying irony and sarcasm in satirical news articles; however, their annotations also demonstrate that this property can be observed in multiple categories, namely in opinion news articles and conspiracy theories, as previously mentioned. Furthermore, the fallacious arguments typically used in conspiracy (namely, personal attacks and appeal to fear) can also be found in satirical and opinion articles.

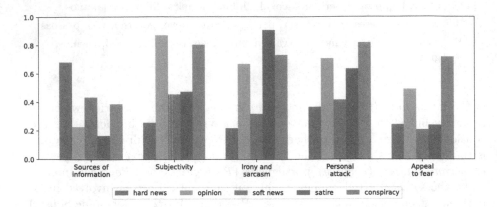

Fig. 1. Relative frequency to the dichotomous questions for each MINT category.

5   Conclusion

This paper presented MINT, a corpus comprising news articles published by different Portuguese mainstream and independent sources. MINT was developed to fill a need in misinformation research, providing annotated resources to enable studies ranging from social sciences to computational journalism. In particular, the MINT corpus can help answering research questions involving the study of news credibility, and support the development of several NLP tasks, including the automatic identification of misinformation and authorship attribution, through the ground truth labels provided. Also, both the news articles and crowdsourced annotations in MINT corpus offer valuable resources for research in the linguistic and communication fields, allowing, for example, the study of fallacies supporting conspiracy theories that surround the COVID-19 pandemic.

MINT was developed in compliance with the Directive 2019/790 of the European Parliament and of the Council on copyright and related rights in the Digital Single Market under the exception for Text and Data Mining used for scientific research. The corpus materials are shared with the research community at https://github.com/dcaled/mint.

Acknowledgement. This work was produced with the support of INCD funded by Fundação para a Ciência e a Tecnologia (FCT) and FEDER under the project 01/SAICT/2016 No. 022153. We also acknowledge the support from Portugal2020 under Project No. POCI-05–5762-FSE-000217, and FCT through grants No. PTDC/ CCI-CIF/32607/2017, UIDB/50021/2020, and SFRH/BD/145561/2019.

References

1. Aker, A., et al.: Corpus of news articles annotated with article level sentiment. In: NewsIR@ SIGIR (2019)
2. Carvalho, P., Caled, D., Silva, M.J., Martins, B.: Annotation and assessment of news credibility. Tech. rep., INESC-ID (2021)
3. Carvalho, P., et al.: Assessing news credibility: misinformation content indicators (2021)
4. Carvalho, P., Martins, B., Rosa, H., Amir, S., Baptista, J., Silva, M.J.: Situational irony in farcical news headlines. In: Proceedings of the International Conference on Computational Processing of Portuguese (2020)
5. Fuhr, N., et al.: An information nutritional label for online documents. In: SIGIR Forum, vol. 51 (2018)
6. Golbeck, J., et al.: Fake news vs satire: a dataset and analysis. In: Proceedings of the ACM Conference on Web Science (2018)
7. Hardalov, M., Koychev, I., Nakov, P.: In search of credible news. In: Artificial Intelligence: Methodology, Systems, and Applications (2016)
8. Holt, K., Figenschou, T.U., Frischlich, L.: Key dimensions of alternative news media. Digital J. **7**(7), 860–869 (2019)
9. Horne, B., Adali, S.: This just in: Fake news packs a lot in title, uses simpler, repetitive content in text body, more similar to satire than real news. In: Proceedings of the International AAAI Conference on Web and Social Media, vol. 11 (2017)
10. Koetsenruijter, A.W.M.: Using numbers in news increases story credibility. Newspaper Res. J. **32**(2), 74–82 (2011)
11. Lehman-Wilzig, S.N., Seletzky, M.: Hard news, soft news, 'general' news: The necessity and utility of an intermediate classification. Journalism **11**(1), 37–56 (2010)
12. Molina, M.D., Sundar, S.S., Le, T., Lee, D.: Fake news is not simply false information: a concept explication and taxonomy of online content. Am. Behav. Sci. **65**(2), 180–212 (2021)
13. Monteiro, R.A., et al.: Contributions to the study of fake news in Portuguese: New corpus and automatic detection results. In: Proceedings of the International Conference on Computational Processing of Portuguese (2018)
14. Moura, R., Sousa-Silva, R., Cardoso, H.L.: Automated fake news detection using computational forensic linguistics. In: Progress in Artificial Intelligence (2021)
15. Nakamura, K., Levy, S., Wang, W.Y.: Fakeddit: A new multimodal benchmark dataset for fine-grained fake news detection. In: Proceedings of the Language Resources and Evaluation Conference (2020)
16. Nørregaard, J., Horne, B.D., Adalı, S.: NELA-GT-2018: a large multi-labelled news dataset for the study of misinformation in news articles. Proceedings of the International AAAI Conference on Web and Social Media, vol. 13 (2019)
17. Pérez-Rosas, V., Kleinberg, B., Lefevre, A., Mihalcea, R.: Automatic detection of fake news. In: Proceedings of the International Conference on Computational Linguistics (2018)
18. Potthast, M., Kiesel, J., Reinartz, K., Bevendorff, J., Stein, B.: A stylometric inquiry into hyperpartisan and fake news. In: Proceedings of the Annual Meeting of the Association for Computational Linguistics (2018)
19. Rubin, V.L., Chen, Y., Conroy, N.K.: Deception detection for news: three types of fakes. In: Proceedings of the Association for Information Science and Technology, vol. 52 (2015)

20. Shahsavari, S., Holur, P., Wang, T., Tangherlini, T.R., Roychowdhury, V.: Conspiracy in the time of corona: automatic detection of emerging COVID-19 conspiracy theories in social media and the news. J. Comput. Soc. Sci. **3**(2), 279–317 (2020). https://doi.org/10.1007/s42001-020-00086-5
21. Shoemaker, P.J.: News values: reciprocal effects on journalists and journalism. American Cancer Society (2017)
22. Silva, M.J., Carvalho, P., Sarmento, L.: Building a sentiment lexicon for social judgement mining. In: Proceedings of the International Conference on Computational Processing of Portuguese (2012)
23. Silva, R.M., Santos, R.L., Almeida, T.A., Pardo, T.A.: Towards automatically filtering fake news in Portuguese. Exp. Syst. Appl. **146**, 113199 (2020)
24. Spradling, M., Straub, J., Strong, J.: Protection from 'fake news': the need for descriptive factual labeling for online content. Future Int. **13**(6), 142 (2021)
25. Tacchini, E., Ballarin, G., Della Vedova, M.L., Moret, S., de Alfaro, L.: Some like it hoax: automated fake news detection in social networks. In: Proceedings of the Workshop on Data Science for Social Good, CEUR-WS (2017)
26. Zhang, A.X., et al.: A structured response to misinformation: defining and annotating credibility indicators in news articles. In: Proceedings of the Web Conference (2018)
27. Zhou, L., Burgoon, J.K., Twitchell, D.P., Qin, T., Nunamaker, Jr., J.F.: A comparison of classification methods for predicting deception in computer-mediated communication. J. Manag. Inf. Syst. **20**(4), 139–166 (2004)
28. Zhou, X., Zafarani, R.: A survey of fake news: fundamental theories, detection methods, and opportunities. ACM Comput. Surv. **53**(5), 1–40 (2020)

Fakepedia Corpus: A Flexible Fake News Corpus in Portuguese

Anderson Cordeiro Charles[1]([⊠]) [iD], Livia Ruback[2] [iD], and Jonice Oliveira[1] [iD]

[1] Universidade Federal do Rio de Janeiro (UFRJ), Rio de Janeiro, Brazil
andersoncordeiro@ppgi.ufrj.br, jonice@dcc.ufrj.br
[2] Universidade Federal Rural do Rio de Janeiro (UFRRJ), Rio de Janeiro, Brazil
liviaruback@ppgi.ufrj.br

Abstract. In recent years, fake news has been massively propagated, causing different damages in society, such as impacting democracy processes and the management of health crises. In this context, automatic fake news classification systems have been profitably created to tackle this problem. These systems require balanced corpus to be used as training data for the machine learning models. In this article, we present a flexible corpus of fake news in Portuguese. To balance our corpus, besides the fake news, we also collected and processed content from real news, extracted from trustable web portals. We also present an automatic process for the corpus creation, which allows keeping it constantly updated. To validate our results and methodology, we performed a news classification experiment using the LSTM model, and we achieved great results, with a precision of 97% on classifying fake news and 92% on classifying real news.

Keywords: Fake news · Real news · Fact checking · Corpus · Machine learning

1 Introduction

In recent years, the growth in the use of social media has transformed human interaction on the Internet, allowing for the rapid dissemination of information and reaching a wide and diverse audience. In this context, fake news is often - and easily - propagated, representing a risk not only to journalistic integrity but also reaching all sectors of society, impairing decision-making or generating embarrassment, loss, and damage to society that is sometimes irreparable [21]. During the 2016 presidential election in the United States, for example, fake news on Facebook was more consumed than real news circulating in the mainstream media [18], which demonstrates its influence on democratic processes, directly impacting the lives of millions of people.

In Brazil, a similar phenomenon could be seen during the 2018 presidential elections, when people also massively used social media, in addition to messaging apps, such as WhatsApp [15], to spread fake news, encouraging the dissemination of this type of content by other actors in the network, motivated by political, philosophical and religious issues [7]. During the COVID-19 pandemic, the Ministry of Health of Brazil needed to develop a specific channel to transmit real information about the new coronavirus and

© Springer Nature Switzerland AG 2022
V. Pinheiro et al. (Eds.): PROPOR 2022, LNAI 13208, pp. 37–45, 2022.
https://doi.org/10.1007/978-3-030-98305-5_4

deny the fake news circulating on the network, which directly impacted the management of the pandemic. This crisis faced by the healthcare area is one of the consequences of fake news dissemination and demonstrates how important and urgent it is to promote debates and develop techniques to reduce the spreading of fake news online, to mitigate some of the harmful consequences of this problem on society.

One of the efforts to tackle this problem is the investigative process performed by fact-checking agencies. However, this process can be compromised if a clear and transparent verification protocol [8] is not adopted. And, even following all the checking practices established by these protocols, human news classification processes are slower compared to the fake news spreading. In this context, automated classification processes become the more suitable strategy to fight fake news. However, automated processes use previously defined linguistic patterns to detect if the news is fake or real, and this language dependency is one of the great difficulties of this type of approach, especially if we consider languages other than English.

In this article, we present a flexible corpus of fake news in Portuguese, developed using an automatic creation process, which allows its easy maintenance. We describe the strategy used for balancing the corpus, to ensure it can be used as training data by classification models without the risk of potential bias. To evaluate the applicability of the corpus, and validate our methodology, we performed a news classification experiment using the LSTM model and we achieved good results. To the best of our knowledge, our corpus is the first flexible corpus of fake and real news in Portuguese, that can be constantly updated and easily used to build increasingly efficient fake news classifiers. It can also be used as an important source for studying fake news dissemination in Brazil.

2 Related Work

Identifying fake news has proven to be a complex challenge [9]. To combat its dissemination and its mass effects, different approaches have been developed using methods that involve manual, automatic or hybrid processes. Different automatic news checking and content validation techniques emerged, as demonstrated by Conroy et al. [1], Shao et al. [17] and Moraes et al. [11]. Other approaches, as in Reis et al. [13], consider that the detection of fake news can be based on a hybrid model addressing content, source reputation and the environment (e.g., social network structure).

Despite the different techniques, characteristics and strategies of automatic classification of news, it can be noted that all these methods have in common the use of pre-classified corpus for training learning algorithms. The work by Rubin et al. [16], for example, gathered 240 texts in English, from different domains, classified as fake or real, and served as a reference for many other works, such as the corporas created by Ferreira & Vlachos [4] and Wang [22]. This type of approach often faces problems related to universalization, since countries do not share the same language and are inserted in different contexts. This limitation makes it difficult to reuse a labelled corpus as training data by a model tring to classify news written in other languages.

Due to the importance of studying fake news produced in different languages and contexts, some corpus have been developed, enabling the study and the automatic classification of fake news in different countries and languages, such as Italian [5], Dutch

[20] and Chinese [23]. In Brazil, with the purpose of filling an important gap for the development of a fake news corpus in Portuguese [14], the work of Monteiro et al. [10] became a reference, presenting a corpus with more than 4000 news in Portuguese classified as fake or not, using a mixed approach, between manual observations and automatic processes for the construction of the corpus.

Despite the efforts in the construction of the corpus and the undeniable contribution to the development of learning algorithms in the Portuguese language, it must be considered that the production of fake news is also evolutionary and tries to circumvent automatic classification methods. In some scenarios, such as epidemics and elections, where there is a rapid proliferation of fake news and the time to fight them is emergency, the method of updating a corpus manually can disrupt the entire process of recognizing and combating fake news. For this reason, it is essential to make making the corpus out of date, and offer there is, for example, relevant news on recent political and health crises in the country.

In this work, we propose a flexible corpus of fake and real news in Portuguese, that can be easily used to build increasingly efficient fake news classifiers. To the best of our knowledge, our work is the first initiative that provides a corpus that can be constantly updated, playing an important role in fighting fake news. In this paper, we do not discuss how the definitions of "fake news" and "disinformation" are related or how these definitions can impact on the identification and awareness of such a broad spectrum problem, instead, we treat the terms in this work as synonyms, knowing that, with this, only a part of a broader phenomenon is being addressed.

Section 3 presents the steps for creating the corpus, detailing the automated processes of news gathering and data balancing. In Sect. 4, we use the corpus in a news classification experiment to verify its viability, presenting the results and in Sect. 5 we bring our conclusions highlighting the contributions of our work.

3 Our Proposal: Fakepedia Corpus

In a previous work (omitted), we developed a database composed of fake news, which is created and maintained automatically through crawlers that capture validated news in specialized portals (e.g.: fact-checking sites, such as Boatos.org[1], Lupa[2], Aos Fatos[3]).

This database is part of a broader platform (omitted) that uses crowdsourcing and media literacy to distribute fact checking tasks among users. In this environment, users are grouped by affinity and collaboratively classify a news as fake or real. We developed this platform to allow the topic to be debated and promote digital literacy.

In this work, we proposed a flexible corpus of fake news in Portuguese, created using an automatic process that allows its easy maintenance. We used part of the mentioned database and we followed the precautions suggested by Rubin et al. [16] in creating a corpus, commonly used to produce training data to be used by machine learning models.

We balance the corpus to ensure that machine learning classifiers can correctly extract patterns to differentiate between true and fake news, avoiding possible classification

---

[1] https://www.boatos.org.
[2] https://piaui.folha.uol.com.br/lupa.
[3] https://www.aosfatos.org.

bias. In this way, for each fake news, we automatically collect a corresponding real news which, if it does not refute the fake news, at least is related.

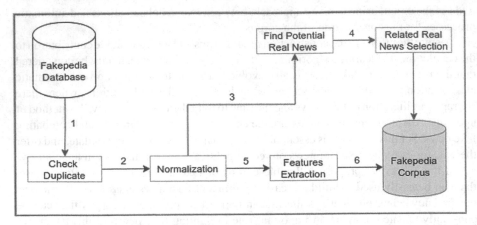

Fig. 1. Automatic corpus creation process

Figure 1 shows the automatic corpus creation process. The Fakepedia platform's database consists of the fake news that was checked in the crowdsourcing process and the news from fact-checking portals, automatically extracted by the crawlers [2] e. For each news stored in the platform's database, we check if it does not yet exist in the corpus (Fig. 1.1). If it is a new news, it is stored and also submitted to the next steps in the process.

We normalize the news content, placing all words in lowercase so that all news items have the same format (Fig. 1.2), and, finally, we extract some features from the news, such as the number of nouns and adjectives (Fig. 1.5).

We then balance the corpus - by adding real news - to ensure it can be used as training data by classification models without the risk of a warning bias due to unbalanced classes (Fig. 1.3 and 1.4). We perform this corpus balancing using Google searches on daily newspaper sites such as 'Globo'[4], 'UOL'[5], 'Extra'[6] and 'Folha de São Paulo'[7], in a way that we can find a real news that match a fake news, using some of its keywords.

To find and choose real related news, we adopt the same technique described in [3] that uses the python library googlesearch[8] to perform Google queries through scripts and google dorks techniques [21] to perform advanced Google queries. For example, in search of real news that demystifies the efficacy of the drug ivermectin in the treatment of COVID, we use the search string: "inurl:uol + intext: ivermectina + supera + eficácia + vacinas", at UOL website. We have limited the search results to the top 5 stories, which represent the potential related news to be added to the corpus. We calculate the

---

[4] https://www.globo.com.

[5] https://www.uol.com.br.

[6] https://extra.globo.com.

[7] https://www.folha.uol.com.br/.

[8] https://pypi.org/project/googlesearch-python.

similarity between the fake news and the 5 potential related real news and we choose the most similar real news. We use the spaCy[9] library and the Word2vec[10] algorithm, which generates a vector representation of each word in a set of words, using neural networks, to predict the closest semantic neighbors of a word.

The resulting similarity score, based on the cosine distance, ranges from 0, when the news compared are completely different, to 1, when the news have exactly the same content.

The corpus brings together fake news collected between 2013 and 2021, on various topics such as politics, health and technology, and covers various moments in Brazil, such as the presidential elections in 2018, totaling 8,589 fake news. Out of the fake news present in the corpus, we found 6,199 corresponding real news (2,390 fake news items did not have equivalent real news and were excluded from the corpus, to ensure the corpus is balanced).

Our resulting corpus, freely available for research purposes[11], including fake news and real news, is composed of 12,398 news (6,199 fake news and 6,199 real news), published online between 2013 and 2021. Table 1 shows an example of fake news - and a related real news - present in the corpus, that was massively spread in Brazil during the COVID pandemic. They are related to the use of Ivermectin, an anti-parasitic drug commonly used for livestock, to treat COVID.

The fake news claims that a study demonstrates that Ivermectin would be more effective than vaccines, and alleges that vaccines are dangerous and would cause people's death. The related real news, instead, mentions the same study, but it presents a series of problems in its development that affects its credibility. In fact, different versions of this fake news has been widely spread all over the world during the pandemic.

Table 1. Example of fake news and true equivalent in the corpus

Fake	True
"IVERMECTINA supera vacinas: mais de 83% de eficácia contra a Covid-19, revela a ciência. Um estudo do Reino Unido revela que a ivermectina promove uma taxa de sobrevivência acima de 83 por cento contra o coronavírus Covid-19, superando as vacinas Covid-19 que são experimentais e perigosas, que tem induzido mais infecção e mortes do que proteção"	*"Um estudo publicado na plataforma Research Square indica que a ivermectina, remédio geralmente usado no combate de piolhos, pode reduzir risco de morte em até 75% para pacientes infectados pelo novo coronavírus (Sars-CoV-2). A pesquisa, no entanto, tem problemas. "É tão mal feito que não dá para tirar qualquer conclusão, o que os próprios autores reconhecem no fim do artigo", aponta Marcio Sommer Bittencourt, cardiologista no Hospital Universitário da USP e editor do periódico científico Circulation:Cardiovascular Imaging"*

---

[9] https://spacy.io.
[10] https://pypi.org/project/word2vec.
[11] https://bit.ly/FkpdCorpus.

Besides the metadata present in the news we collected, we also added new text characteristics into the corpus (Fig. 1.5), such as the url with fact check result (url_review) and the author of the check (source). Table 2 lists and describes these characteristics. We also provide a detailed documentation of these characteristics, together with the corpus.

Table 2. Characteristics present in the corpus

Text characteristic	Description
title	Original title of the news
title_norm	News headline normalized
message	Original news content
message_norm	News content normalized
tokens	Keywords extracted from the news
features	Grammar classes present in the news
entities	People or entities mentioned in the news
class	Indicates if the news is fake or real
source	Indicates the author of the check
url_review	Check url
url_true	Real news related url
real_news_related	Equivalent real news text

4 Experiments and Results

To evaluate the applicability of the corpus created by our automated approach, and to validate our methodology, we performed a news classification experiment using the LSTM model. For the classification, we used the following attributes: message_norm, which contains the normalized texts of news classified as fake; real_news_related, which represents related real news; and class, which indicates whether the news is fake or real. We splitted the corpus into 70% for training the algorithm, and 30% for testing. It is important to highlight that we kept the same proportion of real and fake news in the training and testing sets, keeping the original data balance.

We used the Long Short-Term Memory LSTM [6] deep learning model for the classification of news in this corpus, as this approach has already shown good results in solving similar problems involving NLP [12]. The way LSTM performs the learning process allows the algorithm to capture all the meaning and context of a long article from the stream of incoming words and, therefore, they are very suitable for problems involving contextual features. For this experiment, we used a two-layer LSTM network and trained the model 10 times using cross-validation.

Table 3 details the confusion matrix for the classification model. It is important to mention that, in our classification, we classify a fake news as 1 (positive) and a real news as 0 (negative). The true positives (TP) are news that were correctly classified as fake; false positives (FP) are news classified as fake news but are real; false negatives (FN) are news items that were classified as real but are fake; and finally the true negatives (TN) are real news that are correctly classified by the model.

Table 3. LSTM model confusion matrix

		Actual classes	
		Fake	Real
Model classificaion	Fake	2217 (TP)	60 (FP)
	Real	184 (FN)	1854 (TN)

To evaluate how good the model performs, we consider the metrics accuracy, precision, recall, and f1-score. Table 4 shows the results, considering these metrics. We achieved 94% of f1-score for classifying fake news and 95% of f1-score for classifying real news.

Table 4. Model performance measure

	Precision	Recall	F1-score	Support
True	0.92	0.97	0.95	2277
Fake	0.97	0.91	0.94	2038
Accuracy			0.94	4315

We achieved very good results with the experiment, considering the metrics shown in Table 4. With these results, we believe we offer an important contribution to mitigate the dissemination of fake news in Portuguese.

5 Conclusion

The dissemination of false news represents a risk for society, often causing irreparable loss and damage. These consequences are especially aggravated in times of crisis, demonstrating the importance of developing techniques to reduce the dissemination of fake news quickly and assertively.

Automatic processes for classifying fake news, compared to manual processes, tend to be used due to their agility and processing capacity. However, the need to use linguistic standards is one of the great difficulties of this type of approach, especially if we consider languages other than English. This happens because the creation of corpus with these patterns is still done manually, making its creation and updating process difficult. The constant textual improvement applied by those who intentionally produce false content makes it necessary that this set is always up to date so that new features of the text can be cataloged and presented to classification models.

In this article we presented a flexible corpus of fake news in Portuguese that can be constantly updated. Result of an automated process, our corpus gathers news collected from portals and fact-checking agencies in Brazil between 2013 and 2021. To validate the results of our methodology and the applicability of the generated corpus, we performed a news classification experiment using the LSTM model in the corpus, which was able to correctly classify 94% of the fake news and 92% of the real news, proving to be a successful approach. t is important to emphasize that the results of this experiment may have been influenced by limitations that were not deepened, as the focus of the work was to present the automatic collection of news and corpus creation, even so, we applied techniques such as class balancing to reduce the bias of the classification.

In addition to being one of the few fake news corpuses in Portuguese, available for use at https://bit.ly/FkpdCorpus, we can highlight as another contribution of this work the description of a flexible process of creating and automatically updating the corpus. We believe this work represents an important step to debate fake news dissemination and towards the fighting of fake news in Portuguese.

Acknowledgement. This work was supported in part by Oracle Cloud credits and related resources provided by the Oracle for Research program (award number CPQ-2160239). Also, we would thank CNPq and CAPES for all support.

References

1. Conroy, N.J., Rubin, V.L., Chen, Y.: Automatic deception detection: methods for finding fake news. Proc. Assoc. Inf. Sci. Technol. **52**, 1–4 (2015)
2. Charles, A.C., de Oliveira Sampaio, J.: Checking fake news on web browsers: an approach using collaborative datasets. In: Workshop on Big Social Data and Urban Computing (2018)
3. Cordeiro, A., de Oliveira Sampaio, J., Ruback, L.: FakeSpread: Um framework para análise de propagação de fake news NA Web. In: Anais do XI Workshop sobre Aspectos da Interação Humano-Computador Para a Web Social, pp. 9–16 (2020)
4. Ferreira, W., Vlachos, A.: Emergent: a novel data-set for stance classification. In: Proceedings of the 2016 Conference of the North American Chapter of the Association for Computational Linguistics: Human language technologies (2016)
5. Fornaciari, T., Poesio, M.: Automatic deception detection in Italian court cases. Artif. Intel. Law **21**(3), 303–340 (2013)
6. Hochreiter, S., Schmidhuber, J.: Long short-term memory. Neural Comput. **9**, 1735–1780 (1997)
7. Isaac, M., Roose K.: Disinformation Spreads on WhatsApp Ahead of Brazilian Election, vol. 19. New York Times (2018)
8. Ireton, C., Posetti, J.: Journalism, Fake News and Disinformation: Handbook for Journalism Education and Training. Unesco Publishing, Paris (2018)
9. Lazer, D.M., et al.: The science of fake news. Science **359**(6380), 1094–1096 (2018)

10. Monteiro, R.A., Santos, R.L., Pardo, T.A., De Almeida, T.A., Ruiz, E.E., Vale, O.A.: Contributions to the study of fake news in portuguese: new corpus and automatic detection results. In: International Conference on Computational Processing of the Portuguese Language, pp. 324–334. Springer, Cham (2018). https://doi.org/10.1007/978-3-319-99722-3_33
11. Moraes, M.P., de Oliveira Sampaio, J., Charles, A.C.: Data mining applied in fake news classification through textual patterns. In: Proceedings of the 25th Brazilian Symposium on Multimedia and the Web, pp. 321–324 (2019)
12. Rajendran, G., Chitturi, B., Poornachandran, P.: Stance-in-depth deep neural approach to stance classification. Proc. Comput. Sci. **132**, 1646–1653 (2018)
13. Reis, J.C., Correia, A., Murai, F., Veloso, A., Benevenuto, F.: Supervised learning for fake news detection. IEEE Intell. Syst. **34**(2), 76–81 (2019)
14. Silva, R.M., Santos, R.L., Almeida, T.A., Pardo, T.A.: Towards automatically filtering fake news in Portuguese. Exp. Syst. Appl. **146**, 113199 (2020)
15. Resende, G., Messias, J., Silva, M., Almeida, J., Vasconcelos, M., Benevenuto, F.: A system for monitoring public political groups in WhatsApp. In: Proceedings of the 24th Brazilian Symposium on Multimedia and the Web, pp. 387–390 (2018)
16. Rubin, V.L., Conroy, N., Chen, Y., Cornwell, S.: Fake news or truth? Using satirical cues to detect potentially misleading news. In: Proceedings of the Second Workshop on Computational Approaches to Deception Detection, pp. 7–17 (2016)
17. Shao, C., Ciampaglia, G.L., Flammini, A., Menczer, F.: Hoaxy: A Platform for Tracking Online Misinformation (2016)
18. Silverman, C.: This analysis shows how viral fake election news stories outperformed real news on Facebook. BuzzFeed (2016)
19. Toffalini, F., Abbà, M., Carra, D., Balzarotti, D.: Google dorks: analysis, creation, and new defenses. In: International Conference on Detection of Intrusions and Malware, and Vulnerability Assessment, pp. 255–275 Springer, Cham (2016). https://doi.org/10.1007/978-3-319-40667-1_13
20. Verhoeven, B., Daelemans, W.: CLiPS Stylometry Investigation (CSI) corpus: a Dutch corpus for the detection of age, gender, personality, sentiment and deception in text. In: LREC, pp. 3081–3085 (2014)
21. Vosoughi, S., Roy, D.: Rumor gauge: predicting the veracity of rumors on Twitter. ACM Trans. Knowl. Discov. Data **11**, 1–38 (2017)
22. Wang, W.Y.: "liar, liar pants on fire": a new benchmark dataset for fake news detection. arXiv: 1705.00648 (2017)
23. Zhang, H., Tan, H.Y., Zheng, J.H.: Deception detection based on SVM for Chinese text in CMC. In: 2009 Sixth International Conference on Information Technology: New Generations IEEE, pp. 481–486 (2009)

A Targeted Assessment of the Syntactic Abilities of Transformer Models for Galician-Portuguese

Marcos Garcia[✉][iD] and Alfredo Crespo-Otero

CiTIUS - Centro Singular de Investigación en Tecnoloxías Intelixentes,
Universidade de Santiago de Compostela, Santiago de Compostela, Galiza, Spain
marcos.garcia.gonzalez@usc.gal, alfredo.crespo@rai.usc.es

Abstract. This paper presents a targeted syntactic evaluation of Transformer models for Galician-Portuguese. We defined three experiments that allow to explore how these models, trained with a masked language modeling objective, encode syntactic knowledge. To do so, we created a new dataset including test instances of number (subject-verb), gender (subject-predicative adjective), and person (subject-inflected infinitive) agreement. This dataset was used to evaluate monolingual and multilingual BERT models, controlling for various aspects such as the presence of attractors or the distance between the dependent elements. The results show that Transformer models perform competently in many cases, but they are generally confounded by the presence of attractors in long-distance dependencies. Moreover, the different behavior of monolingual models trained with the same corpora reinforces the need for a deep exploration of the network architectures and their learning process.

Keywords: Language models · Syntax · Targeted syntactic evaluation.

1 Introduction

The use of modern artificial neural networks gave rise to significant improvements on most NLP tasks [4, 23], many of them requiring deep linguistic knowledge, such as machine translation [6] or natural language understanding [21]. This great performance of deep neural networks, together with the fact that they learn from text with no linguistic annotation, has provoked the interest of researchers from different areas, including linguistics and cognitive science. In this regard, there have been several studies that explore how different neural network architectures capture linguistic—mainly syntactic—knowledge [8,11,16].[1]

One of the most prevalent experiments to analyze the syntactic generalizations induced by artificial neural networks is the agreement prediction task, which evaluates whether a model is able to learn a hierarchical morphosyntactic dependency. Therefore, if in a sentence like

---

[1] See [15] and [2] for a review on the syntactic evaluation of neural networks, and on its relation to theoretical linguistics, respectively.

© Springer Nature Switzerland AG 2022
V. Pinheiro et al. (Eds.): PROPOR 2022, LNAI 13208, pp. 46–56, 2022.
https://doi.org/10.1007/978-3-030-98305-5_5

"O *rapaz$_i$* que jogava com as suas *amigas$_j$ está$_i$|*estão$_j$* bem."
'The *boy$_i$* who was playing with his *friends$_j$ is$_i$|*are$_j$* happy.'

a model gives a higher probability to the singular form ("está", 'is') than to the plural ("estão", 'are') it may be an indication that the network is using the hierarchical (syntactic) structure of natural languages instead of a linear one (which would establish an agreement between "amigas" and "estão", both in plural). In this example, the noun "amigas" is used as an *attractor* which may confound the model's behavior with respect to the prediction of the subsequent verb form [3,11].

Inspired by this type of analysis, a new line of research, often dubbed Target Syntactic Evaluation (TSE) [18], has recently emerged defining a variety of analytical probes and releasing datasets in various languages (although mainly in English). In this respect, some authors train *ad-hoc* long short-term memory networks (LSTMs) to observe whether they can generalize syntactic knowledge from raw text [16], while others assess whether models trained on generic language modeling objectives induce syntactic structures [11].

However, to the best of our knowledge, there is no such syntactic evaluation of Language Models (LMs) for Galician-Portuguese.[2] This paper presents a TSE of Galician and Portuguese models based on Transformer [25], one of the best-performing architectures for NLP. We created a dataset to evaluate number, gender, and person agreement dependencies, using instances of subject-verb (e.g., "O rapaz [...] *está*|*estão"), subject-predicative adjective (e.g., "A *rapariga* [...] é *alta*|*alto"), and subject-inflected infinitive (e.g., "Preparei a carne para *tu*|*ele|*nós|...a *comeres"), respectively. We evaluate monolingual and multilingual models, showing that they behave competently, especially for number and gender, but are unstable regarding the person agreement. Furthermore, the results call for an in-depth analysis of the network architecture and learning process, as different models trained with the same corpus show opposite trends.

The rest of the paper is structured as follows: Sect. 2 presents related work on the evaluation of the syntactic abilities of neural language models. Then, Sect. 3 introduces the experiments and the dataset, while the results are discussed in Sect. 4. Finally, the conclusions of this study are drawn in Sect. 5.

2   Related Work

In their seminal paper, Linzen *et alii* assessed whether LSTMs (a type of recurrent neural networks, RNNs) capture syntactic structure from sequential data in English [16]. They presented the *number prediction task*, where a model should encode both the number and the 'subjecthood' between a long-distance subject-verb dependency (e.g., "The *keys* to the cabinet *is|are on the table"), and found

---

[2] Galician and Portuguese are usually considered varieties of a single language [7,14], but the recent standardization of the former adopting a Spanish-based orthography [22] makes difficult to process it using resources and tools built for Portuguese. Thus, our division of Galician and Portuguese is based solely on their different spellings.

that, while a generic language modeling objective is not enough to generalize syntax, supervised LSTMs adequately identify this type of structures. However, a subsequent study analyzing 4 languages (Italian, English, Hebrew, and Russian) showed that carefully constructed LSTM-based LMs are able to induce syntactic generalizations in the number prediction task, with only a moderately lower performance than humans, and performing well in non-sensical sentences [11]. Following this path, the authors of [18] presented a test set for TSE in English, including not only instances of subject-verb agreement but also other syntactic phenomena. Several experiments using both RNN language models and syntax-aware supervised RNNs showed that despite performing well in various scenarios, the models' performance is far from that of human annotators.

The impressive results obtained by Transformer-based BERT models [5] in most NLP tasks also aroused the interest in exploring the syntactic knowledge induced by the self-attention mechanism of this architecture [25]. Using previous subject-verb agreement data in English, the results presented in [10] suggest that the non-recurrent architecture of BERT is able to induce long-distance syntactic agreement. Then, Mueller *et alii* evaluated both LSTM and BERT models in a multilingual scenario [19], using a cross-linguistic dataset of subject-verb agreement in English, French, German, Hebrew, and Russian. Their results show that the models use the cues provided by morphologically-rich languages to learn syntactic generalizations and that multilingual models do not seem to transfer syntactic information across languages.

More recently, [20] discussed different approaches to TSE other than using manually selected verb pairs (e.g., "is|are"), while Hall *et alii* [12] questioned the claims about the syntactic generalization capabilities of current LMs, after obtaining lower results on semantically non-sensical sentences.

In this paper, we follow this line of research and create a new dataset to evaluate number, gender, and person agreement in Galician-Portuguese (Gl and Pt). This manually created dataset includes tens of target pairs, and contains lexical variants to minimize the impact of collocational or statistical cues.

3   Materials and Methods

Here we present the experiments, data, and models used in the evaluation.

3.1   Experiments and Data

We performed three experiments to explore how Transformer models identify the dependency between a subject and its syntactic head, focusing on the following morphosyntactic features: number and gender, on the one hand, and an additional experiment on the person feature using the inflected infinitive, on the other. Gender and number were evaluated in Gl and Pt, while person agreement was only tested in Galician. The latter decision was made mainly because verbal agreement presents a large variation in Brazilian varieties (e.g., second person pronouns can agree with verb forms in both second and third person) [17], and this may complicate the analysis and interpretation of the results.[3]

To create the dataset, we selected as target (masked) words only those forms appearing in the vocabulary of both monolingual and multilingual models, so that the evaluations of all models can be done on the same number of instances.[4]

Number Agreement: For number agreement, we use subject-verb sentences with a relative clause, e.g., "O $rapaz_i$ que jogava com as $raparigas_j$ $está_i$| *$estão_j$ bem" ('The boy who played with the girls is|*are fine'), where we mask the main verb ("está"), which should have the same number as the subject of its clause ("rapaz"). For each of the verbs with singular and plural forms in the mentioned vocabularies (26 for Galician, and 18 for Portuguese), we created a simple sentence with an embedded relative clause, generating new instances with the following conditions: (i) singular and plural subjects (e.g., "o rapaz", "os rapazes"); (ii) masculine and feminine subjects (e.g., "a(s) rapariga(s)"); (iii) 3 variants for each subject (e.g., "a moça", "o menino", etc.); (iv) an attractor, both in masculine and feminine, with a different number (which may confound a sequential model) as the last noun of the relative clause (e.g., "o menino" vs. "os meninos" and vs. "as meninas");[5] (v) 3 variants of the attractors (as in subject); and (vi) sentences with a longer dependency (e.g., "O rapaz que jogava ontem no parque que foi inaugurado recentemente [...]"). This allowed us to create a total of 4,368 (Gl) and 3,024 (Pt) test items.

Gender Agreement: Here we evaluate the gender agreement between the subject and a predicative adjective, e.g., "Os $rapazes_i$ que jogavam com as $raparigas_j$ são $altos_i$| *$altas_j$" ('The boys who played with the girls are tall$_{Masc}$|*tall$_{Fem}$'), where we mask the adjective ("altos"). As in the first scenario, we assess the impact of attractors, and of the distance of the dependency relation. We used all adjectives with both masculine/feminine and singular/plural forms in the vocabulary (e.g., "alto|alta|altos|altas"), totaling 22 for Galician and 23 for Portuguese. Besides, we generated the same sentence variants as in the first experiment, adapted to gender instead of number agreement. However, in this case, we did not use the number variation for attractors (i.e., both the subject and the attractor have the same number), as the verb inflection would behave as a cue (e.g., "O $rapaz_i$ [...] as $raparigas_j$ $é_i$|$são_j$ masked adjective$_i$"). Therefore, this subset is smaller than the one used for number agreement, having a total of 2,112 instances in Galician, and 2,304 instances in Portuguese.

Person Agreement: We observe if the models identify the person (and number) agreement between an inflected infinitive and its subject, e.g., "Preparei a carne para $vós_i$| *eu| *$nós$... a $comerdes_i$" ('I prepared the meat for you$_{2ndPl}$|*us...to

---

[3] As this variation hardly exists in European Portuguese, the analysis of the person feature can be easily done for this variety, and we leave this for further work. It is worth mentioning, however, that most neural language models for Portuguese are trained using large amounts of Brazilian data.

[4] Data available at https://github.com/crespoalfredo/PROPOR2022-gl-pt.

[5] Note that we also included sentences without attractors to observe their impact.

eat$_{2ndPl}$'), masking the subject ("vós") of the infinitive ("comerdes"). To create this subset we avoided the 1st and 3rd person singular pronouns ("eu", "el|ela", "vostede"), as the inflected infinitive has the same form as the non-inflected one in these persons. Then, we selected the nominative pronouns which appear in the vocabulary of mBERT: 2nd person singular ("ti|tu"), 1st person plural ("nós"), and 3rd person plural ("eles|elas"). We chose 27 verbs and created the following variants: (i) long and short contexts (which here do not modify the distance between the target dependency); (ii) 2 tenses of the main verb (past and future, e.g., "Preparei|Prepararei"); (iii) 2 persons of the main verb (1st and 3rd singular, e.g., "Preparei|Preparou"); (iv) position of the masked pronoun (before/after the infinitive, e.g., "[. . .] para a *comerdes vós*"). This subset has 1,296 instances (Gl).

Table 1. Average sizes (in number of tokens) of the short and long contexts. *Number* and *Gender* include the distances between the dependent elements, where *No* and *Att* refer to contexts without and with attractor, and *Mi* and *Ma* are micro-average and macro-average values, respectively. For person, the values are the length of the sentences, as the distance between the target elements is the same in both contexts.

	Galician								Portuguese							
	Short				Long				Short				Long			
	No	Att	Mi	Ma	No	Att	Mi	Ma	No	Att	Mi	Ma	No	Att	Mi	Ma
Number	4.0	7.1	6.6	5.5	6.1	9.1	8.7	7.6	4.1	8.1	7.5	6.1	6.1	10.1	9.5	8.1
Gender	5.1	7.0	6.5	6.1	9.1	11.0	10.5	10.1	5.1	7.9	7.2	6.5	9.0	11.7	11.0	10.3
Person	3.0				9.5				—				—			

Table 1 includes the size of short and long contexts in all subsets. For number and gender, it shows the distances between the dependent elements with and without attractors, along with their averages. For the person agreement task we show the sentence length, as the distance between the target dependent elements is the same in both contexts.

3.2 Models

We used the official multilingual BERT model (base cased, mBERT) [5] as a baseline, which was trained on Wikipedia's of 101 languages (including Galician and Portuguese), with a cross-lingual vocabulary of 119,547 tokens. Besides, we evaluated the following BERT models (using the *Transformers* library [27]):

Galician: We used the *base* (12 layers) and *small* (6 layers) models described in [9], with 119,547 and 52,000 cased tokens, respectively.[6]

Portuguese: We evaluated the *large* (24 layers) and *base* (12 layers) variants of BERTimbau [24], both of them with a vocabulary size of 30,000 cased tokens.

It is worth noting that the monolingual models were trained with the same corpora for each language, so that differences in the results will be due to the architecture of the networks, or to the different vocabularies of the Galician LMs.

---

[6] We also evaluated the Bertinho models [26], with lower results not discussed here.

3.3 Evaluation

We performed the most common method for TSE in masked language models [10, 19], which involves computing the accuracy by selecting, from the alternatives provided by each instance in the dataset, the one to which the model assigns the highest probability. In the number and gender agreement dependencies, each example includes a pair of alternatives (correct|incorrect, e.g., "is|are"), while for person we may have one or two alternatives as correct, and all the other nominative pronouns as incorrect. For instance, in the following sentence:

"Preparei a carne para a *comeren*$_{3rdPlur}$ *eles*$_{3rdPlurMasc}$|*elas*$_{3rdPlurFem}$."[7]

in which the inflected infinitive ("comeren") is in the 3rd person plural, both masculine and feminine pronouns with the same person are correct, while all the other nominative pronouns are wrong. We compare the sum of the probabilities of both classes (correct and incorrect), and select the highest one.

4 Results and Discussion

Table 2 shows the average results of the three experiments. In Galician, the models followed the same trend in all cases, with BERT-base obtaining the higher results followed by the small and multilingual models. However, in Portuguese, BERT-base has on average slightly better performance than the large model, and mBERT obtained competitive results. Overall, the accuracy values for number and especially for gender are markedly higher than for person agreement (in Gl).

Table 2. Micro-average accuracy in the whole dataset for Galician and Portuguese.

	Galician			Portuguese		
	BERT-base	BERT-small	mBERT	BERT-large	BERT-base	mBERT
Number	0.97	0.95	0.80	0.90	0.91	0.88
Gender	0.98	0.97	0.94	0.95	0.96	0.96
Person	0.73	0.65	0.32	—	—	—

Number Agreement: Figure 1 compares the impact of the attractors in both short and long dependency contexts for number agreement. The first two columns of each model indicate that the attractor produces a low effect in short dependencies (except for mBERT), suggesting that in these cases the model may be identifying the relation between the subject and the verb. The comparison between short and long contexts without attractors (columns 1 and 4) reinforces this finding, as there are no remarkable differences between these values in the

---

[7] "Vostedes" (formal pronoun in the 2nd person plural, agreeing with the 3rd person plural) is not used as it does not appear in the mBERT vocabulary.

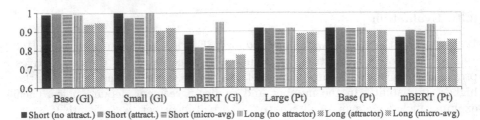

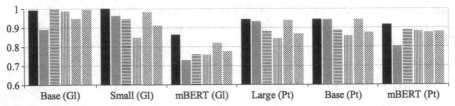

Fig. 1. Accuracy on number agreement in Galician (Gl, left) and Portuguese (Pt, right) for short and long dependencies vs. presence/absence of attractors. For each model, we show six results: first representing short contexts (three bars columns: without attractor, with attractor, and micro-average), and then for long dependency distances.

Fig. 2. Accuracy on number agreement in Galician (Gl, left) and Portuguese (Pt, right) for short and long dependencies vs. number of the main verb. There are 6 results per model: the first pair of columns display singular and plural in short dependencies with attractors; then, the same for plural number; last two columns are the micro-average results (with and without attractors) for singular and plural.

monolingual models. However, columns 4 and 5 in Fig. 1 indicate that the performance of the models (especially mBERT and the Galician monolingual models) in long-distance dependencies is affected by the presence of attractors.

The results in Fig. 2 allow us to compare the performance of the models with respect to the number of the verb of the main clause. The last two columns of BERT-base (Gl) show that it has some bias towards the plural, while the other models (in Gl and Pt) obtain better results with the singular number. Again, this variation is higher in long-distance dependencies (except for mBERT).

Gender Agreement: Overall, the results of gender agreement are higher than those of number, also for the multilingual model (Fig. 3). As expected, the results are slightly lower in long-distance dependencies (columns 1 and 2), and without attractor (columns 3 and 4), except for BERT-base in Portuguese. Regarding the gender of the target relation, BERT-base (Gl) and BERT-large (Pt) show low biases (0.03) towards feminine and masculine, respectively, while the other models seem more stable.

Person Agreement: Concerning subject-inflected infinitive agreement, the results in Table 3 show that BERT-base performs noticeably better in the 1st plural, and similarly in the two other cases. Nevertheless, the small model pro-

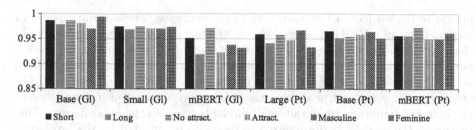

Fig. 3. Accuracy on gender agreement (Gl at left, Pt at right). Each pair of columns on each model displays, respectively, the following scenarios: short and long-distance dependencies; absence and presence of attractors; masculine and feminine subjects.

duced very similar results for the 2nd singular and 1st plural, obtaining higher results in the 3rd person plural. mBERT had relatively similar results in the 1st and 3rd persons of the plural, and an extremely low accuracy in the 2nd singular (0.003, with only 3 correct answers out of 960 instances). Even though further analyses are needed to understand the variation between the base and small models (which were trained on the same corpora), the performance of mBERT on the 2nd singular may be due to the low frequency of this person in writing [1], particularly in the Wikipedia corpus used to train this model.

Table 3. Accuracy vs. person of the inflected infinitive (and its subject) in Galician.

	BERT-base	BERT-small	mBERT
2nd Sing	0.61	0.55	0.00
1st Plur	0.93	0.57	0.42
3rd Plur	0.66	0.81	0.53

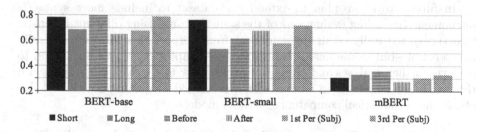

Fig. 4. Accuracy vs. sentence properties in the person agreement test. The variation regarding the tense of the main verb is not shown as it is marginal (average of 0.004).

Finally, Fig. 4 shows pairs of columns to allow for comparisons in the following scenarios: (a) short and long sentences, (b) subject-verb order, and (c) person of the subject of the main verb of the sentence. These variations are in general lower in mBERT, probably due to the low performance of this model in this experiment. Regarding the length of the sentence, both monolingual models perform notoriously better in short contexts, even though context length does not affect the distance of the target dependency. BERT-base (and mBERT) obtains better results at predicting the subject pronoun when it occurs before the inflected infinitive, while the small model behaves in the opposite way. Furthermore, the models' performance also seems to be affected by the properties of the main clause ver—which does not affect morphosyntactically the target relation—, as all the models have higher accuracies with a 3rd singular person. These results may be due to the higher frequency of the 3rd singular person in writing, but further research is needed to explain this behavior.

In summary, these results show that Transformer models, especially monolingual ones, generalize number and gender agreement even in long-distance dependencies, or with the presence of attractors. However, both conditions seem to mislead the models, whose performance drops significantly in this scenario.

5   Conclusions and Further Work

This paper has presented an evaluation of the syntactic capabilities of Transformer models for Galician-Portuguese. The results of the three experiments conducted here, analyzing number, gender, and person features, show that monolingual and multilingual models perform well on number and gender agreements, while person, assessed using inflected infinitives, seems harder to generalize.

Even if the performance in this last evaluation may be influenced by the relatively low frequency of the inflected infinitive in Galician corpora, the differences of the monolingual models (trained on the same corpora) in the three experiments suggest that the models' architecture is crucial, as previous studies have shown [11,13]. In this regard, Baroni proposes careful analyses of the network architectures, treating them as algorithmic linguistic theories instead of empty devices with no priors [2].

In future work, we plan to extend the dataset to include more syntactic phenomena (including evaluations of the same features using different linguistic structures), naturally occurring sentences from corpora, and also semantically non-sensical—but syntactically well-formed—examples. Moreover, we intend to perform further analyses and evaluations that allow to compare our results with those of other languages in similar scenarios, aimed at gaining new knowledge about the grammatical competence of these models.

Acknowledgments. This research is funded by a *Ramón y Cajal* grant (RYC2019-028473-I), by the Galician Government (ERDF 2014-2020: Call ED431G 2019/04, and ED431F 2021/01), and by a summer internship of the CiTIUS Research Center.

References

1. Ariel, M.: The development of person agreement markers: from pronouns to higher accessibility markers. Usage-based models of language, pp. 197–260 (2000)

2. Baroni, M.: On the proper role of linguistically-oriented deep net analysis in linguistic theorizing (2021). arXiv preprint arXiv:2106.08694
3. Bock, K., Miller, C.A.: Broken agreement. Cogn. Psychol. **23**(1), 45–93 (1991)
4. Collobert, R., Weston, J.: A unified architecture for natural language processing: Deep neural networks with multitask learning. In: Proceedings of the 25th International Conference on Machine Learning, pp. 160–167 (2008)
5. Devlin, J., Chang, M.W., Lee, K., Toutanova, K.: BERT: pre-training of deep bidirectional transformers for language understanding. In: Proceedings of the 2019 Conference of the North American Chapter of the Association for Computational Linguistics: Human Language Technologies, vol. 1, pp. 4171–4186. Association for Computational Linguistics, Minneapolis, Minnesota (2019)
6. Edunov, S., Ott, M., Auli, M., Grangier, D.: Understanding back-translation at scale. In: Proceedings of the 2018 Conference on Empirical Methods in Natural Language Processing, pp. 489–500. Association for Computational Linguistics, Brussels, Belgium (2018)
7. Freixeiro Mato, X.R.: Gramática da Lingua Galega IV. Gramática do texto. A Nosa Terra, Vigo (2003)
8. Futrell, R., Wilcox, E., Morita, T., Qian, P., Ballesteros, M., Levy, R.: Neural language models as psycholinguistic subjects: representations of syntactic state. In: Proceedings of the 2019 Conference of the North American Chapter of the Association for Computational Linguistics: Human Language Technologies, vol. 1, pp. 32–42. Association for Computational Linguistics, Minneapolis, Minnesota (2019)
9. Garcia, M.: Exploring the representation of word meanings in context: a case study on homonymy and synonymy. In: Proceedings of the 59th Annual Meeting of the Association for Computational Linguistics and the 11th International Joint Conference on Natural Language Processing, vol. 1, Long Papers, pp. 3625–3640. Association for Computational Linguistics, Online, August 2021
10. Goldberg, Y.: Assessing BERT's Syntactic Abilities (2019). arXiv preprint arXiv:1901.05287
11. Gulordava, K., Bojanowski, P., Grave, E., Linzen, T., Baroni, M.: Colorless green recurrent networks dream hierarchically. In: Proceedings of the 2018 Conference of the North American Chapter of the Association for Computational Linguistics: Human Language Technologies, vol. 1, pp. 1195–1205. Association for Computational Linguistics, New Orleans, Louisiana (2018)
12. Hall Maudslay, R., Cotterell, R.: Do syntactic probes probe syntax? Experiments with jabberwocky probing. In: Proceedings of the 2021 Conference of the North American Chapter of the Association for Computational Linguistics: Human Language Technologies, pp. 124–131. Association for Computational Linguistics (2021)
13. Hu, J., Gauthier, J., Qian, P., Wilcox, E., Levy, R.: A systematic assessment of syntactic generalization in neural language models. In: Proceedings of the 58th Annual Meeting of the Association for Computational Linguistics, pp. 1725–1744. Association for Computational Linguistics (2020)
14. Lindley Cintra, L.F., Cunha, C.: Nova Gramática do Português Contemporâneo. Livraria Sá da Costa, Lisbon (1984)
15. Linzen, T., Baroni, M.: Syntactic structure from deep learning. Ann. Rev. Linguist. **7**, 195–212 (2021)
16. Linzen, T., Dupoux, E., Goldberg, Y.: Assessing the ability of LSTMs to learn syntax-sensitive dependencies. Trans. Assoc. Comput. Linguist. **4**, 521–535 (2016)
17. Lucchesi, D., Baxter, A., da Silva, J.A.A.: A concordância verbal. In: O português afro-brasileiro, pp. 331–371. SciELO Books (2009)

18. Marvin, R., Linzen, T.: Targeted syntactic evaluation of language models. In: Proceedings of the 2018 Conference on Empirical Methods in Natural Language Processing, pp. 1192–1202. Association for Computational Linguistics, Brussels, Belgium (2018)
19. Mueller, A., Nicolai, G., Petrou-Zeniou, P., Talmina, N., Linzen, T.: Cross-linguistic syntactic evaluation of word prediction models. In: Proceedings of the 58th Annual Meeting of the Association for Computational Linguistics, pp. 5523–5539. Association for Computational Linguistics, July 2020
20. Newman, B., Ang, K.S., Gong, J., Hewitt, J.: Refining targeted syntactic evaluation of language models. In: Proceedings of the 2021 Conference of the North American Chapter of the Association for Computational Linguistics: Human Language Technologies, pp. 3710–3723. Association for Computational Linguistics (2021)
21. Radford, A., Narasimhan, K., Salimans, T., Sutskever, I.: Improving language understanding by generative pre-training (2018). https://openai.com/blog/language-unsupervised
22. Samartim, R.: Língua somos: A construção da ideia de língua e da identidade coletiva na Galiza (pré-)constitucional. In: Actas do IX Congreso Internacional de Estudos Galegos. Novas achegas ao estudo da cultura galega II: enfoques socio-históricos e lingüístico-literarios, pp. 27–36. Universidade da Coruña (2012)
23. Schnabel, T., Labutov, I., Mimno, D., Joachims, T.: Evaluation methods for unsupervised word embeddings. In: Proceedings of the 2015 Conference on Empirical Methods in Natural Language Processing, pp. 298–307. Association for Computational Linguistics, Lisbon, Portugal (2015)
24. Souza, F., Nogueira, R., Lotufo, R.: BERTimbau: pretrained BERT models for Brazilian Portuguese. In: Cerri, R., Prati, R.C. (eds.) BRACIS 2020. LNCS (LNAI), vol. 12319, pp. 403–417. Springer, Cham (2020). https://doi.org/10.1007/978-3-030-61377-8_28
25. Vaswani, A., Shazeer, N., Parmar, N., Uszkoreit, J., Jones, L., Gomez, A.N., Kaiser, L., Polosukhin, I.: Attention is All You Need (2017). arXiv preprint arXiv:1706.03762
26. Vilares, D., Garcia, M., Gómez-Rodríguez, C.: Bertinho: Galician BERT representations. Procesamiento del Lenguaje Natural **66**, 13–26 (2021)
27. Wolf, T., et al.: Transformers: state-of-the-art natural language processing. In: Proceedings of the 2020 Conference on Empirical Methods in Natural Language Processing: System Demonstrations, pp. 38–45. Association for Computational Linguistics (2020)

FakeRecogna: A New Brazilian Corpus for Fake News Detection

Gabriel L. Garcia(✉) ⓘ, Luis C. S. Afonso ⓘ, and João P. Papa ⓘ

School of Sciences, São Paulo State University, Bauru, Brazil
{luis.afonso,joao.papa}@unesp.br

Abstract. Fake news has become a research topic of great importance in Natural Language Processing due to its negative impact on our society. Although its pertinence, there are few datasets available in Brazilian Portuguese and mostly comprise few samples. Therefore, this paper proposes creating a new fake news dataset named FakeRecogna that contains a greater number of samples, more up-to-date news, and covering a few of the most important categories. We perform a toy evaluation over the created dataset using traditional classifiers such as Naive Bayes, Optimum-Path Forest, and Support Vector Machines. A Convolutional Neural Network is also evaluated in the context of fake news detection in the proposed dataset.

Keywords: Fake news · Corpus · Portuguese

1 Introduction

Fake news has a significant impact on society, as it affects people's education, decision-making, and attitudes [5]. According to Rubin [27], fake news can be categorized into three main groups: (i) hoaxes, (ii) serious fabrications, and (iii) humorous fakes. Hoaxes are intended to mislead the audience by posing themselves as genuine news. They may cause material damage or even harm to the victim. Serious fabrications stand for articles written by the so-called "yellow press". They can use "clickbait", i.e., a lying headline that does not match the content or hype to get traffic and financial gain. Last but not least, humorous fakes are distinguished from fabricated news, for a reader aware of the satirical intent of the content will not be willing to believe the information.

To reduce the spreading of fake news, news agencies have created and supported many fact-checking pages to verify the veracity of news and explain why the news is fake. Also, many works using Natural Language Processing (NLP) have addressed such a problem. Aphiwongsophon [6] proposed the use of machine learning techniques to detect fake news using three popular methods in the experiments. Ahmed [4] introduced a fake news detection model that uses n-gram analysis and machine learning techniques. Gilda [14] explored term frequency-inverse document frequency (TF-IDF) of bi-grams and probabilistic context-free grammar detection in a corpus of about $11,000$ articles. Jain [17] proposed a

© Springer Nature Switzerland AG 2022
V. Pinheiro et al. (Eds.): PROPOR 2022, LNAI 13208, pp. 57–67, 2022.
https://doi.org/10.1007/978-3-030-98305-5_6

combination of two datasets that contain an equal number of both true and fake news articles on politics. The work extracted linguistic/stylometric features, a bag of words, and TF-IDF features to feed different machine learning models.

Brazil is no different. We can mention the works of Silva et al. [28], which proposed a dataset of labeled real and fake news in Portuguese and performed a comprehensive analysis of machine learning methods for fake news detection. Queiroz et al. [3] compared machine learning algorithms in three languages (English, Portuguese, and Spanish) describing how the results are successful in describing false, satirical, and legitimate news in three different languages. Souza et al. [29] proposed an extended method that, in addition to the grammatical classification and polarity-based sentiment analysis, also applied the analysis of emotions to detect fake news.

However, to tackle such a problem in Brazil, we must have a dataset of local news. Currently, there are only a few datasets in Brazilian Portuguese, which are mostly outdated and not large enough. As an example, one of the most used ones is the *Fake.Br Corpus*, with news dating back from 2016 to 2018. This work proposes building up a new fake news dataset focusing on Brazilian news. The main idea is to collect the most updated news (real and fake ones) from well-known agency news web pages, such as G1, UOL, and Extra, and to increase the number of samples for research. Hence, the main contributions of this work are three-fold:

- A new fake news corpus in Brazilian Portuguese called *FakeRecogna*;
- A larger and updated corpus;
- To foster the research on fake news in Brazilian Portuguese.

The remainder of this paper is organized as follows: Sect. 2 provides a review of related works, while Sect. 3 describes the proposed dataset. Sections 4 and 5 present the methodology and results of a toy-evaluation performed over the proposed dataset, respectively. Finally, Sect. 6 states conclusions.

2   Related Works

This section presents and describes the primary datasets concerning fake news in Brazilian Portuguese.

- Fake.Br: This corpus [20] figures as one of the first and most used datasets concerning fake news in Brazil comprising 7,200 news where 3,600 are fake, and the remaining 3,600 are real ones. The collection was manually analyzed, and only those that were entirely fake were kept in the dataset. An interesting characteristic of this dataset is that for each fake news, a real one was searched by performing a lexical similarity measure using keywords from the fake ones.

– FACTCK.BR: The FACTCK.BR [21] corpus is a dataset in Portuguese structured according to the ClaimReview framework, which was created to ease the sharing of verified news among technological companies. The dataset comprises 1,309 claims with non-binary labels, which are: false, true, impossible to prove, distorted, exaggerated, controversial, without context, and inaccurate, among others. However, the claims in FACTCK.BR are divided between False, Half True, and True.

– Boatos.org: The Kaggle platform[1] provides a dataset comprised of 1,900 fake news verified by Boatos.org, which are either in Portuguese or Spanish. For each fake news, there is a link to a page rebutting it.

– Covid-19 Rumor: The dataset comprises rumors and non-rumors related to COVID-19 collected from three sources: (i) the Brazilian Ministry of Health official website, (ii) a journalistic initiative named Boatos.org focused on debunking online rumors, including COVID-19, and (iii) the O Globo news agency. The COVID-19 RUMOR dataset has 1,291 rumors and 8 non-rumors [12] labeled by the teams of journalists from the sources.

3 FakeRecogna Corpus

This section presents the details behind the design of the proposed corpus. FakeRecogna is a dataset comprised of real and fake news. The real news is not directly linked to fake news and vice-versa, which could lead to a biased classification. The news collection was performed by crawlers developed for mining pages of well-known and of great national importance agency news. The web crawlers were developed based on each analyzed webpage, where the extracted information is first separated into categories and then grouped by dates. The plurality of news on several pages and the different writing styles provide the dataset with great diversity for natural language processing analysis and machine learning algorithms.

The fake news mining was mainly focused on pages created between 2019 and 2021 and mentioned by the Duke Reporters Lab[2], which provides a list of pages that verify the veracity of news worldwide. There were 160 active fact-checking agencies in the world in 2019, and Brazil figures as a growing ecosystem with currently 9 initiatives. Table 1 presents the current initiatives as well as the number of fake news collected from each source. Due to content restrictions, there were considered 6 out of the 9 pages during search with a great variation in the number of fake news extracted from each one, ending in 5,951 samples.

Concerning the real news, the crawlers searched portals such as G1[3], UOL[4] and Extra[5], which are publicly recognized as reliable news outlets, besides the

---

[1] https://www.kaggle.com/rogeriochaves/boatos-de-whatsapp-boatosorg.
[2] https://reporterslab.org/fact-checking/.
[3] https://g1.globo.com/.
[4] https://www.uol.com.br/.
[5] https://extra.globo.com/.

Table 1. Fact-checking agencies in Brazil.

Agency	Web address	# news
AFP checamos	https://checamos.afp.com/afp-brasil	509
Agência Lupa	https://piaui.folha.uol.com.br/lupa/	–
Aos fatos	https://aosfatos.org	–
Boatos.org	https://boatos.org	2,605
Estadão Verifica	https://politica.estadao.com.br/blogs/estadao-verifica	–
E-farsas	https://www.e-farsas.com	812
Fato ou Fake ("Fact or Fake")	https://oglobo.globo.com/fato-ou-fake	1,055
Projeto comprova	https://projetocomprova.com.br	388
UOL confere	https://noticias.uol.com.br/confere	582
total		5,951

Ministry of Health of Brazil[6] home page, resulting in a collection of over $100,000$ samples. From this set, there were filtered out $5,951$ samples to keep the balance between classes and, thus, resulting in a dataset comprised of $11,902$ samples. Each sample has 8 metadata fields, as described in Table 2.

Table 2. Metadata used to describe each sample.

Columns	Description
Title	Title of article
Sub-title (if available)	Brief description of news
News	Information about the article
Category	News grouped according to your information
Author	Publication author
Date	Publication date
URL	Article web address
Class	0 for fake news and 1 for real news

The collected texts are distributed into six categories in relation to their main subjects: Brazil, Entertainment, Health, Politics, Science, and World. These categories are defined based on the journal sections where the news were extracted. The distribution of news by category and its percentages are described in Table 3.

Table 4 provides a comparison among FakeRecogna dataset and the ones mentioned in Sect. 2. Notice that only FACTCK.BR makes uses of a third class, i.e., half true, that considers that a piece of news may contain facts to support a fake idea. However, the class "half true" is not used in the experiments. The FakeRecogna[7] dataset is available as a single XLSX file that contains 8 columns for the metadata, and each row stands for a sample (real or fake news).

---

[6] https://www.gov.br/saude/pt-br.

[7] https://github.com/recogna-lab/datasets/tree/master/FakeRecogna.

Table 3. Amount of news per category in the FakeRecogna.

Category	# news	%
Brazil	904	7.6
Entertainment	1,409	12.0
Health	4,456	37.4
Politics	3,951	33.1
Science	602	5.1
World	580	4.9
total	11,902	100.0

Table 4. Comparison between datasets.

datasets	# news	# real	# fake	# half true
FakeRecogna	11,902	5,951	5,951	—
Fake.Br	7,200	3,600	3,600	—
FACTCK.BR	1,309	411	528	370
Boatos.org	1,900	—	1,900	—
Covid-19 rumor	1,299	8	1,291	—

4 Methodology

This section presents a toy evaluation employed over the proposed dataset.

4.1 Pre-processing

The preprocessing step comprises four steps:

1. Truncation: this step is essential to avoid any classification bias due to the significant variation in size among sentences, especially between fake and real ones. The latter tend to be much longer than the former.
2. Standardization of terms: removal of words that may bias the news, such as, "enganoso", "boato", "#fake" and, so on. Punctuation, special characters, and URLs were also removed and the standardization to lowercase letters.
3. Lemmatization: The lemmatization comprises the morphological analysis of the words resulting in their canonical form [15]. Lemmatization also considers the context of the word to solve other problems, such as disambiguation, that is, differentiating the meaning of identical words depending on the context.
4. Removal of stop words: removal of words considered irrelevant for the understanding of the news, such as articles and prepositions.

All pre-processing steps were performed using the SpaCy library [16], as it uses state-of-the-art approaches for such a purpose. Its performance is usually superior when compared to the Natural Language Toolkit, a.k.a. NLTK [7]. SpaCy also builds up a syntax tree for each sentence, a more robust method that produces much more information about the text.

4.2   Text Representation

The experiments considered two techniques to compute the text representation: (i) Bag-of-Words (BoW) [18], and (ii) FastText [8]. Bag-of-Words computes the text representation as a bag (multiset) of words, disregarding the grammar and even the order of the words, but maintaining the multiplicity, that is, the frequency of each word in the text. The FastText extends the Word2Vec model by representing each word as an n-gram of characters, thus helping to capture the meaning of shorter words and allows embeddings to understand suffixes and prefixes. The parameter values for FastText were: embedding size equals to 200 dimensions, maximum number of unique words as 4,000, and the maximum amount of tokens for each sentence equals to 1,000. Since BoW is a simple text representation, we did not perform experiments using CNN.

4.3   Classifiers

The experiments were performed using the following classifiers:

- Multi-Layer Perceptron (MLP) [2]
- Naive Bayes (NB) [19]
- Optimum-Path Forest (OPF) [23,24]
- Random Forest (RF) [10]
- Support Vector Machines (SVM) [9]
- Convolutional Neural Networks (CNN): [11,13]

Concerning the implementation and parameters, all classifiers but OPF[8] and CNN[9] used the Scikit-learn library [25] with their default parameter values. Regarding the CNN training procedure, the following setup was used: Adam as the optimizer[10] and the Binary Cross Entropy as loss function[11].

4.4   Evaluating Measures

The classifiers were evaluated over four measures: (i) precision, (ii) recall, (iii) f1-score, and (iv) accuracy. The average results over a 5-fold cross-validation are presented in the next section.

---

[8] We used an implementation provided by OPFython library [26].
[9] We used the well-known TensorFlow library [1].
[10] https://keras.io/api/optimizers/adam/.
[11] https://keras.io/api/losses/probabilistic_losses/.

4.5   Additional Experiments

No Removal of Words. One of the preprocessing steps perform the removal of words that might bias the news (e.g., "enganoso", "boato", and "#fake"). This experiment evaluates whether removing the standardization of terms step from the workflow has any influence in the classification process and the lemmatization step. The experiment is performed using all aforementioned text representation techniques and classifiers.

Data Augmentation. The second additional experiment studies the impact of adding the data from FakeRecogna to other datasets. This experiment uses the Fake.Br and FACTCK.BR datasets being classified by the CNN and Fast-Text for text representation in two rounds. The first round classifies the original datasets, whereas the second round merges the datasets mentioned above with FakeRecogna. Notice that the experimental protocol is the same as discussed in the following section.

5   Experimental Results

Table 6 presents the average results for each text representation and classification techniques, with the best results in bold. A more in-depth analysis shows us that the best result with the BoW was achieved by the MLP classifier, followed by RandomForest and SVM, with results that surpassed more than 90% of correct answers. The outcomes show that even using a standard natural language processing technique, i.e., BoW, the achieved results were very interesting (Table 5).

Table 5. Experimental results over FakeRecogna corpus.

Classifier	Precision		Recall		F1-score		Accuracy	
	BoW	FastText	BoW	FastText	BoW	FastText	BoW	FastText
MLP	**0.931**	**0.850**	**0.931**	**0.848**	**0.930**	**0.848**	**93.1%**	**84.8%**
NB	0.896	0.712	0.898	0.680	0.897	0.666	89.7%	68.1%
OPF	0.834	0.784	0.834	0.784	0.834	0.782	83.4%	78.4%
RF	0.924	0.840	0.922	0.840	0.922	0.840	92.3%	84.0%
SVM	0.926	0.832	0.925	0.810	0.926	0.804	92.5%	80.8%
CNN	-	**0.942**	-	**0.942**	-	**0.942**	-	**94.28%**

On the other hand, using a more robust text pre-processing architecture like FastText and the Convolutional Neural Network, the best results surpassed 94%. FastText was considered here for its enriched representations where each word is represented by an embedding of the entire word itself plus its n-grams. Skip-Gram, for example, provides simpler presentations that take into account only the word itself.

5.1 No Removal of Words

This experiment evaluates the influence of both keeping words and terms that may bias the classification and removing the lemmatization step. By the results, FastText provided a slight increase in precision and accuracy. However, BoW as text representation faced a degradation in its precision. We believe the experiments using BoW were deeply affected by the removal of the lemmatization step, since that words and its variations are kept. For instance, the words *playing*, *plays*, and *played* all become *play* after lemmatization.

Table 6. Experimental results over FakeRecogna corpus without pre-processing.

Classifier	Precision		Recall		F1-score		Accuracy	
	BoW	FastText	BoW	FastText	BoW	FastText	BoW	FastText
MLP	**0.926**	**0.848**	**0.926**	**0.844**	**0.926**	**0.844**	**92.6%**	**84.3%**
NB	0.896	0.730	0.896	0.688	0.896	0.674	89.6%	69.1%
OPF	0.680	0.778	0.660	0.776	0.652	0.776	65.9%	77.7%
RF	0.918	0.840	0.918	0.840	0.918	0.840	91.8%	84.0%
SVM	0.918	0.820	0.918	0.796	0.918	0.786	91.8%	79.5%
CNN	–	**0.942**	–	**0.942**	–	**0.942**	–	**94.26%**

5.2 Augmentation Study

As mentioned earlier, the experiments concerning data augmentation were performed using the same CNN from the previous section since it achieved the best results. The main goal of this experiment is to evaluate how much the accuracy can be increased when the FakeRecogna dataset is used to augment Fake.Br and FACTCK.BR datasets. Table 7 presents the experimental results for the original and augmented datasets.

Table 7. Experimental results concerning data augmentation.

Dataset	Precision	Recall	F1-score	Accuracy
Fake.Br	**0,954**	**0,954**	**0,954**	**95.4%**
Fake.Br+FakeRecogna	0.946	0,946	0,946	94.6%
FACTCK.BR	0,871	0,871	0,871	87.7%
FACTCK.BR+FakeRecogna	**0,933**	**0,933**	**0,933**	**93.3%**

According to the results, the best outcome (95.4%) was achieved over the original Fake.Br dataset. By joining Fake.Br to FakeRecogna, the accuracy has a minor decrease. One reason for such a decrease is that each fake news has some level of similarity to some real news, which is a characteristic that is not present in the FakeRecogna dataset. Notice that a few other works, such as one of Okano et al. [22], achieved a higher accuracy (96%) but using the raw text, which may bias the results since real news are usually much longer than fake ones. Regarding the FACTCK.BR dataset, we obtained 87.7% of accuracy over the original data and 93.2% by merging it with FakeRecogna, an improvement of more than 5%. This scenario would be the closest to reality since both datasets' real and fake news do not share any similar relationship between them.

6 Conclusions and Future Works

In this paper, we proposed a new corpus for fake news detection in Brazilian Portuguese called FakeRecogna. The proposed corpus presents a series of advantages over the existing ones, which include:

- Up-to-date news (2019–2021);
- Greater number of categories;
- Greater number of news;
- It covers current issues, such as the Covid-19 pandemic;
- Multiple sources;
- Internationally recognized sources.

By building up the dataset, we hope to foster the research on fake news detection over texts in Brazilian Portuguese since the low number of samples available drives most works to English-based datasets.

Additionally, we performed experiments in which we managed to produce interesting results considering the problem's difficulty. There were employed two text representation techniques and six classifiers, with accuracies higher than 90% in some cases.

As future works, we intend to extract more fake news from other sources to increase the dataset size and use other word embeddings. Regarding deep learning, we intend to consider new architectures such as attention models and BERT.

Acknowledgments. The authors are grateful to FAPESP grants #2013/07375-0, #2014/12236-1, and #2019/07665-4, and CNPq grants #307066/2017-7 and #427968/2018-6.

References

1. Abadi, M., et al.: TensorFlow: a system for large-scale machine learning. In: Proceedings of the 12th USENIX Conference on Operating Systems Design and Implementation, pp. 265–283. OSDI 2016, USENIX Association, USA (2016)
2. Abirami, S., Chitra, P.: Energy-efficient edge based real-time healthcare support system. In: Raj, P., Evangeline, P. (eds.) The Digital Twin Paradigm for Smarter Systems and Environments: The Industry Use Cases, Advances in Computers, vol. 117, pp. 339–368. Elsevier, Amsterdam (2020)

3. Abonizio, H.Q., de Morais, J.I., Tavares, G.M., Barbon Junior, S.: Language-independent fake news detection: English, Portuguese, and Spanish mutual features. Future Internet **12**(5), 87 (2020)
4. Ahmed, H., Traore, I., Saad, S.: Detection of online fake news using N-gram analysis and machine learning techniques. In: Traore, I., Woungang, I., Awad, A. (eds.) ISDDC 2017. LNCS, vol. 10618, pp. 127–138. Springer, Cham (2017). https://doi.org/10.1007/978-3-319-69155-8_9
5. Allcott, H., Gentzkow, M.: Social media and fake news in the 2016 election. J. Econ. Perspect. **31**, 211–236 (2017)
6. Aphiwongsophon, S., Chongstitvatana, P.: Detecting fake news with machine learning method. In: 2018 15th International Conference on Electrical Engineering/Electronics, Computer, Telecommunications and Information Technology (ECTI-CON), pp. 528–531 (2018)
7. Bird, S., Klein, E., Loper, E.: Natural Language Processing with Python: Analyzing Text with the Natural Language Toolkit. O'Reilly Media Inc., Sebastopol (2009)
8. Bojanowski, P., Grave, E., Joulin, A., Mikolov, T.: Enriching word vectors with subword information. Trans. Assoc. Comput. Linguist. **5**, 135–146 (2017)
9. Boser, B.E., Guyon, I.M., Vapnik, V.N.: A training algorithm for optimal margin classifiers. In: Proceedings of the Fifth Annual Workshop on Computational Learning Theory, pp. 144–152. COLT 1992, Association for Computing Machinery, New York, NY, USA (1992)
10. Breiman, L.: Random forests. Mach. Learn. **45**(1), 5–32 (2001)
11. Dalto, M., Matuško, J., Vašak, M.: Deep neural networks for ultra-short-term wind forecasting, pp. 1657–1663 (2015)
12. Endo, P.T., et al.: Covid-19 rumor: a classified dataset of covid-19 related online rumors in Brazilian Portuguese. In: Mendeley Data V3 (2021)
13. Ferreira, A., Giraldi, G.: Convolutional neural network approaches to granite tiles classification. Expert Syst. App. **84**, 19–29 (2017)
14. Gilda, S.: Evaluating machine learning algorithms for fake news detection. In: 2017 IEEE 15th Student Conference on Research and Development (SCOReD), pp. 110–115 (2017)
15. Hippisley, A.: Lexical analysis. In: Indurkhya, N., Damerau, F.J. (eds.) Handbook of Natural Language Processing, 2nd edn., pp. 31–58. Chapman and Hall/CRC, Boca Raton (2010)
16. Honnibal, M., Montani, I.: spaCy 2: natural language understanding with Bloom embeddings, convolutional neural networks and incremental parsing. To Appear **7**, 411–420 (2017)
17. Jain, M.K., Gopalani, D., Meena, Y.K., Kumar, R.: Machine learning based fake news detection using linguistic features and word vector features. In: 2020 IEEE 7th Uttar Pradesh Section International Conference on Electrical, Electronics and Computer Engineering (UPCON), pp. 1–6 (2020)
18. Mikolov, T., Chen, K., Corrado, G., Dean, J.: Efficient estimation of word representations in vector space. In: Bengio, Y., LeCun, Y. (eds.) 1st International Conference on Learning Representations, ICLR 2013, Scottsdale, Arizona, USA, 2–4 May 2013, Workshop Track Proceedings (2013)
19. Mitchell, T.M.: Machine Learning. McGraw-Hill, New York (1997)
20. Monteiro, R.A., et al.: Contributions to the study of fake news in Portuguese: new corpus and automatic detection results. In: Villavicencio, A., et al. (eds.) PROPOR 2018. LNCS (LNAI), vol. 11122, pp. 324–334. Springer, Cham (2018). https://doi.org/10.1007/978-3-319-99722-3_33

21. Moreno, J.a., Bressan, G.: Factck.br: a new dataset to study fake news. In: Proceedings of the 25th Brazillian Symposium on Multimedia and the Web, pp. 525–527. WebMedia 2019, Association for Computing Machinery, New York, NY, USA (2019)
22. Okano, E.Y., Liu, Z., Ji, D., Ruiz, E.E.S.: Fake news detection on Fake.Br using hierarchical attention networks. In: Quaresma, P., Vieira, R., Aluísio, S., Moniz, H., Batista, F., Gonçalves, T. (eds.) PROPOR 2020. LNCS (LNAI), vol. 12037, pp. 143–152. Springer, Cham (2020). https://doi.org/10.1007/978-3-030-41505-1_14
23. Papa, J.P., Falcão, A.X., Albuquerque, V.H.C., Tavares, J.M.R.S.: Efficient supervised optimum-path forest classification for large datasets. Pattern Recogn. **45**(1), 512–520 (2012)
24. Papa, J.P., Falcão, A.X., Suzuki, C.T.N.: Supervised pattern classification based on optimum-path forest. Int. J. Imaging Syst. Technol. **19**(2), 120–131 (2009)
25. Pedregosa, F., et al.: Scikit-learn: machine learning in python. J. Mach. Learn. Res. **12**(Oct), 2825–2830 (2011)
26. de Rosa, G.H., Papa, J.P., Falcão, A.X.: OPFython: a python-inspired optimum-path forest classifier (2020). https://arxiv.org/abs/2001.10420
27. Rubin, V.L., Chen, Y., Conroy, N.J.: Deception detection for news: three types of fakes. In: Proceedings of the 78th ASIST Annual Meeting: Information Science with Impact: Research in and for the Community, ASIST 2015, American Society for Information Science, USA (2015)
28. Silva, R.M., Santos, R.L., Almeida, T.A., Pardo, T.A.: Towards automatically filtering fake news in Portuguese. Expert Syst. App. **146**, 113199 (2020)
29. de Souza, M.P., da Silva, F.R.M., Freire, P.M.S., Goldschmidt, R.R.: A linguistic-based method that combines polarity, emotion and grammatical characteristics to detect fake news in Portuguese. In: Proceedings of the Brazilian Symposium on Multimedia and the Web, pp. 217–224. WebMedia 2020, Association for Computing Machinery, New York, NY, USA (2020)

Implicit Opinion Aspect Clues in Portuguese Texts: Analysis and Categorization

Mateus Tarcinalli Machado[1]([⊠])[iD], Thiago Alexandre Salgueiro Pardo[1][iD],
Evandro Eduardo Seron Ruiz[2][iD], Ariani Di Felippo[3][iD],
and Francielle Vargas[1][iD]

[1] Interinstitutional Center for Computational Linguistics (NILC),
Institute of Mathematical and Computer Sciences, University of São Paulo,
São Carlos, Brazil
{mateusmachado,francielleavargas}@usp.br, taspardo@icmc.usp.br
[2] Department of Computing and Mathematics, University of São Paulo,
Ribeirão Preto, Brazil
evandro@usp.br
[3] Interinstitutional Center for Computational Linguistics (NILC),
Department of Language and Literature, Federal University of São Carlos,
São Carlos, Brazil
arianidf@gmail.com

Abstract. Although very useful, aspect-based sentiment analysis shows several challenges. The occurrence of implicit aspects is one of them. To improve our understanding of implicit aspects, this work analyzes their composition and categorizes the implicit aspect clues found in two corpora of opinionated texts of different domains in the Portuguese language. As results of this work, in addition to the implicit aspect typology, we present four lexicons of implicit aspect clues for different domains and the annotation of implicit aspect clues in an existing corpus.

Keywords: Sentiment analysis · Implicit aspects · Lexicon · Corpus annotation

1 Introduction

Sentiment analysis is a growing research area of natural language processing, at the intersection between Linguistics and Computer Science. It aims to automatically determine sentiments in texts [19], analyze people's opinions, feelings, assessments, attitudes, and emotions concerning entities such as products, services, organizations, individuals, issues, events, topics, and their attributes [9].

The most refined sentiment analysis level is the aspect-based one, which must determine people's opinion about specific features (the aspects) of an entity [11, 16,25]. To do this, it is necessary to identify the entities, their respective aspects,

© Springer Nature Switzerland AG 2022
V. Pinheiro et al. (Eds.): PROPOR 2022, LNAI 13208, pp. 68–78, 2022.
https://doi.org/10.1007/978-3-030-98305-5_7

and the so-called opinion-words related to each aspect. Most systems that perform aspect-based sentiment analysis divide the problem into three steps [14]:

- **Aspect term extraction**: this step identifies the aspect terms. For example, analyses of opinionated texts about a smartphone might reveal "measurements", "volume", and "response time" aspects [9,10,18,26].
- **Aspect Term Sentiment Estimation**: this step estimates the polarity and/or the intensity of opinion for each aspect term of the entity [9,13,20].
- **Aspect Aggregation**: some systems group aspect terms that are synonymous or near synonymous (e.g., "price" and "cost") or group aspect terms ("chicken", "steak" and "fish" can be replaced by "food") [9,10,27,28].

A challenging issue related to the aspect term extraction step is how the aspects appear in the texts. They may be explicit or implicit aspects. Explicit aspects are those directly mentioned in the text, such as the aspect "size" in "The size of the smartphone is adequate". On the other hand, implicit aspects are not directly referenced, as in the examples "The smartphone is too small" and "The smartphone barely fits in my pocket", where "size" is signaled by the adjective "small" and the expression "fits in my pocket". These terms or expressions that refer to implicit aspects are called Implicit Aspect Clues (IACs). We use a definition similar to that established by Cruz, Gelbukh, and Sidorov [1], where, from a predefined set of aspects, we find the related IACs, differing from Liu [9] that defined explicit aspects as nouns and noun phrases and other expressions as implicit aspects. According to Zhang and Zhu [29], about 30% of the reviews in their corpus contain implicit aspects. Panchendrarajan et al. [12] says that over 15% of the sentences in their corpus had one or more implicit aspects and that 92% of the aspects related to restaurant employees were implicitly mentioned. Such numbers show the relevance of the phenomenon.

Given the difficulty of dealing with implicit aspects, most of the researches in the area addresses only explicit aspects. A survey done by K. Ravi and V. Ravi [17] evaluated 160 papers on sentiment analysis and reported that 23 performed aspect extraction and only 4 analyzed implicit aspects. Rana and Cheah [16] evaluated 45 researches related to aspect extraction and found only 7 studies that analyzed the issue of the implicit aspects. Besides the difficulty, one may also explain the lack of researches that deal with implicit aspects by the high frequency of the explicit ones, which are enough for several applications.

Another important issue to be addressed is the language. Most works analyze texts written only in English or Chinese. In the papers of Tubishat, Idris, and Abushariah [21] and Ganganwar and Rajalakshmi [5], 53 articles dealing with implicit aspects were analyzed, of which 33 applied to texts in English, 19 in Chinese, and 1 in French. In Portuguese, the number of works is scarce. In the survey carried out by Pereira [15], the author found only two papers dealing with implicit aspects, namely, Freitas and Vieira [3] and Vargas and Pardo [22].

In order to better understand the issue, this paper presents a deep analysis and categorization of the IACs found in two corpora of opinionated texts of different domains in the Portuguese language, analyzing the composition of IACs and the necessary inferences to identify the corresponding aspects. As far as we know, there is no other initiative that does a similar work. We also introduce four lexicons of IACs and annotate a corpus with the related aspects. We hope that such effort and the resources that it brings may contribute to improve sentiment analysis applications for Portuguese.

In what follows, we briefly introduce the main related work, especially the ones that present corpus analyses for Portuguese. In Sect. 3, we present the analyzed data and the methods that we used, introducing our lexicons of IACs. In Sect. 4, we report a summary of everything that we found in our corpus analysis. Finally, in Sect. 5, we present some final remarks.

2   Related Work

As commented before, few works deal with implicit aspects. Fundamental to any work is the existence of a corpus containing annotated implicit aspects. We selected some of these few works that present this type of dataset.

In Cruz, Gelbukh, and Sidorov [1], the authors argue about the scarcity of resources and, to solve this gap, they manually annotated IACs in Hu and Liu [8] corpus for English. The authors implemented four methods to identify IACs, three simpler methods to serve as baselines, and a fourth based on supervised machine learning.

Vargas and Pardo [22] organized and clustered aspects in opinions in Portuguese. As a result, the authors presented one of the few existent corpora with identified implicit aspects for this language. The authors [23] also investigated methods for grouping explicit and implicit aspects in opinion texts, using the previous corpus. They compared six clustering methods: four linguistic methods, one statistical, and a new one that analyzes the relations between detected aspects, such as synonyms, hypernyms and diminutives, among others. Finally, the authors [24] describe a set of rules for extracting explicit and implicit aspects using psychological verbs and semantic relations.

Freitas and Vieira [3] evaluated available resources for the analysis of feelings in the Portuguese language. For this, they formed a dataset with reviews about hotels, manually marking the explicit aspects, the existence of implicit ones, and the related feeling. The authors compare different part of speech taggers, sentiment lexicons, the impact of linguistic rules, and the position of adjectives. The authors [4] also present a method for aspect-based sentiment analysis, in which the identification of explicit and implicit aspects is based on a domain ontology.

3   Data and Methods

3.1   Methods

As mentioned before, the resources that incorporate the identification of implicit aspects are scarce. To improve this scenario, we analyzed the dataset presented by Freitas and Vieira [3] and performed the identification of the IACs in this corpus, thus creating another dataset suitable for this type of task. We also categorized all IACs and those present in the research of Vargas and Pardo [22], creating a typology related to the composition of each term and the necessary inferences to identify the aspects.

3.2   Datasets

We analyzed the datasets of Vargas and Pardo [22] and Freitas and Vieira [3]. The first one has 180 reviews of cameras, books, and smartphones extracted from Buscapé [6] and ReLi [2] corpora. The authors manually marked the explicit and implicit aspects and grouped the similar ones. The second corpus has 194 reviews about hotels collected from the TripAdvisor website. The explicit aspects and the presence of implicit aspects in the texts were manually annotated, but IACs were not tagged.

3.3   Identification of IACs

We initially analyzed the 194 reviews from Freitas and Vieira [3], and located the respective IACs in the texts. To do this, we aimed to get the smallest number of terms or words that might identify the implicit aspect. For this purpose, a human annotator marked all the terms that implicitly referred to the aspects in the corpus.

For example, the review that contains the sentence "*O preço indica o que receberá como serviço: um hotel simples*" (The price indicates what you will receive as a service: a simple hotel.) was already marked with the presence of an implicit aspect related to "instalation" and, in this case, the annotator marked the expression "*hotel simples*" (simple hotel) as the related IAC. In a second step, the IACs were checked for cases of dubiousness (when they appeared related to other aspects) and minimality (if they were in their shortest viable form). For example, it was checked whether "*hotel simples*" appeared related to some other aspect and also whether the expression could be reduced to "hotel" or "simples" in a way that it would indicate only one aspect. For example, if we consider only the word "*hotel*" as IAC, we can find it related to other aspects, such as "cleanliness" in "*o hotel é limpo*" (the hotel is clean), or not related to any aspect, as in "*tive que ficar neste hotel*" (I had to stay at this hotel). The same happens with the word "*simples*" (simple) in "*café da manhã simples*" (simple breakfast), where the word is related to the aspect "meal", and in "*uma variedade de locais simples para comer*" (a variety of simple places to eat), where it is not related to any aspect. Therefore, only the complete expression ("hotel simples") is related to the aspect "installation". After these identification steps, the list of IACs was once more reviewed by other humans (also from the Computational Linguistics area), in order to possibly refine it.

3.4 Lexicons of IACs

After the identification of IACs, we analyzed the datasets to create lexicons of IACs. These resources may be very useful for developing tools for identifying implicit aspects and improving the results of sentiment analysis tasks.

We analyzed the IACs and grouped them by domain, removing and correcting any eventual spelling errors. We could then create four lexicons, one for each domain. IACs were grouped according to the aspects they refer to. A summary of the composition of the corpora and lexicons of IACs is shown in Table 1.

Table 1. Statistics for corpora and lexicons

Domains	Reviews	Words	Aspects	Explicit aspects		Implicit aspects		Lexicon
Cameras	60	3,997	352	299	84.94%	53	15.06%	39
Books	60	5,515	330	304	92.12%	26	7.88%	24
Smartphones	60	6,210	455	387	85.05%	68	14.95%	48
Hotels	194	13,940	1,417	999	70.50%	415	29.50%	213

As illustration, Fig. 1 shows part of our lexicon of IACs for camera domain. In the example, the IACs *"filma em hd"* (shots in hd) and "megapixels" are related to the aspect "resolution" of the camera.

```
<Resolution>
  <item>filma em hd (shoots in hd)</item>
  <item>megapixels</item>
</Resolution>
<Weight>
  <item>leve (weightless)</item>
  <item>leveza (weightlessness)</item>
</Weight>
```

Fig. 1. Part of the lexicon of IACs related to cameras

In a second analysis, we verified the part of speech tags of the terms identified as aspects. For this, we used the tagger in spaCy [7]. Table 2 presents these results, and we can see a dominance of nouns for the explicit aspects. For the implicit ones, this distribution is more diversified, but we can observe a higher frequency of NOUNs, ADJs, and VERBs. We also noticed that there are terms of different part of speech tags that refer to the same aspects, such as the nouns *"pagamento"* (payment) and *"custo"* (cost), the adjectives *"caro"* (expensive) and *"barato"* (cheap) and the verb *"pagar"* (to pay), all related to "price".

Table 2. The part of speech tags of the aspect terms

Explicit aspects

Camera			Book			Smartphone			Hotel		
TAG	QTY	%	TAG	QTY	%	TAG	QTY	%	TAG	QTY	%
NOUN	337	73.4%	NOUN	228	64.4%	NOUN	358	70.1%	NOUN	835	81.1%
ADP	56	12.2%	PROPN	99	28.0%	PROPN	78	15.3%	ADP	91	8.8%
PROPN	42	9.2%	ADP	10	2.8%	ADP	34	6.7%	PROPN	71	6.9%
ADJ	17	3.7%	VERB	7	2.0%	ADJ	33	6.5%	ADJ	30	2.9%
X	3	0.7%	DET	6	1.7%	X	2	0.4%	VERB	2	0.2%

Implicit aspects

NOUN	28	32.2%	VERB	18	28.6%	ADJ	35	31.8%	NOUN	494	49.1%
ADJ	24	27.6%	NOUN	16	25.4%	VERB	25	22.7%	ADJ	134	13.3%
VERB	13	14.9%	ADP	8	12.7%	NOUN	23	20.9%	ADP	111	11.0%
SCONJ	9	10.3%	DET	5	7.9%	ADP	9	8.2%	VERB	95	9.4%
PROPN	6	6.9%	PRON	4	6.3%	SCONJ	8	7.3%	ADV	69	6.9%

3.5 Categorization of IACs

To better understand the composition of implicit aspects and the necessary inference to identify them, we analyzed each of the IACs. In particular, we aimed to identify what type of information, or characteristics of the text, led to the identification of the aspects. For example, in the sentence "*A camera é muito fácil de usar*" (The camera is very easy to use), we have the IAC "*fácil de usar*" (easy to use) related to the "usability" aspect. Here, we can see that the IAC makes use of an action that refers to the implicit aspect. In other situations, the identification of this relationship can be more complicated, as in the IAC "*auto explicativa*" (self-explanatory), also related to the "usability" aspect.

A human annotator made an initial categorization of the IACs. Other annotators (computational linguists) then reviewed the identified categories. After this step, the annotator made a second round of annotation, refining the categories into subcategories, and the discussion and review process was repeated. With this analysis, we came with four main categories of IACs: event, features, qualification and contextual-related IACs. Table 3 presents these categories, possible subcategories that we also identified, and examples. We explain the categories in what follows.

Event (Action/Process/State): The identification of IACs takes place through the identification of actions, processes, or states related to the aspect. It is not necessarily a verb; it can be a term that refers to the verb tha it is related to the aspect. Here, the IAC may be sub-classified as "non-verbal form", or, when this type of IAC is directly identified by the verb, we classified them as "verb". For this category, it is necessary that the person use, in addition to knowledge about the context, some knowledge about the language. For example, in "*pagamento*" (payment), it is necessary to identify that the noun is related to the verb "to pay", and that both are actions related to the "price" aspect.

In other situations, this relationship is not so clear, for example, in *"recebi chamadas até na beira do rio"* (received calls even on the riverbank), the expression refers to the aspect "signal" of a smartphone and its main part is the expression "to receive calls".

Feature: The IACs of this type are directly related to the aspect or part of the aspect. They can be found as "attributes", or related to the aspects in the following relations: "equivalence", "is-a", or "part-of". For the attribute subcategory, the person needs to know the characteristics of the aspect, for example, the IACs *"material"* (related to the "design" aspect) and *"a recepção é muito boa"* (the reception is very good) ("signal" aspect). In the equivalence relationship, the IAC has a very similar meaning to the aspect, as in *"higiene"* (hygiene) ("cleanliness" aspect) and in *"cada centavo investido"* (every penny invested) ("price" aspect). In the is-a subcategory, we have items related to the aspect, such as the IAC *"café da manhã"* (breakfast), which is a type of "food", or *"pessoal que atende na portaria"* (people who work at the concierge), where the person refers to the concierge staff who is a type of "employee". Lastly, in the part-of case, the IAC is part of the aspect, as in *"banheiro"* (bathroom) or *"local para guardar roupas"* (place to store clothes), both related to hotel "facilities".

Qualification: The IAC is presented as a quality or sentiment about the aspect, without directly mentioning it. In most of the cases, the IAC contains an "adjective" as its major component. In other cases, the IAC appears in an "equivalence" relation to an adjective related to the aspect. We also found IACs represented by adjectives converted to "nominal forms". To differentiate adjectives and nominal forms, it is necessary to make use of knowledge about the language. We have, for example, the IAC *"bonita"* (beautiful), that is an adjective, and *"beleza"* (beauty), that is a nominal form, both related to "design". In the equivalence subcategory, we find IACs as *"hotel simples"* (simple hotel), where the combination of the adjective and the noun refers to the aspect (in this case, "facilities").

Contextual: To relate an IAC of this category to its respective aspect, it is necessary to access world knowledge about the product or service being analyzed, such as its operation, modes of use, or content. We have subdivided this category into "location" and "related". In the "location" subcategory, we classified the IACs related to the place where the product is located. This reference to location can be direct as in *"fica na região central"* (is in the center of the region) or indirect as in *"consegue ir a pé até o mercado público"* (can walk to the public market). In any case, the reader must access knowledge of expressions related to places in order to correctly identify the aspect. The "related" subcategory includes other difficult cases that do not refer to location. For example, in *"sociedade do big brother"* (big brother society), some knowledge about the content of a book is required. In the case of *"cheiro de mofo"* (musty smell), the person needs to be aware that the lack of cleaning causes such smell in order to be able to relate the IAC to the cleanliness aspect.

Table 3. Categories, subcategories, aspects and examples of IACs

Category	Subcategory	Aspect	Corresponding IAC
Event	Non-verbal form	Usability	*fácil de usar* (ease of use)
		price	*pagamento* (payment)
	Verb	Subject	*fala de* (talks about)
		battery	*descarrega* (discharge)
Feature	Attribute	Design	*material* (material)
		image	*modo noite* (night mode)
	Equivalence	Employee	*equipe* (team)
		cleanliness	*higiene* (hygiene)
	Is-a	Food	*pratos* (dishes)
		employee	*recepcionista* (receptionist)
	Part-of	Facilities	*banheiro* (bathroom)
		attendance	*atendentes* (attendants)
Qualification	Adjective	Design	*elegante* (elegant)
		installation	*mobiliado* (furnished)
	Equivalence	Installation	*hotel simples* (simple hotel)
		price	*diárias acessíveis* (affordable rates)
	Nominal form	Design	*beleza* (beauty)
		speed	*rapidez* (rapidity)
Contextual	Location	Location	*fácil acesso ao centro* (easy access to downtown)
		Location	*consegue ir a pé até o mercado público* (can walk to the public market)
	Related	Installation	*infiltrações* (infiltrations)
		cleanliness	*cheira a mofo* (musty smell)

4   Results

Analyzing the data from the lexicons of IACs, we noticed that the studied domains are very different, resulting in difficulties for building domain-independent tools for extracting aspects. However, we did find some common terms, mainly for the camera and smartphone domains, as they are both electronic products. Table 4 presents these common IACs. It is worth mentioning the IAC "*barata*", which is a homograph case that may be translated to "cheap" (not expensive) or "cockroach" (the insect) in English, depending on the context where it is used. For instance, in the Table 4, when it is used for camera domain, it refers to the "price" aspect; when it is used to hotel domain, it refers to "cleanliness".

Table 5 shows the percentage of categories and subcategories in each domain. Cameras and smartphones showed some similar tendencies, in particular, the qualification category prevailed, with 47% and 51%, respectively. For books, the most frequent one was "event", with 52%. For hotels, "feature" was the most frequent one.

Table 4. Common identified IACs

IAC	Domain	Aspect	Domain	Aspect
barata (cheap/cockroach)	Camera	Price	Hotel	Cleanliness
barato (cheap)	Hotel	Price	Smartphone	Price
beleza (beauty)	Camera	Design	Smartphone	Design
demora a responder (delay to respond)	Camera	Velocity	Smartphone	Velocity
fácil de usar (easy to use)	Camera	Usability	Smartphone	Usability
leve (lightweight)	Camera	Weight	Smartphone	Weight
leveza (lightness)	Camera	Weight	Smartphone	Weight
versátil (versatile)	Camera	Design	Smartphone	Design

Table 5. Distribution of categories and subcategories of IACs in the domains

Category	Subcategory	Books	Cameras	Smartphones	Hotels
Event	Non-verbal form	0%	11%	4%	1%
	Verb	**52%**	17%	26%	1%
Feature	Attribute	0%	15%	3%	0%
	Equivalence	20%	2%	0%	19%
	Is-a	4%	0%	1%	13%
	Part-of	0%	0%	0%	**30%**
Qualification	Adjective	0%	**47%**	51%	11%
	Equivalence	0%	0%	0%	2%
	Nominal form	0%	6%	9%	0%
Contextual	Local	0%	0%	0%	9%
	Related	24%	2%	4%	14%

5   Final Remarks

This paper presented a deep study of implicit aspects and how to categorize them according to the necessary inferences for their identification. We hope that such characterization, together with the IAC lexicons and the annotated corpora, may foster the development of better sentiment analysis applications for Portuguese.

It is important to notice that the categories that we propose have some overlapping characteristics. For instance, it is not only the "contextual" category that makes use of "world knowledge", but some predominant characteristic may be found in order to categorize the cases. However, we do acknowledge the fact that, depending on the analysis style, different categorizations might be proposed. The categorization in this paper is one possible proposal among other possibilities.

The interested reader may find more information at the web portal of the POeTiSA project (*POrtuguese processing - Towards Syntactic Analysis and parsing*)[1] or in our repository at GitHub[2].

Acknowledgement. The authors are grateful to the Center for Artificial Intelligence (C4AI), with support of the São Paulo Research Foundation (grant #2019/07665-4) and IBM Corporation.

References

1. Cruz, I., Gelbukh, A.F., Sidorov, G.: Implicit aspect indicator extraction for aspect based opinion mining. Int. J. Comput. Linguist. App. **5**(2), 135–152 (2014)
2. Freitas, C., Motta, E., Milidiú, R.L., César, J.: Vampiro Que Brilha... Rá! Desafios Na Anotação De Opinião Em Um Corpus De Resenhas De Livros. In: XI Encontro de Linguística de Corpus (ELC 2012). São Paulo (2012)
3. d. Freitas, L.A., Vieira, R.: Exploring resources for sentiment analysis in Portuguese language. In: 2015 Brazilian Conference on Intelligent Systems (BRACIS), pp. 152–156, November 2015
4. Freitas, L.A.D., Vieira, R.: Ontology-based feature-level sentiment analysis in Portuguese reviews. Int. J. Bus. Inf. Syst. **32**(1), 30–55 (2019)
5. Ganganwar, V., Rajalakshmi, R.: Implicit aspect extraction for sentiment analysis: A survey of recent approaches. Proc. Comput. Sci. **165**, 485–491 (2019)
6. Hartmann, N., et al.: A large corpus of product reviews in Portuguese: tackling out-of-vocabulary words. In: LREC, pp. 3865–3871 (2014)
7. Honnibal, M., Montani, I., Van Landeghem, S., Boyd, A.: spaCy: industrial-strength Natural Language Processing in Python (2020)
8. Hu, M., Liu, B.: Mining and summarizing customer reviews. In: Proceedings of the tenth ACM SIGKDD International Conference on Knowledge Discovery and Data Mining, pp. 168–177. ACM (2004)
9. Liu, B.: Sentiment analysis and opinion mining. Synth. Lect. Human Lang. Technol. **5**(1), 1–167 (2012)
10. Long, C., Zhang, J., Zhu, X.: A review selection approach for accurate feature rating estimation. In: Coling 2010: Posters, pp. 766–774 (2010)
11. Medhat, W., Hassan, A., Korashy, H.: Sentiment analysis algorithms and applications: a survey. Ain Shams Eng. J. **5**(4), 1093–1113 (2014)
12. Panchendrarajan, R., Ahamed, N., Murugaiah, B., Sivakumar, P., Ranathunga, S., Pemasiri, A.: Implicit aspect detection in restaurant reviews using co-occurence of words. In: Proceedings of the 7th Workshop on Computational Approaches to Subjectivity, Sentiment and Social Media Analysis, pp. 128–136 (2016)
13. Pang, B., Lee, L.: Seeing stars: exploiting class relationships for sentiment categorization with respect to rating scales. In: Proceedings of the 43rd Annual Meeting on Association for Computational Linguistics, pp. 115–124 (2005)
14. Pavlopoulos, J., Androutsopoulos, I.: Aspect term extraction for sentiment analysis: new datasets, new evaluation measures and an improved unsupervised method. In: Proceedings of the 5th Workshop on Language Analysis for Social Media (LASM)@ EACL, pp. 44–52 (2014)

---

[1] https://sites.google.com/icmc.usp.br/poetisa.

[2] https://github.com/mtarcinalli/Implicit-opinion-aspect-clues-in-Portuguese-texts.

15. Pereira, D.A.: A survey of sentiment analysis in the Portuguese language. Artif. Intell. Rev. **54**, 1–29 (2020)
16. Rana, T.A., Cheah, Y.-N.: Aspect extraction in sentiment analysis: comparative analysis and survey. Artif. Intell. Rev. **46**(4), 459–483 (2016). https://doi.org/10.1007/s10462-016-9472-z
17. Ravi, K., Ravi, V.: A survey on opinion mining and sentiment analysis: tasks, approaches and applications. Knowl. Based Syst. **89**, 14–46 (2015)
18. Snyder, B., Barzilay, R.: Multiple aspect ranking using the good grief algorithm. In: Human Language Technologies 2007: The Conference of the North American Chapter of the Association for Computational Linguistics, Proceedings of the Main Conference, pp. 300–307 (2007)
19. Taboada, M.: Sentiment analysis: an overview from linguistics. Ann. Rev. Linguist. **2**, 325–347 (2016)
20. Tsytsarau, M., Palpanas, T.: Survey on mining subjective data on the web. Data Mining Knowl. Disc. **24**(3), 478–514 (2012)
21. Tubishat, M., Idris, N., Abushariah, M.A.: Implicit aspect extraction in sentiment analysis: review, taxonomy, oppportunities, and open challenges. Inf. Process. Manage. **54**(4), 545–563 (2018)
22. Vargas, F.A., Pardo, T.A.S.: Clustering and hierarchical organization of opinion aspects: a corpus study. In: Proceedings of the 14th Corpus Linguistics Meeting, pp. 342–351 (2017)
23. Vargas, F.A., Pardo, T.A.S.: Aspect clustering methods for sentiment analysis. In: 13th International Conference on the Computational Processing of Portuguese. pp. 365–374. Canela, RS, Brazil (2018)
24. Vargas, F.A., Pardo, T.A.S.: Linguistic rules for fine-grained opinion extraction. In: the Workshop Proceedings of the 14th International AAAI Conference on Web and Social Media, pp. 1–6 (2020)
25. Yadollahi, A., Shahraki, A.G., Zaiane, O.R.: Current state of text sentiment analysis from opinion to emotion mining. ACM Comput. Surv. (CSUR) **50**(2), 1–33 (2017)
26. Yu, J., Zha, Z.J., Wang, M., Chua, T.S.: Aspect ranking: identifying important product aspects from online consumer reviews. In: Proceedings of the 49th Annual Meeting of the Association for Computational Linguistics: Human Language Technologies, pp. 1496–1505 (2011)
27. Zhai, Z., Liu, B., Xu, H., Jia, P.: Grouping product features using semi-supervised learning with soft-constraints. In: Proceedings of the 23rd International Conference on Computational Linguistics (Coling 2010), pp. 1272–1280 (2010)
28. Zhai, Z., Liu, B., Xu, H., Jia, P.: Clustering product features for opinion mining. In: Proceedings of the Fourth ACM International Conference on Web Search and Data Mining, pp. 347–354 (2011)
29. Zhang, Y., Zhu, W.: Extracting implicit features in online customer reviews for opinion mining. In: Proceedings of the 22nd International Conference on World Wide Web, pp. 103–104 (2013)

CRPC-DB a Discourse Bank
for Portuguese

Amália Mendes(✉) and Pierre Lejeune

Center of Linguistics, School of Arts and Humanities, University of Lisbon,
Lisbon, Portugal
{amaliamendes,lejeune}@letras.ulisboa.pt

Abstract. We present a new resource for discourse studies in Portuguese,
the CRPC Discourse Bank (CRPC-DB). CRPC-DB follows the Penn Discourse Treebank style of annotation. The annotation is performed on the
PAROLE corpus, a free subset of the Reference Corpus of Contemporary
Portuguese (CRPC) that includes news, fiction and didactic/scientific
texts. The discourse bank covers explicit and implicit relations at intra
and inter-sentential levels, and includes for now a total of 14,436 discourse
relations. We present the main guidelines of our annotation and discuss
specific cases. An experiment in inter-annotator agreement was performed
and holds results of 0.88 F1-score for discourse relation identification, 0.71
Cohen's K for the classification of discourse relation types, and 0,75 for
top-level sense classification. The CRPC-DB will be distributed free of
charge through the PORTULAN CLARIN infrastructure.

Keywords: Discourse bank · Discourse relations · Text coherence ·
PDTB-style of annotation

1 Introduction

We introduce the CRPC-DB, a Discourse Bank for Portuguese annotated according to the Penn Discourse Treebank (PDTB) scheme [22]. The corpus is labeled
for discourse relations (also referred to as rhetorical relations or coherence relations), such as cause and condition, that hold between two spans of text and
contribute to ensure the overall cohesion and coherence of the text. The scheme
follows the principles of the PDTB annotation proposal and includes the updates
of the PDTB 3.0 version [29]. The annotation is applied over the PAROLE corpus, a written subset of the Reference Corpus of Contemporary Portuguese
(CRPC) [13] available on the ELRA catalogue[1]. The CRPC-DB, as a new
resource for Portuguese in the PDTB framework, can be easily compared with
similar projects for other languages, as well as compared with resources in other
frameworks. It is also a source of linguistic insight into discourse relations and
discourse connectives, and has immediate applications for discourse parsing, as

---

[1] http://catalogue.elra.info/en-us/repository/browse/ELRA-W0024_01.

© Springer Nature Switzerland AG 2022
V. Pinheiro et al. (Eds.): PROPOR 2022, LNAI 13208, pp. 79–89, 2022.
https://doi.org/10.1007/978-3-030-98305-5_8

well as texts related tasks, such as summarization, argumentation mining and identification of complexity levels. In Sect. 2 we revise work on discourse banks in several languages and different frameworks, and we specifically address resources that have been developed for the Portuguese language. We introduce the contents of the corpus in Sect. 3.1, the annotation scheme in Sect. 3.2 and the annotation process in 3.3. The results of an inter-annotator agreement experiment are presented in Sect. 4 and we conclude in Sect. 5.

2   Related Work

As semantics, pragmatics and discourse are increasingly the focus of linguistics and NLP, several discourse banks marking coherence relations have been created for different languages and in different discourse frameworks such as Rhetorical Structure Theory or RST [12], Segmented Discourse Representation Theory or SDRT [5], the Penn Discourse Treebank or PDTB [22], and the Cognitive approach to Coherence Relations or CCR [25]. The model of the PDTB has been applied to English [22] and used with many other languages, such as Arabic [1], Chinese [33], Hindi [20], Italian [28], Tamil [24], and Turkish [32]. Some of these discourse banks cover all or part of the components of the PDTB scheme, and some adaptations have been made to accommodate specific linguistic properties of certain languages [23], but the core of discourse types is quite stable and makes it possible to use PDTB as a source of contrastive studies. The PDTB style of annotation has been applied to Portuguese to a small sample of TED Talks in the TED multilingual Discourse Bank - TED-MDB [31]. This multilingual and parallel discourse bank includes 6 talks that were annotated with explicit intra and inter-sentential relations, and with explicit inter-sentential relations. It follows the PDTB 2.0 scheme in terms of discourse relations types (Explicit, Implicit, AltLex, EntRel and NoRel) but adopts the PDTB 3.0 sense hierarchy [29]. To deal with the specific nature of the TED Talks transcripts, a new top-level sense named Hypophora was added to the hierarchy, in order to annotate contexts where the speaker asks a question and answers it himself to appeal to the public. Other discourse annotation efforts have produced resources for Brazilian Portuguese in the RST framework: corpora annotated with discourse information (CSTNews [3], CorpusTCC [19], Rhetalho [21], Summ-it [11]) and discourse parsing tools (RST Toolkit, DiZer, CSTParser) [2,17]. However, the number of resources for discourse studies is still scarce for Portuguese, especially European Portuguese, and are very much needed for the development of parsing tools.

3   The CRPC-DB

3.1   Raw Corpus and Pre-processing

The corpus is composed of written texts from different genres: newspapers, fiction and didactic/scientific texts taken from the PAROLE corpus, a subset of the CRPC [13]. The texts were tokenized using the LX-tokenizer which separates punctuation marks from words, detects sentence boundaries and deals with contracted forms and clitics in Portuguese [10]. The annotation consists of marking the connectives and the arguments of the connective, and consequently text tokenization is required prior to the annotation, in order to isolate connectives that are contracted with the following article or pronoun (e.g., "ao contrário de_ o"). Newspaper articles are usually short and were kept in full, but long texts from the other two genres were reduced to a maximum size of around 10.000 words. The discourse banks contains 65 texts and a total of 85.510 tokens. More information on the corpus is provided in Table 1. The corpus is not balanced in terms of text types. Newspapers is the dominant text type, while fiction is only a small part of our data. This follows from the fact that the PAROLE corpus, and the total CRPC, themselves are not balanced. In the Parole corpus, fiction texts are fewer but much longer. Our decision to select only a sample of the fiction texts (to prevent the inclusion of texts of very different lengths) is also the reason why fiction is underrepresented. This could be mitigated in future versions to provide data for contrastive studies of discourse relations in different text types.

Table 1. Number of files, words and relations per text type in the CRPC-DB

Genre	No. of files	No. of tokens	No. of relations
Newspaper	308	177,457	11,232
Didactic/scientific	4	38,566	2,452
Fiction	3	8,255	752
Total	315	224,278	14,436

3.2 Annotation Scheme

The CRPC-DB is annotated according to the PDTB scheme: we consider that discourse relations are relations that ensure coherence and hold between two arguments that have properties of abstract objects [6], such as eventualities. As a result, we annotate verbal predicates but also nominalizations that are part of a discourse relation. The PDTB-style of annotation follows a lexicalist approach, as each discourse relation is marked by a connective. This connective is either explicit in the context, or the sense is inferred and a connective is supplied by the annotator. Contrary to RST, the two arguments of a relation are not distinguished in a structure Nucleus-Satellite. The decision as to which is argument 1 and which is argument 2 follows from the lexicalist approach of PDTB: the second argument is the one introduced by the connective. The annotation of the CRPC-DB applies at intra and inter-sentential levels and uses the relation types of the PDTB 3.0 (Explicit, Implicit, Alternative Lexicalization (AltLex), Alternative LexicalizationC (AltLexC), Entity Relation and No Relation. The only exception is the new relation type Hypophora, which is not considered in our scheme (see treatment of Question-Answer pairs in this section). We follow the sense hierarchy of the PDTB 3.0 version [29], extended with additional senses that will be discussed in this section.

The relation is considered Explicit when there is an overt connective that denotes the meaning of the relation, as in Example 1 hereunder. For readability, we present the examples as non-tokenized text. In all examples, we underline the connective and render arg1 in italics and arg2 in bold. Connectives include (single or multi word) conjunctions, prepositions and adverbs, and also parallel connectives, i.e., pairs of connectives which are discontinuous and function as a single connective unit (e.g. *não só... mas também* 'not only... but also'). The discourse relation may also be lexically expressed by elements that do not fall into the category of connectives. These are alternative lexicalizations (AltLex) such as "the reason for this is that", "an example is" (Example 2). Another type of relation is expressed by lexico-syntactic constructions (AltLexC) that signal specific coherence relations, such as the inversion of the auxiliary expressing condition, or constructions "so (Adj/Adv) that" expressing result (Example 3). When no connective or alternative lexicalization is found, the relation is considered Implicit and the annotator has to supply a connective that could occur in that context (Example 4). Entity Relations (EntRel) are used when an Entity is introduced in the first argument and the second argument provides additional information on that entity, frequently as a parenthetical segment in the flow of discourse. NoRel is applied when there is no visible relation between two sentences (typically cases of topic shift). Both EntRel and NoRel apply specifically at inter-sentential level, between sentences.

For each relation of the type Explicit, Implicit, AltLex and AltLexC, a sense is provided, out of the sense hierarchy of the PDTB 3.0. The set of senses is divided in 4 top-level senses: Temporal, Contingency, Comparison and Expansion, further subdivided in a two or three-level set of senses. For instance, one subsense of Contingency is Contingency:Cause:Reason, and one subsense of Expansion is Expansion:Conjunction. In cases of ambiguity, the annotator may label the relation with two senses. In the CRPC-DB, both explicit and implicit relations are annotated, at both intra-sentential (Examples (1) and (2)) and inter-sentential levels (Example (4)). Contrary to the PDTB, we do not mark attribution (information related to the source and degrees of factuality of the abstract objects) at this stage of our work.

1. *A situação poderá mesmo agravar-se,* <u>pois</u> **passados os primeiros dias de Janeiro não se vislumbram sensíveis alterações** [Explicit; Contingency:Cause+Belief:Reason+Belief (The situation may even get worse, since after the first days of January no significant changes are expected)

2. *No caso daqueles situados entre a Terra e o Sol - Mercúrio e Vénus - essas "laçadas", como em tempos se lhes chamava, envolvem o Sol,* <u>razão por que</u> **se avistam ora à esquerda ora à direita do Sol (...)** [AltLex; Contingency:Cause:Result] (In the case of those located between the Earth and the Sun - Mercury and Venus - those 'loops' - as they used to be called - circle the Sun, reason why they are visible either on the left or on the right of the Sun)

3. *faz logo de início considerações* <u>*tão tão óbvias*</u>, **que parecem lugares comuns (...)** [AltLexC; Contingency:Cause:Result] ([He/she] makes from the very beginning considerations that are so obvious that they seem commonplaces

4. *Este ano, a Primavera chegou mais cedo.* [Implicit = <u>de facto</u> 'indeed'] **Estamos, em Março, a viver alegremente o clima de Maio.** [Implicit; Expansion:Specification: arg2-as-detail] (This year, spring came earlier. We are, in March, happily enjoying the climate of May.)

During the annotation, we apply several principles that define the extension of the arguments of a relation and the annotation of conjoined structures, noun phrases and relative clauses.

Extension of the Arguments. The extension of the arguments follow the minimality principle: an argument contains the minimal and sufficient amount of information required for the interpretation of the relation. If there is another span of text related to the arguments, they may be annotated as supplementary information (Sup1 and Sup2, for Arg1 and Arg2 respectively). Except for EntRel and NoRel relations, the minimality principle allows the annotator to select parts of the sentences as arguments of the relation. Or instead, to select multiple sentences as an argument if such information is required, for instance, when arg2 expresses a summary of a previous set of sentences.

Conjoined Elements. In cases of conjoined verbal phrases (VPs), only constituents not shared by both arg1 and arg2 are considered in the relation. For instance, in the example "os agricultores *olham para o céu* e *desesperam* (farmers look at the sky and despair), none of the arguments include the subject "the farmers" because it is shared by both arguments. VP coordination only applies to cases where both arg1 and arg2 include a verb. When the second argument is verbless, the coordinated spans are not annotated. For instance, in the sentence "Depois de amanhã, Viana Batista discutirá o problema com Alberto João Jardim e, no dia seguinte, com Mota Amaral" (after tomorrow, Viana Batista will discuss the problem with Alberto João Jardim and, the day after, with Mota Amaral) we don't consider that the span "and the day after" is an argument because it lacks the verb. An exception to the previous rule, and to our option to avoid interpreting contexts as involving elided linguistic material, are cases where each of the conjoined arguments has its own subject but arg2 lacks a verb. These cases are understood as a clause with an elided verb and are annotated. For instance, the sentence "Os anticiclones estão associados a condições de bom tempo e os sistemas depressionários ou frontais, à chuva" (Anticyclones are associated with good weather conditions and low-pressure or frontal systems with rain) is interpreted as equivalent to "and low-pressure or frontal systems [are associated] with rain".

Noun Phrases. A noun phrase (NP) is annotated as an argument of a connective when: (i) there is an existential interpretation (e.g. Dada a grande diversidade de fontes sonoras, a resolução dos problemas (...) 'Given the great diversity of sound sources, the resolution of problems' is interpreted as "Given the [existence] of a great diversity"; (ii) when the head noun is a nominalization (e.g. "utilização" 'utilization').

Question-Answer Pairs. We encountered in our corpus several contexts containing questions. This is the case of newspaper articles, when transcribing an interview, but also of newspaper articles that inform about an event and include part of the declarations made by an intervening party. Furthermore, in fiction texts, it is frequent to find dialogues that include questions and responses. Other discourse banks had to deal with question-answer (QA) pairs in different types of data. Most include a specific set of senses to label those contexts. For instance, the STAC corpus, a corpus of situated multiparty dialogues [4,7] annotated in the style of the SDRT [5], uses labels such as Question-Answer Pair (QAP). The section of the Wall Street Journal that has been annotated in the RST framework [12] labels QA pairs with specific senses combined with the concepts of nucleus and satellite (e.g., Question-Answer-N). In the TED-MDB (a corpus of transcriptions of TED Talks), cases where the speaker asks a question and answers it are labelled with a new top-level sense Hypophora, the name of a pragmatic figure of speech with an appealing function [15,16]. Contrary to these perspectives, the PDTB 2.0 [22] doesn't treat QA pairs with any special sense but the annotation of QA pairs has been revised in the PDTB 3.0 [30]: a new relation type Hypophora is added.

The contexts of QAP found in the CRPC-DB can involve truly interactive contexts (interviews), with two speakers, and contexts with a single speaker, as in phatic contexts of hypophora, frequent for instance in textbooks: the author presents a question that does not, of course, constitute a true request for information, but rather constructs what could be the question of a "second virtual speaker" [14]. The question frequently establishes a break in the flow of discourse with a topic-comment function. Contrary to RDT, the PDTB doesn't include topic-commment relations. Also, in QA pairs there is a single proposition instead of two abstract objects required in a relation in the PDTB: the answer to a global question provides the truth value of the proposition and the answer to a partial question provides the value of the variable identified in the question. In the CRPC-DB, we annotate QA pairs as other sentence sequences in the discourse bank, similarly to the PDTB 2.0 approach. For example, there is an implicit relation in the QA pair: "Quais as razões deste facto? Vamos procurá-las através de um estudo pormenorizado de cada continente." (What are the reasons for this fact? We will try to find them through a detailed study of each continent.) The answer provides additional information and allows the development of a topic, so the meaning of Specification is assigned (Expansion:Level-of-detail:arg2-as-detail) (see [7]). But to be able to identify the QA contexts all QA pairs that are truly interactive are labelled with a new top-level sense QAP, and cases of hypophora are labelled with the subsense QAP-Hypophora. In cases of doubt as to whether there are one or two speakers, the annotation is conservative and the QAP tag is chosen. When there is no relationship between the question and the next segment (that is, when the next segment does not directly refer to the question), it is noted as NoRel. The diversity of contexts of enunciation and the different functions performed at the textual level by QA pairs is a natural area to explore the concept of Attribution and its future application within the CRPC-DB.

3.3 Annotation Process

The corpus is manually annotated at the discourse level by one trained annotator, who follows the principles of the PDTB [23], and is then revised by an experienced annotator. After the discussion of remaining differences between the two annotators and a third experienced member of the team, the final annotation is adjudicated by the experienced annotator.

Contrary to the PDTB, where connectives were annotated one at a time throughout the corpus, here the annotator reads all the text and annotates all the relations that are found, without pre-annotation of lexical cues. This methods guarantees that the annotator is not conditioned to identify certain relations and ignore others. An assessment of 3 different workflow strategies is reported in [26]: they conclude that an approach that proceeds one text at the time (either by annotating the relations sequentially as they appear in the text or by annotating first explicit and then implicit relations in one text) performs better than the PDTB approach. We apply the full text approach and annotate all the relation types sequentially. However, in especially difficult texts, what proved useful was to annotate first intra-sententially and then inter-sententially, to deal with one level at a time. An annotation manual has been elaborated for the Portuguese discourse bank, and is followed by the annotators. The manual is frequently revised after the discussion of differences between annotators.

Results. The total number of discourse relations in the CRPC-DB is 14,436. There are 365 segments marked as NoRel, and 53 marked as EntRel. The remaining relations are Explicit, Implicit and Alternative Lexicalizations (AltLex and AltLexC), to which a sense is attributed. We provide information on the distribution of the relations per type and per top-level sense in Table 2. One interesting result, that can be compared with other discourse banks, is the fact that implicit relations are more frequent than explicit ones. For instance, in the parallel corpus TED-MDB Portuguese stands out due to the higher number of implicits, compared to other languages. Also, when comparing the aligned data of TED-MDB, the authors found that Portuguese showed a stronger tendency to implicitation (translating an explicit relation in the source language as an implicit one in the target language). A comparison with the PDTB shows a different pattern in English, where explicit relations are more frequent (18,459) than implicit ones (16,224). Nevertheless, in the Portuguese CRPC-DB only the top-level sense Expansion occurs more frequently as an implicit relation, suggesting that implicitness may be strongly linked to rhetorical senses.

Table 2. Frequency of discourse relations per text type and top-level sense in the CRPC-DB (Expl. = Explicit; AL = AltLex; ALC = AltLexC; Impl. = Implicit)

Sense	News				Did./sc.				Fiction				Total
	Expl.	AL	ALC	Impl.	Expl.	AL	ALC	Impl.	Expl.	AL	ALC	Impl.	
Temporal	702	47	0	211	77	7	1	29	86	0	0	67	1,227
Contingency	1,006	113	26	473	199	39	2	161	32	1	3	29	2,084
Comparison	892	18	6	403	171	4	0	75	30	0	0	28	1,627
Expansion	2,057	63	0	4,941	432	22	1	1115	178	0	0	286	9,095
Total	4,657	241	32	6,028	879	72	4	1,380	326	1	3	410	14,033

4   Inter-Annotator Agreement Experiment

In order to check the consistency of the annotations in the CRPC-DB, we performed an inter-annotator agreement (IAA) experiment. In our experiments, we selected three texts from the CRPC-DB, which were coded by a second experienced annotator. We then use the data coded by the two raters to evaluate three aspects: identification of discourse units, classification of relations and classification of senses. For the identification of units, we calculate agreement on discourse relation spotting, i.e. whether or not the annotators identified a relation between the same discourse units. As in [31], we do not adopt a strict approach in terms of arguments spans. We only require a match between the selected connectives (for the Explicits and AltLexes), and a match of the end point of the first text span and the beginning of the second span point. Following [18], we computed results of 0.8 for precision, 0.86 for recall and 0.88 for F1 score. To perform the calculations, we consider as "correct" the annotations of the first annotator.

For the classification of relations, we measured agreement among the common annotations on the discourse relation type (whether or not the discourse relation identified in two sets of annotations is of the same type, e.g. Explicit, AltLex, etc.). We also measured agreement on the sense of the discourse relation, i.e., whether or not the discourse relation identified in two sets of annotations is of the same top-level sense of PDTB's relation hierarchy. We report observed agreement and Cohen's kappa in Table 3. Annotating discourse relations is a complex task as the annotator has to infer semantic and pragmatic values from the connective and the context, and has to be aware of relations that hold at intra and also at inter sentential levels. Taking into account these challenges, we consider that the F1 score of 0.88 indicates a high similarity in terms of spotting discourse relations. For IAA values, similar to [31], we consider a kappa of 0.70

Table 3. Agreement on classification of discourse relation and top-level sense

	Observed agreement	Cohen's k
Classification of discourse relations	0.83	0.71
Classification of top-level senses	0.84	0.75

as a good standard [27] and Table 3 shows that this level is reached for the classification of both discourse relations and senses, suggesting a consistent and reliable annotation in the CRPC-DB.

5 Final Remarks

A survey of available language resources and tools for Portuguese pointed out that, while tagged and parsed corpora were available, few resources existed at the discourse level [8]. The results of this survey are still valid today, and the CRPC-DB addresses this shortage of data for discourse studies and applications in Portuguese, especially in what concerns European Portuguese by offering a corpus annotated with a set of 14,436 discourse relations. The CRPC-DB provides annotated data in a widely used format, the PDTB scheme, that enables contrastive linguistic studies of different languages in what concerns the nature of the connectives, the frequency of explicit and implicit relation types, and also the challenges that language properties impose on the annotation scheme.

We reported an experiment in inter-annotator agreement that provided good results, considering the challenging task of discourse annotation: we obtained 0.88 F1-score for discourse relation identification, 0.71 Cohen's K for the classification of discourse relation types, and 0,75 for top-level sense classification. In the future, we plan to address attribution, as a crucial part of discourse studies. Another important aspect will be to parse our corpus to cross-reference the coherence relations with the syntactic relations that hold between the arguments (e.g., the different syntactic patterns to express Cause: subordination, conjunction, juxtaposition). Our goal in preparing this new resource is two-fold: to make available real contexts annotated with discourse relations that provide data for the linguistic analysis of cohesion and coherence relations in Portuguese; and to provide training data for the development of automatic tagging systems of discourse relations. We believe it might prove equally useful for linguistics and NLP. The CRPC-DB will be distributed free of charge through the PORTULAN CLARIN infrastructure[2] [9].

Acknowledgements. This work was partially supported by PORTULAN CLARIN-Research Infrastructure for the Science and Technology of Language, funded by Lisboa2020, Alentejo2020 and FCT-Fundação para a Ciência e Tecnologia under the grant PINFRA/22117/2016, and by FCT under the project UIDP/00214/2020. Some of its developments were implemented in the scope of the COST Action TextLink - Structuring Discourse in Multilingual Europe. We wish to thank the anonymous reviewers for their helpful comments.

References

1. Al-Saif, A., Markert, K.: The leeds arabic discourse treebank: annotating discourse connectives for Arabic. In: Proceedings of LREC 2010, pp. 2046–2053 (2010)

---

[2] https://portulanclarin.net.

2. Aleixo, P., Pardo, T.A.: CSTTool: um parser multidocumento automático para o português do Brasil. In: Proceedings of the IV Workshop on MSc Dissertation and PhD Thesis in Artificial Intelligence – WTDIA, pp. 140–145 (2008)
3. Aleixo, P., Pardo, T.A.: CSTNews: Um córpus de textos jornalísticos anotados segundo a teoria discursiva multidocumento CST (cross-document structure theory). Technical report NILC-TR-08-05, Núcleo Interinstitucional de Lingüística Computacional NILC, Universidade de São Paulo (2008)
4. Asher, N., Hunter, J., Morey, M., Farah, B., Afantenos, S.: Discourse structure and dialogue acts in multiparty dialogue: the STAC corpus. In: The Tenth International Conference on Language Resources and Evaluation (LREC 2016) (2016)
5. Asher, N., Lascarides, A.: The semantics and pragmatics of presupposition. J. Semant. 15(2), 239–299 (1988)
6. Asher, N.: Reference to Abstract Objects in Discourse. Kluwer, Dordrecht (1993)
7. Asher, N., et al.: ANNODIS and related projects: case studies on the annotation of discourse structure. In: Ide, N., Pustejovsky, J. (eds.) Handbook of Linguistic Annotation, pp. 1241–1264. Springer, Dordrecht (2017). https://doi.org/10.1007/978-94-024-0881-2_47
8. Branco, A., et al.: The Portuguese Language in the Digital Age / A Língua Portuguesa na Era Digital. Springer, Heidelberg (2012)
9. Branco, A., Mendes, A., Quaresma, P., Gomes, L., Silva, J., Teixeira, A.: Infrastructure for the science and technology of language PORTULAN CLARIN. In: LREC 2020 Worskhop IWLTP 2020–1st International Workshop on Language Technology Platforms, pp. 1–7. ELRA (2020)
10. Branco, A.H., Silva, J.R.: Contractions: breaking the tokenization-tagging circularity. In: Mamede, N.J., Trancoso, I., Baptista, J., das Graças Volpe Nunes, M. (eds.) PROPOR 2003. LNCS (LNAI), vol. 2721, pp. 167–170. Springer, Heidelberg (2003). https://doi.org/10.1007/3-540-45011-4_24
11. Carbonel, T., Fuchs, J.T., Rino, L.: Anotação parcial de estruturas retóricas (RST) do Corpus Summ-it. Technical report, NILC-TR-04-07, Núcleo Interinstitucional de Lingüística Computacional NILC, Universidade de São Paulo (2007)
12. Carlson, L., Marcu, D.: Discourse tagging reference manual. Technical report ISI-TR-545 (2001)
13. Généreux, M., Hendrickx, I., Mendes, A.: Introducing the reference corpus of contemporary Portuguese on-line. In: Calzolari, N., et al. (eds.) LREC'2012 - Eighth International Conference on Language Resources and Evaluation, pp. 2237–2244. European Language Resources Association (ELRA), Istanbul, Turkey (2012)
14. Grésillon, A., Lebrave, J.L.: Qui interroge qui et pourquoi? In: La langue au ras du texte, pp. 57–132. Presses Universitaires de Lille (1984)
15. Lanham, R.: A Handlist of Rhetorical Terms. University of California Press, Berkeley (1991)
16. Mayoral, J.A.: Figuras Retóricas. Editorial Sintesis, Madrid (1994)
17. Maziero, E., Pardo, T.A.: CSTParser - a multi-document discourse parser. In: Proceedings of the PROPOR 2012 Demonstration, pp. 1–3 (2012)
18. Mírovský, J., Mladová, L., Zikánová, Š.: Connective-based measuring of the inter-annotator agreement in the annotation of discourse in PDT. In: COLING 2010: Posters, pp. 775–781. Coling 2010 Organizing Committee, Beijing, China, August 2010. https://www.aclweb.org/anthology/C10-2089
19. Nunes, M.V., Pardo, T.A.: A construção de um corpus de textos científicos em português do Brasil e sua marcação retórica. Technical report, NILC-TR-03-08, Núcleo Interinstitucional de Lingüística Computacional NILC, Universidade de São Paulo (2003)

20. Oza, U., Prasad, R., Kolachina, S., Sharma, D.M., Joshi, A.: The Hindi discourse relation bank. In: Proceedings of the 3rd Linguistic Annotation Workshop, pp. 158–161. Association for Computational Linguistics (2009)
21. Pardo, T., Seno, E.: Rhetalho: Um corpus de referência anotado retoricamente. In: Anais do V Encontro de Corpora (2005)
22. Prasad, R., et al.: The Penn discourse treebank 2.0. In: Proceedings of LREC 2008, pp. 2961–2968 (2008)
23. Prasad, R., Webber, B., Joshi, A.: Reflections on the Penn discourse treebank, comparable corpora, and complementary annotation. Comput. Linguist. **40**(4), 921–950 (2014)
24. Rachakonda, R.T., Sharma, D.M.: Creating an annotated Tamil corpus as a discourse resource. In: Proceedings of the 5th Linguistic Annotation Workshop, pp. 119–123. Association for Computational Linguistics, Portland, Oregon, USA, June 2011. https://www.aclweb.org/anthology/W11-0414
25. Sanders, T., Spooren, W., Noordman, L.: Toward a taxonomy of coherence relations. Disc. Process. **15**, 1–35 (1992)
26. Sharma, H., Dakwale, P., Sharma, D.M., Prasad, R., Joshi, A.: Assessment of different workflow strategies for annotating discourse relations: a case study with HDRB. In: Gelbukh, A. (ed.) CICLing 2013. LNCS, vol. 7816, pp. 523–532. Springer, Heidelberg (2013). https://doi.org/10.1007/978-3-642-37247-6_42
27. Spooren, W., Degand, L.: Coding coherence relations: reliability and validity. Corpus Linguist. Linguist. Theory **6**(2), 241–266 (2010)
28. Tonelli, S., Riccardi, G., Prasad, R., Joshi, A.: Annotation of discourse relations for conversational spoken dialogs. In: Calzolari, N., et al. (eds.) Proceedings of the Seventh International Conference on Language Resources and Evaluation (LREC 2010), European Language Resources Association (ELRA), Valletta, Malta, May 2010
29. Webber, B., Prasad, R., Lee, A., Joshi, A.: A discourse-annotated corpus of conjoined VPs. In: Proceedings of the 10th Linguistics Annotation Workshop, pp. 22–31 (2016)
30. Webber, B., Prasad, R., Lee, A., Joshi, A.: The Penn Discourse Treebank 3.0 annotation manual. Technical report, Institute for Research in Cognitive Science (2019)
31. Zeyrek, D., Mendes, A., Grishina, Y., Kurfalı, M., Gibbon, S., Ogrodniczuk, M.: TED multilingual discourse bank (TED-MDB) a parallel corpus annotated in the PDTB style. Lang. Resour. Eval. **54**, 587–613 (2020)
32. Zeyrek, D., Webber, B.L.: A discourse resource for Turkish: annotating discourse connectives in the METU corpus. In: IJCNLP, pp. 65–72 (2008)
33. Zhou, Y., Xue, N.: PDTB-style discourse annotation of Chinese text. In: Proceedings of the 50th Annual Meeting of the Association for Computational Linguistics: Long Papers, vol. 1, pp. 69–77. Association for Computational Linguistics (2012)

Challenges in Annotating a Treebank of Clinical Narratives in Brazilian Portuguese

Lucas Ferro Antunes de Oliveira[1]([✉]) [iD], Adriana Pagano[2] [iD],
Lucas Emanuel Silva e Oliveira[1] [iD], and Claudia Moro[1] [iD]

[1] Pontifical Catholic University of Paraná, Curitiba, PR, Brazil
`lucas.ferro@pucpr.edu.br`, {`lucas.emanuel,c.moro`}`@pucpr.br`
[2] Federal University of Minas Gerais, Belo Horizonte, MG, Brazil
`apagano@ufmg.com`

Abstract. Dependency parsing can enhance the performance of Named Entity Recognition (NER) models and can be leveraged to boost information extraction. NER tasks are essential to deal with clinical narratives, but models for Brazilian Portuguese dependency parsing are scarce, even less for clinical texts and its specificities. This paper reports on the development of a treebank of clinical narratives in Brazilian Portuguese and the drafting of guidelines. Based on a corpus of 1,000 clinical narratives manually annotated with semantic information, split into 12,711 sentences, we identified some characteristics of these texts that differ from traditional domains and have a deep impact on the annotation process, such as extensive use of acronyms and abbreviations, words not recognized by POS taggers, misspelling, special use of some symbols, different uses for numerals, heterogeneity of sentence sizes, and coordinated phrases without any punctuation. We developed a document to describe the annotation types and to explain how difficult cases should be treated to ensure consistency, including examples that could be found in this kind of texts. We created a Tag versus Frequency relation to justify some of the characteristics and challenges of the corpus. The corpus when completely annotated will be made available to the entire scientific community that performs research with clinical texts.

Keywords: Clinical narratives · Treebank development · Annotation guidelines

1 Introduction

Clinical text is a rich source of information to be tapped for the purposes of problem-solving related to quality of care, clinical decision support and safe information flow among all the parties involved in healthcare. Clinical texts present great challenges in their handling, even greater challenges than the texts found in medical literature. In these texts, health professionals describe the patient's

© Springer Nature Switzerland AG 2022
V. Pinheiro et al. (Eds.): PROPOR 2022, LNAI 13208, pp. 90–100, 2022.
https://doi.org/10.1007/978-3-030-98305-5_9

entire health history, vital signs, relevant clinical findings and procedures performed. Because they are written in a patient care environment, where there is a time pressure involved, they are more susceptible to errors. Furthermore, they are texts that do not have a formal structure, have high variability and heterogeneity, and may contain highly complex vocabulary [7].

Information extraction in this domain is usually carried out by means of Named Entity Recognition (NER), relation extraction, temporal expression identification, negation detection and terminology mapping [2,15]. These tasks rely on models built on corpora, which can be enriched by annotation at different linguistic levels. In the case of dependency parsing, morphology and syntax annotations can enhance the performance of NER models and can be leveraged to boost information extraction [1].

Although several annotated corpora of clinical texts are available in languages such as English, French, German, English, Spanish and Chinese among others, corpora for Portuguese are very scarce (see [8]). Moreover, there are few resources that can be used to adapt general domain corpora to clinical text in Portuguese.

In this paper, we report on a syntactically-annotated corpus of clinical narratives and describe the lessons learned in annotating dependency relations, considering the particularities and complexities of the clinical text. We report our experience and findings within a collaborative institutional setting for guideline development and corpus annotation. The guidelines and annotations will be made available for download, with instructions on how to load and visualize the syntactic parses.

This article is organized as follows. Section 2 briefly presents available corpora in the biomedical domain and related research on clinical notes. Section 3 describes the design and development of our corpus annotation, including the scheme, guidelines, and the training of annotators. Section 4 shows the results achieved in the annotation process with statistical information. Section 5 discusses implications of our statistics and results and summarizes the faced challenges. Finally, Sect. 6 concludes the paper and considers possible future directions.

2   Related Work

In the field of medical NLP research, size and availability of clinical text corpora is dependent on the type and the language of a corpus. While raw text corpora are large in size and available [3,4,19], annotated corpora are much smaller in size and scarcer in under-represented languages. Among annotated corpora, part-of-speech (POS) [14,18] and named entity recognition (NER) [9] are the most common type of annotation. Corpora of clinical texts annotated for syntactic structure (treebanks) are still emergent and largely concentrated on English, Spanish and Chinese. In the case of Portuguese, to the best of our knowledge there is only a single corpus in European Portuguese [6] and one in Brazilian Portuguese [11] annotated for NER, and explored in [17]. Another initiative contemplates the development of a morphological corpus (i.e., POS tags) for clinical texts in Portuguese, which was recently applied in [13]. No treebank of clinical text, which includes dependency relations, is available in Portuguese, which motivated the creation of our corpus.

A common issue raised by all treebank development projects are the challenges posed by the very nature of clinical texts [10], which we will detail in the following section together with the decisions made in our project to meet those challenges.

3   Materials and Methods

This section presents the main characteristics of the texts compiled in our corpus, the creation and evolution of annotation guidelines, and the corpus development process.

3.1   Data Preparation

The texts used to create our corpus were retrieved from SemClinBr [11], a corpus of 1,000 clinical narratives manually annotated with semantic information[1]. As SemClinBr aimed to support NLP tasks in several medical specialties, it compiled clinical narratives from distinct medical areas (e.g., cardiology, nephrology, orthopedy).

The 1,000 narratives have been split into 12,711 segments relying on periods and blank spaces as indicators for boundaries. 177 sentences having more than 50 tokens were set aside for future annotation. The time to annotate sentences varies according to their size; therefore it was necessary to separate the large sentences to minimize the time invested in the annotation until a sufficiently large corpus for training was obtained. As a first stage in our annotation project, we selected 2,955 sentences (approximately 25%).

In order to create our treebank, we pre-annotated our corpus using the Stanza toolkit [16]. The model Stanza uses by default for Portuguese is the pt-bosque model trained, using UD-Bosque[2], a treebank containing annotated news texts in Brazilian and European Portuguese following the Universal Dependencies (UD) guidelines, which is the standard adopted in our project. The output CoNLL-U files were imported in ArboratorGrew[3] to be annotated by two independent annotators and curated by a third one. We developed our own guidelines for annotation drawing on the UD principles and documentation[4] and available guidelines for Portuguese by Souza et al. (2020) (unpublished work).

---

[1] The use of SemClinBr texts was approved by the Ethics Committee in Research (CEP) of PUCPR, under register n⁰. 1,354,675.
[2] https://universaldependencies.org/treebanks/pt_bosque/index.html.
[3] https://arboratorgrew.elizia.net/#/.
[4] https://universaldependencies.org.

3.2 Corpus Characteristics

The corpus is composed of several types of clinical narratives, such as nursing notes, discharge summaries, and ambulatory notes, which required to be tokenized differently. The tokenization process yielded sentences with large variation in size, ranging from 2 and 3 token segments to over 260 token ones. Segments with 50 or more tokens proved very difficult to annotate in our annotation interface due to the need to use horizontal scroll bar to draw arcs between distant tokens.

Table 1. Segments illustrating size variation

Size	Example
Long (78 tokens)	Às 15:27: CLIENTE ALERTA, CONSCIENTE, PUPILAS ANISOCORICAS E) D, COMUNICATIVA, DISCRETA DISPNEIA AOS ESFORÇOS,COM SUPORTE DE OXIGENOTERAPIA EM CATETER NASAL A 2 /L, MANTENDO OXIMETRIA DE PULSO SAT: 96 %, REPOUSO NO LEITO, ACEITANDO POUCO A DIETA, ACESSO PERIFÉRICO EM MSE SALINIZADO, ABDOMEN GLOBOSO E FLÁCIDO, APRESENTANDO HIPEREMIA EM REGIÃO SACRA, MANTENDO COLCHÃO DE AR, ELIMINAÇÕES PRESENTES
Medium (18 tokens)	sem deficit de força, sem rigidez em membros, sem bradicinesia, sem alterações de pares cranianos
Short (3 tokens)	Marevan 5mg

Table 1 shows three tokenized sentences that are very different in size and in capitalization. The longest sentence have 78 tokens and all words are upper cased, while the medium is composed of 18 and all tokens are lower cased, and the shortest one is 3 token long and capitalized.

It is possible to notice that in the first example in Table 1, there are some different kinds of usage of numbers. "15:57:" appears as an event, with the following tokens describing the state of a patient. The number 2 and the number 96, appearing in "[...] NASAL A 2 /L [...]" ("nasal at 2 /L") and "[...] PULSO SAT: 96 %[...]" ("pulse sat: 96%"), respectively, mean number measurements, quantity, dosage. These examples illustrate the problems posed by numbers in our corpus and their joint use with symbols.

Table 1 also shows that some sentences have subject ("CLIENTE" "client") and predicate with non finite verbs ("MANTENDO" "maintaining", "ACEITANDO" "accepting", and "APRESENTANDO" "presenting"), while others (examples 2 and 3 in Table 1) have neither subject nor verb. Each case demands a decision as regards its "root", which was carried out following the UDs guidelines. Table 2 shows further recurrent characteristics of our corpus and illustrates them.

Table 2. Corpus characteristics and examples

Characteristic	Example
Words not recognized by POS taggers/lemmatizers	Hidantalizado
	Facietomia
	flutter atrial
Extensive use of acronyms and abbreviations	mantendo monitorização p 81, pa 103/74, sat o2 97% po le + ladf em 01/12/15
	colar cervical c/ queixas de dor
Misspelling	em repoiso em o leito
	outras inetrcorrências
Numerical expressions	ssvv a as 05:45 h pa = 133/74 mmhg , fc = 114 bpm, spo2 = 93%
	glasgow: 9
	mantendo monitorização p 81, pa 103/74, sat o2 97%
No punctuation	dois ave um há 1 ano e outro 2 anos
Special use of symbols	hma: inchaço, principalmente em o peridodo de a manha e em mmii (++++/++++), piora de o quadro ha 15 dias, estagio ii de irc
	solicitada svd + coleta de gasometria arterial
	# 61 # professora
	a as 11:30hs: realizado endoscopia digestiva + broncoscopia, sem intercorrência durante o exame e transporte.
	antes 2 carteiras/dia
Coordination	apresenta curativo + tala gessada em mse, referindo algia moderada, edema distal, mobilidade diminuida, apresentou 1 episodio de emese, sendo medicada, diurese presente, segue cuidados
Parenthetical comments	refere cx em a bexiga devido a tumor (sic) em 2013
	hmp : pais falecidos po ca (em a o soube especificar)
	controle glicêmico com glicemia em jejum abaixo de 100 (não costuma anotar)
Reduction	# retorno 7 dias
Ellipsis	apresentou problemas
	aceitando pouco a dieta vo

Characteristics in Tables 1 and 2 have a deep impact on the annotation process.

Words wrongly tagged and lemmatized by the Bosque model (news texts) have to be manually corrected, delaying the annotation process. Most sentences have abbreviations and acronyms; Therefore an abbreviation list had to be created aiming to help annotators with the healthcare terminology and vocabulary.

Additionally, a frequent problem found in the narratives is reiterated misspelled words, misuse of symbols and lack of punctuation to mark off sections. This may be accounted for by the fact that health professionals need to produce text quickly and often resort to "copying and pasting" from previous notes.

Symbols are used for a variety of purposes. Sometimes they can be used as a markup in the text, indicating the beginning of a section (e.g. "#"); other times they can be used to signal coordination as equivalent to "and" (e.g. "+"); further they can indicate operations with numbers as "+" ("plus") or "−" ("minus") and result or comparisons like "=" or "<" and ">". Some punctuation marks are very frequent in clinical text, as is the case for colons and dashes, and they demand an interpretation regarding their function (explanation, rephrasing, equation, etc.)

Bearing in mind all these characteristics of clinical narratives, we developed a document to describe the annotation types and explain how complex cases should be treated to ensure consistency. We adopted an iterative process of annotation, evaluation, and refinement of the annotation scheme and guidelines. Batches of 200 sentences were made available to the annotators and upon their annotation, their results were analyzed to improve the guidelines. The updated guidelines led to significantly better results on subsequent batches.

3.3 Decisions Made in the Annotation Process

The corpus was annotated for POS, lemma and dependency relations following the Universal Dependencies (UDs) guidelines as adopted by the Brazilian and European Portuguese treebanks adhering to UDs. In addition, available guidelines for clinical text in other languages (see Related Work) were consulted in order to decide how to handle particular specs of clinical text in Brazilian Portuguese.

As Table 1 illustrates, our corpus consists of a significant number of segments that can be characterized as fragments. There are instances of medical dosage, description of patient status, etc., which are mostly isolated noun phrases. In these cases, those phrases were annotated having the main noun as root. Most sentences are subject-less sentences, particularly those referring to the patient. Incomplete sentences due to line break or transcription errors were annotated as they were, without any insertion or editing.

A major decision had to do with how to handle ellipsis of major syntactic functions in our corpus. Annotating elliptical sentences implicates deciding whether a sentence will be analyzed considering elided functions or not, which

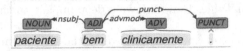

Fig. 1. Annotation presupposing a copula relation

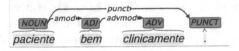

Fig. 2. Annotation of noun modified by adjective

has been shown to have a significant impact on the final results [5]. For instance, "paciente bem clinicamente" ("patient well clinically") can be annotated either as having "bem" ("well") or "paciente" ("patient") as root, as shown below.

In Fig. 1, an elliptical copula relation is presupposed. In Fig. 2, the noun "paciente" ("patient") is taken as the main head being modified by an adjective. We opted for the latter in order to avoid relying on annotators' interpretation of elided functions.

Variation for the same type of information was also an issue regarding prepositional phrases, particularly because comparable functions exhibited different realizations. This was particularly noticeable for temporal expressions. Thus, the time at which entries were recorded in the narratives and notes could be equally expressed as "ás 01:30 horas" ("at one hour thirty"), "ás 01:30" ("at one thirty"), "01:30 horas" ("one hour thirty"), "01:30" ("one thirty"), and "01h30" ("one hour thirty"). To ensure consistency in annotation and aid temporal information retrieval, all forms were annotated as an oblique relationship to the main root.

Clinical text contains abbreviations indicating dose or procedures. We adopted a principle to annotate the abbreviation based on the Part-of-Speech category of the words as they would be written in their full-form (e.g. "rx" -> "raio x" ("x-ray") (NOUN)).

As a result of corpus anonymization, names of physicians and nurses were rendered as "Doutor Vital Brasil" ("Doctor Vital Brasil") and "Enfermeira Florence Nightingale" ("Nurse Florence Nightingale"). These names were annotated as Proper Nouns in the corpus.

In the case of terms quoted from the Portuguese version of the International Classification of Diseases (ICD), their English counterparts were checked so that the annotation would be comparable in both languages.

4   Results

We annotated 2,901 sentences out of 2,955 available ones. 54 sentences remained unannotated due to errors in their CoNLL-U files that prevented the file to be

Table 3. Frequency of annotated dependency and POS tags

DEP tag	Frequency	DEP tag	Frequency	DEP tag	Frequency	POS tag	Frequency
punct	7818	xcomp	248	aux	23	NOUN	12564
case	6094	flat	214	ccomp	20	PUNCT	7919
nmod	4460	advcl	206	iobj	14	ADP	6141
conj	4414	discourse	179	dep	6	ADJ	5779
amod	4402	parataxis	153	subj:pass	4	VERB	2774
root	2928	compound	143	csubj	3	DET	1894
obl	2092	mark	108	nsubj:agent	2	NUM	1329
det	1876	nsubj:pass	107	subj	2	CCONJ	839
obj	1217	cop	73	advmod:part	1	ADV	688
cc	966	flat:name	68	csubj:pass	1	SYM	471
nummod	915	fixed	53	obl:pass	1	PROPN	354
advmod	552	aux:pass	47	orphan	1	X	151
acl	520	acl:relcl	31	reparandum	1	PRON	148
goeswith	476	flat:foreign	31	vocative	0	SCONJ	112
appos	465	obl:agent	25	dislocated	0	AUX	94
nsubj	287	expl	24			PART	15
						INTJ	0

uploaded in ArboratorGrew, the graphic interface used for annotation. Out of 2,901 sentences, 824 (28.4% of annotated sentences) were less or equal to 5 token long. The average number of tokens per sentence is 14.23.

Table 3 shows the frequency of each Dependency tag and Part-of-Speech tag annotated in the 2,901 sentences.

As regards inter annotator agreement, the highest results were 99.78 for the POS-Tagging and 97.23 for the Dependency Parsing. The lowest scores were 88.22 and 69.69 for POS-Tagging and Dependency Parsing, respectively.

5   Discussion

Regarding POS-tagging, the high number of "NOUN" tags can be accounted for the narratives mentioning conditions, drugs, medical procedures and facilities, as "CC" ("Centro Cirúrgico" or "Surgery Center"), and medical exams details and descriptions. This proves an important characteristic of the clinical narratives, which describe patients' health conditions.

Approximately 48.6% of all annotated sentences had no "VERB" tags (1,409 sentences); however the number of "VERB" tags is high, which can be accounted for this POS operating in dependency relationships such as modifiers ("acl" and "acl:relcl"). This is probably explained by the specific characteristics of each section of the clinical text. For example, in defining comorbidities and current health status, the focus will likely be on "coding" the patient's diagnoses, without using verbs. On the other hand, when the continuity of care is informed, verbs are usually used, as seen in [12] (e.g., visit the cardiologist in 10 d).

The high frequency of the POS tag "PUNCT" can be accounted for by the different uses of punctuation in the corpus, as is also the case of the tag "SYM".

As regards the tag "X", this can be accounted for by parsing errors due to typos. This is illustrated by the example in Fig. 3. Here the word "não" had been mistyped as "nao" in the clinical narrative and was wrongly parsed as "em a o". Following UD, the three tokens were annotated with the "goeswith" relation and the POS of the correct word is assigned to the first token, the remaining two receiving the X tag.

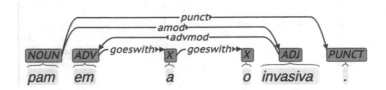

Fig. 3. Annotation of typo and incorrectly parsing

Regarding dependency relations, the most frequent tag is "punct", which can be accounted for the high number of punctuation marks in our corpus, followed by "case", which is typically realized by the "ADP" POS tag. Worth highlighting are the tags "nmod" and "conj". The former can be linked to the high number of NOUN tags, while the latter reflects a key characteristic of our corpus sentences, which consist of several segments coordinated between each other.

Dependency tags with frequency below 20 have been set aside to be reviewed in the next stage of our project, in order to check whether they are rare categories or should be re-annotated.

We understand that the main contribution of this article lies in the solutions found in carrying out the annotation of clinical texts, which can help other researchers to understand the particularities and complexities of clinical texts, allowing them to build additional resources for the medical informatics community. The corpus has an innovative character, being the only corpus in Brazilian Portuguese with clinical texts annotated with morphological and syntactic information.

6   Conclusion

In this paper, we reported the main challenges in annotating clinical narratives with morphological and syntactic information. Additionally we describe the preliminary results obtained in the first stage of our annotation. We annotated 2,901 sentences that compose a treebank in the CoNLL-U format following the Universal Dependencies guidelines. We achieved high agreement between annotators and overall good results for the present stage in our project. Further steps include reviewing annotated segments to improve our model, annotating the remaining segments, and making the corpus and guideline available for the scientific community. Upon finalizing our treebank, this will used to train another pipeline to be used to enhance the semantic NLP tasks of NER and information extraction targeted by our project.

References

1. Bretonnel Cohen, K., Demner-Fushman, D.: Biomedical Natural Language Processing. John Benjamins (2014). https://www.jbe-platform.com/content/books/9789027271068
2. Dalianis, H.: Basic building blocks for clinical text processing. In: Clinical Text Mining, pp. 55–82. Springer, Cham (2018). https://doi.org/10.1007/978-3-319-78503-5_7
3. Dalianis, H., Hassel, M., Henriksson, A., Skeppstedt, M.: Stockholm EPR corpus: a clinical database used to improve health care. In: Swedish Language Technology Conference, pp. 17–18 (2012)
4. Hao, T., Rusanov, A., Boland, M.R., Weng, C.: Clustering clinical trials with similar eligibility criteria features. J. Biomed. Inf. **52**, 112–120 (2014)
5. Jiang, Z., Zhao, F., Guan, Y.: Developing a linguistically annotated corpus of Chinese electronic medical record. In: 2014 IEEE International Conference on Bioinformatics and Biomedicine (BIBM), pp. 307–310. IEEE (2014)
6. Lopes, F., Teixeira, C.A., Oliveira, H.G.: Contributions to clinical named entity recognition in Portuguese. In: BioNLP@ACL (2019)
7. Meystre, S.M., Savova, G.K., Kipper-Schuler, K.C., Hurdle, J.F.: Extracting information from textual documents in the electronic health record: a review of recent research. Yearbook of Med. Inf. **17**(01), 128–144 (2008)
8. Névéol, A., Dalianis, H., Velupillai, S., Savova, G., Zweigenbaum, P.: Clinical natural language processing in languages other than english: opportunities and challenges. J. Biomed. Semantics **9**(1), 1–13 (2018)
9. Ogren, P.V., Savova, G.K., Chute, C.G., et al.: Constructing evaluation corpora for automated clinical named entity recognition. In: LREC, vol. 8, pp. 3143–3150 (2008)
10. Oinam, N., Mishra, D., Patel, P., Choudhary, N., Desai, H.: A treebank for the healthcare domain. In: Proceedings of the Joint Workshop on Linguistic Annotation, Multiword Expressions and Constructions (LAW-MWE-CxG-2018), pp. 144–155 (2018)
11. Oliveira, L., et al.: Semclinbr-a multi institutional and multi specialty semantically annotated corpus for Portuguese clinical NLP tasks. In: CoRR (2020)
12. Oliveira, L.E.S., de Souza, A.C., Nohama, P., Moro, C.M.C.: A novel method for identifying continuity of care in hospital discharge summaries. In: Zhang, Y.-T. (ed.) The International Conference on Health Informatics. IP, vol. 42, pp. 284–287. Springer, Cham (2014). https://doi.org/10.1007/978-3-319-03005-0_72
13. de Oliveira, L.F.A., e Oliveira, L.E.S., Gumiel, Y.B., Carvalho, D.R., Moro, C.M.C.: Defining a state-of-the-art POS-tagging environment for Brazilian Portuguese clinical texts. Res. Biomed. Eng. **36**(3), 267–276 (2020). https://doi.org/10.1007/s42600-020-00067-7
14. Pakhomov, S.V., Coden, A., Chute, C.G.: Developing a corpus of clinical notes manually annotated for part-of-speech. Int. J. Med. Inf. **75**(6), 418–429 (2006)
15. Percha, B.: Modern clinical text mining: a guide and review. Ann. Rev. Biomed. Data Sci. **4**(1), 165–187 (2021). https://doi.org/10.1146/annurev-biodatasci-030421-030931, pMID: 34465177
16. Qi, P., Zhang, Y., Zhang, Y., Bolton, J., Manning, C.D.: Stanza: a Python natural language processing toolkit for many human languages. In: Proceedings of the 58th Annual Meeting of the Association for Computational Linguistics: System Demonstrations (2020). https://nlp.stanford.edu/pubs/qi2020stanza.pdf

17. Schneider, E.T.R., et al.: BioBERTpt - a Portuguese neural language model for clinical named entity recognition. In: Proceedings of the 3rd Clinical Natural Language Processing Workshop, pp. 65–72. Association for Computational Linguistics, November 2020. https://doi.org/10.18653/v1/2020.clinicalnlp-1.7, https://aclanthology.org/2020.clinicalnlp-1.7
18. Tateisi, Y., Tsujii, J.: Part-of-speech annotation of biology research abstracts. In: LREC (2004)
19. Wu, S.T., Liu, H., Li, D., Tao, C., Musen, M.A., Chute, C.G., Shah, N.H.: Unified medical language system term occurrences in clinical notes: a large-scale corpus analysis. J. Am. Med. Inf. Assoc. **19**(e1), e149–e156 (2012)

PetroBERT: A Domain Adaptation Language Model for Oil and Gas Applications in Portuguese

Rafael B. M. Rodrigues[1], Pedro I. M. Privatto[2], Gustavo José de Sousa[2],
Rafael P. Murari[2], Luis C. S. Afonso[3], João P. Papa[3],
Daniel C. G. Pedronette[2], Ivan R. Guilherme[2]([⊠]), Stephan R. Perrout[4],
and Aliel F. Riente[5]

[1] UNESP - São Paulo State University, School of Technology and Sciences,
Presidente Prudente, Brazil
rafael.rodrigues@unesp.br
[2] UNESP - São Paulo State University, Institute of Geosciences and Exact Sciences,
Rio Claro, Brazil
{pedro.privatto,gustavo.sousa,rafael.murari,daniel.pedronette,
ivan.guilherme}@unesp.br
[3] UNESP - São Paulo State University, School of Sciences, Bauru, Brazil
{luis.afonso,joao.papa}@unesp.br
[4] Petróleo Brasileiro S.A. - Petrobras, Rio de Janeiro, Brazil
sperrout@petrobras.com.br
[5] Centro de Pesquisas da Petróleo Brasileiro S.A. - CENPES/Petrobras,
Rio de Janeiro, Brazil
aliel@petrobras.com.br

Abstract. This work proposes the PetroBERT, which is a BERT-based
model adapted to the oil and gas exploration domain in Portuguese.
PetroBERT was pre-trained using the Petrolês corpus and a private daily
drilling report corpus over BERT multilingual and BERTimbau. The
proposed model was evaluated in the NER and sentence classification
tasks and achieved interesting results, which shows its potential for such
a domain. To the best of our knowledge, this is the first BERT-based
model to the oil and gas context.

Keywords: Oil and gas · BERT · Domain adaption

1 Introduction

The Bidirectional Encoder Representations from Transformers (BERT) [7] is a
transformer-based machine learning technique for natural language processing
(NLP) that overcomes one of the limitations in standard language models, the
unidirectionality. BERT is powerful not only in the sense that is capable of
providing deep bidirectional representations, but it is also capable to adapt itself
to any other domain, which made it the state-of-art in many NLP tasks [14].

© Springer Nature Switzerland AG 2022
V. Pinheiro et al. (Eds.): PROPOR 2022, LNAI 13208, pp. 101–109, 2022.
https://doi.org/10.1007/978-3-030-98305-5_10

Although considered the state-of-the-art in NLP, the original BERT model may not achieve interesting results when applied to certain domain-specific problems, which opens room for improvements. One of the main reasons is linguistic ambiguity or even context-specific words. Hence, many initiatives have raised to generate BERT-based models for specific context, such as BioBERT [10], BioBERTpt [13], COBERT [1], SciBERT [4], FinBERT [3], ClinicalBERT [9], MathBERT [14], among others.

In the context of oil and gas exploration is no different. Oil and gas exploration generates a considerable amount of data originated by sensors and reports, which is an important source of information for tasks such as monitoring of operations, failure prevention, project design, planning, among others. Hence, specialized models are of great aid for information extraction in such a domain.

This work proposes the *PetroBERT*, which is a BERT-based model to the domain of oil and gas by adapting BERT Multilingual Cased and BERTimbau models. To the best of our knowledge, there is no BERT-based model adapted to such a context in the literature and being the main contribution of this work. Another contribution is to foster studies concerning model adaption and information extraction in the domain of oil and gas.

The proposed models were adapted using a repository of artifacts for NLP in the oil and gas domain in Portuguese and over a set of daily drilling reports. The models were evaluated in the tasks of Named Entity Recognition (NER) and sentence classification, which are two relevant tasks and is another contribution of our work.

The first task identifies oil and gas named entities (e.g. units of measure, drilling and pumping tools, geological formations, among others) in unstructured texts. After the NER process, the structured data may feed management processes such as monitoring, well design, lessons learned. Structured texts, especially in this domain, are of great importance as they save time when designing new projects, resulting in safer and cheaper new wells.

The second task is specific for daily drilling reports where the person responsible by the reports must describe all events during well drilling as well as indicate the triplet (activity, operation, step) associated with the described event. The reports meet certain regulations and also allow monitoring drilling activities and their classification in the sentence level (i) provides uniformity in the classification and reliability to data; (ii) removes the subjective aspect present in the manual classification; and (iii) saves a significant amount of time. We can mention the works of Hoffimann et al. [8], Sousa et al. [16], Ribeiro et al. [12], Cinelli et al. [5], etc.

The paper is organized as follows: Sect. 2 presents related work and 3 presents the proposed approach of this work. Experimental results are presented and discussed in Sect. 4. Finally, conclusions and future works are stated in Sect. 5.

2   Related Works

BERT's current models are characterized for being multilingual and of general language domain. As aforementioned, such a generalization may not perform well when working in domain-specific problems. Hence, many works have emerged by proposing pre-trained BERT-based models for specific domains, which outperformed the standard BERT in some NLP tasks. The main steps comprise gathering and pre-training BERT over a very large amount of domain-specific texts.

BioBERT [10] is a BERT model pre-trained on biomedical domain corpora comprised of PubMed abstracts and PMC full-text articles. The authors evaluated different combinations and sizes of both general domain and biomedical domain corpora, and how each corpus affects the pre-training. BioBERTpt [13] shares the same idea as BioBERT, but its corpora is comprised of clinical notes collected from Brazilian hospitals and biomedical data in Portuguese.

SciBERT [4] is a pre-trained language model based on BERT that addresses the lack of high-quality, large-scale labeled scientific data. The pre-training is performed over a large multi-domain corpus of scientific publications to improve performance on downstream scientific NLP tasks. To create the model, the authors created their own vocabulary based on their scientific corpus resulting in cased and uncased vocabularies each of size of 30K.

FinBERT [11] a language model based on BERT to tackle NLP tasks in the financial domain. The proposed model differs from the standard BERT in the pre-training process where it is constructed six self-supervised pre-training tasks that can be learned through multi-task self-supervised learning. According to the authors, the tasks help the model to better capture language knowledge and semantic information.

ClinicalBERT [9] is a pre-trained BERT using clinical notes and fine-tuned for the task of predicting hospital readmission. The model is pre-trained using the same pre-training tasks of the standard BERT over a set of $58,976$ unique hospital admissions from $38,597$ patients in the intensive care unit. The authors state that ClinicalBERT can be extended to other tasks such as diagnosis prediction, mortality risk estimation, or length-of-stay assessment.

MathBERT [14] is a model created by pre-training the $BERT_{BASE}$ model on a large mathematical corpus ranging from pre-kindergarten (pre-k) to highschool, to college graduate level mathematical content. After the pre-training, MathBERT is fine-tuned to a mathematical task-specific text dataset for classification.

As aforementioned, to the best of our knowledge, there is no adapted BERT-based model to the context of oil and gas.

3   Proposed Work

This section describes all steps performed in this work to create and evaluate PetroBERT, as depicted in Fig. 1. The experimental setup is provided in the next section.

The model is based on two pre-trained BERT models, which allows us to investigate whether a BERT model pre-trained on the Portuguese language has

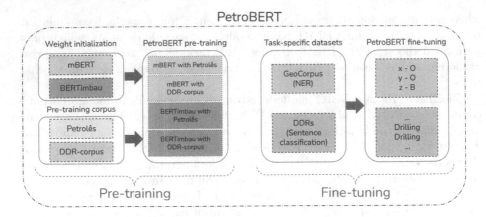

Fig. 1. Overview of the pre-training and fine-tuning of PetroBERT

any advantage in terms of performance over a multilingual one in NLP tasks in Portuguese. The selected models are described next:

- BERT Multilingual Cased (mBERT): It is a pre-trained model on the top 104 languages from Wikipedia using a masked language modeling (MLM). The main idea behind MLM is to randomly mask a few tokens from the input so that the model predicts them based only on the context [7].
- BERTimbau - Portuguese BERT: It is a set of BERT models trained in the Portuguese language. BERT$_{BASE}$ and BERT$_{LARGE}$ Cased variants were trained over the Brazilian Web as Corpus, a large Portuguese corpus, for $1,000,000$ steps, using the whole-word mask (MLM-WWM). The MLM-WWM upgrades MLM by masking all the WordPiece tokens (which form a complete word) if the masked WordPiece token [17] belongs to a whole word.

The pre-training of both models was performed over Petrolês [15] and a private Daily Drilling Reports corpus (DDR-Corpus). Petrolês is a repository of artifacts for NLP in the petroleum domain in Portuguese developed by a partnership of Petrobras Research and Development Center (CENPES), Applied Computational Intelligence Lab (PUC-Rio/ICA), UFRGS, and PUC-RS. The partnership aims at promoting research initiatives related to Natural Language Processing and Computational Linguistic. As aforementioned, DDR-corpus is a private set of daily drilling reports of 302 wells comprised of free-text sentences that describe the whole drilling process of each well. The reports were provided by a multinational corporation in the petroleum industry with over 29k sentences.

The fine-tuning step is performed over GeoCorpus and DDR-Corpus for NER and text classification tasks, respectively. The GeoCorpus [2] is an open dataset of scientific articles, dissertations, theses, and Geosciences Reports from a multinational petroleum company, about Brazilian Sedimentary Basins. This dataset is comprised of over 6 thousand sentences written in Brazilian Portuguese and annotated for the Named Entity Recognition task, with a total of over 5.5 thousand Named Entities divided in 14 different entity types. However, we used the modified version proposed by Consoli et al. [6].

4   Experimental Evaluation and Discussion

This section presents further details of each experiment, which was run using a GeForce RTX 2080 Ti GPU. Each experiment (i.e., NER and text classification) evaluated the impact of adapting each pre-trained model on a specific domain corpus. The performance of the models was measured by the F1-score ($f1$) over a predefined training/testing sets (NER task), and a 5-fold cross-validation (text classification task) where $f1$ is given by:

$$f1 = 2 \times \frac{precision \times recall}{precision + recall}. \tag{1}$$

We also hypothesize if a pre-trained model's performance on the task of Masked Language Modeling indicates its potential for the classification task. For that purpose, we measure the F1-score obtained with each pre-trained model while masking each token of the testing set of GeoCorpus and DDR-corpus and compare them to the results of the classification task. For GeoCorpus we considered all $1,253$ texts, while for DDR-corpus we used a subset of $1,253$ sentences, chosen randomly while maintaining the same class distribution as in the complete dataset, since measuring MLM a token at a time would take too long otherwise.

Table 1 presents the parameters used for both experiments. The columns pre-training and fine-tuning stand for the two steps performed to obtain PetroBERT, as depicted in Fig. 1.

Table 1. General configuration employed in the experiments.

Parameters	Pre-training		Fine-tuning	
	Geocorpus	ddr-corpus	Geocorpus	ddr-corpus
Batch size	2	8	4	12
Gradient accumulation steps	4	–	–	–
Max length	512	256	512	256
Epochs	1	8	4	4
Learning rate	5×10^{-5}	5×10^{-5}	2×10^{-5}	4×-5
Learning rate scheduler	Linear	Linear	Linear	Linear
Running time	48 h	48 h	30 min	5 h

From hereinafter, we mention the four created models as follows:

- $PetroBERT_{multi\_pet}$: BERT Multilingual Cased-based model adapted with Petrolês.

- $PetroBERT_{multi\_ddr}$: BERT Multilingual Cased-based model adapted with DDR-corpus.
- $PetroBERT_{pt\_pet}$: BERTimbau-based model adapted with Petrolês.
- $PetroBERT_{pt\_ddr}$: BERTimbau-based model adapted with DDR-corpus.

4.1   Experiment I - NER

This experiment is focused on the NER task using the GeoCorpus dataset [6], where tokens are categorized in 14 entities as depicted in Fig. 2. We used the split provided in the own dataset page[1] with 75% of samples for training (4,007 samples), 20% of samples for testing (1,128 samples), and 5% of samples for validation (321 samples).

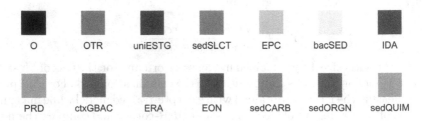

Fig. 2. Named entities of GeoCorpus.

Table 2 reports the results (the best results are shown in bold and our best models are shown underlined) and Fig. 3 presents the recognized entities in one sentence. The domain adaption process did not yield better results for this dataset, as BERTimbau achieved the best result. This indicates that Petrolês and DDR-corpus are not well suited for increasing the performance on GeoCorpus. However, it is interesting to see that BERTimbau outperformed mBERT for over 1% in F1-score, showing the advantage of pretraining BERT using only Portuguese texts when working with tasks in this language.

Table 2. Results for GeoCorpus

Model	Pre-trained model		Fine-tuned model
	MLM	MLM-WWM	NER
mBERT	59.46	29.32	81.63
PetroBERT$_{multi\_pet}$	**59.53**	22.58	<u>77.28</u>
PetroBERT$_{multi\_ddr}$	37.57	19.35	71.67
BERTimbau	53.91	**41.60**	**82.88**
PetroBERT$_{pt\_pet}$	51.79	<u>24.55</u>	76.96
PetroBERT$_{pt\_ddr}$	32.13	21.93	74.81

[1] https://github.com/jneto04/geocorpus.

Ground truth:

O salto positivo acima do intervalo de + 5ppm vem sendo interpretado como a assinatura de um evento isotópico de escala regional , relacionado a uma discordância de primeira ou segunda ordem no interior da Formação Sete Lagoas e , dessa forma , funcionando como marco cronoestratigráfico na Bacia Bambuí .

 O

mBERT, PetroBERT$_{multi\_pet}$, PetroBERT$_{multi\_ddr}$, PetroBERT$_{pt\_ddr}$:

O salto positivo acima do intervalo de + 5ppm vem sendo interpretado como a assinatura de um evento isotópico de escala regional , relacionado a uma discordância de primeira ou segunda ordem no interior da Formação Sete Lagoas e , dessa forma , funcionando como marco cronoestratigráfico na Bacia Bambuí .

 OTR

BERTimbau:

O salto positivo acima do intervalo de + 5ppm vem sendo interpretado como a assinatura de um evento isotópico de escala regional , relacionado a uma discordância de primeira ou segunda ordem no interior da Formação Sete Lagoas e , dessa forma , funcionando como marco cronoestratigráfico na Bacia Bambuí .

 uniESTG

PetroBERT$_{pt\_pet}$:

O salto positivo acima do intervalo de + 5ppm vem sendo interpretado como a assinatura de um evento isotópico de escala regional , relacionado a uma discordância de primeira ou segunda ordem no interior da Formação Sete Lagoas e , dessa forma , funcionando como marco cronoestratigráfico na Bacia Bambuí .

 bacSED

Fig. 3. Example of entity recognition. BERTimbau and PetroBERT$_{pt\_pet}$ were the only ones that misrecognized a few entities.

Another interesting observation is that better performance on the Masked Language Modeling task does not mean greater results on the final task. mBERT, for instance, has very similar MLM results when compared to PetroBERT$_{multi\_pet}$. However, the F1-score on the final task differs by more than 4%.

4.2   Experiment II - Sentence Classification

This experiment focuses on the classification of DDR sentences on the step level. The sentences are categorized in three levels (i.e., multi-label) from top to the bottom: (i) activity, (ii) operation, and (iii) step. As aforementioned, we are dealing with the lowest level which is the most challenging one due to the high number of classes as well (i.e. 204 classes), unbalanced classes, and sentences of different classes may share some textual similarity. Over 130 classes have no more than 100 sentences. Only 3 classes have more than $1,000$ sentences being $1,505$ the maximum.

Table 3 shows the results for DDR-corpus. Here we note that the domain adaption process was effective, especially when done using texts from the very same domain. And again, the performance of the pre-trained model did not correlate to the result obtained after fine-tuning, since PetroBERT$_{multi\_pet}$ was better than mBERT for the sentence classification while having worse results on the MLM task.

It is also interesting that while mBERT and BERTimbau - in their original form - had the same performance after fine-tuning, the domain adaption process over BERTimbau allowed it to achieve a significant greater f1-score.

Table 3. Results for DDR-Corpus

Model	Pre-trained model		Fine-tuned model
	MLM	MLM-WWM	Sentence classification
mBERT	56.28	36.58	47.97
PetroBERT$_{multi\_pet}$	44.35	18.79	48.86
PetroBERT$_{multi\_ddr}$	**87.80**	73.70	50.55
BERTimbau	57.43	46.13	48.24
PetroBERT$_{pt\_pet}$	41.62	21.56	48.83
PetroBERT$_{pt\_ddr}$	87.47	**76.63**	**51.98**

5   Conclusions and Future Works

This work introduced the PetroBERT, a model for the petroleum domain. The work aimed at adapting to pre-trained models for the context of oil and gas using two corpora. The adapted models were evaluated over NER and sentences classification tasks.

It is important to highlight that due to restrictions of time and computational resources, the models were trained with fewer epochs, which may affect the final results. Most proposed models in the literature are trained for several days and use multiple GPUs. In our case, we had only a single GPU available. Nonetheless, the models achieved interesting results in both NLP tasks and demonstrated great potential in such a domain.

Concerning the use of Portuguese-only models, it was observed in both tasks that they outperformed the multilingual ones. Further investigation is needed to determine in which cases the Portuguese models are better, and if there are some scenarios where they are worse, such as sentences with words in other languages.

As future works, besides the investigations already mentioned, we aim at using more powerful computing settings to achieve even better results and also combine Petrolês and our DDR-Corpus on the same adaption process.

Acknowledgments. The authors would like to thank Petróleo Brasileiro (Petrobras) grant 2019/00697-8. The authors are also grateful to FAPESP grants #2013/07375-0, #2014/12236-1, #2018/15597-6, and #2019/07665-4, and CNPq grants #307066/2017-7, #309439/2020-5 and #427968/2018-6.

References

1. Alzubi, J.A., Jain, R., Singh, A., Parwekar, P., Gupta, M.: COBERT: Covid-19 question answering system using Bert. Arabian J. Sci. Eng. 1–11 (2021). https://doi.org/10.1007/s13369-021-05810-5
2. Amaral, D.O.F.: Reconhecimento de entidades nomeadas na área da geologia: bacias sedimentares brasileiras. Ph.D. thesis, Programa de Pós-Graduação em Ciência da Computação (2017). http://tede2.pucrs.br/tede2/handle/tede/8035, escola Politécnica

3. Araci, D.: Finbert: Financial sentiment analysis with pre-trained language models (2019). http://arxiv.org/abs/1908.10063
4. Beltagy, I., Lo, K., Cohan, A.: SciBERT: a pretrained language model for scientific text. In: Proceedings of the 2019 Conference on Empirical Methods in Natural Language Processing and the 9th International Joint Conference on Natural Language Processing (EMNLP-IJCNLP), pp. 3615–3620. Association for Computational Linguistics, Hong Kong, China (2019)
5. Cinelli, L.P.: Automatic event identification and extraction from daily drilling reports using an expert system and artificial intelligence. J. Petrol. Sci. Eng. **205**, 108939 (2021)
6. Consoli, B., Santos, J., Gomes, D., Cordeiro, F., Vieira, R., Moreira, V.: Embeddings for named entity recognition in geoscience Portuguese literature. In: Proceedings of the 12th Language Resources and Evaluation Conference, pp. 4625–4630. European Language Resources Association, Marseille, France, May 2020
7. Devlin, J., Chang, M., Lee, K., Toutanova, K.: BERT: pre-training of deep bidirectional transformers for language understanding. In: Burstein, J., Doran, C., Solorio, T. (eds.) Proceedings of the 2019 Conference of the North American Chapter of the Association for Computational Linguistics: Human Language Technologies, NAACL-HLT 2019, Minneapolis, MN, USA, 2–7 June 2019, Volume 1 (Long and Short Papers), pp. 4171–4186. Association for Computational Linguistics (2019)
8. Hoffimann, J., Mao, Y., Wesley, A., Taylor, A.: Sequence mining and pattern analysis in drilling reports with deep natural language processing. In: SPE Annual Technical Conference and Exhibition, vol. Day 3 Wed, 26 September 2018 (2018)
9. Huang, K., Altosaar, J., Ranganath, R.: ClinicalBERT: modeling clinical notes and predicting hospital readmission (2020)
10. Lee, J., Yoon, W., Kim, S., Kim, D., Kim, S., So, C.H., Kang, J.: BioBERT: a pre-trained biomedical language representation model for biomedical text mining. Bioinformatics **36**(4), 1234–1240 (2019)
11. Liu, Z., Huang, D., Huang, K., Li, Z., Zhao, J.: FinBERT: a pre-trained financial language representation model for financial text mining. In: Bessiere, C. (ed.) Proceedings of the Twenty-Ninth International Joint Conference on Artificial Intelligence, IJCAI 2020, pp. 4513–4519. International Joint Conferences on Artificial Intelligence Organization (2020)
12. Ribeiro, L.C., Afonso, L.C., Colombo, D., Guilherme, I.R., Papa, J.P.: Evolving neural conditional random fields for drilling report classification. J. Petrol. Sci. Eng. **187**, 106846 (2020)
13. Schneider, E.T.R., et al.: BioBERTpt - a Portuguese neural language model for clinical named entity recognition. In: Proceedings of the 3rd Clinical Natural Language Processing Workshop, pp. 65–72. Association for Computational Linguistics, November 2020
14. Shen, J.T., Yamashita, M., Prihar, E., Heffernan, N., Wu, X., Graff, B., Lee, D.: MathBERT: a pre-trained language model for general NLP tasks in mathematics education (2021)
15. da Silva Magalhães Gomes, D., et al.: Portuguese word embeddings for the oil and gas industry: development and evaluation. Comput. Indus. **124**, 103347 (2021)
16. Sousa, G.J., et al.: Pattern analysis in drilling reports using optimum-path forest. In: 2018 International Joint Conference on Neural Networks (IJCNN), pp. 1–8 (2018)
17. Wu, Y., et al.: Google's neural machine translation system: bridging the gap between human and machine translation. CoRR abs/1609.08144 (2016). http://arxiv.org/abs/1609.08144

SS-PT: A Stance and Sentiment Data Set from Portuguese Quoted Tweets

Miguel Won[1]([envelope])[iD] and Jorge Fernandes[2][iD]

[1] INESC-ID, University of Lisbon, Lisbon, Portugal
miguelwon@tecnico.ulisboa.pt
[2] University of Lisbon, Lisbon, Portugal
jorge.fernandes@ics.ulisboa.pt

Abstract. Our contribution presents the first ever stance and sentiment annotated corpus in Portuguese. Using data from Twitter, we annotated a data set with over 15,000 tweets. In building the corpus, we made both random and supervised searches to maximize balance. Using four annotators, we have classified each tweet on four categories: support, against, neutral or inconclusive. Furthermore, we have annotated each tweet for sentiment: positive, negative, neutral, sarcasm or inconclusive. Our annotators yield strong inter-annotator agreement. In addition, we test a baseline model using a pre-trained BERT model for Portuguese. Results suggest that our data set is in line with its counterparts in other languages.

Keywords: Stance detection · Sentiment · Portuguese · Twitter

1 Introduction

Social media dynamics make conditions ripe for polarization. Today, we have access to a vast volume of text data containing pro-and-against style discussions, especially on political issues. The NLP task of Stance Detection is useful to analyze interactions on social media. Its primary goal is to develop methodologies tailored to predict the position for or against a particular target in any given text [12]. The NLP task of Stance Detection aims to develop methodologies tailored to predict the position for or against a particular target in any given text [12]. The task is valuable today, where we have access to a vast volume of text data containing pro-and-against style discussions, especially on political issues. It is, for example, the case of social media, whose dynamics make conditions ripe for polarization.

We turn to the social media Twitter as the source of the data set, where we used Twitter API service.[1] Twitter is well-known to be highly dynamic with respect to political debates. It is frequently a stage of intense interactions with political content, with explicit polarization dynamics, resulting in a rich environment for testing stance position models.

---

[1] https://developer.twitter.com/en/docs/twitter-api.

© Springer Nature Switzerland AG 2022
V. Pinheiro et al. (Eds.): PROPOR 2022, LNAI 13208, pp. 110–121, 2022.
https://doi.org/10.1007/978-3-030-98305-5_11

Traditional stance detection data sets built from tweets are defined based on a structure in which each instance corresponds to one or multiple fixed targets [14,16]. Instead, we build an open-domain stance detection data set [1], in which we do not define a priori a specific target. This type of data set can be used for the development of target-agnostic models, which will allow greater flexibility for production scenarios.

We make available a data set of nearly 15,000 Portuguese tweets annotated with stance position. To our knowledge, it is the first annotated data set of this kind.

Stance Detection is a research problem related to several other NLP tasks. More specifically, it is linked to those that identify or classify text containing some sort of feeling and emotion, for example, of sentiment analysis, emotion recognition, or the detection of irony. Some may argue that political debates hinge on rationality and neutral display of facts. However, many of the opinions relayed on online debates are often accompanied by feelings and emotions, making their classification challenging. For this reason, stance detection is traditionally related to sentiment analysis, and known data sets in the field are also annotated with sentiment [14]. Likewise, we also annotate the sentiment class, allowing future studies on the relationship between both categories. Furthermore, the sentiment category can be used individually to train classifiers focused on short texts with political content.

We present a data set of tweets written in European Portuguese that have been manually annotated for stance position. In what follows, we describe the annotation tasks and the data set.

2 Related Work

Most existing research shows that stance detection focus exclusively on political text as the basis of analysis. One of the firsts works on stance detection tries to infer the "yea" or "nay" position implicit in U.S. Congressional floor debates [23]. In [2], the authors used the online debate platform convinceme.net (currently offline) to build a data set of posts on various themes, including some non-political ones. Their results show that posts with political content generate more engagement and are the most difficult to classify. Other examples of works using similar online debate platforms include [9,10,17,20,21,26,27]. Topics frequently debated in this type of forums are political issues typically known to generate polarized opinions, such as gun rights or abortion.

The need for models fitted to predict stance position has generated a high volume of studies in the field, especially focused on data collected from social media platforms. [14] created the first data set on stance with tweets written in English. They also created a shared task on SemEval-2016, where they registered strong participation of up to 19 teams. Similarly, [32] show a new data set in Chinese. The authors collected publications from the microblogging platform Sina Weibo and proposed a shared task in NLPCC-ICCPOL-2016. A more recent data set and a respective shared task was published by [22]. The corpus contains tweets written in Catalan and, in addition to stance position, is annotated with the author's gender. [16] built a dataset whose tweets contain more than one target while [3] published the first data set annotated with stance for tweets written in Italian.

These data sets paved the way for a growing interest on studies focused on stance detection. The recent surveys [12] and [1] make a detailed overview of these recent works.

Regarding model approaches, stance detection studies have followed similar trends to those of other NLP tasks. Earlier works focused on rule-based approaches [2,26], which search for particular patterns, such as n-grams, punctuation, or particular words. Studies have used feature-based algorithms with the predominant use of SVMs [5,10,26], to which a more recent trend of using deep neural networks ensued, such as LSTM [15,28] and CNN [11,29]. More recently, contextual embeddings such as BERT have been gaining traction in the field [7,24,25].

3   Corpus

3.1   Data Collection

In this work, we use the Portuguese political debate on Twitter as the basis for building the corpus. We adopted as a starting point the accounts of party leaders whose parties garnered parliamentary representation in the 2019 legislative elections. We collected all tweets from their accounts published from 2017 through August 2020. In so doing, our collection yield 8.095 tweets.

The accounts of party leaders are primarily used for political communication. Thus, their tweets focus predominantly on political issues, positions, and propaganda. It is reasonable to assume that interactions from these tweets are somewhat counter-responses, supportive or against, to the positions taken in the original tweet. This dynamic is particularly strong in the case of quoted tweets. In a quoted tweet, users share the original tweet while adding a personalized message related to the original tweet. In quoting tweets from political leaders, users typically position themselves with respect to the original political message. Consequently, we argue, a quoted tweet and the respective original tweet with political content constitute a stance-target style text pair without a pre-defined and fixed target.

We begin by identifying all quoted tweets originated from the political leaders' tweets. Our sample contains only quoted tweet with some form of text (some quotes are an image only) and written in Portuguese. This compilation resulted in a total of 111,762 quoted tweets.

Some accounts receive significantly more attention than others, which results in an unbalanced data set. For example, the *@andrecventura* account, leader of a recent extreme right-wing party, has been gaining traction over the past years. Like other nationalism-populist European parties, André Ventura has recently registered significant vote intentions. Hundreds of quoted tweets usually target his tweets, often with an against stance position and negative sentiment. From our collection of quoted tweets, more than 50% (64,624) are quotes of his tweets. In order to create a more balanced annotated corpus, we took special care in selecting the quoted tweets used for the annotation process (see below).

3.2 Guidelines

For the annotation step, we begin by defining a set of rules to be used as guidelines by the human annotators. For the stance label, we considered the previous work of [14], which, similar to our work, created a manually annotated data set on stance from tweets. Like their work, we do not want to restrict a stance position to an explicit form of expression towards the target. Therefore, in annotating the stance position, we require annotators to classify between one the labels *Support/Against/Neutral/Inconclusive*, based on the following guidelines:

Support

- *The tweet explicitly supports the quoted tweet.*
- *The tweet supports something/someone aligned with the quoted tweet, from which we can infer that the tweeter supports the quoted tweet.*
- *The tweet is against something/someone other than the quoted tweet, from which we can infer that the tweeter supports the quoted tweet.*
- *The tweet is NOT in support of or against anything, but it has some information, from which we can infer that the tweeter supports the quoted tweet.*
- *We cannot infer the tweeter's stance toward the quoted tweet, but the tweet is echoing somebody else's favorable stance towards the quoted tweet (this could be a news story, quote, retweet, etc.).*

Against

- *The tweet is explicitly against the quoted tweet.*
- *The tweet is against someone/something aligned with the quoted tweet, from which we can infer that the tweeter is against the quoted tweet.*
- *The tweet is in support of someone/something other than the quoted tweet, from which we can infer that the tweeter is against the quoted tweet.*
- *The tweet is NOT in support of or against anything, but it has some information, from which we can infer that the tweeter is against the quoted tweet.*
- *We cannot infer the tweeter's stance toward the quoted tweet, but the tweet is echoing somebody else's negative stance towards the quoted tweet (this could be a news story, quote, retweet, etc.).*

Neutral

- *The tweet must provide some information that suggests that the tweeter is neutral towards the quoted tweet – the tweet being neither favorable nor against the quoted tweet is not sufficient reason for choosing this option. One reason for choosing this option is that the tweeter supports the quoted tweet to some extent, but is also against it to some extent.*

Inconclusive

- *There is no clue in the tweet to reveal the stance of the tweeter towards the quoted tweet (support/against/neutral)*

For the sentiment label annotation, we turn to the work of [13] to write the guidelines. We instructed annotators to pay special attention to the type of language used, both positive or negative, and try not to be influenced by the stance position. Also, since many tweets are often subject to mockery, we added the Sarcasm and Irony category. In many cases, Twitter users resort to sarcasm as an indirect way of displaying their negative sentiments. This category can be further used for possible studies on irony detection. In the end, annotators were told to label the tweet with one of the labels *Positive/Negative/Sarcasm/Inconclusive*, based on the following guidelines:

- **Positive**: *The tweet uses positive language, for example, admiration, positive attitude, forgiveness, fostering, success, positive emotional state (happiness, optimism, pride, etc.).*
- **Negative**: *The tweet uses negative language, for example, judgment, negative attitude, questioning validity/competence, failure, negative emotional state (anger, frustration, sadness, anxiety, etc.).*
- **Neutral**: *The tweet is neither using positive language nor using negative language.* Sarcasm/Irony
- **Sarcasm/Irony**: *The tweet uses expressions of sarcasm, ridicule, or mockery.*
- **Inconclusive**: *The tweet uses positive language in part and negative language in part.*

3.3   Annotation Procedure

We recruited four political science students for the annotation process. Additionally, we coded a web application on which each annotator was shown the tweet and the respect labels to annotated. The use of this web application allowed a fast and efficient annotation process.

In order to create a data set as unbiased as possible, we randomly generated our samples based on the user. Each user has its ideological position, and by randomly selecting quoted tweets based on account, we are equitably collecting quoted tweets from different regions of the ideological map.

With this in mind, we begin by randomly selecting accounts that have quoted at least one tweet from the party leaders' accounts and select randomly one quoted tweet from the said account. We also added the original tweet, which can correspond to several quoted tweets (one tweet generates multiple quoted tweets). This collection resulted in a sample of 2,510 tweets of which 1,896 are quoted tweets.

After this first batch was completed, we manually inspected and debated several instances that did not gather consensus with the annotators. This debate was followed by a second annotation step, wherein we have shown each annotator the tweets where she is in the minority and asked if they want to change the answer. In order to prevent peer-pressure bias, we explicitly instructed coders to be wary of the type of possible bias and only to change the annotation if they were sure their initial labeling is incorrect.

This last reviewing step allows each annotator to access their peers' opinions, to understand the group knowledge better, and improve their fit about the decision process, resulting in a broader perspective of annotation goals. Such learning is especially relevant at the beginning of the annotation process, during which each annotator is still learning what is more relevant when selecting the labels.

Next, annotators had access to a second batch of tweets. We continued with the same type of sampling and retrieved tweets from the poll of users not seen in the first batch. Again, it followed a reviewing process that, unlike the first batch, was faster. At this stage of the annotation process, annotators registered better agreement rates. The second batch resulted in a sample of 9,619 tweets of which 8,055 are quoted tweets.

At the end of these first two batches, we registered an unbalanced data set for the stance position, with 68% of the tweets with a majority labeled as *Against* and 22% as *Support*.

3.4   Balancing the Corpus

In order to create a more balanced corpus, we generated a third batch of tweets, where now we sampled the users' accounts based on their ideological proximity. We used the method proposed in [31] that uses a graph embeddings framework to encode each account into a high-dimension dense vector. The authors showed that such embedding is politically meaningful and that distance measures such as a cosine similarity correlate with ideological proximity.

We collected approximately 706,618 tweets from a poll of accounts of Portuguese political actors, such as opinion-makers and legislators, institutional accounts, in particular political parties. We identified the respective retweets and built a weighted graph, where the weight accounts for the number of times both users retweeted the same tweet. In order to prevent isolated nodes, we considered users that retweet at least five retweets. The final graph contains 40,132 nodes and 1,981,770 edges. We then used Node2Vec [8] to estimate embeddings of size 10^2.

Next, we identified all accounts with a cosine similarity higher than 0.75 to each political leader account. We expect these accounts to be more likely to generate support quotes from the respective political leader account. This third batch resulted in 4,526 tweets, and after the annotation process of labeling and reviewing, it registered 88% of the tweets with a majority labeled as *Support*.

---

[2] We use Node2Vec's package **nodevectors** (https://github.com/VHRanger/nodevectors) with the following parameters. $n\_components = 10$, $walklen = 50$, $epochs = 20$, $window = 10$, $negative = 20$, $iter = 10$, $batch\_words = 128$.

3.5   Descriptive Statistics

The final corpus contains 16,655 annotated tweets of which 14,477 are quoted tweets annotated with stance position and sentiment. We make the annotated corpus publicly available at https://github.com/miguelwon/SS-PT/[3]. Table 1 shows descriptive statistics. We can see that we have a balanced data set with 47% of the quoted tweets with majority were labeled as *Against* and 43% as *Support.*

Table 1 shows inter-annotator agreement coefficient, for which we used Fleiss kappa [6]. We report two agreements for the sentiment class: the first in which we consider all classes described in the guidelines, and the second in which we merge the sarcasm class with the negative class. All annotators reported that the most challenging class to label was sarcasm. Tweets annotated with sarcasm often contain negative language, which has led to frequent indecision in classifying the tweet as sarcasm or negative. Others works report similar issues [14]. Typically, a frequent solution is to merge the classes. As expected, in merging sarcasm and negative sentiment classes, we obtain an improvement in inter-coder agreement.

Table 2 shows a type of confusion matrix between stance and sentiment labels. It suggest a strong correlation between a negative sentiment and against stance position. Furthermore, note that 98% of labels with against correspond to a negative and sarcasm sentiment. This correlation results from the against position itself since it is unlikely to tweet positively and not agree with the target. However, the opposite is not valid, showing that there is no symmetry in a stance position. Roughly 50% of support contains positive sentiment, and a relevant share of 25% shows negativity (35% if we account for the sarcasm class).

Table 1. Tweets annotated for stance and sentiment and the respective Fleiss' kappa inter-annotator agreement coefficients. $\kappa*$ was calculated when considering negative and sarcasm in a single class.

	Stance	Sentiment
N$^{\underline{o}}$ of tweets	14477	16655
With majority	14070	15791
Against	6616	–
Support	6051	–
Neutral	44	1459
Inconclusive	1359	521
Positive	–	3601
Negative	–	7090
Sarcasm	–	3120
κ	0.77	0.64
$\kappa*$	0.77	0.70

---

[3] We publish the data in agreement with Twitter API terms and conditions.

These negative and supportive quotes are usually instances where the original tweet shows a solid position or criticizing a particular policy. Additionally, these tweets show more negativity. We measure that 77% of these original tweets were labeled with a negative sentiment. The result suggests that some negativity of the original tweet influence also the creation of quotes with negative sentiment.

4   Baseline Experiment

We show the details of a baseline experiment we performed with the annotated corpus. We test how well the known state-of-the-art BERT model [4] performs in the data set. We used the pre-trained model for Portuguese [18,19], in particular the base-cased version. We used HuggingFace's Transformers [30] library with a classification head composed of two linear and tanh layers that encode each instance to a size of 1.536 (768×2), followed by a final linear layer that outputs according to the number of possible labels.

Table 2. Number of tweets with respect to stance position and the respective sentiment label.

	Support	Against	Neutral	Inc.
Positive	2796	46		16
	49.1%	0.7%		1.2%
Negative	1461	4532	13	289
	25.6%	71.9%	31.7%	22.2%
Neutral	588	48	3	298
	.3%	0.7%	7.3%	22.9%
Sarcarm	494	1622	3	679
	.6%	25.8%	7.3%	.2
Inc.	361	51	22	19
	6.3%	0.8%	5.4%	1.5%

All instances were subject to a pre-processed step, wherein URLs, mentions, and hashtags have been removed. An additional cleaning step was implemented to deal specifically with quotes or mentions to *@andrecventura* account. As mentioned above, his account is intensively targeted with negative sentiment and against quotes. Such a trend could bias the training process by classifying an against a position or negative sentiment, just by the presence of his name. Consequently, we removed any text containing his name as well his party's name. As a last step, we considered consider annotated examples where we have registered a majority. Table 3 shows precision, recall, and f-measures results for stance label when evaluating the model in a stratified test set with a size of 10% of the data set and 90% for training. The f-measure result of 0.75 compares with other studies that measure the performance of BERT models in the task of stance prediction [7,25]. Table 3 also shows the equivalent results for the sentiment class. This experiment shows that the sentiment class is more challenging to predict. The poorer performance stems primarily from the ambiguity that the sarcasm class introduces in the classifications. From Table 3 we see that both positive and negative classes show better f-measure. Furthermore, if we merge both sarcasm and negative class, we register an f-measure of 0.82, which is a significant improvement.

Table 3. Precision, recall and F-Measure for sentiment and stance prediction.

(a) Sentiment

	P	R	F	Support
Positive	0.81	0.81	0.81	357
Negative	0.77	0.83	0.80	708
Neutral	0.52	0.49	0.50	126
Inconclusive	0.26	0.41	0.32	51
Sarcasm	0.62	0.46	0.53	312
Weigh Avg	0.71	0.71	**0.71**	

(b) Stance

	P	R	F	Support
Against	0.75	0.84	0.80	662
Support	0.82	0.73	0.77	580
Inconclusive	0.45	0.38	0.41	127
Neutral	0.00	0.00	0.00	4
Weigh Avg	0.75	0.75	**0.75**	

5   Conclusion

This work contributes to the literature by offering a new data set manually annotated for stance position and sentiment, the first of its kind for the Portuguese language. Data collection was based on the online debate that takes place daily on Twitter. We used the accounts of multiple Portuguese party leaders as a reference. The data set mainly comprises quoted tweets from leaders' tweets, which can be considered open-domain stance-target text pairs. In order to create a balanced corpus for the stance label, we implemented a partially biased search, in which we used a graph embeddings formalism to estimate ideological proximity. Using a partially biased search permits us to overcome prior biases. We observed a high ratio of against positions on the collected tweets, mainly associated with a negative or sarcasm sentiment. Our baseline model shows that the sarcasm category is the most difficult to predict, in line with the annotation difficulties aforementioned. By contrast, the support positions are distributed with positive and negative sentiments. These results confirm that negative emotions intensively characterize the online debate.

We performed a baseline experiment to test the performance of the state-of-the-art pre-trained BERT models. Results show that the data set allows a learning process that outputs comparable performances with equivalent corpora.

Acknowledgements. This research was supported by the Portuguese Science and Technology Foundation (FCT), as part of the "Into the 'Secret Garden' of Portuguese Politics: Parliamentary Candidate Selection in Portugal, 1976-2015" project

(PTDC/CPO-CPO/30296/2017), and the project with ref UIDB/50021/2020. We also thank BioData.pt for the computer resources.

References

1. AlDayel, A., Magdy, W.: Stance detection on social media: state of the art and trends. Inf. Process. Manage. **58**(4), 102597 (2021)
2. Anand, P., Walker, M., Abbott, R., Tree, J.E.F., Bowmani, R., Minor, M.: Cats rule and dogs drool!: classifying stance in online debate. In: Proceedings of the 2nd Workshop on Computational Approaches to Subjectivity and Sentiment Analysis (WASSA 2011), pp. 1–9 (2011)
3. Cignarella, A.T., Lai, M., Bosco, C., Patti, V., Paolo, R., et al.: Sardistance@ EVALITA2020: overview of the task on stance detection in Italian tweets. In: EVALITA 2020 Seventh Evaluation Campaign of Natural Language Processing and Speech Tools for Italian, pp. 1–10. CEUR (2020)
4. Devlin, J., Chang, M.W., Lee, K., Toutanova, K.: BERT: pre-training of deep bidirectional transformers for language understanding. In: Proceedings of the 2019 Conference of the North American Chapter of the Association for Computational Linguistics: Human Language Technologies (2019)
5. Dias, M., Becker, K.: INF-UFRGS-OPINION-MINING at SemEval-2016 task 6: automatic generation of a training corpus for unsupervised identification of stance in tweets. In: Proceedings of the 10th International Workshop on Semantic Evaluation (SemEval 2016), pp. 378–383 (2016)
6. Fleiss, J.L., Cohen, J.: The equivalence of weighted kappa and the intraclass correlation coefficient as measures of reliability. Educ. Psychol. Measur. **33**(3), 613–619 (1973)
7. Ghosh, S., Singhania, P., Singh, S., Rudra, K., Ghosh, S.: Stance detection in web and social media: a comparative study. In: Crestani, F., et al. (eds.) CLEF 2019. LNCS, vol. 11696, pp. 75–87. Springer, Cham (2019). https://doi.org/10.1007/978-3-030-28577-7_4
8. Grover, A., Leskovec, J.: node2vec: scalable feature learning for networks. In: Proceedings of the 22nd ACM SIGKDD International Conference on Knowledge Discovery and Data Mining, pp. 855–864. ACM (2016)
9. Hasan, K.S., Ng, V.: Predicting stance in ideological debate with rich linguistic knowledge. In: Proceedings of COLING 2012: Posters, pp. 451–460 (2012)
10. Hasan, K.S., Ng, V.: Stance classification of ideological debates: data, models, features, and constraints. In: Proceedings of the Sixth International Joint Conference on Natural Language Processing, pp. 1348–1356 (2013)
11. Igarashi, Y., Komatsu, H., Kobayashi, S., Okazaki, N., Inui, K.: Tohoku at SemEval-2016 task 6: feature-based model versus convolutional neural network for stance detection. In: Proceedings of the 10th International Workshop on Semantic Evaluation (SemEval 2016), pp. 401–407 (2016)
12. Küçük, D., Can, F.: Stance detection: a survey. ACM Comput. Surv. (CSUR) **53**(1), 1–37 (2020)
13. Mohammad, S.: A practical guide to sentiment annotation: challenges and solutions. In: Proceedings of the 7th Workshop on Computational Approaches to Subjectivity, Sentiment and Social Media Analysis, pp. 174–179 (2016)
14. Mohammad, S., Kiritchenko, S., Sobhani, P., Zhu, X., Cherry, C.: A dataset for detecting stance in tweets. In: Proceedings of the Tenth International Conference on Language Resources and Evaluation (LREC 2016), pp. 3945–3952 (2016)

15. Siddiqua, U.A., Chy, A.N., Aono, M.: Tweet stance detection using an attention based neural ensemble model. In: Proceedings of the 2019 Conference of the North American Chapter of the Association for Computational Linguistics: Human Language Technologies, Volume 1 (Long and Short Papers), pp. 1868–1873 (2019)
16. Sobhani, P., Inkpen, D., Zhu, X.: A dataset for multi-target stance detection. In: Proceedings of the 15th Conference of the European Chapter of the Association for Computational Linguistics: Volume 2, Short Papers, pp. 551–557 (2017)
17. Somasundaran, S., Wiebe, J.: Recognizing stances in ideological on-line debates. In: Proceedings of the NAACL HLT 2010 Workshop on Computational Approaches to Analysis and Generation of Emotion in Text, pp. 116–124 (2010)
18. Souza, F., Nogueira, R., Lotufo, R.: Portuguese named entity recognition using BERT-CRF. arXiv preprint arXiv:1909.10649 (2019). http://arxiv.org/abs/1909.10649
19. Souza, F., Nogueira, R., Lotufo, R.: BERTimbau: pretrained BERT models for Brazilian Portuguese. In: 9th Brazilian Conference on Intelligent Systems, BRACIS, Rio Grande do Sul, Brazil, 20–23 October (2020, to appear)
20. Sridhar, D., Foulds, J., Huang, B., Getoor, L., Walker, M.: Joint models of disagreement and stance in online debate. In: Proceedings of the 53rd Annual Meeting of the Association for Computational Linguistics and the 7th International Joint Conference on Natural Language Processing (Volume 1: Long Papers), pp. 116–125 (2015)
21. Sridhar, D., Getoor, L., Walker, M.: Collective stance classification of posts in online debate forums. In: Proceedings of the Joint Workshop on Social Dynamics and Personal Attributes in Social Media, pp. 109–117 (2014)
22. Taulé, M., et al.: Overview of the task on stance and gender detection in tweets on catalan independence at Ibereval 2017. In: 2nd Workshop on Evaluation of Human Language Technologies for Iberian Languages, IberEval 2017, vol. 1881, pp. 157–177. CEUR-WS (2017)
23. Thomas, M., Pang, B., Lee, L.: Get out the vote: determining support or opposition from congressional floor-debate transcripts. arXiv preprint cs/0607062 (2006)
24. Toutanova, K., et al.: Proceedings of the 2021 conference of the North American chapter of the association for computational linguistics: human language technologies. In: Proceedings of the 2021 Conference of the North American Chapter of the Association for Computational Linguistics: Human Language Technologies (2021)
25. Vamvas, J., Sennrich, R.: X-stance: a multilingual multi-target dataset for stance detection. arXiv preprint arXiv:2003.08385 (2020)
26. Walker, M., Anand, P., Abbott, R., Grant, R.: Stance classification using dialogic properties of persuasion. In: Proceedings of the 2012 Conference of the North American Chapter of the Association for Computational Linguistics: Human Language Technologies, pp. 592–596 (2012)
27. Walker, M.A., Anand, P., Abbott, R., Tree, J.E.F., Martell, C., King, J.: That is your evidence?: classifying stance in online political debate. Decis. Support Syst. 53(4), 719–729 (2012)
28. Wei, P., Mao, W., Chen, G.: A topic-aware reinforced model for weakly supervised stance detection. In: Proceedings of the AAAI Conference on Artificial Intelligence, vol. 33, pp. 7249–7256 (2019)
29. Wei, W., Zhang, X., Liu, X., Chen, W., Wang, T.: pkudblab at SemEval-2016 task 6: a specific convolutional neural network system for effective stance detection. In: Proceedings of the 10th International Workshop on Semantic Evaluation (SemEval 2016), pp. 384–388 (2016)

30. Wolf, T., et al.: Huggingface's transformers: state-of-the-art natural language processing. arXiv preprint arXiv:1910.03771 (2019)
31. Won, M., Fernandes, J.M.: Analyzing twitter networks using graph embeddings: an application to the British case. J. Comput. Soc. Sci., 1–11 (2021)
32. Xu, R., Zhou, Yu., Wu, D., Gui, L., Du, J., Xue, Y.: Overview of NLPCC shared task 4: stance detection in Chinese microblogs. In: Lin, C.-Y., Xue, N., Zhao, D., Huang, X., Feng, Y. (eds.) ICCPOL/NLPCC -2016. LNCS (LNAI), vol. 10102, pp. 907–916. Springer, Cham (2016). https://doi.org/10.1007/978-3-319-50496-4_85

Natural Language Processing Tasks

ZeroBERTo: Leveraging Zero-Shot Text Classification by Topic Modeling

Alexandre Alcoforado[1]([✉]) [ID], Thomas Palmeira Ferraz[1,2] [ID], Rodrigo Gerber[1] [ID],
Enzo Bustos[1] [ID], André Seidel Oliveira[1] [ID], Bruno Miguel Veloso[3] [ID],
Fabio Levy Siqueira[1] [ID], and Anna Helena Reali Costa[1] [ID]

[1] Escola Politécnica, Universidade de São Paulo (USP), São Paulo, Brazil
{alexandre.alcoforado,rodrigo.gerber,enzobustos,andre.seidel,
levy.siqueira,anna.reali}@usp.br
[2] Télécom Paris, Institut Polytechnique de Paris, Palaiseau, France
thomas.palmeira@telecom-paris.fr
[3] Universidade Portucalense and INESC TEC, Porto, Portugal
bruno.m.veloso@inesctec.pt

Abstract. Traditional text classification approaches often require a good amount of labeled data, which is difficult to obtain, especially in restricted domains or less widespread languages. This lack of labeled data has led to the rise of low-resource methods, that assume low data availability in natural language processing. Among them, zero-shot learning stands out, which consists of learning a classifier without any previously labeled data. The best results reported with this approach use language models such as Transformers, but fall into two problems: high execution time and inability to handle long texts as input. This paper proposes a new model, ZeroBERTo, which leverages an unsupervised clustering step to obtain a compressed data representation before the classification task. We show that ZeroBERTo has better performance for long inputs and shorter execution time, outperforming XLM-R by about 12% in the F1 score in the FolhaUOL dataset.

Keywords: Low-resource NLP · Unlabeled data · Zero-shot learning · Topic modeling · Transformers

1 Introduction

The current success of supervised learning techniques in real-world Natural Language Processing (NLP) applications is undeniable. While these techniques require a good set of labeled data, large corpora of annotated texts are difficult to obtain, as people (sometimes experts) are needed to create manual annotations or revise and correct predefined labels. This problem is even more critical in languages other than English: statistics[1] show that English is used by 63.1%

---

[1] Statistics available at: https://w3techs.com/technologies/overview/content_language.

V. Pinheiro et al. (Eds.): PROPOR 2022, LNAI 13208, pp. 125–136, 2022.
https://doi.org/10.1007/978-3-030-98305-5_12

of the population on the internet, while Portuguese, for instance, is only used by 0.7%. This scenario has contributed to the rise of Low-Resource NLP, which aims to develop techniques to deal with low data availability in a specific language or application domain [12].

Recently, the concept of *zero-shot learning* emerged in NLP: a semi-supervised approach in which models can present results equivalent to those of supervised tasks, such as classification in the absence of labeled data. Current approaches to the zero-shot text classification task (0SHOT-TC) make use of the good performance that *Transformers* have demonstrated in text entailment tasks [30]. In order to be able to process text in a way that is not uniquely suited to any specific task or data-set, these Transformers are first pre-trained in large general databases (usually taken from Wikipedia) and then fine-tuned into a small mainstream dataset for the natural language inference task (such as GLUE [28] and XNLI [7]). However, the use of models based entirely on Transformers falls into two critical problems: (i) limitation of the maximum size of the input text, and (ii) long run-time for large volumes of data. While there are transformer-based solutions to these problems individually [1, 24, 31], to the best of our knowledge, there is no solution that addresses both, nor even in the context of 0SHOT-TC.

In this paper, we propose a new hybrid model that merges Transformers with unsupervised learning, called ZeroBERTo – Zero-shot BERT based on Topic Modeling –, which is able to classify texts by learning only from unlabeled data. Our contribution not only handles long inputs – not limiting the input size and considering every input token to encode the data – but also offers a faster execution time. We propose an experimental setup with unlabeled data, simulating low-resource scenarios where real-life NLP researchers may find themselves. Then, we compare ZeroBERTo to a fully-Transformer-based zero-shot on a categorization dataset in Portuguese, FolhaUOL[2]. Our results show that our model outperforms the previous one, in the best scenario, with about 12% better *label aware weighted F1-score* and around 13 times faster total time.

The paper is structured as follows: Sect. 2 presents a background of how it is possible to move from data scarcity to zero-shot learning, as well as the related work on getting the best model for the 0SHOT-TC task. Section 3 formalizes the ZeroBERTo task and describe its training and inference procedures. Then, Sect. 4 describes the experimental setup that makes it possible to simulate low-resource scenarios to evaluate the proposed model. Finally, the discussion of the results of the experiments along with our final remarks is in Sect. 5.

2   Background and Related Work

The first approach to overcome the shortage of labeled data for classification suggests adopting data augmentation strategies [13], relying on methods to generalize from small sets of already annotated data. Still, the problem persists when there is an extreme lack of data. An alternative approach is to treat the task as a topic modeling problem. Topic modeling is an unsupervised learning

---

[2] Available at: https://www.kaggle.com/marlesson/news-of-the-site-folhauol.

technique capable of scanning a set of documents, detecting patterns of words and phrases within them, and automatically clustering groups of similar words and expressions that best characterize a set of documents [5]. There is usually a later labeling step for these clusters, which can be a problem as their interpretation is sometimes challenging, and a labeling error can affect the entire process. An automatic method for this is in our interest.

The context presented helps explain the growing interest in the field of Low-Resource NLP [4,12], which addresses traditional NLP tasks with the assumption of scarcity of available data. Some approaches to this family of tasks propose semi-supervised methods, such as adding large quantities of unlabeled data to a small labelled dataset [21], or applying cross-lingual annotation transfer learning [2] to leverage annotated data available in languages other than the desired one. Other approaches try to eliminate the need for annotated data for training, relying, for example, on pre-trained *task-agnostic* neural language models [20], which may be used as language information sources, as well as representation learning models [14] for word, sentence or document classification tasks.

Recent breakthroughs in pre-trained neural models have expanded the limits of what can be done with data shortage. The Transformer model [27], which relies solely on attention mechanisms for learning, followed by BERT [8] – a pre-trained Transformer encoder capable of deep bidirectional encoding – offered the possibility of using general-purpose models with previous language understanding. With little to no fine-tuning, BERT-like models have been successfully applied to most natural language comprehension tasks [17], and also show a significant reduction in the need for training data [3]. Such models tend to work better for the 0SHOT-TC task, as they carry information about the context and semantic attributes within their pre-trained parameters. On the downside, pre-trained Transformers are complex, with millions of trainable parameters and slow processing of large quantities of data, and due to memory issues, most pre-trained Transformers cannot process inputs larger than 512 tokens at a time. Also, attention models have another problem related to input size: attention cannot keep track of all information present in a large text, worsening the performance of the models.

In this context, zero-shot learning approaches stand out [25]. A simple way to explain zero-shot is to compare its paradigm with humans' ability to recognize classes of objects by having a high-level description of them without seeing an example of the object previously. [30] defines that 0SHOT-TC aims to learn a classifier $f : X \rightarrow Y$, whereas classifier $f(.)$, however, does not have access to data X specifically labeled with classes from Y. We can use the knowledge that the model already has to learn an intermediate layer of semantic attributes, which is then applied at inference time to recognize unseen classes during the training stages [32].

Several works that seek to improve the performance of zero-shot learning inspired ours. [16] worked in the image domain, seeking to develop a two-stage model that first learns to extract relevant attributes from images automatically and then learns to assign these attributes to labels. Our proposal performs the same two steps for the text classification problem but does not use any specific knowledge of external data or require any labelled data.

In the text domain, [19] defines weak-supervised learning similar to our definition of zero-shot learning. With unlabeled data and a list of classes as inputs, it applies seed word lists to guide an interactive clustering preview. [20] uses topic mining to find out which words have the same semantic meaning as the proposed labels, and with that makes a fine-tuning of the language model assuming the implicit category as the presence of these words in the text. Unlike these approaches, our model does not require the user to have any seed word for the labels, and instead of automatically learning them from the labels themselves, ZeroBERTo discovers them from the input data through topic modeling and then assigns them to the labels based on the language model used.

3   Proposed Method

In this section, we introduce ZeroBERTo which leverages Topic Modeling and pre-trained Language Models (LMs) for the task of zero-shot multi-class text classification (0SHOT-TC).

3.1   0SHOT-TC Task Formalization

Given a set of unlabeled documents $\mathcal{D} = \{d_1, d_2, \ldots, d_n\}$ and a set of m semantically disjoint and relevant label names $\mathcal{L} = \{l_1, l_2, \ldots, l_m\}$, 0SHOT-TC aims to learn $f : \mathcal{D} \times \mathcal{L} \to \Theta$, $|\Theta| = |\mathcal{L}|$ and Θ defines a probability $\theta_j^i \in [0,1]$ for each label l_j being the label for d_i [30]. A single-label classification of a document d_i may then be carried out as $l_j \in \mathcal{L} \mid j = argmax_{(j)}(\theta_1^i, \theta_2^i, \ldots, \theta_m^i)$ – as a notation simplification, for now on, we mention this as $argmax_{(l \in \mathcal{L})}(\Theta_i)$.

Standard approaches to the 0SHOT-TC task treat it as a *Recognizing Textual Entailment (RTE)* problem: given two documents d_1, d_2, we say "d_1 *entails* d_2" ($d_1 \Rightarrow d_2$) if a human reading d_1 would be justified in inferring the proposition expressed by d_2 (named *hypothesis*) from the proposition expressed by d_1 [15]. In the case of 0SHOT-TC, d_2 is the hypothesis $\mathcal{H}(l_j)$, which is simply a sentence that expresses an association to l_j. For example, in a news categorization problem, a label could be "**sports**" and a hypothesis for it could be "This news is about **sports**". Creating the hypothesis is essential to make it understandable by a Language Model, and allows us to discover the probability $P(l_j|d_i) = P(d_i \Rightarrow \mathcal{H}(l_j))$, as $P(d_i \Rightarrow \mathcal{H}(l_j))$ can easily be inferred by a LM, using d_i and $\mathcal{H}(l_j)$ as inputs. For the zero-shot text classification task, it calculates the textual entailment probability of each possible label. This inference, however, is quite demanding computationally.

3.2   ZeroBERTo

ZeroBERTo works differently: instead of processing the entire document in the LM, it learns a compressed data representation in an unsupervised way and only processes this representation in the LM. Thus, it is possible to obtain better performance with large inputs and shorter total time than the standard model, even considering the training time added by the unsupervised step.

To learn this representation, ZeroBERTo uses a statistical model, named **Topic Modeling** (TM), which examines documents and discovers, from the statistics of the words that occur in them, which abstract "topics" are covered, discovering hidden semantic structures in a text body. Given a set of unlabeled documents $\mathcal{D}$, TM aims at learning a set of topics $\mathcal{T}$. A topic $t \in \mathcal{T}$ is a list of q words or n-grams that are characteristic of a cluster but not of the entire documents set. Then, TM also learns how to represent any document $d_i \in \mathcal{D}$ as a composition of topics expressed by $\Omega_{TM}(d_i) = (\omega_1^i, \omega_2^i, \ldots, \omega_k^i)$, such that ω_k^i denotes the probability of a document d_i belonging to a topic t_k.

With this in place, instead of analyzing the relation between document d_i and label l_j, we determine the entailment between the learned topic representation $\Omega_{TM}(d_i)$ of each document and each label l_j. Topics found are given as input to the LM, as a text list of words/expressions that represent the topic, in order to infer entailment probabilities. If the topic representation was learnt properly, then we can assume independence between l_j and d_i given a topic t_k, therefore $P(l_j|t_k, d_i) = P(l_j|t_k) = P(t_k \Rightarrow \mathcal{H}(l_j))$. We then solve the 0SHOT-TC task by calculating the compound conditional probability

$$\theta_i^j = P(l_j|d_i) = \sum_{t_k \in \mathcal{T}} P(l_j|t_k) * P(t_k|d_i) = \sum_{t_k \in \mathcal{T}} P(t_k \Rightarrow \mathcal{H}(l_j)) * \Omega_{TM}^k(d_i) \quad (1)$$

for each label l_j to determine $\Theta_i = (\theta_i^1, \theta_i^2, \ldots, \theta_i^m)$. Classification is then carried out by selecting $argmax_{(l \in \mathcal{L})}(\Theta_i)$.

Algorithm 1: Given a set of documents $\mathcal{D}$, a set of labels $\mathcal{L}$, a hypothesis template $\mathcal{H}$, a topic model TM and a Language model LM as input, ZeroBERTo-training (see Algorithm 1) returns a trained model $\mathcal{Z}$. For that, it trains TM on $\mathcal{D}$ using TM.FIT (line 2), that learns the topic representation of those documents. Then, it applies LM.PREDICT for all topics learned in TM (lines 4 to 7). This function, given a topic t_k, returns the set of probabilities $P(t_k \Rightarrow \mathcal{H}(l_j))$ for all $l_j \in \mathcal{L}$. In the end, the model $\mathcal{Z}$ gathers all information learned from $\mathcal{D}$.

Algorithm 2: ZeroBERTo-prediction leverages a trained model $\mathcal{Z}$ and a specific document d_i to return the predicted label $l \in \mathcal{L}$ (see Algorithm 2). For this, it uses $\mathcal{Z}.TM$.TOPICENCODER (line 1), that returns the topic representation $\Omega_{TM}(d_i)$ of d_i. This was learned by $\mathcal{Z}.TM$ in Algorithm 1. Then, it calculates the Eq. (1) for all candidate labels (lines 2 to 8), returning the one with maximum probability.

Algorithm 1. ZeroBERTo-training	**Algorithm 2.** ZeroBERTo-prediction
Require: $\mathcal{D}, \mathcal{L}, \mathcal{H}, TM, LM$	**Require:** $\mathcal{Z}, d_i$
Ensure: $\mathcal{Z}$	**Ensure:** l
1: **create** $\mathcal{Z}$ ▷ Instantiate ZeroBERTo	1: $\Omega^i_{TM} \leftarrow \mathcal{Z}.TM.\text{TOPICENCODER}(d_i)$
2: $TM.\text{FIT}(\mathcal{D})$ ▷ Topic Model Training	2: $\Theta_i \leftarrow \{\}$
3: $\mathcal{P} \leftarrow \{\}$	3: **for each** $l_j \in \mathcal{Z}.\mathcal{L}$ **do**
4: **for each** $t_k \in TM.topics$ **do**	4: $\theta^i_j \leftarrow 0$
5: $p_k \leftarrow LM.predict(t_k, \mathcal{H}(\mathcal{L}))$	5: **for each** $t_k \in \mathcal{Z}.TM.topics$ **do**
6: $\mathcal{P} \leftarrow \mathcal{P} \cup \{p_k\}$	6: $\theta^i_j \leftarrow \theta^i_j + (\mathcal{P}(t_k) * \Omega^i_{TM}(t_k))$
7: **end for**	7: **end for**
8: $\mathcal{Z}.TM \leftarrow TM$	8: $\Theta_i \leftarrow \Theta_i \cup \{\theta^i_j\}$
9: $\mathcal{Z}.\mathcal{P}, \mathcal{Z}.\mathcal{L} \leftarrow \mathcal{P}, \mathcal{L}$	9: **end for**
10: **return** $\mathcal{Z}$	10: **return** $argmax_{(l \in \mathcal{L})}(\Theta_i)$

4   Experiments

In this section, we present the experiments performed to validate the effectiveness of `ZeroBERTo`. Considering that it would be difficult to evaluate our model in a real low-resource scenario, we propose an experimental setup to simulate low-resource situations in labeled datasets. We compare `ZeroBERTo` with the XLM-R Transformer, fine-tuned only on the textual entailment task. To perform the unsupervised training and evaluation, we use FolhaUOL dataset[3].

Dataset. The FolhaUOL dataset is from the Brazilian newspaper "Folha de São Paulo" and consists of 167,053 news items labeled into journal sections (categories) from January 2015 to September 2017. Categories too broad, that do not have a semantic meaning associated with a specific context (as the case of "editorial" and "opinion"), were removed from the dataset keeping only the categories presented in Table 1. For each news article, we take the concatenation of its title and content as input. Table 1 presents the data distribution by category.

Table 1. Number of articles by news category within FolhaUOL dataset after cleaning and organizing the data.

Category	# of articles	Category	# of articles
Poder e Política	22022	Educação	2118
Mercado	20970	Turismo	1903
Esporte	19730	Ciência	1335
Notícias dos Países	17130	Equilíbrio e Saúde	1312
Tecnologia	2260	Comida	828
TV, Televisão e Entretenimento	2123	Meio Ambiente	491

---

[3] Available at: https://www.kaggle.com/marlesson/news-of-the-site-folhauol.

Models. We compare our proposal to the XLM-R model.

XLM-R is the short name for XLM-RoBERTa-large-XNLI, available on Hugging Face[4], which is state of the art in Multilingual 0SHOT-TC. It is built from XLM-RoBERTa [6] pre-trained in 100 different languages (Portuguese among them), and then fine-tuned in the XNLI [7] and MNLI [29] datasets (which do not include the Portuguese language). It is already in the zero-shot learning configuration described by [30] with template hypothesis as input. The template hypothesis used was "*O tema principal desta notícia é {}*" and texts larger than the maximum size of XLM-R (512 tokens) are truncated.

ZeroBERTo. The implementation of our model here makes use of BERTopic [11] with M-BERT-large (Multilingual BERT) [8] as topic modeling step, and the same XLM-R described above as the Transformer for associating the topic representation of each document to labels. Repeating the use of XLM-R seeks to make the comparison fair. BERTopic's hyperparameters are: interval n for n-grams to be considered in the topic representation (n_grams_range $\in \{1, 2, 3\}$); number of representative words/n-grams per topic (top_n_words = 20); and minimum amount of data in each valid topic (min_topic_size = 10). The XLM-R template hypothesis used is "*O tema principal desta lista de palavras é {}*".

Evaluation. To simulate real-world scenarios, we propose a variation of stratified k-fold cross-validation [23]. First, we split the data into k disjoint stratified folds, *i.e.* the data were evenly distributed in such a way as to make the distribution of the classes in the k folds follow the distribution in the entire dataset. Next, we use these k-folds to perform the following 4 experiment setups:

Exp. 1 - Labeling a dataset: Simulates a situation where one needs to obtain the first labeling of a dataset. ZeroBERTo is trained in $(k-1)$ folds and has the performance compared to XLM-R in the same $(k-1)$ folds, in order to assess its ability to label data already seen. Since this is unsupervised learning, evaluating the model's labeling ability in the training data makes sense as it was not exposed to the ground truth labels.

Exp. 2 - Building a model for additional inferences: Simulates a situation where the researcher wants to create a current model in a real-life application without having data labeled for it. ZeroBERTo is trained in $(k-1)$ folds and can infer new data compared to XLM-R on the remaining fold.

Exp. 3 - Labeling a smaller dataset: Simulates situation of scarcity of data in which, besides not having labeled data, little data is present. ZeroBERTo is trained in one fold and compared to XLM-R in the same fold. Considering the topic-representation learning stage, the presence of little data could be a bottleneck for ZeroBERTo since the topic representation may not be properly learned.

---

[4] Available at: https://huggingface.co/joeddav/xlm-roberta-large-xnli.

Exp. 4 - Building model for additional inferences but with a scarcity of training data: simulates again how the model would behave in a real-life application with few training data. ZeroBERTo is trained in 1 fold and compared to XLM-R in the remaining $k - 1$ folds.

We evaluated the performance of both models for each experiment with the following label-aware metrics: weighted-average Precision (P), weighted-average Recall (R), and weighted-average F1-score (F1). For the k-fold CV, we use $k = 5$. Experiments were run on an Intel Xeon E5-2686 v4 2.3 GHz 61 GiB CPU and an NVIDIA Tesla K80 12 GiB GPU using the PyTorch framework. To run XLM-R, we use batches sized 20 to prevent GPU memory overflow.

Table 2. Table shows the results of the experiments for the FolhaUOL dataset. P is weighted-average precision, R is weighted-average Recall, and F1 is weighted-average F1-score.

	Exp. 1		Exp. 2		Exp. 3		Exp. 4	
	XLM-R	ZeroBERTo	XLM-R	ZeroBERTo	XLM-R	ZeroBERTo	XLM-R	ZeroBERTo
P	0.47 ± 0.00	**0.66 ± 0.01**	0.46 ± 0.01	0.16 ± 0.08	0.46 ± 0.01	**0.64 ± 0.01**	0.47 ± 0.00	0.29 ± 0.17
R	0.43 ± 0.00	**0.54 ± 0.01**	0.43 ± 0.00	0.21 ± 0.05	0.43 ± 0.00	**0.56 ± 0.02**	0.43 ± 0.00	0.31 ± 0.12
F1	0.43 ± 0.00	**0.54 ± 0.01**	0.42 ± 0.01	0.15 ± 0.07	0.42 ± 0.01	**0.52 ± 0.02**	0.43 ± 0.00	0.19 ± 0.17
Time	61 h 30 min	**9 h 21 min**	15 h 22 min	**6 h 20 min**	15 h 22 min	**1 h 10 min**	61 h 30 min	**2 h 25 min**

Results. Table 2 shows the results of the proposed experiments. Time for ZeroBERTo considers unsupervised training time and inference time. Further, as no training is required, only a single run of XLM-R was done on all data. Thus, the times for XLM-R are estimated. Nevertheless, in all experiments, the total time (training + execution) of ZeroBERTo was much lower than the execution time of XLM-R. Our model surpassed XLM-R in all metrics in the experiments in which the evaluation was performed on the data used in the unsupervised training (Exp. 1 and 3). Figure 1 presents a visualization for the entailment mechanism between topics and labels represented by term $P(l_j|t_k) = P(t_k \Rightarrow \mathcal{H}(l_j))$ in Eq. (1). The darker the green, the greater the conditional odds.

Fig. 1. Figure shows text entailment results between topics (X-axis) and labels (Y-axis) for the first 50 Topics (sorted by size) in fold 0 from Experiment 3. In total, 213 topics were generated in this experiment.

5   Discussion and Future Work

The experiments simulated low-resource scenarios where a zero-shot text classifier can be useful. The results showed that it is possible to obtain a better performance in the 0SHOT-TC task with the addition of an unsupervised learning step that allows a simplified representation of the data, as proposed by ZeroBERTo. Moreover, the proposed model presents itself as an excellent tool to help researchers deal with low-resource scenarios, such as the need to label an entire dataset without any previously labeled training data. Another interesting feature is that the model showed evidence of robustness for smaller amounts of data. In experiment 3, it was trained with 25% of the data from experiment 1 and got similar performance metrics in lower time, refuting our concern that little data could be a bottleneck in the model.

However, for configurations where ZeroBERTo was tested simulating real-life applications (Exp. 2 and 4), being exposed to new data, the performance was worse than XLM-R. The results suggest it occurs due to the inability of the embedded topic model to adequately represent new data as a composite of previously learned topics, overfitting training data. This is clear from observing the high variance of the metrics among the k-folds. It allows us to conclude that, for now, the scenarios presented in experiments 1 and 3 are more suitable for using the model.

We have 0.54 of F1-score in the best scenario regarding the metrics obtained. Despite being a positive result considering that it is a multi-class classification, there is much room for improvement. The main reason to be pointed out for low performances is the use of multilingual models that were not fine-tuned in the Portuguese language, which is quite impressive.

A critical remark to be made is concerning the memory and time trade-off. For example, ZeroBERTo was more than 10x faster than XLM-R in Exp. 3. However, the topic model used by ZeroBERTo bases its clustering on the HDBSCAN method, which reduces time taken for data processing but increases the need for memory [18], which XLM-R does not do. As the size of input data grows, processing may become unfeasible. XLM-R, on the other hand, does not use any interaction between data and can be processed in parallel and distributed without any negative effect on the final result. It should be noted, however, that ZeroBERTo does not depend on BERTopic and can use other Topic Modeling techniques that address this issue more adequately in other scenarios.

A significant difficulty of this work was that, as far as the authors are aware of, there are no large benchmark datasets for multi-class text classification in Portuguese, nor general use datasets with semantically meaningful labels. In this sense, some future work directions involve the production of benchmark datasets for Portuguese text classification (and 0SHOT-TC). It would also be interesting to produce Natural Language Inference datasets in Portuguese, which could, in addition to the existing ones [10,22], enable fine-tuning of Transformers 100% in Portuguese. Then, it would be possible to compare the performance of the models using BERTimbau (BERT-Portuguese) [26] both in clustering and classifying. It would also be worthwhile to test the proposed model in other domains: to name one, legislative data present similar challenges [9]. Another interesting future work would be to enable ZeroBERTo to deal with multi-label classification, where each document can have none, one or several labels.

Acknowledgments. This research was supported in part by *Itaú Unibanco S.A.*, with the scholarship program of *Programa de Bolsas Itaú* (PBI), and by the Coordenação de Aperfeiçoamento de Pessoal de Nível Superior (CAPES), Finance Code 001, CNPQ (grant 310085/2020-9), and USP-IBM-FAPESP *Center for Artificial Intelligence* (FAPESP grant 2019/07665-4), Brazil. Any opinions, findings, and conclusions expressed in this manuscript are those of the authors and do not necessarily reflect the views, official policy, or position of the financiers.

References

1. Beltagy, I., Peters, M.E., Cohan, A.: Longformer: the long-document transformer. arXiv preprint arXiv:2004.05150 (2020)
2. Bentivogli, L., Forner, P., Pianta, E.: Evaluating cross-language annotation transfer in the MultiSemCor corpus. In: Proceedings of the 20th International Conference on Computational Linguistics, COLING 2004, p. 364-es. ACL (2004)
3. Brown, T.B., et al.: Language models are few-shot learners. arXiv preprint arXiv:2005.14165 (2020)
4. Chang, M.W., Ratinov, L.A., Roth, D., Srikumar, V.: Importance of semantic representation: dataless classification. In: Proceedings of the 23rd AAAI Conference on Artificial Intelligence, vol. 2, pp. 830–835 (2008)
5. Chen, Q., Yao, L., Yang, J.: Short text classification based on LDA topic model. In: 2016 International Conference on Audio, Language and Image Processing (ICALIP), pp. 749–753. IEEE (2016)
6. Conneau, A., et al.: Unsupervised cross-lingual representation learning at scale. In: Proceedings of the 58th Annual Meeting of the Association for Computational Linguistics, pp. 8440–8451 (2020)
7. Conneau, A., et al.: XNLI: evaluating cross-lingual sentence representations. In: Proceedings of the 2018 Conference on Empirical Methods in Natural Language Processing, pp. 2475–2485. Association for Computational Linguistics (2018)
8. Devlin, J., Chang, M.W., Lee, K., Toutanova, K.: BERT: pre-training of deep bidirectional transformers for language understanding. In: Proceedings of the 2019 Conference of the North American Chapter of the Association for Computational Linguistics: Human Language Technologies, Volume 1 (Long and Short Papers), pp. 4171–4186 (2019)
9. Ferraz, T.P., et al.: DEBACER: a method for slicing moderated debates. In: Anais do XVIII Encontro Nacional de Inteligência Artificial e Computacional, pp. 667–678. SBC (2021)
10. Fonseca, E., Santos, L., Criscuolo, M., Aluisio, S.: ASSIN: avaliacao de similaridade semantica e inferencia textual. In: 12th International Conference on Computational Processing of the Portuguese Language, PROPOR, pp. 13–15 (2016)
11. Grootendorst, M.: BERTopic: leveraging BERT and c-TF-IDF to create easily interpretable topics (2020). https://doi.org/10.5281/zenodo.4381785
12. Hedderich, M.A., Lange, L., Adel, H., Strötgen, J., Klakow, D.: A survey on recent approaches for natural language processing in low-resource scenarios. In: Proceedings of the 2021 Conference of the North American Chapter of the Association for Computational Linguistics: Human Language Technologies, pp. 2545–2568 (2021)

13. Jacobs, P.S.: Joining statistics with NLP for text categorization. In: Third Conference on Applied Natural Language Processing, pp. 178–185 (1992)
14. Ji, Y., Eisenstein, J.: Representation learning for text-level discourse parsing. In: Proceedings of the 52nd Annual Meeting of the Association for Computational Linguistics (Volume 1: Long Papers), pp. 13–24 (2014)
15. Korman, D.Z., Mack, E., Jett, J., Renear, A.H.: Defining textual entailment. J. Am. Soc. Inf. Sci. **69**(6), 763–772 (2018)
16. Li, X., Guo, Y., Schuurmans, D.: Semi-supervised zero-shot classification with label representation learning. In: 2015 IEEE International Conference on Computer Vision (ICCV), pp. 4211–4219. IEEE (2015)
17. Logeswaran, L., Lee, A., Ott, M., Lee, H., Ranzato, M., Szlam, A.: Few-shot sequence learning with transformers. arXiv preprint arXiv:2012.09543 (2020)
18. McInnes, L., Healy, J.: Accelerated hierarchical density based clustering. In: 2017 IEEE International Conference on Data Mining Workshops (ICDMW), pp. 33–42. IEEE (2017)
19. Mekala, D., Shang, J.: Contextualized weak supervision for text classification. In: Proceedings of the 58th Annual Meeting of the Association for Computational Linguistics, pp. 323–333 (2020)
20. Meng, Y., et al.: Text classification using label names only: a language model self-training approach. In: Proceedings of the 2020 Conference on Empirical Methods in Natural Language Processing (EMNLP), pp. 9006–9017 (2020)
21. Nigam, K., McCallum, A.K., Thrun, S., Mitchell, T.: Text classification from labeled and unlabeled documents using EM. Mach. Learn. **39**(2), 103–134 (2000)
22. Real, L., Fonseca, E., Gonçalo Oliveira, H.: The ASSIN 2 shared task: a quick overview. In: Quaresma, P., Vieira, R., Aluísio, S., Moniz, H., Batista, F., Gonçalves, T. (eds.) PROPOR 2020. LNCS (LNAI), vol. 12037, pp. 406–412. Springer, Cham (2020). https://doi.org/10.1007/978-3-030-41505-1_39
23. Refaeilzadeh, P., Tang, L., Liu, H.: Cross-validation. Encycl. Database Syst. **5**, 532–538 (2009)
24. Sanh, V., Debut, L., Chaumond, J., Wolf, T.: DistilBERT, a distilled version of BERT: smaller, faster, cheaper and lighter. arXiv preprint arXiv:1910.01108 (2019)
25. Socher, R., Ganjoo, M., Manning, C.D., Ng, A.: Zero-shot learning through cross-modal transfer. In: Advances in Neural Information Processing Systems, pp. 935–943 (2013)
26. Souza, F., Nogueira, R., Lotufo, R.: BERTimbau: pretrained BERT models for Brazilian Portuguese. In: Cerri, R., Prati, R.C. (eds.) BRACIS 2020. LNCS (LNAI), vol. 12319, pp. 403–417. Springer, Cham (2020). https://doi.org/10.1007/978-3-030-61377-8_28
27. Vaswani, A., et al.: Attention is all you need. In: Advances in Neural Information Processing Systems, pp. 5998–6008 (2017)
28. Wang, A., Singh, A., Michael, J., Hill, F., Levy, O., Bowman, S.R.: GLUE: a multitask benchmark and analysis platform for natural language understanding. In: 7th International Conference on Learning Representations, ICLR 2019 (2019)
29. Williams, A., Nangia, N., Bowman, S.: A broad-coverage challenge corpus for sentence understanding through inference. In: Proceedings of the 2018 Conference of the North American Chapter of the Association for Computational Linguistics: Human Language Technologies, Volume 1 (Long Papers), p. 1112 (2018)

30. Yin, W., Hay, J., Roth, D.: Benchmarking zero-shot text classification: datasets, evaluation and entailment approach. In: Proceedings of the 2019 Conference on Empirical Methods in Natural Language Processing and the 9th International Joint Conference on Natural Language Processing (EMNLP-IJCNLP), pp. 3914–3923 (2019)
31. Zaheer, M., et al.: Big bird: transformers for longer sequences. Adv. Neural. Inf. Process. Syst. **33**, 17283–17297 (2020)
32. Zhang, J., Lertvittayakumjorn, P., Guo, Y.: Integrating semantic knowledge to tackle zero-shot text classification. In: Proceedings of NAACL-HLT, pp. 1031–1040 (2019)

Banking Regulation Classification
in Portuguese

Rafael Faria de Azevedo[✉] , Tiago Nunes Silva ,
Henrique Tibério Brandão Vieira Augusto , Paulo Oliveira Sampaio Reis ,
Isadora Bastos Chaves , Samara Beatriz Naka de Vasconcellos ,
Liliany Aparecida dos Anjos Pereira , Mauro Melo de Souza Biccas ,
André Luiz Monteiro , and Alexandre Rodrigues Duarte

Banco do Brasil S.A, SAUN Quadra 5, Lote B, s/n, Asa Norte, Brasília/DF
70.040-912, Brazil
rafael.f.azevedo@outlook.com, {almonteiro,arduarte}@bb.com.br

Abstract. Products, services, among many other things in life have
a quality standard, are inclusive, or do not harm customers. Regulations required from their manufacturers or providers make it possible.
This type of requirement also exists in the finance sector. Governments,
international agencies, or civil institutions are responsible for creating,
applying, and inspecting these regulations. Regulators from all spheres
(federal, state, and municipal) constantly demand changes in the finance
sector to meet current needs adequately. This paper presents the constant evolution of a banking compliance application in Brazil. It aims to
classify the relevance or irrelevance of regulatory documents published
by more than 100 Brazilian regulators, affecting the businesses of more
than 40 departments of Banco do Brasil. The application uses a hybrid
strategy, combining machine learning and rules for a binary classification
challenge involving each company department. This work also presents a
particular type of corpus imbalance called The Imbalance Within Class.

Keywords: Banking compliance · Finance sector regulation · Machine
Learning · Rules · Imbalance within class

1 Introduction

Have you ever thought about why companies are regulated? We mean in the
sense of following rules, norms, and standards established by the government
or civil institutions. An example is the FDA (Food and Drug Administration)
in the United States (US). Some businesses are more regulated than others.
The most regulated ones have a broader and more profound impact on society,
like the finance industry. It is highly regulated because it deals with everyone's
money and taxes related to financial transactions - banking (finance) regulation
changes almost every day. It reflects the current situation a city, a region, or a
country is passing through. Suppose a country is in an ideal economic situation,

© Springer Nature Switzerland AG 2022
V. Pinheiro et al. (Eds.): PROPOR 2022, LNAI 13208, pp. 137–147, 2022.
https://doi.org/10.1007/978-3-030-98305-5_13

for example. In that case, the finance regulation is adjusted to keep the economy growing and control inflation. However, suppose the economy of the country is terrible. In that case, the finance regulation will be continuously adjusted to find the path of prosperity. Not only the economy can affect the banking regulation, but a pandemic, an earthquake, a political change, advances in technology, and the risks of the banking business itself [1–4]. For years, finance institutions have manually handled the constant changes in financial regulations.

This paper presents a finance (banking) regulation classification application called Radar Regulatório (Regulatory Radar) (RR). It has eliminated most of the manual process previously done at Banco do Brasil related to regulatory monitoring. Before the application, the regulatory monitoring was made manually by each company department (decentralized), without patterns and protocols. As far as we know, RR is the first application that classifies regulatory documents by departments in Brazilian Portuguese.

Currently, the application classifies up to 1,000 documents per day. RR classifies each one according to its relevance to more than 40 departments. If the document is classified as relevant, it is forwarded to the respective department. The tool processes documents from more than 100 regulatory sites, covering municipal, state, and federal regulators. Examples of regulators are Banco Central do Brasil (BACEN) (Brazilian Central Bank), Receita Federal do Brasil (RFB) (like Internal Revenue Service - IRS in the US), Assembleia Legislativa de São Paulo (ALESP) (Legislative Assembly of São Paulo) among others. RR has prevented department workers from looking for relevant documents, like a needle in the hay, among other irrelevant ones. The application is a hybrid solution that uses machine learning and rules to classify the documents. It is also a tool that centralized the regulatory monitoring process at the company. It also settled standards to the process. The Artificial Intelligence (AI) part of the application was built by Diretoria de Tecnologia (DITEC) (Board of Technology) of Banco do Brasil. The rest of the paper is organized as follows. Section two presents the related works. Section three is about the developed application. Section four presents the discussion, results, and future work, and section five presents the paper's conclusions.

2   Related Works

Although there are plenty machine learning applications in the financial domain [5,6], no application was found that does what Radar Regulatório does for Portuguese. This section presents the most similar approaches we have found with our application; some belong to the legal field. The oldest study found was made by Gonçalves and Quaresma [7]. They classified juridical documents from the Portuguese Attorney General's Office in a multi-label approach using binary models created with Support Vector Machine (SVM). Araujo et al. [8] created and tested VICTOR, a large dataset of legal documents belonging to the Brazilian Supreme Court. The dataset can be used to document type classification (6 classes) and theme assignment (29 classes), a multi-label problem. Rodríguez and Bezerra [9] presented a study about Named Entity Recognition (NER) using the Natural Language Toolkit (NLTK)[1] over Ordinances, a type of regulatory document found at Diário Oficial da União (DOU), one of the Brazilian documents which are classified by the application presented in this article. Azevedo et al. [10] developed an application for a Brazilian bank to classify emails from a general email box into four classes. Each class is related to one of four specific email boxes. They reached an F1-score of 0.9048 using an SVM with a linear kernel.

Considering works that do not process Portuguese texts, O'Halloran et al. [11] presented a work that combines observational methods with Machine Learning (ML) classifiers to infer the level of agency discretion in a given law that belongs to a financial regulation database. The authors' aim was to understand the design of the financial regulatory structure in the US. They used different Naive Bayes (NB) approaches in their study. Neill et al. [12] proposed a method to classify sentences in legal language as one of three deontic classes: obligation, prohibition, or permission (deontic modalities). Their gold standard test set had some regulatory documents; a couple belongs to the financial sector. Their best result reached an accuracy of 82.33%, achieved by a bidirectional Long Short-Term Memory (LSTM) classifier compared to other inductors. Wong [13] presents a thesis called Learning Regulatory Compliance Data for Data Governance in Financial Services Industry. The study compares ML and Deep Learning (DL) algorithms to predict data quality. The work also evaluates the prediction of information security compliance levels. The data used is an integrated dataset in English which is assembled with four types of risk: market risk, credit risk, operational risk, and liquidity risk.

Gogas et al. [14] tested an SVM approach to forecasting bank failure using data from US banks during the 2007–2013 period, which reached 99.22% of accuracy. They also proposed a new form of stress-testing to simulate bank failure based on the SVM model. Suss and Treitel [15] developed an early warning system for UK bank distress. Their main input variables came from confidential supervisory assessments of firm risk and regulatory returns data. To implement the system, they tested different statistical and ML approaches, finding that Random Forest (RF) outperformed other algorithms results. Petropoulos et al. [16] applied six modeling techniques to predict bank insolvency in data from US-based financial institutions. An RF model achieved its best result. Jagtiani et al. [17] presented a study mentioning different applications of Big Data/ML techniques related to regulations in different areas of different banks around the world. The article also presents a clear view of challenges faced by those who use ML in the finance industry. The article is outstanding in its pedagogical approach. Polyzos et al. [18] proposed temporary deregulation (among other hypotheses) of the bank sector in the US as part of an agent-based model, which was complemented by a Random Regression Forest (RRF) and an LSTM algorithm. The article aims to study the expected consequences of the COVID-

---

[1] http://www.nltk.org/howto/portuguese_en.html.

19 pandemic on the banking sector and proposed ways to stimulate government responses to the COVID-19 crisis.

Howe *et al.* [19] made a comparative study between relatively recent ML classifiers (BERT, ULMFiT, and Glove) and traditional statistical models (like SVM) using a small dataset of lengthy judgments from the Singapore Supreme Court. In classifying judgments, they found that the recent classifiers were outperformed by the traditional models, mainly because of the small dataset size and the extended size of the documents. Park *et al.* [20] presented a sentiment analysis study in Monetary Policy Board minutes of the Bank of Korea (a type of regulatory document), among other texts about the finance sector.

3   The Application

This section presents the corpus and the architecture of Radar Regulatório.

3.1   The Corpus

An annotated corpus is the fuel needed to train and test a supervised machine learning algorithm to do the classification task. In Natural Language Processing (NLP), a dataset is called corpus. RR uses a corpora (collection of corpus) as it classifies documents by department, where each department has its corpus. Only expert analysts who work with regulatory compliance issues in a specific department were annotators of the corpus. Usually, only one expert checks a document (norm, rule, Etc.), making inviable an evaluation of agreement between annotators. A mistake in the annotation process could lead the enterprise to suffer sanctions from regulators. The annotation process is correlated to creating an action plan in the case of a relevant document to the department. Each corpus of each department has been built once regulators publish new documents. Some departments are more impacted than others because the regulators that regulate their business publish more norms and rules than the regulators that regulate other departments. Some departments have to deal with tens of regulatory publications daily, while others are impacted weekly, monthly, or even annually. There were 48 departments registered in the application up to September/2021. However, only 23 departments had prediction models. This difference will be explained in Subsect. 3.2. On the same date, 109 regulators' websites were registered in the application (federal, state, and municipal regulators). The shortest document in the corpora had two words, "Conteúdo restrito" (Restricted content), while the longest had 233,342 words. The corpora currently has 153.766 documents (up to September/2021).

3.2   The Architecture

This subsection presents the architecture of Radar Regulatório (RR). Figure 1 presents the details. The daily execution of RR starts when the application collects all regulatory documents of all regulators' websites registered in the application (step 1 of Fig. 1). A third-party company makes the web scraping (web crawling) of all regulators' websites.

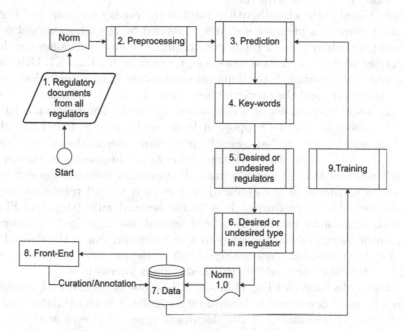

Fig. 1. Radar Regulatório architecture. Each document (norm, rule, etc.) passes through for each department.

The **preprocessing** consists of the removal of numbers, special characters, and NLTK stopwords list for Portuguese. The remaining tokens of each department dataset are turned into features for the inductor (classifier) via the TF-IDF algorithm. Only lowercase ASCII characters are kept (step 2 of Fig. 1). The same preprocessing is used in the training part (step 9 of Fig. 1) and in the classification (prediction) part of the application.

The classification part of RR has four steps, where each document is classified at a time (steps 3 to 6 in Fig. 1). In order to use RR, a department must have at least the prediction model or one rule filled in the application. Nevertheless, the department can have both the prediction model and all rules filled in the application. As indicated by the arrows in Fig. 1, the classification part is a continuous flow, meaning the document will first be evaluated in step 3, then follows to step 4, and so on. Notwithstanding, if the department did not fill one step, the empty step will not alter the prediction value of a previous steps (this behavior also happens when a rule finds no match in the document). Step 6 is an exception because it is correlated to step 5 (in Fig. 1). Steps 5 and 6 have two lists (desired and undesired), which a department can fill one, both, or none of them. Experts of the department create all rules according to their experience.

The different frequency regulators publish documents and the different regulators that matter to each department creates the situation that some departments built a prediction model much earlier than others. So, many departments use RR for a long period only with rules.

The first step of the **classification part** is the prediction (step 3 of Fig. 1). Once the document is preprocessed, it is classified by the binary model of the department if it already has a prediction model. The model classifies the document as relevant if the prediction score is equal to or higher than 0.7. Otherwise, it is classified as irrelevant. If the department does not have a prediction model, this step is skipped, and the prediction score remains 0. The next three steps in the classification part consist of a rule-based approach. The **first rule** (step 4 of Fig. 1) is about key-words. Suppose at least one keyword is found (matched) in the document's body. In that case, the prediction score is altered to 1, meaning there is a high chance the document impacts the businesses of the department. RR receives daily documents from all regulators' websites desired by all departments registered in the application. However, not all regulators impact the businesses of all departments. It is in the **second rule** (step 5 of Fig. 1), where each department can fill the lists of desired and undesired regulators. If the document being evaluated belongs to a regulator present in the desired regulators list, the prediction score is altered to 1. If the publisher of the document is in the undesired regulators' list, the prediction is altered to 0.

The **last rule** (step 6 of Fig. 1) has two lists, one of desired and another of undesired types of documents published by a regulator, once regulators publish different types of documents. If the document type being evaluated is in the desired types list, its prediction score is altered to 1. If the document type is in the undesired types list, the prediction score is changed to 0.

When the classification part of RR ends, the document with its prediction score is saved in the database (step 7 of Fig. 1). The front-end of the application (step 8 of Fig. 1) receives the newly processed regulatory documents once a day and distributes the relevant and irrelevant ones of each department registered at RR. The analysts of each department usually check only the documents predicted as relevant. They first check if the document inferred as applicable is relevant to the department businesses. If so, she or he clicks in an "agree" button to add the document in the relevant class of the corpus. In the negative case, the "disagree" button is hit to add the document in the irrelevant class of the corpus (annotation/curation process - steps 8 and 7 of Fig. 1). If the document is relevant to the department, the analyst creates an action plan to adequate the impacted business (product, service, process, or channel) to fulfill the document requirements.

When needed, the prediction models are retrained (step 9 of Fig. 1). The training step of RR first selects documents with at least 20 words (separated by whitespace). Afterward, RR deals with imbalance problems. **The imbalanced classes problem** present in many corpus of our corpora is solved with the undersampling technique. A corpus is trained when each class has at least 20 samples. However, we also had to cope with what we called **the imbalance within class**

problem. This problem happens because regulators publish different documents in different frequencies. Some regulators publish tens of documents daily, while others publish few documents per week, month, or year. For example, consider the relevant class in the department A corpus; there are 100 documents published by BACEN, 50 documents published by RFB, and 15 published by ALESP. It is a problem of imbalance within the class.

A model trained with **the imbalanced classes problem** and **the imbalanced within class problem** tends to classify more accurately the majority class and the dominant type of data within the class (the regulators that publish more frequently), respectively. To solve it, we built each class of the dataset by picking one document of one regulator at a time and stopped picking when the regulator with fewer documents had no more documents to add in that class (undersampling strategy). With the corpus balanced, an SVM algorithm with a linear kernel is used to train the model of each department. The parameters used in the GridSearchCV[2] algorithm with the SVC[3] (SVM) algorithm are: gamma: auto, kernel: [linear, poly, RBF, sigmoid] and C: [0.025, 0.08, 0.1, 0.5, 0.8, 1, 2]. The stratified 10-fold cross-validation approach prevented the bias problem. Each time the training is applied, parameters can vary for each corpus of each department, as the corpora is in a constant increasing process, which keeps it changing. Once a model is trained, it is deployed to production; this decision will be explained in the next section.

4   Discussion, Results and Future Work

Perhaps, the main lesson we have learned with the development of RR is the need to adapt the application to the current data available. When stakeholders looked for us to explain their pain, they practically required a machine learning solution. The AI hype influenced them as many people in many areas of the industry. However, the data was "telling" us that there were few samples to enable a satisfactory result with this approach. As they insisted on their position, we defined that the minimum quantity of samples per class to train a model would be 20 samples. We knew that in most cases, this number was insufficient. At that moment, few departments would have this prerequisite to train a model (less than five departments). The quantity of irrelevant documents published is much higher than the relevant ones. At that moment, RR was a minimum viable product (MVP). No matter what we did, accuracy, precision, and recall did not increase sufficiently. Each corpus/inductor presented an underfitting or overfitting result. When stakeholders finally came to reality, we proposed adding a rule-based approach to the application. The new idea was a success, but with a side effect. With the addition of the key-words rule, a single word match in a regulatory document potentially increased the false-positive cases. However, this situation was not considered a serious issue by the business analysts. From a

---

[2] https://scikit-learn.org/stable/modules/generated/sklearn.model_selection.GridSearchCV.html.

[3] https://scikit-learn.org/stable/modules/generated/sklearn.svm.SVC.html.

compliance point of view, it is preferred to have some false-positive occurrences instead of any false-negative. In other words, it is preferred an analyst evaluates a document that does not affect the department business than not to read a document that affects the department business.

RR finally pleased the departments that had to do the regulatory screening manually. However, the stakeholders' insistence on using machine learning is becoming more realistic as the corpus of departments gets larger with time. Some departments are no longer having underfitting or overfitting results, as shown in Table 1. It presents the results of six departments, two of them with

Table 1. Evolution of models up to September/2021

	Beginning			Current			Current quantity of relevant samples	Current quantity of irrelevant samples	Corpus beginning
	F1 model	F1 relevant class	F1 irrelevant class	F1 model	F1 relevant class	F1 irrelevant class			
Department A	1	1	1	0.8641	0.8495	0.8772	432	1626	17/07/2020
Department B	0.99	0.9903	0.9897	0.8483	0.8364	0.8571	214	1714	17/07/2020
Department C	0.8182	0.6667	0.875	0.9833	0.9836	0.9831	271	2877	16/10/2020
Department D	1	1	1	0.9615	0.962	0.961	154	165	17/07/2020
Department E	0.9309	0.9333	0.9286	0.9075	0.9124	0.9026	562	1036	21/11/2020
Department F	0.99	0.9903	0.9897	0.9609	0.9639	0.9577	155	345	17/07/2020

overfitting results (departments D and F) and four departments with typical results. To reduce the effects of underfitting and overfitting in each model, we have bet on the increase of samples of each department's dataset. The application needed to be in production for around a year to start having non-underfitting or overfitting results (September/2021). The underfitting problem was detected when the same samples were used in the training and testing steps. If the model had learned how to generalize the patterns found in the classes appropriately, the prediction error would be around zero. However, the error score was much higher than that. The overfitting problem was detected when the F1 prediction metric of the test set (samples not used in training) was 1 or very close to it. F1-score records over time registered in Table 2 show the overfitting situation for Department D (F1 is 1 from time to time).

The stakeholders' insistence on using machine learning taught us that an application not thought capable of using machine learning might do it indeed (deep study is needed). It might be a matter of building a corpus with time. The departments with the biggest corpus have reported increased satisfaction with RR. The application has validated the possibility of using a hybrid strategy (machine learning and rules) once the most important result is the solution of a business problem, no matter the technique.

We intend to test different classifiers per corpus in future work instead of using the same one in the corpora. Initial tests with the larger corpus of the

Table 2. Evolution of Department D's F1

Training date	Model F1	Relevant class F1	Irrelevant class F1
17/07/2020	1	1	1
13/08/2020	0.998	0.998	0.998
18/08/2020	0.983	0.9829	0.983
22/08/2020	0.9475	0.9461	0.949
06/03/2021	0.8927	0.8966	0.8889
13/03/2021	0.8927	0.8966	0.8889
20/03/2021	0.8927	0.8966	0.8889
24/07/2021	0.9857	0.987	0.9841
27/07/2021	1	1	1
03/08/2021	1	1	1
10/08/2021	1	1	1
17/08/2021	0.9867	0.988	0.9851
24/08/2021	0.9601	0.963	0.9565
31/08/2021	0.9734	0.9706	0.9756
07/09/2021	1	1	1
14/09/2021	0.9744	0.975	0.9737
21/09/2021	0.9615	0.962	0.961

corpora using BERT [21] have shown similar results to machine learning algorithms, which can be an indication that part of the corpora is becoming more suitable to machine learning and deep learning. The hypothesis is that the machine learning results overcome the rules results in the future, contrasting with the current results that rely more on rules. The BERTimbal [22] (base and large) configuration we have tested is the default one of the Simple Transformers[4] library, inspired by the binary classification in the work of Leite *et al.* [23]. A future article will present results and other details of BERT experiments. Another point to be studied is the **imbalance of types of documents of the same regulator in the same class**, what is an imbalance problem within the **imbalanced within class problem**.

5 Conclusions

This paper presents Radar Regulatório, a hybrid application (SVM + rules) that automatically classifies documents of more than 100 regulators as relevant or irrelevant to the business field of each of more than 40 departments of Banco do Brasil. The article shows that if the technical decisions in the research of

---

[4] https://simpletransformers.ai/.

AI applications are influenced mainly through data, in the industry, the business features and expectations of business people might influence the technical decisions either. The development of RR has shown that even applications that seem not to fit the use of a machine or deep learning might be capable of using these techniques once its dataset grows with time. RR is an example that most applications developed nowadays must be built with the use of AI in mind.

References

1. O'Halloran, S., Maskey, S., McAllister, G., Park, D.K., Chen, K.: Data science and political economy: application to financial regulatory structure. RSF Russell Sage Found. J. Soc. Sci. **2**, 87–109 (2016)
2. Morgan, D.P.: Rating banks: risk and uncertainty in an opaque industry. Am. Econ. Rev. **92**, 874–888 (2002)
3. de Lima, A.J.D., Ferreira, L.N., Brandi-vinicius, V.R.: The rise of risk: a word on financial stability regulation
4. Leo, M., Sharma, S., Maddulety, K.: Machine learning in banking risk management: a literature review. Risks **7**, 29 (2019)
5. Kumar, B.S., Ravi, V.: A survey of the applications of text mining in financial domain. Knowl.-Based Syst. **114**, 128–147 (2016)
6. El-Haj, M., Rayson, P., Walker, M., Young, S., Simaki, V.: In search of meaning: lessons, resources and next steps for computational analysis of financial discourse. J. Bus. Finance Account. **46**, 265–306 (2019)
7. Gonçalves, T., Quaresma, P.: A preliminary approach to the multilabel classification problem of Portuguese juridical documents. In: Pires, F.M., Abreu, S. (eds.) EPIA 2003. LNCS (LNAI), vol. 2902, pp. 435–444. Springer, Heidelberg (2003). https://doi.org/10.1007/978-3-540-24580-3_50
8. de Araujo, P.H.L., de Campos, T.E., Braz, F.A., da Silva, N.C.: VICTOR: a dataset for Brazilian legal documents classification. In: Proceedings of The 12th Language Resources and Evaluation Conference, pp. 1449–1458 (2020)
9. Rodríguez, M.M., Bezerra, L.D.: Processamento de linguagem natural para reconhecimento de entidades nomeadas em textos jurídicos de atos administrativos (portarias). Revista de Engenharia e Pesquisa Aplicada **5**, 67–77 (2020)
10. Faria de Azevedo, R., et al.: Screening of email box in Portuguese with SVM at Banco do Brasil. In: Quaresma, P., Vieira, R., Aluísio, S., Moniz, H., Batista, F., Gonçalves, T. (eds.) PROPOR 2020. LNCS (LNAI), vol. 12037, pp. 153–163. Springer, Cham (2020). https://doi.org/10.1007/978-3-030-41505-1_15
11. O'Halloran, S., Maskey, S., McAllister, G., Park, D.K., Chen, K.: Big data and the regulation of financial markets. In: Proceedings of the 2015 IEEE/ACM International Conference on Advances in Social Networks Analysis and Mining 2015, pp. 1118–1124 (2015)
12. Neill, J.O., Buitelaar, P., Robin, C., Brien, L.O.: Classifying sentential modality in legal language: a use case in financial regulations, acts and directives. In: Proceedings of the 16th edition of the International Conference on Artificial Intelligence and Law, pp. 159–168 (2017)
13. Wong, K.Y.: Learning regulatory compliance data for data governance in financial services industry by machine learning models (2020)
14. Gogas, P., Papadimitriou, T., Agrapetidou, A.: Forecasting bank failures and stress testing: a machine learning approach. Int. J. Forecast. **34**, 440–455 (2018)

15. Suss, J., Treitel, H.: Predicting bank distress in the UK with machine learning (2019)
16. Petropoulos, A., Siakoulis, V., Stavroulakis, E., Vlachogiannakis, N.E.: Predicting bank insolvencies using machine learning techniques. Int. J. Forecast. **36**, 1092–1113 (2020)
17. Jagtiani, J., Vermilyea, T., Wall, L.D.: The roles of big data and machine learning in bank supervision. Forthcoming, Banking Perspectives (2018)
18. Polyzos, S., Samitas, A., Kampouris, E.: Economic stimulus through bank regulation: government responses to the COVID-19 crisis. J. Int. Fin. Mark. Inst. Money, 101444 (2021)
19. Howe, J.S.T., Khang, L.H., Chai, I.E.: Legal area classification: a comparative study of text classifiers on Singapore supreme court judgments. arXiv preprint arXiv:1904.06470 (2019)
20. Park, K.Y., Lee, Y.J., Kim, S.: Deciphering monetary policy board minutes through text mining approach: the case of Korea. Bank of Korea WP 1 (2019)
21. Devlin, J., Chang, M.-W., Lee, K., Toutanova, K.: BERT: pre-training of deep bidirectional transformers for language understanding. arXiv preprint arXiv:1810.04805 (2018)
22. Souza, F., Nogueira, R., Lotufo, R.: BERTimbau: pretrained BERT models for Brazilian Portuguese. In: 9th Brazilian Conference on Intelligent Systems, BRACIS, Rio Grande do Sul, Brazil, 20–23 October (2020, to appear)
23. Leite, J.A., Silva, D.F., Bontcheva, K., Scarton, C.: Toxic language detection in social media for Brazilian Portuguese: new dataset and multilingual analysis. arXiv preprint arXiv:2010.04543 (2020)

Automatic Information Extraction: A Distant Reading of the Brazilian Historical-Biographical Dictionary

Suemi Higuchi[1]([⊠]) [iD], Claudia Freitas[2] [iD], and Diana Santos[3] [iD]

[1] Fundação Getulio Vargas, Rio de Janeiro, Brazil
suemi.higuchi@fgv.br
[2] Pontifícia Universidade Católica do Rio de Janeiro, Rio de Janeiro, Brazil
claudiafreitas@puc-rio.br
[3] Linguateca and University of Oslo, Oslo, Norway
d.s.m.santos@ilos.uio.no

Abstract. We present some results of applying natural language processing (NLP) techniques in the domain of History, having as object of investigation the Brazilian Historical-Biographical Dictionary (*Dicionário Histórico-Biográfico Brasileiro*, DHBB). After improving or adding annotation of specific fields, information extraction techniques based on manually derived patterns were applied to three relevant problems: the age of entrance in Brazilian politics, the academic background of Brazilian politicians, and family ties among the political elites.

Keywords: Corpus linguistics · Information extraction · Distant reading · Brazilian politics

1 Introduction

Dicionário Histórico-Biográfico Brasileiro (Brazilian Historical-Biographical Dictionary or DHBB for short), an encyclopedic work conceived by Centro de Pesquisa e Documentação de História Contemporânea do Brasil (CPDOC) from Fundação Getulio Vargas (FGV), gathers more than 7,500 biographical and thematic entries on the contemporary history of Brazil, and contains information ranging from the life trajectory, education and career of individuals, to the relationships built between the characters and events that the country hosted [1].

Our goal with the present work was to create, from the DHBB, an annotated corpus for automatic information extraction's purpose, enabling "distant readings" of Brazilian contemporary political history [5]. In 2018, the DHBB corpus was thus integrated into the AC/DC[1] collection and can be freely consulted by the linguistic and NLP communities. In its present version 7.3, it contains 457,101 sentences, almost 16 million tokens and about 14 million words. As it is an organic work, in constant updating, new versions of

---

[1] Available at https://www.linguateca.pt/acesso/corpus.php?corpus=DHBB.

© Springer Nature Switzerland AG 2022
V. Pinheiro et al. (Eds.): PROPOR 2022, LNAI 13208, pp. 148–155, 2022.
https://doi.org/10.1007/978-3-030-98305-5_14

the corpus may be created and released from time to time. Furthermore, DHBB is also available to the research community in an open repository under version control[2] [6].

The complete process of creating the DHBB corpus includes the morphosyntactic analysis of the material, the identification of domain relevant entities, the addition of semantic annotation to the corpus, the definition of semantic relations of interest and the mapping of lexical-syntactic patterns expressing these relations. These steps prepare the texts for the identification of the structures of interest, which are then extracted and presented in a structured way. We evaluate here a set of textual patterns according to their productivity in the DHBB, for the following topics: age of the politicians when entering public life, their academic training and family ties.

Our assumption is that by using specifically designed lexical-syntactic patterns it is possible to extract high quality information from an annotated corpus, at least in an encyclopedic genre in the History domain.

The main motivation to explore the DHBB through computational linguistic tools arose from the need to search for certain kinds of information without closely reading a large number of entries. A survey carried out with researchers who frequently consult the Dictionary asked them which questions they would have liked to have answered automatically. From this survey, questions emerged such as: How is the educational background of political cadres characterized over time? How old were Supreme Court ministers when they were nominated? Who are the politicians who have family ties to other politicians? Which ties?

The answers to these questions are found dispersed in the entries and are not indexed in metadata fields. An information extraction system (IE) helps to overcome this challenge, as it aims to select and obtain specific information from large volumes of text.

2 Information Extraction

When we talk about information extraction (IE) we are referring to the process of automatically obtaining structures – such as entities, relationships between entities and attributes that describe entities – from unstructured sources. An IE system can, for example, identify and extract from a collection of texts the name of all the mentioned organizations - including those that the user had no prior knowledge of -, the name of all the people who have any link with these organizations, and the type of link.

Among the strategies adopted in these systems, there are those that use inference rules from linguistic clues and those that use lexical lists. The clues enable the identification of patterns and can be based on different features, such as morphosyntactic, orthographic, context and so on, and may be language dependent or not. Lexical lists are simpler and do not consider the contexts in which the terms appear; one of the motivations for its use is the fact that parsers are not able to identify with 100% accuracy certain entities, even with the help of morphosyntactic heuristics applied in named entity recognition (NER). As for computational methods, we can roughly classify them into rule-based approaches and machine learning approaches (supervised, semi-supervised and unsupervised), and there are those that combine both.

---

[2] Available at https://github.com/cpdoc/dhbb.

Since we use the first approach, we are only going to describe it here, not the second. Extraction rules are developed manually and mainly relies on lexical-syntactic aspects of sentences. Although at first sight they are constructions that are presented in a very simple way in the language, the formalization of these patterns brings positive results as they serve as clues for the automatic discovery of information structures in the text. According to Hearst [3], different relationships can be expressed using a small number of lexical-syntactic patterns. Her work to extract *is-a* relationships is widely known and cited. These patterns are constructed from phrases containing clues such as "and", "such as", "like", "or", etc., combined with punctuation marks, placeholders for named entities, and regular expression elements. For example, the pattern "such NP as {NP,}*{(or | and)} NP" can be applied to examples like "...works by such authors as Herrick, Goldsmith, and Shakespeare", and extract the following relations: is-a ("author", "Herrick"), is-a ("author", "Goldsmith"), is-a ("author", "Shakespeare") [4, 8]. The main advantage of rule development is that, due to their declarative nature, these patterns are understandable by humans and the effects of change are directly visible when compared to a machine learning model, which requires a training phase and an extraction phase. In general, the quality of the information extracted is quite high, but recall is usually low [9]. This approach has as its main issues scalability - given the high cost of developing rules -, and managing large sets of rules.

3   Methodology

The strategy we adopted for extracting information is the one identified by the work developed by Marti Hearst [3], where information is extracted with help of a set of lexical-syntactic patterns. This choice is due, among other factors, to the predictability of the DHBB texts, whose writing follows a fairly standardized structure. Furthermore, the AC/DC workflow allows us to improve the identification of certain types of information in the corpus through the creation of rules and lexicons of different semantic fields. Thus, new annotations are progressively incorporated into the corpus, to be accessed in search expressions.

The parser used was PALAVRAS, chosen for a number of reasons. The main ones are that this analyzer is specially designed for the Portuguese language, being considered one of the best within the chosen approach, with good syntactic and semantic analysis quality, and is also adopted by Linguateca for processing all corpora included in the AC/DC project [10]. PALAVRAS is rule-based, following constraint grammar (CG) and also performs NER. The tagging of candidate named entities is made in three levels: i) known lexical entries and lists of additional terms; ii) pattern-based prediction (morphological module); and iii) context-based inference for unknown words. Furthermore, the parser joins fixed expressions with the non-compositional semantic-syntactic function for MWEs, creating composite tokens and facilitating token-based CG syntactic rules [2].

The corpus is available through AC/DC, a service developed by Linguateca to make annotated corpora accessible through a web interface. The system employs the IMS Open Corpus Workbench (CWB), a collection of open source tools aimed at questioning corpora enriched with linguistic annotation. CWB sees the corpus as an entity with its own integrity that can be interrogated but never changed, allowing for several different levels of annotation [12]. By being included in the AC/DC environment, queries to the DHBB – expressed through the CQP (Corpus Query Processor) language – can return different types of information, such as concordances or distributions, using extended regular expressions over linguistic annotation and other information present in the corpora.

A predetermined set of semantic tags assigned by PALAVRAS was used to identify some classes of entities in the corpus that we were interested on, namely <hum> for person, <org> and <inst> for organization/institution, <party> for political party, <occ> and <event> for event, <civ> for place, <tit> for document/work and <hprof> for professional role. A class able to bring together instances related to government plans, programs, agreements, treaties, laws, decrees, codes and all sorts of political formulations was missing, so we created a new class for this purpose: <titfpol>. The annotation of this class was made from a list containing instances that belong to it.

After the analysis made by PALAVRAS and other common processing by the AC/DC project, the structure of each entry is now in a pseudo-xml format, with segmented paragraphs and sentences, embedded metadata, and syntactic and semantic tags assigned to tokens. The result is a corpus containing annotation of words, lemmas, grammatical categories (pos), verb tenses, syntactic function and additional semantic information.

To improve NER, we created lists of entities obtained from three sources: i) instances existing in categories on Wikipedia; i) instances found with the AntConc concordancer using lexical clues applied to the corpus; and iii) instances identified by PALAVRAS and manually reviewed. These lists comprise 25,970 organizations, 1,250 policy formulations, 18,488 persons, 350 events and 1,011 political parties.

An extra layer of semantic annotation was then added with help of the *corte-e-costura* (cut-and-sew) tool developed for this purpose [11]. In general terms, the process starts from an initial lexicon whose correspondences in the corpus are noted as belonging to the target semantic field. Through context analysis of the annotated words, specialization or elimination rules are created to correct ambiguous cases. Using the same tool, we tackle two problems that affect the identification of some entities in the corpus. The first is due to errors in the segmentation of proper names, as in the case of *Eugênia Lopes de Oliveira Prestes de Macedo Soares*, which was automatically recognized as being two proper names instead of one: *Eugênia Lopes de Oliveira Prestes* and *Macedo Soares*. Adding some manual rules in the *corte-e-costura* we were able to join the two segments. The second problem is related to the various forms of writing the names of the biographees. It was necessary to both identify these variations in the corpus (lemmas) and their posterior unification. So we retrieved all proper names that PALAVRAS annotated as being "human" and that were not identical to any entry name, checked manually this list, and created a correspondence table indicating which lemmas corresponded to which biographees (called "grounding" in [7]). This is an iterative process: the list of lemmas is obtained, the correspondences are made; we get a new list, new matches, and so on.

After these preprocessing tasks, whose goal is to perfect the annotation in the corpus, we proceed to the IE stage proper, where we identify a set of patterns that can be tested and evaluated regarding their productivity in relation to the DHBB. We can summarize this new process as follows: for each theme, we observe in a sample of entries how the sentences that bring the desired information are constructed and we separate as many of them as possible, considering diversity and scope. We then translate these constructions into lexical-syntactic patterns with regular expressions, iteratively testing them until we get the sentences we are interested in. Finally, we concatenate all expressions, query the corpus, and postprocess the results using R. The excerpts of interest are isolated and synthesized, and the specific information is extracted with finer rules, to be then crossed with metadata.

4 Extraction Evaluation

The first information to be extracted was the year of birth of the biographees. Only one pattern was needed, because the context in which this information appears in the entries follows a certain pattern: it is always located in the first paragraph, and is preceded by the character's name, with few variations. For example: "Moroni Bing Torgan was born in Porto Alegre on June 10, 1956" or "Álvaro Francisco de Sousa was born on February 28, 1903" The pattern created was:

[classe = "bio.*" & dicionario = "dhbb" & pos = "PROP.*"] + [: pos! = "PROP.*":][]{0,1} [lema = "nascer" & word! = "nascido|nascer"] [pos = "PRP.*"][]{0,21} [pos = "NUM.*|ADJ.*"] [word = "de"]? [pos = "N.*"]? [word = "de"]? [pos = "NUM.*"]? [pos = "PU"].

Basically, it means: "if the DHBB entry is biographical, find a compound proper name, followed by the lemma 'born' and a preposition. Keep going until find the first number or modifier of the sentence (day, year or month) and continue to the next comma or period; in this range there may or may not be another number (possibly the other part of the date)". This pattern brought 6,455 occurrences, which were checked manually. Overall, the rate of correct answers was around 98%, considering the entries that were not retrieved due to the absence of this information in the text (true-negative ones).

The same procedure was applied to extract information about the education background of the biographees and their family ties. In the first case, 11 patterns retrieved 10,565 excerpts from 5,627 entries, which represent around 83% of the total DHBB biographical entries. Each of the occurrences was manually checked to identify cases in which the lexical-syntactic construction met one of the defined patterns, but the information contained therein was not valid. If the extracted sentence mentions attended courses, obtained titles, admission to universities and related events, then it is valid, otherwise it is not. It is not possible to know how many and which occurrences were not recovered throughout the corpus, so the assessment does not include a measure for recall. But we considered that 99.1% precision was quite promising.

In the case of family relationships, we searched for patterns in a selection of ten entries whose holders are already known to have family ties with other politicians. The first step was to look for sentences where family ties occur. Looking closely at each of them, it was possible to classify them into valid and non-valid relationships, based on both a supposed family relationship of the politician with other people, and relationships of third parties mentioned in the entries. Relationships that were considered not valid are cases in which the family term does not represent a direct link with anyone or does not demonstrate any family relationship, as in "...feeding pregnant women, young *mothers* and children". In addition to a perfect identification among biographees that uncovered 35 cases already grounded, we created rules to identify other family relations. We created thus 33 patterns that retrieved 6,220 such relationships in the corpus. Manual verification[3] was restricted to 198 random cases, yielding an average precision of .59. It is important to say that our interest here was not to know whether family ties were correctly identified using these patterns (and most of them were), but rather to measure the proportion of family relationships among politicians that can be found in the corpus. Furthermore, not all biographies can be considered politicians. In our understanding, a politician is someone who is invested in his position through election, nomination or designation, usually members of the executive and legislative branches. Positions that serve merely for bureaucratic jobs, such as technical advisers and consultants, whether executive, legislative, judiciary branches or military, are generally not considered politicians, although they are involved in government decision-making processes. Ordinary citizens such as activists and civic leaders are not considered politicians, even though they may be public opinion makers.

Summing up, to extract the year of birth of the biographees, the F-measure was .99 (their date of their first position is included in the metadata), to extract family relationships among politicians, the (estimated) precision was .59 and for information on education training, the precision reached .991.

These extractions, in turn, allow us to make a distant reading of DHBB that shows i) a drop in the average age in the entry of politicians into the public career, who start to position themselves more and more under 40 years of age, mainly those born from the 1960s; ii) a sharp decline in military training, especially for the post-1920 generations, showing that civilian training replaced military training as the preferred path to reach important political positions; and iii) family ties in politics as a phenomenon that remains over time at very significant rates, often representing more than half of the members of certain categories.

5 Distant Reading DHBB

With the data obtained in the extraction, we can carry out some distant reading about the domain of the corpus. The distribution of ages ranging from the generation born before 1920 to the beginning of the 2000s showed us that those aspiring to political careers are getting in the public service steadily younger. The difference in the average between the so-called generation 1 (born before 1900) and generation 6 (born after the 1980s) falls almost by half, that is, if it was more common to start a public career around the age of 50 years old hundred years ago, over time this changed until it reached an average of 27 years old in the last generation (see Fig. 1).

Regarding the education background of the politicians, among the 48 found areas, in the overall reckoning law school appears preponderant in all generations, followed by military training, with just one third of the first. Degrees in engineering, medicine, administration and economics come next, the latter two being practically tied. Across times, we found that the most significant transformation was the decline in military training from the second (born between 1901 and 1920) to the third generation (born between 1921 and 1940), decreasing almost by half. In fact, the lower presence of

---

[3] Which can be inspected at: https://www.linguateca.pt/acesso/dhbb/verifFamiliaDez2021.html.

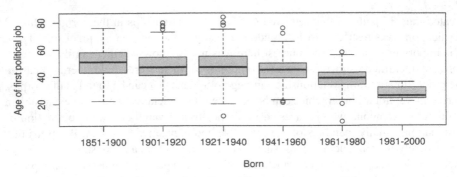

Fig. 1. The age of starting public careers, per generation

politicians with military training from the third generation onwards suggests that civilian training replaced the military career as the most suitable way to reach important political positions.

About family ties in politics, although it is not possible to determine how deeply entrenched Brazilian politics is with regard to family dynasties, since the logic of domination by kinship occurs also in other branches that the DHBB does not cover (like states and municipalities, Executives and Legislative branches), it is possible to see that it is a phenomenon that persists over time, at very significant rates. Presidents and senators are the politicians who most appear with family ties, 50% and 35% respectively, this being most perceived in the first generations (in the present version of DHBB). Ministers and deputies follow with 18%, keeping a stable average over generations. Unfortunately, most of the politicians elected in 2018 have not yet been included in DHBB, and therefore there is no way to study the current context, which would be quite interesting.

6   Final Considerations

Our aim in this paper was to investigate the possibility of extracting useful, diverse and high-quality information from a corpus of encyclopedic text. We explored some approaches to automatic information extraction and described a methodology based on the use of textual patterns, where extraction rules are manually created and rely mainly on lexical-syntactic aspects and semantic annotation of the corpus. We tested the proposed approach in three cases. In general, the results showed high accuracy in the quality of the information extracted.

One big challenge we became aware of during this investigation was how to find a balance between a sufficient number of patterns and a good enough coverage. This is about the quantity – and consequently, the manual work required – of expressions that should be created and applied, which is not easy to predict because of the language's own natural expressiveness.

Although the methodology itself is not new, this study explored issues that have been addressed in debates where the humanities disciplines have been modified with the use of computational techniques, in order to assess the opportunities that open up in this potentially innovative scenario. In our view, these new tools can indeed lead to the expansion of academic research along various alleys, both in terms of methods renewal and knowledge production. Certainly difficulties exist and the challenges are many, but the possibilities open by innovation scenarios lead to a continuous and deserved effort to try to overcome them, if we invest enough work in tailoring the material to our research needs.

The main contributions of this work are: the creation of an annotated encyclopedic corpus made available for language and humanities studies; the presentation of a methodology based on a philosophy of cyclical enrichment: the more information is obtained, the more it is added to the corpus itself; and the compilation of a set of patterns that can be adapted to other corpora containing a similar type of annotations [5].

References

1. Abreu, A., Lattman-Weltman, F., de Paula, C.J. (eds.): Dicionário Histórico-Biográfco Brasileiro pós-1930. CPDOC/FGV, 3 edn. Rio de Janeiro, Brazil (2010)
2. Bick, E.: Functional aspects on Portuguese NER. In: Santos, D., Cardoso, N. (eds.) Reconhecimento de entidades mencionadas em português: Documentação e actas do HAREM, a primeira avaliação conjunta na área. Linguateca, pp. 145–155 (2007)
3. Hearst, M.: Automatic acquisition of hyponyms from large text corpora. In: Proceedings of the 14th Conference on Computational Linguistics, Vol. 2, Coling 1992, pp. 539–545. Stroudsburg, PA, USA (1992)
4. Hearst, M.: Automated discovery of WordNet relations. In: Fellbaum, C. (ed.) WordNet: An Electronic Lexical Database, pp. 131–151. MIT Press (1998)
5. Higuchi, S.: Extração automática de informações: uma leitura distante do Dicionário Histórico-Biográfico Brasileiro (DHBB). Thesis. PUC-Rio. Rio de Janeiro, Brazil (2021)
6. Higuchi, S., Freitas, C., Cuconato, B., Rademaker, A.: Text mining for history: first steps on building a large dataset. In: Calzolari, N., et al. (eds.) Proceedings of the Eleventh International Conference on Language Resources and Evaluation (LREC 2018), Miyazaki, Japan (2018)
7. Higuchi, S., Freitas, C., Santos, D.: Distant reading Brazilian politics. In: Proceedings of 4th Conference of the Association Digital Humanities in the Nordic Countries, pp. 190–200. Copenhagen, Denmark (2019)
8. Jurafsky, D., Martin, J.H.: Speech and Language Processing: An Introduction to Natural Language Processing, Computational Linguistics, and Speech Recognition. Upper Saddle River, USA: Pearson/Prentice Hall (2009)
9. Makarov, P.: Automated acquisition of patterns for coding political event data: two case studies. In: Proceedings of Workshop on Computational Linguistics for Cultural Heritage, Social Sciences, Humanities and Literature, pp. 103–112. Santa Fe, New Mexico, USA (2018)
10. Santos, D., Bick, E.: Providing Internet access to Portuguese corpora: the AC/DC project. In: Gavrilidou, M., Carayannis, G., Markantonatou, S., Piperidis, S., Stainhauer, G. (eds.) Proceedings of the Second International Conference on Language Resources and Evaluation (LREC 2000), pp. 205–210. Athens, Greece (2000)
11. Santos, D., Mota, C.: Experiments in human-computer cooperation for the semantic annotation of Portuguese corpora. In: Calzolari et al. (eds.) Proceedings of LREC 2010, pp. 1437–1444. Valetta, Malta (2010)
12. Santos, D., Ranchhod, E.: Ambientes de processamento de corpora em português: Comparação entre dois sistemas. In: Rodrigues, I., Quaresma, P. (eds.) Actas do IV Encontro para o Processamento Computacional da Língua Portuguesa Escrita e Falada (PROPOR'99), pp. 257–268. Évora, Portugal (1999)

Automatic Recognition of Units of Measurement in Product Descriptions from Tax Invoices Using Neural Networks

Lucas Fernandes Lucena$^{(\boxtimes)}$ ⓘ, Telmo de Menezes e Silva Filho ⓘ,
Thaís Gaudencio do Rêgo ⓘ, and Yuri Malheiros ⓘ

Universidade Federal da Paraíba, Joao Pessoa, PB 58051-900, Brazil
{thais,yuri}@ci.ufpb.br

Abstract. Tax evasion is a problem that affects our society, costing billions of Brazilian reais of public funds every year. Stopping this practice is a complex challenge that involves analyzing a large and diverse volume of data. In this work, we propose an approach to analyze invoices and extract information about measures and units from product descriptions using a neural network with the BiLSTM-CRF architecture. Our method can validate product quantity information to, for instance, check whether any product was bought or sold by a business without issuing an invoice. The results were evaluated according to precision, recall, and f-score. The proposed approach can correctly detect more than 90% of cases of each type of information, showing its feasibility to process invoice data.

Keywords: Named-Entity Recognition · Neural networks · BiLSTM-CRF

1 Introduction

In Brazil, the issuing of Decree nº 6.022, from January 22nd, 2007, created the Public System of Digital Bookkeeping (Sistema Público de Escrituração Digital, Sped), which regulates the informatization of the relation between official fiscal agencies and taxpayers, starting with the Electronic Tax Invoice (Nota Fiscal Eletrônica, NFe). This made it viable to apply Artificial Intelligence (AI) and other data analysis methods to the Brazilian Tax System.

Some information fields which are provided in the NFe include the issuer's name and address, issuing date, and nature of the transaction. Additionally, product descriptions must detail the amount, brand, type, model, number, quality, and other characteristics that allow for easy identification. Information contained in these documents can prove the veracity of transactions and help to ensure tax collection.

The digitization of fiscal documents enabled better integration between the tax system and existing digital technologies. Descriptions in tax invoices are often manually typed, with the level of detail about the products depending on

ⓒ Springer Nature Switzerland AG 2022
V. Pinheiro et al. (Eds.): PROPOR 2022, LNAI 13208, pp. 156–165, 2022.
https://doi.org/10.1007/978-3-030-98305-5_15

the person who provides them. Therefore, there is a wide variety in the way these descriptions are written, making it necessary to apply pre-processing methods in order to use these data as input for a neural network. Processes that can be optimized by this include inventory control, cash flow and fiscal, and accounting declarations. Thus, businesses have modernized themselves in this area and the Federal Department of Revenue and every State Department of Revenue has also adapted to better detect tax evasion using these documents, in an effort to prevent the yearly evasion of around 390 billion Brazilian reais.[1]

By analyzing data taken from fiscal documents, it is possible to verify the balance between products bought and sold by a company. Any discrepancies between these quantities and the inventory declared by the company could mean that there were transactions that were not recorded in tax invoices, which represents a form of tax evasion. The amount of products per transaction is one of the fields in NFe, but it can be filled with incomplete or incorrect information, which motivates a solution that can extract these data from the product description. This could benefit society by increasing tax collection without increasing the actual taxes, ensuring more public funds are available to be invested by the government.

Therefore, the goal of this work is to implement and evaluate an approach to extract values and units of measurement from product descriptions from tax invoices. To that end, we used regular expression (RegEx) and deep learning techniques for natural language processing, focusing on information extraction using Named-Entity Recognition (NER). First, we used regular expressions to automatically label the dataset, in order to train a bidirectional long short-term memory (BiLSTM) architecture with a CRF layer, which has shown good results in the related literature. The model had its performance compared to using only RegEx in the identification of values and measures in the description of the products in tax documents.

The rest of the paper is organized as follows. Section 2 presents related works, comparing them with our proposed approach. Section 3 explains the methodology used in this work, including the steps of the proposed solution, data pre-processing, evaluation metrics, and the chosen neural network architecture. Section 4 presents experimental results and analyses. And lastly, Sect. 5 brings some final remarks and future works.

2   Related Works

Feature extraction from product descriptions has been studied in various contexts. [6] proposed extracting features from product titles, by identifying brand information, type, style, size, and color. The authors used NER techniques applied to their own dataset, taken from the clothing and shoe sections of eBay and composed of 177,963 entries, which were labeled using dictionaries. Their experiments compared several algorithms, including Support Vector Machines, Maximum Entropy Classifiers, Hidden Markov Models, and Conditional Random

---

[1] https://ibpt.com.br/sonegacao-fiscal-da-empresas/.

Fields (CRF). Finally, they analyzed model performance according to precision, with CRF obtaining the best results.

In [5], the authors also focused on feature extraction with the goal to improve product metadata in eCommerce catalogs. Their approach used NER to extract brand data in order to use it in marketing campaigns, making it easier to use search filters. The work was developed by Walmart researchers who used their own data for training and testing. However, little was disclosed about the dataset. Experiments considered various classifiers, including k-nearest neighbors, dictionary-based approaches, Hidden Markov Models, Structured Perceptrons, and Linear Chain CRF, which were evaluated using f-score. The last two models showed satisfactory results.

In the Portuguese language, [7] proposed a process for title generation of products for sale in Brazilian marketplaces. The authors use two natural language processing tasks: NER and template-based generation (TBG). The main goal is to have a quickly implemented pipeline that assures quality to the titles of fashion products.

The authors of [10] proposed a new feature extraction model. For that, they used a BiLSTM architecture, in order to capture context and semantics, and a CRF to increase labeling consistency. Additionally, the solution employed an attention mechanism, aiming to select the main parts of the input sequence when making a decision. The dataset was built from public pages taken from Amazon, focusing on three types of products: dog food, detergents, and cameras. There were 1,180 instances, with attributes defined by domain, including brand, taste, aroma, and size. This approach was validated using precision, recall, and f-score.

The chosen architecture in this work is similar to the last work discussed in this Section [10], however, we do not use the attention method, because the BiLSTM-CRF architecture already has a similar characteristic and considers the whole sentence as the context in order to classify a specific token, where the token is any character set which is separated from others by at least one space. Another difference is the diversity of the dataset, as it is not restricted to any categories. In the first papers mentioned in this Section [5,6], the feature extraction is similar to our proposed method, but their architectures are limited to solutions using only CRF.

3   Methodology

3.1   Materials

This work was developed using an Anaconda environment containing the Python programming language (version 3.7.3). In addition, the following packages helped to implement the experiments: Gensim [8], to perform word vectorization, Keras (version 2.2.4) with TensorFlow 1.14 [1], for tokenization and to define the neural network model, and Scikit-learn [2], which provided the evaluation metrics. Experiments ran on an AMD Ryzen^{TM} 5 3600 CPU @ 3.60 GHz × 6, with 16 GB of 3200 MHz RAM and 1 TB of disk space, as well as an Nvidia GTX 970 with 4 GB of RAM.

3.2   Dataset

The data contain information from tax invoices generated in the Brazilian state of Paraíba. All sensitive data were removed from the dataset, as they were not important for the development of this work. The set contains 11 million records, with columns including Common Mercosul Nomenclature (Nomenclatura Comum do Mercosul, NCM) and product description (xProd). It is worth mentioning that the dataset does not contain the necessary information in order to perform the recognition of units of measurement, i.e. the product descriptions are not labeled. The xProd column is the most important information for this work. Thus, out of the original 10,751,853 instances, we selected 217,413 unique product descriptions, where the pre-processing steps were applied. With regard to tokens (any character set between spaces), we have a total of 1,196,950 tokens out of which 71,727 are unique.

3.3   Data Preparation

The dataset contains tax invoices with product descriptions that may contain errors. Thus, the same word appears in many different ways, which can be treated by a pre-processing step, reducing the number of unique tokens, facilitating the process at the embedding layer of the neural network.

We converted all descriptions to lower case and used Unicode standardization for accents. Some products are recorded with '.' or '+' in lieu of spaces or with brackets in their descriptions. These characters were substituted by spaces. After the initial data treatment, we extracted information about units of measurement in order to classify each token. For that, we used regular expressions (RegEx) to search for patterns. First we used RegEx to find measures with the following pattern: a number followed by grams or liters and any variation thereof.[2] When this pattern is found, the corresponding value is saved. Secondly, in order to extract information about product quantity, the RegEx searches for a number followed by information about units, boxes, bottles, or packages.[3] Similarly, if this pattern is found, the corresponding characters are saved for the next step.

After saving the results of the RegEx, the process iterates over each token. When the first token of a measure is found, it is classified as 'B-M', then any token belonging to the same measure is classified as 'I-M'. When the process finds the first token belonging to a quantity, it classifies it as 'B-U' and the following tokens in the pattern are classified as 'I-U'. Other tokens that are not part of any patterns according to the RegEx are classified as 'O'. When these patterns appear separately, the first class, be it 'B-M' or 'B-U', tends to concentrate the numerical information. On the other hand, the secondary classes, 'I-M' and 'I-U', tend to contain more units and measures (gram, liter, boxes, bottles), depending on the primary class. The use of RegEx has limitations to produce the labels

---

[2] $(? : \ \backslash s\rlap{\vert})((\backslash d*?))\backslash s?(\backslash d+)\backslash s?((? : k|kilos|kilo|gr|kg|mg|g|grs|gramas|l|ml))(? = \backslash s|\$)$.

[3] $(? : \backslash s|\backslash) \backslash b \backslash d + \backslash s?(? : caixas|caixa\backslash b|un\backslash b|o\backslash b|bdj\backslash b|und\backslash b|comp\backslash b|grfs\backslash b|grrf\backslash b| pct\backslash b)(? = \backslash s|\$)$.

used to train and test the model, however, it would be unfeasible to manually label the whole set.

Next, we removed all descriptions that did not contain at least one token belonging to the unit and measure classes, so false-positive errors are less likely to occur, though such inputs are likely to happen in the real world. This was done in order to optimize the training by using only data containing classes of interest for the network.

The last pre-processing procedure was tokenization. Each set of characters between spaces is considered a token and receives a unique numeric identifier. Then, a vector of size 25 is generated with the token identifiers, because none of the descriptions in the dataset were longer than 25 tokens. Each identifier occupies a position in the vector, with empty positions in descriptions shorter than 25 tokens receiving the value zero. Since zeroed tokens are different from all the others, they were labeled with a new class, called 'PAD'. Table 1 presents the resulting class distribution.

Table 1. Number of tokens per class present in the final dataset and their respective percentages.

	B-M	I-M	B-U	I-U	O	PAD
Number of tokens	179,043	15,927	9,494	4,878	987,608	4,238,375
Percentage (%)	3.30	0.30	0.17	0.09	18.17	77.97

3.4   Training and Test

As mentioned above, we chose the BiLSTM-CRF architecture, which takes as input the vectorized data produced by the process discussed in the previous Section. The training set is the result of the application of RegEX and thus, descriptions that deviate from the patterns used in regular expressions were also not captured by the BiLSTM model. The BiLSTM-CRF architecture starts with an embedding layer, followed by a bidirectional LSTM layer and, finally, a CRF layer with sequential dependencies, which returns a confidence score for each class, predicting the class with the highest confidence for each token. Figure 1 presents this architecture.

In addition to the network architecture, some parameters were manually adjusted. In the embedding layer, the 'mask zero' parameter was set as 'True'. With that, the padding tokens are ignored and are not used in order to build the vocabulary of this layer and all the following layers of the model discard the information about these padding tokens. Additionally, in the LSTM layer, the 'recurrent dropout' parameter was set to 0.1.

The chosen optimizer was Adam [3], with the negative log-likelihood cost function and the time-wise marginal argmax precision function. Another important parameter for training is the batch size, which we defined as 32 [4].

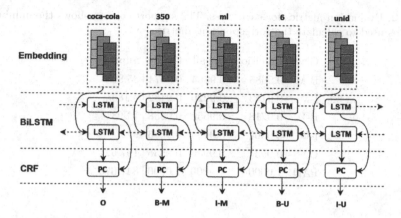

Fig. 1. BiLSTM-CRF architecture – the network input is shown at the top of the image and the output is shown in the bottom.

The model was trained for a maximum of 20 epochs, with an early stopping criterion, if the validation loss reduces by less than 0.1 for at most two epochs. Finally, it was necessary to split the data into training and test datasets. Thus, we performed a 5-fold cross-validation for the experiments. There is no comparison to a baseline as our "baseline" would be RegEx. In this way, the test dataset was created using RegEx.

4 Results and Discussion

We analyzed two types of divergences in the results: the first type happens when the labels used during training, which were produced by the RegEx, did not contain the correct class information, but the trained model was able to correctly classify the tokens; the second type is the opposite, i.e. the input data were correctly labeled, but the model failed to recognize the correct classes. Thus, the first type contains divergences that can be considered positive for the model and the second type corresponds to poor results produced by the model.

4.1 General Analysis

The following results were obtained by using the trained model to predict the classes of the test dataset. The same pre-processing was applied to the training and test datasets.

Table 2 shows the resulting values of the metrics, corresponding to averages across the 5 folds of the cross-validation. All values were higher than 0.9 for all metrics (precision, recall, and f-score) and for all classes. Table 3 shows an example of a product description where the RegEx failed to recognize a pattern that was correctly detected by the model.

Table 2. Evaluation metrics for each class. The support column shows the number of instances used to calculate the corresponding metrics.

Class	Precision	Recall	f-score	Support
B-M	0.9685	0.9664	0.9674	35.808
I-M	0.9153	0.9220	0.9182	3.185
B-U	0.9718	0.9559	0.9638	1.898
I-U	0.9507	0.9684	0.9593	975
O	0.9934	0.9936	0.9935	197.521
PAD	1.0000	1.0000	1.0000	847.675

In addition to detecting new patterns, the model corrected or complemented information in the input data. Table 4 shows a case, where the description contains erroneous information, which happened because some patterns are not mapped in the training set. Due to this, the trained model is able to learn some patterns that the RegEx was unable to recognize. In this particular description, the RegEx identified the number 503 as the first token of a measure sequence when it actually represents a serial number for the sky blue color.

Table 3. Product description containing a measure pattern that was unrecognized by the RegEx, but was correctly found by the model. 'B-M' means the token begins a sequence containing measurement information. 'O' means the token is not of interest.

Token	arroz	chines	parbolizado	tipo1	1k
RegEx	O	O	O	O	O
Model	O	O	O	O	B-M

The behavior observed above is possible due to the chosen neural network architecture, as it is capable to establish relations between distinct descriptions and learning the probability of occurrence of each class, by taking into account the context of the input text.

Table 4. Incorrectly labeled description that was correctly classified by the model.

Token	tempera	guache	azul	celeste	503	15 ml	acrilex
RegEx	O	O	O	O	B-M	I-M	O
Model	O	O	O	O	O	B-M	O

Additionally, the running times of the model while predicting for 1,000, 10,000, and 100,000 instances were measured at 0.1930, 1.9453, and 20.4615 s respectively, which when compared to the processing times registered for the RegEx method for the same data (1.3257, 13.1803, and 140.1435 s, respectively) represented a 7-fold decrease in computing time.

4.2   Analysis of Errors

Table 5 highlights an error that happens when the RegEx correctly classified the tokens, but the trained model was unable to correctly recognize the class of at least one of the tokens.

Table 5. Product description which was correctly labeled by the RegEx, but was not correctly classified by the model.

Token	amoxi	clavpot	875125 mg	12	cpr	gen	germed
RegEx	O	O	B-M	O	O	O	O
Model	O	O	O	O	O	O	O

The error shown in Table 5 may have been caused by the low frequency of descriptions with similar contexts, i.e. there might be insufficient samples corresponding to certain cases. Another related issue is the fact that the model might not be flexible with regard to uncommon tokens. When it sees tokens that were absent in training, the embedding layer assigns the value 1 to it. Thus, if a description contains too many uncommon tokens, it loses its context and the network predicts class 'O' for all its tokens.

The issue of uncommon tokens is frequent with numerical tokens, as each number is considered a separate token in the dictionary that is produced in the pre-processing step. Thus, one possible solution would be to standardize numerical tokens, by converting all of them into a single token and keeping a reference to the original value. However, this solution can be very computationally demanding, hindering model performance.

5   Conclusions

The proposed solution using BiLSTM presented promising results compared to a RegEx-based approach. In addition to good results according to precision, recall, and f-score, the model was seven times faster than the RegEx process, likely because the neural network can to benefit from highly optimized GPU processing, while the RegEx is sequentially computed using the CPU. In addition, with the NNs, we can observe new patterns not registered in the RegEx rules.

Despite being in an early stage, this work reached its goal. However, there are some limitations, such as the inconsistencies between the model predictions and the RegEx, which can be improved by introducing more diversity into the training data. As mentioned before, the training dataset for the BiLTSM model is defined by using RegEx. Thus, descriptions that differ from the regular expressions used will not be recognized by this model either. However, the model could still learn new contexts, improving its results. By improving the hardware used, it is likely possible to reduce training and inference time. Furthermore, Viterbi decoding could be evaluated in place of time-wise marginal argmax, as the ultimate goal is to make a discriminatory decision.

In the context of the Portuguese language, approaches as the presented can be very valuable, given that annotated resources are scarce but unlabeled text data is plentiful [9]. The results obtained in this initial study, can provide new labeled datasets in Portuguese, contributing to other research in the area. Studies on the impact of the tool in production are still necessary.

Finally, with the values and measurement units of products recognized in their descriptions, in addition to those available in other fields, it is possible to cross-reference data between what is sold and what is actually declared by the companies. Thus, it is possible to recognize tax fraud when what is sold is not declared and the tax on that product is not collected by the government.

References

1. Abadi, M., et al.: TensorFlow: large-scale machine learning on heterogeneous systems (2015). https://www.tensorflow.org/. Software available from tensorflow.org
2. Buitinck, L., et al.: API design for machine learning software: experiences from the scikit-learn project. In: ECML PKDD Workshop: Languages for Data Mining and Machine Learning, pp. 108–122 (2013)
3. Kingma, D.P., Ba, J.: Adam: a method for stochastic optimization (2015). http://arxiv.org/abs/1412.6980
4. Masters, D., Luschi, C.: Revisiting small batch training for deep neural networks. CoRR abs/1804.07612 (2018). http://arxiv.org/abs/1804.07612
5. More, A.: Attribute extraction from product titles in ecommerce. CoRR abs/1608.04670 (2016). http://arxiv.org/abs/1608.04670
6. Putthividhya, D., Hu, J.: Bootstrapped named entity recognition for product attribute extraction. In: Proceedings of the 2011 Conference on Empirical Methods in Natural Language Processing, pp. 1557–1567, Edinburgh, Scotland, UK. Association for Computational Linguistics, July 2011. https://aclanthology.org/D11-1144
7. Real, L., Johansson, K., Mendes, J., Lopes, B., Oshiro, M.: Generating e-commerce product titles in Portuguese. In: Anais do XLVIII Seminário Integrado de Software e Hardware, Porto Alegre, RS, Brasil, pp. 299–304. SBC (2021). https://doi.org/10.5753/semish.2021.15835. https://sol.sbc.org.br/index.php/semish/article/view/15835
8. Řehůřek, R., Sojka, P.: Software framework for topic modelling with large corpora. In: Proceedings of the LREC 2010 Workshop on New Challenges for NLP Frameworks, Valletta, Malta, pp. 45–50. ELRA, May 2010. http://is.muni.cz/publication/884893/en

9. Souza, F., Nogueira, R.F., de Alencar Lotufo, R.: Portuguese named entity recognition using BERT-CRF. CoRR abs/1909.10649 (2019). http://arxiv.org/abs/1909.10649

10. Zheng, G., Mukherjee, S., Dong, X.L., Li, F.: OpenTag: open attribute value extraction from product profiles. CoRR abs/1806.01264 (2018). http://arxiv.org/abs/1806.01264

Entity Extraction from Portuguese Legal Documents Using Distant Supervision

Lucas M. Navarezi[1]($\boxtimes$) (iD), Kenzo Sakiyama[1] (iD), Lucas S. Rodrigues[2] (iD),
Caio M. O. Robaldo[3] (iD), Gustavo R. Lobato[3] (iD), Paulo A. Vilela[3] (iD),
Edson T. Matsubara[1] (iD), and Eraldo R. Fernandes[1] (iD)

[1] Universidade Federal de Mato Grosso do Sul, Campo Grande, Brazil
{lucas.navarezi,kenzo.sakiyama}@ufms.br, {edsontm,eraldo}@facom.ufms.br
[2] Instituto Federal de Mato Grosso do Sul, Dourados, Brazil
lucas.rodrigues@ifms.edu.br
[3] Ministério Público do Estado de Mato Grosso do Sul, Campo Grande, Brazil
{caiorobaldo,gustavolobato,paulovilela}@mpms.mp.br

Abstract. Most approaches to role-filler entity extraction (REE) rely on large labeled training corpora in which entity mentions are directly annotated in the input document. In this work, we leverage an existing knowledge base (KB) of entities to perform document-level REE from drug seizure petitions. We propose a system that learns to extract entities from petitions to fill 29 roles of a drug seizure event. Although we have access to a KB covering more than 170 thousand entities and six thousand petitions, such that each entity in the KB is linked to a specific petition, the mentions to an entity within a petition's text are not annotated. The lack of these annotations brings challenges related to mismatches between entity values in the KB and entity mentions in the documents. Additionally, there are entities with same type or same value. Thus, we propose a distant annotation method to overcome these challenges and automatically label petition documents using the available KB. This annotation method includes a parameter that controls the balance between precision and recall. We also propose a strategy to effectively tune this parameter in order to optimize a given metric. We then train a BERT-based sequence labeling model that learns to identify entity mentions and label them. Our system achieves an F_1 score of 78.59 with precision over 82%. We also report ablation studies regarding the distant annotation method.

Keywords: NLP · Entity extraction · BERT

1 Introduction

Template filling is a classic formulation of event extraction that comprises filling slots (roles) of a frame (template) with entities extracted from segments (entity mentions) of a given document [2]. This task is usually split in two sub-tasks:

© Springer Nature Switzerland AG 2022
V. Pinheiro et al. (Eds.): PROPOR 2022, LNAI 13208, pp. 166–176, 2022.
https://doi.org/10.1007/978-3-030-98305-5_16

Template Recognition and Role-filler Entity Extraction (REE). Template recognition comprises identifying events within the document, and each event type is associated to a template. Then, REE consists of extracting entities mentioned in the document to fill the roles within the identified template. In this work, we focus on the latter sub-tasks: REE. Currently, the best performing REE systems rely on deep learning, which usually requires large annotated corpora [19]. This kind of data is not available in most cases, and its creation is expensive.

On the other hand, it is possible to create training data through existing knowledge bases [6, 9]. This is the case for thousands of legal petitions filed by the Ministério Público do Estado de Mato Grosso do Sul (MPMS)[1] regarding illegal drug seizures. In such petitions, a public prosecutor charges one or more people due to a drug seizure performed by law enforcement agents. In this document, the prosecutor describes, among other information, the seizure procedure (location, time, etc.), people charged (names, addresses, IDs), and seized drugs (name, quantity). Thus, we have only one type of event (drug seizure) and there is no need to perform template recognition since there is only one template of interest. Afterwards, a specialist reads the petition, fills the template, and inserts this information in a knowledge base (KB). In Fig. 1, we present a fragment of an illustrative drug seizure petition, in which we highlighted mentions to seven entities. It is important to notice that only the entities themselves are included in the KB, i.e., the spans within the petition's text that mention the entities are not annotated.

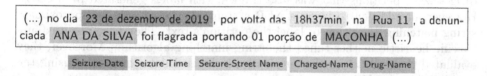

Fig. 1. *Top*: fragment of a drug seizure petition (anonymized) with entity mentions highlighted accordingly. *Bottom*: legend of highlighting colours to entity labels.

In this work, we develop a REE system that extracts entities from a petition to fill a template comprising 29 roles related to a drug seizure. Since we do not have labeled text for this task, we propose a method to annotate entity mentions in a petition's text using a distant supervision approach. This annotation method makes use of the petition's document and its corresponding entries in the KB. The labeled corpus is then used to train a sequence labeling model based on BERT [3]. During prediction, we make use of the learned model to label a given petition text with entity mentions. Then, through simple standardization approaches, the labeled mentions are converted to unique entities resulting in a filled template that can be inserted in the KB (or compared to the entities already in the KB for validation).

---

[1] MPMS is a public institution whose duties include criminal prosecution in the Brazilian state of Mato Grosso do Sul.

In general, when dealing with noisy labels, higher recall is beneficial even when it hurts precision a bit. Later, the training of the BERT-based model should be able to ignore most noise while still benefiting from the larger training signal. The proposed distant annotation method includes a parameter to control the balance between precision and recall. To tune this parameter is tricky because there are more than twenty roles in the template and each role can be affected by the parameter in different ways. We thus propose a technique to efficiently tune this parameter for all considered roles. We experimentally evaluate the impact of this tuning technique on system performance, and the obtained results indicate an increase in recall of 4.67 points, with minimal drop in precision. We also report on other ablation studies to assess different aspects of the proposed distant annotation method. The final system achieves an F_1 score of 78.59 on the test set, with precision over 82%.

The main contributions of this paper are: (i) We propose a REE system based on a KB but no manually labeled text; (ii) We propose a technique to tune the distant annotation method in order to optimize for recall while not hurting precision too much; and (iii) We present ablation studies to assess different aspects of the proposed annotation method.

2   Related Work

Bonifacio *et al.* [1] presented a Named Entity Recognition (NER) system for drug seizure petitions that was also trained with labels generated from a KB. However, in addition to being a NER system, they used only an approximate string matching algorithm to label the petition's text. They have not used any specific heuristic neither tuned the string matching algorithm. Moreover, they evaluated their model on the automatically labeled data, instead of using the manually created KB.

There are just a few works that deal with document-level role-filler entity extraction [4] and template filling [5,7]. Du et al. [4] proposes a modified BERT, called Generative Role-Filler Transformer (GRIT), to access the entire document and map extraction decisions. The GTT framework [5], from same authors, is a modification of GRIT to account for event types. Also a BERT-based framework, the Cross-Attention Guided Template Generation (TEMPGEN) [7] applies a novel copy technique that leverages only the k most important attention heads. All these previous works are based on manually annotated events comprising both the KB entries *and the exact mentions in the documents*. The task tackled in our work, on the other hand, does not include annotations of entity mentions in the documents. And, although we could compare our labeling-based system with these previous methods, by using the distant annotated mentions generated by our heuristics, these methods were not available when we conducted our experiments. This comparison is an obvious future work though. Another important difference between these previous methods and ours is the number of roles in our dataset. While most previous works use the MUC-4 dataset, which includes only five roles, our dataset comprises 29 roles.

As far as we know, there is no previous work that deal with document-level entity extraction using distant supervision. Most work using the technique on information extraction [12, 15, 20] does not consider that each entry in the KB is associated with a specific document to be labeled. Thus, these methods, given an entry in the KB, need to retrieve supporting documents before labeling them. In our method, each KB entry is naturally associate with a document simply because every entry has been extracted from a document and this association is stored in the KB. Thus, we understand that our automatic annotation method uses a supervision signal that is not *that* distant. However, since an entity from the KB frequently does not match any mention in the corresponding document, we still consider it a distant supervision method.

3 Entity Extraction System

The proposed system comprises two phases: training and prediction. In the training phase, the system applies a Distant Annotation Method (DAM) that leverages the KB to create a labeled corpus and then trains a BERT Sequence Labeling Model (BSLM) to label a petition text with the mentioned entities. In the prediction phase, given a petition text, the BSLM is employed to label the text with possible entity mentions and then a standardization procedure is applied to extract unique entities. In the following, we describe each phase in detail.

Training. The training phase comprises two procedures: Distant Annotation Method and Supervised Training. The DAM takes a petition document and its corresponding entities from the KB and automatically labels mentions to these entities in the petition text. The corpus comprising all labeled petitions is then used to supervisedly train the BERT Sequence Labeling Model.

DAM's first step consists of, for each entity in the KB, generating one or more patterns to be searched for in the petition's text. Each pattern represents a possible phrasing for the entity, i.e., a possible mention to the entity. A string matching algorithm is then used to search for all matches of each pattern in the petition's text. We make use of three string matching algorithms: *Simple Match* (SM), *Regular Expression* (REGEX), and *Fuzzy Search* (FS). SM is the exact string matching algorithm. REGEX is the ordinary string matching based on regular expressions. FS is an approximate string matching algorithm based on the Levenshtein distance or edit distance [8]. FS returns a match whenever the edit distance between the pattern and a substring of the text is less than or equal to a given threshold L. This threshold is tuned individually for each role as described in Sect. 4.3.

We denote the pattern generating and string matching algorithms as *Heuristics*. The proposed heuristics also depend on the role and are described in the following.

- • Drug-Quantity: We use the REGEX algorithm to search for two patterns: one using '.' (dot) as decimal separator and the other using ',' (comma).

- • Charged-Birth date, Seizure-Date: We use the FS algorithm to search for three patterns: the KB string as in 'DD/MM/YYYY', the KB string with '/' characters replaced by '.', and the date in full.
- • Charged-CPF: These IDs are stored as eleven digits in the KB, but are represented by different formats in petition documents. We use the FS algorithm to search for two patterns: the KB string and a formatted string: 'XXX.XXX.XXX-XX', where 'X' is a digit of the CPF.
- • Seizure-Legal authority: Legal authorities are stored in the KB as acronyms (e.g. 'PM' for 'Polícia Militar'). We use the FS algorithm to search for two patterns: the acronym and the expanded form.
- • Seizure-Time: This entity is stored in the KB as in the form 'HH:MM'. We use the FS algorithm to search for four patterns: 'HHhMMmin', 'HHh', 'HH horas', and 'HH horas e MM minutos'.
- • Charged-St.Number, Charged-State, Drug-Qty.Unit, Seizure-St.Number, Seizure-Origin state, Seizure-Destination state: These entities are usually represented by very short string (one to three characters). We use the SM algorithm to search for a pattern equal to the value in the KB.
- • *Remaining entities*: For all other entity types, we use the FS algorithm to search for one pattern: the value in the KB.

For a given entity in the KB, all matches of all patterns are annotated in the petition text with the entity type. The generated labels are illustrated by the highlighted spans in Fig. 1. For example, spans of text corresponding to mentions to the entities *Street Name* and *Street Number* of a seizure procedure are labeled as Seizure-St.Name and Seizure-St.Number, respectively. This annotation is then encoded as IOB2 tags [13]. Thus, there are 29 IOB2 types, one for each role, totaling 59 tags (one pair of tags B- and I-for each role plus one O tag).

Our sequence labeling models are supervisedly trained by finetuning a BERT language model [3] called *BERTimbau* [16]. This model has been pretrained on brWaC [17], a Portuguese-based corpus comprising 2.86B tokens. Other BERT based models like Roberta [10], DistilBERT [14] and Multilingual [3] showed little to no difference, sometimes even worse performance, in the target domain. We have trained all models using the Transformers library [18]. We have performed preliminary experiments to tune both the learning rate and the number of epochs. The optimal learning rate was the default one $(5 \cdot 10^{-5})$ and the number of epochs was set to five.

During training, we evaluate the current model on the dev set after each epoch and, in the end, return the model with the highest F_1 score. For most settings, we executed five independent training runs using the same hyperparameters and data. In these cases, we report the average performance over the five models and the corresponding standard deviation. When performance is reported in plots, lines are average values and shadowed areas around them are standard deviations.

Prediction. The prediction phase of our system is mainly comprised by two procedures: Sequence Labeling and Standardization. In the first procedure, we make use of the learned BSLM to label a given petition text. It is important to recall that our evaluation data does not include all mentions of an entity in a document, as is the case in most previous work. Thus, in the second procedure, we employ a standardization method to convert all mentions labeled by BSLM to the expected formats in the KB. Examples of standardization procedures include: removing alphanumeric characters (Charged-CPF and Charged-RG), converting number in full to numerical format (Drug-Quantity and Seizure-Date) and removing ordinal number indicators 'º' and 'ᵒ' (Seizure-Date). After standardization, duplicate values labeled with the same role are removed.

4   Experimental Results

We now present our experimental setup and the achieved results. We also describe the proposed technique to tune the fuzzy search parameter in the distant annotation method.

4.1   Dataset and Evaluation Metric

Our corpus includes 6,664 drug seizure petitions, filed by MPMS from 26 February 2012 to 9 October 2020, comprising more than 225 thousand sentences and almost seven million tokens. The manually-created KB includes entities 170,642 entities. We divide this dataset into three splits: train, test and development, the latter being used to perform hyperparameter tuning and model selection. The train set comprises the first 5,268 petitions, the next 606 petitions were allocated to the dev set, and finally the most recent 790 petitions were put in the test set.

The 29 roles considered in this work are related to three aspects of a seizure procedure: the charged people, the seized drugs, and the procedure itself. Regarding the charged people, the considered roles are (number of entries between parentheses): name (9,003), nickname (1,349), CPF (6,962), RG (7,724), nationality (7,225), mother's name (9,484), phone number (7,648), birth date (8,678), street name (8,701), street number (6,776), neighborhood (7,140), city (6,169), and state (5,823). Regarding the seized drugs, the roles are: name (7,735), quantity (7,717), and quantity unit (6,803). And regarding the seizure procedure itself, the roles are: date (6,711), time (6,630), legal authority (6,740), street name (6,897), street number (2,405), complement (526), neighborhood (4,448), city (6,634), state (6,569), origin city (2,043), origin state (2,028), destination city (2,045), and destination state (2,029).

We report all results considering the CEAF-REE metric [4] which is an entity-based metric, instead of previously used mention-based metrics. CEAF-REE is inspired by the popular entity-based CEAF metric [11] for coreference resolution. CEAF-REE considers that the system should extract only one mention for each role-filler entity, i.e., if the system extracts more than one mention for the same entity, it will get penalized for the extra mentions.

4.2   Best Model Results

When using the best performing BSLM model, our system achieves an F_1 score of 78.59 on the test set, with precision of 82.13% and recall of 75.35%. For most roles, our system achieves an F_1 score over 70 points. We identified different reasons for the low-performing roles. For instance, the state where the charged person resides and the source and destination states of the drug are frequently the same in a petition, which causes issues for the standardization method. Regarding the Charged-City role, when a charged person lives in the same city where the prosecutor's office is, the entity is often mentioned as "nesta cidade" (i.e. "in this city"). Regarding the Charged-Phone number role, there are many entities in the KB that are not mentioned in the petition text (they have been extracted from other sources). For the street name and neighborhood of the charged person, we could verify a great amount of errors in the KB. Finally, for the Seizure-Complement role, there are very few entities in the KB.

4.3   DAM: Role-Specific Threshold

As described in Sect. 3, the FS algorithm used in the Distant Annotation Method depends on a threshold L that controls the maximum edit distance between the given pattern and a substring of the text. We first reparameterize the *absolute* threshold L as $L = \lfloor (1 - S) \cdot |p| \rfloor$, where $|p|$ is the character-wise length of the pattern p and $S \in [0.0, 1.0]$ is the *relative* minimum similarity for p. For example, if we set the minimum similarity to 75% (i.e. $S = 0.75$) and the given pattern is 100-character long, we will have $L = 25$ (maximum edit distance is 25 characters). Although the relative similarity is important to generalize DAM, the optimal S is role dependent. For instance, the dates 10/01/1981 and 10/01/2981 are completely different, although only one character differs one from another. On the other hand, the names Pedro R. Silva and Pedro Roberto Silva are probably mentions to the same person.

Note that the lower the minimum similarity the higher the recall of the Distant Annotation Method but, on the other hand, the lower its precision. We hypothesize that it should be beneficial to have high recall even if it hurts precision a bit. The underlying assumption is that more labeled data is better even if it means some noisy labels. BSLM training should be able to learn to ignore some noise while still benefits from the larger training signal. However, the optimal recall level is unknown and DAM employs the FS algorithm for 22 out of 29 entity types. It is virtually impossible to consider all different combinations of role-specific S values even if we keep to a small set of possible values. If we consider three possible values, for instance, there are 3^{22} combinations. Even if we vary the S value for only one role while keep all the other fixed, the number of possible values considered would be limited because each combination would require three steps to be evaluated: (i) label the data using DAM with the corresponding S values; (ii) train a BSLM using the labeled data; and (iii) evaluate the final system using the learned BSLM. By far, the most time consuming step is the training of BSLM, and for only three possible values of S, we would need to train 66 $(3 \cdot 22)$ models. This is definitely possible, but we would be considering only three different values for S.

Instead, we propose a tuning method based on the F_β metric that allows us to experiment with a great number of possible values for role-specific similarities. F_β is a generalization of the F_1 metric that allows to weight the importance of recall over precision. It is defined as $F_\beta = (1 + \beta^2) \cdot \frac{P \cdot R}{\beta^2 \cdot P + R}$, where P denotes precision, R recall, and β is the weight of recall. Our tuning method consists of, for each $S \in \{0.40, 0.45, \ldots, 0.95, 1.00\}$ and each role for which FS is used, running DAM to label mentions on the dev dataset and then computing precision and recall of these mentions. Later, for each role, we select the similarity value S that maximizes F_β, for $\beta \in \{1, 2, 4, 6\}$ (i.e. different "recall levels"), and evaluate the resulting full system on the dev dataset. In that way, we need to train only four models ($\beta = 1, 2, 4, 6$), although we have considered a plenty number of possible values of S for each role.

We present in Fig. 2 (*left*) the values of precision, recall and F_1 score for the labels generated by DAM in function of β. We can see the expected results: the higher the β the higher the recall and the lower the precision. In Fig. 2 (*right*), we present the performance metrics for the corresponding systems. We can observe that our hypothesis holds: recall and F_1 grow with β. If we compare the precision curves in both figures, we can see that BSLM training is indeed robust to noisy labels.

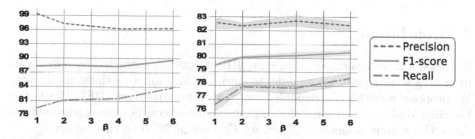

Fig. 2. *Left*: performances of DAM per β. *Right*: performances of the resulting systems.

4.4 Assessment of DAM Components

To assess different components of DAM, we evaluate the following variations: (i) *SM*: use Simple Match for all roles (no heuristic); (ii) *FS*: use Fuzzy Search for all roles with fixed similarity ($S = 0.75$ was tuned to maximize F_1 on the dev set); (iii) *SM+H*: use Heuristics for the respective roles and SM for the remaining; (iv) *FS+H*: use Heuristics for the respective roles and FS (with $S = 0.75$) for the remaining; and (v) *FSRS+H*: our full system with Heuristics and FS with role-specific similarity. (S set according to $\beta = 6$).

In Table 1, we show performance metrics for the corresponding systems on the dev set. We performed a Kruskal-Wallis test on F_1 results, and the obtained p-value was 0.0002074. Therefore we can reject the null hypothesis that the F_1 samples are equal. Proceeding with multiple comparisons using Bonferroni correction $\frac{\alpha}{n} = \frac{0.05}{5} = 0.01$, all pairs of methods present a statistically significant difference, except (*SM+H*, *FS+H*). Consequently, the differences between pairs (*SM*, *SM+H*) and (*FS*, *FS+H*) are significant, indicating that heuristics significantly improved the results. Another important result is that the full system (*FSRS+H*) is significantly better than all other versions, indicating that the proposed similarity tuning method brings significant improvement.

Table 1. Performances on the dev set of systems obtained by different versions of DAM. Averages among five runs. Standard deviations are between parentheses.

DAM version	Precision	Recall	F_1-score
SM	74.78 (1.52)	54.28 (0.45)	62.89 (0.35)
FS	74.10 (1.09)	59.36 (0.49)	65.91 (0.49)
SM+H	82.16 (1.19)	74.33 (0.98)	78.04 (0.35)
FS+H	**82.84 (0.45)**	73.92 (0.53)	78.13 (0.23)
FSRS+H	82.41 (0.43)	**78.59 (0.49)**	**80.45 (0.23)**

5   Conclusion

In this work, we leveraged an existing KB of entities, extracted by specialists from drug seizure petitions, in order to automatically annotate these documents. We proposed a method for role-filler entity extraction based on a BERT Sequence Labeling Model trained using this distant-annotated corpus of drug seizure petitions. Our system achieved a per-entity F_1 score of 78.59 on the test set.

As future work, we plan to cooperate with MPMS in order to further improve our system, the quality of heuristics and evaluation methods. One interesting question to be answered in the future is whether more complex models, like the ones based on the transformer architecture [4,5,7], can outperform the simpler labeling method employed here in this task. Remembering that the REE task tackled in our work differs from the REE task tackled in these previous works, mainly because the former lacks annotated mentions in the documents.

References

1. Bonifacio, L.H., Vilela, P.A., Lobato, G.R., Fernandes, E.R.: A study on the impact of intradomain finetuning of deep language models for legal named entity recognition in Portuguese. In: Cerri, R., Prati, R.C. (eds.) BRACIS 2020. LNCS (LNAI), vol. 12319, pp. 648–662. Springer, Cham (2020). https://doi.org/10.1007/978-3-030-61377-8_46

2. Chelba, C., Mahajan, M.: Information extraction using the structured language model. CoRR cs.CL/0108023 (2001)
3. Devlin, J., Chang, M., Lee, K., Toutanova, K.: BERT: pre-training of deep bidirectional transformers for language understanding. CoRR abs/1810.04805 (2018)
4. Du, X., Rush, A.M., Cardie, C.: Document-level event-based extraction using generative template-filling transformers. CoRR abs/2008.09249 (2020)
5. Du, X., Rush, A.M., Cardie, C.: Template filling with generative transformers. In: Proceedings of the 2021 Conference of the North American Chapter of the Association for Computational Linguistics: Human Language Technologies, NAACL-HLT 2021, Online, 6–11 June 2021 (2021)
6. Hedderich, M.A., Lange, L., Klakow, D.: ANEA: distant supervision for low-resource named entity recognition. CoRR abs/2102.13129 (2021). https://arxiv.org/abs/2102.13129
7. Huang, K., Tang, S., Peng, N.: Document-level entity-based extraction as template generation. CoRR abs/2109.04901 (2021)
8. Levenshtein, V.I.: Binary codes capable of correcting deletions, insertions, and reversals. Sov. Phys. Dokl. **10**(8), 707–710 (1966)
9. Liang, C., Yu, Y., Jiang, H., Er, S., Wang, R., Zhao, T., Zhang, C.: BOND: BERT-assisted open-domain named entity recognition with distant supervision. CoRR abs/2006.15509 (2020)
10. Liu, Y., et al.: RoBERTa: a robustly optimized BERT pretraining approach. CoRR abs/1907.11692 (2019)
11. Luo, X.: On coreference resolution performance metrics. In: Proceedings of Human Language Technology Conference and Conference on Empirical Methods in Natural Language Processing, pp. 25–32. Association for Computational Linguistics, Vancouver (2005)
12. Reschke, K., Jankowiak, M., Surdeanu, M., Manning, C., Jurafsky, D.: Event extraction using distant supervision. In: Proceedings of the Ninth International Conference on Language Resources and Evaluation, pp. 4527–4531. European Language Resources Association (ELRA), Reykjavik, Iceland, May 2014
13. Sang, E.F.T.K., Meulder, F.D.: Introduction to the CONLL-2003 shared task: Language-independent named entity recognition. In: Daelemans, W., Osborne, M. (eds.) Proceedings of the Seventh Conference on Natural Language Learning, CoNLL 2003, Held in cooperation with HLT-NAACL 2003, Edmonton, Canada, May 31–June 1 2003. pp. 142–147. ACL (2003). https://aclanthology.org/W03-0419/
14. Sanh, V., Debut, L., Chaumond, J., Wolf, T.: DistilBERT, a distilled version of BERT: smaller, faster, cheaper and lighter. CoRR abs/1910.01108 (2019)
15. Sarwar, S.M., Allan, J.: SearchIE: a retrieval approach for information extraction. In: Proceedings of the 2019 ACM SIGIR International Conference on Theory of Information Retrieval, ICTIR 2019, pp. 249–252. Association for Computing Machinery, New York (2019)
16. Souza, F., Nogueira, R., Lotufo, R.: BERTimbau: pretrained BERT models for Brazilian Portuguese. In: Cerri, R., Prati, R.C. (eds.) BRACIS 2020. LNCS (LNAI), vol. 12319, pp. 403–417. Springer, Cham (2020). https://doi.org/10.1007/978-3-030-61377-8_28
17. Wagner Filho, J.A., Wilkens, R., Idiart, M., Villavicencio, A.: The brWaC corpus: a new open resource for Brazilian Portuguese. In: Proceedings of the Eleventh International Conference on Language Resources and Evaluation (LREC 2018). European Language Resources Association (ELRA), Miyazaki, May 2018

18. Wolf, T., et al.: HuggingFace's transformers: state-of-the-art natural language processing. CoRR abs/1910.03771 (2019)
19. Xiang, W., Wang, B.: A survey of event extraction from text. IEEE Access **7**, 173111–173137 (2019)
20. Yao, X., Van Durme, B.: Information extraction over structured data: question answering with Freebase. In: Proceedings of the 52nd Annual Meeting of the Association for Computational Linguistics (Volume 1: Long Papers), pp. 956–966. Association for Computational Linguistics, Baltimore, June 2014

Sexist Hate Speech: Identifying Potential Online Verbal Violence Instances

Brenda Salenave Santana[1](✉) [iD], Aline Aver Vanin[2] [iD],
and Leandro Krug Wives[1] [iD]

[1] Postgraduate Program in Computing, Federal University of Rio Grande do Sul,
Porto Alegre, Brazil
{bssantana,wives}@inf.ufrgs.br
[2] Department of Education and Humanities, Federal University of Health Sciences
of Porto Alegre, Porto Alegre, Brazil
alinevanin@ufcspa.edu.br

Abstract. Online communication provides space for content dissemination and opinion sharing. However, the limit between opinion and offense might be exceeded, characterizing hate speech. Moreover, its automatic detection is challenging, and approaches focused on the Portuguese language are scarce. This paper proposes an interface between linguistic concepts and computational interventions to support hate speech detection. We applied a Natural Language Processing pipeline involving topic modeling and semantic role labeling, allowing a semi-automatic identification of hate speech. We also discuss how such speech qualifies as a type of verbal violence widespread on social networks to reinforce a sexist stereotype. Finally, we use Twitter data to analyze information that resulted in virtual attacks against a specific person. As an achievement, this work validates the use of linguistic features to annotate data either as hate speech or not. It also proposes using fallacies as a potential additional feature to identify potential intolerant discourses.

Keywords: Hate speech · Linguistic features · Natural Language Processing

1 Introduction

Online communication has brought new possibilities for expressing what we think and act in daily life. The Internet has opened space for content dissemination, representing changes in the communication paradigm. It has also given a sense of being part of a community, and it opened a window for free-thinking—and free speech. In line with [12], the Internet provides an environment where groups with common affinities can meet. Numerous platforms, resources, and social networks have opened up new content production and sharing channels. As a result, it represents a powerful tool for the most diverse forms of expression, including the ones that, in other circumstances, would not have much visibility. However, it is often the case that discourse disseminated in social networks

© Springer Nature Switzerland AG 2022
V. Pinheiro et al. (Eds.): PROPOR 2022, LNAI 13208, pp. 177–187, 2022.
https://doi.org/10.1007/978-3-030-98305-5_17

allows intolerant discourses to spread hateful points of view, encouraging acts of violence [15].

According to [7], on the one hand, people are more likely to engage in aggressive behavior on the Web, particularly social networks, due to the sense of privacy provided by these ecosystems. On the other hand, people are more willing to express their opinions publicly, thereby leading to the dissemination of hate speech. The dynamics of hate speech involve the occurrence of triggers that favor their manifestation [1]. Such triggers are usually socially polarizing issues involving debates about elections, abortion, racial quotas, etc. Manifestation of this kind of speech might then consist of an identity attack, i.e., based on the interests and perspectives of social groups with which target citizens identify.

Gender discourses, particularly those with sexist content, can be found in various social contexts and political spheres. Sexist[1] speeches are linked to stereotypes and gender roles and might include the belief that one sex or gender is inherently superior. However, sexism is not just about statements that seem to excessively focus on gender when it is not relevant [11]. In this work, we consider sexist speech as a form of verbal violence. Taking the episodes of verbal violence towards Patricia Campos Mello after her journalistic denunciation work as an example of intolerant speech related to gender issues, in this work we use three characteristics already pointed out in the literature (Sanction Speech, Passionate Hate and Aversion to the Different ones, and Themes and Figures of Opposition) [2] as potential identifiers of such speech. We ally these characteristics to key introductory Natural Language Processing (NLP) tools to state these as forms to provide computational support for this process. Also, we intend to raise a discussion of a fourth characteristic: fallacious speech.

The rest of this paper is organized as follows. Section 2 overviews the characteristics related to the identification of potentially intolerant/hate speech and also provides a brief description of the case in focus in this study. Next, Sect. 3 describes an empirical linguistic-computational interface designed to support the identification of sexist hate speech. Section 4 presents a way of applying computational approaches to support hate speech identification through linguistic characteristics. Finally, Sect. 5 concludes this paper by presenting the final remarks of this study.

2   Background

Intolerant discourse is established in terms of three fundamental characteristics [2], based mainly on the Brazilian scenario.

First, such discourses intend to sanction subjects that are considered bad complaints of certain social contracts. Therefore, people who do not fit the rules must be punished (e.g., losing rights). Those who defend a homogeneous society, an immigrant-free country, or a heterosexual-based family constitution are examples of ideologies that emerge through hate speech.

---

[1] Sexism or gender discrimination is prejudice and, sometimes, discrimination based on a person's gender or sex.

The second characteristic appears in speeches in which hatred and fear prevail concerning those who are considered different. These may occur from antipathy to homophobia, xenophobia, misogyny, among others. In this view, hate against the different ones justifies that someone expels another person just because this person does not fit in the imagined ideal of society. According to [8], violent reaction is most likely caused by the fear that minorities are causing. Thus, they are targeted as enemies, and hate speech, then, is justified. Such a viewpoint contradicts democratic values, which entail the coexistence of differences. When we label the other as an enemy, we mischaracterize that another one as non-human, thus becoming someone erasable, or killable [8].

The third characteristic refers to speeches that develop themes and figures from the opposition between equality or identity and difference [2]. In this sense, the other is dehumanized so that one can eliminate them. Such type of hate speech diminishes or makes someone invisible. Also, the Intolerant speech occurs when someone claims that another person lacks ethics, morals, or virtues (e.g., when accusing homosexuals of promiscuity, black people of lack of education, or claimed that white people are more evolved than black people).

It should be noted that the frontiers among these characteristics are blurred and they may overlap in discourse (and in definition). In addition, we bring to the discussion the presence of a fourth characteristic: the use of fallacies, in particular *ad hominem*, where one tends to attack the interlocutor rather than refute their ideas. This study analyzes how misogynistic speech qualifies as a form of verbal violence and how social network scenario has been utilized to reproduce this type of violence while taking these characteristics into account. We focused on virtual attacks against Brazilian journalist Patrícia Campos Mello, linked to a case of information published in a CPI in 2020, to search verbal violence on social networks as reinforcement of a sexist stereotype.

2.1 The Campos Mello Case

In 2018, the Brazilian journalist Patrícia Campos Mello denounced a fraudulent scheme of massive sending of WhatsApp messages using old-aged people's CPF (Brazilian official physical person registration). At that moment, Hans River do Rio Nascimento, the whistleblower, did not confirm what he revealed to the journalist when she had been investigating. Instead, he affirmed that the journalist had tried to get proofs "in exchange for sex". On Twitter, a common theme was that a leftist journalist had offered her body to a man in exchange for information that would harm the government. Suddenly, the investigation about election campaign crimes began to doubt the journalist's credibility. The Brazilian president, Jair Bolsonaro, has given a collective interview some days later, in which he made fun of the situation, playing with the meaning of words: "*Ela [a reporter] queria um furo. Ela queria dar o furo a qualquer preço contra mim.*" ("She wanted a journalistic scoop"). In Brazilian Portuguese, "*dar um furo*" is a journalistic jargon that means to get exclusive news and publish them before any other. However, after Nascimento's testimony, Bolsonaro's later declaration carried a double meaning: "dar o furo", using a definite article, implied that the journalist wanted to have sex with her whistleblower. Even though Patrícia Campos Mello exposed the dialogues between her and the whistleblower, proving that he lied, there was a massive reaction against her. On Twitter, supporters of Nascimento's and Bolsonaro's version started attacking the journalist virtually. Discourses on social networks started to be used to explore the sexist character of the population in a virtual environment, reinforcing the role of victims of a press chase and concluding that the journalist's complaint was false. However, this conclusion was not based on arguments provided by the journalist, but on pejorative characteristics associated with the subject by whom she uttered them.

Given the repercussion that the case gained among social networks, we analyze the speeches related to the case on Twitter to observe how sexist speech behaves and how it is supported in such a social network. In conducting the present study, we collected 20,215 tweets from February 11 to February 20th of 2020[2], through the Twitter API[3]. To observe attacks directly sent to the journalists Patrícia Campos Mello and her colleague Vera Magalhães (who showed support), we kept only tweets directed at the journalists' personal accounts.

3   The Linguistic-Computational Interface

Although there are promising approaches [3,17] that use machine learning (ML) techniques to classify textual context as hate speech, these rely on the limitation that the decisions they make can be ambiguous, making it difficult for humans to understand why the decision was made. This is a practical concern because systems that automatically censor people's speech will almost certainly need a manual review process [10]. Exploring textual data requires intensive linguistic analysis based on computational methods. In this sense, we propose to explore the dataset interdisciplinary.

Our methodology consists of two different observational approaches: topic modeling and semantic role labeling (SRL). The first one, topic modeling, involves counting words and grouping similar word patterns to infer topics within unstructured data. This approach seeks to determine which topics are present in the corpus documents and how strong that presence is. This is performed by observing the dataset over an initial topic modeling to help us analyze relationships between the set of the tweets and the terms they contain. Thus, it is possible to produce a set of concepts related to the documents and terms, enabling us to redirect the focus to more potentially hateful topics.

SRL captures predicate-argument relations, such as "who did what to whom" [9]. We consider what the properties assigned to the journalists might imply in this scenario. We intend to observe the SRL-provided structure to extract latent arguments produced. The objective is to evaluate the possibility of creating heuristics for more accurate annotation of data to develop a language model for hate speech detection in Portuguese. In developing this work, two SRL models were used, one in Portuguese (SRL_BERT_PT) and another one in English

---

[2] Available in https://github.com/brendasalenave/sexist_hate_speech.
[3] https://developer.twitter.com.

(AllenNLP). Currently, the work of [13] presents the state-of-the-art on Semantic Role Labeling for Portuguese, achieved through the use of Transfer Learning and BERT-based models. Following the guidelines pointed out by that study, we decided to make use of the `srl-enpt_xlmr-large` model. The analysis of the data was carried out directly in Portuguese. However, due to the similarity in the findings obtained using SRL_BERT_PT and the translated version utilized in AllenNLP, the latter is used for viewing purposes only.

4   Computational Approaches to Support Hate Speech Identification Through Linguistic Characteristics

We analyze the data using Latent Dirichlet Allocation (LDA) to recover the central topics. LDA is a fully generative model for describing the latent topics of documents [14]. This technique is particularly useful for finding reasonably accurate mixtures of topics within a given document set. After testing different values, we chose four topics due to the coverage achieved. *Topic 0* centralizes terms relating to the integrity of the journalist participating in the case, as well as the reliability of the information she provides. In *Topic 1*, the main terms reflect the issue of the scoop, with the word *furo* [scoop] being used in some cases with ambiguity. In *Topic 2*, terms relating to the journalist's reputation and information legitimacy are emphasized, highlighting the ambiguity once more: as aforementioned, journalistic scoop is here linked to "hole", having a sexual connotation because the same term is used to refer to two different things in Portuguese. Such an intentional ambiguity focuses the attention on the degradation of the journalist's image. Finally, *Topic 3* includes terms that mention the journalist's attempts to publish news as a way of accusing the president of being part of the fraudulent scheme.

Based on topics highlighted by topic modeling, the attention was redirected to some empirically associated main points by observing the characteristics of hate speech (see Sect. 2 for more details.). The next step was to select sentences related to words previously highlighted, which might carry hate speech content.

In the following tweet, for example:

4.a. *Que vergonha hein @camposmello, tu viste o que falaram de ti na cpmi!? O Hans River falou até em sexo, fiquei surpresa c tua atitude, afinal eras uma jornalista 'conceituada', meu Deus qta decepção!! Estou cancelando assinatura da @folha, cambada vermelha, só petralha!?Ecca #forapt*
[English version] What a shame huh @camposmello, did you see what they said about you at cpmi !? Hans River even talked about sex, I was surprised by your attitude, after all you were a 'reputable' journalist, my God, what a disappointment !! I'm canceling subscription to @Folha, red bunch, just petralhada[4]!? Eww

---

[4] Pejorative reference to a person who is affiliated to the Brazilian Worker's Party, i.e., Partido dos Trabalhadores.

It is possible to notice the premise that the journalist targeted in the case is a bad observant of social contracts. In this cultural imagination, the body is expected to be used as a bargaining tool in a profession like this, in this case, in getting information.

Applying SRL to a sentence from this post, it is possible to observe the developed semantic role by the stretched parts. SRL provides a structure where we can automatically extract the arguments used in the speech, creating heuristics for more accurate data annotation. The SRL model used [13] was designed taking as base PropBank Br [5] roles. According to the PropBank Br guidelines, Argument 0 (Arg 0) and Argument 1 (Arg 1) are, respectively, the Agent and the Patient (the participant who changes state) predicates. Figure 1 presents the semantic role labeling attributed to this tweet.

Fig. 1. Semantic role labelling to the 4.a tweet's sentence

Speeches that fulfill the second hate speech criteria [2] (aversion to a different one) can also be observed. This can be seen in the following tweet:

4.b. *A casa Petralha da @folha e de sua jornalista Pinóquio @camposmello caiu de vez. Serve pra jornalista que tenta ganhar um furo dando o seu (isso na minha época era outra profissão). Aí vem ob acéfalo do @gugachacra fazer aqueles prólogos chatos sobre a tal @camposmello, falar de socialismo e vivendo com os benefícios do país mais capitalista do mundo é fácil.*
[English version] The Petralha's house of @folha and its journalist Pinocchio @camposmello fell for good. It is for journalists who try to win a scoop by giving theirs (that, in my time, was another profession). Here comes the headache of @gugachacra making those boring prologues about the @camposmello, talking about socialism and living with the benefits of the most capitalist country in the world is easy.

where a different political ideology is seen as an unacceptable opposition.

Observe the following fragment:

4.c. *Reputação zeroooooooo. Jornazista fake News*
[English version] Reputation zeroooooooo.Journazist fake News

In 4.c, the third characteristic pointed by [2] is present in the attribution of a bad reputation when associated with aspects that remind Nazism, as expressed in the suffix of *journazist*. Forms of disqualification of the subject are present in this example and in so many other variants employed for journalists to enforce directed verbal violence.

The word *furo* (hole) appears several times in the data set, as demonstrated by the LDA technique application, and it draws attention due to the intended pun presented in its use, as seen in the following tweet:

4.d. *Deu o furo em troca do furo*
     [English version] Gave the hole in exchange for the hole.

In this case, such as in other similar tweets, the term appears both with a sexual connotation (first occurrence), and it is linked to journalistic jargon that refers to a scoop/hole (second occurrence). Cases like this are often studied in sense disambiguation area [16] as resources used in hate speech. Figure 2 presents the semantic role labeling attributed to excerpts from the tweet.

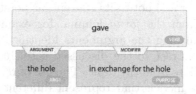

Fig. 2. Semantic role labeling to the 4.d tweet's sentence

Identifying such characteristics in this type of speech reinforces the attribution of misogynist discourse as hate speech. In this way, the conversion of such characteristics in linguistic heuristics allows the annotation of data to verify whether they represent hate speech. Rules like these make associations with Semantic Role Labeling strategies based on language models trained to represent online interactions through texts.

Observing the discursive and situational context data, we sought to explore the variation of meanings expressed through some of the most common terms found. Avoiding expressions genuinely related to the journalism profession (e.g., journalist, journalism, journal, etc.), Fig. 3 presents 10 most common expressions derived from the Portuguese form *jorna* but 31 different expressions were found. The occurrence of such expressions presents direct attacks to the journalist, not related to the central case.

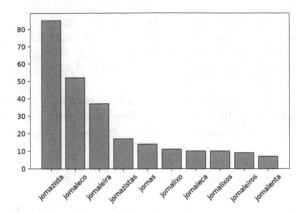

Fig. 3. Most common expressions derived from *Jorna** found in the dataset.

In this sense, one of the most remarkable exposed by the composition of all features previously pointed is the *ad hominem* fallacy, i.e., denying a proposition with criticism to its author and not to its content, as pointed by the various uses of expressions derived from the *jorna* lemma, for example. Computationally, one can verify it by analyzing the arguments identified by applying semantic role labeling tasks, in contrast to the discussed case. In all the instances, the identified arguments deviate from the topic. The use of representation structures associated with language models that represent different domains appears as a proposal to identify this characteristic (semi-) automatically.

4.1 Fallacies in Intolerant Speech

Despite the manifestation of intolerant speech been directly linked to triggering events, the disseminated hate is aimed at people connected to the framed scene. When observing lexical attributes in the dataset, different words used to defame the journalist involved were found. In this sense, we chose to investigate other characteristics present in the data.

Among existing tools for computational analysis, we highlight the Perspective API[5]. This is not a tool created to detect hate speech; however, it is relevant to identify texts with symbolically harmful potential. Using ML models, Perspective aims to determine how a comment has a perceived effect on a conversation. Portuguese texts can be analyzed considering six metrics[6]: (1) *Toxicity*: used to identify a "rude, disrespectful or unreasonable comment that is likely to make one leave a discussion"; (2) *Identity Attack*: Negative or hateful comments targeting someone because of their identity; (3) *Insult*: Insulting, inflammatory, or negative comment towards a person or a group of people; (4) *Profanity*: Swearing words, cursing words, or other obscene or profane languages; (5) *Severe Toxicity*: rude,

---

[5] Available in: https://www.perspectiveapi.com.
[6] There are additional metrics offered for other languages.

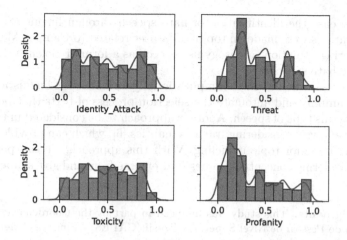

Fig. 4. Distribution of the values extracted through the use of perspective API.

disrespectful, or unreasonable comments that are very likely to make people leave a discussion; and (6) *Threat*: an intention to inflict pain, injury, or violence against an individual or group.

Figure 4 presents the distribution of values obtained when using this API. Densest values were found to be small values (<3) of *Threat* and *Profanity* metrics, indicating a low probability of the presence of these characteristics. However, to *Identity Attack* the distribution is more uniform, indicating a moderate presence of such feature. Nonetheless, in upper ranges of values, it was where most of derogatory words previously indicated in Fig. 3.

Throughout observations performed, it is possible to note that the correlation between the lexicon presented and the case is distant, i.e., the case and its mentions widely diverge, the latter used in most cases to defamation. From this, we raise the hypothesis of considering the presence of fallacies in texts, initially the *ad hominem* fallacy, as an important characteristic to detect intolerant speeches disseminated online when it comes to Brazilian Portuguese. The detection of this type of fallacy has already been studied [4] and presents significant results; however, no related works were found for Portuguese. Therefore, we suggest, for future work, a deeper evaluation by extending the testing to other data sets.

5   Final Remarks

Automatic hate speech detection is still challenging for NLP tasks. Linguistics makes little use of computational methods in the data observation process, making it even more arduous and extensive. Nevertheless, with the help of characteristics provided by linguistics, we believe that it is possible to strengthen ties between areas by semi-automating the identification of this kind of discourse, making it more accessible to scholars who are more familiarized with the use of established linguistic precepts. This work suggested the use of NLP methods as a way to ease the identification of hate speech through linguistics analysis. Our observations were made on top of a dataset related to Campos Mello's case aiming to bring attention to misogynist speech as a form of violence that might characterize hate speech.

In future work, we intend to computationally formalize the linguistic features in order to amplify and automate the selection process of texts that potentially characterize this type of speech. Another approach to be considered in the future is a further analysis considering frame semantics [6], which can provide valuable insights and tools for topic modeling. With this approach, we can perform an analysis considering conceptual frames that emerge from and give shape to sexist hate speech.

Acknowledgments. This study was financed in part by the Coordenação de Aperfeiçoamento de Pessoal de Nível Superior - Brasil (CAPES) - Finance Code 001.

References

1. Almeida, G., Cunha, J.: curso discurso de ódio, tô fora: ferramentas para uma internet cordial (2020, unpublished)
2. de Barros, D.L.P.: O discurso intolerante na internet: enunciação e interação. In: Proceedings of XVII CONGRESO INTERNACIONAL ASOCIACIÓN DE LINGÜÍSTICA Y FILOLOGÍA DE AMÉRICA LATINA (ALFAL 2014) (2014)
3. Davidson, T., Warmsley, D., Macy, M., Weber, I.: Automated hate speech detection and the problem of offensive language. In: Proceedings of the International AAAI Conference on Web and Social Media, vol. 11 (2017)
4. Delobelle, P., Cunha, M., Cano, E.M., Peperkamp, J., Berendt, B.: Computational ad hominem detection. In: Proceedings of the 57th Annual Meeting of the Association for Computational Linguistics: Student Research Workshop, pp. 203–209 (2019)
5. Duran, M.S., Aluísio, S.M.: Propbank-Br: a Brazilian treebank annotated with semantic role labels. In: Proceedings of the Eighth International Conference on Language Resources and Evaluation (LREC 2012), Istanbul, Turkey, pp. 1862–1867. European Language Resources Association (ELRA), May 2012. http://www.lrec-conf.org/proceedings/lrec2012/pdf/272_Paper.pdf
6. Fillmore, C.J.: Frames and the semantics of understanding. Quaderni di semantica **6**(2), 222–254 (1985)
7. Fortuna, P., Nunes, S.: A survey on automatic detection of hate speech in text. ACM Comput. Surv. (CSUR) **51**(4), 1–30 (2018)
8. Gallego, E.S., et al.: O ódio como política: a reinvenção das direitas no Brasil, pp. 33–40. Boitempo, São Paulo (2018)
9. He, L., Lee, K., Levy, O., Zettlemoyer, L.: Jointly predicting predicates and arguments in neural semantic role labeling. In: Proceedings of the 56th Annual Meeting of the Association for Computational Linguistics (Volume 2: Short Papers), Melbourne, Australia, pp. 364–369. Association for Computational Linguistics, July 2018. https://doi.org/10.18653/v1/P18-2058. https://www.aclweb.org/anthology/P18-2058
10. MacAvaney, S., Yao, H.R., Yang, E., Russell, K., Goharian, N., Frieder, O.: Hate speech detection: challenges and solutions. PLoS One **14**(8) (2019)

11. Mills, S.: Language and Sexism. Cambridge University Press, Cambridge (2008). https://doi.org/10.1017/CBO9780511755033
12. Nemer, D.: The three types of Whatsapp users getting Brazil's Jair Bolsonaro elected. The Guardian 25 (2018)
13. Oliveira, A.S.M.: Semantic role labeling in portuguese: improving the state of the art with transfer learning and BERT-based models. M.s. thesis, Faculdade de Ciências. Universidade do Porto, Porto, Portugal (2020). https://repositorio-aberto.up.pt/bitstream/10216/130371/2/431435.pdf
14. Ostrowski, D.A.: Using latent dirichlet allocation for topic modelling in twitter. In: Proceedings of the 2015 IEEE 9th International Conference on Semantic Computing (IEEE ICSC 2015), pp. 493–497, February 2015. https://doi.org/10.1109/ICOSC.2015.7050858
15. Santana, B.S., Vanin, A.A.: Detecting group beliefs related to 2018's Brazilian elections in tweets: a combined study on modeling topics and sentiment analysis. In: Proceedings of the Workshop on Digital Humanities and Natural Language Processing (DHandNLP 2020) co-located with International Conference on the Computational Processing of Portuguese (PROPOR 2020) (2020)
16. Warner, W., Hirschberg, J.: Detecting hate speech on the world wide web. In: Proceedings of the Second Workshop on Language in Social Media, pp. 19–26. Association for Computational Linguistics (2012)
17. Zimmerman, S., Kruschwitz, U., Fox, C.: Improving hate speech detection with deep learning ensembles. In: Proceedings of the Eleventh International Conference on Language Resources and Evaluation (LREC 2018) (2018)

Book Genre Classification Based on Reviews of Portuguese-Language Literature

Clarisse Scofield, Mariana O. Silva(ID), Luiza de Melo-Gomes,
and Mirella M. Moro(✉)(ID)

Universidade Federal de Minas Gerais, Belo Horizonte, Brazil
{clarissescofield,mariana.santos,luizademelo,mirella}@dcc.ufmg.br

Abstract. Automatic book genre classification is a hard task as it requires the whole book's content or a high-quality summary, which is challenging to write automatically. On the other hand, online reviews are an accessible resource for readers to evaluate a book or even get a general sense about it, including its genre. As the amount of book reviews is always increasing, using such information to genre classification needs a robust solution to deal with high volumes of data. In such a context, we introduce a model for automatically classifying book genres by analyzing online text reviews. We build a dataset of compiled texts from online book reviews. Then, we use multiple machine learning algorithms to categorize a book into a specific genre. Such a process enables to compare algorithms and detect the best classifiers. Hence, the most efficient machine learning algorithm completed the task with an accuracy of 96%; i.e., the proposed model is convenient for various information retrieval systems due to its high certainty and efficiency.

Keywords: Text classification · Book genre classification · Online reviews · Multiclass classification

1 Introduction

Genre classification plays an essential role in the book industry ecosystem as a whole. For publishers, it may help to associate manuscripts with a publishing house's readership. Also, such categorization supports sellers to lead readers to books they may like based on past purchases. Finally, not only does genre classification help readers to find a book, but it also assists in identifying a book's competitors and audience, directly impacting both marketing and sales.

Although important, classifying a book's literary genre is not trivial as there is no universal procedure to define or classify literary texts. Given this lack of standard, such a task has traditionally been tackled through a philological method, i.e., by a researcher reading printed materials and a personal intuitive abstraction of generalizations [10]. Still, being a method based on external criteria, the categories and genres suggested tend to be inconsistent and unreliable.

© Springer Nature Switzerland AG 2022
V. Pinheiro et al. (Eds.): PROPOR 2022, LNAI 13208, pp. 188–197, 2022.
https://doi.org/10.1007/978-3-030-98305-5_18

On the other hand, with the advancement of Natural Language Processing (NLP) techniques and the high availability of literary works in digital format, there are new approaches for book genre automated classification. A solution is usually: processing the entire book or chunks of it, extracting words and textual structure, then feeding everything into clustering or classification models. There are also few alternative efforts using more straightforward ways to represent the book's content, including books' summaries [11] and short descriptions [15].

The limited length and lack of information needed to classify a book's genre are critical challenges in such studies, which then generally reflect into ineffective results. To overcome such challenges, we explore **book reviews** as a valuable resource for book genre classification. The reasons for such choice are summarized as: reviews are written opinions about a particular book, they are short pieces of texts (especially when compared to the whole text of a book), they are written by both book experts (i.e., editors, critics, publishers, and other professionals) and book readers in general, and they typically include comments on the author's writing style as well as the book's themes, quality, meaning, and other features.

Next, Sect. 2 goes over related work and emphasizes our contributions within the current state-of-the-art. Section 3 introduces our methodology for classifying book genres based on book reviews (considering only Portuguese literature). Then, Sect. 4 validates our solution through a set of experimental evaluations that include: results from six specialized classifier algorithms and a naïve one, and deeper comparison using the best classifier. Section 5 concludes this text with a brief review of main insights and some directions for future work.

2   Related Work

Text classification is a fundamental task in NLP, as it classifies documents into a set of predefined categories. It is also tackled by studies in different contexts such as music [1], sentiment [8] and mood [18]. Classification is also a general task of data mining and machine learning [19], which sometimes requires tailoring for different languages. For Portuguese, examples include Hartman et al. [7] classifying children's school books by reading complexity, and Veiga et al. [16] classifying speech styles into "prepared" or "unprepared". Regarding text genre (in any language), Xu et al. [17] use words and text structure to classify it in a particular genre; whereas Rinaldi et al. [12] takes a different perspective by using text semantics instead of its structure to find web documents genre.

A specific context is *book genre classification*, whose input is usually the whole text of a book or a high quality summary. Despite its relevance, few works tackle it in the literary context, mostly because book genres are not precisely defined, making classification more complex. Also, as a book may have more than one genre, classifying it into a one category is practically impossible (even for a human) without reading it. Few efforts use machine learning algorithms and text processing to predict the genre of a book based on its title or summary [11] and book descriptions on websites [15]. Specifically, Ozsarfati et al. [11] use a

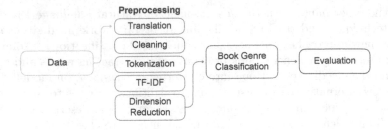

Fig. 1. Book genre classification process overview.

deep learning approach based only on the title to classify books into 32 different genres. In total, five architectures were trained using a large dataset retrieved from Amazon library. Despite their low accuracy, the paper presents the first instance of a book genre classification approach only based on title. Sobkowicz et al. [15] identify the genre of a book by using a deep learning method to analyze the description from the book cover, which is usually a small text.

On datasets of book evaluations and reviews, Freitas et al. [5] present *ReLi* as a set of book reviews posted on Skoob platform, which is manually annotated regarding opinion about the books. It is composed of 1600 reviews, but limited to 13 books from seven authors only. On a different perspective, Lozano and Plannels [9] introduce a dataset of 52,478 records of books on the "GoodReads Best Books Ever List". However, its users' evaluation information is limited to ratings, number of ratings, and ratings by stars without any textual review. Using book reviews has also other challenges that are out of the scope here, as for example finding the opinion target or subject [3].

Compared to the aforementioned literature, this paper proceeds with the following **contributions and novel aspects**: we propose a methodology for book genre classification that relies on book reviews and classification algorithms; our solution does not need the whole book text – an advantage per se; it does not rely on complex algorithms or a small piece of information from the book (e.g., deep learning as [15], and only book title as [11]), but rather on off-the-shelf classifiers over actual book reviews; the dataset is robust, with almost 3,800 reviews, from 24 distinct genres and 325 books written in **Portuguese**; and our solution classifiers reach an almost perfect accuracy in some cases (96%).

3   Genre Classification Methodology

The genre classification starts from the data (i.e., set of book reviews), which is processed to get into a computable input format for the book genre prediction; at the end, the result of such prediction must also be evaluated. Figure 1 illustrates such classification model in its four mains steps, which are detailed next.

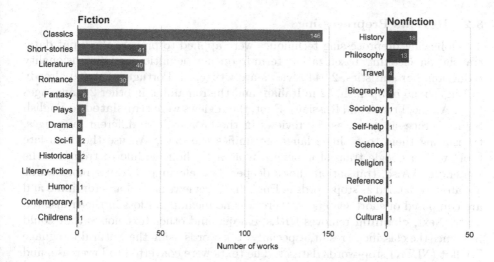

Fig. 2. Available book genres divided into fiction and nonfiction.

3.1 Data

In this study, we use PPORTAL, a dataset of public domain literature written in Portuguese [13,14]. PPORTAL is composed of three digital libraries for public domain works mainly from Brazil and Portugal: Domínio Público,[1] Projecto Adamastor,[2] and Biblioteca Digital de Literatura de Países Lusófonos (BLPL).[3] Such heterogeneous information was integrated using the Goodreads API and a fuzzy matching approach, which results in 2,388 unique works. The works' IDs in the integrated dataset allows collecting additional information from essential elements of the book industry ecosystem: works, authors, readers, and reviews.

For classifying literary genres, we use compiled texts from online reviews. There are 325 works with online reviews in the dataset, each with up to 30 reviews that vary in length and idiom. We also use the main genres of each book to form the labeled data, needed for testing purposes. Such genres come from Goodreads users' bookshelves.[4] For example, if multiple users shelve a book using the *Science* tag, that genre is assigned to the book. Hence, we set works' genres as the most voted tag, included in the *Fiction* and *Nonfiction* related genres list. The final dataset has 3,790 reviews, 325 works with 24 distinct genres. Figure 2 shows the genre distribution for the dataset, with a predominance of Fiction works, with more works of the genres *Classics*, *Short-stories* and *Literature*.

---

[1] Domínio Público: https://www.dominiopublico.gov.br.

[2] Projecto Adamastor: https://projectoadamastor.org.

[3] BLPL: https://www.literaturabrasileira.ufsc.br.

[4] On Goodreads, a bookshelf is a list where one can add or remove books to facilitate reading, similar to a real-life bookshelf where one keeps books.

3.2 Reviews Preprocessing

The following preprocessing techniques were applied to prepare the input data: translation, cleaning, tokenization, term frequency definition and dimensionality reduction. For statistics, 2,044 reviews are written in Portuguese, 1,499 already in English, 95 in Spanish, 52 in Italian, and the remaining in other 24 languages (e.g., Arabic, French and Russian). First, the reviews were **translated** to English for fair processing; i.e., as the reviews in the dataset have different languages, translating them to a single language unifies the data. We use the Translate tool[5] with a google translator behind it as a Python module to translate the sentences. AAlso, translation allows deeper data cleaning, because more words are already defined as stop-words in English. As reviews have character limits and are composed of short sentences, there was no meaningful loss in the translated texts. Next, **cleaning** removes URLs, emojis, and other text noises that could influence the classifier's result, especially stop-words using the Natural Language Toolkit (NLTK) stop-words dataset. The texts were converted to lowercase, and numbers and punctuation were deleted. Here, the words removed were present in most reviews (e.g., 'a' and 'the') and thus are irrelevant for categorization.

Then, **tokenizing** (and normalizing) the data is needed to create a custom dictionary for the unique words. For feature representation, we use **TF-IDF**[6] (Term frequency-inverse document frequency) to compute the weight for each term, based on the importance of a term compared to the hole text.

Genre classification also needs **reducing the data dimensionality**. Even after the aforementioned processing, many unique words may still be redundant. Thus, this phase applies the Latent Semantic Analysis (LSA) [4], which is a dimensionality reduction technique. LSA uses SVD or Singular Value Decomposition (particularly Truncated SVD) to reduce the number of dimensions and select the best ones. We use LSA method after analyzing the results obtained by Altszyler et al. [2]. Their research compares LSA capabilities to learn accurate word embeddings in small text corpora and show it to be more appropriate for a not very large corpus also outperforming Word2Vec in such a context.

3.3 Book Genre Classification

We tackle the book genre classification as a multiclass classification problem, in which instances are classified into one of many potential classes. Here, the feature matrix is divided into two parts, training and testing: 70% of data set is used to train the model and evaluate the training score; and 30% is used to test the accuracy of the model (test score). Then, the classifiers are applied to the training set to learn from it. We consider the following classifiers:[7] Naïve Classifier,[8]

---

[5] https://pypi.org/project/translate.

[6] TF-IDF is a numerical statistic that reflects how important a word is to a document within a collection or corpus. Its value increases proportionally to the number of times a word appears in the document and is offset by the number of documents that contain it (source: wikipedia).

[7] Most classifiers are described in Data Mining textbooks such as [6,19].

[8] As implemented by sklearn.dummy.DummyClassifier using *prior* as strategy.

Decision Tree Classifier, Random Forest, Stochastic Gradient Descent, Gaussian Naive Bayes, and K Nearest Neighbor. Such classifiers are among the most known ones, and we use their implementations from the scikit-learn[9] version 1.0.1 with default parameter settings. Also, we use AdaBoost Classifier [6, Chapter 8] to improve the accuracy of Decision Tree by reducing bias and variance. After the model is trained on the training set, it classifies genre on the test set. Note that we are interested in investigating whether we can classify book genres based mainly on online reviews with high accuracy, rather than looking for the best performance or comparing the models' performance with existing works.

3.4 Evaluation

For evaluating all classifiers performance, we consider four well-known evaluation metrics: Accuracy, Precision, Recall and F1-score.[10] Moreover, we use a confusion matrix to show the combination of the actual and predicted classes.

4 Experiments and Results

Our data is highly unbalanced because there are more books categorized as a couple of genres than others (see Figure 2). Hence, a proper evaluation is critical to determine the performance of the proposed model for each class and the test set performed as a whole. Table 1 presents the classification results comparison on the test data between the several classifiers. Notably, Random Forest (RF) yields the best performance for most of the evaluation metrics considered, except Recall, reaching 96% on Accuracy. Compared to the Naïve Classifier, which serves as baseline, such results for book genre classification based on the compiled reviews' text are very impressive. The second best classifier is the Decision Tree, also showing high accuracy and significant values for the other metrics.

To better explain the methodology, we plot a confusion matrix to identify which book genres are erroneously categorized. Figure 3 shows the matrix that compares the values obtained by the RF classifier with the actual values. Overall, the classification model had relatively few errors. As expected, the diagonal values correspond to the genres that the classifier correctly predicted and are more prominent than the rest of the matrix. However, the class imbalance misclassified some genres, which were conveniently treated as the majority class (i.e., 'Classics'). The following errors are of interest.

- Genres totally misclassified – all *Historical* and all *Reference* books were classified as 'Classics', mostly due to their insignificant number of instances in the dataset (2 and 1 respectively);

---

[9] Scikit Learn: https://scikit-learn.org/stable.

[10] Standard metrics for evaluating models, common in Information Retrieval. Precision $= truePositive/predictedPositive$. Recall $= truePositive/totalActualPositive$. Accuracy $= (truePositive + trueNegative)/(Positive + Negative)$. F1 $= 2 \times ((Precision \times Recall)/(Precision + Recall))$.

Table 1. Experimental results from classifier algorithms, sorted by F1.

Classifier	Accuracy	Precision	Recall	F1-score
Random Forest	**0.96**	**0.87**	0.74	**0.79**
Decision Tree	0.94	0.84	**0.76**	0.78
Gaussian Naive Bayes	0.88	0.61	0.61	0.59
K Nearest Neighbor	0.78	0.66	0.61	0.58
Stochastic Gradient Descent	0.83	0.48	0.38	0.41
AdaBoost	0.69	0.17	0.17	0.17
Naïve (baseline)	0.45	0.06	0.06	0.06

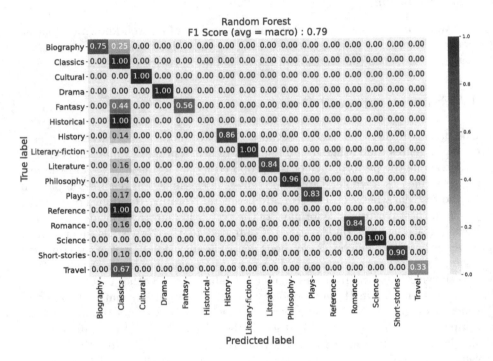

Fig. 3. Normalized confusion matrix of random forest classifier results on test set.

- Genres with major errors – 67% of *Travel*, 44% of *Fantasy*, and 25% of *Biography* were classified as 'Classics', again due to their small amounts of instances in the dataset (from 4 to 6);
- Genres with minor errors – 17% of *Plays*, 16% of *Literature* and *Romance*, 14% of *History*, and 10% of *Short-Stories* were classified as 'Classics', and these cases need further study to justify such errors because, except for *Play* with 5 instances, all the other genres have between 18 and 41 instances within the dataset, which are relative good numbers.

Now, we claim the main reason for misclassifying such books as 'Classics' is their small amount of instances and the predominance of such category within the dataset. The question then becomes: how other genres with equally low number of instances were correctly classified as *Cultural, Drama, Literary-fiction* and *Science*? The answer is probably due to *specific terms* within their reviews that were **not** close enough to 'Classics', as given by the following examples.

We now discuss three examples of how the methodology works by applying it to three books *not seen* by the Random Forest algorithm already trained, one nonfiction and two fictions. First, we analyzed an example of a book with only one instance: *"As Máscaras do Destino"* (The Masks of Destiny) by Florbela Espanca classified as a book of 'cultural' genre. The book reviews contain terms such as: series, diary, women, reflection, eternity, topic, poetic, emotion, extraordinary, contextualization, prayer, terrestrial, country, enriching. The Random Forest classifier applied to such instance returned the correct answer, 'Cultural'.

Then, the book *"Os Lusíadas"* (The Lusiads) by Luís Vaz de Camões is originally classified as 'classic fiction', and its reviews include terms such as: surprise, perform, literature, Portuguese, epic, poem, Iliad, fantastical, adventure, art, bard, pioneer, grandeur, national. When performing the individual prediction of the work, the classifier returns the expected genre result: 'Classics'.

Another case also served to evaluate the prediction: *"Primeiro Fausto"* (First Fausto) by Fernando Pessoa. The book is primarily classified as 'philosophy', and its reviews include terms such as: dramatic, remain, unique, drama, struggle, intelligence, life, inspire, philosophical, think, thought, clarity, tragedy, paradoxical, analogy, intense, evidence, explore, thought, understand, debating, consciousness. Applying the trained Random Forest Classifier also returned the expected 'Philosophy' genre as a result.

5   Conclusion and Future Work

The present study proposes a methodology composed of multiple machine learning algorithms for classifying book genres based on their reviews. The experimental results show impressive performance by Random Forest Classifier. This state-of-the-art machine learning model trained on the <dataset> was able to achieve an average accuracy of 96%. In other words, reviews written by online users have enough information to successfully predict the genre of a book, without the burden of processing its entire text or using complex solutions, such as deep learning algorithms for example. Also, the dataset used considers Portuguese written books with reviews written in Portuguese and other languages.

Regarding future work, as the classification model was significantly impacted by class imbalance, we plan to expand the dataset by considering a larger set of books labeled with the least-represented classes. As a result, we can perform the required class balance to improve the classifiers' performance. We also plan to assess the effect of the reviews' language on the classification performance by comparing results using other languages to unify reviews during the translation stage, such as Portuguese. Finally, we also plan to extend the dataset to Spanish Literature, allowing us to expand our analyses to Ibero-American Literature.

196   C. Scofield et al.

Acknowledgments. This work was funded by CNPq and FAPEMIG, Brazil.

References

1. Akalp, H., Cigdem, E.F., Yilmaz, S., Bölücü, N., Can, B.: Language representation models for music genre classification using lyrics. In: ISEEIE - International Symposium on Electrical, Electronics and Information Engineering, pp. 408–414. ACM, Seoul, Republic of Korea (2021). https://doi.org/10.1145/3459104.3459171
2. Altszyler, E., Sigman, M., Fernández Slezak, D.: Comparative study of LSA vs Word2Vec embeddings in small corpora: a case study in dreams database, October 2016
3. Catharin, L.G., Feltrim, V.D.: Finding opinion targets in news comments and book reviews. In: Villavicencio, A., et al. (eds.) International Conference on Computational Processing of the Portuguese Language (PROPOR). LNCS, vol. 11122, pp. 375–384. Springer, Canela, Brazil (2018). https://doi.org/10.1007/978-3-319-99722-3_38
4. Dumais, S.T., Furnas, G.W., Landauer, T.K., Deerwester, S.C., Harshman, R.A.: Using latent semantic analysis to improve access to textual information. In: SIGCHI Conference on Human Factors in Computing Systems, pp. 281–285. ACM, Washington, D.C. (1988). https://doi.org/10.1145/57167.57214
5. Freitas, C., Motta, E., Milidiú, R., César, J.: Sparkling vampire... lol! annotating opinions in a book review corpus. In: Aluisio, S.M., Tagnin, S.E. (eds.) New Language Technologies and Linguistic Research: A Two-Way Road, pp. 128–146. Cambridge Scholars Publishing, Newcastle upon Tyne (2014)
6. Han, J., Kamber, M., Pei, J.: Data Mining Concepts and Techniques, 3rd edn. Morgan Kauffman Publishers, Waltham (2012)
7. Hartmann, N., Cucatto, L., Brants, D., Aluísio, S.: Automatic Classification of the Complexity of Nonfiction Texts in Portuguese for Early School Years. In: Silva, J., Ribeiro, R., Quaresma, P., Adami, A., Branco, A. (eds.) PROPOR 2016. LNCS (LNAI), vol. 9727, pp. 12–24. Springer, Cham (2016). https://doi.org/10.1007/978-3-319-41552-9_2
8. Jelodar, H., et al.: A NLP framework based on meaningful latent-topic detection and sentiment analysis via fuzzy lattice reasoning on youtube comments. Multim. Tools Appl. **80**(3), 4155–4181 (2020). https://doi.org/10.1007/s11042-020-09755-z
9. Lozano, L.C., Planells, S.C.: Best Books Ever Dataset. Zenodo, November 2020. https://doi.org/10.5281/zenodo.4265096
10. Omar, A.: Classificação de gêneros literários: uma sinergia metodológica de modelagem computacional e semântica lexical. Texto Livre: Linguagem e Tecnologia **13**, 83–101 (2020). 10.35699/1983-3652.2020.24396
11. Ozsarfati, E., Sahin, E., Saul, C.J., Yilmaz, A.: Book genre classification based on titles with comparative machine learning algorithms. In: IEEE International Conference on Computer and Communication Systems (ICCCS), pp. 14–20 (2019). https://doi.org/10.1109/CCOMS.2019.8821643
12. Rinaldi, A.M., Russo, C., Tommasino, C.: Web document categorization using knowledge graph and semantic textual topic detection. In: Computational Science and Its Applications (ICCSA). Springer, Cham (2021). https://doi.org/10.1007/978-3-030-24311-1

13. Silva, M., Scofield, C., Moro, M.: PPORTAL: public domain Portuguese-language literature Dataset. In: Anais do III Dataset Showcase Workshop, Brazilian Symposium on Databases, pp. 77–88. SBC, Rio de Janeiro, Brazil (2021). https://doi.org/10.5753/dsw.2021.17416

14. Silva, M.O., Scofield, C., Moro, M.M.: PPORTAL: Public domain Portuguese-language literature Dataset, August 2021. https://doi.org/10.5281/zenodo.5178063

15. Sobkowicz, A., Kozłowski, M., Buczkowski, P.: Reading book by the cover - book genre detection using short descriptions. In: Gruca, A., et al. (eds.) Man-Machine Interactions 5. ICMMI 2017. Advances in Intelligent Systems and Computing, vol. 659, pp. 439–448. Springer (2018)

16. Veiga, A., Candeias, S., Celorico, D., Proença, J., Perdigão, F.: Towards automatic classification of speech styles. In: de Medeiros Caseli, H., et al. (eds.) International Conference on Computational Processing of the Portuguese Language (PROPOR). LNCS, vol. 7243, pp. 421–426. Springer, Coimbra, Portugal (2012). https://doi.org/10.1007/978-3-642-28885-2_47

17. Xu, Z., Liu, L., Song, W., Du, C.: Text genre classification research. In: International Conference on Computer, Information and Telecommunication Systems (CITS), pp. 175–178 (2017). https://doi.org/10.1109/CITS.2017.8035329

18. Ying, T.C., Doraisamy, S., Abdullah, L.N.: Genre and mood classification using lyric features. In: International Conference on Information Retrieval & Knowledge Management, pp. 260–263. IEEE, Kuala Lumpur, Malaysia (2012). https://doi.org/10.1109/InfRKM.2012.6204985

19. Zaki, M.J., Meira Jr, W.: Data Mining and Machine Learning: Fundamental Concepts and Algorithms. 2nd edn. Cambridge University Press, London (2020)

Combining Word Embeddings
for Portuguese Named Entity Recognition

Messias Gomes da Silva(ID) and Hilário Tomaz Alves de Oliveira(⊠)(ID)

Programa de Pós-graduação em Computação Aplicada (PPComp), Instituto Federal
do Espírito Santo (IFES), Serra, Brazil
hilario.oliveira@ifes.edu.br

Abstract. Named Entity Recognition (NER) is the task of identifying
textual elements and categorizing them into predefined classes, such as
names of people, locations, organizations, and others. Recently, NER
systems based on neural networks have obtained state-of-the-art results.
One of the main components of this kind of system is the word embeddings representation adopted that can be static (traditional) or contextual trained in language models. This work analyzes the strategy of combining traditional and contextual embeddings to obtain richer representations for Portuguese NER. We adopt a Bidirectional Long Short-Term
Memory (BiLSTM) as a classification model integrated with the Conditional Random Fields (CRF) algorithm. Experiments were carried out
in different corpora, and the results obtained demonstrate that the combination strategy of word embeddings models is viable and led to results
comparable with state-of-the-art NER systems in Portuguese.

Keywords: Named Entity Recognition · Word embeddings ·
Language model · Neural networks

1 Introduction

Named Entity Recognition (NER) is a Natural Language Processing (NLP) task
that consists of identifying and categorizing textual fragments into predefined
semantic categories, such as mentions of names of people, places, organizations,
among others [13,25]. Depending on the context and particularities of the domain
of interest, there is the possibility of using more specific entity categories, such
as proteins, genes, enzymes, among others [13]. The NER is a complex task
and presents many challenges. For instance, the category of a named entity is
very dependent on the surrounding context, and different categories can occur
in similar contexts. Furthermore, identifying the boundaries of named entities
composed of multiple words is challenging. The NER task plays an important
role for many NLP applications, such as information extraction [11], information
retrieval [14], automatic text summarization [5,16], and others.

© Springer Nature Switzerland AG 2022
V. Pinheiro et al. (Eds.): PROPOR 2022, LNAI 13208, pp. 198–208, 2022.
https://doi.org/10.1007/978-3-030-98305-5_19

Generally, approaches employed for NER can be classified into four major categories [13]: (i) Rule-based approaches that extract entities using a set of handcrafted lexical and syntactic rules or predefined lists (gazetteers); (ii) Unsupervised approaches that do not require labeled data and, in general, adopt clustering or similarity algorithms to identify the entities of interest; (iii) Supervised approaches that rely on labeled data and a set of features to represent the words. The Conditional Random Fields (CRF) is an example of a supervised learning algorithm commonly applied; and (iv) Approaches based on Deep Learning (DL) models that extract representations needed to identify and classify the entities from raw input.

Recently, DL-based architectures have been successfully applied in several NLP applications, including for NER [13,25]. DL models are based on neural networks and do not require handcrafted features or rules. Furthermore, these neural NER systems have adopted word and character embeddings to create rich representations of the inputs [21]. These embedding models are trained to generate word representations both statically (e.g., Word2Vec [15]) or contextually using neural Language Models (LM) (e.g., BERT [8]).

The most recent NER systems have applied contextual embeddings obtained from neural LM with DL architectures, especially using a Long Short-Term Memory (LSTM) with the CRF algorithm [13,21,23]. Contextual embeddings differ from traditional (static) ones, as each token is assigned a representation that considers the sentence in which it is included. In this way, it is possible to capture semantic and syntactic characteristics of the use of words and how they vary depending on the context in which the word is being used (polysemy) [18].

In this work, we investigate the efficiency of combining traditional and contextual embeddings for NER in Portuguese. We adopted an LSTM-CRF architecture and evaluated the combination of two traditional word embedding models, Word2Vec [15], and Glove [17], with the BERT [8], ELMO [18], and FLAIR [2] models, all pre-trained for Portuguese. Experiments were carried out using three corpora: HAREM [20], Paramopama [12] and LeNER-BR [4]. Different scenarios were assessed, ranging from using a single embedding model to combining traditional and contextualized embeddings. The experimental results demonstrated that the architecture using the LSTM-CRF with the Word2vec skip-gram and BERT model obtained the best results in most evaluated scenarios. The implementation and data used in our experiments are available at[1].

2 Related Work

Since the first mention of the term *named entity* in the Message Understanding Conference (MUC-6) [9] in 1996, the NER task has gained great interest from the NLP community. Early systems were based on classical approaches using handcrafted rules or predefined lists known as gazetteers. More recently, neural architectures based on deep neural networks have become standard due to the state-of-the-art results obtained. In this section, we focused on NER systems for

---

[1] https://github.com/messias077/ner_pt.

Portuguese. For a more comprehensive overview of the area, we suggest references [13, 25] that present a survey of the most recent advances, especially DL-based architectures.

The Conditional Random Fields (CRF) is a probabilistic algorithm commonly adopted in sequential classification as the NER task. Amaral et al. (2014) [3] developed a system called NERP-CRF that uses the CRF algorithm trained with 15 handcrafted features for identification and classification of named entities. In reference [19], the authors presented a NER system based on a deep neural network that adopts word- and character-level embedding representations to perform sequential classification. Experiments were performed using the Harem corpus [20] considering two scenarios (Total and Selective). The selective scenario contains annotations of five entity categories: Date, Location, Organization, Person, and Value. The Total scenario has the previous five categories plus the following classes: Abstraction, Event, Thing, Title, and Other.

Castro et al. (2018) [6] presented a neural architecture based on a Bidirectional Long Short-Term Memory (BiLSTM) network connected to the traditional CRF. The BiLSTM is responsible for extracting features at the word- and characters-level. Afterward, a CRF algorithm layer is responsible for the sequential classification. Several traditional embedding models were evaluated, including Word2vec [15] and Glove [17]. The First Harem and Mini Harem corpora [20] were used for training and testing, respectively, considering the two available scenarios (Total and Selective).

More recently, contextualized embedding has been explored in many works. Castro et al. (2019) [7] propose a NER system based on the BiLSTM-CRF architecture. The model receives contextual word representations from the ELMO language model [18], combined with character-level representations obtained from a Convolutional Neural Network (CNN). The proposed system was evaluated using different corpora in diverse domains. Santos et al. (2019) [21] analyzed the combination of contextual embedding based on the FLAIR Embedding Language Model (LM) [2] with traditional embedding models. The authors trained the Flair Embedding LM (FlairBBP) in a corpus with 4.9 billion words, containing texts written in Brazilian Portuguese. The FlairBBP was combined with the Word2Vec Skip-gram embedding [15] and used as input to an architecture based on a BiLSTM-CRF. Souza et al. (2019) [23] evaluated different architectures based on the Bidirectional Encoder Representation from Transformers (BERT) models for the NER task in Portuguese. The authors compared different training strategies based on features and fine-tuning in their evaluations.

3   Resources

This section presents the corpora adopted in the experiments (Sect. 3.1), the traditional and contextual embedding models analyzed (Sect. 3.2), and the Flair framework employed as the basis for our NER classification model (Sect. 3.3).

3.1   Corpora

We adopted the following corpora in the experiments performed.

Harem [20]. One of the main datasets used for evaluating NER systems in Portuguese is the HAREM collection. The first version of HAREM was divided into two subsets known as First HAREM and MiniHAREM. Each set was annotated manually and had two evaluation scenarios. The first scenario, named Total, has annotations for ten categories of entities: Location, Person, Organization, Value, Date, Title, Thing, Event, Abstraction, and Other. The second scenario, known as Selective, has annotations of only five classes: Person, Organization, Location, Value, and Date.

Paramopama [12]. This corpus was created from the extension of another corpus called WikiNER, which has versions in several languages, including Portuguese. Initially, a review and reclassification of the incorrect annotations of the Portuguese WikiNER were carried out. In addition, the corpus size was increased by incorporating texts obtained from news sites on economics, sports, politics, technology, among other subjects. The texts were annotated in four categories: Person, Location, Organization, and Time. The authors performed several experiments combining the Paramopama corpus with different versions of the HAREM corpora.

LeNER-BR [4]. It is a domain-specific corpus built from 70 legal documents, including 66 documents from several Brazilian courts and four legislation documents. The documents were manually annotated, taking into account the following categories of entities: Organization, Person, Time, Location, Legislation, and Jurisprudence.

As in [6,21,23], the First HAREM was used as a training set and the Mini-HAREM as a test set. We adopted the preprocessed version of the HAREM corpus made available by [23] at[2]. The Paramopama combined with the Second version of HAREM made available at[3] was adopted here. In this corpus, we divided sentences, keeping the proportion among the entity categories, being 60% for training, 20% for validation, and 20% for testing. Also, duplicated sentences were removed. Finally, we removed some duplicate sentences observed among the training, testing, and validation sets identified in the LeNER-BR corpus. Table 1 presents some basic statistics of the corpora versions used in this work.

3.2   Word Embedding Models

The use of pre-trained word representations is one of the fundamental components of a neural NER approach. In this work, we evaluate the Word2vec [15], and Glove [17] models, briefly described following.

Word2vec [15] is a statistical technique used to learn distributed representations of words from texts. It is based on neural networks and has two models: Continuous Bag Of Words (CBOW) and Skip-gram. The CBOW

---

[2] https://github.com/jneto04/ner-pt.

[3] https://github.com/davidsbatista/NER-datasets/tree/master/Portuguese.

Table 1. Basic statistics of adopted corpora.

Corpora		Sentences	Tokens	Entities
HAREM (Total)	Train	4,505	93,627	1,402
	Validation	237	4,685	113
	Test	3,393	66,547	1,111
HAREM (Selective)	Train	4,506	93,470	1,182
	Validation	238	4,830	94
	Test	3,393	66,572	945
Paramopama + Second Harem	Train	9,374	230,497	4,112
	Validation	3,125	76,235	1,752
	Test	3,125	76,428	1,698
LeNER-BR	Train	5,897	203,379	1,771
	Validation	888	34,636	303
	Test	1,169	43,727	358

model is trained to predict a target word w_t from a context word window $w_{t-2}, w_{t-1}, w_{t+1}, w_{t+2}$. Meanwhile, the Skip-gram model aims to predict context words $w_{t-2}, w_{t-1}, w_{t+1}$, w_{t+2} given a target word w_t. Both models aim to learn an n-dimensional word representation considering the context in which they are inserted.

Glove [17] is a model used to create distributed word representations by creating a square matrix of word co-occurrences and computing the number of times each word occurs in the same context. The model aims to build a distributed representation of the words so that the learned characteristics reflect the relevance between words according to the conditional probability rates of occurrences between them.

In this work, we adopt the Word2vec and Glove pre-trained models made available by [10] for Portuguese at[4]. A major limitation of both models is that they generate static vectors to represent the words. Thus, phenomena such as polysemy are not taken into account. Therefore, the application of contextual embeddings generated from language models has grown in recent years. In this work, the following models were evaluated.

BERT [8]. The Bidirectional Encoder Representation from Transformers (BERT) is a language-based model based on the Transformer architecture [24]. The model generates bidirectional representations analyzing the contexts of the left and right sides of the words. The model has two basic architectures (Base and Large) that differ by some parameters. The BERT Base comprises 12 encoder layers, 12 attention heads, and 768 hidden dimensions. Meanwhile, BERT Large

---

[4] http://www.nilc.icmc.usp.br/embeddings.

has 24 encoder layers, 16 attention heads, and 1024 hidden dimensions. We used the models trained and made available by [22] at[5].

Elmo [18]. The Embeddings from Language Models (ELMO) generate deep contextual representations from a Bidirectional Language Model (biLM) based on a Bidirectional Long Short-Term Memory (BiLSTM) network. The model input is a character-level representation extracted by a Convolutional Neural network (CNN). We adopted the model trained by [7] for Portuguese and made it available at[6].

Flair [2]. The Flair Embedding is a word-level model that handles both words and characters sequences. Thus, this model can analyze the context of neighboring words at the character level. The embeddings are extracted from a Neural Character-level Language Modeling (CharLM). The Flair combines two models, one trained in the forward direction and one trained in the backward direction. In this work, we use the models trained by [21] and made available at[7] for Portuguese.

3.3 NER Classification Model

We applied the open-source FLAIR framework [1] to perform the classification of the named entities. FLAIR implements a BiLSTM-CRF sequence labeling model, which has been successfully used in several previous works for the NER task [7, 21]. Besides, the FLAIR framework enables the concatenation of different types of embeddings to create a combined representation. This strategy referred to as Stacking Embeddings, has been shown to be effective and has shown promising results in previous works [2,21]. Thus, the combined embedding used in this work is given by:

$$w_{comb} = \begin{bmatrix} w^T \\ w^C \end{bmatrix} \tag{1}$$

Here, w^T is extracted from the traditional embedding (here Word2vec or Glove), and w^C is obtained from a contextualized embedding (here BERT, ELMO, or Flair). The combined embedding representation w_{comb} is passed as input to the BiLSTM-CRF to perform the sequential labeling. The CRF model then gives the final sequence probability over the possible sequence labels.

4   Experiments

Experiments were performed to address the following issues: (i) evaluate the strategy of combining traditional and contextual embeddings; and (ii) comparing the results obtained by the best found configuration against some state-of-the-art NER systems for Portuguese. Before discussing the obtained results, a

---

[5] https://github.com/neuralmind-ai/portuguese-bert.
[6] https://allennlp.org/elmo.
[7] https://github.com/jneto04/ner-pt.

brief description of the experimental environment and implementation details are presented in the next section.

4.1 Experimental Setup

Table 2 presents the hyperparameters employed with the BiLSTM model adopted in the performed experiments. During training, a checkpoint was set to monitor and persist only the model with the best performance (minimum loss) based on the validation set. In addition, due to the learning rate decay strategy, training is stopped if it reaches a value lower than 0.002.

Table 2. Hyperparameters adopted in our experiments.

Hyperparameters	Value
Initial learning rate	0.1
Optimizer	SGDW[a]
Hidden layers	256
Mini batch size	32
Max number of epochs	100

[a]Stochastic gradient descent with weight decay.

Evaluation Measures. All evaluation measures used in the experiments were computed using the CoNLL 2002 evaluation script[8]. We adopted the micro evaluation measures (Precision, Recall, and F1 score) at the entity level, considering only exact matches.

The experiments were executed on a computer with an Intel Core i9 CPU, 32 GB of memory RAM, an Nvidia GeForce RTX 2060 GPU, and running the Ubuntu 20.04 operational system.

4.2 Experimental Results

In this first experiment, we evaluated different application scenarios (single and combined) of traditional (Glove and Word2vec Skip-gram) and contextual (BERT base, BERT Large, ELMO, and Flair) embedding models. Table 3 presents the results obtained in this experiment based on the F1 score considering the evaluation scenarios for each of the adopted corpora: Harem Total and Selective, Paramopama + Second Harem (referred only as Paramopama for the sake of simplicity), and LeNER-BR.

Regarding the scenarios using only the traditional embeddings, it is possible to observe that Word2vec Skip-gram obtained the best results in Harem corpus in both Total and Selective scenarios, while Glove presented the top performance in

---

[8] https://www.clips.uantwerpen.be/conll2002/ner/.

Table 3. The experimental results (%) of the embeddings combinations evaluation based on the F1 score. The highest result in each corpus is highlighted in bold.

Traditional	Contextualized	Harem total	Harem selective	Paramopama	LeNER-BR
-	$BERT_{Base}$	75.95	82.96	87.87	91.08
	$BERT_{Large}$	77.20	82.58	88.07	91.95
	ELMO	73.62	80.17	88.99	88.61
	FLAIR	73.48	79.74	86.74	89.52
Glove	-	60.45	64.97	82.75	84.89
	$BERT_{Base}$	78.02	81.31	88.51	90.53
	$BERT_{Large}$	77.76	82.89	88.53	92.45
	ELMO	74.81	80.40	88.71	88.57
	FLAIR	72.91	78.85	88.22	90.93
Word2vec Skip	-	62.34	66.69	82.26	83.98
	$BERT_{Base}$	78.09	83.32	88.29	92.11
	$BERT_{Large}$	**78.40**	**83.88**	88.08	**92.71**
	ELMO	75.26	79.96	**89.14**	89.39
	FLAIR	74.29	80.43	88.18	90.68

Paramopama and LeNER-BR. Considering the adoption of only the contextual embedding, the $BERT_{Base}$ and $BERT_{Large}$ models obtained the best performance in the Selective and Total Harem corpus, respectively. The $BERT_{Large}$ also achieved top performance in the LeNER-BR and the ELMO presented the best results in the Paramopama. Overall, contextual embeddings achieved superior results than traditional ones in all corpora, demonstrating that considering the context in which the words are mentioned is important for the NER task.

Analyzing the 16 evaluated scenarios considering only the contextual embeddings (4 corpora × 4 embedding models), it is possible to see that the combination with Glove led to better results in 10 of the 16 scenarios (62.5%). Meanwhile, the integration with the Word2vec Skip-gram improved in 15 out of 16 scenarios (93.75%). Overall, the architecture using the $BERT_{Large}$ combined with the Word2vec Skip-gram performed best in both Harem scenarios and the LeNER-BR while combining the ELMO with the Word2vec Skip-gram achieved the top performance in the Paramopama.

Based on the experimental results obtained, we conclude that: (i) Combining traditional and contextual embedding led to improved results in most of the evaluated scenarios, especially using Word2vec Skip-gram; and (ii) The architecture using $BERT_{Large}$ with Word2vec Skip-gram (BiLSTM-CRF $BERT_{Large}$-W2V) achieved the best overall performance considering all corpora.

Table 4 presents the results based on the Precision (P), Recall (R), and F1 score (F1) measures of the comparison among the best architecture identified in this work (BiLSTM-CRF $BERT_{Large}$-W2V) with state-of-the-art NER systems for Portuguese. We carried out this experiment only on the Harem corpus in both scenarios because this corpus was also adopted in the experiments carried out in some previous works [19,21,23]. We also included, as a baseline, the results of the CRF algorithm trained with handcrafted features and considering the neighboring words (if any) similarly as proposed in [3].

Table 4. Comparison results (%) with state-of-the-art Portuguese NER systems. The highest result in each measure and corpus is highlighted in bold.

Systems	Harem total			Harem selective		
	Precision	Recall	F1	Precision	Recall	F1
CRF	59.43	50.66	54.69	66.76	51.86	58.38
CharWNN [19]	67.16	63.74	65.41	73.98	68.68	71.23
BiLSTM-CRF [6]	72.28	68.03	70.33	78.26	74.39	76.27
BiLSTM-CRF+FlairBBP [21]	74.91	74.37	74.64	83.38	81.17	82.26
PT-$BERT_{Large}$-CRF [23]	**80.08**	77.31	**78.67**	84.82	81.72	83.24
BiLSTM-CRF $BERT_{Large}$-W2V	79.29	**77.53**	78.40	**85.14**	**82.65**	**83.88**

The $PT - BERT_{Large} - CRF$ [23] presented the best performance in the precision and F1 score for the Total scenario of Harem, whereas the BiLSTM-CRF $BERT_{Large} - W2V$ obtained the best recall results in the Harem (Total scenario) and all measures considering the Selective scenario. Thus, in general, the $BiLSTM - CRFBERT_{Large} - W2V$ outperformed the considered state-of-the-art NER systems, especially in the Selective scenario, and achieved competitive performance with the $PT - BERT_{Large} - CRF$ in the Total scenario.

5   Conclusion

In this work, we assess the feasibility of combining traditional and contextual embeddings for named entity recognition in Portuguese. The Glove and Word2vec Skip-gram word embeddings and the contextual ones generated from BERT (Base and Large), Elmo, and Flair were evaluated. An architecture based on a BiLSTM-CRF was employed as a classification model. Experiments were carried out considering the First and MiniHarem in the Total and Selective scenarios, Paramopama combined with the second version of the Harem and LeNER-BR. The experimental results obtained demonstrate that the embeddings combination strategy led to improved performance in most evaluated scenarios. In particular, the combination of Word2vec Skip-gram with BERT Large presented competitive results with state-of-the-art NER systems.

As future work, we intend to evaluate whether the combination of embeddings trained in specific domains with general embeddings can improve results in specific scenarios, such as law or biomedicine.

References

1. Akbik, A., Bergmann, T., Blythe, D., Rasul, K., Schweter, S., Vollgraf, R.: FLAIR: an easy-to-use framework for state-of-the-art NLP. In: Proceedings of the 2019 Conference of the North American Chapter of the Association for Computational Linguistics (Demonstrations), pp. 54–59. Association for Computational Linguistics, Minneapolis, June 2019
2. Akbik, A., Blythe, D., Vollgraf, R.: Contextual string embeddings for sequence labeling. In: Proceedings of the 27th International Conference on Computational Linguistics, pp. 1638–1649. Association for Computational Linguistics, Santa Fe, New Mexico, August 2018
3. do Amaral, D.O.F., Vieira, R.: NERP-CRF: uma ferramenta para o reconhecimento de entidades nomeadas por meio de conditional random fields. Linguamática 6(1), 41–49 (2014)
4. Luz de Araujo, P.H., de Campos, T.E., de Oliveira, R.R.R., Stauffer, M., Couto, S., Bermejo, P.: LeNER-Br: a dataset for named entity recognition in Brazilian legal text. In: Villavicencio, A., Moreira, V., Abad, A., Caseli, H., Gamallo, P., Ramisch, C., Gonçalo Oliveira, H., Paetzold, G.H. (eds.) PROPOR 2018. LNCS (LNAI), vol. 11122, pp. 313–323. Springer, Cham (2018). https://doi.org/10.1007/978-3-319-99722-3_32
5. Baralis, E., Cagliero, L., Jabeen, S., Fiori, A., Shah, S.: Multi-document summarization based on the yago ontology. Exp. Syst. Appl. 40(17), 6976–6984 (2013)
6. Quinta de Castro, P.V., Félix Felipe da Silva, N., da Silva Soares, A.: Portuguese named entity recognition using LSTM-CRF. In: Villavicencio, A., Moreira, V., Abad, A., Caseli, H., Gamallo, P., Ramisch, C., Gonçalo Oliveira, H., Paetzold, G.H. (eds.) Computational Processing of the Portuguese Language, pp. 83–92. Springer, Berlin (2018). https://doi.org/10.1007/978-3-540-85980-2
7. de Castro, P.V.Q., da Silva, N.F.F., da Silva Soares, A.: Contextual representations and semi-supervised named entity recognition for Portuguese language. In: IberLEF@SEPLN. CEUR Workshop Proceedings, vol. 2421, pp. 411–420. CEUR-WS.org (2019)
8. Devlin, J., Chang, M.W., Lee, K., Toutanova, K.: BERT: pre-training of deep bidirectional transformers for language understanding. In: Proceedings of the 2019 Conference of the North American Chapter of the Association for Computational Linguistics: Human Language Technologies, vol. 1 (Long and Short Papers), pp. 4171–4186. Association for Computational Linguistics, Minneapolis, June 2019
9. Grishman, R., Sundheim, B.: Message understanding conference-6: a brief history. In: Proceedings of the 16th Conference on Computational Linguistics, COLING 1996, vol. 1, p. 466–471. Association for Computational Linguistics (1996)
10. Hartmann, N., Fonseca, E.R., Shulby, C., Treviso, M.V., Rodrigues, J.S., Aluísio, S.M.: Portuguese word embeddings: evaluating on word analogies and natural language tasks. In: Symposium in Information and Human Language Technology (STIL) (2017)
11. Jiang, J.: Information extraction from text. In: Aggarwal, C., Zhai, C. (eds.) Mining Text Data, pp. 11–41. Springer, Boston (2012). https://doi.org/10.1007/978-1-4614-3223-4_2
12. Júnior, C.M., Macedo, H., Bispo, T., Santos, F., Silva, N., Barbosa, L.: Paramopama: a Brazilian-Portuguese corpus for named entity recognition. Encontro Nac. de Int, Artificial e Computacional (2015)

13. Li, J., Sun, A., Han, J., Li, C.: A survey on deep learning for named entity recognition. IEEE Trans. Knowl. Data Eng. **34**, 50–70 (2020)
14. Liu, X., Gao, J., He, X., Deng, L., Duh, K., Wang, Y.y.: Representation learning using multi-task deep neural networks for semantic classification and information retrieval. In: Proceedings of the 2015 Conference of the North American Chapter of the Association for Computational Linguistics: Human Language Technologies, pp. 912–921. Association for Computational Linguistics, Denver, Colorado, May–June 2015
15. Mikolov, T., Sutskever, I., Chen, K., Corrado, G., Dean, J.: Distributed representations of words and phrases and their compositionality. In: Proceedings of the 26th International Conference on Neural Information Processing Systems, NIPS 2013, vol. 2. pp. 3111–3119. Curran Associates Inc., Red Hook (2013)
16. Oliveira, H., et al.: Assessing shallow sentence scoring techniques and combinations for single and multi-document summarization. Exp. Syst. Appl. **65**, 68–86 (2016)
17. Pennington, J., Socher, R., Manning, C.: GloVe: global vectors for word representation. In: Proceedings of the 2014 Conference on Empirical Methods in Natural Language Processing (EMNLP), pp. 1532–1543. Association for Computational Linguistics, Doha, Qatar, October 2014
18. Peters, M.E., et al.: Deep contextualized word representations. In: Proceedings of the 2018 Conference of the North American Chapter of the Association for Computational Linguistics: Human Language Technologies, vol. 1 (Long Papers), pp. 2227–2237. Association for Computational Linguistics, New Orleans, Louisiana, June 2018
19. dos Santos, C., Guimarães, V.: Boosting named entity recognition with neural character embeddings. In: Proceedings of the Fifth Named Entity Workshop, pp. 25–33. Association for Computational Linguistics, Beijing, China, July 2015
20. Santos, D., Seco, N., Cardoso, N., Vilela, R.: HAREM: an advanced NER evaluation contest for Portuguese. In: Proceedings of the Fifth International Conference on Language Resources and Evaluation (LREC 2006). European Language Resources Association (ELRA), Genoa, Italy, May 2006
21. Santos, J., Consoli, B., dos Santos, C., Terra, J., Collonini, S., Vieira, R.: Assessing the impact of contextual embeddings for Portuguese named entity recognition. In: 2019 8th Brazilian Conference on Intelligent Systems (BRACIS), pp. 437–442 (2019)
22. Souza, F., Nogueira, R., Lotufo, R.: BERTimbau: pretrained BERT models for Brazilian Portuguese. In: 9th Brazilian Conference on Intelligent Systems, BRACIS, Rio Grande do Sul, Brazil, October 20–23 (to appear 2020)
23. Souza, F., Nogueira, R.F., de Alencar Lotufo, R.: Portuguese named entity recognition using BERT-CRF. CoRR abs/1909.10649 (2019)
24. Vaswani, A., et al.: Attention is all you need. In: Guyon, I., et al. (eds.) Advances in Neural Information Processing Systems, vol. 30, pp. 5998–6008. Curran Associates Inc. Long Beach (2017)
25. Yadav, V., Bethard, S.: A survey on recent advances in named entity recognition from deep learning models. In: Proceedings of the 27th International Conference on Computational Linguistics, pp. 2145–2158. Association for Computational Linguistics, Santa Fe, New Mexico, August 2018

BERT for Sentiment Analysis:
Pre-trained and Fine-Tuned Alternatives

Frederico Dias Souza(✉) and João Baptista de Oliveira e Souza Filho(✉)

Electrical Engineering Program, Federal University of Rio de Janeiro,
Rio de Janeiro, Brazil
{fredericodspoli,jbfilhopoli}@ufrj.br

Abstract. BERT has revolutionized the NLP field by enabling transfer learning with large language models that can capture complex textual patterns, reaching the state-of-the-art for an expressive number of NLP applications. For text classification tasks, BERT has already been extensively explored. However, aspects like how to better cope with the different embeddings provided by the BERT output layer and the usage of language-specific instead of multilingual models are not well studied in the literature, especially for the Brazilian Portuguese language. The purpose of this article is to conduct an extensive experimental study regarding different strategies for aggregating the features produced in the BERT output layer, with a focus on the sentiment analysis task. The experiments include BERT models trained with Brazilian Portuguese corpora and the multilingual version, contemplating multiple aggregation strategies and open-source datasets with predefined training, validation, and test partitions to facilitate the reproducibility of the results. BERT achieved the highest ROC-AUC values for the majority of cases as compared to TF-IDF. Nonetheless, TF-IDF represents a good trade-off between the predictive performance and computational cost.

Keywords: Sentiment analysis · Natural language processing · Machine learning · Transfer learning · Transformers

1 Introduction

Text classification (TC) is one of the most widely studied natural language processing (NLP) tasks, exploring a range of methods. More recently, the Transformers architecture [21], replacing the recurrence with the self-attention mechanism, enabled that large pre-trained language models could now be used to address several NLP tasks, leading to the state-of-the-art in many of these applications [11].

BERT (Bidirectional Encoder Representations from Transformers) [3] represents the most prominent Transformer-based model, extensively studied and evaluated in most NLP problems and benchmark datasets. However, more studies are required regarding pre-trained BERT approaches to identify the best manner of aggregating the multiple embeddings generated, especially for the Brazilian Portuguese language.

© Springer Nature Switzerland AG 2022
V. Pinheiro et al. (Eds.): PROPOR 2022, LNAI 13208, pp. 209–218, 2022.
https://doi.org/10.1007/978-3-030-98305-5_20

Typically, classification models based on BERT embeddings use the output corresponding to the first token of the sequence (CLS). However, what if the multiple embeddings produced at this layer are combined to define a new document embedding? Would this procedure bring us some significant performance gain in the sentiment analysis scenario? To answer this question, we analyzed three different BERT variants: the *BERTimbau* Base and Large [3], a Portuguese BERT variant trained with the *Brazilian Web as Corpus* (BrWaC) [22], and the *Multilingual BERT* (m-BERT) [5], trained on about 100 different languages, and considered a range of aggregation strategies over BERT outcomes to produce a single document embedding that is classified by a Logistic Regression (LR). The experiments included BERT models with and without fine-tuning, assuming different learning and dropout rates.

Another research question was how do these models generalize to other contextual settings? For this analysis, five open-source datasets with pre-defined training, test, and validation set partitions were considered in a cross predictive performance experiment, i.e., embedding and/or classification models finetuned to a particular dataset were evaluated with instances from another one. In addition, a generalist model, developed with all datasets concatenated, was produced to infer if database specif models were significantly more accurate than a unique general embedding-classification model. To better position the results, the experiments also included the most classical embedding approach: the *term frequency-inverse document frequency* (TF-IDF) [19] followed by a LR as a baseline.

The main paper contribution is proposing different ways of using BERT for sentiment classification in Brazilian Portuguese texts. This analysis considered cost-benefit aspects, covering from more straightforward solutions to more computationally demanding approaches.

2   Related Work

The most classical approach for text classification consists of extracting basic corpus statistics such as the word frequency or TF-IDF [19] to generate large sparse embedding vectors with a size equal to the vocabulary size. In these cases, Latent Semantic Analysis [8] may be useful for reducing the dimensionality of such vectors through the Singular Value Decomposition (SVD). As shown by Zhang et al. [24], on some occasions, models using TF-IDF, despite being simpler and unable to capture complex text patterns, can achieve better results than more complex neural-based approaches.

Devlin et al. [3] proposed the BERT (Bidirectional Encoder Representations from Transformers), one of the most popular Transformer-based architectures. Transfer-learning with BERT may consider two design options: pre-trained and fine-tuning. The pre-trained approach assumes BERT as a large fixed model for producing "unsupervised" features; therefore, only the model stacked over it is trained for a target application. Conversely, the fine-tuning strategy focus on updating BERT weights using labelled data from a specific task. Surprisingly, the authors presented competitive results in the named entity recognition (NER) task compared to the state-of-art just by exploiting the pre-trained approach.

BERT's authors also open-sourced [5] a variant with a multilingual purpose (m-BERT), trained on more than 100 languages, including Portuguese. In 2019, Souza et al. [16] open-sourced BERTimbau Base and Large, trained exclusively on Brazilian Portuguese corpora. This work focus on how to better explore m-BERT and BERTimbau in the sentiment analysis task.

Despite being a recent model, BERTimbau has already being applied to other tasks. Lopes et al. [10] fine-tuned m-BERT and BERTimbau to an aspect extraction task, whereas Leite et al. [9] to toxic sentence classification, outperforming other bag-of-words solutions. Jiang et al. [7] and Neto et al. [12] evaluated fine-tuning BERTimbau to an irony detection task. Carriço and Quaresma et al. [2] exploited different ways of extracting features from its output layer (CLS token, vector maximum and vector average), considering a semantic similarity task.

Additionally, other authors considered producing large language models for the Brazilian Portuguese language. Paulo et al. [4] developed the BERTaú, a BERT Base variant trained with data from Itaú (the largest Latin American bank) virtual assistant, and reported better results than BERTimbau and m-BERT for the NER task. Carmo et al. [1] open-sourced the PTT5 model, a T5 model trained on the BrWac corpus, the same used to train BERTimbau, achieving similar results to BERTimbau in a semantic similarity task.

3   Datasets

This work considered five user reviews datasets: *Olist* [13], *B2W* [14], *Buscapé* [6], *UTLC-Apps*, and *UTLC-Movies* [15], available in a public repository [17], with predefined training, test, and validation set partitions. We also examined the results for all of them concatenated. In all evaluations, we considered the binary polarity target feature. Table 1 summarizes the number of samples, document length, vocabulary size, and the polarity distribution of each dataset.

4   Models

The experiments included two base models: m-BERT and BERTimbau, and two design strategies: pre-trained and fine-tuned. The pre-trained solution considered just using BERT for producing document embeddings, subsequently fed to a LR model. The fine-tuned model considered adjusting the BERT weights to the sentiment analysis task. In both cases, the models adopted the *AutoTokenizer* from *Huggingface* [23], padding the sentences to 60 tokens and no extra processing was conducted over the documents.

The baseline adopted in this work was based on the results of Souza and Filho [18], wherein TF-IDF and alternative word embedding strategies were evaluated in the same datasets and partitions. Therefore, this baseline considered the TF-IDF embedding followed by a LR, which performed best in all cases. The figure of merit was the ROC-AUC inferred over the test set.

Table 1. Summary of the datasets used in this work: number of samples, mean/median document length, vocabulary size, and the polarity distribution.

Dataset	Training/ Validation/ Test samples	Mean/median length	Vocab size (1 gram)	Labels distribution (Positive)
Olist	30k/4k/4k	7/6	3.272	70.0%
Buscapé	59k/7k/7k	25/17	13.470	90.8%
B2W	93k/12k/12k	14/10	12.758	69.2%
UTLC Apps	775k/97k/97k	7/5	28.283	77.5%
UTLC Movies	952k/119k/119k	21/10	69.711	88.4%
All	1909k/239k/239k	15/7	86.234	82.8%

4.1 Pre-trained BERT

Previous works [3] reported that creative combinations of the token representations provided by the BERT outputs might lead to a significant performance improvement in the NER task, even without any fine-tuning of model parameters. Such findings strongly motivated the present work.

The evaluated BERT models assumed documents constituted by one to the sixty tokens. To each token, this model produces a representation, having 768 or 1024 dimensions, in the case of Base and Large models, respectively, referred to as layers. In the following, we described the different approaches evaluated in this work to combine these embeddings. In parenthesis, the number of vector concatenations of each case is exhibited. Thus, the size of the vectors used for document representations have from 768 (768×1) up to 3072 (1024×3) dimensions.

1. **first** (1): layer corresponding to the first token, the [CLS] special token, created with the purpose of sentence classification, considered as the default BERT embedding;
2. **second** (1): layer corresponding to the 2nd token;
3. **last** (1): layer corresponding to the last (60th) token;
4. **sum all** (1): sum of all 60 layers;
5. **mean all** (1): average of all 60 layers;
6. **sum all except first** (1): sum of all 59 layers, ignoring the first one;
7. **mean all except first** (1): average of all 59 layers, ignoring the first one;
8. **sum + first** (2): concatenation of the first layer with the sum of the remaining 59 layers;
9. **mean + first** (2): concatenation of the first layer with the average of the remaining 59 layers;
10. **first + mean + std** (3): concatenation of the first layer, the average and the standard deviation of the last 59 layers;
11. **first + mean + max** (3): concatenation of the first layer, the average and the maximum of the last 59 layers;

12. **mean + min + max** (3): concatenation of the average, minimum and maximum of the last 59 layers;
13. **quantiles 25, 50, 75** (3): concatenation of the quantiles 25%, 50%, and 75% of the last 59 layers.

For all these aggregations modalities, we also evaluated three different BERT models: BERTimbau Base and BERTimbau Large, trained exclusively with Brazilian Portuguese corpus, and m-BERT Base, trained in a multilingual schema.

4.2   Fine-Tuned BERT

For BERT fine-tuning, a linear network was added on the top of the layer associated with the [CLS] token, targeting to predict one of the two sentiment classification classes, i.e., assuming as target-values 0 or 1. Network training adopted the Adam optimizer with weight decay, slanted triangular learning rates with a warm-up proportion of 0.1, and a maximum number of epochs equal to 4.

Design choices, such as the training and model hyperparameters, were based on Sun et al. [20]. Two base learning rates (2.5e–5 and 5e–5) and dropout rates (0 and 10%) were evaluated considering the log-loss observed in the validation set. Experiments for hyperparameters' tuning restricted only to the *Olist*, *Buscapé*, and *B2W*, due to the expressive computational efforts required for conducting this analysis in the significantly bigger remaining datasets. The best combination of the learning rate, dropout rate, and number of epochs were 2.5e–5, 10%, and one, for the BERTimbau models; whereas 2.5e–5, no dropout, and two, for the m-BERT. As expected, the m-BERT required one more training step to learn Portuguese language patterns.

5   Results and Discussion

5.1   Pre-trained BERT

Figure 1 compares the ROC-AUC values considering different pre-trained BERT models and aggregation strategies discussed in Sect. 4.1, including TF-IDF (horizontal red lines) and fine-tuned (to be discussed later). For all datasets and aggregations methods, m-BERT Base is worse than BERTimbau Base, which is inferior to BERTimbau Large. In addition, except for UTLC-Movies and All-Combined datasets, these BERT embedding can outperform all previous approaches.

Table 2 summarizes the average rankings restricted to the BERTimbau models for different datasets. The model Large performs better than the model Base in all cases. For both models, the best aggregations are: "first + mean + std", "first + mean" and "first + mean + max". These findings confirm that the first layer (CLS) carries, in fact, important information for classification, but such task can largely benefit from the remaining layers. Quantiles-based aggregations performed poorly, possibly due to not including the first layer content.

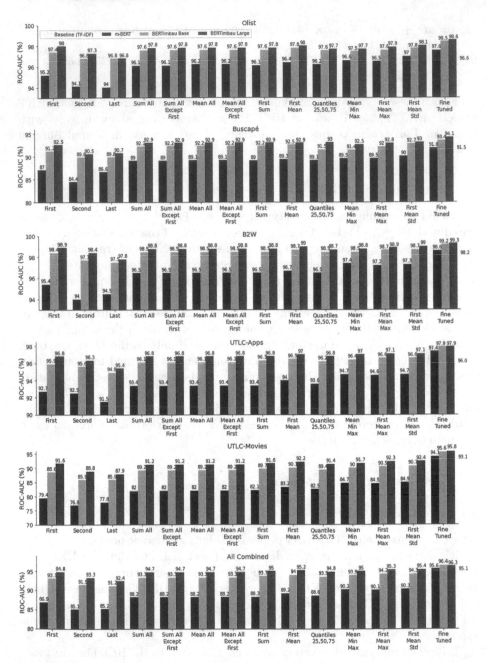

Fig. 1. ROC-AUC (%) per BERT type, embedding type, and dataset. The figure also includes the results for fine-tuned BERT models. The horizontal line corresponds to the baseline model (TF-IDF with logistic regression).

Table 2. Average ranking (avg. rank) according to BERTimbau size and aggregation modality

BERT size	Aggregation modality	Avg. rank	BERT size	Aggregation modality	Avg. rank
Large	first + mean + std	1.0	Base	first + mean + max	13.8
Large	first + mean	2.4	Base	first + sum	15.0
Large	first + mean + max	3.8	Base	sum all except 1st	16.0
Large	first + sum	4.6	Base	mean all except 1st	16.0
Large	sum all except 1st	5.2	Base	mean all	16.0
Large	mean all except 1st	5.2	Base	quantiles 25,50,75	16.8
Large	mean all	5.2	Base	sum all	16.8
Large	sum all	5.2	Base	mean + min + max	17.4
Large	first	5.2	Large	second	21.4
Large	mean + min + max	7.0	Base	first	22.4
Large	quantiles 25,50,75	7.2	Large	last	24.0
Base	first + mean + std	10.0	Base	second	24.6
Base	first + mean	11.0	Base	last	25.2

Previous results also bring us some important practical guidelines in operational scenarios with limited computational resources, for instance, those which restrictions over vRAM GPUs availability hinder the Large model usage: a simple aggregation of the type "first + mean + std" or even "first + mean" with the Base model can significantly boost its performance, reducing the gap between both. Additionally, all BERT embeddings evaluated here used numbers in 16 bits (dtype = "float16" in NumPy) precision, instead of 32 bits (the default). A quick analysis over the influence of using 16 and 32 bits in model training for BERTimbau Base and Large models with an aggregation of the type "first" has shown no significant impact on model performance. Nonetheless, the reduction in the computational time and RAM usage with 16 bits of precision was impressive. Therefore, a useful practical lesson learned is to adopt numbers with 16 bits precision when dealing with pre-trained BERT models.

5.2   Fine-Tuned BERT

Figure 1 also exhibits the results for fine-tuned BERT models exclusively for the aggregation of the type "first + mean + std". For all datasets, the fine-tuning allowed the new models to surpass all the pre-trained and baseline alternatives. The *UTLC-Movies* dataset was the one that most benefited from fine-tuning, presenting relative gains for the ROC-AUC of 10%, 4.9%, and 3.4%, considering m-BERT, BERTimbau Base, and BERTimbau Large, respectively. Moreover, for this dataset, BERT models only surpass the TF-IDF baseline by fine-tuning. The BERT model that most benefited from fine-tuning was the m-BERT, despite not being able to reach the BERTimbau performance after retraining. Therefore, the large dataset used to pre-train BERTimbau seems to contribute to its significant predictive power.

5.3   Cross-model Comparison

Cross-model comparisons were restricted to the BERTimbau Large models and "first + mean + std" embedding. Table 3 summarizes the results.

Table 3. Cross-comparison of ROC-AUC (%) values for the BERTimbau pre-trained and fine-tuned models for different datasets (see text).

Model		Olist	Buscapé	B2W	UTLC Apps	UTLC Movies
BERTimbau fine-tuned with	Olist	97.9	93.4	99.1	97.4	93.2
	Buscapé	98.3	93.9	99.0	97.3	93.3
	B2W	98.2	93.4	99.2	97.5	93.7
	UTLC-Apps	98.4	93.8	99.1	97.9	92.7
	UTLC-Movies	98.2	93.7	99.1	97.4	95.9
	All-Combined	98.4	93.7	99.0	97.5	95.3
Pre-trained BERTimbau		98.1	93.0	99.0	97.1	92.4

Except for the Olist, the smallest dataset, specifically fine-tuning models to each dataset resulted in higher performance, as expected. The most extensive and complex content dataset, the *UTLC-Movies*, exhibited the highest gains with retraining. The general fine-tuned model obtained with the All-Combined dataset performed better than the pre-trained alternative but worse than the specialized models. Some datasets also seemed to benefit from fine-tuning, even if this procedure is conducted with another dataset. A notable example is again the *UTLC-Movies*, when the retraining considered the *B2W* dataset, resulting in a gain of 1.3% percentage points as compared to the pre-trained model. However, the gains observed with retraining to most datasets were inferior to 1%, which might not be cost-effective for some applications.

6   Conclusion

This work analyzed different ways of exploiting the BERT model for sentiment analysis on Brazilian Portuguese user reviews. An important finding is that the pre-trained BERTimbau embeddings performed much better than those related to the multilingual m-BERT. Additionally, the proposed aggregation approach over BERT outputs also brought considerable gains over the more conventional scheme of selecting the first layer, i.e., the output related to the [CLS] token. For all datasets, except UTLC-Movies, some BERT embeddings configurations achieved the highest results among all evaluated models. Nonetheless, the fine-tuning allowed BERT models to surpass all other alternatives, resulting in a significant m-BERT performance gain, despite it still performs worse than the BERTimbau model. Therefore, BERTimbau represents the best BERT variant for Brazilian Portuguese text classification tasks.

As following steps, we intend to evaluate the performance of other deep learning models, more complex than the TF-IDF baseline and simpler than BERT, such as CNNs and LSTMs. Furthermore, an interesting point for further studies is the fine-tuning schema, which may be modified to exploit better the large amount of annotated data available in the dataset considered in this work.

References

1. Carmo, D., Piau, M., Campiotti, I., Nogueira, R., Lotufo, R.: PTT5: pretraining and validating the T5 model on Brazilian Portuguese data (2020)
2. Carrico, N., Quaresma, P.: Sentence embeddings and sentence similarity for Portuguese FAQs. In: IberSPEECH 2021, pp. 200–204, March 2021
3. Devlin, J., Chang, M.W., Lee, K., Toutanova, K.: BERT: pre-training of deep bidirectional transformers for language understanding. In: Proceedings of the 2019 Conference of the North American Chapter of the Association for Computational Linguistics: Human Language Technologies, vol. 1 (Long and Short Papers), pp. 4171–4186. Association for Computational Linguistics, Minneapolis, June 2019. https://doi.org/10.18653/v1/N19-1423, https://aclanthology.org/N19-1423
4. Finardi, P., Viegas, J.D., Ferreira, G.T., Mansano, A.F., Carid'a, V.F.: BERTaú: Itaú BERT for digital customer service. ArXiv abs/2101.12015 (2021)
5. Google: BERT. https://github.com/google-research/bert (2019)
6. Hartmann, N., et al.: A large corpus of product reviews in Portuguese: tackling out-of-vocabulary words. In: Proceedings of the Ninth International Conference on Language Resources and Evaluation (LREC 2014). Reykjavik, May 2014. European Language Resources Association (ELRA), Reykjavik (2014)
7. Jiang, S., Chen, C., Liu, N., Chen, Z., Chen, J.: Irony detection in the Portuguese language using BERT. In: Iberian Languages Evaluation Forum 2021, pp. 891–897 (2021)
8. Landauer, T.K., Foltz, P.W., Laham, D.: An introduction to latent semantic analysis. Discourse Process. **25**(2–3), 259–284 (1998). https://doi.org/10.1080/01638539809545028
9. Leite, J.A., Silva, D.F., Bontcheva, K., Scarton, C.: Toxic language detection in social media for Brazilian Portuguese: new dataset and multilingual analysis. CoRR abs/2010.04543 (2020). https://arxiv.org/abs/2010.04543
10. Lopes, E., Correa, U., Freitas, L.: Exploring BERT for aspect extraction in Portuguese language. The International FLAIRS Conference Proceedings 34, April 2021. https://doi.org/10.32473/flairs.v34i1.128357, https://journals.flvc.org/FLAIRS/article/view/128357
11. Minaee, S., Kalchbrenner, N., Cambria, E., Nikzad, N., Chenaghlu, M., Gao, J.: Deep learning based text classification: a comprehensive review. arXiv preprint arXiv:2004.03705 (2020)
12. Neto, A.M.S.A., et al.: SiDi-NLP-Team at IDPT2021: Irony detection in Portuguese 2021. In: Montes, M., et al. (eds.) Proceedings of the Iberian Languages Evaluation Forum (IberLEF 2021) co-located with the Conference of the Spanish Society for Natural Language Processing (SEPLN 2021), XXXVII International Conference of the Spanish Society for Natural Language Processing. Málaga, Spain, September 2021. CEUR Workshop Proceedings, vol. 2943, pp. 933–939. CEUR-WS.org (2021), http://ceur-ws.org/Vol-2943/idpt_paper6.pdf

13. Olist: Brazilian e-commerce public dataset by Olist, November 2018. https://www. kaggle.com/olistbr/brazilian-ecommerce
14. Real, L., Oshiro, M., Mafra, A.: B2W-Reviews01 - an open product reviews corpus. In: STIL - Symposium in Information and Human Language Technology (2019). https://github.com/b2wdigital/b2w-reviews01
15. Sousa, R.F.d., Brum, H.B., Nunes, M.d.G.V.: A bunch of helpfulness and senti- ment corpora in Brazilian Portuguese. In: Symposium in Information and Human Language Technology - STIL. SBC (2019)
16. Souza, F., Nogueira, R., Lotufo, R.: BERTimbau: Pretrained BERT Models for Brazilian Portuguese. In: Cerri, R., Prati, R.C. (eds.) BRACIS 2020. LNCS (LNAI), vol. 12319, pp. 403–417. Springer, Cham (2020). https://doi.org/10.1007/ 978-3-030-61377-8_28
17. Souza, F.: Brazilian Portuguese sentiment analysis datasets, June 2021. https:// www.kaggle.com/fredericods/ptbr-sentiment-analysis-datasets
18. Souza, F., Filho, J.: Sentiment analysis on Brazilian Portuguese user reviews. In: IEEE Latin American Conference on Computational Intelligence 2021 (preprint), December 2021. https://arxiv.org/abs/2112.05459
19. Sparck Jones, K.: A statistical Interpretation of Term Specificity and Its Applica- tion in Retrieval, pp. 132–142. Taylor Graham Publishing, GBR, San Diego (1988)
20. Sun, C., Qiu, X., Xu, Y., Huang, X.: How to fine-tune BERT for text classification? In: Sun, M., Huang, X., Ji, H., Liu, Z., Liu, Y. (eds.) CCL 2019. LNCS (LNAI), vol. 11856, pp. 194–206. Springer, Cham (2019). https://doi.org/10.1007/978-3- 030-32381-3_16
21. Vaswani, A., et al.: Attention is all you need. In: Proceedings of the 31st Inter- national Conference on Neural Information Processing Systems. NIPS 2017, pp. 6000–6010. Curran Associates Inc., Red Hook (2017)
22. Wagner Filho, J.A., Wilkens, R., Idiart, M., Villavicencio, A.: The brWaC corpus: a new open resource for Brazilian Portuguese. In: Proceedings of the Eleventh International Conference on Language Resources and Evaluation (LREC 2018). European Language Resources Association (ELRA), Miyazaki, Japan, May 2018, https://aclanthology.org/L18-1686
23. Wolf, T., et al.: HuggingFace's transformers: state-of-the-art natural language pro- cessing (2020)
24. Zhang, X., Zhao, J., LeCun, Y.: Character-level convolutional networks for text classification. In: Cortes, C., Lawrence, N., Lee, D., Sugiyama, M., Gar- nett, R. (eds.) Advances in Neural Information Processing Systems, vol. 28. Curran Associates, Inc. (2015). https://proceedings.neurips.cc/paper/2015/file/ 250cf8b51c773f3f8dc8b4be867a9a02-Paper.pdf

Fostering Judiciary Applications with New Fine-Tuned Models for Legal Named Entity Recognition in Portuguese

Luciano Zanuz(✉) and Sandro José Rigo

Applied Computing Graduate Program, University of Vale do Rio dos Sinos (UNISINOS), São Leopoldo, Brazil

rigo@unisinos.br

Abstract. Artificial Intelligence applied to Law is getting attention in the community, both from the Judiciary and the lawyers, due to possible gains in procedural celerity and the automation of repetitive tasks, among other use cases. Many of its benefits can be derived from Natural Language Processing since legal proceedings are textual document-based. Named Entity Recognition is the NLP task of identifying and classifying named entities in unstructured text to help achieve these goals. In recent years, transformers emerged as the new state-of-the-art architecture for some tasks in NLP systems. NLP resources in Portuguese, such as models and datasets, are needed to allow Portuguese speaking countries to benefit from this new NLP level. This paper presents the first fine-tuned BERT models trained exclusively on Brazilian Portuguese for Legal NER. The models achieved new state-of-the-art on LeNER-Br dataset, a Portuguese NER corpus for the legal domain. We also built a prototype application for Judiciary users to evaluate how the model performed with authentic law documents. The results showed that the models were able to extract information with good quality. Both the models and the prototype application are publicly available for the community.

Keywords: Natural Language Processing · Named Entity Recognition · Artificial Intelligence · Law

1 Introduction

Named Entity Recognition (NER) is the problem of locating and categorizing important nouns and proper nouns in a text [12], being one of the leading Natural Language Processing (NLP) tasks. NER has great importance in real applications in the Law field due to the large amount of unstructured data usually written by lawyers in petitions or by judges in orders, decisions, and sentences [4]. Advances in NLP based on traditional word embedding such as Word2Vec [11] and GLoVE [14] and more recently contextualized word embeddings based on pre-trained neural language models built from deep learning such as ELMo [15], ULMFit [6] and transformer-based architectures [18, 21] such as BERT [3] quickly leverage the State-Of-The-Art (SOTA) in NLP tasks [16].

© Springer Nature Switzerland AG 2022
V. Pinheiro et al. (Eds.): PROPOR 2022, LNAI 13208, pp. 219–229, 2022.
https://doi.org/10.1007/978-3-030-98305-5_21

Although far away from the amount available in English and other languages, resources in Portuguese are rapidly becoming available, supporting the NLP research in countries like Brazil and Portugal. The Brazilian Portuguese brWaC Corpus [19] was recently made available with a resulting corpus including 145 million sentences and 2,7 billion tokens, based on 38 million URLs of.*br* top-level domain pages. First HAREM [16] and Second HAREM [5] were respectively the first and second evaluation contest for named entity recognizers for Portuguese. Both corpora are manually labeled with ten named entities. Paramopama [9] is a tagged Brazilian Portuguese corpus for named entity recognition, extending the PtBR version of WikiNER corpus [13], revising incorrect assigned tags to improve corpus quality and extend the corpus size. WikiNER is a multilingual silver-standard corpus for named entity recognition, automatically built by exploiting the text and structure of Wikipedia. Another silver-standard corpus is SESAME (Silver-Standard Named Entity Recognition dataset) [10], a massive dataset built on the Portuguese Wikipedia and DBpedia. LeNER-Br [7] is the first Portuguese language dataset for named entity recognition applied to legal documents, and consists entirely of manually annotated legislation and legal cases texts and contains tags for persons, locations, time entities, organizations, legislation, and legal cases. Table 1 presents a comparison between NER datasets available in Portuguese.

Table 1. Comparison between available NER datasets for Portuguese

Corpus	Sentences	Tokens	Year
First HAREM	5.000	80.000	2006
Second HAREM	3.500	100.000	2008
WikiNER	125.821	2.830.000	2013
Paramopama	12.500	310.000	2015
LeNER-Br	10.392	318.073	2018
SESAME	3.650.909	87.769.158	2019

NER is a token classification task, which usually has good results in BERT based models. According to the best of our knowledge, there was no Legal Named Entity Recognition in Portuguese using a BERT model pre-trained exclusively on Portuguese texts when we started this work. Considering our research in AI applied to Law and the resources currently available, we decided to train BERT models in Brazilian Portuguese for Legal NER and compare them with previous benchmarking to evaluate improvements in the use of BERT models in the development of applications for the Judiciary and for the legal domain in general.

In this work, we fine-tuned a BERT model pre-trained on Brazilian Portuguese for the NER task in the legal domain, achieving new state-of-the-art performance on the LeNER-Br corpus. We also built a prototype application so that Judiciary users could try out the model with real documents. We discuss the results and suggest future work to support the development of real and effective applications for the Judiciary.

The remainder of this paper is structured as follows. Related work is presented in Sect. 2. Then, we detail the model and prototype application in Sect. 3, and in Sect. 4 we present the obtained results. Lastly, final considerations are presented.

2 Related Work

The following works are directly related to ours and contribute to reach the SOTA of Legal Named Entity Recognition in Portuguese.

BERTimbau [17] is the first pre-trained BERT model for Brazilian Portuguese. It achieves SOTA performances on three downstream NLP tasks: Named Entity Recognition, Sentence Textual Similarity, and Recognizing Textual Entailment. The model was trained on the brWaC Corpus [19] for 1.000.000 steps, using a whole-word mask. The fine-tuning approach obtained new state-of-the-art results on the HAREM I dataset (using First HAREM as training set and MiniHAREM as test set).

LeNER-Br [7] is the first dataset for Named Entity Recognition in Brazilian Legal Text, and it is the current baseline for comparison on legal entities recognition in Portuguese. The authors trained a LSTM-CRF machine learning model on this dataset and achieved an average F1-score of 92.53% on token-level evaluation.

The impact of fine-tuning a language model on a large intradomain corpus of unlabeled text before training it on the final task is investigated by [1]. This aspect is not well explored in the current literature. Different scenarios were explored considering two Portuguese ELMo models (Wikipedia and brWaC corpus) and the official BERT Multilingual model, pre-trained on the 100 largest Wikipedias, including Portuguese. To derive legal-domain language models, the authors fine-tuned the BERT Mutilingual and ELMo brWaC language models on the Acordaos TCU corpus[1], which comprises judgments from the Brazilian Federal Court of Accounts during the period from 1992 to 2019. The intradomain fine-tuned BERT-based model improved LeNER-Br results by 3.97 points.

BertBR [2] also performed additional BERT training for the legal language, by fine-tuning BERTimbau [17] on the Iudicium Textum Dataset [20], as a step prior to fine-tuning for the NER task. The dataset was generated through the scraping process of Supreme Federal Court Agreements, resulting around 20 gigabytes and 50.928 lawsuits between 2010 and 2018. The fine-tuned model on LeNER-Br [7] achieved F1-score of 95.25%. As not mentioned by the author, we believe it had been used token-level evaluation, the same as the LeNER-Br paper.

We identified an opportunity to train a specific NER model for the legal field based on a BERT architecture and compare it with the existing benchmarking [1], in addition to evaluating the model in real legal documents through a prototype application.

3 Materials and Methods

This section presents details on the construction of the models and on the prototype application. We emphasize the hyperparameters used and the tokenization process of the fine-tuning, as well the functionalities of the application.

---

[1] https://www.kaggle.com/ferraz/acordaos-tcu.

3.1 Fine-Tuned Legal NER

We trained two models by fine-tuning both the bert-base-portuguese-cased (BERTimbau Base[2]) and the bert-large-portuguese-cased (BERTimbau Large[3]) pre-trained models [17]. We trained it on the LeNER-Br[4] dataset [7], generating two legal fields domain-specific BERT models for the NER task. The BERT Base model has 12 layers, 768 hidden dimensions, 12 attention heads, and 110M parameters. The BERT Large has 24 layers, 1024 hidden dimensions, 16 attention heads, and 330 M parameters. For both, the maximum sentence length is 512 tokens, and the vocabulary size is 29794 words.

In general, the main technical aspects of the models are the same as the BERTimbau [17], considering that the former is a fine-tuning of the latter. The following hyperparameters were used to build the models: learning_rate = 2e-05; weight_decay = 0.01; lr_scheduler_type = linear; optimizer = Adam with betas = (0.9,0.999) and epsilon = 1e-08; gradient_accumulation_steps = 1. The only difference between the fine-tuned base and large versions is the batch size (train_batch_size and eval_batch_size), respectively 8 and 4.

We used a single Tesla P100-PCIE 16GB GPU. The GPU limited the batch size of large version in 4. The base version accepted a batch size of 16, but better results were obtained with 8. To build the models, we used the Transformers library [21]. This is a powerful tool for developing transformer-based models and supports a great variety of architectures (almost 70) like BERT, DistilBERT, RoBERTa, BART, ELECTRA, GPT-2, T5, etc.

The tokenizer is an important component of the solution. We used a fast version of the BERT tokenizer with a subword tokenization algorithm. The fast version allows a significant speed-up in particular when doing batched tokenization. Subword tokenization relies on the principle that frequently used words should not be split into smaller subwords, but rare words should be decomposed into meaningful subwords. It allows the model to have a reasonable vocabulary size while being able to learn meaningful context-independent representations. It also enables the model to process words it has never seen before by decomposing them into known subwords. In our case, as the dataset is already splitted into words, the tokenizer splitted each of those words again. We had also used the tokenizer to add the special tokens [CLS] and [SEP] to identify the start and the separation of the sentences. Due to added special tokens and possible splits of words in multiple tokens, the tokenizer return is longer than the dataset sentence, so we had to do some postprocessing to align the labels after the tokenization.

Figure 1 shows a sentence in the dataset and the result of its tokenization. As we can see, some words considered rare by the tokenizer, such as "indemnity" ("indenizatória", in Portuguese), were divided into subwords.

The fine-tuning performed 10 epochs over the training data. At the end of the training, the best model considering the F1-score metric was loaded to evaluate the results in the

---

[2] https://huggingface.co/neuralmind/bert-base-portuguese-cased.

[3] https://huggingface.co/neuralmind/bert-large-portuguese-cased.

[4] https://huggingface.co/datasets/lener_br.

```
['-', 'Tratando-se', 'de', 'ação', 'indenizatória', 'ajuizada', 'por',
'pessoa', 'incapaz', ',', 'é', 'obrigatória', 'a', 'intervenção', 'do',
'Ministério', 'Público', 'na', 'condição', 'de', 'fiscal', 'da',
'ordem', 'jurídica', '.']
['[CLS]', '-', 'Trata', '##ndo', '-', 'se', 'de', 'ação', 'inden',
'##iza', '##tória', 'aju', '##izada', 'por', 'pessoa', 'incapaz', ',',
'é', 'obrigatória', 'a', 'intervenção', 'do', 'Ministério', 'Público',
'na', 'condição', 'de', 'fiscal', 'da', 'ordem', 'jurídica', '.',
'[SEP]']
(In the case of an indemnity action filed by an incapable person, the
intervention of the Public Prosecutor's Office as supervisor of the
legal system is mandatory.)
```

Fig. 1. Example of the subword tokenization.

test set. The trained models bertimbau-base-lener_br[5] and bertimbau-large-lener_br[6] were made freely available for the community on HuggingFace's model hub.

3.2 Prototype Application

A Proof of Concept (POC) application was developed and made available[7], allowing an evaluation of users from the Judiciary considering a real context of use. After using the POC application, users from the Court of Justice of the State of Rio Grande do Sul answered a questionnaire, evaluating the application about the perceived usefulness.

A NER system would be useful in several use cases in the Judiciary. For instance, it could be applied to all petitions received from lawyers to identify entities of interest, which could be used to facilitate human analysis or as input to automations. It could also be used to process text from hearings transcripts and identify people, places and other entities mentioned, which could be presented in a graphical user interface. Among other useful use cases.

The application enables users to test the extraction of entities from text and directly from PDF files. Figure 2 illustrates the main app screen. The app has two legal texts as examples presented in a text area, where users can make changes or type in a new text. The POC presents the possibility for users to upload their documents in PDF. The entities extraction is presented in visual markups on the text and in a table format, and it is possible to download the extractions in CSV format.

To allow users to work with real documents that are usually larger than the model's limit of 512 tokens, the strategy adopted was to split the document into sentences. For this, we used the Spacy library[8] along with the pt_core_news_sm Portuguese model. The aggregation strategy used to fuse tokens based on the model prediction into group entities follows the default schema ((A, B-TAG), (B, I-TAG), (C, I-TAG), (D, B-TAG2)

---

[5] https://huggingface.co/Luciano/bertimbau-base-lener_br.

[6] https://huggingface.co/Luciano/bertimbau-large-lener_br.

[7] https://share.streamlit.io/lucianozanuz/streamlit-lener_br/main.

[8] https://spacy.io/.

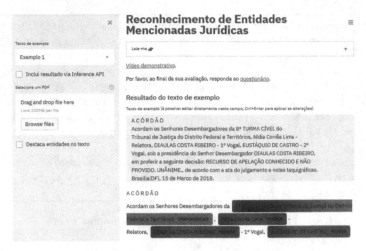

Fig. 2. Main prototype application interface.

(E, B-TAG2) will end up being [{"word": ABC, "entity": "TAG"}, {"word": "D", "entity": "TAG2"}, {"word": "E", "entity": "TAG2"}]). The scores are averaged first across tokens, and then the maximum label is applied, so words don't end up with different tags. This is necessary since subword tokenization was used.

4   Results and Discussion

This section presents the results of the trained models and the evaluation of the prototype application.

4.1   Fine-Tuned Legal NER

The results reported in this section are F1-score averages over five runs and the respective standard deviations obtained on the test set of the dataset. The metrics were computed using the seqeval library[9]. Seqeval is an entity-level evaluation metric, which means that a predicted entity is only considered correct if it matches the exactly chunk and tag. This is different from LeNER-Br [7] and BertBR [2] papers, where the metrics are based on the token-level evaluation.

Table 2 presents the comparison between the results obtained by our models and previous benchmarking [1] on the LeNER-Br dataset. LSTM + CRF is the original model of LeNER-Br paper [7], BERT-Multi and BERT-Acordaos are based on pre-trained BERT Multilingual, which is trained on Wikipedia, and the ELMO model is trained on the brWaC Corpus [19]. Both BERT-Acordaos and ELMo-Acordaos models have an additional step of fine-tuning on the intradomain Acordaos TCU corpus. Our models BERTimbau-Base and BERTimbau-Large are based on pre-trained BERTimbau [17], which is trained on the brWaC Corpus, with no additional intradomain fine-tuning.

---

[9] https://github.com/chakki-works/seqeval.

Table 2. Comparison between our models and previous benchmarking

Entity type	LSTM + CRF	BERT-Multi	BERT-Acordaos	ELMo-Acordaos	BERTimbau-Base	BERTimbau-Large
Person	80.83 ± 1.83	91.38 ± 0.87	93.66 ± 0.21	98.28 ± 0.41	96.91 ± 0.27	97.38 ± 0.44
Time	90.12 ± 2.28	94.43 ± 0.39	92.39 ± 1.82	93.77 ± 1.05	96.01 ± 0.10	96.04 ± 0.58
Location	64.81 ± 3.05	68.67 ± 1.89	65.78 ± 2.26	75.21 ± 1.13	75.39 ± 4.71	75.67 ± 3.18
Organization	84.37 ± 0.62	84.76 ± 0.57	86.43 ± 0.49	86.54 ± 0.74	86.21 ± 0.66	86.66 ± 1.17
Law	93.01 ± 0.61	93.40 ± 1.23	95.48 ± 0.47	88.08 ± 1.18	94.36 ± 1.10	95.90 ± 0.83
Legal case	81.22 ± 1.65	84.04 ± 0.63	83.26 ± 0.73	80.81 ± 1.14	87.32 ± 0.99	87.76 ± 0.87
Overall	85.42 ± 0.61	88.81 ± 0.29	89.39 ± 0.08	88.41 ± 0.41	90.62 ± 0.20	91.14 ± 0.39

As shown in the table, our models defined a new state-of-the-art for Portuguese Legal NER, achieving an overall F1-score of 91.14 on BERTimbau-Large and 90.62 on BERTimbau-Base. Therefore, it increases the previous benchmarking of BERT base version in 1.81 points, or 1.23 points if compared to the intradomain fine-tuned BERT-Acordaos. BERTimbau-Base obtained better results in all entities comparing to BERT-Multi, and only worst in Organization and Law if compared to BERT-Acordaos. Our BERTimbau-Large outperformed the BERT models in all entities, being only smaller than ELMo-Acordaos in entity Person.

The results show the importance of unlabeled data on the model quality. As illustrated in Table 3, brWac is considerably larger than Wikipedia and Acordaos-TCU. Our models, which are based exclusively on brWac corpus, obtained better results even not being fine-tuned in the legal intradomain Acordaos-TCU corpus. On the other hand, agreeing with [1], we believe that we could improve the results by adding a previous step of fine-tuning a general language model with an intradomain context-specific corpus, as it occurred with them.

Table 3. Basic statistics for the unlabeled Portuguese corpora

Corpus	Documents	Sentences	Tokens
brWaC	3,530k	145,000k	2,680mi
Wikipedia	934k	13,900k	1,400mi
Acordaos-TCU	298k	9,000k	912mi

4.2 Prototype Application

The application has been made available for about ninety users from the Brazilian Judiciary, including judges and office servers. The users evaluated the application and answered a questionnaire[10] based on the Technology Acceptance Model (TAM) [8] by Fred Davis, which is a dominant model in investigating factors affecting users' acceptance of the technology. Although TAM assesses perceived ease of use and usefulness, in this case we were interested only in the latter, regarding the goals of the POC.

---

[10] https://forms.gle/ZsFCGFasarkchR6SA.

The questionnaire had ten statements with a positive bias, in which users answered their level of agreement. The answers were standardized on a five-point Likert scale ("Strongly agree", "I agree", "I neither agree nor disagree", "I disagree" and "Strongly disagree"). The statements were: Q1. The use of AI applied to Law is useful for the Judiciary; Q2. AI can help automate and speed up legal proceedings; Q3. AI can be an important decision support tool for magistrates and civil servants; Q4. AI can be an important tool for extracting information from legal texts; Q5. NER in legal texts is useful for legal activity; Q6. The entities recognized by the trained model are relevant in the legal context; Q7. It would be useful to train models capable of extracting other entities, including those based on specific contexts, such as health; Q8. The resulting quality (accuracy) of the extractions was acceptable; Q9. It would be useful to assess whether models trained in specific contexts are more accurate in extracting entities from those contexts (for instance, if models trained with petition texts are more accurate in extracting entities from petition texts); Q10. It would be useful to automatically apply NER to the textual documents of legal proceedings, such as petitions from lawyers and transcripts of hearings, for extraction and structured storage of entities.

As shown in Fig. 3, the results were very encouraging. Twenty-eight users answered the questionnaire with no negative response (Strongly disagree or disagree). In the first four questions, we took the opportunity to verify the user's opinion about AI and Law in general. The results indicate that this group of people from Judiciary believe in AI as a useful and important tool for decision support and information extraction to increase automation and celerity of legal proceedings. The last six questions are specific about NER and the prototype application. The results show that Judiciary users perceived the usefulness of the NER application in the real-world.

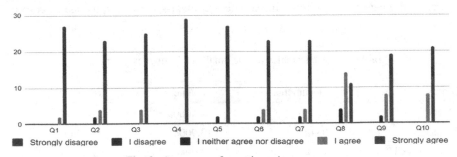

Fig. 3. Summary of questionnaire responses

The less positive rating was on Q8, about the accuracy of the extractions (Strongly agree: 10; I agree: 14; I neither agree nor disagree: 4), in which we received some interesting feedback from the users: "Nothing escapes!"; "The identification of Law and Location presented some confusion. The identification of people seemed correct in most cases."; "It was quite acceptable, only getting a little confused in Legal Case that sometimes separates the case numbers into several parts."; "Overall it works fine. But I could see that there is room for improvement. Long dates it identifies well but lacks in other date formats. I also noticed that it can't capture complete addresses as a single token.". User feedback is in line with our tests. Although the model obtained very good results in the dataset, the real-world documents are more diverse. Some results clearly reflect a probable underfitting caused by few samples used in training.

5 Conclusion

The Legal domain is an important field of research in Natural Language Processing. It handles a large number of textual documents and unstructured data, and the Named Entity Recognition task is a necessity. In recent years, transformers-based architectures, like BERT, are becoming the base of the new NLP systems. This paper presents the first fine-tuned BERT models trained exclusively on Brazilian Portuguese for Legal NER.

The models obtained new state-of-the-art on LeNER-Br dataset, achieving an overall F1-score of 91.14 in the large version and 90.62 in the base version, considering the seqeval entity-based evaluation metric. We also built a prototype application for Judiciary users to evaluate how the model performed with real documents. User evaluation results showed that the models were able to extract information with good quality. However, there could be gains with the training of models on a new corpus containing a greater amount and variety of legal texts, more adherent to the context where they would be applied, for instance, using text documents by lawyers. Both the models and the application were made publicly available to the community.

As future work, we intend to do new experiments on Legal NER, including a step of fine-tuning a BERT model with an intradomain corpus and making available new annotated datasets and trained models.

References

1. Bonifacio, L.H., Vilela, P.A., Lobato, G.R., Fernandes, E.R.: A study on the impact of intradomain finetuning of deep language models for legal named entity recognition in Portuguese. In: Cerri, R., Prati, R.C. (eds.) BRACIS 2020. LNCS (LNAI), vol. 12319, pp. 648–662. Springer, Cham (2020). https://doi.org/10.1007/978-3-030-61377-8_46
2. Ciurlino, V.H.: BertBR : a pretrained language model for law texts. Trabalho de Conclusão de Curso (Bacharelado em Engenharia Eletrônica). Universidade de Brasília (2021)
3. Devlin, J., et al.: BERT: Pre-training of deep bidirectional transformers for language understanding. In: Proceedings of the 2019 Conference of the North American Chapter of the Association for Computational Linguistics: Human Language Technologies, Vol. 1 (Long and Short Papers), pp. 4171–4186. Association for Computational Linguistics, Minneapolis, Minnesota (2019). https://doi.org/10.18653/v1/N19-1423
4. Dozier, C., Kondadadi, R., Light, M., Vachher, A., Veeramachaneni, S., Wudali, R.: Named entity recognition and resolution in legal text. In: Francesconi, E., Montemagni, S., Peters, W., Tiscornia, D. (eds.) Semantic Processing of Legal Texts. LNCS (LNAI), vol. 6036, pp. 27–43. Springer, Heidelberg (2010). https://doi.org/10.1007/978-3-642-12837-0_2
5. Freitas, C., et al.: Second HAREM: advancing the state of the art of named entity recognition in Portuguese. In: Proceedings of the Seventh International Conference on Language Resources and Evaluation (LREC'10). European Language Resources Association (ELRA), Valletta, Malta (2010)
6. Howard, J., Ruder, S.: Universal language model fine-tuning for text classification. In: Proceedings of the 56th Annual Meeting of the Association for Computational Linguistics (Volume 1: Long Papers). pp. 328–339. Association for Computational Linguistics, Melbourne, Australia (2018). https://doi.org/10.18653/v1/P18-1031

7. Luz de Araujo, P.H., de Campos, T.E., de Oliveira, R.R.R., Stauffer, M., Couto, S., Bermejo, P.: LeNER-Br: a dataset for named entity recognition in brazilian legal text. In: Villavicencio, A., et al. (eds.) PROPOR 2018. LNCS (LNAI), vol. 11122, pp. 313–323. Springer, Cham (2018). https://doi.org/10.1007/978-3-319-99722-3_32

8. Marangunić, N., Granić, A.: Technology acceptance model: a literature review from 1986 to 2013. Univ. Access Inf. Soc. **14**(1), 81–95 (2014). https://doi.org/10.1007/s10209-014-0348-1

9. Mendonça Júnior, C., et al.: Paramopama: a Brazilian-Portuguese corpus for named entity recognition. Presented at the XII Encontro Nacional de Inteligência Artificial e Computacional (ENIAC) (2015)

10. Menezes, D.S., et al.: Building a Massive Corpus for Named Entity Recognition using Free Open Data Sources. arXiv:190805758Cs (2019)

11. Mikolov, T., et al.: Efficient Estimation of Word Representations in Vector Space. arXiv:130 13781Cs (2013)

12. Mohit, B.: Named entity recognition. In: Zitouni, I. (ed.) Natural Language Processing of Semitic Languages. TANLP, pp. 221–245. Springer, Heidelberg (2014). https://doi.org/10.1007/978-3-642-45358-8_7

13. Nothman, J., et al.: Learning multilingual named entity recognition from Wikipedia. Artif. Intell. **194**, 151–175 (2013). https://doi.org/10.1016/j.artint.2012.03.006

14. Pennington, J., et al.: GloVe: global vectors for word representation. In: Proceedings of the 2014 Conference on Empirical Methods in Natural Language Processing (EMNLP). pp. 1532–1543. Association for Computational Linguistics, Doha, Qatar (2014). https://doi.org/10.3115/v1/D14-1162

15. Peters, M.E., et al.: Deep contextualized word representations. In: Proceedings of the 2018 Conference of the North American Chapter of the Association for Computational Linguistics: Human Language Technologies, Volume 1 (Long Papers). pp. 2227–2237. Association for Computational Linguistics, New Orleans, Louisiana (2018). https://doi.org/10.18653/v1/N18-1202

16. Santos, D., Cardoso, N.: A golden resource for named entity recognition in Portuguese. In: Vieira, R., Quaresma, P., Nunes, M.D.G.V., Mamede, N.J., Oliveira, C., Dias, M.C. (eds.) PROPOR 2006. LNCS (LNAI), vol. 3960, pp. 69–79. Springer, Heidelberg (2006). https://doi.org/10.1007/11751984_8

17. Souza, F., Nogueira, R., Lotufo, R.: BERTimbau: pretrained BERT models for Brazilian Portuguese. In: Cerri, R., Prati, R.C. (eds.) BRACIS 2020. LNCS (LNAI), vol. 12319, pp. 403–417. Springer, Cham (2020). https://doi.org/10.1007/978-3-030-61377-8_28

18. Vaswani, A., et al.: Attention is all you need. In: Proceedings of the 31st International Conference on Neural Information Processing Systems. pp. 6000–6010. Curran Associates Inc., Red Hook, NY, USA (2017)

19. Wagner Filho, J.A., et al.: The brWaC corpus: a new open resource for Brazilian Portuguese. In: Proceedings of the Eleventh International Conference on Language Resources and Evaluation (LREC 2018). European Language Resources Association (ELRA), Miyazaki, Japan (2018)

20. Willian Sousa, A., Fabro, M.: Iudicium textum dataset uma base de textos jurídicos para NLP. In: 2nd Dataset Showcase Workshop at SBBD (Brazilian Symposium on Databases). Fortaleza, Brazil (2019)
21. Wolf, T., et al.: Transformers: state-of-the-art natural language processing. In: Proceedings of the 2020 Conference on Empirical Methods in Natural Language Processing: System Demonstrations. pp. 38–45. Association for Computational Linguistics, Online (2020). https://doi.org/10.18653/v1/2020.emnlp-demos.6

Natural Language Processing Applications

Using Topic Modeling in Classification of Brazilian Lawsuits

André Aguiar[1](✉) , Raquel Silveira[2] , Vasco Furtado[1,3] , Vládia Pinheiro[1] , and João A. Monteiro Neto[1]

[1] University of Fortaleza, Fortaleza, Brazil
andrewescley@edu.unifor.br, {vasco,vladiacelia,
joaoneto}@unifor.br
[2] Federal Institute of Education, Science and Technology of Ceará, Fortaleza, Brazil
raquel_silveira@ifce.edu.br
[3] ETICE - Information Technology Company of Ceará, Fortaleza, Brazil

Abstract. Legal text processing is a challenging task for modeling approaches due to the peculiarities inherent to its features, such as long texts and their technical vocabulary. Topic modeling consists of discovering a semantic structure in the text. This paper investigates the application of topic modeling and the use of information about the legislation cited in identifying the subject of legal documents and evaluating its applicability in the classification of Brazilian lawsuits. The models were trained with a Golden Collection of 16 thousand initial petitions and indictments from the Court of Justice of the State of Ceará, in Brazil, whose lawsuits were classified in the five more representative National Council of Justice (CNJ) of Brazil classes - Common Civil Procedure, Execution of Extrajudicial Title, Criminal Action - Ordinary Procedure, Special Civil Court Procedure, and Tax Enforcement. The results obtained outperform the baseline, achieving 0.89 of F1 score (macro). Our interpretation is that the representation of the document through contextual embeddings generated by BERT, as well as the architecture of the model with bidirectional contexts, makes it possible to capture the specific context of the domain of legal documents. Thus, the use of the legislation mentioned in the representation of documents can improve the accuracy of the classification task.

Keywords: Topic modeling · Text classification · Legal domain · Brazilian lawsuits

1 Introduction

Topic Modeling has been successfully applied to Natural Language Processing (NLP) and it is frequently used when a huge textual collection cannot be reasonably read and classified by one person. Given a set of text documents, a topic model is applied to find out interpretable semantic concepts, or topics, present in documents. Topics represent the theme, or subject, of the text and can be used for the elaboration of high-level abstracts

© Springer Nature Switzerland AG 2022
V. Pinheiro et al. (Eds.): PROPOR 2022, LNAI 13208, pp. 233–242, 2022.
https://doi.org/10.1007/978-3-030-98305-5_22

considering a massive collection of documents, research documents of interest, and also for grouping similar documents [1].

An approach using topic modeling in the Brazilian legal framework can be explored. It is possible to notice the strong semantic context present in legal documents, which directs the studies to an applicability analysis and thus have a text classification with a desirable precision.

In this article we investigate stochastic topic modeling approaches for legal documents, using BERTopic [2], and we extend the semantic representation of the document with the cited laws in the body of the text.

7,103 legal processes were selected, distributed in 6 different classes, where the processes had a total of 16,668 petitions. Classes were defined as priority by the Court of Justice of the State of Ceará, in Brazil. We then evaluated the approach in the task of classifying lawsuits for these classes selected. The approach achieves results of 0.89 F1 Score, outperforming baselines that use supervised algorithms in classifying legal documents.

2 Related Works

Many works use Topic Modeling with satisfactory results in solving problems in the area of Natural Language Processing (NLP) and it is frequently used to help with the difficulty in textual classification of large collections, which would be read and classified by a person. Until now, the LDA is still the preferred model for modeling topics, inclusive em model legal corpora [3–5]. Despite its popularity, LDA has several weaknesses. Distributed representations of documents and words are gaining popularity due to their ability to capture the semantics of words and documents [1]. Pre-trained language models based on transformers, such as BERT [6] and its variants, have achieved state-of-the-art results in several downstream NLP tasks.

BERTopic is a topic modeling technique that leverages models based on transformers to achieve robust text representation, HDBSCAN to create dense and relevant clusters, and class-based TF-IDF (c-TF-IDF) to allow easy interpretable topics, while keeps important words in topic descriptions [2].

Text classification methods are investigated and applied with commercial or forensic goals [7–10]. However, in the legal domain, these methods have been under-explored, mainly in Brazilian lawsuits [11–14]. Since topics make it possible to group similar documents semantically, some strategies apply topic modeling in the classification of texts from generic domains [15, 16].

However, we are not aware of publications that use topic modeling in legal documents in classifying lawsuits. An approach using topic modeling in the Brazilian legal framework can be explored for classifying legal proceedings.

3 Corpus and Data Preparation

In this section, we will present the data used in the experiments collected in lawsuits from the Court of Justice of the State of Ceará, in Brazil, and the process of recognition of citations of legislation in legal documents.

3.1 Corpus and Golden Collection

The corpus was formed by 7,103 lawsuits totaling 16,668 petitions, the processes are divided into 6 different classes. The 6 classes selected were defined as priority by the Court of Justice of the State of Ceará, in Brazil. These classes express the type of lawsuits and were defined by the National Council of Justice (CNJ) of Brazil[1]. Table 1 shows the name of the lawsuit classes of the dataset and the number of the National Council of Justice of Brazil (informed in parentheses in the Class column), and the distribution of dataset lawsuits in the 6 classes.

Table 1. Distribution of lawsuits in legal classes.

Classes	Number of lawsuits	Number of petitions
Others (*)	1,486	3,286
Common Civil Procedure (17)	2,466	6,678
Execution of Extrajudicial Title (12154)	471	1,092
Criminal Action - Ordinary Procedure (283)	772	2,511
Special Civil Court Procedure (436)	824	1,637
Tax Enforcement (1116)	1,084	1,464
Total	7,103	16,668

* This class represents a mix of several classes.

3.2 Integration with the Brazilian Legal Knowledge Graph

Considering that legal documents have the characteristic of presenting legal citations and understanding that legislation can be important to classify lawsuits, we use a Named Entity Recognizer (NER) in order to identify the legislation mentioned in the text of the lawsuits. The NER we use was structured in the Stanford JavaNLP API Conditional Random Field model (CRF) Classifier and trained with the LeNER-BR dataset [17].

A knowledge graph with federal and regional legislation in the state of Ceará, Brazil was constructed, where the laws were taken from the Federal Government Legislation Portal, Legislative and Legal Information Network and the Legislative Assembly of Ceará. The legislation identified by NER in the legal texts that are present in the knowledge graph were validated as a "legislation" entity.

4 Topic Modeling in Legal Documents

At its most basic level, topic modeling aims to group a set of documents according to contextual similarity and identify the words that represent the main theme of each group of documents.

---

[1] https://www.cnj.jus.br/sgt/consulta_publica_classes.php.

4.1 Pre-processing

Our data are defined in terms of documents $D = \{d_1, d_2, ..., d_N\}$. Initially, each document is pre-processed, in order to form the set of words that represent the document $W_{di} = \{w_1, w_2, ..., w_n\}$, following the steps: (P1) tokenization (separating the text into words), (P2) lowercasing, (P3) PoS tagging, (P4) PoS tagging filter (removing words whose PoS tagging is neither verb or noun) (P5) lemmatization[2] (P6) non-ASCII character removal and (P7) addition of the cited legislation. In the case of legal documents, citations to pre-existing laws are as important as the content of the document itself. In this way, in step P7, for each document d, we check if it contains a citation for Brazilian legislation (according to the procedure described in Sect. 3.2). If it contains, we add the legislation identification to the set of words of the document.

4.2 Topic Generation

The approach presented in this paper identifies the document topics using BERTopic [2], a topic modeling technique that takes advantage of BERT embeddings [6], dimensionality reduction and clustering algorithms, as well as a class-based TF-IDF to create dense clusters, allowing interpretable topics from the extraction of the most important words from the clusters. In the following, we explain the topic modeling process, as well as some of the specific features of BERTopic.

We convert the elements of the sets of words that represent each document in contextualized numerical vector representations, $EMB_D = \{emb_{d1}, emb_{d2}, ..., emb_{dN}\}$. We used the Sentence Transformer [18] with the BERTimbau model [2] (an extended model of Bidirectional Encoder Representations from Transformers (BERT) [6] pre-trained specifically for the portuguese language) for this purpose, as it extracts different embeddings based on the context of the legal texts. In this way, we obtain the vector representation of 768 units (according architecture BERTimbau), emb_{di}, for each W_{di}, where $d_i \in D$.

Before using a clustering algorithm, we first need to reduce the dimensionality of the embeddings of the documents, since many clustering algorithms deal poorly with the high dimensionality. We used Uniform Manifold Approximation and Projection (UMAP) [19] and reduced the dimensionality to 5. UMAP has several hyperparameters that determine how it performs the dimension reduction. Possibly the most important parameter is the number of nearest neighbors. We set the number of nearest neighbors to 15.

After having reduced the dimensionality of the embeddings of the documents, we can cluster them. The goal of density-based clustering is to find areas of highly similar embeddings in the semantic space, which indicate an underlying topic. We used Hierarchical Density-Based Spatial Clustering of Applications with Noise (HDBSCAN) [20] to find dense areas of embeddings without forcing data points into clusters, as we consider them outliers. The number of clusters has not been defined, while the minimum size of documents in each cluster has been set to 5. In this way, the algorithm will try

---

[2] The lemmatization process and PoS tagging were based on what is available in the spaCy library for Portuguese language (https://spacy.io/).

to find the ideal number of clusters, grouping similar documents, whose clusters must represent the topics of the documents.

Then, we identified a set of words that represent the content of each cluster. For this, a variant of the TF-IDF (Term Frequency - Inverse Document Frequency) is structured in clusters, named c-TF-IDF, calculated according to Eq. (1) below:

$$c - TF - IDF = \frac{f_i}{wd_i} \times log \frac{m}{\sum_j^n f_j},$$ (1)

where the frequency of each word f is extracted from each cluster i and divided by the total number of words w_d of cluster i. This action can be seen as a way of normalizing the frequency of words in the cluster. Then the number of clusters m is divided by the total frequency of the word f across all clusters.

To create a topic representation, we obtain the top-10 most representative words of each topic, $t_i = \{w_{t1}, w_{t2}, ..., w_{t10}\}$, $ti \in T$, where t_i is one of the topics generated by the approach and T is the set of all topics. The most representative words of each topic are identified based on their scores in c-TF-IDF.

4.3 Converting Topics to Feature Vectors

After grouping similar documents and identifying the most representative words for each topic, we characterize each document from a vector of features using the topic distribution and we use this vector as input to the classification algorithm, in order to evaluate the presented topic approach in this paper in the task of classifying lawsuits.

We represent a lawsuit as a feature vector structured in the topics. In other words, given a vocabulary $V = \{w_1, w_2, ..., w_k\}$ formed by all the most representative words of the T topics, we represent each lawsuit d_i as a length-$|V|$ vector $F(d_i)$, conforme a equação (2):

$$F(d_i)_j = prob(t_x|d_i) * PWI(d_i, w_j), \text{ with } t_x \in T, j = 0 \text{ to } |V| - 1 \text{ and } w_j \in V,$$ (2)

where the word w_j is one of the most representative words of the topic t_x, $prob(t_x|d_i)$ sents the probability of the document d_i belonging to the topic t_x and $PWI(d_i, w_j)$ is the probability-weighted amount of information (PWI) d_i and w_j contribute to the total amount of information, proposed in [1], calculated according to Eq. (3):

$$PWI(d_i, w_j) = P(d_i, w_j) \times log(\frac{P(d_i, w_j)}{P(d_i)P(w_j)})$$ (3)

5 Experiments

The approach presented in this paper for modeling topics in legal documents was evaluated in the task of classifying legal cases. In this section, initially, we define the scenarios and algorithms used in the experiments for classifying lawsuits. Then, we present and discuss the results achieved.

5.1 Experimental Setup

Lawsuit classification experiments were conducted in different scenarios, which include two baseline models proposed by [21].

Baseline 1 - Embeddings of the Lawsuit/Case Text (S1). In this scenario proposed by [21], the lawsuit is represented by the embedding of the lawsuit text, generated from the pre-trained model BERTimbau [2] (a pre-trained model BERT for Brazilian Portuguese).

Baseline 2 - Embeddings of the Lawsuit and Topics (S2). In this scenario proposed by [21], the LDA runs on corpus D to find 6 topics. To each document, the top-10 words more representative to the lawsuit's topic are chosen. Each lawsuit is represented by: (i) embedding of the lawsuit text, generated according to S1, and (ii) bag-of-words with the word distribution of the topics.

Embeddings of Topics of the Lawsuit (S3). Initially, we apply the pre-processing steps (P1) to (P6) described in Sect. 4.1. After, the documents are represented following the steps described in Sects. 4.2 and 4.3.

Embeddings of Topics of the Lawsuit With Cited Laws (S4). Initially, we apply the pre-processing steps (P1) to (P7) described in Sect. 4.1. Step (P7) was included to evaluate our hypothesis that the laws are cited as important as the text of the lawsuit. After, the documents are represented followings the steps described in Sects. 4.2 and 4.3.

5.2 Models

We train the models on split-of-the-data training in the scenarios presented in Sect. 4.1 as a multiclass classification task, using the following parameters:

Bidirectional Encoder Representations from Transformers (BERT). We use this model for scenario (S1), as proposed by [21]. Given the specifics of the BERT's original architecture, this model was trained only in scenario (S1). We used the fine-tuning-based approach with the pre-trained model BERTimbau [3], 4 epochs and batch size of 4 samples for the classification task. For the optimizer, we used the ADAM optimizer with a learning rate of $1e-5$.

Extreme Gradient Boosting (XGBoost). We use this model for scenarios (S2) (as proposed by [21]), (S3) and (S4). We applied the XGBoost algorithm using XGBoost Classifier package[3]. We trained 1,000 trees with a maximum depth of 4 and a learning rate of 0.1.

---

[3] https://xgboost.readthedocs.io/en/latest/python/python_api.html.

5.3 Experimental Results and Analysis

The evaluation of topic modeling quality involves quantifying how good is the final model generated given the observed data. Table 2 shows the top-10 representative words (according to c-TF-IDF described in Sect. 4.2) extracted by the topic modeling approach presented in this paper for a subset of the dataset with ten legal documents of different thematic. The words listed for each topic appear in descending order, from the highest to least c-TF-IDF.

Table 2. Topics modeled to legal documents.

ID	Topics
t1	Ministério Público, maconha, Promotoria Justiça, polícia, denunciar, promotoria, prisão, Lei 11.343 de 23/08/2006, tráfico, drogas
t2	fornecimento, tratamento, medicamentar, direito saúde, doença, leito, saúde, leito UTI, UTI, saúde
t3	Lei 8.078 de 11/09/1990, abusividade, contrato, taxar juro, capitalização juro, comissão permanência, contratar, taxar, juro, capitalização
t4	Fortaleza, Lei 13.105 de 16/03/2015, contratar, consumidor, justiça, ação, dever, lei, Ceará, direito
t5	membro GAECO, combate organizações, especial combate organizações, atuação especial, especial combate, atuação especial combate, criminosas, organizações criminosas, organizações, GAECO

One way to evaluate topic modeling is to analyze how well the topics describe the documents. This assessment measures how informative the topics are to a user. Thus, when inspecting the topic model, we can confirm that some topics provide information about the document, that is, the words of the topic associated to the document are semantically related to the thematic of that legal document, making it possible to identify the subject of the document. For example, the words "Ministério Público, maconha, Promotoria Justiça, polícia, denunciar, promotoria, prisão, Lei 11.343 de 23/08/2006, tráfico, drogas" allow us to summarize the subject of "drug traffic". This example of a summary allows a user to identify the subject related to certain legal matters or simply summarize the content of a legal document by analyzing the topic of the document.

We assess the quality of the topic model, using them in the representation of legal documents and applying them to the task of classifying lawsuits. To carry out the experiments in the scenarios and models described in Sects. 4.1 and 4.2, we divided the dataset into 85% for the train set and 15% for the test set. Table 3 shows the performance of each experiment scenario, in terms of F1 score (macro) for the test set.

The S4 scenario that includes the laws mentioned in the documents in the pre-processing stage and uses the embeddings generated by the topic model outperforms the other scenarios, achieving the best result of 0.89 of F1 score (macro). Legal documents have specific characteristics such as long documents, specialized vocabulary, formal syntax, semantics based on a broad specific domain of knowledge, and citations to laws.

Table 3. Results in terms of Precision, Recall and F1 Score macro for lawsuit classification.

Experiments scenario	Precision	Recall	F1 score
S1 (Baseline - Embeddings of the Lawsuit + BERT)	0.86	0.88	0.87
S2 (Baseline - Embeddings of the Lawsuit and Topics + XGBoost)	0.81	0.75	0.77
S3 (Embeddings of Topics of the Lawsuit + XGBoost)	0.87	0.88	0.88
S4 (Embeddings of Topics of the Lawsuit With Cited Laws + XGBoost)	0.89	0.88	**0.89**

Our interpretation is that (i) the legislation cited informs about the class, helping to classify the lawsuits, and (ii) the topics may suggest the main theme of the document, making it possible, therefore, to help infer the class of lawsuits.

The model presented in this paper outperforms baselines. Compared with S1, our interpretation is that topics capture the most representative words of the document and therefore represent the documents from the topics reducing the size of the text, but keeping only the excerpts that present reasons for the content of the lawsuit, which is therefore relevant for the classification of lawsuits. Compared with S2, our interpretation is that the topic model generated from BERTopic allows the representation of the document through contextual embeddings generated by BERT, as well as the architecture of the model with bidirectional contexts, makes it possible to capture the specific context of the domain of legal documents.

The approach presented in this paper offers an attractive way to automate the summary of legal documents quickly. It can be useful when we have a large amount of text data and we want to identify the subject of a particular legal document. This strategy can be used to enhance the task of classifying legal proceedings.

6   Conclusions

In this paper we propose the use of BERTopic to build thematic models of legal documents and use this structure together with the legislation cited in the legal documents for classifying legal texts using a dataset of lawsuits from the Court of Justice of the State of Ceará, in Brazil.

The legal text has specific characteristics, in this way, we represent the text contextually from the BERTimbau (pre-trained model for Brazilian Portuguese) and provide the Brazilian laws mentioned in the lawsuits. We argue that the contextual representation of the text and the citation to legislation help to identify the classes of a lawsuit.

In the future, we intend to investigate other features to characterize the lawsuits from topics and quantitatively evaluate the interpretability and coherence of the topics and to compare the proposed approach with other approaches of the state of the art. We also intend to investigate the accuracy in the application of topic modeling with other features to classify lawsuits.

References

1. Angelov, D.: Top2Vec: Distributed Representations of Topics. arXiv:2008.09470v1 (2020)
2. Grootendorst, M.: BERTopic: leveraging BERT and c-TF-IDF to create easily interpretable topics (2020). https://doi.org/10.5281/zenodo.4381785
3. Remmits, Y.: Finding the Topics of Case Law: Latent Dirichlet Allocation on Supreme Court Decisions, Thesis. Radboad Universiteit (2017)
4. Araújo, P.H.L., Campos, T.: Topic Modelling Brazilian Supreme Court Lawsuits. JURI SAYS, vol. 113 (2020)
5. Neill, J.O., Robin, C., Brien, L.O., Buitelaar, P.: An Analysis of Topic Modelling for Legislative Texts. ASAIL 2017, London, UK (2017)
6. Devlin, J., Chang, Ming-Wei, Lee, K., Toutanova, K.: BERT: pre-training of deep bidirectional transformers for language understanding. In: Proceedings of the 2019 Conference of the North American Chapter of the Association for Computational Linguistics: Human Language Technologies, Volume 1 (Long and Short Papers), pages 4171–4186, Minneapolis, Minnesota. Association for Computational Linguistics (2019)
7. Sumner, C., Byers, A., Boochever, R., Park, G.J.: Predicting dark triad personality traits from Twitter usage and a linguistic analysis of Tweets. In: Proceedings of ICMLA (2012). https://doi.org/10.1109/ICMLA.2012.218
8. Pérez-Rosas, V., Mihalcea, R.: Experiments in open domain deception detection. In: Màrquez, L., Callison-Burch, C., Su, J., Pighin, D., Marton, Y. (eds.) Proceedings of EMNLP. Association for Computational Linguistics (2015). http://aclweb.org/anthology/D/D15/D15-1133.pdf
9. Pinheiro, V., Pequeno, T., Furtado, V., Nogucira, D.: Information extraction from text based on semantic inferentialism. In: Andreasen, T., Yager, R.R., Bulskov, H., Christiansen, H., Larsen, H.L. (eds.) FQAS 2009. LNCS (LNAI), vol. 5822, pp. 333–344. Springer, Heidelberg (2009). https://doi.org/10.1007/978-3-642-04957-6_29
10. Justin, C., Cristian, D.-N.-M., Jure, L.: Anti-social behavior in online discussion communities. In: Proceedings of ICWSM (2015)
11. Katz, D.M., Bommarito, I.I., Michael, J.I., Blackman, J.: Predicting the Behavior of the Supreme Court of the United States. A General Approach. arXiv:1407.6333 (2014)
12. Aletras, N., Tsarapatsanis, D., Preotiuc-Pietro, D., Lampos, V.: Predicting judicial decisions of the european court of human rights: a natural language processing perspective. PeerJ Comput. Sci. 10 (2016)
13. Sulea, O. M., Zampieri, M., Vela, M., vanGenabith, J.: Predicting the law area and decisions of French Supreme Court cases. In: Proceedings of the International Conference Recent Advances in Natural Language Processing, RANLP, pp. 716–722. INCOMA Ltd. (2017)
14. Araújo, P.H.L., Campos, T.E., Braz, F.A., Silva, N.C.: VICTOR: a dataset for Brazilian legal documents classification. In: Proceedings of the 12th Conference on Language Resources and Evaluation (LREC 2020), pp. 1449–1458. Marseille (2020)
15. Neogi, P.P.G., Das, A.K., Goswami, S., Mustafi, J.: Topic modeling for text classification. In: Mandal, J.K., Bhattacharya, D. (eds.) Emerging Technology in Modelling and Graphics. AISC, vol. 937, pp. 395–407. Springer, Singapore (2020). https://doi.org/10.1007/978-981-13-7403-6_36
16. Ge, J., Lin, S., Fang, Y.: A Text classification algorithm based on topic model and convolutional neural network. J. Phys.: Conf. Ser. 1748, 032036 (2021). https://doi.org/10.1088/1742-6596/1748/3/032036
17. Luz de Araujo, P.H., de Campos, T.E., de Oliveira, R.R.R., Stauffer, M., Couto, S., Bermejo, P.: LeNER-Br: a dataset for named entity recognition in brazilian legal text. In: Villavicencio, A., et al. (eds.) PROPOR 2018. LNCS (LNAI), vol. 11122, pp. 313–323. Springer, Cham (2018). https://doi.org/10.1007/978-3-319-99722-3_32

18. Reimers, N., Gurevych, I.: Sentence-BERT: Sentence Embeddings using Siamese BERT-Networks (2019). https://arxiv.org/pdf/1908.10084.pdf
19. McInnes, L., Healy, J.: UMAP: Uniform manifold approximation and projection for dimension reduction, J. Open Source Softw. **3**(29), 861 (2018). arXiv:1802.03426 (2018)
20. McInnes, L., Healy, J., Astels, S.: hdbscan: hierarchical density based clustering. J. Open Source Softw. **2**(11), 205 (2017). https://doi.org/10.21105/joss.00205
21. Aguiar, A., Silveira, R., Pinheiro, V., Furtado, V., Neto, J.A.: Text classification in legal documents extracted from lawsuits in brazilian courts. In: Britto, A., Valdivia Delgado, K. (eds.) BRACIS 2021. LNCS (LNAI), vol. 13074, pp. 586–600. Springer, Cham (2021). https://doi.org/10.1007/978-3-030-91699-2_40

PortNOIE: A Neural Framework for Open Information Extraction for the Portuguese Language

Bruno Cabral[✉][iD], Marlo Souza[iD], and Daniela Barreiro Claro[iD]

FORMAS Research Group, Federal University of Bahia, Salvador, Brazil
{bruno.cabral,msouza,dclaro}@ufba.br

Abstract. Open Information Extraction (OpenIE) is the task of extracting structured information from text. Recent advances in applying Deep Learning to OpenIE tasks have improved the state of the art for the task, although few works have been produced for languages other than English. In this work, we propose PortNOIE, a neural framework for open information extraction for the Portuguese language. We evaluate our method on a manually annotated corpus of Open IE extractions, obtaining better performance than the current state of the art for OpenIE for Portuguese, both based on rule-based approaches or neural methods.

Keywords: Open Information Extraction · OpenIE · Portuguese

1 Introduction

With the increasing digitalization of processes, a huge and growing amount of data is generated every day in various fields. However, it is not always possible to use this data as it is often unstructured data in the form of natural language texts, such as books, blogs, articles, etc.

We need tools that help extract information from texts efficiently and reliably. Open Information Extraction (OpenIE) as introduced by Banko et al. [3], is a promising approach to this problem, as it aims at extracting knowledge from large collections of text documents regardless of the domain.

By extracting information, we mean that these systems generate a structured representation of the information in the original documents, usually in the form of relational tuples, such as (arg_1, rel, arg_2), where arg_1 and arg_2 are the discourse entities, usually described by noun phrases, and rel is a textual descriptor of the semantic relation between arg_1 and arg_2. For example, consider the sentence *"Peter studies Math."* An OpenIE system can produce valid extractions such as *(Peter, studies, Math)*.

Since 2007, several OpenIE methods have been proposed for many different languages [3,12,15], mostly based on manually-crafted rules. However, recent

V. Pinheiro et al. (Eds.): PROPOR 2022, LNAI 13208, pp. 243–255, 2022.
https://doi.org/10.1007/978-3-030-98305-5_23

innovations in applying Deep Learning techniques to Natural Language Processing (NLP) tasks have led to excellent results on various NLP tasks. This is also true for OpenIE, where neural networks have recently been used for supervised OpenIE [7,34,35], achieving state-of-the-art results for English. For the Portuguese language, the only neural-based OpenIE extractor available in the literature, that we are aware, is Multi2OIE [29], a multilingual OpenIE extractor trained with an English dataset translated into other languages. It is important evaluate whether such improvements could also improve Portuguese OpenIE systems by using Deep Learning methods

In this work, we analyze the application of Deep Learning specifically for Portuguese Open Information Extraction. The main contributions of this work are (i) the introduction the problem and existing works, and analysis of the challenges of using existing neural architectures for Portuguese. (ii) the proposition of PortNOIE, a method of neural open information extraction for the Portuguese language (iii) an open source neural framework for open information extraction (OpenIE) with a modular architecture that allows rapid experimentation and (iv) an empirical evaluation of PortNOIE with the actual state of art Portuguese systems on several datasets.

This article is organized as follows: Sect. 2 presents some related work. Section 3 describes our approach and methodology. Section 4 shows our experiments, results, and discussions. Finally, Sect. 5 concludes our paper.

2   Related Work

Early work on OpenIE for the Portuguese language employ manually-crafted rules based on either dependency [12], or shallow syntactic information and lexical constraints [27]. Later works such as [11] and [15,25] improve this strategy by using state-of-the-art dependency parsing technology for the Portuguese language and linguistically inspired extraction rules, achieving high results on the task [6].

While machine learning techniques have been used within OpenIE methods, both for teach English [10] and Portuguese languages [30–32], they are mainly used as a post-processing technique to increase the quality of the extractions. Work focused on machine learning techniques to extract relations for Portuguese has only recently appeared in the literature.

In this latter line, the work of de Abreu and Vieira [1] model the problem of identifying relations between named entities in an organizational domain as a sequence labeling problem and apply a Conditional Random Fields classifier to perform the extraction.

Recently, new machine learning-based approaches for OpenIE [7,34,35] have been proposed, leading to a new generation of OpenIE systems. While these systems represent the state-of-the-art, their focus on the English language and the need for annotated data make it hard to generalize their results to other languages.

Works such as that of [7] employ machine translation machinery by modeling OpenIE as a sequence-to-sequence learning problem and training a neural model over a corpus of examples. Other work such as that of Stanovsky et al. [34], on the other hand, model OpenIE as a sequence labeling problem, employing sequence classification techniques such as a Recursive Neural Networks (RNN) architecture to perform OpenIE for English. Considering the limitations in modeling this task, Shengbin and Yang [21] introduced a tagging scheme to consider multiple overlapping relation triples.

From 2020, several works, such as [18,19,29] start to use Transformer architectures directly or using BERT embedding [9] to construct neural-based OpenIE systems. For example, Multi2OIE [29] used multilingual BERT for feature embedding and a multi-head attention block for argument extraction.

For the Portuguese language, due to the lack of resources for this task, new data-oriented methods have been proposed as cross-lingual approaches. The authors in [4,5] employ multilingual language models to perform quality assessment and classification of OpenIE extractions. Similarly, Multi2OIE [29] used M-BERT for feature embedding and as a predicate extractor, and used Multihead attention blocks for argument extraction. Their system was able to create extractors for multiple languages (English, Portuguese and Spanish). As far as we know, it was the first Deep Learning extractor for Portuguese. However, it used an English dataset that was automatically translated into Portuguese.

In this paper, we have proposed a method called PortNOIE. We compared it with the existing state-of-the-art for Portuguese, namely DptOIE, Linguakit [13] - a new implementation of ArgOE - and Multi2OIE, a method that also uses Deep Learning. Our proposed method uses a set of techniques similar to those of [34], as a sequence learning problem with a combination of modifications and improvements for Portuguese.

3 PortNOIE

3.1 Problem Definition

Let $X = \langle x_1, x_2, \cdots, x_n \rangle$ be a sentence composed of tokens x_i, an Open IE triple extractor is a function that maps X into a set $Y = \langle y_1, y_2, \cdots, y_j \rangle$ as a set of tuples $y\_i = \langle rel_i, arg1_i, arg2_i, \cdots, argn_i \rangle$, which describe the information expressed in sentence X.

In this work, we consider that the tuples are in the format of $y = \langle arg_1, rel, arg_2 \rangle$, where $arg1$ and $arg2$ are noun phrases, formed from tokens in X, and rel is a descriptor of a relation holding between arg_1 and arg_2. We do not consider extractions describing n-nary relations or composed of tokens that are not present in the input sentence. These types of extractions, however, are present in our dataset and are considered in our evaluation.

We consider the OpenIE problem as a sequence labeling task, so elements in Y are sequences of BIO [28] tags, that correspond to tokens. Given X and Y, the OpenIE problem consists of labeling the elements of Y by assigning the BIO [28] tags to the tokens in X. However, unlike the method proposed in Stanovsky et al. [34], which uses a custom BIO tagging scheme to extract multiple tuples from a single sentence, we use a regular BIO scheme with the following tagset: $[ARG1, REL, ARG2]$. We have chosen to simplify the tagset and treat the multiple extraction problem as a separate problem. We will return to this problem later when we introduce the Variant Generation module.

3.2   Architecture

Our general architecture and classifier are illustrated in Fig. 1. It is constituted of the following components: a preprocessing step, a tokenizer, a feature extraction module, a variant generator, and an encoder-decoder architecture that takes the features produced as input and decodes it to produce a triple. Further, we discuss these components in more detail.

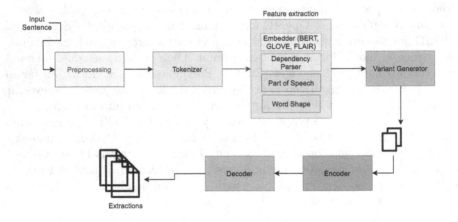

Fig. 1. Architecture overview

The **Preprocessing** module converts a sentence to a standard format. We remove duplicate punctuation and spaces at the end and perform expansion of preposition and determiner contractions, common in Portuguese, using a manually created table. For example, the Portuguese contraction '*num*' is split into preposition+article '*em um*'. This is necessary because different parts of a token can occur in different parts of an extraction. The **Tokenization** step splits the sentence into tokens.

The **Feature Extraction** component takes a sequence of tokens as input and outputs a vector of features describing the information about each token. It facilitates the creation and use of new features and performs all the necessary steps to transform any type of feature into a vector representation, such as learnable embedding or one-hot encoding. We use a total of four features: *Part-of-speech (POS)*, *Dependency tree categories* (such as nominal subject or adverbial modifier), *Word shape* (a condensed representation of the word to capture orthographic features, for example, the word "1FastFox!" would be represented as $dXx!$) and vector representation of the word, based on language models such as GloVe [26], Flair [2] and BERT [9]).

The **Variant Generation** component performs multiple extractions from a single sentence. The first step identifies all tokens marked as verbs in POS using the features from the previous step and uses them as predicate candidates. Second, we combine consecutive tokens that are marked as predicates into a single example, e.g., the sentence "Apple está querendo comprar uma startup" (*Apple wants to buy a startup*) in our POS would be tagged: "PROPN AUX VERB VERB DET NOUN". The words "está querendo" are considered as a single predicate, since the POS tagged them as verbs (namely, AUX as an auxiliary verb and VERB).

In the last step, we create a new extraction candidate for each predicate and check if it fits the binary $\langle arg_1, rel, arg_2 \rangle$ structure. This process is illustrated in Fig. 2. In the sentence "Her name is Joanna and she likes to dance", we identify as candidates : 'is' (AUX), 'likes' (VERB), and 'dance' (VERB). The token 'dance' is discarded because the predicate is the last word of the sentence.

All these candidates are considered as inputs to our model and the model will generate a BIO tag for each token in the input. The chosen VERB/AUX will not necessarily be part of the extraction.

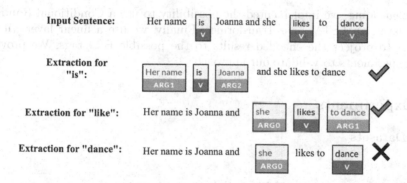

Fig. 2. Example of extractions for a sentence. Here, we identify the predicate candidates (blue boxes) and then generate a candidate triple ($<arg_1$, arg_2, $rel>$) for each verb. If the extraction does not contain all the constituent elements, it is considered an invalid extraction. (Color figure online)

During the training phase, all possible candidates are generated and matched with the corresponding triple in the training set. If there is no match, the variant is included in the training set as a negative example. This can also be considered as a way of augmenting the dataset. During prediction, all candidates are used and duplicate matches are merged.

This method started as an adaptation of Stanovsky et al. [34] to the Portuguese language, but it has greatly departed from it and became a new implementation with some important differences. Unlike us, in their work the authors introduced a custom BIO tagging scheme, do not perform verb merging, do not use negative examples in training, and use a different representation for this problem (the feature representation for each word is concatenated with the predicate representations, i.e. a single word). These differences emerged during the design and evaluation process, where we tried different approaches to maximize performance for Portuguese.

The last modules, **Encoder** and **Decoder**, employ the Semantic Role Labeling Encoder by He et al. [17] as a basis, as it has a similar requirement for the use of additional features and the output constraints that reject sequences that do not produce valid BIO transitions. The encoder block is given a dense vector representing the features from the previous module. For each candidate predicate p we obtain the feature vector for each word w_i in the sentence by concatenating the features generated for each extraction with predicate p_vec represented as a one-hot vector as follows:

$$
\begin{aligned}
F(w_i, p\_vec) = &\ Word\_Embedding(w_i) \oplus .Pos\_tag\_Embedding(w_i) \\
&\oplus Dependency\_tag\_Embedding(Emb\_rel) \\
&\oplus Word\_Shape\_Embedding(w_i) \oplus p\_vec
\end{aligned}
$$

$$(1)$$

For encoding, we implemented the possibility to use a Conditional Random Fields layer, an LSTM or a Transformer. Finally, we use a linear layer with a softmax to project the encoded results to the possible BIO tags. We provide some experiments to validate our approach.

4   Experiments

4.1   Datasets

Table 1. Dataset statistics

	# Sentences	# Extractions
Gamalho	103	346
Pragmatic	400	485
PUD 200	200	337
PUD 100	100	136

We use four different datasets: **Pragmatic**, a human annotated dataset from a news corpus [31]; **Gamalho**, a set of relations extracted from Portuguese texts by five different Open IE systems, and marked as valid by human judges [8,11]; **PUD 100 and PUD 200**, a set of sentences from news sources and Wikipedia of the Portuguese part of the Parallel Universal Dependencies (PUD) corpus [24] manually annotated by several academic OpenIE experts from the FORMAS

Research Group[1]. The PUD 100 is constituted by 100 sentences obtained by multiple rounds of annotation and reaching consensus among the annotators and PUD 200 a set of 200 sentences annotated in one round. Dataset statistics are summarized in Table 1.

4.2   Experimental Design

Our framework was developed using the AllenNLP [14] Framework with the PyTorch[2] Framework. Our tokenizer, part-of-speech, and dependency tagger uses the SpaCy[3] framework with the *pt_core_news_lg* model. For GloVe embeddings, we have NILC 300-dimensions [16], for Flair embeddings we trained a 1024-dimension model, and for BERT we used the BERTimbau large [33], both trained using the same corpus. We used DptOIE, Linguakit, and Multi2OIE as comparison systems. All systems used the default parameters, and Multi2OIE was trained with 300 epochs and used the same datasets as this work. To select the hyperparameters of the models, we performed a grid search with some possible values. We use three different NN modules for encoding embedded sequences: Transformers (with XTransfomer [36]), Bi-LSTM [20] and SRU++ [23].

For training, we used two strategies. We ran one set of tests with **PUD 100** as the test dataset and the others as training, and another set of tests with **Gamalho** as the test dataset and the others as training. We decided against the use of k-fold cross-validation because we found during dataset creation that the OpenIE task is complex and that there is no consensus on the representation of information between annotators, which means that such corpora may not agree with each other on what they consider to be a valid relation. By separating two datasets created in different but consistent ways, we were able to better assess the predictive ability of the extractor

Our evaluation used precision (P), recall (R), and the F1 measure as quality measures for our extractor. We adapted the evaluation proposed by Stanovsky et al. [34] as it has been widely used in the literature [22,29]. However, we introduced a new evaluation strategy called **Perfect match**. By default, their benchmark uses a scoring method that simply considers if there is at least a 50% match between tokens in triples, regardless of order, called **Lexical match**. Perfect match takes into account that the strings are identical after removing punctuation.

Hyper Parameter Search. We performed a grid search to determine the best hyperparameters for the model and examined four hyperparameters with 54 possible combinations:

- **Encoder** - [LSTM, SRUPP and Transformer]
- **Embedding dimension** - [384, 512, 768]
- **Number of layers** - [2, 3]
- **Word embedding** - [GloVe, BERT, Flair]

---

[1] http://formas.ufba.br/.

[2] https://pytorch.org/.

[3] https://spacy.io/.

Table 2. Metrics scores for a hyper-parameter search testing different combinations of encoders and embeddings

Encoders - Using BERT	AUC	Precision	Recall	F1
SRUPP (2 layers)	0.0752	0.2345	0.1218	0.1603
LSTM (3 layers)	**0.1150**	**0.3292**	**0.1730**	**0.2269**
Transformer (3 layers)	0.0593	0.1568	0.1026	0.1240
Embeddings - Using LSTM				
GLOVE - 300 dimensions	0.0807	0.1447	0.1410	0.1428
FLAIR - 1024 dimensions	0.0817	0.2142	0.1346	0.1653
BERT - Large	**0.1150**	**0.3292**	**0.1730**	**0.2269**

Table 2 shows the results for the best encoder tested and the best word embedding, along with the average precision, recall, and F1 measure. The best combination was a LSTM with a hidden size of 384 and 3 layers using the Portuguese BERT Large.

4.3   Results

For the first comparison, the **PUD 100** was used as the test dataset and the others as the training dataset using Perfect Match scoring. Table 3 summarizes the results of our comparative study, with the highest scores highlighted in bold. The PortNOIE performed best on all metrics, with an F1 of 0.22, followed by the Multi2OIE with an F1 of 0.05. These results are visually represented in Fig. 3(a).

Table 3. Perfect Match scores using the dataset Pud 100

	AUC	Precision	Recall	F1
DPTOIE	0.0133	0.0560	0.0252	0.0347
Linguakit	0.0098	0.0263	0.0192	0.0222
Multi2OIE	0.0238	0.0630	0.0448	0.0524
PortNOIE	**0.1150**	**0.3292**	**0.1730**	**0.2268**

The results of the second comparison are shown in Table 4. In this comparison, we used the **Gamalho** as the test dataset and all others as the training dataset. In this comparison, we also used the Lexical Match since it is a less strict metric. In this comparison, PortNOIE was also the best performing system, followed by Mult2OIE. In contrast to the previous test, the Linguakit performed better than DPTOIE. Figure 3(b) shows the results with Perfect Match and Lexical Match.

Table 4. Metrics scores using lexical match and Perfect Match against Gamalho dataset

	Lexical match				Perfect match			
	AUC	Precision	Recall	F1	AUC	Precision	Recall	F1
DPTOIE	0.0143	0.1520	0.0248	0.0426	0.0033	0.0400	0.0065	0.0112
Linguakit	0.0236	0.1181	0.0422	0.0622	0.0073	0.0393	0.0140	0.0207
Multi2OIE	0.0701	0.1520	0.1217	0.1352	0.0238	0.0642	0.0448	0.0528
PortNOIE	**0.1271**	**0.4579**	**0.1743**	**0.2525**	**0.0398**	**0.1775**	**0.0676**	**0.0979**

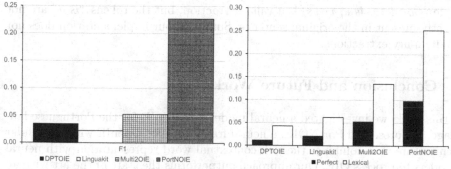

(a) Pud 100 F1 results using Perfect Match   (b) Gamalho F1 results using Perfect and Lexical Match

Fig. 3. Evaluation results of PUD 100 and Gamalho datasets

4.4   Ablation and Discussion

In this paper, we have proposed a model employing rich features and a variant generation procedure. To evaluate the impact of each component, we performed two ablation studies using the PUD 100 as a test dataset. In the first study, we evaluate the rich features, and in the second study, we investigate the influence of the variant generation. Finally we observe the influence of disabling both. The results can be seen on Table 5. From this analysis, we conclude that both components have a significant impact on the final performance, with a 42% reduction in F1 when both are disabled.

Table 5. Ablation evaluation

	AUC	F1
Original	**0.1730**	**0.2268**
Disable rich features	0.0675 (−41%)	0.1497 (−34%)
Disable variant generator	0.0869 (−24%)	0.1619 (−29%)
Disable both	0.0635 (−45%)	0.1317 (−42%)

The results show that PortNOIE outperforms the other systems on both datasets. Even on a very small dataset, the machine learning model was able to achieve good results.

Despite these promising results, we should be aware of the limitations of this method. We use a BIO tagging with which it might be difficult to represent more complex extractions. Thus, our method cannot handle multiple extractions with the same predicate. Stanovsky et al. [34] introduces a custom tagging scheme to handle these cases. Although our method does not forbid it, our current implementation requires that the triple constituents be subsequences of the input. In the sentence *"There is now a vaccine for the Covid-19 virus"* for example, the triple *(Covid-19, is a, virus)* is a valid extraction, but the tokens *"is a"* are not directly present in the original sentence. Similarly, our implementation does not handle n-ary extractions.

5   Conclusion and Future Work

In this work, we investigated a neural model for OpenIE for the Portuguese language. We presented PortNOIE, a neural framework for OpenIE with a modular architecture that combines the rich contextual word representation with neural encoders to process OIE. Our approach outperforms the state of the art with an F1 of 0.22, a 340% improvement over the second-best result.

In the future, we plan to extend the system to other languages and make it a multilingual OpenIE system. We believe that this will increase the reliability of this work and also the possibility to compare the results with other languages. Another issue that should be adapted in future work is the limitations of extracting triples with the same predicate or implicit relations. Finally, we could consider the possibility of fine-tuning BERT directly on the OpenIE extraction task.

We believe that our system provides a solid foundation for the research community to use and test new approaches to OpenIE in Portuguese. PortNOIE is freely available at *https://github.com/FORMAS/dptoie-neural*.

Acknowledgement. We would like to thank FAPESB for financial support.

References

1. de Abreu, S.C., Vieira, R.: Relp: Portuguese open relation extraction. Knowl. Organ. **44**(3), 163–177 (2017)
2. Akbik, A., Bergmann, T., Blythe, D., Rasul, K., Schweter, S., Vollgraf, R.: Flair: an easy-to-use framework for state-of-the-art NLP. In: Proceedings of the 2019 Conference of the North American Chapter of the Association for Computational Linguistics (Demonstrations), pp. 54–59 (2019)
3. Banko, M., Cafarella, M.J., Soderland, S., Broadhead, M., Etzioni, O.: Open information extraction for the web. In: IJCAI, vol. 7, pp. 2670–2676 (2007)

4. Cabral, B.S., Glauber, R., Souza, M., Claro, D.B.: CrossOIE: Cross-Lingual Classifier for Open Information Extraction. In: Quaresma, P., Vieira, R., Aluísio, S., Moniz, H., Batista, F., Gonçalves, T. (eds.) PROPOR 2020. LNCS (LNAI), vol. 12037, pp. 368–378. Springer, Cham (2020). https://doi.org/10.1007/978-3-030-41505-1_35

5. Cabral, B.S., Souza, M., Claro, D.B.: Explainable OpenIE classifier with Morphosyntactic rules. In: HI4NLP@ ECAI, pp. 7–15 (2020)

6. Collovini, S., et al.: IberLEF 2019 Portuguese named entity recognition and relation extraction tasks. In: Proceedings of the Iberian Languages Evaluation Forum, vol. 2421, pp. 390–410. CEUR-WS.org (2019)

7. Cui, L., Wei, F., Zhou, M.: Neural open information extraction. arXiv preprint arXiv:1805.04270 (2018)

8. Del Corro, L., Gemulla, R.: Clausie: clause-based open information extraction. In: 22nd International Conference on World Wide Web, pp. 355–366. ACM (2013)

9. Devlin, J., Chang, M.W., Lee, K., Toutanova, K.: Bert: pre-training of deep bidirectional transformers for language understanding. arXiv preprint arXiv:1810.04805 (2018)

10. Fader, A., Soderland, S., Etzioni, O.: Identifying relations for open information extraction. In: Proceedings of the 2011 Conference on Empirical Methods in Natural Language Processing,, Edinburgh, Scotland, pp. 1535–1545. Association for Computational Linguistics, July 2011

11. Gamallo, P., Garcia, M.: Multilingual open information extraction. In: Pereira, F., Machado, P., Costa, E., Cardoso, A. (eds.) EPIA 2015. LNCS (LNAI), vol. 9273, pp. 711–722. Springer, Cham (2015). https://doi.org/10.1007/978-3-319-23485-4_72

12. Gamallo, P., Garcia, M., Fernández-Lanza, S.: Dependency-based open information extraction. In: Joint Workshop on Unsupervised and Semi-supervised Learning in NLP, pp. 10–18. Association for Computational Linguistics (2012)

13. Gamallo, P., Garcia, M., Pineiro, C., Martinez-Castano, R., Pichel, J.C.: LinguaKit: a big data-based multilingual tool for linguistic analysis and information extraction. In: Fifth International Conference on Social Networks Analysis, Management and Security, pp. 239–244. IEEE (2018)

14. Gardner, M., et al.: AllenNLP: a deep semantic natural language processing platform (2017)

15. Glauber, R., Claro, D.B., de Oliveira, L.S.: Dependency parser on open information extraction for Portuguese texts - DptOIE and dependentie on IberLEF. In: Proceedings of the Iberian Languages Evaluation Forum (IberLEF 2019), vol. 2421, pp. 442–448. CEUR-WS.org (2019)

16. Hartmann, N.S., Fonseca, E.R., Shulby, C.D., Treviso, M.V., Rodrigues, J.S., Aluísio, S.M.: Portuguese word embeddings: evaluating on word analogies and natural language tasks. In: XI Simpósio Brasileiro de Tecnologia da Informação e da Linguagem Humana, Porto Alegre, RS, Brasil, pp. 122–131. SBC (2017)

17. He, L., Lee, K., Lewis, M., Zettlemoyer, L.: Deep semantic role labeling: what works and what's next. In: Proceedings of the 55th Annual Meeting of the Association for Computational Linguistics, Vancouver, Canada, pp. 473–483. Association for Computational Linguistics, July 2017. https://doi.org/10.18653/v1/P17-1044

18. Hohenecker, P., Mtumbuka, F., Kocijan, V., Lukasiewicz, T.: Systematic comparison of neural architectures and training approaches for open information extraction. In: Conference on Empirical Methods in Natural Language Processing (EMNLP), pp. 8554–8565 (2020)

19. Hu, X., Zhang, C., Xu, Y., Wen, L., Yu, P.S.: Selfore: self-supervised relational feature learning for open relation extraction. arXiv preprint arXiv:2004.02438 (2020)
20. Huang, Z., Xu, W., Yu, K.: Bidirectional LSTM-CRF models for sequence tagging. arXiv preprint arXiv:1508.01991 (2015)
21. Jia, S., Xiang, Y.: Hybrid neural tagging model for open relation extraction. arXiv preprint arXiv:1908.01761 (2019)
22. Kolluru, K., Adlakha, V., Aggarwal, S., Chakrabarti, S., et al.: OpenIE 6: Iterative grid labeling and coordination analysis for open information extraction. arXiv preprint arXiv:2010.03147 (2020)
23. Lei, T.: When attention meets fast recurrence: training language models with reduced compute (2021)
24. Nivre, J., et al.: Universal dependencies v2: an evergrowing multilingual treebank collection. In: Proceedings of the 12th Language Resources and Evaluation Conference, Marseille, France, pp. 4034–4043. European Language Resources Association, May 2020
25. de Oliveira, L.S., Glauber, R., Claro, D.B.: DependentIE: an open information extraction system on Portuguese by a dependence analysis. Encontro Nacional de Inteligência Artificial e Computacional (2017)
26. Pennington, J., Socher, R., Manning, C.: GloVe: global vectors for word representation. In: Conference on Empirical Methods in Natural Language Processing, Doha, Qatar, pp. 1532–1543. Association for Computational Linguistics, October 2014
27. Pereira, V., Pinheiro, V.: Report-um sistema de extração de informações aberta para língua portuguesa. In: X Simpósio Brasileiro de Tecnologia da Informação e da Linguagem Humana, pp. 191–200. SBC (2015)
28. Ramshaw, L.A., Marcus, M.P.: Text chunking using transformation-based learning. In: Natural Language Processing Using Very Large Corpora, pp. 157–176. Springer, Dordrecht (1999). https://doi.org/10.1007/978-94-017-2390-9
29. Ro, Y., Lee, Y., Kang, P.: Multi2OIE: multilingual open information extraction based on multi-head attention with BERT. arXiv preprint arXiv:2009.08128 (2020)
30. Sena, C.F.L., Claro, D.B.: InferPortOIE: a Portuguese open information extraction system with inferences. Nat. Lang. Eng. **25**(2), 287–306 (2019)
31. Sena, C.F.L., Claro, D.B.: PragmaticOIE: a pragmatic open information extraction for Portuguese language. Knowl. Inf. Syst. **62**(9), 3811–3836 (2020)
32. Sena, C.F.L., Glauber, R., Claro, D.B.: Inference approach to enhance a Portuguese open information extraction. In: Proceedings of the 19th International Conference on Enterprise Information Systems - Volume 3: ICEIS. pp. 442–451. INSTICC, SciTePress (2017)
33. Souza, F., Nogueira, R., Lotufo, R.: BERTimbau: pretrained BERT models for Brazilian Portuguese. In: 9th Brazilian Conference on Intelligent Systems (2020)
34. Stanovsky, G., Michael, J., Zettlemoyer, L., Dagan, I.: Supervised open information extraction. In: Proceedings of the 2018 Conference of the North American Chapter of the Association for Computational Linguistics: Human Language Technologies, vol. 1 (Long Papers), pp. 885–895 (2018)

35. Sun, M., Li, X., Wang, X., Fan, M., Feng, Y., Li, P.: Logician: a unified end-to-end neural approach for open-domain information extraction. In: Eleventh ACM International Conference on Web Search and Data Mining, pp. 556–564. ACM (2018)
36. Sun, M., Li, X., Wang, X., Fan, M., Feng, Y., Li, P.: Logician: a unified end-to-end neural approach for open-domain information extraction. In: Eleventh ACM International Conference on Web Search and Data Mining, pp. 556–564. ACM (2018)

Tracking Environmental Policy Changes in the Brazilian Federal Official Gazette

Flávio Nakasato Cação[1]([⊠])(iD), Anna Helena Reali Costa[1](iD),
Natalie Unterstell[2](iD), Liuca Yonaha[2](iD), Taciana Stec[2](iD), and Fábio Ishisaki[2](iD)

[1] Escola Politécnica, Universidade de São Paulo, Sao Paulo, Brazil
{flavio.cacao,anna.reali}@usp.br
[2] Política por Inteiro, Sao Paulo, Brazil
{natalie,liuca,taciana,fabio}@politicaporinteiro.org

Abstract. Even though most of its energy generation comes from renewable sources, Brazil is one of the largest emitters of greenhouse gases in the world, due to intense farming and deforestation of biomes such as the Amazon Rainforest, whose preservation is essential for compliance with the Paris Agreement. Still, regardless of lobbies or prevailing political orientation, all government legal actions are published daily in the Brazilian Federal Official Gazette (BFOG, or "Diário Oficial da União" in Portuguese). However, with hundreds of decrees issued every day by the authorities, it is absolutely burdensome to manually analyze all these processes and find out which ones can pose serious environmental hazards. In this paper, we present a strategy to compose automated techniques and domain expert knowledge to process all the data from the BFOG. We also provide the fff, a highly curated dataset, in Portuguese, annotated by domain experts, on federal government acts about the Brazilian environmental policies. Finally, we build and compared four different NLP models on the classification task in this dataset. Our best model achieved a F1-score of 0.714 ± 0.031. In the future, this system should serve to scale up the high-quality tracking of all official documents with a minimum of human supervision and contribute to increasing society's awareness of government actions.

Keywords: Document classification · BERT model · Brazilian government acts

1 Introduction

Brazil has one of the largest reserves of biodiversity in the world, such as the Amazon Rainforest, Cerrado and Atlantic forest. The preservation of these biomes is essential for the country to be able to fulfill the objectives of the Paris Agreement [12], since 78% of greenhouse gas emissions in Brazil come from land use and cover change [20]. In 2020, while global emissions fell as a

© Springer Nature Switzerland AG 2022
V. Pinheiro et al. (Eds.): PROPOR 2022, LNAI 13208, pp. 256–266, 2022.
https://doi.org/10.1007/978-3-030-98305-5_24

result of the coronavirus pandemic, in Brazil they grew substantially driven by deforestation and farming [17]; the Amazon Rainforest deforestation rate was the greatest of the decade [15]. At the same time, the country is an agribusiness powerhouse, with 26.6% of the GDP related to it [3]. Despite this complex and dynamic environment, governments at all hierarchical levels of the nation are required to record all their legal actions in the Official Gazette. Thus, one can infer potentially harmful directions for the environmental policy from the systematic scrutiny of these documents. This makes tracking government acts a powerful tool to alert journalists and empower civil society with qualified and clear information [13]. However, this is an arduous task for manual work alone [6]: hundreds of highly technical documents are issued every day by the Legislative and the Executive branches, at the federal, state and municipal levels. According to the Brazilian Institute of Geography and Statistics (IBGE), Brazil has 5570 municipalities and 26 states in addition to its Federal District[1], and typically each of these federative entities has its own Official Gazette.

Therefore, this scenario represents a yet underexplored opportunity for the most recent pre-trained language models, particularly for the Brazilian Portuguese language. Pretrained language models, such as BERT [4] and T5 [11], have started to become popular in recent years and have set new quality standards in virtually all natural language processing (NLP) tasks, such as classification, translating and question answering. They have millions or billions of parameters and are built upon the Transformer architecture [19], which leverages self-attention mechanisms and eliminates the need for recurrent neural networks. This allows models to be trained in parallel in a self-supervised way over huge databases, such as the entire Wikipedia. Finally, the parametric knowledge accumulated in its parameters can thus be transferred efficiently to general language tasks after minor fine-tunings on smaller domain-specific datasets. The results obtained in this way usually outperform models trained solely on the aforementioned smaller dataset [11].

Work presented in [18] draws attention to the existing opportunities for collaboration between the NLP community and social scientists in studies related to climate change, such as tracing political discourses, topic modeling, and extracting insights when there is not "Big Data" – which is often a prerequisite in machine learning. *ClimateQA* is one of the most recent initiatives to tackle public and open data with advanced NLP models [10]. It consists of a RoBERTa model [9] that can be adjusted in any company's reporting database to answer questions about sustainability by consulting the company's unstructured files. Other works, such as [8], address the lack of accountability of politicians by providing a topic modeling system to aggregate policy makers' speeches from multiple data sources, such as Twitter and Facebook. Such systems have the potential to help the public more clearly discern opinions that are currently in vogue in public debate.

---

[1] IBGE: https://cidades.ibge.gov.br/brasil/panorama.

In the Portuguese language, the scarcity of resources, datasets or models, is even more striking. Among the initiatives, DEBACER is an algorithm developed to automatically segment blocks of speeches by politicians registered in the minutes of the Portuguese Parliament [5]. On the environmental side, Pirá is the first Portuguese-English bilingual question answering (QA) dataset on the Brazilian coast and oceans in general; it was crowdsourced and contains 2,261 question answer pairs on these subjects [1]. In the same direction, DEEPAGÉ is a QA system dedicated to answer questions about the Brazilian environment in Portuguese. It runs over news and Wikipedia articles on the subject and was fine-tuned on QA pairs filtered and translated from a massive open-domain QA dataset, due to the lack of Portuguese QA datasets on the topic [2].

To cover the gap of approaches like those mentioned above in the case of the Portuguese language and address important federal government acts, in this work, we collected thousands of historical documents from the Brazilian Federal Official Gazette (BFOG) – or, as it is known in Brazil, "Diário Oficial da União" (DOU) – and compared multiple NLP models to classify changes in environmental policies. In order to do so, we first built a rule-based robot to scrap all the official documents from the BFOG, filter and pre-classify based on keywords defined by domain experts. Thus, the same domain experts reviewed and enriched a share of this initial data specifically related to environmental issues. Finally, this curated dataset was splitted and used to train and compare multiple NLP models on the classification task of federal government acts. We tested 4 models: from a traditional Naive Bayes and BiLSTMs to two state-of-the-art techniques, based on BERT [4], a bidirectional Transformer encoder architecture. To summarize, our main contributions are:

- **A new approach to collecting and classifying Brazilian Federal Official Gazette data**, that takes advantage of automatic pre-classification techniques and knowledge from domain experts;
- The *Government Actions Tracker* (GAT), an ever-increasing highly curated dataset, in Portuguese, of federal government acts related to the main Brazilian environmental policies – the dataset is made available at https://www.politicaporinteiro.org/monitor-de-atos-publicos/;[2]
- **Comparison among multiple NLP models**, from LSTMs to BERT, designed to classify the acts aforementioned;
- A **BERT model fine-tuned** on a Masked Language Model (MLM) task over a corpus of 500k raw documents (not included in GAT) from the BFOG. It is made available at https://huggingface.co/flavio-nakasato/berdou_500k.

It is noteworthy that the system formed only by the rule-based robot followed by a layer of human supervision today feeds one of the largest newspapers in the country with daily monitoring of acts by the Brazilian government that may have negative consequences for the preservation of the country's native forests and

---

[2] The version of the GAT dataset used specifically in this work can be downloaded from: https://github.com/nakasato/gat.

wildlife[3]. Thanks to this, it was possible to identify massive repeals of protection laws moved by the Federal Government in 2020, with the potential increase in deforestation[4]. However, since this current process requires the evaluation of human experts, a more effective classification system, such as these presented in this work, could eliminate the need for human supervision in the vast majority of cases, allowing their efforts to be redirected to new challenges, and dramatically scaling the model's tracking capability.

In the next sections, we will cover the construction strategy of the datasets, highlighting the domain experts' role in this effort and how the rule-based robot performed the initial classifications. Thus, we present GAT, the dataset used for training our models, as well as their main settings. Finally, we discuss our results, presenting future work perspectives.

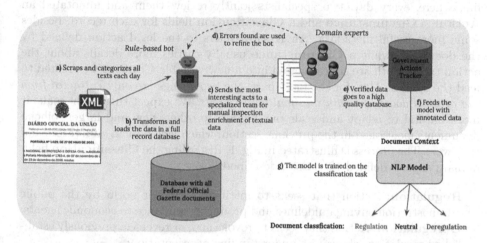

Fig. 1. The operational flow of the data pipeline. A rule-based robot scrapes and pre-classifies all official documents released every day (step *a*), and loads them into a general database (step *b*). The most relevant acts related to the environment are sent to a team of domain experts (step *c*), who manually reviews the robot's classifications and enriches the database with new information. Errors found by annotators are regularly used to improve the rule-based robot (step *d*). This filtered and verified subset of data is loaded into the *Government Actions Tracker* database (step *e*), which is used to train the NLP models. These models receive a *Context* variable for each document and are trained/fine-tuned to classify it as a Regulation/Deregulation/Neutral action (step *g*). The system over the gray area represents the Política Por Inteiro's system currently deployed in production.

---

[3] The Environmental Policy Monitor can be accessed here: https://arte.folha.uol.com. br/ambiente/monitor-politica-ambiental.

[4] A newspaper article reporting this can be found here: https://www1.folha.uol.com. br/ambiente/2020/07/governo-acelerou-canetadas-sobre-meio-ambiente-durante-a-pandemia.shtml.

2   Methods

2.1   Data Preparation

Every morning, a robot scrapes all documents published in the Federal Official Gazette[5] and pre-classifies them under "Themes", based on rules defined by domain experts and refined over the years. These rules are based mainly on keywords and more complex expressions to include or exclude a document from a given theme. So far, there are 22 possible themes like *Climate Change*, *Amazon Region* and *Environmental Disasters*, and this pre-tagging helps the robot and domain experts to make an initial filter of the most pertinent documents. All official document data is transformed and loaded into a database.

The most relevant documents filtered by the robot are also sent to a separate file, where, every day, two specialists jointly review them and annotated an **Action**, a **Circumstance** and a **Classification** fields for each record, besides some more useful metadata. An **Action** refers to the legal action defined by the document, while a **Circumstance** usually carries more details about the action taken. Both are concatenated into a new variable **Context** we created to feed the models. Also, for the most part, the two strings are only *extracted from the original document with minimal adjustments*. We expect this might make it more natural to adapt and scale our models to other, new and larger, official documents mentioned in the previous section, which lack human annotators and reviewers. The process is illustrated in Fig. 1. Regarding the **Classification** field, domain experts defined 12 classes, described below:

- **Regulation:** Action that seeks to institute a rule or norm by the public administration, giving guidelines and producing guidance to economic agents;
- **Deregulation:** Action that seeks to revoke and/or reverse a previously established regulation, change its understanding or orientation;
- **Institutional reform:** Change in structure, skills and institutional arrangement related to public policy;
- **Response:** Action that aims to respond to a significant external event, such as a natural disaster or a major accident;
- **Flexibilization:** Alteration, temporary or not, of deadlines or conditions for compliance with environmental rules, norms and legislation;
- **Neutral:** Action with no significant impact when considered in isolation, but cataloging assessed as necessary because it addresses topics on relevant agendas or with indications of becoming relevant in the medium and long terms;
- **Retreat:** Action that seeks to revoke, replace or modify previously established regulations, due to political or popular pressure;
- **Law consolidation:** Result of regulatory review, with no impact on content;
- **Revocation:** Batch revisions or acts associated with the full revision process;

---

[5] The official documents of the federal government, originally in PDF, are also published in a machine readable format – in this case, XML. These are the files processed by the robot.

- **Privatization:** Action that seeks the alienation of business rights under the competence of the Union; the transfer, to the private sector, of the execution of public services operated by the Union; or the transfer or grant of rights over movable and immovable property of the Union;
- **Legislation:** Action that seeks to agree a new law before society, giving guidelines and providing guidance to economic agents;
- **Planning:** Action that does not institute regulatory processes per se, but discloses documents and guiding strategies, such as management plans, creation of committees and working groups, approval of programs and policies that have not yet been defined, among others.

Misclassifications found by the annotators are also used regularly to refine the rule-based robot, in a process of continuous feedback adjustment via active learning. In the curation process of the GAT dataset, specialists even regularly double-checked the original BFOG documents themselves, which substantially improved the rule-based robot recall over time, minimizing the chances of loss of relevant material.

Table 1. *Theme, Action* and *Circumstance* and its and respective *Classification* for three examples of instances from the Government Actions Tracker database. The *Context* feature was omitted here because it is simply the concatenation of the second and third columns.

Theme	Action	Circumstance	Classification
Environment	*Estabelece os procedimentos administrativos no âmbito do Ibama para a delegação de licenciamento ambiental de competência (...) ou Municipal*	*Autoriza o IBAMA a repassar para Estados e municípios qualquer processo de licenciamento ambiental de sua responsabilidade, incluindo empreendimentos em terras indígenas, áreas protegidas e na costa brasileira. Entende-se como desregulação porque (...) Lei Complementar n $\underline{o}$ 140/2011 (Art. 2 $\underline{o}$ §2$\underline{o}$)*	Deregulation
Institutional	*Revoga atos normativos (...) Fundação Nacional do Índio - Funai, conforme Decreto (...)*	*Declara revogados os atos normativos da Procuradoria Federal Especializada junto à Fundação Nacional do Índio: Ordem de Serviço (...) setembro de 2008, p. 5-7*	Revocation
Energy	*Recomenda (...) de energia no âmbito do Programa de Parcerias de Investimentos*	*Opina favoravelmente e submeter (...) no âmbito do Programa de Parcerias de Investimentos - PPI (...) no ano de 2021*	Privatization

After the human supervision stage, the verified and enriched data are sent to a separate database, the *Government Actions Tracker* (GAT) database. Table 1 shows the **Theme**, **Action**, **Circumstance** columns and their respective **Classification** column for three examples of instances, obtained from the GAT database (held in the original language). The version of GAT dataset we used in this work has 1,181 instances and no missing data in the Theme or Classification variables. Figure 2 shows their distributions in the dataset used. The *Action* feature has 29.1 ± 19.6 words on average; the *Circumstance* one, 70.0 ± 54.0 words. The first record dates from January 1, 2019; the last, July 12, 2021.

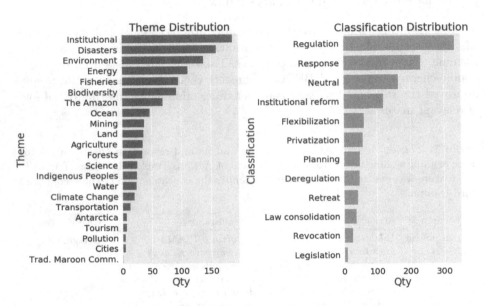

Fig. 2. Distribution of teme and cassification variables in the GAT dataset we used.

Due to the small size of the GAT database, the training with the original 12 classes proved to be very unstable, since the objective was to predict the **Classification** of a document given only its **Context**. Thus, we regrouped the previous classes of the **Classification** variable into three major classes, as follows:

- **Regulation:** Regulation, Planning and Response;
- **Neutral:** Neutral, Retreat and Legislation;
- **Deregulation:** Privatization, Deregulation, Flexibilization, Institutional reform, Law consolidation and Revocation.

Therefore, the dataset ended up with the following proportions: Regulation (52.0%), Neutral (18.5%) and Deregulation (29.5%).

2.2   Experiment Description

In order to discover the most suitable model for classifying the Acts in the BFOG, we built and compared four models. We start with two simpler models, based on Naive Bayes [21] and Bidirectional LSTMs (BiLSTMs) [14]. We also fine-tuned a BERTimbau Base model [16] (we call "BERT1") directly on the classification task of GAT. Finally, our fourth model ("BERT2") was also based on the BERTimbau Base model, but in this case we performed two subsequential fine-tunings: first on 500k documents from the entire (and unprocessed) BFOG database since 2002[6] (the blue database in Fig. 1), and then on the GAT database to classify the government acts.

All models were trained under a stratified cross-validation with k-$folds = 10$. We also performed different strategies for data augmentation with sequence-to-sequence models, such as T5 [11] and Pegasus [22]. However, as none of them outperformed the models without data augmentation, we left them out of the scope of this work. Further, we describe our four models in more details below:

Simpler Models: Naive Bayes and BiLSTM. As our first models, we trained a Multinomial Naive Bayes (NB) model and a bidirectional LSTM (BiL-STM) network with 32 LSTM units, with batch size of 32, maximum sequence length of 50 for 4 epochs - a Gridsearch was performed to select these hyperparameters. The net weights were initialized from a previously trained matrix (CBOW) of 300 dimensions [7].

BERT1. We also fine-tuned a BERTimbau Base model, a pretrained BERT model in Portuguese with 12 layers and 110 million parameters, on the GAT classification task. After multiple inspections, we trained the model for 15 epochs, with 512 as the maximum sequence length, a learning rate of 5e-5, a batch size of 128 and an Adam's optimizer algorithm with weight decay.

BERT2. As Table 1 illustrates, the sentences in the BFOG have a very characteristic writing style, with many technical terms and legal jargon. Hence, instead of fine-tuning BERTimbau Base directly on the GAT classification task, we first trained it on a Masked Language Model (MLM) task on a dataset of 500k documents, since 2002, from the BFOG, scraped from the official websites. We only use the body of the documents (the "*ementa detalhada*"), with minimal text processing – basically the removal of special characters like "\n" or "\t". The final file was 1.5 GB of plain text and we trained the MLM model for 10 epochs. Finally, the model was then fine-tuned in the classification problem of the GAT dataset, as in the previous case and with the same hyperparameters as BERT1, as both responded in a similar way to the tests.

---

[6] For the Executive branch, it is available at: https://www.politicaporinteiro.org/base-de-atos-do-executivo/.

3   Results

Table 2 summarizes the results obtained for each model. Pre-trained models were superior to baselines in all metrics, and BERT2 performed slightly above BERT1, although the difference is not statistically relevant. Among the baseline models, even with the LSTM network having been initialized with an already trained weight matrix and after a careful choice of parameters, its results in general were still inferior to the NB, which reinforces the idea that, without pre-trained models based on the Transformer architecture, recurrent networks can be quite limited in offering a substantial improvement over simpler models.

Considering the proportions of each class in each experiment, one can see that specially the first two models, BERT1 and BERT2, are promising, despite the challenges of dealing with a small database for the current standards of the state-of-the-art pretrained models and also despite of the imbalanced classes.

Table 2. Summary of the Matthews Correlation Coefficient (MCC), Accuracy (Acc) and weighted F1-score for each model in the task of classifying the *Context* information into one of the three classes: *Regulation, Neutral* or *Deregulation*. Results were cross-validated with *k-fold = 10*. In bold, the best ones.

Model	MCC	Acc	F1-score
BERT2	**0.538 ± 0.046**	**0.725 ± 0.027**	**0.714 ± 0.031**
BERT1	0.530 ± 0.050	0.716 ± 0.031	0.710 ± 0.032
BiLSTM (CBOW 300)	0.401 ± 0.090	0.644 ± 0.055	0.618 ± 0.059
Naive Bayes	0.429 ± 0.032	0.658 ± 0.019	0.601 ± 0.030

4   Conclusion and Future Work

In this work, we present strategy to leverage automated techniques and expert knowledge to track and classify potentially harmful changes in environmental policies directly from texts in Brazilian Federal Official Gazette. In addition to this strategy, we contribute with the Government Actions Tracker, a new challenging curated dataset, in Portuguese, of federal government acts related to Brazilian environmental policies. Also, we designed and compared four different NLP models on the classification task posed by this dataset, from the simpler models to the state-of-the-art ones. Monitoring each act published by the government in order to inform civil society is an extremely challenging task and there is still no single practical solution to solve it. While a rule-based system working jointly with domain experts already deliver immeasurable value when it comes to policy monitoring, it is also paramount that the latest NLP technologies be considered to increase the scalability and performance of these systems. Hence, among the future work are the expansion of the annotated datasets, as well as the improvement of the best models presented here so that they can keep the quality and stability of the classification for a greater number of classes.

Acknowledgement. This work is the result of an academic partnership between the Escola Politécnica of Universidade de São Paulo (EP-USP) and *Política Por Inteiro*. Without the data curation efforts of Política Por Inteiro experts, building these NLP models would not have been possible. Also, this work was financed in part by the *Coordenação de Aperfeiçoamento de Pessoal de Nível Superior* (CAPES, Finance Code 001), the *Itaú Unibanco S.A.*, through the *Programa de Bolsas Itaú* (PBI) of the Centro de Ciência de Dados (C2D) of EP-USP, and by the *Conselho Nacional de Desenvolvimento Científico e Tecnológico* (CNPq) (grant 310085/2020-9). We also thank the *Center for Artificial Intelligence* (C4AI-USP), with support by the *Fundação de Amparo à Pesquisa do Estado de São Paulo* (FAPESP, grant 2019/07665-4) and by the *IBM Corporation*. The data, views and opinions expressed in this article are those of the authors and do not necessarily reflect the official policy or position of the financiers.

References

1. André F., et al.: Pirá: A Bilingual Portuguese-english dataset for question-answering about the ocean. In: 30th ACM International Conference on Information and Knowledge Management (CIKM'21) (2021). https://doi.org/10.1145/3459637.3482012

2. Cação, F.N., José, M.M., Oliveira, A.S., Spindola, S., Costa, A.H.R., Cozman, F.G.: DEEPAGÉ: answering questions in Portuguese about the Brazilian environment. In: Britto, A., Valdivia Delgado, K. (eds.) BRACIS 2021. LNCS (LNAI), vol. 13074, pp. 419–433. Springer, Cham (2021). https://doi.org/10.1007/978-3-030-91699-2_29

3. CEPEA-ESALQ: PIB do Agronegócio Brasileiro - Centro de Estudos Avançados em Economia Aplicada - CEPEA-Esalq/USP (2021)

4. Devlin, J., Chang, M.W., Lee, K., Toutanova, K.: BERT: pre-training of deep bidirectional transformers for language understanding. In: Proceedings of the 2019 Conference of the North American Chapter of the Association for Computational Linguistics: Human Language Technologies, vol. 1, Long and Short Papers, pp. 4171–4186. Association for Computational Linguistics, Minneapolis, Minnesota (2019). https://doi.org/10.18653/v1/N19-1423

5. Ferraz, T., et al.: DEBACER: a method for slicing moderated debates. In: Anais do XVIII Encontro Nacional de Inteligência Artificial e Computacional, pp. 667–678. SBC, Porto Alegre, RS, Brasil (2021). https://doi.org/10.5753/eniac.2021.18293. Evento Online, ISSN 0000-0000

6. Grimmer, J., Stewart, B.M.: Text as data: the promise and pitfalls of automatic content analysis methods for political texts. Political Anal. **21**(3), 267–297 (2013). https://doi.org/10.1093/pan/mps028

7. Hartmann, N.S., Fonseca, E.R., Shulby, C.D., Treviso, M.V., Rodrigues, J.S., Aluísio, S.M.: Portuguese word embeddings: evaluating on word analogies and natural language tasks. In: Anais do XI Simpósio Brasileiro de Tecnologia da Informação e da Linguagem Humana, pp. 122–131. SBC, Porto Alegre, RS, Brasil (2017). https://sol.sbc.org.br/index.php/stil/article/view/4008

8. Hätönen, V., Melzer, F.: From talk to action with accountability: Monitoring the public discussion of policy makers with deep neural networks and topic modelling (2021). https://www.climatechange.ai/papers/icml2021/75

9. Liu, Y., et al.: Roberta: a robustly optimized BERT pretraining approach (2019). http://arxiv.org/abs/1907.11692

10. Luccioni, A., Baylor, E., Duchene, N.: Analyzing sustainability reports using natural language processing http://arxiv.org/abs/2011.08073 (2020)
11. Raffel, C., et al.: Exploring the limits of transfer learning with a unified text-to-text transformer. J. Mach. Learn. Res. **21**(140), 1–67 (2020). http://jmlr.org/papers/v21/20-074.html
12. Rochedo, P.R.R., et al.: The threat of political bargaining to climate mitigation in Brazil. Nat. Clim. Chang. **8**(8), 695–698 (2018). https://doi.org/10.1038/s41558-018-0213-y. ISSN 1758-678X
13. Rolnick, D., et al.: Tackling climate change with machine learning. arXiv (2019)
14. Schuster, M., Paliwal, K.K.: Bidirectional recurrent neural networks. IEEE Trans. Sig. Process. **45**(11), 2673–2681 (1997). https://doi.org/10.1109/78.650093
15. Silva Junior, C.H., Pessôa, A.C., Carvalho, N.S., Reis, J.B., Anderson, L.O., Aragão, L.E.: The Brazilian Amazon deforestation rate in 2020 is the greatest of the decade. Nat. Ecol. Evol. **5**(2), 144–145 (2021). https://doi.org/10.1038/s41559-020-01368-x
16. Souza, F., Nogueira, R., Lotufo, R.: BERTimbau: pretrained BERT models for Brazilian Portuguese. In: Cerri, R., Prati, R.C. (eds.) BRACIS 2020. LNCS (LNAI), vol. 12319, pp. 403–417. Springer, Cham (2020). https://doi.org/10.1007/978-3-030-61377-8_28
17. Spring, J.: Deforestation boosts Brazil greenhouse gas emissions as global emissions fall — Reuters (2020). https://www.reuters.com/article/us-brazil-environment-emissions-idUSKBN22X2AA
18. Stede, M., Patz, R.: The climate change debate and natural language processing. In: Proceedings of the 1st Workshop on NLP for Positive Impact, pp. 8–18 (2021)
19. Vaswani, A., et al.: Attention is all you need. In: Guyon, I., Luxburg, U.V., Bengio, S., Wallach, H., Fergus, R., Vishwanathan, S., Garnett, R. (eds.) Advances in Neural Information Processing Systems, vol. 30. Curran Associates, Inc. (2017)
20. West, T.A.P., Börner, J., Fearnside, P.M.: Climatic benefits from the 2006–2017 avoided deforestation in Amazonian Brazil. Front. Forests Global Change **2**(September), 1–11 (2019). https://doi.org/10.3389/ffgc.2019.00052
21. Zhang, H.: Exploring conditions for the optimality of Naïve Bayes. Int. J. Pattern Recogn. Artif. Intell. **19**(2), 183–198 (2005). https://doi.org/10.1142/S0218001405003983
22. Zhang, J., Zhao, Y., Saleh, M., Liu, P.: Pegasus: pre-training with extracted gap-sentences for abstractive summarization. In: Daumé III, H., Singh, A. (eds.) Proceedings of the 37th International Conference on Machine Learning. Proceedings of Machine Learning Research, 13–18 July, vol. 119, pp. 11328–11339. PMLR (2020). https://proceedings.mlr.press/v119/zhang20ae.html, http://proceedings.mlr.press/v119/zhang20ae/zhang20ae.pdf

A Transfer Learning Analysis of Political Leaning Classification in Cross-domain Content

Danielle Caled[(✉)] and Mário J. Silva

INESC-ID, Instituto Superior Técnico, Universidade de Lisboa, Lisbon, Portugal
{dcaled,mjs}@inesc-id.pt

Abstract. This work presents an analysis of Brazilian political discourse from speeches and social media posts, focusing on the ability to transfer learned models' knowledge between different contexts. The analysis is conducted through PoliS, a new resource containing two datasets of political discussions labeled for party and ideological leaning from congressional speeches and social media posts by political influencers. The transfer learning experiments are performed using the transcripts of the congressional speeches to train a model used to predict the political leaning of social media influencers. To evaluate the robustness of the model, the analysis includes a time-lag study of the performance degradation of the transferred model. We find that relatively little social media data (about one hour) is needed to achieve reasonable performance in classification, and that performance does not degrade significantly over time.

Keywords: Political dataset · Social media · Polarization · Cross-domain

1 Introduction

Disinformation has been plaguing social media for years, and the room for new strategies for promoting it now appear to be inexhaustible. Prevention of disinformation spreading in present social environments is becoming increasingly harder. We believe that automatic methods for identification of media bias, leveraging existing labeled discourse, could contribute to inform news consumers about the nature of social media posts, even while publishers portray themselves as impartial. To address this problem, we research how text and metadata collected from transcripts of parliamentary speeches could be used for political bias detection in social media.

For our research, we created a new linguistic resource, the *PoliS* collection, addressing the Brazilian Political Scenario. PoliS is a vast linguistic resource, containing 31,101 transcripts of speeches held by parliamentarians in the Brazilian Chamber of Deputies. We have supplemented this collection by adding over 450,000 Twitter posts published by 100 federal deputies over two years. Both speeches and Twitter posts were labeled at two levels: (i) political party-level,

© Springer Nature Switzerland AG 2022
V. Pinheiro et al. (Eds.): PROPOR 2022, LNAI 13208, pp. 267–277, 2022.
https://doi.org/10.1007/978-3-030-98305-5_25

considering the party affiliation of each deputy, and (ii) political leaning-level, considering the political alignment (*left* or *right*) of the deputy's party.

This article studies the effectiveness of transferring a model learned for the classification of political leaning in parliamentary speeches records to social media posts by political influencers. The transfer learning analysis considered two temporal settings. First, a model was trained and tested on temporally aligned content (congressional speech records and the social media posts, respectively). Then, the same model was used for classifying social media content published in a later time window. The results of our cross-domain experiments suggest that it is possible to transfer the learning from a model trained on parliamentary speeches to social media, thus allowing the identification of the political bias of public entities through social media messages. It is worth noting that the performance of the transferred classification model, as the temporal distance from the training data and the object data increases, remains high with a lag of up to ten months.

2   Related Work

Modeling the political alignment of legislators, parties, and voters is a vast research area, with applications in electorate behavior analysis, online political campaigning, and advertising [18]. Previous works have studied congressional speeches, social media messages, and press releases focused on political framing [10,19], polarization prediction [6,12], and agenda setting [7]. Regarding the Brazilian political scenario, few works are available. Colliri and Zhao proposed a network-based technique to analyze bills-voting data comprising the votes of Brazilian congressmen [4]. The authors explored temporal networks mapping voting similarities between pairs of congressmen, finding out that such networks can be used to identify convicted politicians.

Souza et al. conducted a study to estimate the ideological position of political influencers on social media platforms [17]. They also rely on social network structure, first identifying the Twitter profile of Brazilian federal deputies, and discovering relevant political actors, followed by a number of congressmen. The results of this work reflect the polarization of the Brazilian political scenario during the 2014 Legislative and Presidential Elections. Brito et al. also focused on understanding the political polarization in social media context [3]. They observed how the 2018 Brazilian Presidential Election results correlate with the interactions between candidates and citizens. Their findings show that candidates heavily used social media throughout the election year, focusing on engaging words and avoiding sensitive topics. Also, a strong correlation between votes and followers was identified.

Recuero et al. examined the role of hyperpartisanship and polarization on Twitter during the 2018 Brazilian Presidential Election [13]. According to their work, as the centrality of hyperpartisan outlets on Twitter grew, conversations became more polarized. Their study also suggests that hyperpartisan outlets often share disinformation or biased information, presented as a "truth-telling"

Table 1. Examples of how deputies from opposing leanings addressed the trial for corruption of the former Brazilian President Lula.

Speech data	Speech summary
Date: 2018-02-17 Speaker: Zé Geraldo Party: PT Leaning: Left	*"[...] Alegação de ocorrência de perseguição judicial contra o ex-Presidente da República Luiz Inácio Lula da Silva. Críticas à atuação do Supremo Tribunal Federal. Defesa da participação de Lula nas eleições presidenciais de 2018."* ([...] Allegation of judicial persecution against the former President of the Republic Luiz Inácio Lula da Silva. Criticism of the actions of the Supreme Federal Court. Defense of Lula's participation in the 2018 Presidential Elections.)
Date: 2018-02-07 Speaker: Onyx Lorenzoni Party: DEM Leaning: Right	*"Condutas criminosas praticadas pelo ex-Presidente Luiz Inácio Lula da Silva e pelo ex-Deputado José Dirceu, do PT. Acerto da condenação judicial dos líderes petistas. Expectativa de derrota da Esquerda brasileira nas eleições de 2018."* (Criminal conducts practiced by the former President Luiz Inácio Lula da Silva and by the former Deputy José Dirceu, from PT. Agreement with the judicial condemnation of PT leaders. Expectation of the Brazilian left-wing parties being defeat in the 2018 Elections.)

alternative to traditional media outlets. Sales et al. resorted to news stories from the politics section of four popular Brazilian news organizations to predict media bias across three consecutive elections years (2010, 2014, and 2018) [14]. The authors introduced new methods for assessing coverage, association, and subjective bias, signaling an escalation of polarization even in mainstream news sources from 2018 onwards.

3   Data Collection

PoliS (Political Scenario) is composed of two datasets, including *congressional speeches*, and *social media messages* from political influencers. The collection process is described below. We made our datasets public at https://github.com/dcaled/polis.

The *congressional speeches* dataset contains the transcripts of political speeches held in the Brazilian Chamber of Deputies[1] from January 1, 2018 to February 2, 2020. It includes 31,101 transcribed statements by 793 deputies affiliated with 25 different political parties. The speeches were web scraped and, for each record, we collected the text, and the metadata (i.e., speaker name, political party, federated state of the speaker, date, plenary session, summary, and url). This dataset allows a two-level political text classification. At a specific level, it uses party affiliations of speakers as labels. At a general level, it differentiates parties according to their political leaning (*left* vs. *right*).

---

[1] https://bit.ly/2Zqk9Ic.

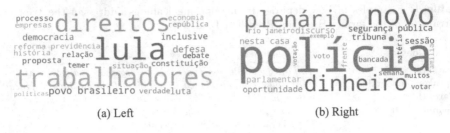

(a) Left   (b) Right

Fig. 1. Diverging terms among the top 150 unigrams and bigrams for left and right-aligned speeches.

For the political leaning labeling, we relied on a manual consolidation of the previous labeling proposed by four sources (BBC [16], Congresso em Foco [15], O Globo [20] and Wikipedia[2]). Accordingly, each party was assigned to a leaning label only if at least three sources agreed on it. Following this labeling scheme, six political parties could not be labeled regarding their political leaning, either because the sources indicated contradictory alignments, do not have labels for all the parties, or classified them as center parties. As a result, the *congressional speeches* dataset has 15,731 documents labeled as *left* and 11,238 documents labeled as *right*. Table 1 presents examples of speeches addressing the same topic but issued by deputies with opposing political leanings.

To understand the differences in topics present in the left and right speeches, we identified the divergent terms among the top 150 unigrams and bigrams of each subset (Fig. 1). As expected, left-aligned speeches focus on topics related to (i) the workers and human rights, addressed through terms like *direitos* (*rights*), *trabalhadores* (*workers*), *reforma [da] previdência* (*social security reform*), (ii) the defense of the democratic processes and the Brazilian constitution, through terms like *democracia* (*democracy*), *constituição* (*constitution*), *república* (*republic*), and (iii) on individuals with great political relevance for the Brazilian context, e.g., *[Luiz Inácio] Lula [da Silva]*, and *[Michel] Temer*, both former Brazilian Presidents. On the other hand, right-aligned speeches have agendas addressing to (i) public security issues, observed through terms like *polícia* (*police*), *segurança pública* (*public security*), and (ii) defense of traditional institutions of western society, addressed by the preservation of family (*família*) values.

The *social media* dataset was assembled by scraping Twitter posts published by Brazilian political figures whose political leaning is known. To this end, we crawled posts from 389 Twitter profiles (144 left-aligned and 245 right-aligned) belonging to federal deputies active during 2020. The list of Twitter accounts was compiled by the non-profit organization Auditoria Cidadã da Dívida[3], supported by different Brazilian labor unions. The political leaning of each deputy was again inferred according to the political party affiliation already labeled in

---

[2] https://bit.ly/3vG8ilf.
[3] https://bit.ly/3GdeXIi.

congressional speeches dataset. As not all Twitter profiles posted new messages regularly, we only selected the 100 profiles (50 left-aligned, and 50 right-aligned) with the highest number of posts. We segmented the *social media* dataset into two samples, according to Table 2. Table 3 illustrates how deputies from opposite leanings address another controversial topic (homosexuality) in social media.

Table 2. *Social media* dataset *left* vs. *right* distribution.

	Collection period	*Left*	*Right*	Total
Tweets Sample 1	Jan 1, 2018–Feb 2, 2020	171,010	120,586	291,596
Tweets Sample 2	Feb 3, 2020–Dec 31, 2020	92,885	68,661	161,546

4 Experiments

To test the feasibility of learning a model for party identification, we first performed the classification of congressional speeches. Then, we analyzed whether a model trained on the speeches dataset could be employed to classify texts from a different domain, as the Twitter collection. We did two sets of transfer learning experiments: i) considering tweets timely aligned with the speeches dataset (Tweets Sample 1) and, ii) analyzing posts made in a lagged period in relation to the training data (Tweets Sample 2).

4.1 Congressional Speeches Classification

The classification of congressional speeches was performed at two levels: i) a multi-class classification (political party classification) and ii) a binary classification (political leaning classification) of the speech records. For both sets of experiments, we separated 80% of our dataset for training and used a 5-fold cross-validation for tuning. We evaluated our models on a separate test collection.

The models were evaluated using the term frequency-inverse document frequency (TF-IDF) representation, considering the 5,000 most frequent words in the dataset. Any reference to the speaker's name was removed from the texts in the preprocessing phase. We did not apply any stemming or lemmatization technique before training our models to avoid losing important aspects or rhetorical strategies employed by the speaker. We made this decision based on previous research, which identified differences in discourse according to the political alignment of the speaker (e.g., the usage of first person plural subjects [6]).

We performed experiments with the following baseline classification methods: support vector machines (SVMs) [2,5] with a linear kernel, logistic regression (LR) [21], and a multi-layer perceptron classifier (MLP) [9]. As the performance of SVM and MLP can be highly affected by the choice of parameters, we resorted to a grid search considering the following range of values for the regularization parameter of SVM and MLP: $[2^{-5}, 2^{-3}, ..., 2^{13}, 2^{15}]$. For the MLP, we also considered architectures comprising one to three hidden layers with 100 neurons each. For the LR, we set the parameters to the default values.

Table 3. Examples of tweets extracted from the PoliS collection.

Leaning: Left.	Leaning: Right.
Marcelo Freixo ✔ @MarceloFreixo · Jun 13, 2019 ··· No mês do orgulho LGBT, o STF aprova a criminalização do homofobia e transfobia. Ainda há muito o que se lutar contra o ódio e discriminação, mas é um momento histórico a ser comemorado. Consideramos justa toda forma de amor! ▬ ♥	**Eduardo Bolsonaro** 🔘 ✔ @Bolsonaro... · Feb 19, 2018 ··· Só eu q acho incoerente? 1) Hétero quer virar gay e procura psicólogo > ok, é ciência, é medicinal, pode ter tratamento. 2) Gay quer virar hétero e procura psicólogo > preconceito, cura gay, retrógrado, proibido pelo CRP.
Translation: In the month of LGBT pride, the STF [Supreme Federal Court] approves the criminalization of homophobia and transphobia. There is still a lot to fight against hatred and discrimination, but it is a historic moment to be celebrated. We consider every form of love fair!	Translation: Only I find it inconsistent? 1) Heterosexual wants to become gay and seeks a psychologist > ok, it's science, it's medicinal, it can be treated. 2) Gay wants to become straight and seeks psychologist > prejudice, gay cure, retrograde, banned by CRP [Regional Psychology Association].

We also experimented a deep learning approach for the speeches classification through an attention-based bidirectional Long Short-Term Memory network (BiLSTM) [22]. The BiLSTM was fed with a Word2Vec distributed text representation of the speeches, mapping each word into a low dimension vector [11]. We generated the word embeddings by using the 300-dimensional Word2Vec CBOW model, pre-trained on a large Portuguese corpus [8]. We used the grid search to find the best dropout rates (ranging from 0.1 to 0.5) and number of epochs (ranging from 5 to 20) to train the model.

Tables 4a and 4b respectively present the precision, recall, macro F_1, and accuracy scores for the political party classification and for the classification regarding the political leaning of the political parties. As expected, classifying the political party is considerably more complex than identifying the political leaning of speech records. This reflects the current scenario of Brazilian politics, which has many different political parties representing similar ideologies. Consequently, classifying the political leaning of speech records becomes a more feasible task. Therefore, our transfer learning experiments only consider the political leaning prediction.

4.2 Transfer Learning Classification

In this set of experiments, we investigated whether a model trained on congressional speeches could be used to identify political bias in social media. Although the topics addressed in these two channels may be similar, the rhetorical devices used in the two domains differ. For example, speeches are delivered in spoken language, using formal terms and specific terminology (jargon), and with a specific target audience (mostly other deputies, senators, and politicians, in general). In turn, social media encourage a more informal and accessible written communication. In addition, these platforms provide a channel to politicians to address their constituency.

A model able to transfer learning would be useful to predict the political bias of a given source in scenarios where there is a shortage of labeled data, or even to identify the political leaning of social media influencers who pretend being impartial. Thus, we made the transfer learning assessment using Tweets Sample 1, considering the content produced in periods overlapping the collected speeches. In this case, we assumed that the topics discussed by both datasets would be similar.

Since Twitter posts are considerable shorter than speech records, we grouped the tweets into time-ordered sets. More specifically, for each Twitter profile, we modeled a message timeline by dividing the ordered set of messages into discrete, ordered intervals. We considered time intervals (Δt) of different sizes, ranging from 30 min to a week. To assess the ability to transfer learning, we used the BiLSTM classifier, which achieved the best results in the political leaning classification task. We trained a model on the entire speeches dataset and then predicted the labels for the tweets considering different configurations of the temporal groupings. In the training phase, we again used CBOW word embeddings as input features and optimized the parameters of the BiLSTM estimator by 5-fold cross-validated grid search over a parameter grid to find the best dropout rates and number of epochs as in the previous experiments. The tweets were preprocessed by replacing the most frequent mentions and hashtags by equivalent terms (e.g., *#LulaPresidente* by *Lula presidente*).

Table 5a presents the scores for the cross-domain classification, with the models trained on the speeches dataset and evaluated on the Tweets Sample 1. As expected, longer texts lead to a better classification performance. Even though our model is not able to have the same results as in the in-domain experiments, with only one hour we can already achieve an accuracy of 70% when predicting the political leaning of social media influencers.

Table 4. Political party/leaning classification results on *congressional speeches*.

	(a) Political party level.					(b) Political leaning (*left* vs. *right*) level.			
Approach	Prec.	Rec.	F_1 (macro)	Acc.	Approach	Prec.	Rec.	F_1 (macro)	Acc.
LR	0.512	0.499	0.499	0.540	LR	0.818	0.824	0.819	0.822
MLP	0.571	0.471	0.508	0.563	MLP	0.825	0.826	0.826	0.830
SVM	**0.639**	**0.503**	**0.544**	**0.594**	SVM	0.823	0.821	0.822	0.827
BiLSTM	0.607	0.441	0.489	0.553	BiLSTM	**0.888**	**0.895**	**0.890**	**0.892**

4.3   Transfer Learning Decay over Time

The last round of experiments assessed the deterioration over time of the performance of a model trained on the speeches dataset in a cross-domain configuration. For this, we considered the Tweets Sample 2 dataset. What is interesting about these experiments is that the social and political context of the country has changed, becoming dominated by new public health concerns, especially about COVID-19. During the collection period of the speeches and Tweets Sample 1, little was said about the disease in Brazil. This issue only gained great repercussion in the country as of February 2020, with the arrival of the epidemic to the American continent. From this period, a dispute of political narratives began around the disease. We believe, therefore, that the Twitter posts would reflect this change in the Brazilian political scenario.

To assess whether our classification performance on Twitter posts would deteriorate because of the time lag between the collection period of the training and test datasets, we grouped the tweets by daily periods using the tweets' timestamps. These groupings were used as test sets. Then, we ran the model trained on the speeches dataset and tested it using monthly subsets of daily groupings of tweets. The model used in this experiment was the same BiLSTM model used in the previous cross-domain classification analysis. Table 5b shows the classification scores for the Tweets Sample 2 dataset, showing the performance for monthly lags.

As one can observe, the decline in the classification was not constant in all the analyzed months. On the contrary, the trained model seems sufficiently robust to classify content published up to ten months ahead of the training set. However, ten months of lag may still be a period close enough not to indicate any deterioration in the classification results. Therefore, further analysis is still needed to draw more reliable conclusions.

Table 5. Cross-domain classification experiments, having a model trained on the speeches dataset and evaluated on tweets.

(a) Tweets Sample 1.

Δt	Prec.	Rec.	F_1 mac	Acc.
1 h	0.70	0.68	0.69	0.70
4 h	0.72	0.70	0.70	0.72
8 h	0.73	0.71	0.71	0.73
12 h	0.74	0.72	0.73	0.74
1 day	0.77	0.75	0.75	0.76
2 days	0.81	0.78	0.78	0.79
7 days	0.86	0.84	0.84	0.84

(b) Tweets Sample 2 ($\Delta t = 1$ *day*).

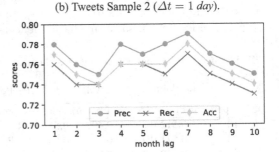

5   Discussion

While natural language processing (NLP) research has often considered political text analysis in the United States, less work has been done to understand political expression in other contexts. This study presents an analysis of Brazilian political discourse from speeches and social media posts, focusing on the ability to transfer learned models' knowledge between the different contexts.

The PoliS collection includes two datasets of political discussions labeled for party and ideological leaning, from congressional speeches and from social media posts published by political influencers. Using a variety of classifiers, our study first finds that it is easier to identify ideological leaning as compared to political party in the *congressional speeches* data. Building on this finding, we then attempt to transfer the learned models from the domain of political speeches to social media. We find that relatively little social media data (about one hour) is needed to achieve reasonable performance in classification, and that performance does not degrade significantly over time. Our study overall contributes a new data collection of politically aligned Portuguese texts, having the ideology confirmed by external organizations.

Even though our paper focuses on political leaning prediction for both congressional speeches and social media posts, our approach can be generalized to other media, e.g., news. Furthermore, our analysis suggests that political ideology prediction is more flexible than expected in terms of data requirements, and this could prove useful for "now-casting" political sentiment changes in response to breaking news events [18].

6   Limitations and Future Work

The major limitations in our study refer to the lack of diversity of Twitter accounts considered in the *social media* dataset. Although our Twitter dataset is extensive, containing more than 450 thousand messages, the analyzed accounts belong to players involved in the Brazilian political scenario.

Future work could explore a wider diversity of social media accounts, considering not only the profiles of politicians, but also voters. For this, we could infer the political alignment of social media users from their connections in social networks, taking advantage of the principle of homophily [1].

In addition, while the party-level classification has led to less effective results, our experiments suggest that some signal does exist in the text and may prove useful in a more coarse-grained version of the task. It would therefore be worth exploring the similarities and differences in congressional speeches in order to predict party affiliation for larger party coalitions, and how these coalitions behave in relation to specific agendas, i.e., identify the topics in which there is greater or lesser convergence between the parliamentarians.

Acknowledgment. This work was supported by Portuguese national funds through Fundação para a Ciência e a Tecnologia (FCT) under references UIDB/50021/2020 and SFRH/BD/145561/2019.

References

1. Barberá, P., Jost, J.T., Nagler, J., Tucker, J.A., Bonneau, R.: Tweeting from left to right: is online political communication more than an echo chamber? Psychol. Sci. **26**(10), 1531–1542 (2015). https://doi.org/10.1177/0956797615594620
2. Boser, B.E., Guyon, I.M., Vapnik, V.N.: A training algorithm for optimal margin classifiers. In: Proceedings of the Annual Workshop on Computational Learning Theory, pp. 144–152. Association for Computing Machinery, New York (1992). https://doi.org/10.1145/130385.130401

3. Brito, K., Paula, N., Fernandes, M., Meira, S.: Social media and presidential campaigns - preliminary results of the 2018 Brazilian Presidential Election. In: Proceedings of the 20th Annual International Conference on Digital Government Research, pp. 332–341. dg.o 2019, Association for Computing Machinery, New York (2019). https://doi.org/10.1145/3325112.3325252

4. Colliri, T., Zhao, L.: Analyzing the bills-voting dynamics and predicting corruption-convictions among Brazilian congressmen through temporal networks. Sci. Rep. **9**(1), 1–11 (2019). https://doi.org/10.1038/s41598-019-53252-9

5. Cortes, C., Vapnik, V.: Support-vector networks. Mach. Learn. **20**(3), 273–297 (1995). https://doi.org/10.1007/BF00994018

6. Demszky, D., et al.: Analyzing polarization in social media: method and application to tweets on 21 mass shootings. In: Proceedings of the Conference of the North American Chapter of the Association for Computational Linguistics: Human Language Technologies, pp. 2970–3005. Association for Computational Linguistics, Minneapolis (2019). https://doi.org/10.18653/v1/N19-1304

7. Gilardi, F., Gessler, T., Kubli, M., Müller, S.: Social media and political agenda setting. Polit. Commun. **39**(1), 39–60 (2021). https://doi.org/10.1080/10584609.2021.1910390

8. Hartmann, N.S., Fonseca, E.R., Shulby, C.D., Treviso, M.V., Rodrigues, J.S., Aluísio, S.M.: Portuguese word embeddings: evaluating on word analogies and natural language tasks. In: Anais do Simpósio Brasileiro de Tecnologia da Informação e da Linguagem Humana, pp. 122–131. SBC, Porto Alegre (2017)

9. Haykin, S.S.: Neural Networks and Learning Machines, 3rd edn. Pearson Education, Upper Saddle River (2009)

10. Johnson, K., Goldwasser, D.: Classification of moral foundations in microblog political discourse. In: Proceedings of the Annual Meeting of the Association for Computational Linguistics, pp. 720–730. Association for Computational Linguistics, Melbourne (2018). https://doi.org/10.18653/v1/P18-1067

11. Mikolov, T., Sutskever, I., Chen, K., Corrado, G.S., Dean, J.: Distributed representations of words and phrases and their compositionality. In: Advances in Neural Information Processing Systems, vol. 26, pp. 3111–3119. Curran Associates, Inc. (2013). https://doi.org/10.5555/2999792.2999959

12. Peterson, A., Spirling, A.: Classification accuracy as a substantive quantity of interest: measuring polarization in westminster systems. Polit. Anal. **26**(1), 120–128 (2018). https://doi.org/10.1017/pan.2017.39

13. Recuero, R., Soares, F.B., Gruzd, A.: Hyperpartisanship, disinformation and political conversations on Twitter: the Brazilian Presidential Election of 2018. In: Proceedings of the International AAAI Conference on Web and Social Media, vol. 14, no. 1, pp. 569–578 (2020)

14. Sales, A., Balby, L., Veloso, A.: Media bias characterization in Brazilian Presidential Elections. In: Proceedings of the ACM Conference on Hypertext and Social Media, pp. 231–240. Association for Computing Machinery, New York (2019). https://doi.org/10.1145/3342220.3343656

15. Sardinha, E., Costa, S.: Direita cresce e engole o centro no Congresso mais fragmentado da história. Congresso em Foco (2019). https://bit.ly/3jwMbc8

16. Shalders, A.: Direita ou esquerda? Análise de votações indica posição de partidos brasileiros no espectro ideológico. BBC Brasil (2017). https://bbc.in/3noEkOR

17. de Souza, R.M., Guedes da Graça, L.F., dos Santos Silva, R.: Politics on the web: using Twitter to estimate the ideological positions of Brazilian representatives. Braz. Polit. Sci. Rev. **11**, 1–26 (2017)

18. Tsakalidis, A., Aletras, N., Cristea, A.I., Liakata, M.: Nowcasting the stance of social media users in a sudden vote: the case of the Greek Referendum. In: Proceedings of the ACM International Conference on Information and Knowledge Management, pp. 367–376. Association for Computing Machinery, New York (2018). https://doi.org/10.1145/3269206.3271783

19. Tsur, O., Calacci, D., Lazer, D.: A frame of mind: using statistical models for detection of framing and agenda setting campaigns. In: Proceedings of the Annual Meeting of the Association for Computational Linguistics and the International Joint Conference on Natural Language Processing, pp. 1629–1638 (2015)

20. Vasconcellos, F.: Maioria dos partidos se posiciona como de Centro. Veja quem sobra no campo da Direita e da Esquerda. O Globo (2016). https://glo.bo/3BaP6gj

21. Yu, H.F., Huang, F.L., Lin, C.J.: Dual coordinate descent methods for logistic regression and maximum entropy models. Mach. Learn. **85**(1–2), 41–75 (2011). https://doi.org/10.1007/s10994-010-5221-8

22. Zhou, P., et al.: Attention-based bidirectional long short-term memory networks for relation classification. In: Proceedings of the Annual Meeting of the Association for Computational Linguistics, pp. 207–212. Association for Computational Linguistics, Berlin (2016). https://doi.org/10.18653/v1/P16-2034

Integrating Question Answering and Text-to-SQL in Portuguese

Marcos Menon José[1]([⊠])[iD], Marcelo Archanjo José[2][iD],
Denis Deratani Mauá[3][iD], and Fábio Gagliardi Cozman[1][iD]

[1] Escola Politécnica, Universidade de São Paulo, São Paulo, Brazil
{marcos.jose,fgcozman}@usp.br
[2] Center for Artificial Intelligence (C4AI), São Paulo, Brazil
marcelo.archanjo@usp.br
[3] Instituto de Matemática e Estatística, Universidade de São Paulo, São Paulo, Brazil
denis.maua@usp.br

Abstract. Deep learning transformers have drastically improved systems that automatically answer questions in natural language. However, different questions demand different answering techniques; here we propose, build and validate an architecture that integrates different modules to answer two distinct kinds of queries. Our architecture takes a free-form natural language text and classifies it to send it either to a Neural Question Answering Reasoner or a Natural Language parser to SQL. We implemented a complete system for the Portuguese language, using some of the main tools available for the language and translating training and testing datasets. Experiments show that our system selects the appropriate answering method with high accuracy (over 99%), thus validating a modular question answering strategy.

Keywords: Question answering · Transformers networks · Natural language processing in portuguese · Natural language interfaces to databases

1 Introduction

Question Answering (QA) has undergone a significant evolution over the past few years with the emergence of transformer neural networks [17]. Consider the Stanford Question Answering Dataset (SQuAD) task [13]: state-of-the-art performance increased from about 70% accuracy in 2018 to over 90% in 2020 [23], thus surpassing human performance.

Despite their success, transformer-based neural models pre-trained on massive datasets [12,13] still fail to answer satisfactorily certain types of questions. This is partly because many scalable approaches mostly repeat information in the corpus, and approaches that perform reasoning scale poorly [1].

In practice, it seems that different strategies better address different types of questions. While factual and simple common-sense questions can be properly

© Springer Nature Switzerland AG 2022
V. Pinheiro et al. (Eds.): PROPOR 2022, LNAI 13208, pp. 278–287, 2022.
https://doi.org/10.1007/978-3-030-98305-5_26

answered by neural question answering models with access to sizeable unstructured text corpora, questions that require complex reasoning or chaining of information are best answered by systems based on relational databases.

To exploit the best of both approaches, we propose here a new architecture that combines neural models trained with large, unstructured datasets, and neural models trained to respond to database queries states in natural language (text-to-SQL interfaces). Additionally, we target texts in the Portuguese language, as there has been little effort in developing question answering tools for this language.

The proposed architecture takes natural-language questions and selects the appropriate answerer using a text classifier. We experimented with two popular text classifiers: a naive Bayes classifier and a neural classifier based on the Portuguese pre-trained transformer network BERTimbau (Portuguese BERT model) [16], the latter showing superior performance. Once a question is classified, it is fed either into a neural reader-retriever model composed of a BM25 [14] retriever and a PTT5 (Portuguese T5 model) [3] reader, or into the text-to-SQL model mRAT-SQL (multilingual Relation-Aware Transformer SQL) [7] that uses a mT5 (multilingual T5 model) [20] model to produce a SQL query that is then run to generate an answer.

Our approach differs from previous efforts that combine techniques to QA. For example, in the landmark work on the Watson engine [6], the question is feed to an ensemble of predictors and their confidences scores are then used to decide which answer to return (if any). The work of Li et al. [10] uses BM25 and T5, in which the first select both tables and passages related to the question, and then T5 has to decide and answer in SQL or text, thus using a single model to answer both types of questions.

We evaluated our approach on a new biomedical domain QA benchmark built by combining and translating to Portuguese three publicly available datasets: the MS MARCO dataset with factual questions [12], and the text-to-SQL datasets Spider [21] and MIMICSQL [18]. The use of a closed-domain (biomedicine) ensures that the classifier learns to differentiate between question types and not between different domains. All the relevant code, models and data are publicly available.[1]

2   Background and Tools

In this paper, we resort to text classifiers and question answering methods.

Text classification algorithms can be divided into classical approaches and deep neural networks. In the first case, in general, the text is transformed into a sparse vector and one of the conventional machine learning techniques, such as Support Vector Machines, is used to classify it. The state-of-the-art deep learning approach uses pre-trained transformers networks since they allow the transfer learning, and the encoder layers can make good use of context information in the input text.

---

[1] https://github.com/C4AI/Integrating-Question-Answering-and-Text-to-SQL-in-Portuguese.

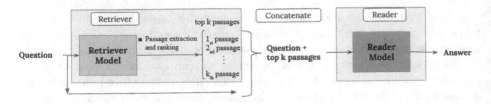

Fig. 1. Neural Question Answering Reasoner using the reader-retriever architecture.

Question Answering systems that deal with factual questions usually resort to two blocks: a retriever and a reader. The retriever gathers passages (small chunks of text) that are concatenated with the question; the reader generates the answer (Fig. 1). Some proposals use neural transformers both in the retriever and the reader [8], while others use keyword-based models for the retriever [4].

For the **translation of textual questions to SQL**, known as NL2SQL, there are rule-based approaches, machine-learning approaches, and mixtures of both. Unlike traditional QA, NL2SQL usually deals with context-specific questions and idiosyncratic patterns. For example, the question *"How many appointments are there?"* is meaningless without context, and must be grounded on the facts and schema of a specified database; e.g., a table named Appointment.

3   Proposed Architecture

Figure 2 summarizes our proposal: a free-form natural language question is fed into a text classifier that outputs a classification of either 1-factual or 2-text-to-SQL, and processed accordingly. Clearly, more classes can be added to the classifier to address other kinds of questions and other domains. Factual questions are sent to a retriever (Fig. 2b), which sends back passages related to the question. The question and the passages go to the reader (Fig. 2c), which finally produces the answer (Fig. 2e).

We tested two text classifiers: a naive Bayes classifier with one-hot encoding of unigrams as features, and the BERTimbau language model, a version of the BERT model [5] that uses a bidirectional attention mechanism, pre-trained on a corpus of Brazilian Portuguese documents.

We used BM25 [14], a keyword-based technique, as retriever, and PTT5 [3], a Portuguese trained transformer-based encoder-decoder neural network model, as reader. BM25 deals with sparse representation text document retrieval by ranking passages based on their similarity with the question text. This pipeline was based on the DEEPAGÉ system, an implementation by Cação et al. [2], which answered questions from the PAQ dataset [9] about the environment translated into Portuguese.

Questions that require relational databases are sent to a dedicated NL2SQL module. One of the most successful techniques for this is the RAT-SQL+GAP[2]

---

[2] Relation-Aware Transformer SQL Generation-Augmented Pretraining.

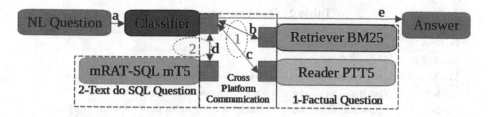

Fig. 2. Proposed architecture that deals both with factual and text-to-SQL questions.

system [15] where, machine learning and a BART-large model are applied. We used a multilingual version of that system, named mRAT-SQL [7], with a mT5-large model (Fig. 2d) for Text-to-SQL, which sends back a query that answers the original question (Fig. 2e).

A significant challenge is integrating these systems; each one has specific libraries, requirements and heavy computational demands. We developed a cross-platform communication scheme through the file system using a shared mount point to send and receive the questions and answers in different machines independent of their operating systems.

4   Question Answering Datasets

In order to build a system in Portuguese, it was necessary to use a dataset with questions and answers in that language. As most of the resources are nowadays available in English, we applied automatic translation to existing datasets in English, thus translating questions using Google Translate and, in the case of MS MARCO, all the contexts and answers for training BM25+PTT5.

The MS MARCO dataset [12] consists of questions that were anonymized from search queries of users of the Bing platform. One of its significant advantages is that it is based on actual questions that people ask in contrast to other artificially created datasets. In the end, human editors wrote down answers to each of the questions with the support of retrieved passages from texts on the internet. To get questions from the closed domain of medicine, a partition created by Ying Xu et al. [19] was used, which separated the question and answer pairs using LDA topic modeling and clustering (they made the data accessible via API[3]). Among the six available domains, the one of interest for this research was biomedicine, with 31620 question/answer pairs. Table 1 shows some examples of translated natural language questions from the MS MARCO dataset.

To build a dataset for the classifier, 112 natural language questions were selected from Spider [21] as training dataset and 100 as testing dataset.[4]

---

[3] The instructions to download can be found in the project github: https://github.com/ibm-aur-nlp/domain-specific-QA.

[4] Spider dataset is a popular resource that contains 200 databases with multiples tables under 138 domains: https://yale-lily.github.io/spider.

Table 1. Questions examples.

Dataset	Translated question
MS MARCO	O que é fístula?
MS MARCO	De onde se ramifica a artéria descendente posterior?
Spider	Quais são os nomes dos pacientes que marcaram uma consulta?
Spider	Quais são os nomes dos cientistas designados para qualquer projeto?
MIMICSQL	quantos pacientes com menos de 45 anos?
MIMICSQL	encontre o número de pacientes únicos com diagnóstico de miopia

Those questions are related to 4 databases[5] about health and medical domains. Together with questions taken from Spider, we added a total of 10,000 questions taken from the MIMICSQL [18] set, a dataset consisting of questions whose answers are SQL queries built automatically and reviewed by human editors. Table 1 shows more examples of natural language questions from Spider and from MIMICSQL,[6] both translated from English to Portuguese.

To conclude this section, we offer a few comments on the datasets. To build a model that correctly classifies each of the classes, the questions must have characteristics that distinguish them. Looking at Table 1, we see that some of the Text to SQL questions are quite specific, like: "Quais são os nomes dos pacientes que marcaram uma consulta?" ("What are names of patients who made an appointment?"). Instead, MS MARCO-derived questions like "O que é fístula?" ("What is fistula?") are much more factual and the answer must be accessed via a knowledge base or corpus. Our dataset is a combination of two different types of datasets. One could argue that this introduces artifacts and trivializes the classification task. While we plan to evolve this research making the dataset ecologically valid [11], we also argue that current QA datasets do share some of the characteristics of our fabricated dataset, with questions that are quite easy for humans to categorize into factual or SQL-based.

5   Experiments

Experiments were run in a number of machines: AMD Ryzen 9 3950X 16-Core Processor, 64 GB RAM, 2 GPUs NVidia GeForce RTX 3090 24 GB running Ubuntu 20.04.2 LTS for both the PTT5 reader and mRAT-SQL; and AMD Ryzen 9 3950X 16-Core Processor, 32 GB RAM, 2 GPUs NVidia GeForce RTX 3080 10 GB running Ubuntu 20.04.2 LTS for the classifier and BM25.[7]

---

[5] hospital_1 100 questions (test), protein_institute 20 questions (train), medicine_enzyme_interaction 44 questions (train), scientist_1 48 questions (train).

[6] Text-to-SQL Generation for Question Answering on Electronic Medical Records Github: https://github.com/wangpinggl/TREQS.

[7] We used well-known implementations of naive Bayes [22] and transformers. In particular, the tranformers HuggingFace library, at https://huggingface.co/transformers/, and also simpletransformers at https://simpletransformers.ai/docs/installation/.

5.1 Classifier

As the construction of each of the original datasets was different, it is possible to notice that there are some differences in the format of the questions. The biggest one is that in the MIMICSQL and Spider datasets, most questions came with punctuation (interrogation or period), while in MS MARCO this did not happen with the same frequency. Therefore, a cleanup was performed, taking away the final punctuation and some special characters so that the datasets would be more similar. This was important because the trained model did not learn to separate by unwanted information but to classify due to the content and type of question.

The team decided to match the instance number between the two dataset classes for classifier training. So, there were 8000 training and 1000 validation MIMIC questions and 112 separate for Spider training (from protein_institute, scientist_1 and medicine_enzyme: the ones related to biomedicine), we separated the first 9112 training questions from the MS MARCO dataset.

In order to obtain a correct evaluation of both models, Naive Bayes Classifier and BERTimbau,[8] and to compare them, cross-validation was performed in the database with 10 folds—dividing the database into 10% pieces and training with the other 90% 10 different times. This allows a comparison between the models and to verify the standard deviation between the pieces of training and thus its generalizability.

Once the best model is decided based on the cross-validation result, it will be tested by checking its performance separately for each dataset. All test questions from MS MARCO biomedical, 4743, all from test MIMIC, 1000, and 100 from the database Hospital_1 from Spider were selected for this step.

5.2 Question Answering Reasoner

MS MARCO is made available with the questions gathered with their respective answers and the context of the answer. In order to simulate a real system, the questions were separated from their contexts, and the joining of all these documents formed the Knowledge Base (KB).

The BM25's function is to search inside this KB to help the reader answer the question. Thus, following the literature, the KB was broken into passages of up to 100 words (respecting punctuation), and when a question arrives, the model removes the K-passages closest to that question. The value of K chosen was 5 following the lighter model of the work by CaÇão et al. [2].

Finally, the PTT5 pre-trained neural network was trained[9] using the questions together with the respective 5 passages selected for the BM25 using the totality of the 22134 training questions of MS MARCO. After training, the model was tested with 4743 test questions and the Exact Match and Macro Average

---

[8] Trained using 5 epochs, learning rate of 5e-5, batch size of 32 and maximum sequence length of 512.

[9] Trained using 25 epochs, learning rate of 2e-5, batch size of 32 and maximum sequence length of 512.

Table 2. Top: results of the classifiers Naive Bayes and BERTimbau in a 10 fold cross validation in the training dataset. Bottom: results of the BERTimbau classifier in the different test datasets.

Classifier Algorithm	Validation F1-Score
Naive Bayes Classifier	98.2 ± 0.3 %
BERTimbau	99.9 ± 0.01 %

MS MARCO Test Accuracy	Spider Test Accuracy	MIMIC Test Accuracy
99.8 %	98.0%	99.6%

F1-Score metrics were verified based on an adaptation of the codes provided by the SQuAD dataset team.

6   Results and Analyses

The entire architecture has inference time that depends on the type of question it receives. While it takes an average of 7.4 s to answer a factual question, questions that are based on SQL tables take only 3.2 s on average. This was expected because the Question Answering Reasoner depends on two subsystems (BM25 and PTT5) while NL2SQL depends only on one (mRAT-SQL).

We start by analyzing the classifiers. Both of them produced high F1-Scores[10] in cross-validation with 10 different folds. While the naive Bayes classifier is faster and lighter than BERTimbau, we decided to adopt the latter for the next steps as it got the best results in the validation (99.9%), as shown in Table 2 (top).

In the testing datasets, BERTimbau kept the best results from the cross-validation, Table 2 (bottom). It is possible to infer that the results of Spider were slightly inferior because there were fewer training instances, but it was still excellent since the model managed to generalize from similar questions MIMIC.

These results demonstrate that questions in different classes are indeed quite different on average. Our proposed modular architecture does not significantly decrease the performance of the techniques that come in the following steps.

As much as the BERTimbau based model has a close-to-perfect result, it is interesting to analyze which of the questions in the test set are wrongly classified. One of the questions in the MIMIC set is "Como os Nephrocaps são administrados" ("*How are Nephrocaps managed*"), which could very well be considered a factual question given that this information could come from a text. MS MARCO's question "Qual é o propósito do pedido de Hektoen Enteric Agar" ("*What is the purpose of Hektoen's request Enteric Agar*") was misclassified, probably because many of the SQL questions are about specific people like "how many patients Doctor X has seen this month".

Overall, results obtained with the MS MARCO Biomedical Dataset (translated into Portuguese) are consistent with the literature [2] with Macro Average

---

[10] This is the standard F1-score for classification, not the Macro Average F1-Score.

F1-Score of 32.0%. It is worth remembering that there is an inevitable variance depending on the dataset used, and, in the case of MS MARCO, there are responses that are longer than the PAQ dataset, which can increase the complexity.

We should note that in our implementation, mRAT-SQL with mT5-large was fine-tuned with a multilingual dataset with four languages: English (original), Portuguese, Spanish, and French (these three translated versions using Google Translator). This extensive training dataset leads to the best results in Portuguese, even better than just training solely with the dataset in Portuguese [7].

In short, the architecture works as expected; we now present some examples that are related to an actual application.

When the model receives the question: "O que causa dor nas costas" (*"What causes back pain"*) that is in the MS MARCO test group, it sends the question to the Question Answering Reasoner since the question seems factual and must look for the answer in texts. So, the final answer you get is: "A dor nas costas é causada por uma queda ou levantamento pesado." (*"Back pain is caused by a fall or heavy lifting."*), since one of the retrieved texts is: "A dor nas costas pode vir de repente e durar menos de seis semanas (aguda), que pode ser causada por uma queda ou levantamento pesado" (*"Back pain can come on suddenly and last for less than six weeks (acute), which can be caused by a fall or heavy lifting."*).

As for the question "Encontre o procedimento mais caro." (*"Find the most expensive procedure."*), the model correctly classifies it as an SQL question. Thus, the mRAT-SQL model returns the answer "SELECT Procedures.Name FROM Procedures ORDER BY Procedures.Cost Asc LIMIT 1" which performs all the queries correctly.

7 Conclusion

This paper proposed and validated a new Question Answering architecture that classifies natural language questions in Portuguese to feed them to appropriate systems, either a neural reader-retriever or a natural language parser to SQL. Experiments with real data demonstrated that a simple classifier can achieve near-perfect results in the closed biomedical domain. The possibility of integrating more subsystems is encouraging; while our original goal has been attained, there is still room for including other models and techniques.

Since the dataset used merges different sources, it is possible that the results are overestimated. Future work to mitigate this is to increase the number of sources and to perform data augmentation.

Acknowledgment. This work was partly supported by Itaú Unibanco S.A. through the *Programa de Bolsas Itaú* (PBI) of the *Centro de Ciência de Dados* da Universidade de São Paulo (C^2D-USP); by the Center for Artificial Intelligence (C4AI) through support from the São Paulo Research Foundation (FAPESP grant #2019/07665-4) and from the IBM Corporation; by CNPq grants no. 312180/2018-7 and 304012/2019-0, and CAPES Finance Code 001.

References

1. Bender, E.M., Gebru, T., McMillan-Major, A., Shmitchell, S.: On the dangers of stochastic parrots: can language models be too big? In: Proceedings of the 2021 ACM Conference on Fairness, Accountability, and Transparency, pp. 610–623. Association for Computing Machinery, New York, NY, USA (2021). https://doi.org/10.1145/3442188.3445922
2. Cação, F.N., José, M.M., Oliveira, A.S., Spindola, S., Costa, A.H.R., Cozman, F.G.: Deepagé: answering questions in Portuguese about the Brazilian environment. In: Britto, A., Valdivia, D.K. (eds.) Intelligent Systems. BRACIS 2021. Lecture Notes in Computer Science, vol. 13074. Springer, Cham (2021). https://doi.org/10.1007/978-3-030-91699-2_29
3. Carmo, D., Piau, M., Campiotti, I., Nogueira, R., de Alencar Lotufo, R.: PTT5: pretraining and validating the T5 model on brazilian portuguese data. CoRR abs/2008.09144 (2020). https://arxiv.org/abs/2008.09144
4. Chen, D., Fisch, A., Weston, J., Bordes, A.: Reading Wikipedia to answer open-domain questions. In: Proceedings of the 55th Annual Meeting of the Association for Computational Linguistics (Volume 1: Long Papers), pp. 1870–1879. Association for Computational Linguistics, Vancouver, Canada (2017). https://doi.org/10.18653/v1/P17-1171
5. Devlin, J., Chang, M., Lee, K., Toutanova, K.: BERT: pre-training of deep bidirectional transformers for language understanding. In: Proceedings of the 2019 Conference of the North American Chapter of the Association for Computational Linguistics: Human Language Technologies, NAACL-HLT 2019, Minneapolis, MN, USA, June 2–7, 2019, Volume 1 (Long and Short Papers), pp. 4171–4186. Association for Computational Linguistics (2019). https://doi.org/10.18653/v1/n19-1423
6. Ferrucci, D., et al.: Building watson: an overview of the deepQA project. AI Mag. **31**(3), 59–79 (2010). https://doi.org/10.1609/aimag.v31i3.2303
7. José, M.A., Cozman, F.G.: mRAT-SQL+GAP: a Portuguese text-to-SQL transformer. In: Britto, A., Valdivia Delgado, K. (eds.) BRACIS 2021. LNCS (LNAI), vol. 13074, pp. 511–525. Springer, Cham (2021). https://doi.org/10.1007/978-3-030-91699-2_35
8. Lewis, P., et al.: Retrieval-augmented generation for knowledge-intensive NLP tasks. In: Advances in Neural Information Processing Systems. vol. 33, pp. 9459–9474. Curran Associates, Inc. (2020). https://doi.org/10.48550/arXiv.2005.11401
9. Lewis, P., et al.: Paq: 65 million probably-asked questions and what you can do with them. Trans. Assoc. Comput. Linguis. **9**, 1098–1115 (2021). https://doi.org/10.1162/tacl_a_00415
10. Li, A.H., Ng, P., Xu, P., Zhu, H., Wang, Z., Xiang, B.: Dual reader-parser on hybrid textual and tabular evidence for open domain question answering. In: Proceedings of the 59th Annual Meeting of the Association for Computational Linguistics and the 11th International Joint Conference on Natural Language Processing, ACL/IJCNLP 2021, (Volume 1: Long Papers), Virtual Event, August 1–6, 2021, pp. 4078–4088. Association for Computational Linguistics (2021). https://doi.org/10.18653/v1/2021.acl-long.315
11. McCallum, A., Penn, G., Munteanu, C., Zhu, X.: Ecological validity and the evaluation of speech summarization quality. In: Proceedings of the 2012 IEEE Workshop on Spoken Language Technology, SLT 2012, pp. 467–472 (2012). https://doi.org/10.1109/SLT.2012.6424269

12. Nguyen, T., et al.: MS MARCO: a human generated Machine reading Comprehension dataset. In: CEUR Workshop Proceedings, vol. 1773, pp. 1–10 (2016)

13. Rajpurkar, P., Zhang, J., Lopyrev, K., Liang, P.: SQuAD: 100,000+ questions for machine comprehension of text. In: Proceedings of the 2016 Conference on Empirical Methods in Natural Language Processing, pp. 2383–2392. Association for Computational Linguistics, Austin, Texas (2016). https://doi.org/10.18653/v1/D16-1264

14. Robertson, S., Zaragoza, H.: The probabilistic relevance framework: Bm25 and beyond. Found. Trends Inf. Retr. **3**(4), 333–389 (2009). https://doi.org/10.1561/1500000019

15. Shi, P., et al.: Learning contextual representations for semantic parsing with generation-augmented pre-training. Proc. AAAI Conf. Artif. Intell. **35**(15), 13806–13814 (2021). https://doi.org/10.48550/arXiv.2012.10309

16. Souza, F., Nogueira, R., Lotufo, R.: Bertimbau: pretrained BERT models for Brazilian Portuguese. In: Cerri, R., Prati, R.C. (eds.) Intelligent Systems. BRACIS 2020. Lecture Notes in Computer Science, vol. 12319. Springer, Cham (2020). https://doi.org/10.1007/978-3-030-61377-8_28

17. Vaswani, A., et al.: Attention is all you need. In: Proceedings of the 31st International Conference on Neural Information Processing Systems, pp. 6000–6010. Curran Associates Inc., Red Hook, NY, USA (2017)

18. Wang, P., Shi, T., Reddy, C.K.: Text-to-SQL generation for question answering on electronic medical records. In: WWW '20: The Web Conference 2020, Taipei, Taiwan, April 20–24, 2020, pp. 350–361. ACM/IW3C2 (2020). https://doi.org/10.1145/3366423.3380120

19. Xu, Y., Zhong, X., Yepes, A.J.J., Lau, J.H.: Forget me not: reducing catastrophic forgetting for domain adaptation in reading comprehension. In: 2020 International Joint Conference on Neural Networks (IJCNN), pp. 1–8 (2020). https://doi.org/10.1109/IJCNN48605.2020.9206891

20. Xue, L., et al.: mT5: a massively multilingual pre-trained text-to-text transformer. In: Proceedings of the 2021 Conference of the North American Chapter of the Association for Computational Linguistics: Human Language Technologies, pp. 483–498. Association for Computational Linguistics (2021). https://doi.org/10.18653/v1/2021.naacl-main.41

21. Yu, T., et al.: Spider: a large-scale human-labeled dataset for complex and cross-domain semantic parsing and text-to-SQL task. In: Proceedings of the 2018 Conference on Empirical Methods in Natural Language Processing, pp. 3911–3921. Association for Computational Linguistics, Brussels, Belgium (2018). https://doi.org/10.18653/v1/D18-1425

22. Zhang, H.: The optimality of Naive Bayes. In: Proceedings of the Seventeenth International Florida Artificial Intelligence Research Society Conference, FLAIRS 2004, vol. 2, pp. 562–567 (2004)

23. Zhang, Z., Yang, J., Zhao, H.: Retrospective reader for machine reading comprehension. Proc. AAAI Conf. Artif. Intell. **35**(16), 14506–14514 (2021). https://doi.org/10.48550/arXiv.2001.09694

Named Entity Extractors for New Domains by Transfer Learning with Automatically Annotated Data

Emanuel Matos[1] , Mário Rodrigues[2] , and António Teixeira[1(✉)]

[1] DETI/IEETA, University of Aveiro, Aveiro, Portugal
{easm,ajst}@ua.pt
[2] ESTGA/IEETA, University of Aveiro, Aveiro, Portugal
mjfr@ua.pt

Abstract. Named entity recognition (NER) tasks imply token-level labels. Annotating documents can be time-consuming, costly, and prone to human error. In many real-life scenarios, the lack of labeled data has become the biggest bottleneck preventing NER being effectively used in some domains and with some natural languages, with negative impacts on the quality of some tasks. To overcome the barrier of the lack of annotated data for new application domains in some natural languages, we propose a method that uses the output of an ensemble of NER's to automatically annotate the data needed to train a Bidirectional Encoder Representations from Transformers (BERT) based NER for Portuguese. The performance was assessed using MiniHAREM dataset with promising results. For domain relevant classes such as LOCAL, F1, Precision and Recall above 50% were obtained when training only with automatically annotated data.

Keywords: Named entities · Named Entity Recognition (NER) · Transfer learning · Automatic annotation

1 Introduction

Named Entity Recognition (NER) has application in several domains such as user interest modeling [27] and dialog systems [9], among other. Approaches to NER include training statistical sequential models based on handcrafted features, and more recently, deep learning models [8,14] to ease the burden of designing crafted rules. The models with robust performance are often created based on substantial amounts of labeled training data.

Because NER tasks imply token-level labels, annotating many documents can be time-consuming, and thus costly and prone to human error. In many real-life scenarios, the lack of labeled data has become the biggest bottleneck preventing NER being used in some domains and tasks. To solve the label scarcity problem, [10] proposes a method based on BERT [3] and distant supervision which involves

© Springer Nature Switzerland AG 2022
V. Pinheiro et al. (Eds.): PROPOR 2022, LNAI 13208, pp. 288–298, 2022.
https://doi.org/10.1007/978-3-030-98305-5_27

avoiding the traditional labeling procedure by matching tokens in the target corpus with concepts in knowledge bases such as Wikipedia and YAGO [15].

Our approach is also based on BERT. Instead of annotated data we use as reference the output of an ensemble of 3 general purpose NER developed previously [16] as well as an annotated dataset created by linguists named HAREM [17,20]. The performance was measured using a fully annotated corpus, MiniHAREM, that is not included in the first HAREM. The results show that the proposed method is feasible, and the resulting system was able to annotate previously unseen data.

This document is organized as follows: after this Introduction follows the second section elaborating on the relevant Related Work. In the third section the proposed Method is explained followed by Results in Sect. 4. The paper ends in Sect. 5 with the Conclusion.

2 Related Work

The set of approaches proposed for NER can be classified according to 2 types: Rule-based, covering both systems based in patterns and in lists (the so-called Gazetteers); and machine learning based.

Machine learning methods are more flexible to adapt to distinct contexts if there exists enough data about the target context. Diverse machine learning methods have been applied to NER, such as Support Vector Machines (SVM), Conditional Random Field (CRF) or Neural networks (NN) (e.g., [6]).

In recent years, Deep Learning and the existence of larger datasets resulted in relevant advances in NER with systems based on Long Short-Term Memory (LSTM), Bidirectional LSTMs (Bi-LSTM) and Transformers (e.g., [10,14]). LSTMs are recursive neural networks in which the hidden layers act as memory cells. As a result, they revealed better capabilities to deal with long range dependencies in data [7,8]. Transformers [23], introduced in 2017, are a deep learning model based on the attention mechanism designed to handle sequential input data, such as natural language. Their potential for parallelization enabled training using huge datasets. This created the conditions for the development of pretrained systems such as BERT (Bidirectional Encoder Representations from Transformers) and GPT (Generative Pre-trained Transformer) [18]. Transformers demonstrated their superior efficiency in the recognition of named entities and in a variety of other classification tasks.

Following the general tendency, for Portuguese, the last years main developments on NER were systems featuring machine learning. A representative selection of works is presented in the following paragraphs:

The LeNER-Br system [13], presented in 2018, was developed for Brazilian legal documents. It features LSTM-CRF models trained using the Paramopama data set and achieved F1 scores of 97.0% and 88.8% for legislation and judicial entities, respectively. The results show the feasibility of using NER for judicial applications.

Pirovani and coworkers [19] adopted a hybrid technique combining Conditional Random Fields with a Local Grammar (CRF+LG) for a NER task at IberLEF 2019.

Lopes and coworkers [12] addressed NER for Clinical data in Portuguese showing Bi-LSTM and word embeddings superiority relative to CRF. They obtained F1 scores above 80%.

The first use of BERT in NER for Portuguese appeared in 2020 [21], adopting a BERT-CRF architecture combining transfer capabilities of BERT with the structured CRF forecasts. BERT was pre-trained using the brWac corpus (2.68 billion tokens), and the NER model was trained using the First HAREM and tested with MiniHAREM. This system surpassed the previous state art despite being trained with much less data.

To the best of our knowledge all these machine learning systems were trained with data annotated by humans, at least in a revision stage. This is a major limitation in the development of NER for new domains, which are in large demand by the expansion of potential application areas.

3   Method

The process used to assess the potential of automatically annotated entities is summarized in Fig. 1. Distinct BERT-based NERs were trained with automatically annotated data (BIO annotations) to detect words belonging to entities. The difference between both variants was if they included or not out of domain annotated entities, in this case obtained with the First HAREM dataset. The performance of entity detection of the 2 variants was assessed using a third annotated dataset (MiniHAREM) and by querying DBPedia. The main blocks of the processing are described in the following subsections.

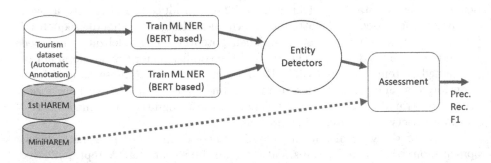

Fig. 1. Overview of the process adopted to assess the potential of automatically annotated data for the development of Named Entity Detection for new domains. The development of Named Entity Detection for new domains implies the use of automatically annotated datasets for training machine learning models.

3.1 Datasets

Three datasets were used, two for training and one for testing, namely:

Automatically annotated dataset − we have used the results of our recent work on automatic annotation [16] as data to train the models. Briefly, a corpus for Tourism domain - a set of more than 300 documents obtained from Wikivoyage [25] - was annotated using a set of 3 NER (Linguakit NER [4,11], Alen NLP [1,5] and a DBPedia-based NER developed by the authors [16]). The output tags of these 3 NERs were combined to tag a word as part of an ENTITY or not, without including classification of the entity. More details can be found in [16].

HAREM datasets − Two HAREM [17,20] datasets were used, the First HAREM and the MiniHAREM, both with their labels annotated manually. The evaluation of the Entity detectors was performed against MiniHAREM. Profiting from the processing and XML made available by authors of [21][1], both text and BIO annotated files were derived.

The number of words annotated as part of Entity are presented in Fig. 2. The automatically annotated dataset for Tourism is the smallest one, being less than half the size of its combination with HAREM.

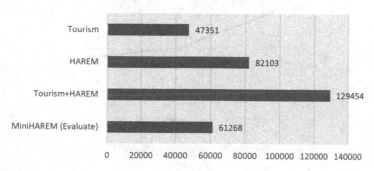

Fig. 2. Number of words annotated as part of an Entity for the 3 datasets used and the combination Tourism+HAREM used for training.

3.2 BERT-Based Classifiers for Entity Detection

Motivated by the recent evolutions highlighted in Sect. 2, a NER based on BERT [3] was selected for our experiments. After tests with several implementations, we have adopted a simple and documented implementation by Tobias Sterbak [22] using the Transformers package by Huggingface [26], Keras and TensorFlow. It uses a BERT case sensitive tokenizer − based on Wordpiece tokenizer − that splits tokens into subwords.

---

[1] https://github.com/neuralmind-ai/portuguese-bert/tree/master/ner_evaluation.

Two base systems were considered for our investigation: one trained using just automatic annotations (called Tourism); a second one trained with these automatic annotations plus the annotations of First HAREM (Tourism+HAREM).

Training

The models were finetuned with AdamW optimizer adopting the default parameters of [22], $\mathtt{lr} = 3 \times 10^{-5}$ and $\mathtt{eps} = 10^{-8}$, in a notebook with GPU NVIDIA GeForce RTX 2060.

The training datasets were split into training and validation, with 90% for training and 10% for validation. The stop criteria adopted were a maximum of 10 epochs or the increase of loss in the validation set.

The variation of loss with epochs is presented in Fig. 3 for the two variants trained. The training process stopped, for both variants, after the third epoch due to the loss increase. The number of epochs needed to finetune the model is aligned with the information in [22] that "a few epochs should be enough ... 3–4 epochs".

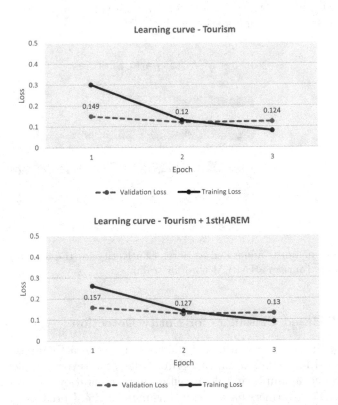

Fig. 3. Loss variation during the training of both system variants.

The information regarding processing time is presented in Fig. 4. It is visible that train and test durations are similar for both variants, and the complete process (train plus test) is under 8 min.

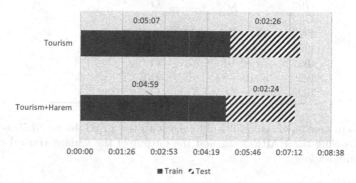

PROCESSING TIME (MINUTES)

Fig. 4. Training and testing times (in minutes) for the two system variants.

4   Results

The output obtained by processing MiniHAREM is exemplified in Fig. 5. The performance was evaluated using the standard metrics (Precision, Recall and F1) considering both the individual words of the entity and the full entity as a single unit (the entity is well detected when all words composing it are correctly tagged).

The results obtained for both variants of the system (trained with and without using First HAREM) are summarized in Table 1.

Table 1. Results of the evaluation of both variants with MiniHAREM, showing word and entity metrics. Acc.* refers to Accuracy calculated excluding all words with tag "O".

Train data	Word-based					Entity-based			
	Acc.	Prec.	Rec.	F1	Acc.*	Acc.	Prec.	Rec.	F1
Tourism only	92.6	90.0	37.3	52.7	35.8	88.6	41.4	26.4	32.2
Tourism + HAREM	94.0	94.0	49.6	64.9	48.0	88.6	56.3	40.4	47.1

Table 1 shows that even testing with an out-of-domain dataset:

- with automatically annotated, tourism domain, data the system could achieve a word-based precision and full entity detection of 90.0% and 41.4%, respectively.

Position	Word	HAREM Tag	BERT NER Output
4702	do	O	O
4703	Porto	B-LOCAL	B-ENT
4704	para	O	O
4705	Nine	B-LOCAL	B-ENT
4706	.	O	O
...			
4925	São	B-LOCAL	B-ENT
4926	João	I-LOCAL	B-ENT
4927	do	I-LOCAL	O
4928	Souto	I-LOCAL	B-ENT
4929	.	O	O

Fig. 5. Two fragments of the results obtained with the BERT-based NER using Mini-HAREM, showing the HAREM tag and the output of the variant trained only with automatic annotations.

- Results improved, as expected, by using first HAREM data to complement domain data in the training process.
- Recall is much lower. Over 50% of the words belonging to entities are not detected even when including HAREM data in the training. The best recall value when considering complete entities is 40.4%.
- The best full entity precision is approx. 56%.

As the test dataset contains several entity classes not annotated in our tourism data, it is worth looking in detail at the performance by class. The split of entity-based Precision, Recall and F1 by entity class is presented graphically in Fig. 6.

Bar-plots show that: 1) LOCAL presents the highest F1, being Precision and Recall above 50% when trained with just automatically annotated data. 2) PERSON obtains the second highest F1 but only when HAREM data is used to complement the domain data. 3) Classes that are not in the domain dataset such as WORK or ABSTRACTION present interesting Precision and Recall, showing some potential of the system to generalize.

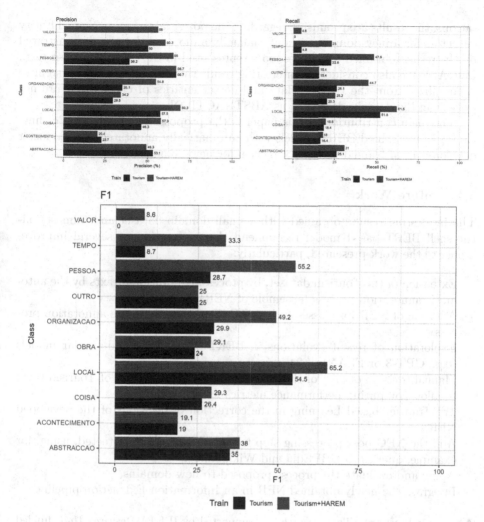

Fig. 6. Entity-based Precision (top left), Recall (top right) and F1 by entity class.

5   Conclusion

Aiming at making possible and simple creation of new NER for domains without annotated data available, **the potential of automatic annotation to
provide the necessary datasets for training of entity detectors by fine-
tuning of BERT models is assessed in this paper**.

A first proof-of-concept of the proposed method was evaluated with an existing manually annotated dataset, MiniHAREM. As the dataset used for testing -
selected by being the only publicly available dataset for NER evaluation in Portuguese - is out-of-domain and integrates several entities without examples in the
domain dataset, the results need to be considered with caution. Admitting limi-

tations, the results are promising regarding the potential to create Named Entity detectors for a new domain without manually annotated data as demonstrated by the results obtained for classes more represented in the domain dataset (e.g., LOCAL). We also consider an interesting result the capability of the system to "generalize" from the training data and detect entities of classes that are not present in the domain data such as ABSTRACTION.

The main contribution of this paper is the proposal and evaluation of fine-tuning of pretrained BERT models with automatically annotated data to foster development of Named Entity Extraction for new domains.

5.1 Future Work

The interesting results obtained with a small domain dataset and (almost) off-the-shelf BERT-based model recommend the exploration of several improvements to the work presented, particularly:

- Extension of the Tourism dataset, by processing additional texts by the automatic annotation process (ensemble of NER).
- Addition of NER for classes such as TIME to the automatic annotation process.
- Exploration of recent evolutions in BERT-based NER and similar models (e.g., GPT-3 or FLAN) [2,24].
- Manual revision of part of the results obtained for a subset of Tourism texts to allow computing performance metrics for domain data.
- Try Transfer based Learning in the correction of decisions of the developed NER.
- Add the NEC post-processing step to classify the entity detected, using, for example, queries to DBPEdia and Wikipedia.
- Apply and evaluate the process proposed to new domains.
- Integrate the newly obtained NER in an Information Extraction pipeline.

Acknowledgement. This research was supported by IEETA Research Unit, funded by National Funds through the FCT - Foundation for Science and Technology, in the context of the project UIDB/00127/2020.

References

1. Allen NLP - An Apache 2.0 NLP research library, built on PyTorch, for developing state-of-the-art deep learning models on a wide variety of linguistic tasks. https://github.com/allenai/allennlp
2. Brown, T.B., et al.: Language models are few-shot learners. arXiv:2005.14165 (2020)
3. Devlin, J., Chang, M.W., Lee, K., Toutanova, K.: BERT: pre-training of deep bidirectional transformers for language understanding. arXiv:1810.04805 (2018)
4. Gamallo, P., Garcia, M.: Linguakit: uma ferramenta multilingue para a análise linguística e a extração de informação. Linguamática **9**(1), 19–28 (2017)

5. Gardner, M., et al.: AllenNLP: a deep semantic natural language processing platform (2018)
6. Goyal, A., Gupta, V., Kumar, M.: Analysis of different supervised techniques for named entity recognition. In: International Conference on Advanced Informatics for Computing Research, pp. 184–195. Springer, New York (2019). https://doi.org/10.1007/978-981-15-0108-1_18
7. Graves, A., Schmidhuber, J.: Framewise phoneme classification with bidirectional LSTM and other neural network architectures. Neural Netw. **18**(5–6), 602–610 (2005)
8. Huang, Z., Xu, W., Yu, K.: Bidirectional LSTM-CRF models for sequence tagging. arXiv:1508.01991 (2015)
9. Ketsmur, M., Teixeira, A., Almeida, N., Silva, S., Rodrigues, M.: Conversational assistant for an accessible smart home: proof-of-concept for portuguese. In: Proceedings of the 8th International Conference on Software Development and Technologies for Enhancing Accessibility and Fighting Info-Exclusion, pp. 55–62. DSAI 2018, Association for Computing Machinery, New York, NY, USA (2018)
10. Liang, C., et al.: Bond: bert-assisted open-domain named entity recognition with distant supervision. In: Proceedings of the 26th ACM SIGKDD International Conference on Knowledge Discovery and Data Mining, pp. 1054–1064. KDD 2020, Association for Computing Machinery, New York, NY, USA (2020)
11. Linguakit full (2020). https://linguakit.com/en/full-analysis
12. Lopes, F., Teixeira, C., Oliveira, H.G.: Contributions to clinical named entity recognition in portuguese. In: Proceedings 18th BioNLP Workshop and Shared Task (2019)
13. Luz de Araujo, P.H., de Campos, T.E., de Oliveira, R.R.R., Stauffer, M., Couto, S., Bermejo, P.: LeNER-Br: a dataset for named entity recognition in Brazilian legal text. In: PROPOR. LNCS, Springer, New York (2018). https://doi.org/10.1007/978-3-319-99722-3_32
14. Ma, X., Hovy, E.: End-to-end sequence labeling via bi-directional LSTM-CNNs-CRF. In: Proceedings of the 54th Annual Meeting of the Association for Computational Linguistics (Volume 1: Long Papers), pp. 1064–1074. Association for Computational Linguistics, Berlin, Germany (Aug 2016)
15. Mahdisoltani, F., Biega, J., Suchanek, F.M.: YAGO3: a Knowledge base from multilingual wikipedias. In: CIDR. Asilomar, United States (2013). https://hal-imt.archives-ouvertes.fr/hal-01699874
16. Matos, E., Rodrigues, M., Miguel, P., Teixeira, A.: Towards automatic creation of annotations to foster development of named entity recognizers. In: Queirós, R., Pinto, M., Simões, A., Portela, F., Pereira, M.J.A. (eds.) 10th Symposium on Languages, Applications and Technologies (SLATE 2021). Open Access Series in Informatics (OASIcs), vol. 94, pp. 11:1–11:14. Schloss Dagstuhl - Leibniz-Zentrum für Informatik, Dagstuhl, Germany (2021). https://drops.dagstuhl.de/opus/volltexte/2021/14428
17. Mota, C., Santos, D. (eds.): Desafios na avaliação conjunta do reconhecimento de entidades mencionadas: O Segundo HAREM. Linguateca (2008), http://www.linguateca.pt/LivroSegundoHAREM, iSBN: 978-989-20-1656-6
18. Patel, A., Arasanipalai, A.: Applied Natural Language Processing in the Enterprise: Teaching Machines to Read, Write, and Understand. O'Reilly Media, Incorporated (2021)
19. Pirovani, J.P., Alves, J., Spalenza, M., Silva, W., da Silveira Colombo, C., Oliveira, E.: Adapting NER (CRF+ LG) for many textual genres. In: IberLEF@ SEPLN, pp. 421–433 (2019)

20. Santos, D., Seco, N., Cardoso, N., Vilela, R.: HAREM: an advanced NER evaluation contest for Portuguese. In: Calzolari, N., et al. (eds.) Proceedings of the 5th International Conference on Language Resources and Evaluation (LREC) (2006)
21. Souza, F., Nogueira, R., Lotufo, R.: Portuguese Named Entity Recognition using BERT-CRF (2020)
22. Sterbak, T.: Named entity recognition with BERT (2018). https://www.depends-on-the-definition.com/named-entity-recognition-with-bert/ last updated: 2020-04-24. Accessed on 24 Oct 2021
23. Vaswani, A., et al.: Attention is all you need. arXiv:1706.03762 (2017)
24. Wei, J., et al.: Finetuned language models are zero-shot learners. arXiv:2109.01652 (2021)
25. Wikivoyage. https://pt.wikivoyage.org/
26. Wolf, T., et al.: Transformers: state-of-the-art natural language processing. In: Proceedings of the 2020 Conference on Empirical Methods in Natural Language Processing: System Demonstrations, pp. 38–45. Association for Computational Linguistics (2020). https://www.aclweb.org/anthology/2020.emnlp-demos.6
27. Zhu, Z., Zhou, Y., Deng, X., Wang, X.: A graph-oriented model for hierarchical user interest in precision social marketing. Electron. Commer. Res. Appl. **35**, 100845 (2019). https://www.sciencedirect.com/science/article/pii/S1567422319300225

PTT5-Paraphraser: Diversity and Meaning Fidelity in Automatic Portuguese Paraphrasing

Lucas Francisco Amaral Orosco Pellicer[1]([⊠]), Paulo Pirozelli[2],
Anna Helena Reali Costa[1], and Alexandre Inoue[3]

[1] Escola Politécnica, Universidade de São Paulo, São Paulo, Brazil
{lucas.pellicer,anna.reali}@usp.br
[2] Institute of Advanced Studies, Universidade de São Paulo, São Paulo, Brazil
paulo.pirozelli.silva@usp.br
[3] Oceanographic Institute, Universidade de São Paulo, São Paulo, Brazil
arinoue@usp.br

Abstract. Paraphrasing is a fundamental technique for many text applications. Typically, this task is performed through models that perform lexical and translation operations, which tend to present a trade-off between meaning preservation and diversity. In this paper, we present a transformer-based approach called *PTT5-Paraphraser*, a PPT5 model fine-tuned on TaPaCo, a large corpus of paraphrases. PTT5-Paraphraser achieves good results according to a number of metrics, showing a good compromise between diversity and fidelity to the original meaning. Two human evaluations are made to explore the paraphrases produced by our model: the first analyzes their quality in terms of preserving the meaning and diversity of sentences, while the second compares automatically generated paraphrases with human-made ones. Finally, we perform a classification task, which shows that datasets augmented with paraphrases can substantially increase the performance of classifiers.

Keywords: Data augmentation · PTT5 · Paraphrases · Text diversity

1 Introduction

Current applications in natural language processing (NLP), particularly those based on neural architectures, demand large amounts of training data. Nonetheless, the addition of new data can represent a considerable issue in some situations: data may be exiguous, costly to acquire, and not very diversified. Depending on the intended use, the new data may also demand additional labeling for supervised learning.

For this reason, automatic data augmentation proves to be a valuable alternative to several NLP applications, by permitting the artificial enlargement of datasets [21]. One particularly interesting form of data augmentation in NLP is *paraphrase generation* [10]. Broadly conceived, paraphrasing involves changing

V. Pinheiro et al. (Eds.): PROPOR 2022, LNAI 13208, pp. 299–309, 2022.
https://doi.org/10.1007/978-3-030-98305-5_28

the lexical and syntactic properties of a text—usually a single sentence or small excerpt—, while keeping its semantic content relatively intact. Paraphrases find several application areas in NLP, such as plagiarism identification [8], dialogue systems [4], and data augmentation for different tasks (e.g., question answering [6]). Paraphrasing techniques can be particularly useful in low resource languages, such as Portuguese [3].

Previously developed paraphrasers make use of lexical or translation operations, or a combination of both techniques. In the first case, words and expressions are replaced by expressions of similar meaning, through a thesaurus or web semantics; as with WordNet [11] and PPDB [7]. The second case depends on back-translation [9,10,22]; i.e., translating a text from a language to another language, and then translating it back to the first language. The result of this process is a new sentence that slightly differs from the original one. This is the case, for example, of ParaNet [10], a neural machine translation paraphraser that back-translates from English to Czech. Finally, models such as ParaBank [8] attempt to combine both approaches, using lexical operations in between translation operations.

In this work, we present *PTT5-Paraphraser*, a paraphraser for Portuguese. PTT5-Paraphraser is based on PTT5 [2], the Portuguese version of T5, a state-of-the-art text-to-text transformer architecture [17]. We fine-tune PTT5 on the Portuguese part of TaPaCo [19], a large corpus collection of paraphrases, in order to improve it to this particular task. PTT5-Paraphraser presents a good compromise between diversity and meaning preservation, providing a great alternative in Portuguese for augmenting NLP datasets.

In Sect. 2, we describe previous works on paraphrasing. Section 3 describes PTT5, as well as the fine-tuning technique and the data used in the fine-tuning process. In Sect. 4, we compare the paraphrases generated with PTT5-Paraphraser with those generated with four other paraphrasers; we also describe the results of two human assessments conducted to evaluate the quality of PTT5-Paraphraser. Finally, Sect. 5 shows the benefits of data augmentation with PTT5-Paraphraser for text classification.

2   Related Work

Low availability of training data is a common problem to many applications in Artificial Intelligence. In these cases, data augmentation can come as a handy solution, which consists of generating synthetic data from the limited original data. Data augmentation is regularly used in several areas, such as image classification [16], object detection [25], and speech recognition [13]. Images are a favorable field for data augmentation—simple heuristics can be applied to pictures, such as rotation and color changes, that produce large amounts of equally adequate data. Data augmentation can be more complicated for NLP tasks, though, since small changes to a text can alter its meaning and introduce unwanted distortions. Despite that, several approaches have been developed in the literature.

A first group of paraphrasers uses lexical resources to generate equivalent texts. In that case, the words and expressions in a text are replaced by words and expressions with similar meaning. Basic implementations of this approach involve the use of thesaurus [8]. More sophisticated versions are based on lexical database, such as WordNet [11], or purposefully developed paraphrase databases, such as PPDB [7].

A second strategy for paraphrase generation is related to translation operations; i.e., translating the original text to a second language and translating it back to the first language; preferably with languages with greater lexical and semantic differences, such as Czech-English or German-Spanish. This solution is employed in ParaNet [10], which is based on neural machine translation. In general, texts produced with translation-based paraphrasers exhibit more diversity than those made with lexical-based ones. Their disadvantage, by contrast, is a greater risk of changing the meaning and context of the original text.

Finally, models such as ParaBank [8] try to combine lexical and translation operations. In between back-translations (usually between Czech and English), ParaBank uses rules and equivalences from lexical models (PPDB or WordNet) [8]. ParaBank offers excellent diversity, but with a higher risk of altering the meaning of texts, when compared to more basic translator paraphrasers.

3   The PTT5-Paraphraser

PTT5-Paraphraser is based on PPT5 [2] – Google's original T5 architecture [17], pre-trained in Portuguese on the BrWac dataset. As the original T5 architecture, PTT5 is a unified text-to-text transformer. It can be used in a number of tasks, such as summarization, machine translation, and question answering.

For the aim of paraphrase generation, we fine-tune PPT5 on TaPaCo [19], a large corpus of paraphrases in 73 languages. The paraphrases in the TaPaCo dataset were obtained from the TaToeba project, a crowdsourcing project for language learners, which offers examples of translations of sentences. Sentences of similar meaning were then grouped together, forming pairs of paraphrases.

For the PTT5 fine-tuning, we select only the paraphrases in Portuguese of TaPaCo. This gives a total of 36,000 pairs of paraphrases, of which 33,000 were used for training and 3,000 for validation. We used the standard maximum likelihood loss function and the AdaFactor optimizer for training. A prefix *parafrase* was created for training and we ran the training in 6 epochs with a batch size equal to 8 observations, similar to project [12]. The model was trained in Google Colab GPU.[1]

At the end of training, PTT5-Paraphraser behaves as a conditional text generator which, when fed with a text marked with the prefix for paraphrase, generates a paraphrase for the input text. PTT5-Paraphraser can be easily put to work, as it is only necessary to load the model and add the prefix for paraphrase to the input text. More importantly, PTT5-Paraphraser is computationally lighter than

---

[1] The codes used for this project are available at https://github.com/lucasfaop/ptt5_paraphraser.

most translators used for paraphrases. Table 1 provides some examples of Pirá questions [1], a dataset of question answering on ocean data, and their respective paraphrases.

Table 1. Examples of paraphrases generated by PTT5 on Pirá dataset

Original question	Paraphrase	Cosine Disim.
O que ocasionou o atraso da construção de tubos na bacia do Espirito Santo que ligariam a região sudeste e nordeste?	O que causou o atraso na construção dos tubos na bacia do Espirito Santo que ligariam as regiões sudeste e nordeste?	0.0043
A produção total na bacia de Campos nos primeiros 4 meses de 2004 equivaleu a quantos % da produção do país?	Qual foi o percentual da produção total na bacia de Campos nos primeiros 4 meses de 2004 comparado com a produção brasileira?	0.0408
A Petrobras criou um programa estratégico para monitorar reservatórios de carbonato. No que esse programa é baseado?	Em que medida foi a criação de um programa estratégico para monitorar reservatórios de carbonato?	0.2247

4   Evaluating Paraphrasers

In this section, we evaluate the paraphrases made by PPT5-Paraphraser, according to computational metrics and human assessments.

4.1   Evaluation by Computational Metrics

We use three different metrics to assess the quality of the paraphrasers: METEOR, BLEU (without brevity penalty), and cosine dissimilarity of sentence embeddings. METEOR and BLEU are both widely used in translation tasks. They indicate how much a candidate text (in our case, a paraphrase) is similar to a reference text. Both metrics, BLEU and METEOR, are indicative of lexical diversity: the higher their score, the more a candidate text is similar in words to the reference text [8]. The main difference between the two metrics is that METEOR is sensitive to word order, while BLEU disregards that information. The third metric, the cosine dissimilarity of sentence embeddings, provides a measure of semantic similarity or, for our purposes, meaning preservation. The embeddings are produced with a multilingual knowledge distillation approach [18]. Ideally, we would like to *minimize* all three metrics: we want a paraphrase that is lexical diverse (low METEOR and BLEU score) and that means the same as the original text (low cosine dissimilarity).

We ran PPT5-Paraphraser on the Pirá [1] and the Assin [5] datasets and compared the generated paraphrases with those generated with four other paraphrasers (WordNet, PPDB, ParaNet, and ParaBank), according to the three aforementioned metrics. The paraphrasers with translation use the M2-M100 model, performing operations in Portuguese and German, while Wordnet for Portuguese was built through Wordnet in NLTK package and PPDB using the lexical model available on the PPDB website.[2] Results can be seen in Table 2.

The lexical paraphraser WordNet generates sentences with a large semantic similarity (low cosine disimilarity), but with low diversity (high METEOR/ BLEU). The translation paraphrasers (ParaNet and ParaBank) and PPDB obtain opposite results: they achieve good lexical diversity (low METEOR/ BLEU) but at the cost of losing some of the original semantic content (high cosine disimilarity).

Table 2. Table of results of paraphrase generation on Pirá and ASSIN datasets (relative position in square brackets, best result in **bold**).

Paraphraser	Pirá			ASSIN		
	METEOR	BLEU w/o bp	Cosine Disim.	METEOR	BLEU w/o bp	Cosine Disim.
WordNet	0.88 [4]	78.9 [5]	**0.042** [1]	0.89 [5]	78.7 [5]	**0.043** [1]
PPDB	0.66 [3]	39.3 [2]	0.099 [4]	0.61 [3]	40.6 [3]	0.132 [5]
ParaNet	0.64 [2]	39.8 [3]	0.08 [3]	0.6 [2]	37.7 [2]	0.096 [3]
ParaBank	**0.62** [1]	**32.8** [1]	0.109 [5]	**0.54** [1]	**31.7** [1]	0.128 [4]
PTT5-Parap.	0.66 [3]	51.3 [4]	0.056 [2]	0.66 [4]	52.2 [4]	0.052 [2]

PTT5-Paraphraser is in an intermediate position in relation to the three metrics. For one side, it scores much better than WordNet in diversity (lower METEOR/BLUE), a paraphraser based on simple lexical operations. At the same time, PTT5-Paraphraser is considerably better in preserving meaning (lower cosine disimilarity) than the more diverse paraphrasers. Overall, PTT5-Paraphraser achieves a good compromise between diversity and semantic fidelity, whereas the other paraphrases seem to lay at one of the extreme poles: low diversity-meaning preserving paraphrasers (WordNet) or high diversity-meaning distorting ones (PPDB, ParaNet, and ParaBank).

4.2 Human Evaluation

The metrics described above provide useful standards to evaluate important aspects of paraphrase generation, such as meaning invariance and sentence diversity. Nonetheless, word matching and dissimilarity of sentence embeddings, the two strategies on which these metrics are based on, may often miss subtler phenomena such as the use of synonymous expressions composed of multiple words, idioms, and substantial syntactic changes. For this reason, we designed two experiments to access the quality of paraphrases from human standards. Each experiment was performed by three annotators.

Experiment 1 aimed to assess the quality of automatically produced paraphrases against the original question they were derived from. For each pair of

---

[2] The lexical model is available at http://paraphrase.org/#/download.

questions, annotators had to answer if the paraphrase was grammatically accept-able. If the answer was affirmative, the paraphrase should be evaluated with respect to "Meaning preservation" and "Diversity". These assessment were made with a Likert scale (1 - Strongly disagree, 2 - Disagree, 3 - Neither agree nor disagree, 4 - Agree, 5 - Strongly agree). 150 evaluations were conducted in this experiment.

Experiment 2 involved comparing the manual paraphrases found in Pirá with the automatically generated ones produced with PPT5-Paraphraser (chosen at random among the k different paraphrases generated by the paraphraser). The annotators had no information of which was which, and the position of the paraphrases (left or right) was randomly assigned. Faced with a question, the annotators had to evaluate which of the two paraphrases was better according to three criteria: "Meaning preservation", "Diversity", and "Clarity". Again, evalu-ations were made according to a Likert scale. Possible answers were: "Paraphrase A", "Paraphrase B" and "Indifferent". 175 evaluations were conducted in this experiment.

Experiment 1 Results: Almost all of the 150 pairs analyzed in Experiment 1 were considered grammatically acceptable by annotators (94.2%).[3] Generally, paraphrases were thought to preserve the original sense of the question: 67.4% of the sentences received a score of 5 and 12.2% a score of 4 regarding mean-ing preservation. As to diversity, most paraphrases were put in the bottom or medium spectrum: 32.4% of the questions received a score of 1, 23.9% a score of 2, and 24% a score of 3.

Not surprisingly, results show an inverse correlation between a paraphrase's ability to preserve the original content and its lexical and syntactic departure from it. Figure 1 displays the diversity of paraphrases for the different scores of meaning preservation. In general, more faithful paraphrases are also more lexical and syntactic similar to the original questions; as they grow in diversity, they tend to become less faithful in meaning. Figure 2 shows the same phenomenon from a different perspective. The more similar in content a paraphrase is to the original question, less diverse it is in average.

Experiment 2 Results: Experiment 2 involved a blind comparison between paraphrases made by humans and with PPT5-Paraphraser. Given a question, annotators had to choose which of the paraphrases: i) Better preserved the orig-inal meaning; ii) Was more diverse; and iii) Exhibited more clarity. If the sen-tences looked similar, annotators could assign "Indifferent" to them.

Meaning preservation had a similar number of positive and indifferent answers: only in 94 (59.6%) of the cases annotators preferred one of the alterna-tives. Although there was a positive preference for human paraphrases concern-ing the preservation of meaning (53.53%), that difference was not statistically

---

[3] Here, we prefer to give simple means of the results. Inter-annotator measures, such as the Fleiss' kappa (for more than two annotators, as in our experiments), operate with nominal variables. Because of that, they tend to underestimate the agreement of ordinal variables.

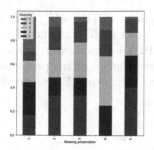

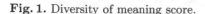

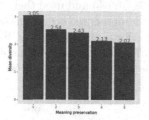

Fig. 1. Diversity of meaning score.   **Fig. 2.** Average diversity.

significant in a two-sided binomial test (5% of significance, p-value = 0.91). In general, paraphrases created with PPT5-Paraphraser seem to match human generated ones, as regards meaning preservation. We must note, however, that results varied considerably for annotators. Whereas of the annotators strongly preferred human paraphrases (61.5%); another showed only a slight preference for human paraphrases (51%); and another showed a slight preference for automatic ones (52.5%).

Assessment of diversity, on the other hand, tended to favor human paraphrases. In 76.5% of the time, annotators were confident enough to choose one of the alternatives; and in 65.1% of the time, they considered human paraphrases as more diverse. This may indicate that, even though PPT5-Paraphraser is able to produce sentences of similar meaning, the model has not yet achieved human-like levels of language creativity.

The last feature analyzed was clarity. Only in 30.3% of the cases, annotators gave a positive answer. Preference leaned to human paraphrases (55.7%), but, as in the case of meaning preservation, the difference was not statistically significant in a two-sided binomial test (5% of significance, p-value = 0.91).

Experiment 2 indicates that PPT5-Paraphraser produces sentences that are capable of preserving meaning, grammatically acceptable, and human-like written. At the same time, the paraphrases show a limited creativity, when compared to human generated ones. This offers a strong suggestions that PPT5-Paraphraser, although not a rule-based approach based on lexical operations, tends to work locally; and that it is successful within this scope.

5   Data Augmentation Experiment

To test the potential use of PPT5-Paraphraser, we decided to conduct a couple of tests, in order to assess its potential for data augmentation. For that, we performed a text classification task on OffComBR [15], a dataset of tweets in Portuguese, which aim to identify offensive language. The distribution of the response variable is 32% of texts with offensive language and 68% without. We randomly separated 3,670 tweets for training and 1,700 for testing.

Next, we created several partitions of the training set (1%, 5%, 10%, 25%, 50%, 75%, 100%) and used them to train a LSTM and a BERT classifier. We also generated augmented sets of these partitions with PPT5-Paraphraser, generating 5 samples for each observation. Finally, we compared the classifier's performance with and without data augmentation on the test set, using F1-macro as an evaluation metric. Figure 3 illustrates the results.

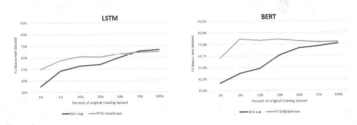

Fig. 3. LSTM and BERT Classifier F1-Macro results for percentage of training dataset.

As the chart indicates, data augmentation is more efficient in scenarios with more data scarcity (1%–10%), with up to 30% gain in the 5% train set for BERT Classifier. On the other hand, the contribution of data augmentation to performance decreases in scenarios with larger amounts, as for BERT; in the case of LSTM, data augmentation may actually lead to worse results when large amounts of data are already available.

As a second test, we compared the results of data augmentation with PPT5-Paraphraser with five other approaches for data augmentation:

- **Keyboard Error** [24]: creates text that simulates typos.
- **EDA** [21]: performs simple operations with words: remove, replace by synonyms or change the order.
- **Embedding Aug** [14]: uses an embedding to change or insert words more similar. In our text, we are using Portuguese Word2Vec.
- **BERT Aug** [23]: similar to the previous one, but uses a BERT embedding. In tests, we are using BERTimbau [20].
- **Back Translation** [3]: uses translation operations. In our tests, we translate from Portuguese to Germany and back to Portuguese.

Augmenters were applied to a 5% partition of the training set. For each observation, 5 new texts were generated. Table 3 shows the F1-macro classification results.

PTT5-Paraphraser achieved the best F1-macro result in the comparison for the two classifiers (LSTM and BERT). Results were especially good when compared to the non-augmented dataset. Overall, PTT5-Paraphraser helped to compensate the lack of data.

Table 3. Text classification model results with 5% of training dataset and F1-macro metric.

Augmenters	LSTM	BERT
W/o Aug	53,4%	49,9%
Keyboard Error	59,3%	73,2%
EDA	53,7%	68,9%
Embedding (Word2Vec)	58,0%	72,0%
Bert Aug	59,2%	62,7%
Back Translation	61,3%	71,3%
PTT5-Paraphraser	62,5%	79,5%

6 Conclusions

In this paper, we present *PTT5-Paraphraser*, a new model for generating paraphrases. This paraphraser presents a balance between fidelity in meaning and lexical and syntactic diversity.

PTT5-Paraphraser can be particularly useful for data augmentation. In a scenario with low availability of data, the addition of synthetic data may considerably improve a model's performance. Compared to other traditional data augmentation algorithms, PTT5-Paraphraser offered the best results in two text classification tasks. Moreover, PTT5-Paraphraser is easy to share and reuse; it also demands less computational resources than most translation paraphrasers.

In future work, we want to use PTT5-Paraphraser for new data augmentation applications, such as question answering. We would also like to explore more specific variations of it, such as sentence-style transformations; e.g., informal to formal sentences. Finally, we hope to better understand the underlying structure learned by the model, concerning locality, lexical change, and syntactic reconstructions.

Acknowledgement. This research was supported in part by the Coordenação de Aperfeiçoamento de Pessoal de Nível Superior (CAPES), Finance Code 001, CNPQ (grant 310085/2020-9). The authors of this work would like to thank the Center for Artificial Intelligence (C4AI-USP) and the support from the São Paulo Research Foundation (FAPESP grant #2019/07665-4) and from the IBM Corporation. Any opinions, findings, and conclusions expressed in this manuscript are those of the authors and do not necessarily reflect the views, official policy, or position of the financiers.

References

1. Paschoal, A.F.A., et al.: A bilingual Portuguese-English dataset for question-answering about the ocean. In: 30th ACM International Conference on Information and Knowledge Management (CIKM'21) (2021). https://doi.org/10.1145/3459637. 3482012

2. Carmo, D., Piau, M., Campiotti, I., Nogueira, R., Lotufo, R.: PTT5: pretraining and validating the t5 model on brazilian portuguese data. arXiv:2008.09144 (2020)
3. Fadaee, M., Bisazza, A., Monz, C.: Data augmentation for low-resource neural machine translation. In: Proceedings of the 55th Annual Meeting of the Association for Computational Linguistics (Volume 2: Short Papers). Association for Computational Linguistics (2017). https://doi.org/10.18653/v1/p17-2090
4. Falke, T., Boese, M., Sorokin, D., Tirkaz, C., Lehnen, P.: Leveraging user paraphrasing behavior in dialog systems to automatically collect annotations for long-tail utterances. In: Proceedings of the 28th International Conference on Computational Linguistics: Industry Track. pp. 21–32. International Committee on Computational Linguistics (2020). https://doi.org/10.18653/v1/2020.coling-industry.3, https://aclanthology.org/2020.coling-industry.3
5. Fonseca, E., Santos, L., Criscuolo, M., Aluisio, S.: Assin: avaliacao de similaridade semantica e inferencia textual. In: Computational Processing of the Portuguese Language-12th International Conference, pp. 13–15. Tomar, Portugal (2016)
6. Gan, W.C., Ng, H.T.: Improving the robustness of question answering systems to question paraphrasing. In: Proceedings of the 57th Annual Meeting of the Association for Computational Linguistics, pp. 6065–6075. Association for Computational Linguistics, Florence, Italy (2019). https://doi.org/10.18653/v1/P19-1610, https://aclanthology.org/P19-1610
7. Ganitkevitch, J., Van Durme, B., Callison-Burch, C.: PPDB: the paraphrase database. In: Proceedings of the 2013 Conference of the North American Chapter of the Association for Computational Linguistics: Human Language Technologies, pp. 758–764. Association for Computational Linguistics, Atlanta, Georgia (2013). https://aclanthology.org/N13-1092
8. Hu, J.E., Rudinger, R., Post, M., Durme, B.V.: PARABANK: monolingual bitext generation and sentential paraphrasing via lexically-constrained neural machine translation, vol. 33, pp. 6521–6528 (2019). https://doi.org/10.1609/aaai.v33i01.33016521
9. Maier Ferreira, T., Reali Costa, A.H.: Deepbt and NLP data augmentation techniques: a new proposal and a comprehensive study. In: Cerri, R., Prati, R. (eds.) Intelligent Systems - BRACIS 2020. Lecture Notes in Computer Science, vol. 12319, pp. 435–449. Springer, Cham (2020). https://doi.org/10.1007/978-3-030-61377-8_30
10. Mallinson, J., Sennrich, R., Lapata, M.: Paraphrasing Revisited with Neural Machine Translation. Association for Computational Linguistics (2017). https://doi.org/10.18653/v1/e17-1083
11. Miller, G.A.: Wordnet: a lexical database for English. Commun. ACM **38**(11), 39–41 (1995)
12. Pandya, H.: Paraphrase datasets and pretrained models (2021). https://github.com/hetpandya/paraphrase-datasets-pretrained-models
13. Park, D.S., et al.: Specaugment: a simple data augmentation method for automatic speech recognition. arXiv:1904.08779 (2019)
14. Park, D., Ahn, C.W.: Self-supervised contextual data augmentation for natural language processing. Symmetry **11**(11), 1393 (2019). https://doi.org/10.3390/sym11111393
15. Pelle, R.P.D., Moreira, V.P.: Offensive comments in the brazilian web: a dataset and baseline results. Sociedade Brasileira de Computação - SBC (2017). https://doi.org/10.5753/brasnam.2017.3260
16. Perez, L., Wang, J.: The effectiveness of data augmentation in image classification using deep learning. arXiv:1712.04621 (2017)

17. Raffel, C., et al.: Exploring the limits of transfer learning with a unified text-to-text transformer. J. Mach. Learn. Res. **21**(140), 1–67 (2020). http://jmlr.org/papers/v21/20-074.html

18. Reimers, N., Gurevych, I.: Making monolingual sentence embeddings multilingual using knowledge distillation. In: Proceedings of the 2020 Conference on Empirical Methods in Natural Language Processing. Association for Computational Linguistics (2020). https://arxiv.org/abs/2004.09813

19. Scherrer, Y.: TaPaCo: a corpus of sentential paraphrases for 73 languages. In: Proceedings of the 12th Language Resources and Evaluation Conference, pp. 6868–6873. European Language Resources Association, Marseille, France (2020). https://aclanthology.org/2020.lrec-1.848

20. Souza, F., Nogueira, R., Lotufo, R.: BERTimbau: pretrained BERT models for brazilian portuguese, pp. 403–417. Springer International Publishing (2020). https://doi.org/10.1007/978-3-030-61377-8_28

21. Wei, J., Zou, K.: EDA: easy data augmentation techniques for boosting performance on text classification tasks. In: Proceedings of the 2019 Conference on Empirical Methods in Natural Language Processing and the 9th International Joint Conference on Natural Language Processing (EMNLP-IJCNLP). Association for Computational Linguistics (2019). https://doi.org/10.18653/v1/d19-1670

22. Wieting, J., Gimpel, K.: ParaNMT-50M: pushing the limits of paraphrastic sentence embeddings with millions of machine translations. In: Proceedings of the 56th Annual Meeting of the Association for Computational Linguistics (Volume 1: Long Papers), pp. 451–462. Association for Computational Linguistics, Melbourne, Australia (2018). https://doi.org/10.18653/v1/P18-1042, https://aclanthology.org/P18-1042

23. Wu, X., Lv, S., Zang, L., Han, J., Hu, S.: Conditional BERT contextual augmentation. In: Rodrigues J., et al. (eds.) Computational - ICCS 2019. ICCS 2019. Lecture Notes in Computer Science, vol. 11539. Springer, Cham (2019). https://doi.org/10.1007/978-3-030-22747-0_7

24. Xie, Z., et al.: Data noising as smoothing in neural network language models. In: 5th International Conference on Learning Representations, ICLR 2017, Toulon, France, April 24–26, 2017, Conference Track Proceedings. OpenReview.net (2017). https://openreview.net/forum?id=H1VyHY9gg

25. Zhong, Z., Zheng, L., Kang, G., Li, S., Yang, Y.: Random erasing data augmentation. In: Proceedings of the AAAI Conference on Artificial Intelligence, vol. 34, pp. 13001–13008 (2020)

Speech Processing and Applications

A Protocol for Comparing Gesture and Prosodic Boundaries in Multimodal Corpora

Camila Barros[1]([📧])[iD] and Saulo Santos[2][iD]

[1] Federal University of Minas Gerais, UFMG, Belo Horizonte, Brazil
`camila-ab@ufmg.br`
[2] Université Paris-Saclay, UPSaclay, Paris, France
`saulo.mendes-santos@universite-paris-saclay.fr`

Abstract. This paper aims to summarize the key points and results of an analysis of the alignment of gesture and prosodic boundaries collected through manual an-notation and automated treatment. For this purpose, we used a multimodal corpus of spontaneous speech, the BGEST corpus [1], part of the C-ORAL-BRASIL language resources [10,23]. Gestures and prosodic boundaries were manually annotated with ELAN. The gestural an-notation followed partly the Linguistic Annotation System for Gestures guidelines [5], whereas the prosodic boundaries followed the perceptual criterion adopted in other C-ORAL resources. The tabular data outputted by ELAN was then analyzed by a script that compares the alignment of gesture phrases and intonation units. The results point to a larger gestural phrase that encompasses the intonation unit, while the stroke is almost always within the intonation unit. Around 85% of all information units align with a gesture. The analysis also points that the time values of alignment are shorter than analyzed by [17] both for initial as well for final boundaries and more complex than proposed by [6]. This indicates that more research is needed before we can set an approximate value for the overlap of larger units.

Keywords: Corpus linguistics · Gesture · Prosody

1 Gesture and Prosody Alignment Background

1.1 The Alignment and Its Types

The alignment of gestures and prosodic boundaries were used initially to indicate how gestures and prosody are functionally coupled [14], and still pose a methodological challenge in data analysis [22,26]. The importance of analyzing this coordination stems from its complexity, since it is multi-level and in different time-scales [22] with implications on a developmental level [11]. In this paper we aim to present a protocol and the resulting tool, which is still under development, for comparing longer stretches (i.e. intonation units and

© Springer Nature Switzerland AG 2022
V. Pinheiro et al. (Eds.): PROPOR 2022, LNAI 13208, pp. 313–322, 2022.
https://doi.org/10.1007/978-3-030-98305-5_29

gesture-phrases) of multi-modal corpora, and to report the results of an analysis. Under our perspective, those longer stretches are useful to understand how information units relate to gestures.

The state-of-the-art methodology for analyzing this coordination relies on either identifying the points of maximum effort of hand movement [17,26], also called kinematic goal, or working with high-quality equipment such as motion-capture devices that are also highly expensive [22]. [22] proposed a framework that uses a video-based motion-tracking algorithm to analyze coordination in a sharper yet accessible way. This is specially addressed to tackle the problem of defining what points of maximum effort are.

The key point of the discussion around a methodology for gesture-speech coordination analysis is the attempt to find a spot to anchor the alignment of gesture and speech. In the literature, this anchorage is usually found to be the apex of the gestural movement under a broad understanding of gesture, as pointed by [22,26]. However, the coordination of gesture and speech is, as already pointed, multilevel: it spreads from biomechanical relations between phonation and speech-gestures [21], to the word-level influencing the perception of stressed syllables [3], see also [11–13], and on a semantical level, when the gesture couples with the content conveyed in speech [4,15,16,19]. [7] proposed that even illocutions are coupled with gestures without providing a specific time constraint to its synchronicity. The aim of this paper is, thus, to provide a protocol to analyze the coordination of gesture and speech by means of the time alignment of intonation units and gesture-phrases, in order to analyze how different information units couple with gestures, following [7].

This protocol takes into consideration the coordination of prosodic boundaries with gesture boundaries rather than with gesture apices for two main reasons: the first is to get around the problem of what precisely are the points of apex that anchor speech [22]. The second reason is to look for larger standards of comparison with larger portions of gesture/speech coupling. The latter point is motivated by an attempt to understand how gestures are linked to the information units defined by the Language into Act Theory [9,20]. To use the Language into Act Theory to analyze gesture, we followed some of the methodological steps of the works of [1,6,7].

1.2   The Language into Act Theory

Information units are referred to here as they are defined within the Language into Act Theory (L-AcT) [9,20] framework. Contrary to other frameworks, which assume the sentence or the turn as the basic reference unit, the L-AcT puts forth that the speech is organized around the terminated sequence, defining it as a speech chunk containing a speech act (thus, pragmatically autonomous) delimited by a terminal prosodic boundary (thus, prosodically autonomous). Terminated sequences are either realized as utterances, where only one speech act is to be found, and Stanzas, where multiple speech acts are juxtaposed and separated by non-terminal boundaries. Stanzas are usually found in monological texts and reflect the flow of thought of the speaker. For the sake of simplicity and economy of space, we only explain and exemplify the utterance. This type of terminated sequence may be either simple or compound. A simple utterance is not segment-ed internally by a non-terminal prosodic boundary. On the other way, a com-pound utterance is segmented by non-terminal boundaries that forms intonation units smaller than the whole utterance. The L-AcT assumes that there is an isomorphism between the prosodic and the informational level. This is to say that the intonation units formed by the non-terminal boundaries matches on the informational level the information units that have, accordingly to their prosodic realization and distribution, different informational statuses. Take for instance the pattern formed by a Topic unit and by the Comment[1]:

Example 1. afammn02
ALN: [79] for this guy /=TOP= he was very successful //=COM=

Here, the Topic is defined by identifying the scope of application of the illocutionary force of the Comment, which, in its turn, carries a prosodic illocutionary nucleus ascribing to the utterance its actional status, thus, whether it is an assertion, a total question, an order, and so forth. The Comment is the sole unit necessary to form an utterance, therefore being the unique unit needed for building a simple utterance. The Topic-Comment pattern is often found accompanied by other information units, such as Parentheticals, Appendices, Locutive Introducers, and discourse markers, all of which are prosodically parsed.

Example 2. afammn04
LAJ: [13] and I know my brother /=TOP= who lives in Dallas /=PAR= &he /=TMT= the one that played football at Perdue /=PAR– he [/1]=EMP= he knew it //=COM=

In the example above, the Topic-Comment pattern is interrupted by a Parenthetical unit that inserts an extra information to the utterance. We refer the reader to [20] for a comprehensive introduction on the information units provided for by the L-AcT framework.

As a data-driven theory, the L-AcT emerged from the observation of the organization of spontaneous speech, as recorded on the C ORAL corpora family. This project was aimed at compiling comparable corpora [10] of the main European romance languages (French, Italian, Portuguese, and Spanish) focusing the diaphasic variation (variation elicited by the context) so as to register the largest number of speech acts and information patterns possible. The project was later extended to encompass Brazilian Portuguese [23], Angolan Portuguese [25] and English [8].

---

[1] All examples are taken of [8]. The transcription conventions can be summarized as follows: the speaker is indicated by an acronym, as "*ABC:" (regex: [A-Z]{3}:) and separated by turns in different line breaks. Each utterance is separated by double dash "//" and intonation units by a single dash "/". The utterance number is indicated by numbers in brackets, as "[3]". The information unit tags are between equal signs, as "=COM=" for the Comment unit. Time taking units are always transcribed as "&he" regardless of the vowels. Further information can be found in [8] and [23], the audios can be accessed in https://www.c-oral-brasil.org.

1.3   BGEST Corpus Overview

Originally the script was designed to process data from the BGEST corpus, a pilot project led by the C-ORAL-BRASIL research group aimed at analyzing the coordination of gestural and prosodic boundaries gesture on an intermediate level: gesture-phrases and intonation units[2]. This follows a similar yet smaller attempt made by [6] to study gesture under the light of the L-AcT. The contribution of her proposal was to find not only a compatible and coherent methodology for segmenting gestures and speech, but also to understand how the information patterning couples with the organization of gestures. This meant to check whether gestures accompany the information unit that is conveyed, both in a temporal and in a functional way. Her focus was much more exploratory and linked to a comparison of recited speech rather than a methodological endeavor.

The BGEST corpus [1] is compound of 10 excerpts of up to three minutes long of monologues of Brazilian Portuguese, having roughly 4,000 words and 450 gestures. They were segmented into utterances, intonation units (and, thus, information units) on the speech level, and in gesture units, phrases, phases, movement, orientation, handshape, and position, in a simplified annotation scheme adapted from the Language Annotation System for Gestures [5] (Table 1).

Table 1. Overview of key features of the BGEST Corpus

File	Length (mm:ss)	# Words	# Utterances
bgest_001	02:24	330	18
bgest_002	02:24	386	33
bgest_003	02:40	417	22
bgest_004	02:11	382	19
bgest_005	02:04	341	19
bgest_006	02:40	375	36
bgest_007	02:39	514	39
bgest_008	02:04	276	18
bgest_009	02:39	545	35
bgest_010	02:43	418	36
Total	24:28	3984	275

We used Praat [2] for the prosodic annotation, and ELAN [27] for the gesture annotation. We decided not to use any automatic annotation tools to avoid as much as possible errors since accuracy was of upmost importance in this trial. The script is intended to be used with the outputs data of Praat and ELAN, in tabular form, without additional layers of annotation or post-processing.

---

[2] As above mentioned, the speech chunk formed by non-terminal boundaries between the beginning and the end of the utterance (marked by a terminal boundary).

2   Script Outline

In order to implement the protocol we developed a tool to calculate the amount of alignment: the script (which is in a beta version) takes into consideration the closest and most overlapping stroke to an intonation unit. This allows to filter the overlap by stroke, initial or final break and information unit. The sole necessary part of the gesture is the stroke. Therefore, iterations are centered around strokes even though the amounts of overlapping are calculated considering the whole gesture-phrase interval. The steps in the script:

- Get the boundary times of each stroke and the boundary times of the corresponding gesture-phrase;
- Iterate through all intonation units to find the unit with which the stroke mostly overlaps. Since hypothetically the stroke might overlap with more than one intonation unit time domain, a brute-force approach was adopted;
- Calculate the amount of overlapping, if any, between the gesture-phrase and intonation units time domain;
- Calculate the proportion of the stroke overlap.

To run the script, two types of files are required: gesture annotation files in .tab format with beginnings and endings of annotations in millisecond and alignment files of the same video file also in a .tab format and the breaks marks in millisecond. Each pair of gesture and prosodic annotation data file should always refer to the same video file.

The script was written in R [24] and it is currently in a beta version. It needs further update to make it more abstract in what concerns not only input format but also and output possibilities. We plan to rewrite it in Python and integrate to it all Praat and ELAN data extraction/exportation routines so that the user do not have to manually manage any raw data file.

3   Results and Discussion

Differently of [17] and [6], we search for overlapping strokes and intonation units before analyzing their synchronicity. This way we would not fall into differences of coordination (how long gesture and speech can be one from each other apart?) or overlap matters. The methodology of [17] is clear about analyzing boundaries in English: after a dispersion analysis, the author considered that intermediate phrases and gesture phrases can be considered coordinated when they are coordinated within a 500 ms frame. This frame is way too large to make further analysis without a strong qualitative component under-lying it, which is provided in our work by the L-AcT. Even though his work was a milestone for peak analysis, different possibilities of functional coupling cannot be fully understood under the analysis of peaks. On the other hand, [6] checked for overlaps of gesture and intonation units for Italian. She found that, within a threshold of 200 ms, all gesture and speech units (terminated or not) overlap, either in the beginning or (preferably with) the end. We argue with those results, firstly because the methods are not as clear as they could be, thus leaving some unanswered questions on how those measurements were made. Secondly, the analysis of [6] does not specify if the stroke is tight with the closest non-terminal speech unit to be relevant to the analysis, even though the synchronicity only makes sense when the peaks are aligned. Both methodologies require a deep and detailed qualitative analysis because the quantitative analysis is not for itself as informative as it could be. Here we argue that the quantitative analysis of gesture and speech should: i) check if strokes and non-terminal units overlap, for they are at a comparable level of analysis, ii) check to which extent their boundaries are overlapping, for this provides a time gap. This time gap should be reasonably short to support the hypothesis of a common conceptualization and performance. And, finally, iii) enable the filtering of data by the information units, since they will support and guide the qualitative analysis.

The tool provides a table with the following information about each gesture-phrase-to-information-unit overlapping (all measurements of time are in milliseconds):

- beginning of the stroke;
- end of the stroke;
- duration of the stroke;
- beginning of the gesture-phrase;
- end of the gesture-phrase;
- duration of the gesture-phrase;
- overlap of gesture-phrase and stroke;
- beginning of the intonation unit;
- end of the intonation unit;
- duration of the intonation unit;
- overlap of gesture-phrase and intonation unit;
- interval time;
- id of the utterance;
- id of the intonation unit;
- difference of beginnings (gesture-phrase - intonation unit);
- difference of endings (gesture-phrase - intonation unit);
- difference of beginnings regarding stroke (gesture-phrase - stroke);
- difference of endings regarding stroke (gesture-phrase - stroke);
- overlapping ratio of gesture-phrase and intonation unit (percent);
- overlapping ratio of stroke and intonation unit (percent).

All data are measured in millisecond and consider the closest pair of gesture and speech.

The tool pre-process the input data files and outputs them in a format that allows for surveys having different purposes. This means that one could analyze different coupling of gesture and speech filtering by information tag. It is noteworthy to stress that for our specific purposes the variables that were more useful were these related to differences of beginnings and endings of strokes, gesture-phrases and intonation units, and durations, which indicate to what extent there is an overlap. Those values indicate that gesture parameters fit to those of L-AcT units: first because they portray the same findings that [14,17,18] achieved by other prosodic parameters, namely that the stroke is within the gesture-phrase and an intermediate prosodic unit, being the latter smaller than the former, refining the methods presented by [6]. Secondly, and more importantly, they also provide a functional background for this kind of coupling, which is concerned with how the information unit affects synchronicity. Further evidence were found regarding the gestural mapping of parentheticals, addressed in [1].

The main finding of our analysis is that the coupling of gesture and speech vary according to the information unit they are synchronous with. Bellow, we provide the main median values for selected information units.

Table 2. Main measures captured in the processed data (Acronyms were used for the sake of readability. They follow this code: B stands for *begin*, E for *end*, D for *duration*, S for *stroke*, GP for *gesture-phrase*, IU *intonation unit*. A code such as GPB-IUB should be read as following: *difference of gesture-phrase beginning and intonation unit beginning*, DS should be read as *duration of the stroke*).

Information unit	DS	GPB-IUB	GPE-IUE	DGP	SB-IUB	SE-IUE	DIU	Overlap ratio of GP and IU	Overlap ratio of S and IU
All information units	747	−260	73	1801	118	−356	1334	0.35	0.99
Comment	733	−286	160	1815	76	−390	1270	0.35	0.94
Parenthetical	704	−290	−4	1768	87	427	1255	0.30	0.91

As it can be seen in Table 2, the results shows that strokes measure approx. 740 ms for the group formed by all information units. The strokes are always within the gesture-phrases and almost always within the intonation unit they are included in, with an overlap rate of over 90%. This indicated that the non-terminated unit is not tied to the whole gesture-phrase, but there is a specific span that is tied to it.

The data point that the gesture-phrase is the first one to take place, followed by the intonation unit 200 ms later. Approx. 70 ms–120 ms after (depending on the information unit), the stroke is performed, ending before the intonation unit. The gesture-phrase end time occurs, with some variation (SD beginning = 754 ms, SD end = 941 ms), after the intonation unit, unless it is a Parenthetical, in which they tend to end together. The standard deviation probably lies on the preparation and retraction phases that occur in some, but not all gesture-phrases.

The data analysis of the BGEST corpus provided important insights on the analysis of larger stretches of speech and gesture. The first of them is to use the annotation process in our favor and apply it to a quantitative data analysis of the agreement and overlap of speech and gesture. The second is to use these longer stretches to consistently analyze boundaries and, by doing so, support the qualitative analysis, which indicated that synchronicity is pivotal to the functional analysis.

Regarding the first point, the results are coherent with the literature: the boundaries are within a 500 ms distance [17] starting with the gesture [21]. This finding indicates the adequacy of the methodology used, i.e. the pairing between gesture-phrase and intonation unit (L-AcT).

Secondly, the results show that an analysis of gesture-phrases and intonation units must take the information unit into consideration. The type of information unit affects the alignment of gesture and prosodic boundaries. [1] provided evidence for the hypothesis that both gesture and speech are guided by actional principles, which modulate their realization. The gestures start the unpacking of the message to be conveyed, followed by the information unit.

Acknowledgement. Both authors acknowledge the support of C-ORAL-BRASIL Research Group, S. M. S. acknowledges the support of CAPES and C. A. B. acknowledges the support of Fapemig.

References

1. Barros, C.: A relação entre unidades gestuais e quebras prosódicas: o caso da unidade informacional Parentético. Ph.D. thesis, Universidade Federal de Minas Gerais, Belo Horizonte (2021). Accessed on 11 May 2021
2. Boersma, P., Weenink, D.: Praat: doing phonetics by computer (2020). Accessed on 07 March 2020
3. Bosker, H.R., Peeters, D.: Beat gestures influence which speech sounds you hear. Proc. Roy. Soc. B: Biol. Sci. **288**(1943), 20202419 (2021). https://doi.org/10.1098/rspb.2020.2419
4. Bressem, J.: 124. repetitions in gesture. In: Müller, C., Cienki, A., Fricke, E., Ladewig, S., McNeill, D., Bressem, J. (eds.) Handbücher zur Sprach- und Kommunikationswissenschaft/Handbooks of Linguistics and Communication Science (HSK) 38/2. DE GRUYTER, Berlin, München, Boston (2014). https://doi.org/10.1515/9783110302028.1641
5. Bressem, J., Ladewig, S., Müller, C.: 71. linguistic annotation system for gestures. In: Müller, C., Cienki, A., Fricke, E., Ladewig, S., McNeill, D., Tessendorf, S. (eds.) Handbücher zur Sprach- und Kommunikationswissenschaft/Handbooks of Linguistics and Communication Science (HSK) 38/1. De Gruyter, Berlin, Boston (2013). https://doi.org/10.1515/9783110261318.1098
6. Cantalini, G.: La gestualitá co-verbale nel parlato spontaneo e nel recitato. Ph.D. thesis, Universitá degli studi Roma Tre, Roma Tre (2018)
7. Cantalini, G., Moneglia, M.: The annotation of gesture and gesture/prosody synchronization in multimodal speech corpora. J. Speech Sci. **9**, 7–30 (2020)
8. Cavalcante, F.A., Ramos, A.C.: The american english spontaneous speech minicorpus. CHIMERA. Romance Corpora Linguis. Stud. **3**(2), 99–124 (2016)
9. Cresti, E.: Corpus del italiano parlato. Accademia della Crusca, Firenze (2000)
10. Cresti, E., Moneglia, M. (eds.): C-ORAL-ROM: Integrated Reference Corpora for Spoken Romance Languages. Studies in corpus linguistics, J. Benjamins, Amsterdam; Philadelphia, PA (2005), oCLC: ocm57506724
11. Esteve-Gibert, N., Guellaï, B.: Prosody in the auditory and visual domains: a developmental perspective. Front. Psychol. **9**, 338 (2018). https://doi.org/10.3389/fpsyg.2018.00338

12. Esteve-Gibert, N., Prieto, P.: Prosodic structure shapes the temporal realization of intonation and manual gesture movements. J. Speech, Lang. Hear. Res. **56**(3), 850–864 (2013). https://doi.org/10.1044/1092-4388(2012/12-0049)

13. Esteve-Gibert, N., Prieto, P.: Infants temporally coordinate gesture-speech combinations before they produce their first words. Speech Commun. **57**, 301–316 (2014). https://doi.org/10.1016/j.specom.2013.06.006

14. Kendon, A.: Some relationships between body motion and speech. In: Seigman, A., Pope, B. (eds.) Studies in Dyadic Communication, pp. 177–216. Pergamon Press, Elsmford, NY (1972)

15. Ladewig, S.: 118. recurrent gestures. In: Müller, C., Cienki, A., Fricke, E., Ladewig, S., McNeill, D., Bressem, J. (eds.) Handbücher zur Sprach- und Kommunikationswissenschaft/Handbooks of Linguistics and Communication Science (HSK) 38/2. DE GRUYTER, Berlin, München, Boston (2014). https://doi.org/10.1515/9783110302028.1558

16. Ladewig, S.: 126. creating multimodal utterances: the linear integration of gestures into speech. In: Müller, C., Cienki, A., Fricke, E., Ladewig, S., McNeill, D., Bressem, J. (eds.) Handbücher zur Sprach- und Kommunikationswissenschaft/Handbooks of Linguistics and Communication Science (HSK) 38/2. DE GRUYTER, Berlin, München, Boston (2014). https://doi.org/10.1515/9783110302028.1662

17. Loehr, D.: Intonation and Gesture. Ph.D. thesis, University of Georgetown, Washington, D.C. (2004)

18. McNeill, D.: Hand and Mind: What Gestures Reveal About Thought. Hand and Mind: What Gestures Reveal About Thought, pp. xi, 416. University of Chicago Press, Chicago, IL, US (1992)

19. Mittelberg, I.: 130. gestures and iconicity. In: Müller, C., Cienki, A., Fricke, E., Ladewig, S., McNeill, D., Bressem, J. (eds.) Handbücher zur Sprach- und Kommunikationswissenschaft/Handbooks of Linguistics and Communication Science (HSK) 38/2. DE GRUYTER, Berlin, München, Boston (2014). https://doi.org/10.1515/9783110302028.1712

20. Moneglia, M., Raso, T.: Appendix: notes on the language into act theory. In: Raso, T., Mello, H. (eds.) Studies in Corpus Linguistics, vol. 61, pp. 468–495. John Benjamins Publishing Company, Amsterdam (2014). https://doi.org/10.1075/scl.61.15mon

21. Pouw, W., Harrison, S.J., Dixon, J.A.: Gesture-speech physics: the biomechanical basis for the emergence of gesture-speech synchrony. J. Exp. Psychol.: General **149**(2), 391–404 (2020). https://doi.org/10.1037/xge0000646

22. Pouw, W., Trujillo, J.P., Dixon, J.A.: The quantification of gesture–speech synchrony: a tutorial and validation of multimodal data acquisition using device-based and video-based motion tracking. Behav. Res. Meth. **52**(2), 723–740 (2019). https://doi.org/10.3758/s13428-019-01271-9

23. Raso, T., Mello, H. (eds.): C-ORAL-BRASIL I: Corpus de referência do português brasileiro falado informal. Editora UFMG, Belo Horizonte (2012)

24. RCoreTeam: R: a language and environment for statistical computing. R Foundation for Statistical Computing, Vienna, Austria (2020)

25. Rocha, B., Mello, H., Raso, T.: Para a compilação do c-oral-angola. Filologia e Linguística Portuguesa **20**(Especial), 139–157 (2018). https://doi.org/10.11606/issn.2176-9419.v20iEspecialp139-157

26. Wagner, P., Malisz, Z., Kopp, S.: Gesture and speech in interaction: an overview. Speech Commun. **57**, 209–232 (2014). https://doi.org/10.1016/j.specom.2013.09. 008
27. Wittenburg, P., Brugman, H., Russel, A., Klassmann, A., Sloetjes, H.: Elan: a professional framework for multimodality research. In: Proceedings of LREC 2006, pp. 1556–1559. Fifth International Conference on Language Resources and Evaluation, Max Planck Institute for Psycholinguistics, The Language Archive, Nijmegen (2006). Accessed on 07 March 2020

Forced Phonetic Alignment in Brazilian Portuguese Using Time-Delay Neural Networks

Cassio Batista$^{(\boxtimes)}$ (iD) and Nelson Neto (iD)

Computer Science Graduate Program, Federal University of Pará, Belém, Brazil
{cassiotb,nelsonneto}@ufpa.br

Abstract. Forced phonetic alignment (FPA) is the task of assessing the time boundaries of phonetic units, i.e., calculating when in the speech utterance a certain phoneme starts and ends. This paper describes experiments on FPA for Brazilian Portuguese using Kaldi toolkit. Based on time-delay neural networks (TDNN), several acoustic models were trained on the top of the combination between hidden Markov models (HMM) and Gaussian mixture models (GMM). The nature of the input features and the topology of the HMMs have been varied in order to analyze each one's influence. Results with respect to the phone boundary metric over a dataset of 385 hand-aligned utterances show that the network is mostly invariant to the input features, while regular HMM topologies do perform better in comparison to a modified version used in chain models. Conversely, the neural network still does not outperform GMM models for phonetic alignment.

Keywords: Forced phonetic alignment · Speech segmentation · Acoustic modeling · Kaldi · Brazilian Portuguese

1 Introduction

Forced phonetic alignment (FPA) is the task of aligning a speech recording with its phonetic transcription, which is useful across a myriad of linguistic tasks. However, annotating phonetic boundaries of several hours of speech by hand is very time-consuming, even for experienced phoneticians. As several approaches have been applied to automate this process, some of them brought from the automatic speech recognition (ASR) domain, the combination of hidden Markov models (HMM) and Gaussian mixture models (GMM) has been for long the most widely explored for FPA.

Before Kaldi's success on ASR [10], mainly due to its efficient implementation of deep neural networks (DNN) for HMM-DNN hybrid acoustic modeling, EasyAlign [4] and UFPAlign [15] were the only ASR-based forced aligners with support to Brazilian Portuguese (BP), based on HTK toolkit [16]. Nowadays, Montreal Forced Aligner (MFA) [8] and an updated version of UFPAlign [1,3] both provide Kaldi-compliant acoustic models for BP.

© Springer Nature Switzerland AG 2022
V. Pinheiro et al. (Eds.): PROPOR 2022, LNAI 13208, pp. 323–332, 2022.
https://doi.org/10.1007/978-3-030-98305-5_30

Hence, this work provides an additional study on phonetic alignment using Kaldi tools, bearing in mind the idea of seeking improvements using the default neural network architecture that achieves state of the art for ASR in Kaldi's nnet3 framework—factorized time-delay neural networks (TDNN-F) [9]. In total, 24 acoustic models were trained by varying i) the GMM model the network was trained upon (monophones, triphones and speaker-adapted triphones, namely mono, tri-deltas and tri-sat); ii) the HMM topology used as reference (single state vs. three-state, namely chain or no-chain); iii) and finally the input features: MFCCs or LDA, with or without stacked i-vectors.

To overcome the time it would take to train all such models, only LaPS-Benchmark dataset was used, which sums up to a total of only 54 min of recorded speech, 700 utterances divided among 10 female and 25 male native BP speakers. Evaluation procedures, on the other hand, were performed over 385 manually aligned audio files, 193 spoken by a male speaker and 192 spoken by a female speaker, which sums up to about 15 min of speech. The similarity measure is given by the absolute difference between the forced alignments with respect to manual ones, which is called phonetic boundary [8]. All scripts and resources have been release under MIT open license on GitHub[1].

2   Model Training and Evaluation Tests

The deep-learning-based training approach in Kaldi actually uses the GMM training as a pre-processing stage. For details on the GMM training pipeline, the reader is referred to [3]. The DNN is trained on the top of the last GMM model of the pipeline, which usually comprises a speaker-adapted triphone training (SAT). However, we experimented with monophones and triphones without SAT as well.

Figure 1 details how the DNN model is obtained as a final-stage acoustic model (AM) by using the neural network to model the state likelihood distributions as well as to input those likelihoods into the decision tree leaf nodes [5]. The implementation in Kaldi uses a sub-sampling technique (with a default factor of 3) that avoids the whole computation of a feed-forward's hidden activations at all time steps and therefore allows a faster training of TDNNs.

Models were trained following Kaldi's LibriSpeech recipe. The hardware setup consists of an Intel® Core™ i7-10700 octa-core processor, 32 GB of RAM and an 10 GB NVIDIA GeForce RTX 3080 GPU running CUDA 11.3. Although in Kaldi the number of epochs actually differs from the number of iterations in which the algorithm "sees" each data point, the former was set to 10 for all simulations. The number of layers was reduced to seven, as opposed to 16 in the default recipe for speeding up purposes. Layers were kept with dimension 1,536 each. Time strides were also left as is, with three past frames and nine future frames (i.e., left and right context w.r.t. the reference frame, respectively.) As the amount of training data was made to be limited, all five HMM-GMM models and 24 HMM-DNN could be trained in less than 12 h.

---

[1] https://github.com/falabrasil.

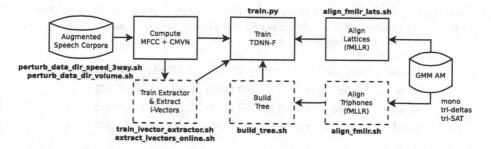

Fig. 1. Stages for training a TDNN-F in Kaldi. On the left side, high-resolution, cepstral-normalized MFCCs (40 features instead of 13) are extracted from an augmented corpora after applying speed and volume perturbation [7], as are the speaker-related 100-dimensional i-vectors [2,14]; to be used as input to the neural network. On the right side, labels are provided by a GMM acoustic model. Dashed blocks may or may not be used. For instance, the tree must only be rebuilt when using **chain** models, in which the HMM topology is modified, whereas i-vectors may be excluded from the network's input as well.

The evaluation procedure takes place by comparing pairs of annotated files: the alignments that we consider as gold standard (hand-aligned reference), and the ones automatically annotated by inference (forced-aligned hypothesis). The phone boundary metric considers the absolute difference between the ending time of both phoneme occurrences [8], as a phone's beginning time is considered the same as its predecessor's ending time. The calculation is performed for each acoustic model, and involves all utterances from the evaluation dataset composed by one male and one female speaker.

2.1   Evaluation Speech Corpus

The automatic alignment was estimated on the basis of the manual segmentation. The original dataset used for assessing the accuracy of the phonetic aligner is composed of 200 and 199 utterances spoken by a male and a female speaker, in a total of 15 min and 32 s of hand-aligned audio, as shown in Table 1. Praat's TextGrid files, whose phonetic timestamps were manually adjusted by a phonetician, are available alongside audio and text transcriptions.

The authors acknowledge that this corpus is rather limited in both its size and speaker variability: 15 min of recorded speech from two speakers is too small indeed. However, we emphasize the difficulty to get access to this kind of labeled data, which very often requires an expert phonetician to spend hours aligning audios by hand.

This dataset was aligned with a set of phonemes inspired by the SAMPA alphabet, which in theory is the same set used by the FalaBrasil's G2P software that creates the lexicon during acoustic model training. Nevertheless, there are some problems of phonetic mismatches, and some cross-word phonemes between

Table 1. Speech corpus used to evaluate the automatic phonetic aligners. Actual duration and number of files after discard are shown between parentheses, as well as the number of unique words.

Dataset	Duration	# Files	# Words	# Tokens
Male	7 m:58 s (7 m:40 s)	200 (193)	1,260 (665)	5,275
Female	7 m:34 s (7 m:18 s)	199 (192)	1,258 (664)	5,262
Total	15 m:32 s (14 m:58 s)	399 (385)	2,518 (686)	10,537

words, which makes the mapping between both phoneme sets challenging, given that FalaBrasil's G2P only handles internal-word conversion [13].

The example in Table 2 shows the phonetic transcription for a sentence given by the original dataset (top) and the acoustic model (bottom) which then suppress vowel sounds altogether due to cross-word rules (usually elision and apocope) when they occur at the end of the current word and at the beginning at the next. Such mismatches occur because the dataset was aligned by a phonetician considering acoustic information (i.e., listening), which cannot be done by the G2P tool that creates the acoustic model's lexicon, since it is provided only with textual information. Situations like these of phonetic information loss led to the removal of such audio files from the dataset before evaluation.

Table 2. Cross-word mismatches between transcriptions manually aligned by a phonetician (top) vs. generated by FalaBrasil's G2P software (bottom). Word boundary losses are represented by the empty set symbol (∅).

(a) "ás novi meia, pairum ar no rio" → "ás nove e meia, paira um ar no rio"

```
6 ∅ Z n O v i ∅ ... p a j 4 ∅ u~ m a h/ ...
a j s n O v i i  ... p a j r a u~ ∅ a X  ...
```

In the end, fourteen files were excluded from the dataset, so about 34 s of audio was discarded, and 193 and 192 utterances remained in the male and female datasets, respectively. The filtering also ignored intra- and inter-word pauses and silences, resulting in 2,518 words (686 unique, since the utterances' transcriptions are identical for both speakers, i.e., they speak the very same sentences) and 10,537 phonetic segments (tokens) (c.f. Table 1).

2.2 Simulation Overview

Figure 2 shows a diagram of the experiments where the input audio files (.wav) with their respective textual transcriptions (.txt) are passed to Kaldi aligner. These are the files whose manual annotation is available. The output is a TextGrid file (.tg) for each audio given as input, which then serve as the inference inputs to the phone boundary calculation. The reference ground-truth annotations, on the

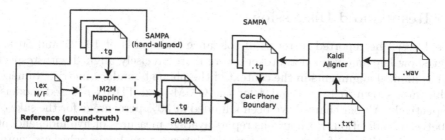

Fig. 2. Evaluation takes place by comparing the output of Kaldi to a hand-aligned ground-truth. The M2M mapping is applied to make different phone sets match the SAMPA version used by FalaBrasil's G2P, which is provided by the lexicon generated over transcriptions of the corpus (`lex M/F`).

other hand, are provided by the 385 TextGrid files that contain the hand-aligned phonemes corresponding to the transcriptions in the evaluation dataset.

However, for computing phone boundaries, there must exist a one-to-one mapping between the reference and the inference phones, which was not possible at first due to the nature of the phonetic alphabets: in our experiments, we used the SAMPA-inspired lexicon generated by FalaBrasil's G2P tool, while the hand-aligned utterances (referred here as "original") are also available in a SAMPA-inspired phonetic alphabet, but not exactly the same as FalaBrasil's.

Apart from the fact that cross-word rules can insert or delete phones, some phonemes do not have an equivalent, such as /tS/ and /dZ/. Besides, there are also usual swaps between phonetically similar sounds: /h//, /h\/, /h/ and /4/, for instance, might be almost deliberately mapped to either /r/, /R/ or /X/.

Thus, since the situation seemed to require a smarter approach than a simple one-to-one tabular, static mapping, it was necessary to employ a many-to-many (M2M) mapping procedure (c.f. dashed blocks on Fig. 2) based on statistical frequency of occurrence, e.g., how many times phones /t/ and /S/ from the original evaluation dataset were mapped to a single phone /tS/ in the `lex M/F` file representing FalaBrasil's G2P SAMPA-inspired alphabet.

By taking another look at Table 2, one might have also reasoned that the mapping between the two sets of phonemes is not always one-to-one. The usual situation is where a pair of phonemes from the dataset (original) is merged into a single one for the AM (FalaBrasil G2P), such as /i~/ /n/ → /i~/ and /t/ /S/ → /tS/. However, a single phoneme can also be less frequently split into two or more, such as /u/ /S/ → /u/ /j/ /s/.

To deal with these irregularities, we used the many-to-many alignment (m2m-aligner) software [6] in the core of a pipeline that converts the original TextGrid from the evaluation dataset to a TextGrid that is compatible with the FalaBrasil's lexicon used to train the acoustic models. The m2m-aligner works in an unsupervised fashion, using an edit-distance-based algorithm to align two strings in order for them to share the same length [6].

3   Results and Discussion

Results will be reported in terms of tolerance thresholds of 10, 25 and 50 ms that show how many phonetic tokens were more precisely aligned with respect to the manual alignments in the context of the phone boundary metric. Numeric values are shown in Figs. 3 and 4 for the GMM- and TDNN-F-based models, respectively. All bar charts have been trimmed at 30% percentage for the sake of a better visualization. Both graphs report average measures of five independent training repetitions of each acoustic model, hence vertical caps/whiskers represent the standard deviation. Blue- and red-shaded bars represent the male and the female speakers from the evaluation dataset, respectively.

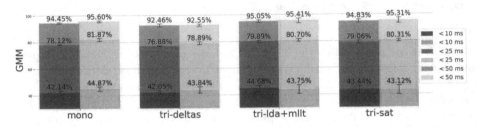

Fig. 3. Cumulative percentage below a tolerance threshold, in milliseconds, of the differences between forced aligned audio and ground-truth (hand aligned) phonemes, also known as phone boundary. Results for monophones and triphones trained with low resolution, MFCCs (deltas), spliced-MFCCs (LDA+MLLT) and speaker adaptation (SAT) within the HMM-GMM framework. (Color figure online)

The performance of the GMM models is shown in Fig. 3. As it can be seen, all four models' behaviors were virtually the very same: there is nearly a 1% difference in tokens correctly aligned within the 10 ms threshold, with an average of ~43% across all models. With respect to the gender of the speaker, there have not been much of a difference either. One could say that tri-SAT and tri-LDA+MLLT contain all the high numbers for phone boundary, but we would rather state their performance is comparable. At the tolerance of 50 ms, more than 90% of the phonemes are correctly aligned with the speech.

Figure 4 shows all results for the TDNN-F models. Again, at the 10 ms threshold, one cannot observe a significant difference among distinct models and input features. Stacking i-vectors on the top or splicing MFCCs with linear discriminant analysis procedures do not seem to improve performance at all. Topology-wise, on the other hand, we can say that the design of the HMMs under the chain modeling framework is not well suited for phonetic alignment. As with regular three-state left-to-right HMM topology (i.e., no chain) [11] the range of the cumulative percentages stayed within the 41%–45%, similar to the obtained with GMM models, it dropped to around the 30% in the chain models. For higher tolerance values, models outside the chain framework achieved the average of 80% and 94% of tokens correctly aligned, while chain models achieved only ~65% and ~90%, respectively.

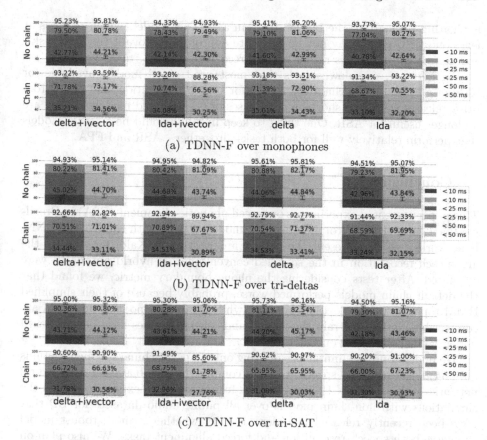

(a) TDNN-F over monophones

(b) TDNN-F over tri-deltas

(c) TDNN-F over tri-SAT

Fig. 4. Results for the TDNN-F trained on the top (hybrid HMM-DNN framework) of the monophones, tri-deltas and tri-SAT GMM-based AMs using either MFCCs (delta) or spliced-MFCCs (LDA) as input, with or without i-vectors. (Color figure online)

Overall, on the chain-free framework, delta features (MFCCs) achieved the highest percentages for both speakers, sometimes combined with i-vectors as well. Regarding the GMM-based model upon which the TDNN-F is trained, tri-SAT models provide the best results for the female speaker, while tri-deltas was best for the male speaker. But once again, as maximum difference observed is 2%, the gains are so marginal that one should avoid using the word "outperform".

An interesting point is that one can achieve good results even with as little as one hour of recorded speech from LaPSBenchmark to train a model for phonetic alignment: past experiments on a dataset of ~170 h of recorded speech also show results floating around the 45% percentage at 10 ms [1]. What we cannot tell, however, is how would the network behave if the training was scaled up to an 1,000 h dataset. MFA, for instance, uses the GlobalPhone dataset [12], which we consider already small although it contains 22 h for Brazilian Portuguese. As a matter of fact, MFA also uses GMM models, which may emphasize that navigating through all the burden to train any DNN model (which requires at least one GPU card) may not be the more appropriate move if the final task's goal is to align phonemes rather than to recognize speech.

Furthermore, one downside is that most pre-trained models available for Kaldi are based on the chain framework for speech recognition, and apart from MFA releases there is a shortage on releases of GMM-based models as they are no longer useful for ASR. One thing to keep in mind would be to train models that perform relatively well for both tasks altogether—ASR and FPA.

4   Conclusion

This paper presented experiments on forced phonetic alignment (FPA) in Brazilian Portuguese (BP). In total, 24 acoustic models trained with Kaldi over TDNN-F networks (which represent the default architecture in Kaldi for state of the art speech recognition in the so-called conventional or hybrid approach) were evaluated. After tests considering the phone boundary metric, we found that the default chain models performed worse, probably because of their simplified HMM topology in the decision tree [11], while chain-free models and GMM are comparable. Scripts to train the models and other resources have been released under MIT open license on GitHub[2].

We understand the limitations of using only LapsBenchmark, which contains only 54 min of recorded speech, to train complex models based on deep neural networks such as TDNN-F. Therefore, as future work, we expect to extend the simulations with non-chain models over all public audio datasets for BP that have been recently released in order to verify whether a more robust model can serve both speech recognition and forced alignment tasks. We also plan on exploring the use of frame-subsampling on chain models, since the TDNN-F is configured to only "see" a third of the frames. We suspect that if this feature is disabled, the alignments could be more accurate. Moreover, other architectures like LSTMs or CNNs in combination with time-delay networks should have its use evaluated.

Finally, the employment of transfer learning techniques could be investigated to take advantage of the abundance of audio data for other languages like English. That way, an acoustic model trained over LibriSpeech dataset, for example, could be trained to serve as a starting point, and GMM-based models would be trained from scratch over the male/female evaluation dataset to play the role of the new tri-SAT reference alignments. Once more, the impediment, however, is that most of the pre-trained TDNN-F-based models available on the Internet are chain models, so a chain-free would have to be trained from scratch. Additionally, other newer toolkits could be explored alongside Kaldi if configured in a phoneme-based setup, like the new K2-Lhotse-Icefall trilogy, ESPnet or SpeechBrain.

---

[2] https://github.com/falabrasil.

Acknowledgment. We gratefully acknowledge NVIDIA Corporation with the donation of the Titan Xp GPU used for this research. The authors also would like to thank CAPES for providing scholarships and FAPESPA (grant 001/2020, process 2019/583359) for the financial support.

References

1. Batista, C., Neto, N.: Experiments on kaldi-based forced phonetic alignment for brazilian portuguese. In: Britto, A., Valdivia Delgado, K. (eds.) Intelligent Systems, pp. 465–479. Springer, Cham (2021). https://doi.org/10.1007/978-3-030-91699-2_32
2. Dehak, N., Kenny, P.J., Dehak, R., Dumouchel, P., Ouellet, P.: Front-end factor analysis for speaker verification. IEEE Trans. Audio Speech Lang. Process. **19**(4), 788–798 (2011). https://doi.org/10.1109/TASL.2010.2064307
3. Dias, A.L., Batista, C., Santana, D., Neto, N.: Towards a free, forced phonetic aligner for brazilian portuguese using kaldi tools. In: Cerri, R., Prati, R.C. (eds.) Intelligent Systems, pp. 621–635. Springer, Cham (2020). https://doi.org/10.1007/978-3-030-61377-8_44
4. Goldman, J.P.: Easyalign: an automatic phonetic alignment tool under praat. In: Proceedings of the Annual Conference of the International Speech Communication Association, INTERSPEECH, pp. 3233–3236 (2011)
5. Guiroy, S., de Cordoba, R., Villegas, A.: Application of the kaldi toolkit for continuous speech recognition using hidden-markov models and deep neural networks. In: IberSPEECH'2016 On-line proceedings, pp. 187–196. IberSPEECH 2016, Lisboa, Portugal (2016)
6. Jiampojamarn, S., Kondrak, G., Sherif, T.: Applying many-to-many alignments and hidden markov models to letter-to-phoneme conversion. In: Human Language Technologies 2007: The Conference of the North American Chapter of the Association for Computational Linguistics; Proceedings of the Main Conference, pp. 372–379. Association for Computational Linguistics, Rochester, New York (2007)
7. Ko, T., Peddinti, V., Povey, D., Khudanpur, S.: Audio augmentation for speech recognition. In: Proceedings of Interspeech (2015)
8. McAuliffe, M., Socolof, M., Mihuc, S., Wagner, M., Sonderegger, M.: Montreal forced aligner: trainable text-speech alignment using kaldi. In: Proceedings of Interspeech, pp. 498–502 (2017). https://doi.org/10.21437/Interspeech.2017-1386
9. Peddinti, V., Povey, D., Khudanpur, S.: A time delay neural network architecture for efficient modeling of long temporal contexts. In: Proceedings of Interspeech, pp. 3214–3218 (2015)
10. Povey, D., et al.: The kaldi speech recognition toolkit. In: In IEEE 2011 workshop (2011)
11. Povey, D., et al.: Purely sequence-trained neural networks for ASR based on lattice-free mmi. In: Interspeech 2016, pp. 2751–2755 (2016). https://doi.org/10.21437/Interspeech.2016-595
12. Schultz, T., Vu, N.T., Schlippe, T.: Globalphone: a multilingual text speech database in 20 languages. In: 2013 IEEE International Conference on Acoustics, Speech and Signal Processing, pp. 8126–8130 (2013). https://doi.org/10.1109/ICASSP.2013.6639248
13. Siravenha, A., Neto, N., Macedo, V., Klautau, A.: Uso de regras fonológicas com determinação de vogal tônica para conversão grafema-fone em português brasileiro (2008)

14. Snyder, D., Garcia-Romero, D., Povey, D., Khudanpur, S.: Deep neural network embeddings for text-independent speaker verification. In: Proceedings Interspeech 2017, pp. 999–1003 (2017). https://doi.org/10.21437/Interspeech.2017-620
15. Souza, G., Neto, N.: An automatic phonetic aligner for brazilian portuguese with a praat interface. In: Silva, J., Ribeiro, R., Quaresma, P., Adami, A., Branco, A. (eds.) Computational Processing of the Portuguese Language, pp. 374–384. Springer, Cham (2016). https://doi.org/10.1007/978-3-319-41552-9_38
16. Young, S., Ollason, D., Valtchev, V., Woodland, P.: The HTK Book. Cambridge University Engineering Department, version 3.4, Cambridge, UK (2006)

Brazilian Portuguese Speech Recognition Using Wav2vec 2.0

Lucas Rafael Stefanel Gris[1]([✉])[iD], Edresson Casanova[2][iD],
Frederico Santos de Oliveira[3][iD], Anderson da Silva Soares[4][iD],
and Arnaldo Candido Junior[1][iD]

[1] Federal University of Technology - Paraná, Medianeira, Brazil
gris@alunos.utfpr.edu.br
[2] University of São Paulo, São Carlos, Brazil
edresson@usp.br
[3] Federal University of Mato Grosso, Cuiabá, Mato Grosso, Brazil
fredoliveira@ufmt.br
[4] Federal University of Goias, Goiânia, Brazil

Abstract. Deep learning techniques have been shown to be efficient in various tasks, especially in the development of speech recognition systems, that is, systems that aim to transcribe an audio sentence in a sequence of written words. Despite the progress in the area, speech recognition can still be considered difficult, especially for languages lacking available data, such as Brazilian Portuguese (BP). In this sense, this work presents the development of an public Automatic Speech Recognition (ASR) system using only open available audio data, from the fine-tuning of the Wav2vec 2.0 XLSR-53 model pre-trained in many languages, over BP data. The final model presents an average word error rate of 12.4% over 7 different datasets (10.5% when applying a language model). According to our knowledge, the obtained error is the lowest among open end-to-end (E2E) ASR models for BP.

Keywords: Speech recognition · Wav2vec 2.0 · Brazilian Portuguese

1 Introduction

Speech is one of the most natural ways of human communication, and the development of systems, known as Automatic Speech Recognition (ASR) Systems, capable of transcribing speech automatically have shown great importance and applicability in various scenarios, as in personal assistants, tools for customer attendance and other products [11,17,31]. The task to transcribe speech can be understood as a mapping of an acoustic signal containing speech to a corresponding sequence of symbols intended by the speaker [11]. The research in the field started with the recognition of spoken digits [10] and has shown great advances recently with the use of E2E deep learning models, especially for the English language.

© Springer Nature Switzerland AG 2022
V. Pinheiro et al. (Eds.): PROPOR 2022, LNAI 13208, pp. 333–343, 2022.
https://doi.org/10.1007/978-3-030-98305-5_31

Despite its progress in the area, the development of robust ASR models for languages other than English can still be considered a difficult task, mainly because state-of-the-art (SOTA) models usually needs many hours of annotated speech for training to achieve good results [3,26]. This can be a challenge for some languages, such as BP, that has just a fraction of open resources available, if compared to the English language [20,21]. In general, the accuracy of Portuguese ASR models are far from researches for more popular languages [1]. To overcome these challenges, self supervised learning, for instance Wav2vec 2.0 [7], can be used to learn representations for posterior use in a fine-tuning process using less labeled data.

Although the original work focused on the English language, [9] pre-trained a new version, called Wav2vec 2.0 XLSR-53, using 56k h of speech audio of 53 different languages, including BP. This work uses the model pre-trained by [9] to build an ASR for BP, using only open available data. The resulting fine-tuned model for BP and code of this work is publicly available[1].

This work is organized as follows: Sect. 2 explains the Wav2vec 2.0 model, Sect. 3 provides details about the best available open model for ASR in BP, Sect. 4 discuss the proposed method and Sect. 5 shows and discusses the obtained results. Finally, Sect. 6 presents conclusions of the work.

2   Wav2vec

Wav2vec 2.0 is an E2E model inspired on the previous works [6,27]. The pre-training uses speech masking in order to solve a contrastive task to differentiate true quantized latent representations from a set of distractors, which allows the model to learn audio representations from speech. During fine-tuning, a projection is added to the last layer of the model containing the respective vocabulary and the model is trained in a supervised way using aligned labeled speech to perform ASR. The model is based on the idea of taking discrete speech representations directly as input to the Transformer [30] (called Context Network).

The architecture of the Wav2vec 2.0 is presented in Fig. 1. It is composed by a multi-layer convolutional encoder $f : X \longmapsto Z$ which maps raw speech X into latent speech representations $z_1, \ldots, z_T$ in T time-steps. The convolutional blocks of the encoder consist of causal convolutions followed by layer normalization [4] and the GELU activation function [15]. The output of the encoder is then provided to the context network $g : Z \longmapsto C$ which maps the latent representations Z into contextualized representations $c_1, \ldots, c_T$. The context network follows the Transformer architecture. In this network, the positional encoding is replaced by a convolutional layer with GELU activation function and layer normalization that acts as a relative positional embedding.

During the pre-training phase, the model has the objective to learn the speech representations solving a contrastive task. This corresponds to the task of identifying a true quantized representation q_t from a set of false examples in a masked

---

[1] https://github.com/lucasgris/wav2vec4bp.

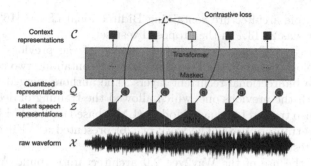

Fig. 1. Wav2vec 2.0 architecture. [7]

time-step context. After pre-training, a projection of n targets is added to the output of the context network and the model is fine-tuned in a supervised task for speech recognition [7]. In this phase, the model is trained using the Connectionist Temporal Classification (CTC) [12] as loss function. An approach similar to SpecAugment [22] is also used, promoting a better generalization to the ASR model.

The authors proposed a series of experiments using two versions of the model, BASE and LARGE (the LARGE has more parameters in the context network) and varying the datasets used to pre-train and fine-tune the model. [7] showed that it is possible to build ASR models even with few labelled data available. The experiments with 10 min of labeled data showed a Word Error Rate (WER) of 4.8% and 8.2% in both LibriSpeech test sets, namely clean and other, respectively. In this work, we use Wav2vec 2.0 XLSR-53 [9], which is based on the LARGE architecture.

3 ASRs for Brazilian Portuguese

The accuracy of ASR systems has been increased with the use of new technologies based on neural networks, in particular, with the development of E2E models, which achieved most of the recent state-of-the-art results [19]. Despite the development of new technologies among ASR researchers, there is still few work related to speech recognition for Brazilian Portuguese.

An important ASR baseline for BP is the work of [8]. The authors developed baseline ASR systems using the Kaldi toolkit [23] by training several acoustic and language models using various free and paid BP datasets (170 h in total). Although the developed systems are not based on the use of deep learning techniques and modern E2E topologies, the results are promising, with the lowest WER being 4.75% against LapsBM Benchmark [20].

In the context of E2E models, the works of [25,26] and [13] can be highlighted as important recent advances. The work of [25] presented a dataset in Portuguese composed by various freely available datasets (SID, VoxForge, LapsBM) and the proprietary dataset CSLU Spoltech [28]. The author proposed an E2E model based on a simple architecture containing Bidirectional LSTM [16] layers. The obtained error was 25.13% in the proposed test set.

More recently, [26] proposed a better version of the previous dataset and trained a topology based on the DeepSpeech 2 [3], containing two convolutional layers and five bidirectional recurrent layers. The authors merged the CETUC [2] dataset with the previous one, which allowed the training of deeper models. The authors also trained Language Models (LMs) based on KenLM [14] for post-processing the transcriptions. The work of [26] presented a WER of 25.45% in the proposed test set.

Regarding the use of the Wav2vec 2.0 architecture to build ASRs for BP, we can cite [13] as an important contribution. In this previous work, we used a low-resource data (LapsBM dataset) to fine-tune the XLSR-53 model for the BP language. We validated and tested the model using the Common Voice dataset, which demonstrated promising results (34% WER) even using only 1 h to fine-tune the model.

4 Datasets and Experiments

This section presents the datasets used to fine-tuning the Wav2vec 2.0 model for Brazilian Portuguese. The proposed datasets are:

- CETUC [2]: contains approximately 145 h of Brazilian Portuguese speech distributed among 50 male and 50 female speakers, each pronouncing approximately 1,000 phonetically balanced sentences selected from the CETEN-Folha[2] corpus;
- LaPS Benchmark [20][3] (LapsBM) is a dataset used by the Fala Brasil group to benchmark ASR systems in Brazilian Portuguese. Contains 35 speakers (10 females), each one pronouncing 20 unique sentences, totalling 700 utterances in Brazilian Portuguese;
- VoxForge[4]: is a project with the goal to build open datasets for acoustic models. The corpus contains approximately 100 speakers and 4,130 utterances of Brazilian Portuguese, with sample rates varying from 16 kHz to 44.1 kHz.
- Common Voice (CV) 7.0: is a project proposed by Mozilla Foundation with the goal to create a wide open dataset in different languages. In this project, volunteers donate and validate speech using the official site[5];
- Multilingual LibriSpeech (MLS) [24]: a massive dataset available in many languages. The MLS is based on audiobook recordings in public domain like LibriVox[6]. The dataset contains a total of 6k h of transcribed data in many languages. The set in Portuguese used in this work[7] (mostly Brazilian variant)

---

[2] https://www.linguateca.pt/cetenfolha/.
[3] "Falabrasil–UFPA" (https://github.com/falabrasil/gitlab-resources).
[4] http://www.voxforge.org/.
[5] https://commonvoice.mozilla.org/pt.
[6] https://librivox.org/.
[7] http://www.openslr.org/94/.

has approximately 284 h of speech, obtained from 55 audiobooks read by 62 speakers;

- Sidney[8] (SID): contains 5,777 utterances recorded by 72 speakers (20 women) from 17 to 59 years old with fields such as place of birth, age, gender, education, and occupation;
- Multilingual TEDx: a collection of audio recordings from TEDx talks in 8 source languages. The Portuguese set (mostly Brazilian Portuguese variant) contains 164 h of transcribed speech.

The assembled dataset is very similar to the base presented by [26]. Besides the data used by these authors, Common Voice (CV), MLS, and Multilingual TEDx (Portuguese audios only) were also included. CSLU Spoltech [21] was not considered, since we opted to use only publicly available datasets.

The majority of audios have short duration (between 1 to 10 s), while MLS tends to have longer audios. Regarding quantity of speakers, CV is the dataset that contains the greatest amount: 2,038 in total. In contrast, MLS has only 62 speakers. Training in data with more variety of speakers is expected to lead to better results if compared to less variety.

Some issues are present in the gathered datasets. For example, TEDx has some audios in European Portuguese and some transcription errors, MLS contains old spellings, before the last BP spelling reform, and SID has audios lacking transcriptions, acronyms instead of spelled words in transcriptions as well as arabic numbers instead of number in full. Additionally, it is expected to have some imbalances in the gathered datasets, especially VoxForge, which has the majority of its non-anonymous speakers identified as males.

We used the original splits of the gathered data on our assembled dataset. For datasets that did not have a subdivision of their data, we created a train and a test set. Table 1 presents the split used for training, validating and testing the final model. Common Voice was selected as validation during training. We also augmented the Common Voice training subset, by selecting all validated instances excepting the speakers and sentences present in the original dev and test sets. Although this might insert some duplicated sentences and speakers to the final subset, it has the potential to increase the size of the dataset, as we are interested to train the model with more data as possible.

The test subsets were created as follows. For VoxForge, SID and LaPS BM, we selected 5% of unique male speakers and 5% of unique female speakers. The CETUC test set was created as proposed by [26]. For the remaining datasets (TEDx, MLS and Common Voice), we used the official test sets. We also performed a filtering to remove sentences of the training data that were also present in the test subsets of the final assembled dataset. This was done in order to provide unbiased training data while preserving the test one. We performed this operation on the final assembled dataset, considering all test sets, to avoid any subset contamination. For the subsets training, we do not perform any filtering besides removal of missing and empty transcriptions.

---

[8] https://igormq.github.io/datasets/.

Table 1. Dataset split in hours. Common Voice dev was selected to validate the model.

Dataset	Train	Valid	Test
CETUC	93.9 h	–	5.4 h
Common Voice*	37.6 h	8.9 h	9.5 h
LaPS BM	0.8 h	–	0.1 h
MLS	161.0 h	–	3.7 h
Multilingual TEDx (Portuguese)	144.2 h	–	1.8 h
SID	5.0 h	–	1.0 h
VoxForge	2.8 h	–	0.1 h
Total	437.2 h	8.9 h	21.6 h

*Augmented training set

Regarding audio preprocessing, we performed some processing using Librosa[9]. All audios were resampled to 16 kHz. We also ignored audio with more than 30 s of our dataset (less than 1% of the total).

For the subsets experiments, we used both a NVIDIA TITAN V 12 GB and a NVIDIA TESLA V100 32 GB, depending on the size of the dataset used for training. The final model was trained in three NVIDIA TESLA V100 32 GB. Fine-tuning parameters were defined using the same configurations of the 100-h experiment proposed by the original Wav2vec 2.0 authors[10], except the number of updates and the max quantity of tokens, which was set to 10^5 and 10^6, respectively. As in the original work, we also used the Adam optimizer. Other parameters include: a 10k initial freeze of the transformer during fine-tuning, an augmentation similar to SpecAugment applied to time-steps and channels, a learning rate of 3×10^{-5} and a gradient accumulation of 12 steps. The model was trained using the Fairseq[11] framework for a total of 117 epochs in approximately 4 days. The batch size during training was defined automatically by the framework depending on the max quantity of predefined tokens (the effective batch size was led to approximately 2,250 s of audio).

During training, the best model was selected based on the lowest WER obtained on the validation set. We do not perform validation for the subsets experiments, as we did not have validation subsets for all the gathered datasets.

We also performed experiments using language models to post-process the ASR model results following the original work of [7], that is, using KenLM and Transformer based LMs. In this sense, we opted to use the KenLM based language models provided by [26], and also to train a new Transformer based LM [5] using portuguese data.

We trained the Transformer LM using a Wikipedia based corpus[12] constructed by [26]. This corpus is composed of over 8 million sentences extracted

---

[9] https://librosa.org/.
[10] https://github.com/pytorch/fairseq/tree/master/examples/wav2vec.
[11] https://github.com/pytorch/fairseq.
[12] Available at https://igormq.github.io/datasets.

from the Wikipedia articles and was pre-processed removing all punctuation and tags, besides converting the numbers into their written form. We opted to use the CV validation set to validate the model while training. We trained this model for 50,000 updates using a gradient accumulation of 32 steps. We also set the max quantity of tokens equal to 1,024. Regarding hyperparameters, the predefined settings of the original repository of Fairseq[13] was used.

The training of the Transformer LM lasted for approximately 12 days using a NVIDIA TESLA V100 32 GB GPU. The measured perplexity of the training and validation data was 29.88 and 144.6, respectively, while the measured average perplexity over the BP test sets was 195.65.

Finally, we also trained a baseline model based on DeepSpeech2 and implemented by [26]. This model was trained using the BP dataset and the configurations proposed by [26]. The model trained for 50 epochs, which seems to be adequate considering the amount of data and the results obtained by the authors.

5   Results and Discussion

The final assembled dataset has approximately 470 h of speech in total. This amount can be considered appropriate, since Wav2vec 2.0 reaches optimal results in English for experiments based on 100 and 960 h of audio. As presented in Table 1, the majority of the dataset is composed by the TEDx, MLS, followed by CETUC and Common Voice. The VoxForge and LapsBM datasets together represented less than 2% of the total, the same for SID. In particular, LapsBM corresponds to less than 1% of the final dataset. This means that this dataset might make little contribution to the final model. Another important aspect is the duration of the audios: the MLS dataset corresponds to approximately 40% of the final dataset, while having only 16% of the total number of audios present in the training set.

The results of this work are presented in Table 2. The lowest WER obtained in the Common Voice test set was 9.2% using a Transformer based language model. Similar results were obtained using KenLM based models trained by [26]. Without LM, the WER was 14%. Both results can be considered promising in the context of the development of ASR models given the SOTA for Brazilian Portuguese. We also tested the final model against all other test sets, obtaining 12.4% of WER on average without LM.

Our more discrepant result is observed against the CETUC test set. Our trained model using only the CETUC subset achieved a WER of 32%, while the final model obtained less than 3% of error, when tested against the same test set. One explanation for this result is that this dataset has a poor variety of vocabulary since the same phrases are repeated by each of the 100 speakers. This provides a difficult train set to generalize while the test set appears to be easier if compared to the others. A similar effect can be observed in the VF subset. In this case, a possible explanation is the dataset imbalance caused by the majority of male speakers present in the training set.

---

[13] https://github.com/pytorch/fairseq/blob/main/examples/language_model.

Table 2. Results and comparison with related works (WER) and baseline. The n-gram models are based on KenLM [26].

Experiment	Train data	LM	Test subset							
			CETUC	CV	LaPS	MLS	SID	TEDx	VF	AVG
Baseline	BP dataset	No	0.307	0.444	0.361	0.442	0.363	0.552	0.467	0.419
1. All data	BP dataset	No	0.052	0.140	0.074	0.117	0.121	0.245	**0.118**	0.124
2. All data + 3-gram	BP dataset	Yes	0.033	0.095	0.046	**0.123**	0.112	0.212	0.123	0.106
3. All data + 5-gram	BP dataset	Yes	0.033	0.094	0.043	**0.123**	**0.111**	**0.210**	0.123	**0.105**
4. All data + Transf	BP dataset	Yes	**0.032**	**0.092**	**0.036**	0.130	0.115	0.215	0.125	0.106
5. Subsets	Subset*	No	0.447	0.126	0.145	0.163	0.124	0.203	0.561	0.258
6. Subsets + 3-gram	Subset*	Yes	0.333	0.097	0.073	0.144	**0.104**	0.203	0.453	0.201
7. Subsets + 5-gram	Subset*	Yes	**0.328**	0.096	0.073	**0.143**	**0.104**	**0.201**	0.450	**0.199**
8. Subsets + Transf	Subset*	Yes	0.400	**0.086**	**0.053**	0.165	0.198	0.204	**0.406**	0.216
Batista et al. [8]	Various**	Yes	–	–	0.047	–	–	–	–	–
Gris et al. [13]	LaPS BM	No	–	0.34	–	–	–	–	–	–
Quintanilha et al. [26]	BRSD v2	Yes	0.254	–	–	–	–	–	–	–

*Train subset respective to the test subset **No name provided

The obtained results of our final model are better than the subsets experiments, as expected. An exception is Experiment 5, which performed better than Experiment 1 against Common Voice. In this case, a small training set leads to a small error. This result is possibly explained due to slight overfitting towards recording conditions. Similar occured to TEDx, another big dataset, but the phenomenon was not verified in smaller datasets.

The LMs used also considerably improved the performance of the trained models. The improvement is more noticeable in the subsets experiments. In some cases, the language models appear to slightly worsen the model performance, which may be explained by the characteristics of the data used to train the language models or some particularities of each subset. The Transformer LM demonstrates better performance on CETUC, CV and LapsBM. We hypothesize that these subsets represents more the data used to train the LM, if compared to the other datasets.

In the context of BP models, there are few works that we can compare with our work. Specifically, we built a test set following [26] to compare this recent work with ours. Using the CV test set, we can compare the obtained results with our previous work [13], and using the LapsBM test subset, we can compare the results against the baseline proposed by [8]. The complete comparison is present in Table 5. Although the baseline proposed by [8] is not based on deep learning, the obtained results against LapsBM seems to be notably competitive to ours. However, we believe that LapsBM does not reflect all the domains of BP data, since the results over the other test subsets diverge considerably.

Regarding E2E models, the results from [26] are interesting, considering that the model training was made entirely in a supervised form. However, the result of 25.45% of WER is above the WER of this work (3.2%). We believe that our results were superior from the work of [26] for two main reasons. First, we used

Wav2vec 2.0, a more modern neural architecture. Second, we trained over more data, since recently several public access dataset were released. This result is also observed with our baseline, where the model trained with BP dataset performed worse against all test sets in all experiments.

Finally, in our previous work [13], we obtained 34% of WER against the CV dataset. Although we used the same model architecture as in this work, the obtained WER is worse than our current result, even without LM (14%). The same behavior is observed in Experiment 5, in which the WER is only 12.6%. Both results demonstrate the importance of the use of more data among in-domain training to achieve better results.

6   Conclusions

In this work we presented a model for Automatic Speech Recognition for the Brazilian Portuguese Language. Our results show that self-supervised learning is a great advance in the development of ASR systems for BP, mainly because it requires less labeled data for training, achieving a better performance if compared to the models trained entirely on a supervised form. On average, our model obtained 10.5% and 12.4% of WER against the proposed test sets, with and without a language model, respectively. According to our knowledge, the model achieves state-of-the-art results among the open available E2E models for the target language.

In addition, our work suggests that the use of datasets with a large variety of vocabulary and speakers are still important to the development of robust models, as well as in-domain training. Besides, it is not clear how much these models are sensitive to noisy data. We also do not investigate the development of robust LM models, which can further improve the results. In this sense, as future work, we plan to train more robusts models with new datasets and to investigate the use of data augmentation techniques, such as additive noise [29] and Room Impulse Response (RIR) simulation [18]. We believe that these approaches can collaborate with the community towards the development of robust ASR models for Brazilian Portuguese.

Acknowledgements. This research was funded by CEIA with support by the Goiás State Foundation (FAPEG grant #201910267000527) (http://centrodeia.org/), Department of Higher Education of the Ministry of Education (SESU/MEC), Copel Holding S.A. (https://www.copel.com), and Cyberlabs Group (https://cyberlabs.ai/). Also, this study was financed in part by the Coordenação de Aperfeiçoamento de Pessoal de Nível Superior – Brasil (CAPES) – Finance Code 001. We also would like to thank Nvidia Corporation for the donation of Titan V GPU used in part of the experiments presented in this research.

References

1. Aguiar de Lima, T., Da Costa-Abreu, M.: A survey on automatic speech recognition systems for Portuguese language and its variations. Comput. Speech Lang. **62**, 101055 (2020). https://doi.org/10.1016/j.csl.2019.101055. https://www.sciencedirect.com/science/article/pii/S0885230819302992
2. Alencar, V., Alcaim, A.: LSF and LPC-derived features for large vocabulary distributed continuous speech recognition in Brazilian Portuguese. In: 2008 42nd Asilomar Conference on Signals, Systems and Computers, pp. 1237–1241. IEEE (2008)
3. Amodei, D., et al.: Deep speech 2: end-to-end speech recognition in English and mandarin. In: International Conference on Machine Learning, pp. 173–182. PMLR (2016)
4. Ba, J.L., Kiros, J.R., Hinton, G.E.: Layer normalization. arXiv preprint arXiv:1607.06450 (2016)
5. Baevski, A., Auli, M.: Adaptive input representations for neural language modeling. In: International Conference on Learning Representations (2018)
6. Baevski, A., Schneider, S., Auli, M.: vq-wav2vec: self-supervised learning of discrete speech representations. In: International Conference on Learning Representations (ICLR) (2020). https://openreview.net/pdf?id=rylwJxrYDS
7. Baevski, A., Zhou, Y., Mohamed, A., Auli, M.: wav2vec 2.0: a framework for self-supervised learning of speech representations. In: Larochelle, H., Ranzato, M., Hadsell, R., Balcan, M.F., Lin, H. (eds.) Advances in Neural Information Processing Systems, vol. 33, pp. 12449–12460. Curran Associates, Inc. (2020). https://proceedings.neurips.cc/paper/2020/file/92d1e1eb1cd6f9fba3227870bb6d7f07-Paper.pdf
8. Batista, C., Dias, A.L., Sampaio Neto, N.: Baseline acoustic models for Brazilian Portuguese using Kaldi tools. In: Proceedings of IberSPEECH 2018, pp. 77–81 (2018). https://doi.org/10.21437/IberSPEECH.2018-17
9. Conneau, A., et al.: Unsupervised cross-lingual representation learning at scale. In: Proceedings of the 58th Annual Meeting of the Association for Computational Linguistics, pp. 8440–8451 (2020)
10. Davis, K.H., Biddulph, R., Balashek, S.: Automatic recognition of spoken digits. J. Acoust. Soc. Am. **24**(6), 637–642 (1952)
11. Goodfellow, I., Bengio, Y., Courville, A.: Deep Learning. MIT Press, Cambridge (2016)
12. Graves, A., Fernández, S., Gomez, F., Schmidhuber, J.: Connectionist temporal classification: labelling unsegmented sequence data with recurrent neural networks. In: Proceedings of the 23rd International Conference on Machine Learning, pp. 369–376 (2006)
13. Gris, L.R.S., Casanova, E., de Oliveira, F.S., da Silva Soares, A., Candido-Junior, A.: Desenvolvimento de um modelo de reconhecimento de voz para o Português Brasileiro com poucos dados utilizando o Wav2vec 2.0. In: Anais do XV Brazilian e-Science Workshop, pp. 129–136. SBC (2021)
14. Heafield, K.: KenLM: faster and smaller language model queries. In: Proceedings of the Sixth Workshop on Statistical Machine Translation, pp. 187–197 (2011)
15. Hendrycks, D., Gimpel, K.: Gaussian error linear units (GELUs) (2020)
16. Hochreiter, S., Schmidhuber, J.: Long short-term memory. Neural Comput. **9**(8), 1735–1780 (1997)

17. Karpagavalli, S., Chandra, E.: A review on automatic speech recognition architecture and approaches. Int. J. Sig. Process. Image Process. Pattern Recogn. **9**(4), 393–404 (2016)
18. Ko, T., Peddinti, V., Povey, D., Seltzer, M.L., Khudanpur, S.: A study on data augmentation of reverberant speech for robust speech recognition. In: 2017 IEEE International Conference on Acoustics, Speech and Signal Processing (ICASSP), pp. 5220–5224. IEEE (2017)
19. Li, J.: Recent advances in end-to-end automatic speech recognition. arXiv preprint arXiv:2111.01690 (2021)
20. Neto, N., Patrick, C., Klautau, A., Trancoso, I.: Free tools and resources for Brazilian Portuguese speech recognition. J. Braz. Comput. Soc. **17**(1), 53–68 (2011)
21. Neto, N., Silva, P., Klautau, A., Adami, A.: Spoltech and OGI-22 baseline systems for speech recognition in Brazilian Portuguese. In: Teixeira, A., de Lima, V.L.S., de Oliveira, L.C., Quaresma, P. (eds.) PROPOR 2008. LNCS (LNAI), vol. 5190, pp. 256–259. Springer, Heidelberg (2008). https://doi.org/10.1007/978-3-540-85980-2_33
22. Park, D.S., et al.: SpecAugment: a simple data augmentation method for automatic speech recognition. In: INTERSPEECH 2019, September 2019. https://doi.org/10.21437/Interspeech.2019-2680
23. Povey, D., et al.: The Kaldi speech recognition toolkit. In: IEEE 2011 Workshop on Automatic Speech Recognition and Understanding, No. CONF. IEEE Signal Processing Society (2011)
24. Pratap, V., Xu, Q., Sriram, A., Synnaeve, G., Collobert, R.: MLS: a large-scale multilingual dataset for speech research. In: INTERSPEECH 2020, October 2020. https://doi.org/10.21437/Interspeech.2020-2826
25. Quintanilha, I.M.: End-to-end speech recognition applied to Brazilian Portuguese using deep learning. MSc dissertation (2017)
26. Quintanilha, I.M., Netto, S.L., Biscainho, L.W.P.: An open-source end-to-end ASR system for Brazilian Portuguese using DNNs built from newly assembled corpora. J. Commun. Inf. Syst. **35**(1), 230–242 (2020)
27. Schneider, S., Baevski, A., Collobert, R., Auli, M.: wav2vec: unsupervised pre-training for speech recognition. In: INTERSPEECH (2019)
28. Schramm, M., Freitas, L., Zanuz, A., Barone, D.: CSLU: Spoltech Brazilian Portuguese version 1.0 ldc2006s16 (2006)
29. Snyder, D., Garcia-Romero, D., Sell, G., Povey, D., Khudanpur, S.: X-vectors: robust DNN embeddings for speaker recognition. In: 2018 IEEE International Conference on Acoustics, Speech and Signal Processing (ICASSP), pp. 5329–5333. IEEE (2018)
30. Vaswani, A., et al.: Attention is all you need. In: Neural Information Processing Systems (NIPS) (2017)
31. Yu, D., Deng, L.: Automatic Speech Recognition. Springer, London (2015). https://doi.org/10.1007/978-1-4471-5779-3

A Corpus of Neutral Voice Speech in Brazilian Portuguese

Pedro H. L. Leite[1,2]($\boxtimes$) (iD), Edmundo Hoyle[2] (iD), Álvaro Antelo[2] (iD), Luiz F. Kruszielski[2] (iD), and Luiz W. P. Biscainho[1] (iD)

[1] Federal University of Rio de Janeiro (UFRJ), Rio de Janeiro, Brazil
{pedro.lopes,wagner}@smt.ufrj.br
[2] Globo Comunicação e Participações S.A., Rio de Janeiro, Brazil
{edmundo.hoyle,alvinho,luiz.fk}@g.globo

Abstract. This work presents a new database containing high sampling rate recordings of a single male speaker reading sentences in Brazilian Portuguese with neutral voice, along with the corresponding text corpus. Intended for synthesis and other speech-oriented applications, the dataset contains text scripts extracted from a popular Brazilian news TV program, read out loud by a trained individual in a controlled environment, resulting in roughly 20 h of audio data. The text was normalized in the recording process and special textual occurrences (e.g. acronyms, numbers, foreign names etc.) were replaced by their phonetic translation to a readable text in Portuguese. There are no noticeable accidental sounds and background noise has been kept to a minimum in all audio samples. To illustrate the potential benefits of having this data available, text-to-speech experiments were conducted using state-of-the-art models for speech synthesis (Tacotron 2 and Waveglow). As a result, we obtained intelligible and natural sounding voices from as few as 8 min of audio samples coming from an unseen target speaker, after having trained over our data; moreover, by increasing the target recording time to 75 min, we have noticeably improved accuracy in pronunciation.

Keywords: Speech syntesis · Automatic speech recognition · Dataset · Brazilian Portuguese · Audio signal processing

1 Introduction

Speech analysis and synthesis algorithms have been in the spotlight for many years in both audio and linguistics research topics, composing building blocks for personal assistants, voice recognition systems, virtual characters and much more. Recently, with the advances in machine learning algorithms, great strides have been made in improving these speech devices, sometimes achieving surprising results. However, regarding the resources available in Brazilian Portuguese, there is still a gap to be filled, as neither the amount nor the quality of data is comparable to those in other languages.

V. Pinheiro et al. (Eds.): PROPOR 2022, LNAI 13208, pp. 344–352, 2022.
https://doi.org/10.1007/978-3-030-98305-5_32

1.1 Related Works

The vast majority of speech data-based algorithms available today are designed to handle varieties of English, due to the universal spread of (and consequent amount of content in) that language. Datasets like LJSpeech [1], Librispeech [2] and CHiME 5 [3] provide different kinds of data, encompassing speech with and without emotion, multiple and single speaker emissions, noisy and noise-free scenarios and a varied set of recording qualities, covering most of the general uses of speech recognition and synthesis in English.

For Brazilian Portuguese, some private entities have proposed to collect data openly through the internet, developing heterogeneous (and hopefully large) datasets (e.g. Mozilla Common Voice (MCV) [4] and VoxForge Speech Corpus [5]) and making them available to the general public. Also, The Open Speech and Languages Resources group has made available two datasets for text/speech applications: Multilingual LibriSpeech (MLS) [6] and Multilingual TEDx (mTEDx) [7]. The MLS dataset is composed of audiobook excerpts, while the mTEDx corpus is built over TED [8] conferences transcripts.

In the academic community, The Fala Brasil Group recorded a dataset of approximately 1 h with 35 speakers reading texts (also available) from the area of Law as well as general benchmark sentences. Also, the CETUC [9][1] dataset provides a large corpus (144 h) of speech and text pairs[2], with 100 speakers, resulting in roughly 1.5 h per speaker. This is the only dataset found in the literature whose environment was described and controlled to maximize recording quality for the intended applications. Recently, the TTS-Portuguese-corpus (TTS-PT) [10] was released, containing around 10 h of sentences read by a single speaker recorded in full-band in a controlled but not professional recording environment. In Table 1, we show a brief comparative description of the datasets cited here.

2 Objectives

The database released with this article meets the need for a large set of sentences read by a single speaker with neutral emotion, recorded under professional and controlled conditions and with text control for phoneme alignment. The goal is to support the research community with a reference voice that enables the pre-training of data-driven speech models for automatic speech recognition (ASR) and speech synthesis in Brazilian Portuguese, providing ways to develop a warm start to transfer learning processes or to deliver a voice that sounds natural as it is.

---

[1] Available from https://igormq.github.io/datasets/.

[2] A new transcript of the sentences read, including punctuation and graphic accentuation, is available from www.smt.ufrj.br/gpa/propor2022/.

Table 1. Text to speech datasets: Lang. = Language, US = U. S. English, BR = Brazilian Portuguese; Hours = Duration in hours; w. = words, u. = unique words, utt. = utterances, sent. = sentences; m = male, f = female; F (kHz) = sampling rate in kHz; Prof. = professional recording, Ctrl. = controlled environment, Unctrl = uncontrolled environment, Het. = heterogeneous conditions.

Dataset	Lang.	Hours	Text count	# Speakers	F (kHz)	Recording
LJSpeech	US	20	226k w., 14k u.	1 m	22.05	Prof., Ctrl.
Librispeech	US	1000	900k u. w.	1,283 m, 1,183 f	16	Prof, Het.
CHiME	US	50	100k utt.	48	16	Parties, Ctrl.
MCV	BR	200	496k w., 33k u.	2038	48	Unctrl., Het.
VoxForge	BR	4	21k w., 729 u.	111	16–44.1	Unctrl., Het.
MLS	BR	200	13.84M w., 383k u.	50	16	Prof., Het.
mTEDx	BR	164	520k w.	316	48	Prof., Het.
Fala BR	BR	1	700 sent.	35	16	Prof., Ctrl.
CETUC	BR	144	1M w., 3.5k u.	50 m, 50 f	16	Prof., Ctrl.
TTS-PT	BR	10.5	71k w., 13k u.	1 m	48	Prof., Ctrl.
Ours	BR	20	180k w., 23k u.	1 m	96	Prof., Ctrl.

3   Dataset

This work provides to the general public an open source dataset that contains audio recordings of Brazilian Portuguese speech paired with the corresponding text. We proceed to describe the structuring methodology and general information over the dataset.

3.1   Text

The text samples are small excerpts from one of the main Brazilian TV news programs, called "Jornal Nacional". Small sentences were obtained by means of web scraping, using the *python* [11] module *selenium* [12] on articles found at the program's website [13]. Around two months of news articles between May and June of 2021 were scanned. Only the net text content of the news articles were retrieved, i.e., advertisements, figures, footnotes etc. were ignored.

The scraped text contained numerals, abbreviations, foreign words, proper names and other occurrences that could disrupt phoneme/grapheme correspondence. To address this issue, such anomalous words were carefully transcribed by hand into the form they would have been written to be read in Brazilian Portuguese, e.g. "2020" was rewritten as "dois mil e vinte", "TV" as "tê vê" and "Biden" as "Baiden".

3.2   Recordings

The recording process was aimed to develop a dataset that could cover a broad, general use. A male speaker was asked to apply a neutral emotion intonation and avoid, as much as possible, regionalisms and/or prosody biases. The microphone used was a Neumann TLM 102 [14], positioned 20 cm from the speaker, to avoid proximity effect. The microphone had a cardioid polar pattern, chosen in this way to avoid any acoustical influence from the recording room. Also, there were no noticeable accidental noises, and the noise floor was kept to a negligible minimum.

The samples were recorded through an Apogee Duet [15] interface, in software Audacity [16], and coded into a broadcast ".wav", 24 bit, 96 kHz format. Although 96 kHz is not considered standard in broadcast or popular AI training, we considered that a higher sample rate could be beneficial for future research, besides the fact that a moderate downsampling would not produce any significant data degradation.

3.3 Data Structure

After the acquisition process, we chose to downsample and convert the files to the standard 16 bit, 44.1 kHz ".wav" format, in order to generate a downloadable version of the dataset and to speed up processing steps. This conversion was done with sox [17] library for linux, resulting in the folder structure as follows: from the root folder, texts are included in the txts folder and the audio files in the wavs folder, with the pair sentence/recording sharing a unique filename in both formats. A spreadsheet file (".csv" format) containing the original and the grapheme corrected sentences, alongside the duration of each matching audio sample is provided in the root folder. Besides, some of the statistics reported in this paper can also be found there, in a text file. This data structure follows the LJSpeech dataset formatting.

3.4 Statistics

Regarding text features, the total number of characters in the transcribed text is 1,113,803, and the total count of words is 178,873, with 23,407 distinct words distributed in 5,484 sequences (an average of 32.6 words per sequence). These quantities were chosen in order to achieve around 20 h of voice recordings, considering an average speech speed of 160 words per minute. To help visualization, a word cloud of the text dataset (without stopwords) is presented in Fig. 1.

The audio samples are presented in 5484 ".wav" files, with an average of 13.04 s, minimum of 4.78 s and maximum of 31.05 s of duration. This results in roughly 20 h of recorded speech, constituting, to the authors knowledge, the largest text-to-speech oriented corpus for a single voice in the Portuguese language.

3.5 Data Access

The final version of the dataset, more details about the construction process, application examples and other information can be found through this link: www.smt.ufrj.br/gpa/propor2022/.

Fig. 1. Word cloud of the provided dataset.

4　Applications

Regarding the speech synthesis problem, the data provided in this work can be useful for the development of different types of systems. As an example, we can mention the automatic generation of informational speech: having a neutral voice to read news, social network content or general text in accessibility systems in Portuguese is an immediate benefit.

Another application can be found in the development of a fast start for voice cloning systems: the initial learning stages of decoding text and prosody construction can be absorbed by models pre-trained with this data, leaving only the features related to the target voice to be learned.

As for ASR, the data made available here can certainly contribute in a multi-speaker context to speech-to-text applications by providing several hours of professional recording quality audio and correspondingly curated text. In addition, more general models such as those employed in representation learning, speech classification and speech clustering can also benefit from this kind of data, as a purposefully neutral voice avoids unwanted biases coming from variations in prosody and accent.

5　Experiments

With the purpose of demonstrating the practical usage of this dataset, we conducted some text-to-speech experiments using deep learning models that reach state-of-the-art performance in similar applications for the English language.

Firstly, Tacotron 2 [18] text-to-mel and Waveglow [19] mel-to-audio models are used with our dataset to develop a natural voice that sounds like our single neutral speaker. After that, the pre-trained models with our dataset are used as a warm start to a voice cloning attempt, in which target speaker data (now with allowed expression and accent) are collected from smaller datasets.

To start training the neutral voice, the audio samples in our dataset were converted to 16-bit/22.05 kHz PCM in order to speed up the processing stages. After that, the initial silence in each audio file was trimmed according to a 40 dB threshold below the maximum signal magnitude. The input sentences used were the raw normalized text transcripts, precisely as described before.

Having the formatted examples in hand, the dataset was split into train, validation and test partitions ($\approx$90%, $\approx$5% and $\approx$5%, respectively). The Tacotron 2 model was then trained in an NVIDIA QUADRO RTX 8000 with 48 GB RAM. With this GPU, the text-to-mel model training stage took approximately 6 full days in 102 k iterations with 32 batch size. For Waveglow, we used the pre-trained model from the English language available from the original repository, speeding up training to about two days of processing in 38 k iterations with 80 batch size on the same GPU. The resulting combined model was able to decode new text samples and generate speech from them without problems, even though some synthesis-related artifacts might be noticed in the audio. Prosody and accent seem natural yet neutral, indicating that the goal of generating a neutral voice for text-to-speech applications has been achieved.

With the neutral voice already trained, two other experiments were conducted, setting aside a small percentage of the data for comparison. In the first one, we use a proprietary dataset with less than 8 min of audio from a male speaker to perform a voice transfer experiment. In this case, both the Tacotron 2 and the Waveglow models started from the pre-trained checkpoints and converged in a few hours. The resulting voice is clearly identifiable as that of the target speaker, with some synthesis artifacts as in the synthesized neutral voice, but this time containing also some mispronunciations. The second experiment resorted to a larger dataset (around 75 min) collected from the CETUC dataset to perform a similar voice transfer procedure. The models took around a day to reach convergence, but the voice obtained seems more natural, with reduced synthesis artifacts and better pronunciations.

To illustrate the results, we resort to a set of audio files generated in each experiment along with audio samples from the original datasets. For a comparative evaluation between synthetic samples, we use ten sequences from the test split of the neutral voice dataset. When assessing synthetic audio against original recordings, we choose some examples from the test split of each target dataset and make a visual comparison between the mel spectrogram representations: Figs. 2, 3 and 4 show one pair of corresponding mel spectrograms to compare original and synthetized examples. All audio signals corresponding to the experiment results are available on our webpage[3].

---

[3] http://www.smt.ufrj.br/gpa/propor2022/audios.

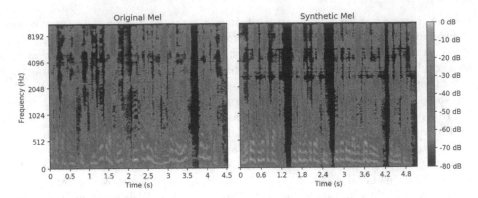

Fig. 2. Original and synthetized mel spectrograms for the 20 h neutral dataset.

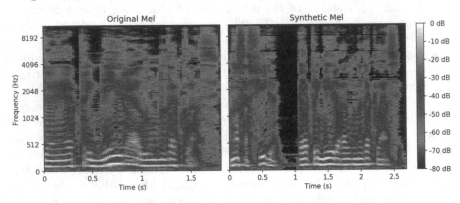

Fig. 3. Original and synthetized mel spectrograms for the 75 min target dataset.

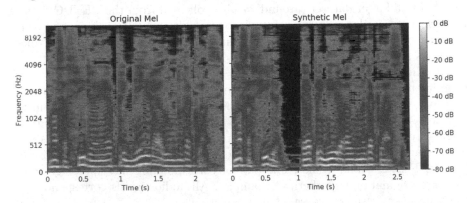

Fig. 4. Original and synthetized mel spectrograms for the 8 min target dataset.

6   Conclusion

This work presented in detail the development of a neutral voice speech database for Brazilian Portuguese. We also provided a brief overview of the similar open source datasets available, showing that there are still gaps to be filled with regard to data resources for speech synthesis and recognition. Three experiments were conducted in order to demonstrate the usability of the presented database. Their results indicated the potential to provide a natural voice in Brazilian Portuguese. In addition, we also showed that it is possible to establish a successful workflow for speaker transfer, trained over a short recording time from the target voice.

We also acknowledge the need for a similar dataset based on a female voice, since learning procedures can become harder in the case of male/female transfer. Also, other data driven models are expected to be developed by the authors for other applications such as automatic captioning, speech-to-speech translation, metadata annotation and many others.

The authors hope that this dataset will enable new developments within the speech processing community.

Acknowledgment. This work is partially funded by the National Council for Scientific and Technological Development – CNPq.

References

1. The LJ Speech Dataset. https://keithito.com/LJ-Speech-Dataset/. Accessed 23 Oct 2021
2. Panayotov, V., Chen, G., Povey, D., Khudanpur, S.: LibriSpeech: an ASR corpus based on public domain audio books. In: 2015 International Conference on Acoustics, Speech and Signal Processing (ICASSP), South Brisbane, Australia, pp. 5206–5210. IEEE (2015)
3. Barker, J., Watanabe, S., Vincent, E., Trmal, J.: The fifth 'CHiME' speech separation and recognition challenge: dataset, task and baselines. In: 19th Annual Conference of the International Speech Communication Association (Interspeech 2018), Hyderabad, India, pp. 1561–1565. ISCA (2018)
4. Ardila, R., et al.: Common voice: a massively-multilingual speech corpus. In: 12th Conference on Language Resources and Evaluation (LREC 2020), Marseille, France, pp. 4211–4215. ELRA (2020)
5. VoxForge. http://www.voxforge.org/home. Accessed 23 Oct 2021
6. Pratap, V., Xu, Q., Sriram, A., Synnaeve, G., Collobert, R.: MLS: a large-scale multilingual dataset for speech research. In: 21st Annual Conference of the International Speech Communication Association (Interspeech 2020), Shanghai, China, pp. 2757–2761. ISCA (2020)
7. Salesky, E., et al.: The multilingual TEDx corpus for speech recognition and translation. In: 22nd Annual Conference of the International Speech Communication Association (Interspeech 2021), Brno, Czech Republic, pp. 3655–3659. ISCA (2021)
8. TED. https://www.ted.com/. Accessed 23 Oct 2021
9. Alencar, V., Alcaim, A.: LSF and LPC - derived features for large vocabulary distributed continuous speech recognition in Brazilian Portuguese. In: Asilomar Conference on Signals, Systems and Computers, California, U.S.A., pp. 1237–1241. IEEE (2008)

10. Casanova, E., et al.: TTS-Portuguese corpus: a corpus for speech synthesis in Brazilian Portuguese. arXiv preprint https://arxiv.org/abs/2005.05144
11. Python Programming Language. https://www.python.org/. Accessed 23 Oct 2021
12. Selenium Framework. https://www.selenium.dev/. Accessed 23 Oct 2021
13. Jornal Nacional Website. https://g1.globo.com/jornal-nacional/. Accessed 23 Oct 2021
14. Neumann TLM 102 Microphone. https://www.neumann.com/homestudio/en/tlm-102. Accessed 23 Oct 2021
15. Apogee Duet Interface. https://www.apogeedigital.com/products/duet. Accessed 23 Oct 2021
16. Audacity Software. https://www.audacityteam.org/. Accessed 23 Oct 2021
17. Sox Software. http://sox.sourceforge.net/. Accessed 25 Oct 2021
18. Shen, J., et al.: Natural TTS synthesis by conditioning WaveNet on MEL spectrogram predictions. In: 2018 IEEE International Conference on Acoustics, Speech and Signal Processing (ICASSP), Calgary, AB, Canada, pp. 4779–4783. IEEE (2018)
19. Prenger, R.J., Valle, R., Catanzaro, B.: WaveGlow: a flow-based generative network for speech synthesis. In: 2019 IEEE International Conference on Acoustics, Speech and Signal Processing (ICASSP), Brighton, UK, pp. 3617–3621 (2019)

Comparing Lexical and Usage Frequencies of Palatal Segments in Portuguese

Luís Trigo[1](✉) [iD] and Carlos Silva[2] [iD]

[1] LIACC Laboratório de Inteligência Artificial e Ciência de Computadores,
University of Porto, Porto, Portugal
[2] CLUP Centro de Linguística, University of Porto, Porto, Portugal

Abstract. Palatal consonants in Portuguese are considered complex or marked segments because they are inherently heavy and restricted in terms of their distribution, in relation to other consonants. Moreover, they appear to display differences between themselves, as first language acquisition and creoles' adaptation suggest that /ʎ/ is more complex than /ɲ/. The arguments for complexity are endorsed by some qualitative studies but are still lacking quantitative support. This paper aims at analyzing the phonological restrictiveness of these consonants by comparing their actual frequency in several different corpora, reporting both lexical entries and usage in discourse. In addition to their context-free frequency, we control for their word position and phonetic adjacency. We find that palatals are less frequent than other consonants. However, relative to each other, they do not display proportional lexical and usage frequencies. These results shed new light not only on the representation of /ɲ/ and /ʎ/ but also on the relation between frequency and markedness in language studies.

Keywords: Phoneme frequency · Palatal consonants · Phonological representation

1 Introduction

The research on Portuguese palatal sonorants, /ɲ/ and /ʎ/, assumes that they are rare and restricted in terms of their distribution [9, 30–32], although it never tells us how restricted they are. The label *restricted* is assigned due to their distributional constraints, once they are constrained to one syllable constituent (the onset) and to one context (between vowels). These constraints motivated several proposals concerning their phonological nature, most of which agree that, although they emerge as singletons, they correspond to more than one unit at the phonological level. Nevertheless, there is still no agreement regarding whether the palatal nasal and the palatal lateral share the same basic structure or not. In order to evaluate these hypotheses, we need to engage in an approach that enables us to take concrete measures of the behavior of /ɲ/ and /ʎ/, relatively to other Portuguese consonants and to each other.

In line with classical criteria for phonological classification [28], Portuguese palatal sonorants display distinctiveness (e.g. /soɲu/ "dream" /soʎu/ "wooden floor"), but their contrastiveness is highly constrained. For instance, unlike their coronal counterparts, palatals sonorants [31]:

© Springer Nature Switzerland AG 2022
V. Pinheiro et al. (Eds.): PROPOR 2022, LNAI 13208, pp. 353–362, 2022.
https://doi.org/10.1007/978-3-030-98305-5_33

1. Are disallowed word-initially ([lama] "mud" ≠ *[ʎama]);
2. Do not admit complex rhymes at their left ([aɾma] "gun" ≠ *[aɾɲa]);
3. Do not occur in the last syllable of proparoxytones ([tuˈaʎa] "towel" ≠ *[ˈtɔaʎa]).

There are three additional arguments which support the idea that palatal consonants are phonologically complex segments, based on phonological processes:

1. *Stress conditioning*: they prevent proparoxytone stress assignment when they occupy the final onset [31,32];
2. *Etymological bimoracity*: they descend from a sequence of CoronalConsonant&PalatalGlide [30];
3. *Dialectal diphthonguization*: they can trigger the diphthongization of the previous syllable (if stressed), generating a palatal glide on the right of the vowel [3,22] or result from merging the standard [lj] or [nj] into a singleton [21,24].

Given these arguments, several linguists suggested that Portuguese palatal sonorants are mentally represented either as geminates [31] (thus, [ʎ] = /ʎ.ʎ/ and [ɲ] = /ɲ.ɲ/), complex segments with a palatal autosegment [30] (hence, [ʎ] = /l |I|/ and [ɲ] = /n |I|/) or a sequence of segments that share the same slot [15] based on the notion of *covert diphthong*, that is, [ʎ] = /(Vowel)jl/ and [ɲ] = /(Vowel)jN/.

These representations agree that palatal sonorants are complex and share a similar internal structure. But, although they seem to capture the notion of palatal complexity, there are reasons to believe that these consonants may differ internally; for instance:

1. *Historical source*: in spite of sharing the historical path mentioned above, they also have unique sources (e.g. *KL > [ʎ] and *GN > [ɲ] [2]);
2. *Typological frequency*: while 42% of the languages have /ɲ/, only 5% have /ʎ/ [13];
3. *First language acquisition*: in European Portuguese, /ɲ/ is acquired earlier than /ʎ/ (2.4–3.4 years old *vs* after 4.0 years old [5]);
4. *Adaptation into creoles*: more than 70% of the Portuguese-based creoles have phonologized /ɲ/, but no creole appears to have a phonological /ʎ/, whose features are partially or totally deleted [23].

Whereas we know more and more about the importance of statistical learning in language acquisition and how statistics may shape the production of speech sounds both in children and adults [6,14], a descriptive statistical analysis is a piece still missing in the discussion about the representation of palatal sonorants in Portuguese. The current study aims at filling this gap, by assessing the frequency of palatal consonants in Portuguese, with these questions in mind:

1. Does the usage frequency of palatal sonorants mirror the lexical frequency patterns in Portuguese?
2. Are there differences in the distribution of palatal sonorants (e.g. quality of the adjacent vowel, word position)?
3. Does this imply any changes to the current representations?

In general, the answer to these questions can open a new window to what we know about the relation between frequency and complexity and, in particular, to the internal structure of palatal consonants. On the one hand, the ease of articulation and perception may determine the usage frequency of a sound pattern, which in turn is a clue to its universal complexity [33]. On the other hand, the frequency of a segment within a language-specific lexicon is constrained by idiosyncratic features, such as historical change, which may mirror a particular interpretation of universal elements by a particular language [20].

2   Methods

In studying phonological frequency patterns, there are at least two very different dimensions one can evaluate: the possibilities of use and the actual use, which mirror long existing dicotomies in linguistics, like *langue vs parole* [19] and *I-language vs E-language* [4]. On orthographic grounds, these dimensions can be translated into dictionary-like corpora, on the one hand, and usage corpora like press or multimedia corpora, on the other. For this work we take both dimensions. Using orthographic corpora for phonological analysis gives us a great advantage in this sense, once it allows us to assess a large and diverse amount of lexical units.

We started by searching for a large dictionary in order to explore the limits of the distribution of palatals and the constraints that condition lexical incorporation within this language. Dicionário Aberto[1] is an online Portuguese dictionary that resulted from the transcription of the 1913 dictionary *Novo Diccionário da Língua Portuguesa*, of Cândido de Figueiredo which is in public domain [25]. These features make it a suitable tool once it is large, reliable, and easily accessible. Another advantage of this dictionary is its time spectrum, in the sense that it includes both archaic and modern vocabulary. There is more spelling variation than in current dictionaries, which demands more data preparation. However, this variation may be also interesting, opening a window for future work. Thus, the main difficulty in the exploration of this dictionary is the more complex outdated spelling. For instance, some archaic spelling entries with *lh* and *nh* consisted of etymological *h* having no palatal value (e.g., *inharmonia, estilhial*) by *l* and *n*. We made a comprehensive spelling homogenization by doing some replacements for orthographic update that were suggested in [25]. It should be pointed that this dictionary already has some redundant entries with alternative orthographic forms (e.g. *f* and *ph*). The pre-processing step resulted in 112.018 words.

As a complement to the exploration of this historical dictionary, we used a contemporary dictionary, although more reduced in the number of entries. Wikcionário[2] is the Portuguese version of the multilingual collaborative web based wiktionary project. Its collaborative nature implies having no fixed structure, usually dependent on the colective user choices for each language, "which are necessary to describe culture- or language-specific information" [11]. It also provides comprehensive language knowledge, including etymology and phonetic information that may be very useful both for synchronic and diachronic analysis. Compared to Dicionário Aberto, this resource also has the big advantage of having an up-to-date spelling and does not need a complex pre-processing step. For this analysis, we considered the words from all Portuguese

---

[1] https://dicionario-aberto.net/.
[2] https://pt.wiktionary.org.

varieties – African, Brazilian and European. The extraction process resulted in 13.983 words.

Regarding the usage corpora, we started by making an exploratory analysis of the CETEMPúblico [18]. This is a freely available and well-known European-Portuguese language corpus that collects 180 million words from published and non-published raw texts provided by the Portuguese newspaper Público that covered the period between 1991 and 1998. We also opted for only processing the raw text with no arabic numerals, no abbreviations nor url and email addresses. Another pre-processing action that we executed was splitting words with clitics – this step had a significant impact in the account of total words (tokens) with /ʎ/ and /m/. After all the pre-processing steps described above we accounted for more than 171 million tokens and almost 611.000 unique words (types).

We also noticed that recent literature considers that traditional corpora written by professionals and specialists, newspapers included, may not reflect the distribution of lexical choice that conversational corpora has [8,26]. Thus, we also explored SUBTLEX-PT corpus[3]. This corpus compiles "132,710 Portuguese words obtained from a 78 million corpus based on film and television series subtitles, offering word frequency and contextual diversity measures" [26]. Beyond the aforementioned benefits, it has also the advantage of being very easy to process.

The additional processing step that we made for all the corpora was word syllabification in the Portulan Clarin platform[4] [16]. The computational processing was made in the Python programming language and is available as jupyter notebooks in a Github repository[5].

3   Results

In this section, we perform a visual inspection of the frequency patterns that characterize palatal sonorants in Portuguese. The relative percentage values are given according to the size of each corpus as described in Sect. 2.

3.1   Context-Free Frequency

Previous studies used to measure the frequency of each segment for the whole phonological inventory of a given language [7,12,27,29]. These studies investigate the frequency patterns of segments or phonological features independently of their context in a single kind of corpus. Here, we take a similar approach. However, instead of measuring the frequency of all segments in a given corpus, we calculate the percentage of some selected segments in different kinds of corpora: lexical, written usage and oral usage. In this section, we compare the frequency of /ɲ/ and /ʎ/ with two near-universal consonants /m/ and /p/, which are considered non-complex, in onset position.

Figure 1 represents the frequencies of the targeted lemmas extracted from lexical corpora. Lemma frequency, as types with no inflection, can better be compared with

---

[3] http://p-pal.di.uminho.pt/about/databases.

[4] https://portulanclarin.net/workbench/lx-syllabifier/.

[5] https://github.com/Portophon/palatal-sonorants-pt.

type frequency from usage corpora. As expected, we find that /m/ and /p/ are about nine/ten times more frequent than the palatal sonorants. Nevertheless, we notice that /ɲ/ is less frequent than /ʎ/, which is contrary to our expectations.

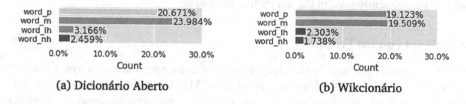

(a) Dicionário Aberto   (b) Wikcionário

Fig. 1. Context-free frequency on dictionaries

In Fig. 2, we display the percentage values for the usage corpora. Again, the palatal sonorants are about 10 times less frequent than /p/ and /m/ in the most informal, oral-like corpus, that is, SUBTLEX-PT (Figs. 2a and 2c). This difference is slightly increased if we consider the formal, written corpus, CetemPúblico (Figs. 2b and 2d). Unlike dictionaries, in usage corpora /ɲ/ is more frequent /ʎ/ both considering types and tokens, especially in the subtitles corpus. These results are in line with the order of acquisition and with the typological frequency of these consonants, although the differences between segment frequency are softer in Portuguese.

We also control for the morphological influence on lexical frequency. We do it by separating the clitic <lh(e)>, which corresponds to the dative form of the 3rd person personal pronoun, and the words ended with <inh(o)>, which are mostly diminutives, from the remaining words with /ʎ/ and /ɲ/. The former is statistically more significant in the oral-like corpus (Fig. 2a, 2c) than in the written corpus especially concerning types

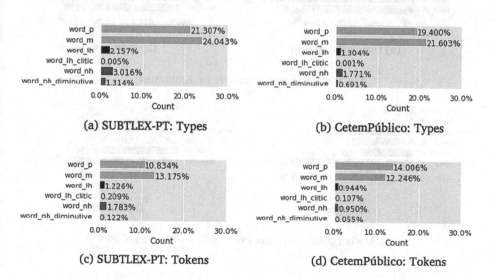

(a) SUBTLEX-PT: Types   (b) CetemPúblico: Types

(c) SUBTLEX-PT: Tokens   (d) CetemPúblico: Tokens

Fig. 2. Context-free frequency on subtitles and newspapers

(Fig. 2b). The latter is again more frequent in SUBLEX-PT in spite displaying similar proportions in both corpora. Hence, when comparing the frequency of the diminutive words and the total amount of words with /ɲ/, we find that they are more significant in terms of types than in terms of tokens. This means that there is a small group of words which are frequently used in the diminutive form only.

3.2 Word Position Frequency

Word position is relevant to the study of palatal consonants in two ways. Firstly, it allows us to assess the word-initially restriction [31]. Secondly, it reveals the proportion of palatals which influence stress assignment, i.e., the palatals occupying the final onset of the words [32]. The results extracted from lexical corpora (Fig. 3) show a small number of words whose initial onset is /ɲ/ or /ʎ/. A closer examination revealed that this group corresponds to loanwords (except the clitic pronoun <lhe>), imported either from neighbour languages, like Mirandese and Spanish (concerning /ʎ/), or from native African and American languages (concerning /ɲ/). Moreover, the graphs indicate that the Portuguese lexicon tends to store words with palatal sonorants occupying the final onset, at the expense of other positions.

Although the usage-based results seems different when we look at the types (Fig. 4a), the actual use represented by the tokens displays results similar to those of the dictionaries (Fig. 4b). The increased percentage of word initial /ʎ/ is an effect of the recurrent presence of the clitic pronoun.

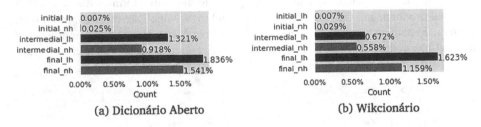

(a) Dicionário Aberto   (b) Wikcionário

Fig. 3. Word position frequency on dictionaries

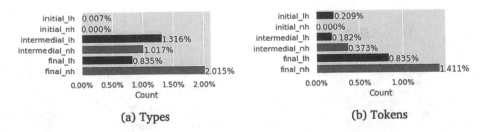

(a) Types   (b) Tokens

Fig. 4. Word position frequency on subtitles – SUBTLEX-PT

3.3 Left Adjacent Vowel Frequency

Knowing the preferred environment of a consonant is crucial to a deep understanding of its internal structure [1]. In this section, we test the idea of *covert diphthongs* [15] by assessing the quality of the vowels on left of palatal sonorants and lexical palatal diphthongs. We do not consider their right adjacency given that these consonants affect or are affected mainly by their left context (see Sect. 1).

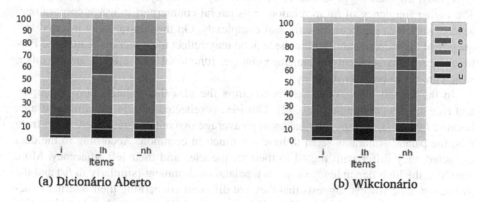

(a) Dicionário Aberto   (b) Wikcionário

Fig. 5. Left adjacent vowel frequency on dictionaries

The results from Figs. 5 and 6 point out that all palatal consonants in Portuguese occur mostly after a palatal vowel, that is, either /i/ or /e/. However, /ɲ/ and /j/ show a higher degree of dependency on such environments than /ʎ/ does. The palatal lateral is also the most tolerant palatal segment in allowing back vowels on its left adjacency in all corpora, while the palatal nasal and the palatal glide are more restrictive.

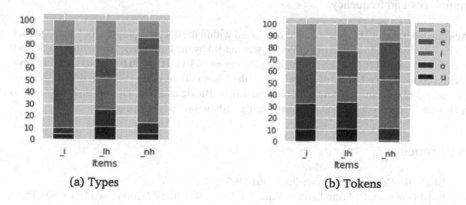

(a) Types   (b) Tokens

Fig. 6. Left adjacent vowel frequency on subtitles – SUBTLEX-PT

4 Discussion

This study investigates the complexity of palatal sonorants by comparing the frequencies in lexical and usage-based corpora. In accord with the observations across previous studies, our results show that palatal sonorants are restricted in Portuguese [9,30,31]. However, the descriptive statistical analysis performed allows us to have a clearer picture of what this restrictiveness means.

Firstly, the data suggests that complexity may not always govern frequency [17]. The higher frequency of /ɲ/ in relation to its lateral counterpart in usage corpora may indeed work as a predictor of universal complexity. On the contrary, the inverted frequency of these consonants within the lexicon may reflect idiosyncratic features of Portuguese, such as accidents in language change, functional load effects, among other, which are yet to be determined.

In the second place, our analysis confirms the idea that palatals play an important role in stress assignment [30,32]. This idea is reflected both in lexicon and usage, because /ɲ/ and /ʎ/ occupy the final onset on average two out of three times. Apart from this, the palatal sonorants seem to have not much in common. According to the data extracted, they differ with regard to their frequencies and their left adjacency. More crucially, the high dependency of /ɲ/ on a palatal environment (similarly to /j/) and the avoidance back vowels suggests that they are different concerning their internal structure. We can speculate that the higher complexity of /ʎ/ is precisely what gives this segment a distributional advantage, which, in turn, makes it more frequent in the lexicon.

We believe that these results will improve the accuracy of the representation of palatals in Portuguese. In addition, the knowledge of the statistical patterns of /ɲ/ and /ʎ/ may help speech therapists find better ways to correct speech disorders, since children are known to track distributional regularities in language acquisition [10]. Future research focusing on the frequencies of palatals in acquisition and in aphasia would be important to evaluate the current results and to shed new light on the relation between complexity and frequency.

Acknowledgment. This research was conducted within the doctoral program of Languages Sciences (Faculty of Arts-University of Porto), was funded by the Portuguese Foundation for Science and Technology (FCT MCTES) through the PhD grant SFRH/BD/2020.07466.BD (Carlos Silva) and supported by the Center of Linguistics of the University of Porto (FCT-UIDB/00022/2020). We would like to thank Steven Moran and Rikke Bundgaard-Nielsen and three anonymous reviewers for the feedback and comments that greatly improved the manuscript.

References

1. Bloch, B.: Contrast. Language **29**, 59–61 (1953)
2. Boyd-Bowman, P.: From Latin to Romance in Sound Charts. Georgetown University Press, Washington, D.C. (1980)
3. Brissos, F.: Proposta de reformulação da caracterização dialetal do noroeste português. Estudos de Lingüística Galega, pp. 193–208 (2018). https://doi.org/10.15304/elg.ve1.3560. https://revistas.usc.gal/index.php/elg/article/view/3560

4. Chomsky, N.: Knowledge of Language: Its Nature, Origin, and Use. Praeger, Westport (1986)
5. Costa, T.: The acquisition of the consonantal system in European Portuguese: focus on place and manner features. Ph.D. thesis, Universidade de Lisboa (2010). https://repositorio.ul.pt/handle/10451/2010
6. Edwards, J., Beckman, M., Munson, B.: Frequency effects in phonological acquisition. J. Child Lang. **42**, 306–311 (2015). https://doi.org/10.1017/S0305000914000634
7. Hayden, R.: The relative frequency of phonemes in general-American English. Word **6**, 217–223 (1950)
8. Herdağdelen, A., Marelli, M.: Social media and language processing: how Facebook and Twitter provide the best frequency estimates for studying word recognition. Cogn. Sci. **41**(4), 976–995 (2017)
9. Mateus, M., Andrade, E.: The Phonology of Portuguese. Oxford University Press, Oxford (2000)
10. Maye, J., Werker, J.F., Gerken, L.: Infant sensitivity to distributional information can affect phonetic discrimination. Cognition **82**(3), B101–B111 (2002). https://doi.org/10.1016/S0010-0277(01)00157-3. https://www.sciencedirect.com/science/article/pii/S0010027701001573
11. Meyer, C.M., Gurevych, I.: Wiktionary: a new rival for expert-built lexicons? Exploring the possibilities of collaborative lexicography. na (2012)
12. Mines, M., Hanson, B.F., Shoup, J.E.: Frequency of occurrence of phonemes in conversational English. Lang. Speech **21**, 221–241 (1978)
13. Moran, S., McCloy, D. (eds.): PHOIBLE 2.0. Max Planck Institute for the Science of Human History, Jena (2019). https://phoible.org/
14. Munson, B.: Phonological pattern frequency and speech production in adults and children. J. Speech Lang. Hear. Res. **44**, 778–92 (2001). https://doi.org/10.1044/1092-4388(2001/061)
15. Pimenta, H.: Nasalité et syllabe: Une étude synchronique, diachronique et dialectologique du portugais européen. Ph.D. thesis, Université de Paris VIII, October 2019
16. Rodrigues, J., Costa, F., Silva, J., Branco, A.: Automatic syllabification of portuguese. In: Actas do XXX Encontro Nacional da Associação Portuguesa de Linguística (ENAPL 2014) (2016)
17. Romani, C., Galuzzi, C., Guariglia, C., Goslin, J.: Comparing phoneme frequency, age of acquisition, and loss in aphasia: implications for phonological universals. Cogn. Neuropsychol. **34**, 449–471 (2017)
18. Santos, D., Rocha, P.: Evaluating cetempúblico, a free resource for Portuguese. In: Proceedings of the 39th Annual Meeting of the Association for Computational Linguistics, pp. 450–457 (2001)
19. Saussure, F.: Cours de linguistique générale. Payot, Paris (1916)
20. Scheer, T., Kula, N.: Government phonology: element theory, conceptual issues and introduction. In: Hannahs, S.J., Bosch, A.R.K. (eds.) The Routledge Handbook of Phonological Theory. Routledge (2018)
21. Segura, L., Saramago, J.: Variedades dialectais portuguesas. In: Caminhos do Português: Exposição Comemorativa do Ano Europeu das Línguas, pp. 221–237. Biblioteca Nacional (2001)
22. Silva, C.: O estranho caso da vogal breathy voiced em pe: evidências a partir de um dos dialetos madeirenses. elingUP 6 (2016). https://ojs.letras.up.pt/index.php/elingUP/article/view/2539
23. Silva, C.: The representation of Portuguese palatal sonorants through the eyes of Portuguese-based creoles. In: Proceedings of the 8th School-Conference Language Issues: A Young Scholars' Perspective. Institute of Linguistics of the Russian Academy of Sciences, Moscow (forc)

24. Silva, P.: Palatalização de laterais por harmonização de elementos. Master's thesis, Universidade do Porto, November 2017
25. Simões, A., Farinha, R.: Dicionário aberto: um recurso para processamento de linguagem natural. Viceversa: revista galega de tradución 16 (2010). https://revistas.webs.uvigo.es/index.php/viceversa/article/view/2569
26. Soares, A.P., et al.: On the advantages of word frequency and contextual diversity measures extracted from subtitles: the case of Portuguese. Q. J. Exp. Psychol. 68(4), 680–696 (2015)
27. Tantibundhit, C., Onsuwan, C., Munthuli, A., Kosawat, K., Wutiwiwatchai, C.: Frequency of occurrence of phonemes and syllables in Thai: analysis of spoken and written corpora. In: ICPhS (2015)
28. Trubetzkoy, N.: Grundzüge der Phonologie. Cercle Linguistique de Prague (1939)
29. Vasilévski, V.: Phonologic patterns of Brazilian Portuguese: a grapheme to phoneme converter based study. In: Proceedings of the EACL 2012 Workshop on Computational Models of Language Acquisition and Loss, pp. 51–60. Association for Computational Linguistics, Avignon (2012)
30. Veloso, J.: Complex segments in Portuguese: the unbearable heaviness of being palatal. In: Zendoia, I.E., Nazabal, O.J. (eds.) Bihotz ahots. M. L. Oñederra irakaslearen omenez, pp. 513–526. Euskal Herriko Unibertsitatea (2019)
31. Wetzels, W.L.: Consoantes palatais como geminadas fonológicas no português brasileiro. Revista de Estudos da Linguagem 9(2), 5–15 (2000). https://doi.org/10.17851/2237-2083.9.2.5-15. http://www.periodicos.letras.ufmg.br/index.php/relin/article/view/2323
32. Wetzels, W.L.: Primary stress in Brazilian Portuguese and the quantity parameter. J. Portuguese Linguist. 5–6, 9–58 (2007)
33. Zipf, G.K.: Human Behaviour and the Principle of Least Effort. Addison-Wesley (1949)

Lexical Semantics

Extracting Valences from a Dependency Treebank for Populating the Verb Lexicon of a Portuguese HPSG Grammar

Leonel Figueiredo de Alencar[1,3]([✉])(iD), Lucas Ribeiro Coutinho[3](iD),
Wellington José Leite da Silva[3](iD), Ana Luiza Nunes[3](iD),
and Alexandre Rademaker[2,3](iD)

[1] Universidade Federal do Ceará, Fortaleza, Brazil
`leonel.de.alencar@ufc.br`
[2] IBM Research, Rio de Janeiro, Brazil
[3] FGV/EMAp, Rio de Janeiro, Brazil

Abstract. We propose a methodology to populate the verb type hierarchy of a deep computational grammar in the HPSG formalism using syntactic and morphological information from Universal Dependencies (UD) treebanks. It is exemplified by means of the UD Bosque corpus and PorGram, a computational grammar for Portuguese constructed in the LinGO Grammar Matrix framework, but it can be applied to analogous grammars of other languages using other UD treebanks. The main component of the methodology is a Python module that extracts from the annotated sentences the core arguments and other features that are relevant to determine verb valence. This module enables the creation of a Python dictionary that maps valence frames to verb objects. This dictionary facilitates not only determining which frames occur with which verbs, but also detecting annotation errors. The potential of the module for rapid expansion of the lexical coverage of PorGram and corpus annotation error detection is illustrated with concrete examples.

Keywords: Verb valence · Grammar engineering · HPSG ·
Dependency treebank · Universal dependencies

1 Introduction

Carefully hand-crafted, linguistically motivated grammars of natural languages have shown to be valuable resources in different contexts where deep syntactic parsing is required. A paramount example is Watson, IBM's Q&A system that gained popularity after winning the Jeopardy! television competition against two human champions. One of the original components of this system is the English Slot Grammar, a manually constructed grammar of English in the Slot Grammar (SG) formalism [15,23].

Differently than the representations generated by shallow parsing techniques, deep syntactic representations are closer to semantic structure. The HPSG formalism, akin to SG, is one of the most widely used frameworks for implementing

© Springer Nature Switzerland AG 2022
V. Pinheiro et al. (Eds.): PROPOR 2022, LNAI 13208, pp. 365–375, 2022.
https://doi.org/10.1007/978-3-030-98305-5_34

large scale grammars for deep syntactic parsing [24]. In comparison to LFG, for example, another popular grammar engineering framework, HPSG has the advantage of facilitating the encoding of semantic structures in parallel to morphosyntactic structures. Another advantage of HPSG is the availability of free, open source (henceforth FOSS) tools and resources, like the LKB development environment [6] and the parsers and wide-coverage grammars of diverse languages distributed within the DELPH-IN Consortium. The English Resource Grammar (ERG) [16], one of the largest computational grammars ever constructed, is one of these grammars. It generates semantic representations in the framework of Minimal Recursion Semantics (MRS) [7]. These representations have shown to be very useful in text understanding tasks (e.g. [12,19,20,29]). As a relatively low-resourced language, Portuguese lacks a wide-coverage computational grammar targeted at deep syntactic parsing distributed under a FOSS license. LXGram [5,8] is a wide-coverage HPSG grammar, but is not FOSS. BrGram is a middle-coverage LFG grammar [1] that depends on the proprietary XLE parser. Available parsers like PALAVRAS [4] and UDPipe [32] produce relatively shallow analyses and/or are not FOSS.

In other to provide a completely FOSS resource for deep syntactic and semantic parsing of Portuguese, PorGram was initiated [25][1]. Analogously to LXGram, PorGram was initially developed using the LinGO Grammar Matrix [2,3]. This system generates a starter grammar from specifications elicited from the user by means of a customization questionnaire. This starter grammar is formalized in the Type Description Language (TDL), which is used by the HPSG grammars of the DELPH-IN Consortium. The common core of this grammar was provided by the ERG and the JACY Japanese HPSG grammar [30]. Grammatical phenomena of Portuguese that are not covered by the customization system have been hand-coded in TDL.

Since HPSG is a lexicalist theory, the bulk of grammatical information is encoded in the lexicon. Therefore, valence properties of verbs play a major role. Modeling this information in a computational grammar, however, is a non-trivial and time consuming task. According to [31], the valence dictionary of Portuguese verbs of [14] contains information on circa 12126 lemmas, 6000 of which are currently used and thoroughly described in [31]. In both dictionaries, almost all verb lemmas are assigned different valence frames. It is not uncommon for a verb to be used in 10 or more frames.

As reported in [31], manually extracting, analyzing and organizing valence information of thousands of verbs demands many man-years of work. Previous studies report on the extraction of valence properties from electronic dictionaries and other sources [34]. Digital dictionaries of Portuguese, e.g., Michaelis[2] and Caldas Aulete[3], do assign each verb one or more basic valence patterns, i.e., whether it is transitive, intransitive or ditransitive. However, this is not sufficient

---

[1] https://github.com/LR-POR/PorGram.

[2] https://michaelis.uol.com.br/.

[3] https://aulete.com.br/.

in a computational grammar, as we will see in Sect. 2. Besides, these on-line materials are subject to copyright.

In the present paper, we propose a methodology to extract valence information from resources distributed under a FOSS license, namely Universal Dependencies treebanks, so as to populate the verb type hierarchy of a computational grammar. The methodology is exemplified by means of UD Portuguese Bosque and PorGram, but it can be applied to other grammars in the spirit of the LinGO Grammar Matrix framework using UD treebanks of other languages.

In the next Sect. 2, we outline the development of PorGram and how valence is encoded therein. Then, in Sect. 3, we explain the annotation format of UD Bosque and show what type of information it contains for valence extraction. Section 4 describes the module we implemented for extracting valences. Finally, in Sect. 5, we summarize our results.

2   Valence Encoding in PorGram

Since its start about 8 months ago, the development of PorGram has followed two parallel paths. On the one hand, the LinGO Grammar Matrix customization system has been used to implement those grammatical phenomena of Portuguese that are covered by the questionnaire. On the other hand, phenomena that fall outside of the scope of this system or seem more easily to implement manually have been hand-coded in TDL.

We focus here on the implementation of valence patterns. The questionnaire only supports the encoding of intransitive and strictly transitive verbs, whereby the object can take the form of a noun phrase, an adpositional phrase or a clause. A clausal complement, on its turn, can represent, e.g., a proposition (1), a polar (2) or a constituent question (3) [33].

(1) Ela insistiu   que ele dormisse.
     she insist:PST;IND;3SG that he sleep:PST;SBJV;3SG
     'She insisted he sleep.'

(2) Ela perguntou   se ele tinha   dormido.
     she ask:PST;IND;3SG if he have:PST;IND;3SG sleep:PTCP
     'She asked if he had slept.'

(3) Ela perguntou   quais ratazanas ele matou.
     she ask:PST;IND;3SG which rats   he kill:PST;IND;3SG
     'She asked which rats he killed.'

Clausal complements with external subjects, however, are not supported by the customization questionnaire. Therefore, subject and object control verbs, as in (4) and (5), cannot be implemented by this means. The questionnaire only allows for the implementation of subject raising verbs, e.g., auxiliaries of compound tenses (2), modals (6) and aspectual verbs (7).

(4) Elas lamentam   ter   chorado.
they regret:PRS;IND;3PL have:INF cry:PTCP
'They regret having cried.'

(5) Convenci   as alunas a concorrerem.
convince:PST;IND;1SG the students to apply:INF:3PL
'I convinced the students to apply.'

(6) Ele precisa   dormir.
he must:PRS;IND;3SG sleep:INF
'He must sleep.'

(7) Ele continua   dormindo.
he continue:PRS;IND;3SG sleep:PROG
'He's still sleeping.'

Note that the verb in (5) is ditransitive, i.e., it governs two complements. The customization questionnaire limits itself to verbs of arity one and two. Besides, the implementation of prepositional objects with this interface revealed to be problematic (8). Raising verbs subcategorizing for a complementizer phrase (CP), as in (9)–(11), also fall outside the sphere of the questionnaire. Therefore, many types were manually encoded, including, e.g., transfer of possession and communication verbs, see (12) and (13).

(8) Ele gosta   do   gato.
he like:PRS;IND;3SG of;the cat
'He likes the cat.'

(9) Ele parou   de chorar.
he stop:PST;IND;3SG of cry:INF
'He stopped crying.'

(10) Ela começou   a rir.
she start:PST;IND;3SG to laugh:INF
'She started to laugh.'

(11) Ele tem   que|de dormir.
he have:PRS;IND;3SG that|of sleep:INF
'He must sleep.'

(12) Ele deu   o livro ao   artista.
he give:PST;IND;3SG the book to;the artist
'He gave the artist the book.'

(13) Ela contou   ao   rapaz que estava   triste.
she tell:PST;IND;3SG to;the boy that be:PST;IND;3SG sad
'She told the boy that she was sad.'

The core component of every grammar produced by the customization system, however, provides abstract types that facilitate the manual encoding of daughter types tailored at the morphosyntactic characteristics of Portuguese. Using these abstract types as templates, we created 38 new verb types in addition to the 27 verb types implemented with the questionnaire. These new types enabled the grammar to parse all the above mentioned examples.

Due to intermediate types that encode the characteristics of subgroups of verbs, the type hierarchy can easily be extended to cover new valence patterns. For example, `ditrans-2nd-arg-ctrl` is the common supertype of a variety of object control verbs. It is inherited by `inf-ditrans-2nd-arg-ctrl`, which, in turn, is a supertype for different classes of verbs governing an infinitival CP headed by prepositional complementizers, e.g., `a-inf-ditrans-2nd-arg-ctrl` as in (5) and `de-inf-ditrans-2nd-arg-ctrl`, exemplified by *impedir alguém de fazer algo* 'prevent someone from doing something'.

The present verb lexicon has just a few instances of each type, which were manually encoded resorting to print grammars [9,22] and valence dictionaries [14,31][4] as well as to our own language intuitions. To expand lexical coverage, we designed a methodology to populate the lexicon using freely available resources. This is the subject of Sect. 4.

3   Universal Dependencies and the UD Bosque Treebank

Universal dependencies (henceforth UD) is "a framework for cross-linguistically consistent morphosyntactic annotation" [21]. Version 2.9, released on November 2021, comprises 217 treebanks, totaling 122 languages[5]. This treebank collection has grown fast, 60 new treebanks and over 30 new languages were added in the last two years. In the present study, we decided to use data from the UD project due to its wide adoption, consistent annotation guidelines and a unique file format across different languages. This means that methodology and tools developed for processing one UD treebank can be used unchanged with other UD corpora.

The UD collection has three Portuguese treebanks: UD Bosque, GSD and PUD. The present work focuses on UD Bosque [27]. Regardless of its limitations, UD Bosque is the authoritative Portuguese corpus in the UD project, since it is adopted for almost all widely used statistical parsers (e.g., Stanza[6], UDPipe[7], Spacy[8]) to train their standard models[9]. Figure 1 illustrates the

---

[4] We consider this to be fair use, due to the small amount of knowledge from these sources that was incorporated into PorGram.

[5] http://hdl.handle.net/11234/1-4611.

[6] http://stanza.run.

[7] http://ufal.mff.cuni.cz/udpipe.

[8] http://spacy.io.

[9] One of the reviewers suggested the newly released BDCamões Treebank, whose dependency graphs are also available in UD format, but with a different tag set [17]. Despite its potential advantages, it mostly a historical corpus, which makes it not immediately useful in our context, since our main concern with PorGram is modern Portuguese. Therefore, we postpone using BDCamões Treebank data for future work.

annotation scheme. It was generated by the UDPipe parser with the model trained with UD Release 2.6.

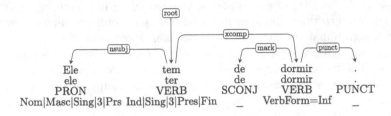

Fig. 1. UD annotation of the variant of (11) with complementizer *de* 'of'

UD representations express dependency relations between words, which are classified into two basic types: content words and functional words. Dependency relations between content words express argument structure and modification, while relations between a content word and a functional word express morphosyntactic properties of the content word. For example, in Fig. 1 the content words are the pronoun and the two verbs. Examples of functional words are adpositions and complementizers, which are structurally similar: via the `case` and `mark` relations, respectively, they specify that the word they attach to is a dependent of another word.

Unlike argument structure (ARG-ST) lists in HPSG, UD does not encode valence explicitly. UD, however, assigns each dependent of a verb head that is one of its core arguments a syntactic relation from a set of six relations: subject (`nsubj`), object (`obj`), indirect object (`iobj`), open clausal complement (`xcomp`), clausal complement (`ccomp`) and clausal subject (`csubj`).

An `obj` can be a direct object (no `case` dependent) or a prepositional object (8) (with a `case` dependent). Typically, the `iobj` corresponds to the recipient of a transfer of possession or communication verb, see (12) and (13). The infinitival complement of a control verb, see (4) and (5), is an `xcomp`. The complement clauses in (1)–(3) and (13) are examples of `ccomp`.

UD's core arguments mostly correspond to what are assumed to be arguments in LFG [13] and ARG-ST elements in HPSG [28]. There is, however, an important exception: while oblique arguments, e.g., of locative verbs, are arguments in these theories, UD treats them as "non-core dependents"[10]. This is because UD abolishes the pervasive distinction between complement and adjuncts [21]. Therefore, one cannot automatically infer from the fact that a PP dependent is analyzed as an `obl` whether it should be treated as an ARG-ST element in PorGram.

---

[10] https://universaldependencies.org/u/dep/.

4   From Dependency Information to Valence Types

This section describes the methodology developed to populate the hierarchy of verb types in PorGram using the information encoded in UD Bosque. The main component is a module implemented in Python on top of the CoNLL-U Parser[11]. It is freely available for use with other UD treebanks to extract valence patterns for analogous computational grammars of other languages[12].

The module consists of three major Python objects that store the syntactic information extracted from a UD treebank: `Relation`, `Valence` and `Verb`. The most basic object is the `Relation`, which stores the information from a token of a sentence: lemma, dependency relation, morphosyntactic features and the token itself. It recursively stores every `mark` and `case` daughter token inside of itself as a `Relation` object.

The `Verb` object stores every `Valence` object associated with the same verb lemma. The `Valence` object, on its turn, stores whatever information is relevant to determine the valence of a verb, i.e., properties of the `VERB` token and any child thereof that is either a core argument or an `expl`, a `subj:pass` or an `aux:pass`. Expletive reflexive clitics are required or licensed by many verbs, e.g. *queixar-se* 'complain' and *abrir-se* 'open'. In PorGram, this expletive is generated by a lexical rule that applies to some verb types, but not to others, e.g. *desaparecer* 'disappear'. Therefore, the information that a verb governs an `expl` is crucial for assigning it the appropriate type in PorGram. Also important for determining valence is whether a subject is a passive one (`subj:pass`) or whether the verb governs a passive auxiliary (`aux:pass`). Passivization means that the verb in the active form governs an `obj`.

An example will help understand how valence information is encoded: the frame `<VERB:act,nsubj,xcomp:de+Inf>` states that *ter* in Fig. 1 is in the active voice and has an infinitival `xcomp` daughter governing the complementizer (i.e., `SCONJ`) *de* 'of'.

With these three objects, we can (i) identify which verbs occur with which valences in which sentences and (ii) detect incorrectly annotated sentences. To illustrate this, we constructed a Python dictionary with the module. It maps valence frames to list of `Verb` objects sharing the same frame.

The snippet in Listing 1.1 extracts all verbs that follow the pattern of *dar* 'give' in (12), whose prepositional object can be pronominalized with a dative clitic. These verbs are associated with the valence frames in lines 3 to 7. These frames correspond to the active and passive usages with a dative clitic `iobj` or a prepositional object `iobj:a` and/or a null subject. The output is a set with 132 lemmas. These are potential candidates for the `nom-acc-dat-ditrans` type in PorGram. In Brazilian Portuguese, the recipient of transfer of possession verbs can be introduced either by the dative preposition *a* or the goal preposition *para* 'to'. This type of verb is assigned the type `nom-acc-rec-ditrans` in PorGram.

---

[11] https://github.com/EmilStenstrom/conllu/.
[12] https://github.com/LR-POR/tools.

Listing 1.1. Extracting accusative-dative verbs

```
1   valences = joblib.load("valences_dict.joblib")
2   acc_dat_verbs=set()
3   for e in ['<VERB:act,nsubj,iobj:a,obj>',
4             '<VERB:act,iobj:a,obj>',
5             '<VERB:pass,nsubj,iobj:a>', '<VERB:pass,iobj:a>',
6             '<VERB:act,nsubj,iobj,obj>','<VERB:act,iobj,obj>',
7             '<VERB:pass,iobj>', '<VERB:pass,nsubj,iobj>']:
8         verbs=valences.get(e)
9         if verbs:
10                  acc_dat_verbs.update(verbs)
```

By contrast, ditransitive verbs which only license *para* 'to' are assigned the type nom-acc-goa-ditrans.

Further developing the basic concept of Listing 1.1, we have implemented Python code that automatically constructed 2059 new lexical entries for 1340 verbs. These entries instantiate 27 types of PorGram, including, besides the three ones above, different types for (i) intransitives, (ii) direct transitives, (iii) transitives with a prepositional object and (iv) transitives and ditransitives with a clausal complement. Classes (i), (iii) and (iv) also include verbs with expletive reflexives. Previously, PorGram only had 227 entries of 167 verbs. The key component of the code is a mapping from valence frames to PorGram types. Only the basic valence frame in each case, e.g., the first frame in Listing 1.1, needs to be manually specified in a two column table in raw text format. A function derives all contextual variants of the basic frame, e.g., the frames in lines 4–7 of Listing 1.1. Another function collapses entries of ditransitives like *dar* 'give' whose prepositional object is headed by *a* or *para* in the corpus into a single entry with the nom-acc-rec-ditrans type.

One could easily define new mappings from frames to types in order to further populate the verb hierarchy of PorGram, but there are some important limitations. First, UD Bosque does not encode deep dependencies [11]. This means that the external subject of an xcomp is not identified. Consequently, it is not possible to decide whether the verb is an object or a subject control verb. This information is encoded in the corpus version in the *Deep Universal Dependencies* collection[13] and could be explored by adding a new functionality to the module. However, it is uncertain how correct these deep annotations are. Besides, the distinction between raising and control is not encoded. Therefore, the extracted results should be inspected by a human expert to decide between these two types of external subjects or more sophisticated processing techniques (e.g., using OpenWordNet-PT data [26]) should be used. Another problem are absolute relative clauses, e.g., (14) from UD Bosque, which are assigned the ccomp function but correspond to a nominal argument in PorGram. Presently,

---

[13] https://ufal.mff.cuni.cz/deep-universal-dependencies.

these cases also require manual revision. We intend to modify the frame extraction module to store information about the relative pronoun.

(14) "cobardia" não se   aplica   a quem enfrenta   toiros
      cowardice not REFL apply:PRS;3SG to who face:PRS;3SG bulls
      '*cowardice* does not apply to those facing bulls'

A more serious type of problem are the annotation errors. But these reveal the usefulness of the module as a helping tool to correct the corpus. We address this issue in the last section.

5 Final Remarks

Although the main goal was the acquisition of verbs and their valences, a very relevant byproduct was the detection of several erroneous annotations in UD Bosque. The problems found will certainly also occur in other Portuguese UD corpora. Below, we highlight the main problems encountered.

It seems that verbs normally have at most three core arguments, tritransitives being exceptional in the world's languages [10,14,18]. Very long frames were detected, inspection of some of them revealed annotation errors. For example, we found some sentences with successively embedded verbs whose complements were assigned to the first verb in the series.

Another problem were valences with both nsubj and csubj. Occurrences of multiple conflicting complementizers were also detected, e.g. xcomp:a:em:a+Inf or xcomp:de:que:a+Inf. An analysis of some examples revealed that these extraneous complementizers result from annotation errors and that they actually belong to other constituents. Finally, the valences extracted revealed a lack of uniformity in the treatment of verbs like *pedir* 'ask' following the pattern of (13), whose recipient is inconsistently analyzed as iobj or obj.

Despite these problems, we are confident that the proposed methodology will enable the rapid expansion of the verb lexicon of PorGram in the near future. In addition, it provides a strong methodology to detect errors and increase the consistency of treebank annotations.

References

1. de Alencar, L.F.: Br Gram: uma gramática computacional de um fragmento do português brasileiro no formalismo da LFG. In: Proceedings of the 9th Brazilian Symposium in Information and Human Language Technology (2013)
2. Bender, E.M., Drellishak, S., Fokkens, A., Poulson, L., Saleem, S.: Grammar customization. Res. Lang. Comput. 8(1), 23–72 (2010)
3. Bender, E.M., Flickinger, D., Oepen, S.: The grammar matrix: an open-source starter-kit for the rapid development of cross-linguistically consistent broad-coverage precision grammars. In: Carroll, J., Oostdijk, N., Sutcliffe, R. (eds.) Proceedings of the Workshop on Grammar Engineering and Evaluation at the 19th International Conference on Computational Linguistics, pp. 8–14. Taipei, Taiwan (2002)

4. Bick, E.: The Parsing System Palavras: Automatic Grammatical Analysis of Portuguese in a Constraint Grammar Framework. Aarhus University Press, Aarhus (2000)
5. Branco, A., Costa, F.: A computational grammar for deep linguistic processing of Portuguese: LXGram (version 5). University of Lisbon, Department of Informatics, Technical Report (2014)
6. Copestake, A.: Implementing typed feature structure grammars. CSLI, Stanford (2002)
7. Copestake, A., Flickinger, D., Pollard, C., Sag, I.A.: Minimal recursion semantics: an introduction. Res. Lang. Comput. **3**(2), 281–332 (2005)
8. Costa, F., Branco, A.: LXGram: a deep linguistic processing grammar for Portuguese. In: Pardo, T.A.S., Branco, A., Klautau, A., Vieira, R., de Lima, V.L.S. (eds.) PROPOR 2010. LNCS (LNAI), vol. 6001, pp. 86–89. Springer, Heidelberg (2010). https://doi.org/10.1007/978-3-642-12320-7_11
9. Cunha, C., Cintra, L.: Nova Gramática do Português Contemporâneo. Nova Fronteira, Rio de Janeiro (1985)
10. Davis, A.R.: Linking by types in the hierarchical lexicon. CSLI, Stanford (2001)
11. Droganova, K., Zeman, D.: Towards deep universal dependencies. In: Proceedings of the Fifth International Conference on Dependency Linguistics (Depling, SyntaxFest 2019), pp. 144–152. Association for Computational Linguistics, Paris, August 2019
12. Emerson, G., Copestake, A.: Leveraging a semantically annotated corpus to disambiguate prepositional phrase attachment. In: Proceedings of the 11th International Conference on Computational Semantics (IWCS), Association for Computational Linguistics (2015)
13. Falk, Y.: Lexical-functional grammar: an introduction to parallel constraint-based syntax. CSLI, Stanford (2001)
14. Fernandes, F.: Dicionário de verbos e regimes, 35th edn. Globo, Rio de Janeiro (1991)
15. Ferrucci, D., et al.: Building Watson: an overview of the DeepQA project. AI Mag. **31**(3), 59–79 (2010)
16. Flickinger, D.: On building a more efficient grammar by exploiting types. Nat. Lang. Eng. **6**(1), 15–28 (2000)
17. Grilo, S., Bolrinha, M., Silva, J., Vaz, R., Branco, A.: The BDCamões collection of Portuguese literary documents: a research resource for digital humanities and language technology. In: Proceedings of the 12th Language Resources and Evaluation Conference, pp. 849–854. European Language Resources Association, Marseille, France, May 2020. https://aclanthology.org/2020.lrec-1.106
18. Helbig, G., Schenkel, W.: Wörterbuch zur Valenz und Distribution deutscher Verben, 8th edn. Niemeyer, Tübingen (1991)
19. Kuhnle, A., Copestake, A.: Shapeworld - a new test methodology for multimodal language understanding (2017). https://arxiv.org/abs/1704.04517
20. Lien, E., Kouylekov, M.: Semantic parsing for textual entailment. In: Proceedings of the 14th International Conference on Parsing Technologies, pp. 40–49. Association for Computational Linguistics, Bilbao, July 2015
21. de Marneffe, M.C., Manning, C.D., Nivre, J., Zeman, D.: Universal dependencies. Comput. Linguist. **47**(2), 255–308 (2021)
22. Mateus, M.H.M., Brito, A.M., et al.: Gramática da língua Portuguesa. Caminho, Lisboa (1989)
23. McCord, M.C., Murdock, J.W., Boguraev, B.K.: Deep parsing in Watson. IBM J. Res. Dev. **56**(3.4), 3-1 (2012)

24. Müller, S.: Grammatical Theory, 4th edn. Language Science Press, Berlin (2020)
25. Nunes, A.L., Rademaker, A., de Alencar, L.F.: Utilizando um dicionário mor-fológico para expandir a cobertura lexical de uma gramática do português no formalismo hpsg. In: Ruiz, E.E.S., Torrent, T.T. (eds.) Proceedings of the XIII Brazilian Symposium in Information and Human Language Technology, pp. 11–18. Departamento de Computação e Matemática, Universidade de São Paulo, Ribeirão Preto (2021)
26. de Paiva, V., Rademaker, A., de Melo, G.: OpenWordNet-PT: an open Brazilian WordNet for reasoning. In: Proceedings of COLING 2012: Demonstration Papers. pp. 353–360. The COLING 2012 Organizing Committee, Mumbai, India, December 2012. http://www.aclweb.org/anthology/C12-3044, published also as Techreport http://hdl.handle.net/10438/10274
27. Rademaker, A., Chalub, F., Real, L., Freitas, C., Bick, E., de Paiva, V.: Universal dependencies for Portuguese. In: Proceedings of the Fourth International Conference on Dependency Linguistics (Depling), pp. 197–206. Pisa, Italy, September 2017
28. Sag, I.A., Wasow, T., Bender, E.M.: Syntactic Theory: A Formal Introduction, 2nd edn. University of Chicago Press, Chicago (2003)
29. Schäfer, U., Kiefer, B., Spurk, C., Steffen, J., Wang, R.: The ACL anthology search-bench. In: Proceedings of the ACL-HLT 2011 System Demonstrations, pp. 7–13 (2011)
30. Siegel, M., Bender, E.M., Bond, F.: JACY: an implemented grammar of Japanese. CSLI (2016)
31. da Silva Borba, F.: Dicionário gramatical de verbos do português contemporâneo do Brasil, 2nd edn. Editora da UNESP, São Paulo (1991)
32. Straka, M., Straková, J.: Tokenizing, POS tagging, lemmatizing and parsing UD 2.0 with UDPipe. In: Proceedings of the CoNLL 2017 Shared Task: Multilingual Parsing from Raw Text to Universal Dependencies, pp. 88–99. Association for Computational Linguistics, Vancouver, August 2017
33. Zamaraeva, O.: Assembling Syntax: Modeling Constituent Questions in a Grammar Engineering Framework. Ph.D. thesis, University of Washington (2021)
34. Čulo, O.: Automatische Extraktion von bilingualen Valenzwörterbüchern aus deutsch-englischen Parallelkorpora: Eine Pilotstudie. Universaar, Saarbrücken (2011)

CQL Grammars for Lexical and Semantic Information Extraction for Portuguese and Italian

Chiara Barbero[✉] [iD]

Linguistic Research Centre of NOVA University Lisbon, Lisbon, Portugal
chiarabarbero@fcsh.unl.pt

Abstract. The anchorage to real data is one of the main parameters that guarantees the quality and the coverage of lexical resources, especially in the context of specialized domains. Thus, lexicon extraction from corpora is a consensual method for building lexical resources. However, given that data validation by experts in specialized contexts is a necessary step, the automatic screening of data becomes fundamental to maximize the informational value of the interaction with experts. In this paper we present and discuss a hybrid methodology, combining linguistic and statistical approaches, focusing on the extraction of specialized lexical units and salient semantic information using CQL grammars. The proposed method involves several steps, from frequency information analyses, concordances and collocations extraction to manual revision and expert validation and encompasses the construction and application of knowledge-based patterns CQL grammars. We present two CQL grammars for lexical and semantic information extraction developed for Portuguese and Italian and evaluate results from its application to specialized corpora on Public Art domain, demonstrating the value of this method for lexicon and semantic information extraction from large data.

Keywords: Semi-automatic lexicon extraction · Knowledge patterns · Lexical-syntactic patterns · Lexicon modelling · CQL grammars

1 Introduction

Large corpora exploration at lexical and conceptual level always represents a challenge for researchers, especially when it involves languages other than English.

This paper presents a hybrid corpus-driven methodology for lexical and semantic information extraction, that combines linguistic filters and statistical measures, oriented to lexical modeling, namely the improving of a relational lexical resource, the WordNet.PT. The proposed method involves sequential steps with a particular focus on the development of Corpus Query Language (CQL)[1] grammars on Sketch Engine, for automatic extraction of lexical items linked through specific semantic relations. The proposed CQL grammars involve both relations conventionally used in lexicon modelling

---

[1] CQL was devised by Schulze and Christ [35].

© Springer Nature Switzerland AG 2022
V. Pinheiro et al. (Eds.): PROPOR 2022, LNAI 13208, pp. 376–386, 2022.
https://doi.org/10.1007/978-3-030-98305-5_35

(generic/specific, whole/part, etc.), but also relations oriented to events description and concepts characterization, particularly relevant in WordNet.PT context.

The paper is organized in 4 main sections concerning: (i) the general framing of the theoretical approach and methodology; (ii) the selection of potential specialized lexical items from unranked wordlists exploiting frequency analysis; (iii) the designing of the CQL grammars for concordance/collocational analysis and the preliminary evaluation of the results; and (iv) the final remarks and reference to future work, namely collocation analysis and attention to specific parts of the documents.

1.1 General Methodology

Automatization in extracting salient lexical items has been one of the crucial challenges explored in terminology associated to computer science knowledge [1]. Current research has been pointing to three main approaches for automatic term extraction (ATE), namely: the linguistic, the statistical and the hybrid approach [2–4].

The methodology presented here involves specialized corpora exploration, applied in comparison to common language reference corpora.

Starting from the data collected from the compilation and treatment of CORPORART [5], a bilingual – European Portuguese/Italian – comparable corpus of specialized texts on Public Art, we focus on two main issues concerning the extraction of viable candidates: i) frequency analysis, to improve the lists extracted from the specialized corpus before submitting it to expert validation; and ii) design, application and testing of lexical-syntactic patterns to isolate specific semantic relations.

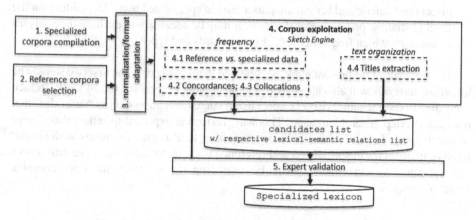

Fig. 1. General methodology for candidates list extraction

Although the process presented in Fig. 1 and already discussed by [6] encompasses two more phases, collocation analysis and titles extraction, these topics are out of the scope of this paper.

2   Specialized Lexical Units Extraction: Frequency Analysis Wrt Reference Corpora

Frequency is an essential parameter in corpora analysis that needs to be considered for lexicon extraction. In particular, in specialized (sub)languages contexts, frequency becomes relevant in contrast to common language, ergo when compared to reference corpora.

To be efficient, the selection of a reference corpora must consider the specific variety in use. For this reason, we used the itTenTen [7] for Italian and the CORLEX [8] for European Portuguese.

To test the workflow for the extraction process, we defined a limited sample considering the most frequent 200 types for each part of speech (POS). The POS considered within the context of this work are nouns, verbs and adjectives, as further discussed in Sect. 2.1. The selection of the items encompasses 3 main steps, considering that all steps can be mutually exclusive.

1. Simple exclusion: lemmas/POS that only occur in the 200 more frequent items of the specialized wordlist and are not in the 200 more frequent items in the wordlist of the reference corpus.
2. Selection of lemmas/POS with relevant differences in frequency in both corpora, considering distinct intervals: high (>300% frequency differences); medium high (>100% <300% frequency differences); medium (>50% <100% frequency differences).
3. Analysis of low frequency lemmas/POS, >1/2 <10, to account for the known-subject effect (and deictic and lexical anaphora use) in specialized texts. Depending on the level of shallow processing of the texts, it may be necessary to exclude the analyses of hapaxes, which frequently reflect fuzzy words and typos).

For the goals of the present work, we selected items using only the first two steps. The identified intervals will also allow us to establish other criteria for future work. In fact, according to several authors [9–11], specialized languages can be seen as "subcodes" that partially overlap general language. This way, lexicon is expected to reflect this degree of overlapping. In this sense, it will be interesting to also examine items with similar relative frequencies in specialized and reference corpora, to see if there are differences in what concerns semantics, in particular, regarding argument structures and complex nominal patterns.

2.1   CORPORART vs Monitor Corpora: Data Analysis and Results

Applying the methodology described above, we achieved the following results.

A) Items extracted following the simple exclusion principle

	CORPORART-PT	CORPORART-IT
Nouns	104/200	83/200

(continued)

(*continued*)

	CORPORART-PT	CORPORART-IT
Verbs	81/200	52/200
Adjectives	94/200	66/200

B) Items extracted considering high frequency differences (>300%):

	CORPORART-PT	CORPORART-IT
Nouns	6/96	7/117
Verbs	2/119	1/148
Adjectives	1/106	4/154

The second step described above for lexical unit extraction shows some very interesting results, since it provides units that are crucial modelling the lexicon of the Public Art domain, such as the nouns *arte* (art); *cidade* (city); *elemento* (element); *espaço* (space); *forma* (form) and *obra* (work); the verbs *apresentar* (present) and *realizar* (realize/make); and the adjectives *público* (public) collected from the Portuguese corpus; or the nouns *città* (city); *cultura* (culture); *forma* (form); *intervento* (intervention); *opera* (work); *processo* (process) and *progetto* (project); the verb *realizzare* (realize/make); and the adjectives *culturale* (cultural); *artistico* (artistic); *differente* (different) and *pubblico* (public), from the Italian.

Contrasting specialized corpora with reference corpora, we reached a first screening of the data, and we gathered, organized, and limited potential specialized wordlists, divided per POS, which are easier to submit to expert validation. We present some illustrative examples in Sect. 3.2.

3 Concordances Analysis Through Lexical-Syntactic Patterns

Concordances are one line length text strings, where specialized lexical units (atomic or multi-words) occur. In other words, concordances reflect real contexts of occurrence of the lexical units under analysis. Concordances provide interesting data about valency properties, namely in what concerns subcategorization and argument selection, that can reflect relevant meaning properties. They also give leads to identify semantically related words, both in a domain and conceptual perspectives, and to infer semantic properties, therefore providing data for lexicon modelling.

However, especially in cases of large corpora, it is necessary to reduce the volume of concordances to the ones containing effective relevant information: "texts are repository of valuable information for information extraction (IE) tasks and for terminology and knowledge extraction. But they can also be unstructured, noisy, ambiguous, contradictory and extended" [12]. Automatic sorting of "knowledge rich contexts" (KRC) guarantee the user a rapid and easy access to this information and prevent waste of time in manual analysis of large amounts of useless text strings [13, 14]. According to distributional theories [15–17] lexical items denoting some semantic proximity tend to occur in similar syntactic and syntagmatic contexts. Distributional theories applied to corpora [18, 19] corroborate the existence of semi-fixed structures that speakers repeat, for syntactic and semantic reasons, but also for ontological ones, i.e. objects that co-occur within the same contexts, or frames, in real world are more likely to be mentioned together [18, 20].

The most common strategy to identify and isolate rich contexts is by filtering concordances through knowledge patterns (KP), that is, linguistic and paralinguistic patterns[2] that convey semantic relations [21–24]. Literature on semantic/conceptual relations extracted from text by applying KP typically focuses on hierarchical relations (hypernymy/ hyponymy and whole/part) for some simple reasons: (i) hypernymy and holonymy stand at the basis of Aristotelian definitions (*genus proximum* + defining characteristics), i.e. static knowledge [12]; (ii) information about hypernymy and holonymy is frequent in texts; (iii) patterns for hypernymy and holonymy are more intuitive than others, especially for structures such as "is a/is a kind of" [21, 24].

Our proposal aims to extend research on automatic semantic relations extraction, systematizing relations for event characterization and for verbs and adjectives description. In particular, we consider the following relations: synonymy, co-hyponymy, cause/agent_effect, location, characterization, instrument, function_result [25, 26].

3.1 Knowledge Patterns and Sketch Grammar

Following Meyer, "knowledge patterns can be of three types, lexical, grammatical, or paralinguistic" [21]. In our perspective, define the KPs used in our work as "lexical-syntactic", since they employ specific words (lexical), but also consider syntactic restrictions (POS) and syntagmatic structures (as compound nouns).

The complexity of the patterns depends, as well, on the degree of sophistication of the corpora analysis tool employed. This way, Sketch Engine allows us to work on POS tagged and lemmatized corpora and to use a large set of query variables (simples word, whole lemma, POS definition, specific word + POS, etc.). The KP developing process can be synthetized in 5 major steps. The sequence of the steps is not necessarily and strictly linear as listed below.

1. Collect KPs already described in literature [14, 21, 22, 24, 27–32] and adapt them to Portuguese and Italian (state-of-art based KPs)
2. Define and add new KPs by identifying and systematizing frequent structures from texts (corpora-driven KPs)
3. Convert the established KPs established into CQL queries
4. Test and analyze the output to evaluate KPs productivity in specialized corpora and reference corpora
5. Revise KPs to customize highly ambiguous patterns and to remove unproductive patterns to lower the error percentage.

Pattern restrictions should be accurate to prevent overgeneration while not excluding valid contexts [21]. In other words, ideally, precision (more than recall) is a key feature

---

[2] According to Meyer, 2001, paralinguistic patterns are not strictly grammatical or lexical and include punctuation and other elements from the general structure of a text.

to get contexts as comprehensive as possible while reducing noisy data. In this sense, adding new patterns increases the number of hits, yet it potentially also increases false positives matches.

Following the EcoLexicon Sketch Grammar [24], we developed two user-friendly grammars for PT and IT[3], to easily extract semantic related items within the word sketch functionality.

3.2 Lexical-Syntactic Patterns Evaluation and Discussion

For purposes of evaluation, we focused on the analysis of highly productive patterns, i.e., patterns whose queries gave numerous results that require substantial manual effort. Since the relations extracted concern two words, the CQL grammars operate on a keyword given to the system. To evaluate precision and recall, we considered cases involving specialized words already validated. In this section we present the CQL patterns used, and discuss the results obtained. For each KP we provide the pattern description with an English equivalence in square brackets (e.g. *enquanto* [as a]) and the elements in the semantic relation expressed by the KP in capital letters (e.g. HYPONYM; HYPERNYM; RESULT etc.). This is followed by the CQL expression of the pattern (e.g. 1:"N.*"[word = "enquanto"]2:"N.*"), the total results obtained and the specific keywords used for the evaluation (e.g. *intervenção* enquanto HYPERONYMY).

- KP1: HYPONYM enquanto [as a] HYPERONYM

  1:"N.*"[tag = "A.*"]?[tag = "S.*"]?[tag = "N.*"]?[tag = "S.*"]?[tag = "N.*"]?[tag = "A.*"]?[tag = "F.*"]?[word = "enquanto"]2:"N.*"[tag = "A.*"]?[tag = "S.*"]?[tag = "N.*"]?[tag = "S.*"]?[tag = "N.*"]?[tag = "A.*"]?

  Total results in CORPORART: 3 530.

  Keyword used for evaluation: *intervenção.*

- KP2: RESULT usarlprecisarlrequererlutilizarlnecessitarlempregar [useldemand lrequirelutilizelneedlemploy] INSTRUMENT

  1:"N.*"[tag = "A.*"]?[tag = "S.*"]?[tag = "N.*"]?[tag = "S.*"]?[tag = "N.*"]?[tag = "A.*"]?[lemma = "usarlprecisarlrequererlutilizarlnecessitarlempregar"][tag = "S.*"]?[tag = "D.*|Z.*"]?2:"N.*"[tag = "A.*"]?[tag = "S.*"]?[tag = "N.*"]?[tag = "S.*"]?[tag = "N.*"]?[tag = "A.*"]?

  Total results in CORPORART: 944.

  Keywords used for evaluation: *obra, artista.*

- KP3: MERONYM farelesserelformare [makelbelform] parte [part] dildell.ldeildegli [of] HOLONYM

[3] These CQL grammars will be available soon through Sketch Engine Sketch Grammars and CLUNL resources webpage (https://clunl.fcsh.unl.pt/en/online-resources/).

1:NOUN[tag = "ADJ"]?[tag = "PRE.*"]?[tag = "NOUN"]?[tag = "PRE.*"]?[tag = "NOUN"]?[tag = "ADJ"]?[lemma = "fare|essere|formare"][lemma = "parte"]?[word = "di|dell.|dei|degli"] [tag = "ART*|NUM"]?[tag = "ADV"]? [tag = "ADJ"]?2:NOUN.

Total results in CORPORART: 137.

Keywords used for evaluation: *museo* (Table 1).

Table 1. Precision and recall values for the keywords defined

	intervenção	*obra*	*artista*	*museo*
Precision	0.4	0.2	0.6	1
Recall	1	1	1	1
F-measure	0.5	0.3	1	1

We calculated precision and recall directly, using the formulae:

$$precision = \frac{true\ positives}{true\ positives + false\ positives}; \quad recall = \frac{true\ positive}{true\ positive + false\ negative}$$

As hinted earlier, in these cases, recall is not a useful evaluation measure since there are no possible false negative results for an isolated pattern: the CQL expression will retrieve all token sequences with the expressed features (POS, lemma, etc.). False negatives are due to POS or lemmatization errors. According to [33] these have accuracy levels of roughly 97%. Although far from ideal trends, precision demonstrates a high degree of improvement in terms of workflow, namely in time saving reading and analyzing concordances to identify hypernyms, meronyms, etc. and also for establishing standards (patterns and criteria) reusable in other contexts and domains. Taking the example of *arte* (art), one of the most productive lemmas in CORPORART-PT (as described in Sect. 2.1), a fully manual concordance analysis would require the revision of 18715 concordances, an extremely time-consuming task. It is hard to accurately estimate the time average required for this task, but it would surely take hours. The application of a CQL grammar based on KPs allows users to isolate, in few seconds, 98 blocks of the most relevant concordances, organized according to its role in a specific semantic relation.

The patterns established are strongly language dependent, both due to the use of specific lexical units and sequences, but also due to the syntactic restrictions and KPs can also in some manner be considered domain-dependent[4]. The analysis of the results shows the differences in the number of results obtained from the Italian corpus, generally lower than the ones obtained from the Portuguese corpus. The Italian corpus is actually smaller, although the degree of saturation and the degree of specialization are equivalent for both [6]. The KPs were first developed for Portuguese and the literature considered

---

[4] Structures that point to instrument_result relations seem very productive within the Public Art domain, but eventually in other domains probably not.

focused on general language. Consequently, this analysis reflects a gap in terms of richness and of degree of specialization of the KPs content for Italian, an area to be further developed.

A general overview of the CQL grammars proposed shows that the lexical-syntactic expressions that compose our grammars focus mostly on nominal nodes. However, we guarantee the identification and modeling of verbal nodes, both because they potentially represent specialized conceptual nodes by itself, but also because verbs are essential in a lexical mapping perspective [29]. Even when expressed by nouns (i.e. deverbal nous), it is possible to precisely extract a verbal node from the deverbal nominal phrase [21].

In terms of a more general evaluation, one significant problem detected in precision improvement is related to texts creativity and language variation, even if specialized contexts are expected to be more circumscribed than general languages. On the other hand, in Sketch Engine, metaphoric senses retrieval, anaphora resolution and crucial elements omission are not automatically treated, requiring manual revision. Also, most false positive matches are traceable to larger structures the pattern does not cover (e.g. prepositional phrases, nominal compounds, passive constructions, etc.). Consequently, the retrieved element (i.e. "N:2") often remains outside the boundaries of the extracted expression, thus out of the scope of the automatic retrieval. For instance, the KP2, sorted by the keyword *artista* extracts results from concordances as *artistas utilizam de forma deliberada* (artists deliberately uses) as the marked expression[5] when the following noun phrase *objetos da cultura popular* (objects from popular culture) should be the N:2 extracted within the agent_instrument relation. The implementation of complex variables in the CQL grammar (ex.: define('np1','1:"NOUN" "ADJ"? "PRE.*"? "NOUN"? "PRE.*"? "NOUN"? "ADJ"?') should be tested to reduce the incidence of this error category.

Considering still precision, other main problems are linked to cases of deduplication, semantic ambiguity, verbs polysemy, expression of uncertainty and expression of negation. For instance, constructions with compositional verbs with the past participle sometimes invert the elements 1 and 2, especially in KPs for instrument_result relation. Polysemic verbs, e.g. *ser* (to be); *usar* (to use); *requerer* (to require")), also leads to ambiguous results (instrument or agent), determined by the feature ± animate of the "N:1".

The expression of uncertainty and negation, as stated by Marshman [14], is also an issue to be considered in semi-automatic lexical and semantic IE from texts, especially for scientific texts. The word sketch of *arte* (art) obtained by the CQL grammar for Portuguese shows emblematic examples of the effects of expressions of negation in automatic IE. The system suggests *produção* (producing) as an hyperonym of *arte* (art), but manual analysis of the concordance revealed that, in fact, it is quite the opposite, because of the presence of an adverb of negation at the beginning of the string.[6] Interrogative propositions, as well, raise some doubts about how to use the sematic relations they point to. The structure *"Design é uma forma de arte?"* (Is design a form of art?),

---

[5] N:1 = "artista" [lemma = "usar"] [tag = "S.*" 'de']? N:2 = "forma" [tag = "A.*" 'deliberada'].

[6] *"Não entendem a arte como produção de obras unitárias"* | They do not understand art as the production of unique works.

for instance, matches perfectly one of the patterns for hypernymy[7] but the interrogation mark adds a relevant degree of uncertainty. These cases need manual revision and retrieving larger contexts to solve the ambivalence and they should be marked for expert evaluation at validation phase.

Negative verbs are also tricky since they have scope over the meaning of the whole sentence and consequently turn null or antithetical the potential relation pointed out by the KP. This is the case of the verb *rejeitar* (reject) in the example extracted for characterization relation between *arte* (art) and *inútil* (useless): "*Armajani rejeita a estética Kantiana e a ideia de que a arte é algo inútil*" (Armajani rejects the Kantian aesthetics and the idea that art is something useless). Adverbs, quantifiers, modal verbs and expressions of negation are elements that have impact in knowledge-rich-context identification and lexicon extraction and account for many unsuccessful correspondences between patterns and texts occurrences, with impact on the extracted data reliability.

4 Final Remarks and Future Work

Tools for semi-automatic corpora exploration are crucial for linguistics analysis at many levels. The application of CQL grammars in Sketch Engine for IE from Portuguese and Italian corpora has shown real improvements in our workflow, both in terms of time and coverage, as commonly accepted by previous works (e.g. [34]) avoiding manual revision of a great amount of non-organized data and maximizing the interaction with experts. On the other hand, the CQL grammars evaluation highlighted some relevant issues, reflecting a reasonable margin for enhancement. As mentioned in 1.1, the semantically based IE method proposed here encompasses some more steps, namely collocation analysis and title extraction. Also, in specialized domains, nominal compounds (including noun phrase or near-noun phrase extraction), is essential to lexicon modelling.

This way, in our future work, we plan to: (i) implement and test CQL grammars with complex variables, to achieve more precise and accurate results; (ii) establish the criteria for collocational analysis and title extraction; (iii) examine items with similar relative frequencies to evaluate the degree of overlapping/disparity in argument structures and complex nominal patterns; (iv) improve the CQL grammars, especially for Italian, to increase the precision.

Acknowledgments. I would like to thank Raquel Amaro for the insights and the discussion of parts of this paper and the anonymous reviewers for all the useful critiques and suggestions.

This research is supported by Portuguese national funding through the FCT – Portuguese Foundation for Science and Technology as part of the project of CLUNL School of Social Sciences and Humanities, NOVA University Lisbon, 1069-061 Lisboa, Portugal (UIDB/LIN/03213/2020 and UIDP/LIN/03213/2020), and by the PhD grant (PD/BD/128131/2016).

---

[7] 1NP + be + punctuation + *portanto|entāo* + 2NP.

References

1. Heylen, K., De Hertog, D.: Automatic term extraction. In: Handbook of Terminology, pp. 203–221. John Benjamins Publishing Company, Amsterdam (2015)
2. Pazienza, M.T., Pennacchiotti, M., Zanzotto, F.M.: Terminology extraction: an analysis of linguistic and statistical approaches. Knowl. Min. **185**, 255–279 (2005)
3. Vu, T., Aw, A.T., Zhang, M.: Term extraction through unithood and termhood unification. In: Proceedings of the Third International Joint Conference on Natural Language Processing, pp. 631–636 (2008)
4. Periñán-Pascual, C., Mestre-Mestre, E.M.: DEXTER: automatic extraction of domain-specific glossaries for language teaching. Procedia - Soc. Behav. Sci. **198**, 377–385 (2015)
5. Barbero, C.: CORPORART - um corpus de arte pública para a extração de léxico: representatividade e comparabilidade em corpora de especialidade. Rev. da APL, pp. 43–57 (2019)
6. Barbero, C., Amaro, R.: Exploração de corpora para extração e descrição de léxico de especialidade: para uma metodologia sólida e sustentada. Linha D'Água. **33**, 69–104 (2020)
7. Jakubíček, M., Kilgarriff, A., Kovář, V., Rychlý, P., Suchomel, V.: The tenten corpus family. In: 7th International Corpus Linguistics Conference, pp. 125–127 (2013)
8. Mendes, A., Généreux, M., Hendrickx, I., Pereira, L., Bacelar do Nascimento, M.F., Antunes, S.: CQPWeb: uma nova plataforma de pesquisa para o CRPC. Textos Selecionados do XXVII Encontro Nac. da APL, pp. 466–477 (2012)
9. León-Araúz, P., Faber, P., Montero Martínez, S.: Specialized language semantics. In: A cognitive linguistics view of terminology and specialized language, pp. 133–211. De Gruyter Mouton (2012)
10. Cabré, M.T.: Terminology: Theory, Methods and Applications. John Benjamins Publishing Company, Amsterdam (1999)
11. Pearson, J.: Terms in Context. John Benjamins Publishing Company, Amsterdam (1998)
12. Barrière, C.: Knowledge-rich contexts discovery. In: Tawfik, A.Y., Goodwin, S.D. (eds.) AI 2004. LNCS (LNAI), vol. 3060, pp. 187–201. Springer, Heidelberg (2004). https://doi.org/10.1007/978-3-540-24840-8_14
13. Marsham, E.: The cause-effect relation in a french-language biopharmaceuticals corpus: some lexical knowledge patterns. In: Workshop Programm, pp. 40–43 (2004)
14. Marsham, E.: Expressions of uncertainty in candidate knowledge-rich contexts: a comparison in English and French specialized texts. Terminol. Int. J. Theor. Appl. Issues Spec. Commun. **14**, 124–151 (2008)
15. Jackendoff, R.: Semantic Structures. MIT Press, Cambridge (1990)
16. Levin, B.: English Verb Classes and Alternations: A Preliminary Investigation. The University of Chicago Press, Chicago (1993)
17. Firth, J.R.: A synopsis of linguistic theory 1930–1955. Studies in Linguistic Analysis, pp. 1–32. Philological Society, Oxford (1957)
18. Sinclair, J.: Corpus, Concordance, Collocation. Oxford University Press (1991)
19. Geeraerts, D.: Theories of Lexical Semantics. Oxford University Press, Oxford (2010)
20. Fillmore, C.J., Baker, C.: A frames approach to semantic analysis. In: The Oxford Handbook of Linguistic Analysis, pp. 313–340 (2010)
21. Meyer, I.: Extracting knowledge-rich contexts for terminography: a conceptual and methodological framework. In: Recent Advances in Computational Terminology, pp. 279–302. John Benjamins Publishing Company (2001). https://doi.org/10.1075/nlp.2.15mey
22. Bowker, L.: Lexical knowledge patterns, semantic relations, and language varieties: exploring the possibilities for refining information retrieval in an international context. Cat. Classif. Q. **37**, 153–171 (2003)

23. León Araúz, P.L., Reimerink, A.: High-density knowledge rich contexts. Argentinian J. Appl. Linguist. **7**, 109–130 (2019)
24. León-Araúz, P., San Martín, A.: The EcoLexicon semantic sketch grammar: from knowledge patterns to word sketches. In: Proceedings of the LREC 2018 Workshop "Globalex 2018 – Lexicography & WordNets.", pp. 94–99 (2018)
25. Mendes, S., Amaro, R.: Modeling adjectives in GL: accounting for all adjective classes. In: Proceedings of GL'2009 - 5th International Workshop on Generative Approaches to the Lexicon, pp. 176–183. Istituto di Linguistica Computazionale del CNR, Pisa (2009)
26. Amaro, R., Mendes, S., Marrafa, P.: Increasing density through new relations and PoS encoding in WordNet.PT. Int. J. Comput. Linguist. Appl. **4**, 11–27 (2013)
27. Sierra, G., Alarcón, R., Aguilar, C., Bach, C.: Definitional verbal patterns for semantic relation extraction. Terminol. Int. J. Theor. Appl. Issues Spec. Commun. **14**, 74–98 (2008)
28. Amaro, R.: Extracting semantic relations from Portuguese corpora using lexical-syntactic patterns. In: Proceedings of the 9th International Conference on Language Resources and Evaluation, pp. 3001–3005 (2014)
29. Faber, P.: A Cognitive Linguistics View of Terminology and Specialized Language. De Gruyter Mouton, Berlin, Boston (2012)
30. Gil-Berrozpe, J.C., León-Araúz, P., Faber, P.: Specifying hyponymy subtypes and knowledge patterns: a corpus-based study. In: Proceedings of the 5th International Conference on Electronic Lexicography, pp. 63–92 (2017)
31. Khoo, C.S.G., Na, J.-C.: Semantic relations in information science. Annu. Rev. Inf. Sci. Technol. **40**, 157–228 (2006)
32. León-Araúz, P., San Martín, A., Faber, P.: Pattern-based word sketches for the extraction of semantic relations. In: Proceedings of the 5th International Workshop on Computational Terminology, pp. 73–82 (2016)
33. Garcia, M., Gamallo, P.: Análise Morfossintáctica para Português Europeu e Galego: Problemas. Soluções e Avaliação. **2**, 59–67 (2010)
34. Sheehan, S., Luz, S.: Text visualization for the support of lexicography-based scholarly work. In: Proceedings of Electronic Lexicography in the 21st Century Conference, pp. 694–725 (2019)
35. Schulze, B.M., Christ, O.: The CQP user's manual. Inst. f ur maschinelle Sprachverarbeitung, Univ. Stuttgart, Version. 1 (1996)

Drilling Lexico-Semantic Knowledge in Portuguese from BERT

Hugo Gonçalo Oliveira(✉) [ID]

CISUC, Department of Informatics Engineering, University of Coimbra,
Coimbra, Portugal
hroliv@dei.uc.pt

Abstract. We compiled a set of patterns that denote lexico-semantic relations in Portuguese, created templates where one argument is fixed and the other is replaced by a mask, and then used BERT for predicting the latter. For most relations and measures, when assessed in a test of lexico-semantic analogies, BERT predictions outperformed those of earlier methods computed from static word embeddings, either with a pattern alone or with a combination of patterns. There is still a large margin of progression, but this suggests that BERT can be used as a source of lexico-semantic knowledge in Portuguese.

Keywords: BERT · Masked language model · Semantic relations ·
Lexico-semantic knowledge · Lexical patterns

1 Introduction

Whether it is for the creation or for the enrichment of lexical knowledge bases (LKBs) like WordNet [8], there is a long research history on the automatic acquisition of lexico-semantic knowledge from textual corpora. Following the seminal work of Hearst [17], much relies on lexico-syntactic patterns where related words tend to co-occur, e.g., "X_1, such as X_2", for hypernymyOf(X_1, X_2). Nowadays, some of those patterns can be easily tested in masked language models (MLMs) like a pre-trained BERT [4], with some authors suggesting that these large models could be used as knowledge bases [22].

In order to analyse to what extent this shortcut works, specifically for Portuguese lexico-semantic relations, we explore BERTimbau [25], a BERT model pre-trained for Portuguese. More precisely, we compiled a set of lexical patterns for the acquisition of such relations, and then created templates by presetting one argument (X_1) and masking the other, to be predicted by BERT. The quality of the predictions, based on three different measures (accuracy, accuracy@10, MAP), was assessed with TALES [14], a dataset of lexico-semantic analogies in Portuguese, and compared with that of two earlier methods, applied on a GloVe model for Portuguese [16]. Besides each pattern individually, we further assessed the benefits of combining the predictions of different patterns, considering their score and rank. Performance varied amongst different relations and patterns, and

© Springer Nature Switzerland AG 2022
V. Pinheiro et al. (Eds.): PROPOR 2022, LNAI 13208, pp. 387–397, 2022.
https://doi.org/10.1007/978-3-030-98305-5_36

was especially high in the acquisition of hypernyms of concrete concepts. Still, for each relation, there was at least one pattern or combination that outperformed both baselines in at least one measure.

The interesting results suggest that a pre-trained BERT is indeed a great source of lexico-semantic knowledge, faster and possibly more focused than raw corpus search. Yet, even if it may boost the search for related words to include in a LKB, for the sake of accuracy, this would still require additional filtering.

In the remainder of the paper, we overview work on the automatic acquisition of lexico-semantic relations; describe the proposed approach and the experimentation setup; and, before concluding, report on the obtained results.

2   Related Work

Early work on the automatic acquisition of lexico-semantic relations from text follows the work of Hearst [17], where a set of lexico-syntactic patterns denoting hyponymy was presented. To minimise human intervention, some proposed to improve precision and recall of the extractions, e.g., by computing the cosine similarity of the arguments [2]; or learning the patterns automatically, not only for hyponymy [24], but also other relations [21], respectively using distant and weak supervision, with seed examples from WordNet [8]. All the previous targeted English, but rule-based approaches for acquiring hyponymy [9], part-of [18], and other relations [13] were also applied to Portuguese text.

In models of distributional semantics, such as word embeddings, relations are not explicit, but analogies [19] have been computed for a broad range of syntactic and semantic relations, including lexico-semantic [5]. Besides the unsupervised discovery of hypernymy instances [3], the performance of simple analogy was improved by learning to compute related words from multiple examples [5]. The previous were also applied to Portuguese word embeddings, and used to solve lexico-semantic analogies in this language [14]. Despite their low accuracy in these relations, predictions can still be useful for enriching wordnets [15].

Currently, transformer-based models, like BERT [4] or GPT [23], are the paradigm in Natural Language Processing. They are also not ready for explicitly retrieving semantic relations, but provide a shortcut for earlier corpora-based approaches, i.e., they are pre-trained in large collections of text and are good at filling blanks [7,22], completing sentences [23], or computing their likelihood [11,20], including of those matching the aforementioned patterns. It is thus no surprise that BERT has been assessed for the presence of relational knowledge [22], having in mind its utilisation as a knowledge base; or for relation induction [1], starting with a small number patterns and seeds; even if it suits better some relations than others [7].

Recent work [20] exploited BERT for detecting hyponymy pairs in Portuguese. This is however slightly different from our goal, because, instead of scoring the likelihood of two words forming a hyponymy pair, we aim to predict hypernyms, as well as other related words, for a given word.

3   Experimentation Setup

To some extent, the process of acquiring relations from corpora based on lexical patterns can be simulated with a masked language model (MLM). This has two main advantages: it does not require to process the full corpus for each pattern; and it will retrieve the most likely words, not any value found.

An important difference is that common MLMs predict a single token, meaning that: (i) predictions will never be multiword expressions; (ii) one relation argument has to be fixed in the pattern. So, the problem is better framed as the acquisition of words x_2, given a template that uses x_1, such that instance $relation(x_1, x_2)$ holds. For instance, the lexical pattern "a x_2 is a type of x_1" typically indicates hypernym(x_1, x_2). Thus, to acquire hyponyms of *animal*, x_1 and x_2 are respectively replaced by the word animal and the [MASK] token. Expected predictions for x_2 would be *dog*, *horse* or *human*.

Following this, we explored BERTimbau [25] (base), a BERT model pretrained for Portuguese, and tested templates based on different lexical patterns for acquiring lexico-semantic relations that one would find in a LKB. This section provides some considerations on the patterns used, and further describes the dataset, the metrics, and the baselines used for evaluation.

3.1   Considerations on the Patterns

Available literature was our starting point [9,13] for compiling useful patterns, but a broader set was crafted to cover different relations, also trying to control some limitations of this approach. Specifically, we avoid patterns that lead to predictions like punctuation signs or non-content words (e.g., determiners, prepositions); or in the plural (e.g., "X_1 e outros [MASK]", for hypernyms of X_1), so that lemmatisation is not necessary. We considered patterns using both the masculine and feminine determiners, and avoided those starting with [MASK].

For instance, pattern "[MASK] ou outro X_1" could be used for acquiring hyponyms of X_1, but with X_1 = *veículo*, we get the top-5 predictions: *Um*, *Gol*, *Moto*, *Uma*, *ou*. The majority is capitalised, and only one is good enough (*Moto*). If we change the pattern to "um [MASK] ou outro X_1", we get: *carro*, *caminhão*, *automóvel*, *veículo*, *ônibus*, where only one is incorrect (*veículo*). Moreover, since starting with the determiner '*um*' constrains the predictions to masculine words, we add a second pattern "uma [MASK] ou outro X_1". This results in additional predictions: *moto*, *bicicleta*, *pessoa*, *van*, *aeronave*, four of which correct (all but *pessoa*). We could further add patterns starting with the definite articles '*a*' and '*o*' but, from our experience, they would not add much.

A similar example is the pattern "o X_1 tem [MASK]" for acquiring parts of X_1. With X_1 = *computador*, we get: ., ?, que, :, *[UNK]*, including punctuation signs, a preposition and the unknown token. Of course we can ignore these, as we did for punctuation signs, but a more fruitful strategy was to include similar patterns with an article before the mask. For instance, "o X_1 tem um [MASK]" results in *teclado*, *computador*, *programa*, *problema*, *processador*; and "o X_1 tem uma [MASK]" in *função*, *tela*, *interface*, *memória*, *câmera*.

An average of 12 patterns were compiled for each of the 14 target relations, totalling 169 patterns. The full list of patterns was made publicly available[1] for anyone willing to use or expand it, and several examples are included in Table 1.

3.2   Dataset

To assess different methods and patterns in the acquisition of lexico-semantic knowledge, we used TALES [14], a dataset originally developed for assessing lexico-semantic analogies in Portuguese, obtained from several LKBs. TALES has the same format as BATS [10], i.e., for each relation, it includes 50 entries with two columns: a word (source) and a list of related words split by a '/' (target). An example for hyponym-of(source, target) is: água líquido/substância.

Patterns were compiled for each of the 14 different relations in TALES, including four symmetric – synonym between nouns, verbs and adjectives; antonyms between adjectives – and ten non-symmetric – purpose-of (e.g., *abrir-chave*) and has-purpose (*lápis-escrever*); abstract (*valor-preço*), concrete (*ave-papagaio*) and verb (*permitir-aprovar*) hypernyms; abstract (*ano-período*), concrete (*arma-instrumento*) and verb (*explicar-dizer*) hyponyms; part-of (*mão-corpo*) and has-part (*casa-sala*). We used version 1.1[2] of TALES, which has the same contents as the original, but target words are re-ordered by the number of LKBs they were found in (roughly, confidence).

3.3   Metrics

A common measure for assessing word embeddings in analogy tasks is the accuracy [5,19]. It computes the proportion of entries x'_1 for which the first prediction x'_2 is correct. However, this is too restrictive for most lexico-semantic relations (e.g., a hypernym has many hyponyms; or an object might have several parts), especially if the final goal is to create or enrich a knowledge base. Therefore, we compute two additional measures that consider the top-10 predictions: Accuracy@10 (Acc@10), more relaxed, which counts the answer as correct as long as one of the top-10 predictions is correct; and Mean Average Precision@10 (MAP), which accounts for the number of correct predictions and their ranking. The latter is especially suitable to a scenario like ours, where more than one correct prediction often exists.

3.4   Baselines

Performance achieved with the patterns was compared with that of 3CosAvg and LRCos [5], two methods with a similar purpose, but applied to word embeddings learned from corpora, here a 300-sized GloVe model for Portuguese [16], which previously showed to be the best in semantic analogies [14,16]. Given any number

---

[1] https://github.com/NLP-CISUC/PT-LexicalSemantics/blob/master/Patterns/
    BERT_patterns_for_TALES.txt.
[2] https://github.com/NLP-CISUC/PT-LexicalSemantics/tree/master/TALESv1.1.

of (x_1, x_2) pairs, such that $relation(x_1, x_2)$ holds, and any argument x'_1, their goal is to find suitable values of x'_2, such that $relation(x'_1, x'_2)$ holds.

3CosAvg (Eq. 1) computes the average vector offset in all other available relations of the same type (in TALES, $50 - 1 = 49$). LRCos (Eq. 2) considers the similarity of x'_2 to x'_1 and the probability of x'_2 belonging to the same class as other target words (x_2), in relations of the same type. We implemented both methods and, as Drozd et al. [5], used a Logistic Regression classifier for computing the probability in LRCos, trained with positive examples taken from the first target word of every entry of the dataset, except x'_2. Pairs of random words were used as negative examples.

$$x'_2 = \operatorname*{argmax}_{w \in V} \cos(w, x'_1 + avg\_offset) \tag{1}$$

$$x'_2 = \operatorname*{argmax}_{w \in V} P(w \in class(x_2)) * cos(w, x'_1) \tag{2}$$

4 Performance with Different Patterns

With TALES as our reference, we select the target relation and: (i) go through each entry; (ii) predict the target word(s), given the source; (iii) compute evaluation scores of predictions against the target word(s). For 3CosAvg and LRCos, the relation is learned from all (x_1, x_2) pairs in TALES, except the current one. Predictions for x'_2 are obtained given the source word x'_1. For the lexical patterns, X_1 is replaced by the source word and BERT predicts tokens for the mask.

Although patterns were compiled for 14 relations, we noted that, for the symmetric (synonym and antonymy), baselines were hard to beat. Exceptions were: "ou X_1 ou [MASK]", for antonymy ($Acc = 0.30$, $Acc@10 = 0.42$, $MAP = 0.33$, against 0.20, 0.46, 0.28 by LRCos); and "X_1 é o mesmo que [MASK]", for synonymy between verbs ($Acc = 0.12$, $Acc@10 = 0.80$, $MAP = 0.28$, against 0.26, 0.62, 0.32 by LRCos). We tested different lexical patterns (e.g., "X_1 é a mesma coisa que [MASK]" or "X_1 é sinónimo de [MASK]" for synonymy), but similarity – better modelled with the cosine of the embeddings of each word than with a single template – plays an important role in these relations.

This section is focused on the other ten (non-symmetric) relations, namely on the best patterns, their performance and of their combination.

4.1 Single Patterns for Non-symmetric Relations

For each non-symmetric relation in TALES, Table 1 reports on a selection of patterns, covering the best for each measure, also including their scores and of the baselines. It is clear that performance varies significantly, depending on the relation and on the pattern. Part, has-part, and purpose-of relations are the most challenging, followed by hyponymy between abstract nouns. This happens both for baselines and lexical patterns. For all but one non-symmetric relation (hypernymy between concrete nouns), there is at least one pattern that outperforms both baselines in at least one measure, suggesting that BERT can be a better source of lexico-semantic knowledge than static word embeddings, at least concerning non-symmetric relations[3].

It is interesting to note that, depending on the type of arguments (abstract or concrete nouns, verbs), the best patterns for hyponymy and hypernymy vary. The top performance is achieved for hyponymy between concrete nouns, namely with the well-known pattern "X_1 é um tipo de [MASK]". This is in line with previous work for English [7], where BERT performed particularly well in the acquisition of hypernyms[4]. Relations of this kind include hyponymOf(*táxi, veículo*) and hyponymOf(*rosa, flor*).

4.2 Combining the Best Patterns

Despite some interesting results, the best pattern is not always the same, not only for different measures, but also for variations of the same relation (hypernymy). So, in order to maximise the outcomes, one would have to combine the predictions of different patterns. This is especially true for patterns that constrain the gender of the predictions (see Sect. 3.1). If there are target words of both genders, we will hardly get them all from a single pattern of those.

We thus tested two different methods of combining predictions by different patterns. Both consider the top-n predictions by the top-m patterns, but differ on the ranking criteria. The Score method ranks all the predictions according to the sum of their BERT-assigned scores[5] with each considered pattern. The Borda method disregards the scores and only considers the ranking of each prediction for each pattern, by applying the Borda [6] voting scheme, i.e., for each pattern, a prediction ranked r will get the score of $n - r + 1$.

Table 2 reports on the performance of both combination methods, with $n = 10$ and two different values for m, $m = 3$ and $m = 5$, considering the best patterns according to the MAP measure. For easier comparison, their scores are put together with those of the best baseline(s) and pattern(s). When there is not a pattern that stands out as the best, we include the scores of the two best. On the right-hand side, a table has the overall performance, based on the average for the 50 entries of each non-symmetric relation in TALES.

There are improvements, but not a straightforward best combination method for every single relation, while overall performance is close for any of the four combinations. When compared to the best patterns, both overall Acc and

---

[3] Even though both the models and the methods applied are significantly different, we note that the BERT model used was pre-trained in a corpus with nearly twice the number of tokens as the GloVe model used. This is still relevant for less experienced users, or when nor time nor resources are available for training of new models, limiting the choice to what is available out-of-the-box.

[4] TALES is organised in files where the source (first column) is related to the target (second). So, in the Hyponymy file, hyponymyOf(source, target) holds, and consequently hypernymOf(target, source). Since we are predicting the targets, this file is used for assessing hypernym prediction.

[5] BERT predictions are always ranked according to a score also given by the model.

Table 1. Performance of different methods and patterns for non-symmetrical relations.

Relation	Method/Pattern	Acc	Acc@10	MAP
Purpose-of	3CosAvg	0.08	0.28	0.12
	LRCos	0.10	**0.32**	**0.16**
	preciso de uma [MASK] para X_1	0.10	0.22	0.13
	uma [MASK] serve para X_1	0.08	0.20	0.11
	preciso de um [MASK] para X_1	**0.12**	0.16	0.13
Has-Purpose	3CosAvg	**0.24**	0.40	**0.29**
	LRCos	**0.24**	0.40	**0.29**
	uma X_1 é usada para [MASK]	0.20	**0.42**	0.26
	um X_1 é usado para [MASK]	0.20	0.38	0.24
	uma X_1 serve para [MASK]	0.06	0.24	0.10
Hypernym-of (abstract)	3CosAvg	0.06	0.58	0.22
	LRCos	0.08	0.56	0.20
	se X_1 é hiperónimo de [MASK]	0.20	**0.66**	0.27
	um [MASK] ou outra X_1	0.22	0.64	**0.31**
	a [MASK] é uma espécie de X_1	**0.24**	0.56	0.28
Hypernym-of (concrete)	3CosAvg	0.16	**0.54**	**0.27**
	LRCos	**0.18**	0.50	0.25
	um [MASK] ou outra X_1	0.14	**0.54**	0.20
	um [MASK] ou outro X_1	0.16	0.46	0.23
	uma [MASK] ou outro X_1	0.14	0.40	0.21
Hypernym-of (verbs)	3CosAvg	0.08	0.46	0.16
	LRCos	**0.20**	0.48	**0.27**
	como [MASK] e outros modos de X_1	0.08	**0.54**	0.18
	como [MASK] e outras maneiras de X_1	0.10	0.48	0.19
	como [MASK] ou outras maneiras de X_1	0.12	0.42	0.17
Hyponym-of (abstract)	3CosAvg	0.06	0.36	0.11
	LRCos	0.08	0.38	0.14
	X_1 é um tipo de [MASK]	**0.14**	**0.52**	**0.23**
	X_1 é hipónimo de [MASK]	**0.14**	**0.52**	0.21
	X_1 ou outro [MASK]	**0.14**	0.42	0.21
Hyponym-of (concrete)	3CosAvg	0.12	0.60	0.26
	LRCos	0.28	0.56	0.34
	X_1 é um tipo de [MASK]	**0.54**	**0.88**	**0.58**
	X_1 ou outro [MASK]	0.20	0.60	0.30
	um [MASK], como X_1	0.22	0.58	0.32
Hyponym-of (verbs)	3CosAvg	0.16	0.52	0.23
	LRCos	0.20	0.54	0.26
	como X_1 ou outras maneiras de [MASK]	**0.24**	**0.64**	**0.30**
	como X_1 e outras maneiras de [MASK]	0.18	0.56	0.23
	como X_1 ou outros modos de [MASK]	0.10	0.44	0.17
Part	3CosAvg	0.02	**0.30**	0.09
	LRCos	0.06	0.28	0.11
	um [MASK] tem X_1	**0.12**	**0.30**	**0.17**
	um [MASK] possui X_1	0.08	0.24	0.14
	o X_1 do [MASK].	**0.12**	0.22	0.15
Has-Part	3CosAvg	0.06	0.22	0.09
	LRCos	0.06	0.24	0.09
	o X_1 possui uma [MASK].	0.08	**0.34**	**0.17**
	um [MASK] é uma parte de X_1	**0.12**	0.28	**0.17**
	a [MASK] é uma parte de X_1	0.06	0.22	0.10

Table 2. Performance of best methods and the combination of patterns for non-symmetrical relations.

Relation	Method	Acc	Acc@10	MAP
Purpose-of	LRCos	0.10	**0.32**	0.16
	Best pattern	0.10	0.22	0.13
	Score-3	0.08	0.30	**0.20**
	Borda-3	0.08	0.30	0.16
	Score-5	**0.14**	0.30	0.16
	Borda-5	0.08	**0.32**	0.14
Has-Purpose	3CosAvg / LRCos	**0.24**	0.40	**0.29**
	Best pattern	0.20	**0.42**	0.26
	Score-3	0.22	0.38	0.26
	Borda-3	0.18	0.40	0.25
	Score-5	0.20	0.34	0.25
	Borda-5	0.20	0.36	0.25
Hypernym-of (abstract)	3CosAvg	0.06	0.58	0.22
	LRCos	0.08	0.56	0.20
	Best pattern	0.20	0.66	0.27
	Best pattern 2	0.22	0.64	0.31
	Score-3	0.28	**0.76**	0.32
	Borda-3	**0.38**	0.74	**0.34**
	Score-5	0.32	0.74	0.31
	Borda-5	0.34	0.74	0.32
Hypernym-of (concrete)	3CosAvg	0.16	0.54	0.27
	LRCos	0.18	0.50	0.25
	Best pattern	0.14	0.54	0.20
	Best pattern 2	0.16	0.46	0.23
	Score-3	**0.26**	0.54	**0.29**
	Borda-3	0.18	**0.56**	0.23
	Score-5	0.22	0.54	0.24
	Borda-5	0.18	0.52	0.23
Hypernym-of (verbs)	LRCos	**0.20**	0.48	**0.27**
	Best pattern	0.08	0.54	0.18
	Best pattern 2	0.10	0.50	0.18
	Score-3	0.10	0.54	0.19
	Borda-3	0.10	**0.56**	0.19
	Score-5	0.12	0.52	0.19
	Borda-5	0.10	0.52	0.19
Hyponym-of (abstract)	LRCos	0.08	0.38	0.14
	Best pattern	0.14	0.52	0.23
	Score-3	**0.22**	0.60	**0.25**
	Borda-3	0.16	0.56	0.24
	Score-5	**0.22**	0.60	0.24
	Borda-5	0.14	**0.68**	0.23
Hyponym-of (concrete)	3CosAvg	0.12	0.60	0.26
	LRCos	0.28	0.56	0.34
	Best pattern	**0.54**	**0.88**	**0.58**
	Score-3	0.50	0.86	0.51
	Borda-3	0.52	0.84	0.54
	Score-5	0.42	0.86	0.46
	Borda-5	0.46	0.86	0.49
Hyponym-of (verbs)	LRCos	0.20	0.54	0.26
	Best pattern	**0.24**	**0.64**	**0.30**
	Score-3	0.20	0.58	0.22
	Borda-3	0.18	0.56	0.23
	Score-5	0.16	0.54	0.20
	Borda-5	0.16	0.52	0.19
Part	3CosAvg	0.02	0.30	0.09
	LRCos	0.06	0.28	0.11
	Best pattern	0.12	0.30	0.17
	Score-3	0.12	0.30	0.17
	Borda-3	**0.16**	0.30	0.18
	Score-5	0.14	**0.40**	**0.20**
	Borda-5	**0.16**	0.30	0.18
Has-Part	LRCos	0.06	0.24	0.09
	Best pattern	0.08	0.34	0.17
	Best pattern 2	0.12	0.28	0.17
	Score-3	**0.14**	0.44	**0.22**
	Borda-3	0.08	**0.46**	0.17
	Score-5	**0.14**	0.40	0.21
	Borda-5	0.10	0.40	0.19

Overall Method	Acc	Acc@10	MAP
3CosAvg	0.11	0.43	0.19
LRCos	0.13	0.44	0.22
Best pattern Acc	0.21	0.45	0.26
Best pattern Acc@10	0.19	0.50	0.25
Best pattern MAP	0.20	0.47	**0.27**
Score-3	**0.22**	**0.52**	**0.27**
Borda-3	0.21	**0.52**	0.26
Score-5	**0.22**	**0.52**	0.26
Borda-5	0.21	0.51	0.25

Acc@10 increase and MAP is matched. There is no relation for which a baseline is the best in the three measures, but, for two (has-purpose and hyponymy verbs), the best Acc and MAP are still by LRCos. Additionally, for three relations, there were no improvements over using the best pattern (has-purpose, hyponym-of concrete and verbs).

5   Conclusions

In what may be seen as yet another contribution for better understanding BERT and what we can do with it, we have explored a Portuguese BERT model in the acquisition of lexico-semantic relations. After manually compiling lexical patterns that denote the relations of interest, templates were obtained by fixing one argument, while the other was a mask, to be predicted by BERT's MLM. Predictions by each pattern were assessed in a dataset of lexico-semantic analogies and compared to baselines that exploit static word embeddings. Either with a single pattern or by a combination, baselines were outperformed for most relations. The best performance was in the acquisition of hypernyms of concrete nouns.

Improvements confirm that a pre-trained BERT can be useful for boosting the creation or enrichment of LKBs, but probably not in a completely automatic fashion, because not all predictions are accurate. This is especially true for parts of concepts, concepts of parts, or concepts with a specific purpose. For better accuracy, results may have to be further filtered by humans or by dedicated automatic procedures.

To improve the current results, compiled patterns can be tested with other models in the future. In fact, we can give a word on two initial experiments with BERT-large and GPT-2 fine-tuned for Portuguese[6]. The former led to improvements in hypernymy and hyponymy between verbs and abstract nouns, also synonymy between verbs, but had even lower performance for part and has-part, while struggling to beat the baselines in the same relations as BERT-base. For GPT-2, templates[7] had to be slightly modified and were more limited – i.e., the prediction is the first generated word – so performances were significantly lower.

We did consider a broad range of patterns, but others, possibly acquired automatically from corpora as in Bouraoui et al. [1], may be tested in the future. It is also in our plans to analyse how well the BERT-computed likelihood of sentences that instantiate semantic relations correlates with relation prototypicality and whether it can be used as a confidence score, e.g., how it correlates with the number of lexical resources where a relation instance is found [12].

Acknowledgements. This work was funded by the project POWER (grant number POCI-01-0247-FEDER-070365), co-financed by the European Regional Development Fund (FEDER), through Portugal 2020 (PT2020), and by the Competitiveness and Internationalization Operational Programme (COMPETE 2020); and by national funds through FCT, within the scope of the project CISUC (UID/CEC/00326/2020) and by European Social Fund, through the Regional Operational Program Centro 2020. It is also based upon work from COST Action CA18209 Nexus Linguarum, supported by COST (European Cooperation in Science and Technology). http://www.cost.eu/.

---

[6] https://huggingface.co/pierreguillou/gpt2-small-portuguese.
[7] Patterns for GPT available from https://github.com/NLP-CISUC/PT-LexicalSema ntics/blob/master/Patterns/GPT_patterns_for_TALES.txt.

References

1. Bouraoui, Z., Camacho-Collados, J., Schockaert, S.: Inducing relational knowledge from BERT. In: Proceedings of the AAAI Conference on Artificial Intelligence, pp. 7456–7463. AAAI Press (2020)
2. Cederberg, S., Widdows, D.: Using LSA and noun coordination information to improve the recall and precision of automatic hyponymy extraction. In: Proceedings of the Seventh Conference on Natural Language Learning at HLT-NAACL 2003, pp. 111–118 (2003)
3. Chang, H.S., Wang, Z., Vilnis, L., McCallum, A.: Distributional inclusion vector embedding for unsupervised hypernymy detection. In: Proceedings of the 2018 Conference of the North American Chapter of the Association for Computational Linguistics: Human Language Technologies, vol. 1 (Long Papers), pp. 485–495 (2018)
4. Devlin, J., Chang, M.W., Lee, K., Toutanova, K.: BERT: Pre-training of deep bidirectional transformers for language understanding. In: Proceedings of 2019 Conference of the North American Chapter of the Association for Computational Linguistics: Human Language Technologies, pp. 4171–4186. ACL (2019)
5. Drozd, A., Gladkova, A., Matsuoka, S.: Word embeddings, analogies, and machine learning: beyond king - man + woman = queen. In: Proceedings the 26th International Conference on Computational Linguistics: Technical papers COLING 2016, pp. 3519–3530. COLING 2016 (2016)
6. Emerson, P.: The original Borda count and partial voting. Soc. Choice Welfare **40**(2), 353–358 (2013)
7. Ettinger, A.: What BERT is not: lessons from a new suite of psycholinguistic diagnostics for language models. Trans. ACL **8**, 34–48 (2020)
8. Fellbaum, C. (ed.): WordNet: An Electronic Lexical Database (Language, Speech, and Communication). The MIT Press, London (1998)
9. de Freitas, M.C., Quental, V.: Subsídios para a elaboração automática de taxonomias. In: Anais do XXVII Congresso da SBC, pp. 1585–1594 (2007)
10. Gladkova, A., Drozd, A., Matsuoka, S.: Analogy-based detection of morphological and semantic relations with word embeddings: what works and what doesn't. In: Procs of NAACL 2016 Student Research Workshop, pp. 8–15. ACL (2016)
11. Goldberg, Y.: Assessing BERT's syntactic abilities. arXiv:1901.05287 (2019)
12. Gonçalo Oliveira, H.: A survey on Portuguese lexical knowledge bases: contents, comparison and combination. Information **9**(2), 34 (2018)
13. Gonçalo Oliveira, H., Costa, H., Gomes, P.: Extracção de conhecimento léxico-semântico a partir de resumos da Wikipédia. In: Proceedings of INFORUM 2010, Simpósio de Informática. Braga, Portugal (September 2010)
14. Gonçalo Oliveira, H., Sousa, T., Alves, A.: TALES: test set of Portuguese lexical-semantic relations for assessing word embeddings. In: Procs of ECAI 2020 Workshop on Hybrid Intelligence for Natural Language Processing Tasks (HI4NLP 2020). CEUR Workshop Proceedings, vol. 2693, pp. 41–47. CEUR-WS.org (2020)
15. Gonçalo Oliveira, H., Aguiar, F.S.d.S., Rademaker, A.: On the utility of word embeddings for enriching OpenWordNet-PT. In: Proceedings of 3rd Conference on Language, Data and Knowledge (LDK 2021). OASIcs, vol. 93, pp. 21:1–21:13. Schloss Dagstuhl - Leibniz-Zentrum für Informatik, Dagstuhl, Germany (2021)
16. Hartmann, N.S., et al.: Portuguese word embeddings: evaluating on word analogies and natural language tasks. In: Proceedings of 11th Brazilian Symposium in Information and Human Language Technology (STIL 2017), pp. 122–131 (2017)

17. Hearst, M.A.: Automatic acquisition of hyponyms from large text corpora. In: Proceedings of 14th Conference on Computational Linguistics, pp. 539–545. COLING 1992, Association for Computational Linguistics, Morristown, NJ, USA (1992)
18. Markov, I., Mamede, N., Baptista, J.: Automatic identification of whole-part relations in Portuguese. In: Proceedings of 3rd Symposium on Languages, Applications and Technologies. OASICS, vol. 38, pp. 225–232. Schloss Dagstuhl-Leibniz-Zentrum fuer Informatik (2014)
19. Mikolov, T., Chen, K., Corrado, G., Dean, J.: Efficient estimation of word representations in vector space. In: Proceedings of Workshop track of ICLR (2013)
20. Paes, G.E.: Detecção de Hiperônimos com BERT e Padrões de Hearst. Master's thesis, Universidade Federal de Mato Grosso do Sul (2021)
21. Pantel, P., Pennacchiotti, M.: Espresso: leveraging generic patterns for automatically harvesting semantic relations. In: Procs of 21st International Conference on Computational Linguistics and 44th Annual Meeting of the Association for Computational Linguistics, pp. 113–120. ACL Press, Sydney, Australia (2006)
22. Petroni, F., et al.: Language models as knowledge bases? In: Proceedings of 2019 Conference on Empirical Methods in Natural Language Processing and 9th International Joint Conference on Natural Language Processing (EMNLP-IJCNLP), pp. 2463–2473. ACL (2019)
23. Radford, A., Wu, J., Child, R., Luan, D., Amodei, D., Sutskever, I.: Language models are unsupervised multitask learners. OpenAI Blog 1(8), 9 (2019)
24. Snow, R., Jurafsky, D., Ng, A.: Learning syntactic patterns for automatic hypernym discovery. Adv. Neural Inf. Process. Syst. 17, 1297–1304 (2005)
25. Souza, F., Nogueira, R., Lotufo, R.: BERTimbau: pretrained BERT models for Brazilian Portuguese. In: Cerri, R., Prati, R.C. (eds.) BRACIS 2020. LNCS (LNAI), vol. 12319, pp. 403–417. Springer, Cham (2020). https://doi.org/10.1007/978-3-030-61377-8_28

Short Papers

The Systematic Construction of Multiple Types of Corpora Through the Lapelinc Framework

Bruno Silvério Costa[1](✉) ⓘ, Jorge Viana Santos[2] ⓘ, Cristiane Namiuti[2] ⓘ,
and Aline Silva Costa[1] ⓘ

[1] Federal Institute of Education, Science and Technology of Bahia, Vitória da Conquista, Brazil
{brunosilverio,alinecosta}@ifba.edu.br
[2] State University of Southwest Bahia, Vitória da Conquista, Brazil
{viana.jorge.viana,cristianenamiuti}@uesb.edu.br

Abstract. The lack of a pattern widely accepted in Corpus Linguistics for the construction of text corpora has resulted in multiple possible paths to compilation, resulting in research products that are difficult to interface and have low continuity. The variety of existing corpora aggravates this problem since individual studies use different forms of expression to describe and solve similar problems. Thus, a gap is identified in the production initiatives to create corpora regarding the "exploratory" way of conducting such initiatives. Based on the Lapelinc Workflow for the construction of historical corpora, the Lapelinc Framework presents a working pattern for construction and research activities involving Portuguese language corpora, thereby establishing a set of steps and by-products common to corpora-based linguistic research. Providing a set of tools in the Import Stage with a reduced learning curve and allowing the convergence of efforts during development, the Lapelinc Framework tools add functionalities for multiple purposes in the construction of corpora, simplifying the construction of multi-type corpora, facilitated by the resources it makes available.

Keywords: Corpus linguistic · Corpora typologies · Lapelinc Framework

1 Introduction

The digital humanities, through the convergence of knowledge and technologies, aggregate knowledge of the humanities and digital technologies in a single area, enabling the development of new methods and techniques for research on linguistic corpora [1]. This development of the linguistic corpus area has, in addition to the solution of known problems, allowed the creation of entirely new research possibilities. Standardizing techniques and procedures allows us to establish a standard way to solve problems with the same typology or similar characteristics, selecting practices that reduce the complexity in performing activities, in addition to reducing the chances of error and rework index [2].

The lack of a widely accepted standard for the construction of corpora has resulted in the development of several different paths that by not talking to each other yield research products that are difficult to interface and lack continuity [3].

© Springer Nature Switzerland AG 2022
V. Pinheiro et al. (Eds.): PROPOR 2022, LNAI 13208, pp. 401–406, 2022.
https://doi.org/10.1007/978-3-030-98305-5_37

The variety of corpora pointed out by Sardinha [4] aggravates this problem, since in addition to the possibility of independent research programs using different methods to describe and solve similar problems, the variety of corpora has naturally led to distinct methodologies to solve associated problems.

Thus, there is a gap in corpus production initiatives resulting from the "exploratory" way in which such initiatives are conducted. Although there are specifics in each study and in the typology of corpora, it is possible to identify a series of common steps in the construction process, establishing an essential shared path. Respecting the need to adapt to the specifics of each research program and at the same time seeking a solution that affords the benefits of standardized construction of corpora, philological consistency, the possibility of directly reducing the cost of implementation of the corpus and promoting the reuse of such corpora, a customizable framework is proposed as a methodology for the creation of linguistic corpora of multiple types for Portuguese that constitutes a snapshot of doctoral research in progress of Costa [4] within the scope of PPGLIN/UESB.

2   The Lapelinc Framework

As part of Lapelinc Workflow [5], the Lapelinc Framework is a work pattern for the construction and research activities involving Portuguese language corpora, establishing a set of steps and by-products common to linguistic research to aid the develop corpora that are designed to correspond with each other from the corpus design process to the analysis and editing phases, in addition to the visualization and exchange of recorded information.

Table 1. Main corpora contributing to the design of the Lapelinc Framework

Language	Corpus name	Project description
English	BNC - British National Corpus [2]	British English, written and spoken
English	PPCME - Penn-Helsinki Parsed Corpus of Middle English [3]	American corpus of Middle English, written
English	OANC - The Open American National Corpus [4]	American English, including all genres and transcripts of spoken data produced from 1990
Portuguese	CRPC [5]	Electronic Corpus of Portuguese of Portugal, Brazil, Angola, Cape Verde, Guinea-Bissau, Mozambique, Sao Tome and Principe, Goa, Macau and Timor-Leste
Portuguese	Corpus de São Carlos (NILC) [6]	Electronic process of Portuguese
Portuguese	Banco de Português [7]	Oral and written excerpts (mostly journalistic), almost entirely of Brazilian origin

Several initiatives for the composition of corpora were studied to establish a common path in light of their typological diversity. Among the corpora studied, those that positively contributed to the development of this work are listed in Table 1.

Studying these initiatives allowed us to identify the essential stages of the construction of these corpora in English and Portuguese. As the objective of the Lapelinc Framework is the production of corpora for the Portuguese language, the knowledge acquired in the study of the corpora of English aided in the design of the steps established for the Portuguese language in the developed Framework.

Each stage consists of fixed points (frozen spots) and flexible points (hot spots) [12]. Fixed points are indispensable guidelines. Contrariwise, the flexible points provide the necessary customization to suit the specifics of each research. Figure 1 presents the stages and the flow between them presented by the Lapelinc Framework [3].

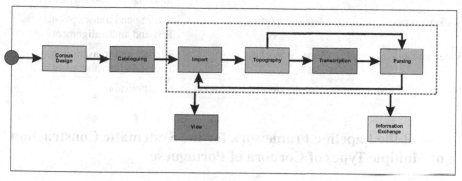

Fig. 1. Lapelinc Framework [3]

According to the stages presented in Fig. 1, the Lapelinc Framework allows the creation of corpora of multiple types and purposes, consisting of both a set of workflows that implement a standard proposal for the construction of corpora and a set of software tools that enable the implementation of corpora in accordance with the proposed standard. Its internally programmed routines allow the establishment of size and scope indicators in the Project Stage, as well as provide a specialized dashboard to present the state of a corpus under development in relation to these indicators. In the Cataloging Stage, the framework allows the composition of a catalog of the collection of implemented corpora, recording and displaying information of a philological nature for the documents related to each corpus, following the Lapelinc Workflow methodology [5]. According to its multi-typological characteristic, the Lapelinc Framework provides tools and functionalities for working with various text media, as shown in Table 2.

Table 2. Tools available by the Lapelinc Framework through the Import and Transcription Stages for the implementation of various types of corpora. Based on Costa, Santos, and Namiuti [5].

Corpus type	Import framework tool	Text transcript framework tool
Historical documents	Image capture, image editing, and image co-indexing	Reading and decryption, paleographic transcription, text and image alignment, dictionary of letters, spellings, abbreviations, and symbols
Digital image text	Digital image import, image editing, and image synthesis (with metadata stamp)	Reading and decryption, paleographic transcription, text and image alignment, dictionary of letters, spellings, abbreviations, and symbols
Spoken corpus	Audio importing	Hearing and transcription, Text and audio alignment
Video and movie corpus	Video importing	Hearing and transcription, Text and video alignment
Native-digital text import	Multiple-format text import	Not applicable

3   Use of the Lapelinc Framework for the Systematic Construction of Multiple Types of Corpora of Portuguese

The construction of each type of corpus is related to the nature of the documents that compose it. Historical corpora require techniques and rigor different from those used in the implementation of corpora based on native-digital texts of the web. However, despite the diversity of paths adopted by each typology, there is a convergence in the representation of texts common to the construction of all digital corpora: the representation of transcriptions in digital text. Thus, although different types of corpora entail different demands in the initial treatment, the subsequent phases of implementation are common, allowing the use of a pattern of representation of the metainformation generated. In addition, the entire structure of analysis, visualization, and exchange of information can be unique, reducing the work and the possibilities of error during the process, since best practices can be used for these activities.

Figure 2 presents the interaction between the initial Design and Cataloguing Stages at the Import Stage and later. We note that the construction of corpora begins without alternative activity flows, dividing into several possibilities at the Import Stage. Depending on the specific type of corpus to be constructed, or in the case of a mixed type, distinct sub-stages for the desired implementation can be selected. Creating corpora of different typologies begins with the Design Stage, which allows parameters to be established beyond a given type, such as extensions and the choice of annotation layers for the analysis. Following the Design Stage is the Cataloguing Stage, allowing textual information and the minimum visuals necessary to register the documents or works to be collected for inclusion in the corpus.

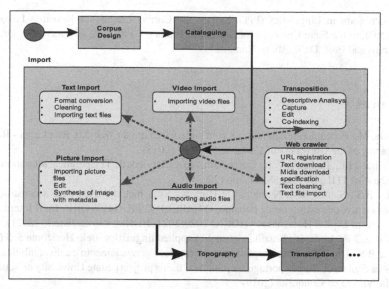

Fig. 2. Lapelinc Framework stages for constructing a multimedia corpus for Portuguese

All artifacts produced in the Import Stage are directed to the Topography Stage, which allows the construction of a topographic analysis of the collected media. If these media comprise native-digital texts, the Transcription Stage can be ignored and the later stages of the framework can be followed. In the case of digital images, videos, and audios, the stream will be forwarded to the Transcription Stage, which allows the final transposition of the obtained media to digital text.

4 Conclusions

The construction of corpora is a complex task that requires rigorous activities to be implemented in accordance with the specific typology of the corpus. The set of stages and activities available in the Lapelinc Framework and the software that implement it enable the controlled construction of corpora in Portuguese, as well as allowing the generation of standardized research artifacts, which enables both the development with reduced rework, as in the sharing of the artifacts generated, and the continuity of research developed by multiple and distinct teams in time.

The Lapelinc Framework allows the elaboration of Portuguese language corpora of multiple typologies, providing a set of software tools that offers a reduced learning curve to facilitate the convergence of development efforts. These characteristics spurred the development of a tool that integrates functionalities for the implementation of multi-typological corpora. As a result, this framework aggregates several computer programs for the implementation of a variety of corpora for the Portuguese language, constituting a potentially useful tool to assist researchers in corpus linguistics in developing corpora.

Acknowledgment. We thank FAPESB and CNPq as this work is linked to thematic projects funded by FAPESB (APP0007/2016 and APP0014/2016) and CNPq (436209/2018-7); the

Graduate Program in Linguistics (PPGLIN); to the Corpus Linguistics Research Laboratory (LAPELINC); to the State University of Southwest Bahia – UESB; and advisors Prof. Dr. Jorge Viana Santos and Prof. Dr. Cristiane Namiuti.

References

1. Portela, M.: Humanidades digitais: as humanidades na era da Web 2.0. Rua Larga - Rectory Magazine of the University of Coimbra, vol. 147 (2013)
2. Magalhães, I.L., Pinheiro, W.B.: Gerenciamento de Serviços de TI na Prática: uma abordagem com base na ITIL. Novatec, São Paulo (2007)
3. Costa, B.S., Santos, J.V., Namiuti, C.: Uma proposta metodológica para a construção de corpora através de estruturas de trabalho: O LAPELINC FRAMEWORK, In: II International Congress of Digital Humanities - HDRIO 2020/2021. HDRio, Rio de Janeiro (2021)
4. Sardinha, T.B., Leila, B.: Brazilian journal in applied linguistics. Belo Horizonte **5**, 5 (2005)
5. Costa, B.S.: Um framework integrado para a criação, o gerenciamento e a disponibilização de corpora digitais em língua portuguesa [Doctoral thesis project]. State University of Southwest Bahia, Vitória da Conquista (2019)
6. Santos, J.V., Namiuti, C.: O futuro das humanidades digitais é o passado. In: V CILH - International Congress of Historical Linguistics, São Paulo (2017)
7. BNC. http://www.natcorp.ox.ac.uk
8. Kroch, A., Taylor, A.: The Penn-Helsinki Parsed Corpus of Middle English (PPCME2). http://www.ling.upenn.edu/ppche-release-2016/PPCME2-RELEASE-4
9. OANC. http://www.anc.org/data/oanc/
10. CRPC. http://www.clul.ulisboa.pt/en/10-research/713-crpc-reference-corpus-of-contemporary-portuguese
11. NILC - São Carlos. http://www.nilc.icmc.usp.br/nilc/index.php
12. Fayad, M.E., Schmidt, D.C., JOHNSON, R. E.: Building Application Frameworks: Object-Oriented Foundations of Framework Design. Wiley, New York (1999)

Revisiting CCNet for Quality Measurements in Galician

John E. Ortega[✉][iD], Iria de-Dios-Flores[iD], José Ramom Pichel[iD], and Pablo Gamallo[iD]

Centro de Investigación en Tecnoloxías Intelixentes (CiTIUS),
Universidade de Santiago de Compostela, Santiago de Compostela, Spain
{john.ortega,iria.dedios,jramon.pichel,pablo.gamallo}@usc.gal

Abstract. In this article, we report the construction of a web-based Galician corpus and its language model, both made publicly available, by making use of CCNet tools and data. An in-depth analysis of the corpus is made so as to provide insights on how to achieve optimum quality through the use of heuristics to lower the perplexity.

Keywords: Galician · Web crawl · Quality estimation · Perplexity

1 Introduction

In recent years, there has been a higher need for quality data to create high performing machine learning models that typically use neural networks. This has especially been the case for languages that have low to medium resources where approaches require an immense amount of digital text. The varieties of such languages that we are concerned with are the Galician-Portuguese branch, which belongs to the Western Ibero-Romance group, spoken in the northwest of the Iberian Peninsula. This article highlights the efforts of a new proposal to increase the use of Galician within a novel project called *Nós*[1], starting off with the first gathering of the CCNet corpus. We report the first of a series of tasks that will attempt to provide higher quality texts in Galician for training both supervised and unsupervised statistical models that will, in turn, be used for various natural language processing tasks. Our work introduces the CCNet corpus for Galician and makes it publicly available for anyone to download in an easy way. Additionally, we provide evidence from a systematic human-based analysis carried out by Galician expert reviewers that the original CCNet corpus contains several caveats. We document those caveats and describe the analysis performed on the CCNet quality. In this article, we report three main contributions: (1) A Galician corpus made available publicly, (2) a Galician language model also made publicly available, and (3) an in-depth analysis of the corpus that provides insight on how to achieve optimum quality through the use of heuristics to lower the perplexity for use in natural language processing (NLP) tasks in future work.

---

[1] https://nos.gal.

© Springer Nature Switzerland AG 2022
V. Pinheiro et al. (Eds.): PROPOR 2022, LNAI 13208, pp. 407–412, 2022.
https://doi.org/10.1007/978-3-030-98305-5_38

2   Background and Related Work

In this article, we present our findings on reproducing the introduction of the common crawl corpus by Facebook, known as the CCNet corpus [11]. The CCNet corpus attempts to comprise monolingual data for 174 languages using a more common corpus known as the Common Crawl[2] corpus based on a "snapshot" of the web at a given time – the work on CCNet is based on the Common-Crawl dataset from February 2019 which is composed of 1.5 billion documents in 174 languages. Documents and languages in the CCNet work as presented on GitHub[3] and in the original paper are limited to a small subset of languages. Statistics are provided by CCNet [1] for 25 of the 174 languages and downloadable language models are only available for 48 languages (see Makefile from GitHub[3]). Unfortunately, language models for Galician and a download-able corpus is not readily available, despite other efforts found online[4] that publish downloadable corpora for several of the missing languages yet do not claim authorship.

We present the CCNet corpus for Galician after processing and also freely provide the language model[5]. This forms part of an initiative to provide more Galician text and work available for wide use in an effort to increase visibility and add authorship to future projects based on the CCNet corpus for Galician. To this effect, we believe that the analysis presented here is unprecedented and will help establish some of the caveats of using the CCNet corpus for localized low-to-medium resource languages that are not included in the 25 to 48 language models currently available for use.

3   Methodology

This work is the first step of several in a multi-part project on Galician[6]. The project will help increase quality for several NLP tasks including machine translation, information extraction, text generation, and more. Since the CCNet corpus is most probably used for unsupervised machine learning (see [11] for an example of an unsupervised implementation), our plan is to create the highest quality corpus possible while at the same time gathering as many sentences, or segments, as possible. This was done by compiling a large Galician corpus of high-quality segments that have been improved using several heuristics. Our method comprised the following tasks: (1) use the CCNet corpus project tools from GitHub to download the de-duplicated Galician text as described in the CCNet article [11]; (2) compile the CCNet corpus and make the de-duplicated text available for public use; (3) create a Galician language model based on

---

[2] https://commoncrawl.org/about.
[3] https://github.com/facebookresearch/cc_net.
[4] http://data.statmt.org/cc-100.
[5] https://github.com/proxecto-nos/propor2022.
[6] https://www.lingua.gal/recursos/todos/_/promovelo/contido_607/nos-intelixencia-artificial-servizo-lingua-galega.

KenLM [4] after tokenizing with SentencePiece [6] as described in the CCNet article and make it available for public use; (4) select 1000 random sentences for a systematic qualitative analysis carried out by two Galician expert reviewers; (5) define several heuristics that can be used to better the already de-duplicated CCNet corpus in turn lowering the perplexity and apply them on 111 sample documents to verify their usefulness by calculating the perplexity before and after applying the heuristic.

Since the de-duplicated corpus and language model are not readily available on-line, the bulk of the work to be performed in order to create the high-quality corpus is related to the downloading of the corpus and creation of its model. On a 2.20 GHz Intel(R) Xeon(R) Silver 4214 CPU, approximately 2,000 documents can be processed in one day using the "debug" execution mode (single-threaded and single-process execution) from CCNet since parallel processing uses Slurm[7] which does not work well in our experiments[8]. Since there are a total of 64,000 crawls to be processed[9], the download and de-duplication process takes nearly a month. After that, the SentencePiece tokenization and KenLM model creation require less time (nearly 5 d on the same architecture) since the CCNet tools include code for training the model.

1000 random segments are chosen and given to two native Galician speakers. Both speakers are trained in Galician linguistics and have some background on NLP. They are asked to mark the original positions of text and provide what text should be modified and how. Patterns are then searched from both annotations which resulted in the heuristics described in the next section.

The final goal for this work is to eventually attain a high-quality Galician corpus. We base our definition of quality on *perplexity* as described in previous work on isolated European languages [3]. In the current work, we use it to measure the distance between noisy and cleaned texts of the Galician corpus. Our word tri-grams perplexity model was trained on Wikipedia data sets similar to previous work [3] for Galician. Tools used to create the model can be found on GitHub.[10]

4   Analysis and Results

We report the error analysis, the heuristics applied to improve the quality of the text and the perplexity scores comparing the two data-sets. After de-duplication, the corpus contains 4,100,006 tokens and 6,496,871 lines.[11] As an aside, the original size reported by CCNet is of 440 MB and around 400k documents, our downloaded corpus is the same size (440 MB), but the number of documents in

---

[7] https://slurm.schedmd.com/.

[8] Similar issues have been reported for other languages at https://github.com/facebookresearch/cc_net/issues.

[9] Each crawl consists of several documents totalling around ≈150 MB in size.

[10] https://github.com/proxecto-nos/propor2022.

[11] In the original CCNet article, the sentence splitting uses Moses but the version is not clear, we report the number of lines here instead.

our experiment is 64k compared to 400k in the CCNet article, this is due to the CCNet system automatic break up of the documents to parallelize processing. The final results left around 11% of the original tokens and less than half of the number of characters – a drastic reduction of the original crawled corpus.

4.1 Error Analysis

Several issues were identified by the two Galician expert reviewers in our experiments. One of the recurring issues, as stated from the original CCNet work [11], was the introduction of other languages, namely English and Spanish. Thus, much like other research on low-resource languages [7,9,10], we found that the higher-resource neighbor, Spanish, was often present within the Galician texts.

The main language error types found in the CCNet de-duplicated corpus were the following: (1) English and Spanish excerpts ranging to as many as 80 words long; (2) book publications along with their titles, authors, and other bibliographical information; (3) bibliographical entries containing mundane punctuation or long alphabetically-sorted lists separated by delimiters; (4) misspelled or non-standarized Galician words; (5) boilerplates and typical errors from web crawls such as the inclusion of HTML tags, Javascript, the combining of two or more words into one, and other non-human readable text.

4.2 Heuristics

In order to mitigate the issues found during error analysis, we propose four heuristics for lowering the perplexity of the Galician corpus. These heuristics cover the main issues discovered during error analysis but further discovery will be considered in future work. **Heuristic 1**. Remove non-Galician words since there are several words in English, Spanish, and other languages. **Heuristic 2**. Words in lists in any language can be removed or broken down into separate words (or tokens). **Heuristic 3**. Splitting of combined words can be performed by using character-level splits along with SentencePiece [6] tokenization and byte-pair encoding [5]. **Heuristic 4**. Replace those words that have been misspelled by making use of a Levenshtein-based [8] character distance between in-vocabulary words found in a Galician word dictionary. An initial threshold such as 90% could be used to measure the distance between the misspelled word and the potentially correct words.

In order to show that the implementation of heuristics could lower complexity of the CCNet Galician corpus, we test Heuristic 1 by removing non-Galician text and measuring the quality of the text before and after the removal by using perplexity. Non-Galician text was removed by making use of QueLingua language detector [2], software originally tuned for Galician. Our results show that the average perplexity of 111 documents before removing the text is 5028.054 and after removing the text is lower, 4988.369. While initially, this is not a huge gain, we note that this was done for 111 documents only. Future work will apply all four heuristics over the entire corpus.

5   Conclusion and Future Work

We believe that the inclusion of all four heuristics introduced over the entire corpus will result in significantly lower perplexity. We have shown that with a small sample of documents the most problematic issue can be resolved to increase the quality. We have downloaded the CCNet Galician corpus and made it publicly available in an easy-to-use format along with its corresponding language model. Future work will include the implementation and evaluation of the other three heuristics proposed in this work along with other heuristics. We also plan on evaluating the model and using both the corpus and model in various NLP tasks for Galician and Portuguese.

Acknowledgements. This research was funded by the project "Nós: Galician in the society and economy of artificial intelligence", agreement between Xunta de Galicia and University of Santiago de Compostela, and grant ED431G2019/04 by the Galician Ministry of Education, University and Professional Training, and the European Regional Development Fund (ERDF/FEDER program).

References

1. Conneau, A., et al.: Unsupervised cross-lingual representation learning at scale. In: Proceedings of the 58th Annual Meeting of the Association for Computational Linguistics, pp. 8440–8451. Association for Computational Linguistics, July 2020. https://doi.org/10.18653/v1/2020.acl-main.747, https://aclanthology.org/2020.acl-main.747
2. Gamallo, P., Alegria, I., Pichel, J.R., Agirrezabal, M.: Comparing two basic methods for discriminating between similar languages and varieties. In: COLING Workshop on NLP for Similar Languages, Varieties and Dialects (VarDial3) (2016)
3. Gamallo, P., Pichel, J.R., Alegria, I.: Measuring language distance of isolated european languages. Information **11**(4), 181 (2020). https://doi.org/10.3390/info11040181, https://www.mdpi.com/2078-2489/11/4/181
4. Heafield, K.: Kenlm: faster and smaller language model queries. In: Proceedings of the sixth workshop on statistical machine translation, pp. 187–197 (2011)
5. Kida, T., Fukamachi, S., Takeda, M., Shinohara, A., Shinohara, T., Arikawa, S.: Byte pair encoding: a text compression scheme that accelerates pattern matching (1999)
6. Kudo, T., Richardson, J.: Sentencepiece: A simple and language independent subword tokenizer and detokenizer for neural text processing. arXiv preprint arXiv:1808.06226 (2018)
7. Lankford, S., Afli, H., Way, A.: Machine translation in the covid domain: an english-irish case study for loresmt 2021. In: Proceedings of the 4th Workshop on Technologies for MT of Low Resource Languages (LoResMT2021), pp. 144–150 (2021)
8. Levenshtein, V.: Binary codes capable of correcting deletions, insertions and reversals. Soviet Phys. Doklady. **10**(8), 707–710 (1966)
9. Ortega, J.E., Castro-Mamani, R.A., Samame, J.R.M.: Love thy neighbor: combining two neighboring low-resource languages for translation. In: Proceedings of the 4th Workshop on Technologies for MT of Low Resource Languages (LoResMT2021). pp. 44–51 (2021)

10. Ortega, J.E., Mamani, R.C., Cho, K.: Neural machine translation with a polysynthetic low resource language. Mach. Trans. **34**(4), 325–346 (2020)
11. Wenzek, G., et al.: CCNet: extracting high quality monolingual datasets from web crawl data. In: Proceedings of the 12th Language Resources and Evaluation Conference, pp. 4003–4012. European Language Resources Association, Marseille, France, May 2020. https://aclanthology.org/2020.lrec-1.494

Identifying Literary Characters in Portuguese
Challenges of an International Shared Task

Diana Santos[1]([✉])(iD), Roberto Willrich[2](iD), Marcia Langfeldt[1](iD),
Ricardo Gaiotto de Moraes[3](iD), Cristina Mota[4](iD), Emanoel Pires[5](iD),
Rebeca Schumacher[1](iD), and Paulo Silva Pereira[6](iD)

[1] Linguateca & University of Oslo, Oslo, Norway
{d.s.m.santos,r.s.e.fuao}@ilos.uio.no
[2] INE-UFSC, Florianópolis, Brazil
roberto.willrich@ufsc.br
[3] DLLV-UFSC, Florianópolis, Brazil
[4] Linguateca & INESC-ID, Lisbon, Portugal
[5] UEMA-UFPI, Caxias, Brazil
[6] Faculdade de Letras, Universidade de Coimbra, Coimbra, Portugal
psilvapereira@sapo.pt

Abstract. We introduce the problem of identifying characters in literary text, and mention some specific issues that are special for Portuguese, in the context of presenting DIP, a shared task to foster work in the area and produce resources for computational literature studies in Portuguese. We describe how the task is organized, the resources that will be created, and how we plan to evaluate the results produced by the participant systems.

Keywords: Lusophone literature · Distant reading · Digital humanities

1 Identifying Characters in Literary Text

We describe here DIP: *Desafio de identificação de personagens* (Character identification challenge), an evaluation contest to foster the development of systems that, given a literary work in Portuguese, identify and characterize literary characters, see https://www.linguateca.pt/DIP/.

We see this as a natural first step of distant reading in Portuguese, given the importance of characters for literary studies. In DIP we will deal with novels (written in the last 250 years), digitized as pdfs, or already in text form.

1.1 Brief Motivation from Literary Studies

A literary character is important in fiction, as it sustains the plot and moves it in a particular direction, and may also organize the discourse (if the narrator is

© Springer Nature Switzerland AG 2022
V. Pinheiro et al. (Eds.): PROPOR 2022, LNAI 13208, pp. 413–419, 2022.
https://doi.org/10.1007/978-3-030-98305-5_39

also a character). Since they are created by the author in an attempt to revive or project experiences, they are ideological products. And characters are then built by the reader depending on her beliefs and context, so their reception can drastically change depending on the audience.

If we can get information on characters from thousands of works, we may be able to read the (character) landscape by epoch, literary genre, and/or author, expanding our base with many works outside the literary canon, which may provide interesting opportunities for postcolonial, gender and queer studies. Specifically in a Brazilian context, the presence (or absence) of slaves as characters in the literature is a most relevant concern.

Finally, the form of the names themselves is relevant, not only because address forms reflect different social status, but because some epithets have relevant interpretations, as the case of *Capitu* and *Bentinho* in Dom Casmurro, see [5].

1.2   Motivation from Computer Science Studies

From a computer science perspective, one can see the problem as a standard information extraction task, that from literary works must populate a knowledge base with characters, their attributes, and relations to other characters, as illustrated in Fig. 1.

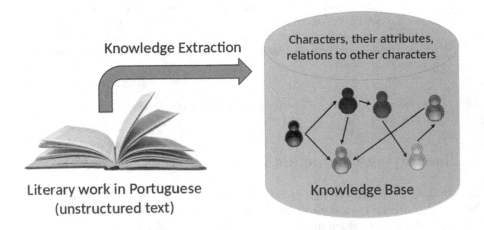

Fig. 1. The task of DIP in a nutshell

In order to perform this extraction task, one may have to use various NLP techniques, which make the challenge more related to (somehow) understanding Portuguese text. Figure 2 presents the main steps in DIP.

The first is named entity recognition of the person names present in the narrative. But it should be noted that DIP is not interested in all person names, only plot characters. Historical people, or characters from other literature should

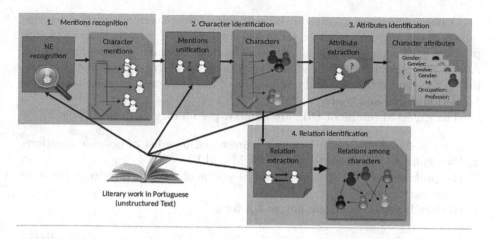

Fig. 2. Different subtasks in DIP (figure adapted from [4])

not be flagged as characters of a given novel. However, it is possible that historical figures appear as fictional characters – as is the case of *D. Pedro II* in *Dom Casmurro*. Note also that novelists always pressupose some shared knowledge by their readers, but this knowledge can be epochal, and/or regional, as the following example illustrates: *A criança ainda vai ficar mais famosa que a Catarina Eufémia*. Although DIP participants do not have to decide whether the book is talking about a historical person or a famous literary character in another work, one might need to access some knowledge base not to mark *Catarina Eufémia* as a character.

As one character is rarely always called the same way throughout a book, we have the widely known coreference problem. This is what the unification step is supposed to solve, identifying all mentions that refer to the same character. Mentions are often depending on the context: depending on who is talking or referring to her, the name may be radically different. So, a serious challenge is to identify the set of (proper noun) denominations by which a novel character is mentioned in a work. By just comparing the two example novels, we see that diminutives may refer to the same person (as in *Guida* for *Margarida*), or to another one named after another character (as in *Capituzinha* and *Capitu*), and that in both books there are characters with the same first name (*João* and *Ezequiel*).

The two last steps presented in Fig. 2, attributes and relation identifications, aim at recognizing the gender, profession/occupation/social status of the detected characters, and the relationship between them. DIP allows the creation of character networks, currently a hot task, as can be seen in the overview by [4]. These can in turn be used for genre prediction, (visual) text summarization, comparing fiction with (social) reality, comparing different literatures, and deciding who are the main characters.

Other applications do not rely on networks, but concern simply the description of large amounts of data: the role of women and men as characters, the professions or social statuses mentioned, the most common relationships found. And it is conceivable that the kind of relations and address forms differ depending on the time of the plot and on the time of the book creation, providing clues for periodization and genre.

The expected results of DIP, are namely, per literary work (see Table 1).

1. a list of characters, each character represented by a list of possible mentions
2. the gender of the character (M, F, or M and F)
3. the profession, or occupation, or social status of the character (can be more than one, or none)
4. the family relations among any characters.

Table 1. Results for *As pupilas do Senhor Reitor* and *Dom Casmurro* (incomplete).

Characters	Sex	Profession
Margarida, Guida, Guida dos Meadas	F	cabreira, professora
Clara, Clarinha, Clarita, Clarita dos Meadas	F	
Daniel, Sr. Daniel, Danielzinho, Daniel do Dornas, Danielzinho do Dornas	M	médico, estudante
Francisca, Chica, Chica da Esquina	F	
Joana, Sra. Joana	F	criada
José das Dornas, Sr. José, Sr. José das Dornas, José, Sr. Zé, Sr. José	F	lavrador
Pedro, Pedro das Dornas, Sr. Pedrinho	M	lavrador
Sr. Reitor, Sr. Padre António, Padre António, Senhor Reitor	M	padre
João Semana, Sr. João Semana, João da Semana	M	médico
João da Esquina, Sr. João da Esquina, Sr. João, João	M	boticário
Sra. Teresa, Sra. Teresa de Jesus	F	
Zefa da Graça, Josefa da Graça, Zefa	F	
Álvaro, Sr. Álvaro	M	
Margarida irmã de Clara		
Daniel irmão de Pedro		
José das Dornas pai de Daniel		
João da Esquina marido de Sra. Teresa		
João da Esquina pai de Francisca		
Doutor João da Costa, João da Costa, Pai João	M	
Cosme, Mano Cosme, Primo Cosme, Tio Cosme	M	advogado
Ezequiel A. de Santiago	M	
D. Glória, Dona Glória, D. Maria da Glória Fernandes Santiago, Prima Glória, mana Glória	F	
Pedro de Albuquerque Santiago	M	fazendeiro, deputado
Sancha, Sanchinha, D. Sancha, Sinhazinha Sancha, sinhazinha Gurgel	F	
Justina, Prima Justina, D. Justina	F	
Padre Cabral, Cabral	M	padre
Pádua, João, Sr. Pádua, Joãozinho, Tartaruga	M	funcionário público
Dona Fortunata	F	

(*continued*)

Table 1. (*continued*)

Characters	Sex	Profession
Bento, Padre Bentinho, Sr. Bentinho, Doutor Santiago, Dom Casmurro	M	
Escobar, Ezequiel de Sousa Escobar	M	investidor em café
José Dias, Sr. José Dias	M	médico, agregado
Capitu, Capitolina	F	
Capituzinha	F	
Miquelina	F	escrava
Maria Gorda	F	escrava
D. Pedro II	M	imperador do Brasil
Bento marido de Capitu		
Capitu mãe de Ezequiel A. Santiago		
D. Glória viúva de Pedro Santiago		
D. Glória mãe de Bento		
D. Fortunata mãe de Capitu		
D. Fortunata esposa de Pádua		

2   Previous Work

There are a number of works on automatic character recognition, see e.g. [1, 2,12]. [6] identify characters in Portuguese children's books to attribute direct speech, while [9] use rules to create character networks for some literary works, distinguishing between plot characters and other named people who are either historical, or characters from other works.

As to named entity recognition in Portuguese, there has been significant work in (among others) person name recognition in HAREM [10], and also some form of identification among different denominations in ReRELEM [3] a decade ago. As to distant reading in Portuguese, cf. [7].

3   The DIP Setup

DIP organization will provide 200 books in digital form (half in text, half in pdf format) to the community, which has 48 h to return the results. This effectively prevents a close reading of the 200 works, ensuring that the analysis is done automatically.

In order to have large numbers of works to process, distant reading of literary collections necessarily includes works from several time periods – after all, one of the goals of distant reading is to address trends and changes in time, see [11]. This means that, specifically for Portuguese, systems will have to process several different ortographies and styles, including different ways to describe professions and relations. For example, *boticário* or *cacaolista* are not exactly modern words to refer to a pharmacist or a cocoa farmer, and there are few *fogueteiros* or *jograis* nowadays. The historical novel subgenre, quite frequent in Portuguese, brings a set of additional problems [8], such as old names, jobs and address forms.

After the submission period is over, the golden collection (containing the right information for 40 out of the 200 books) is made publicly available, and the evaluation results are computed. A workshop presenting the results and the different approaches of the participants will then be organized, followed by the publication of a journal volume. All data amassed about the literary works will also be released.

The systems will be evaluated separately on the five tasks, with the final score per book being the sum of the five measures. The ranking among the systems is done by macro-averaging over the golden collection.

Finally, it was necessary to devise a relativey complex form for evaluating family relationships, inspired by [13], given that e.g. X irmã de Y (X sister of Y) and Y filho de Z (Y son of Z) conveys precisely the same information as Z mãe de X (Z mother of X) and Y irmão de X. (Y brother of X).

References

1. Bamman, D., Popat, S., Shen, S.: An annotated dataset of literary entities. In: Proceedings of NAACL 2019, pp. 2138–2144 (2019)
2. Dekker, N., Kuhn, T., van Erp, M.: Evaluating named entity recognition tools for extracting social networks from novels. Peer J. Comput. Sci. **5**, e189 (2019)
3. Freitas, C., Santos, D., Mota, C., Oliveira, H.G., Carvalho, P.: Detection of relations between named entities: report of a shared task. In: Proceedings of the NAACL HLT Workshop on Semantic Evaluations, SEW-2009, pp. 129–137 (2009)
4. Labatut, V., Bost, X.: Extraction and analysis of fictional character networks: a survey. ACM Comput. Surv. **52**(5), 1–40 (2019)
5. Langfeldt, M.C., Gaiotto de Moraes, R., Pires, E.C.: A importância do Desafio em Identificação de Personagens (DIP) para os estudos literários lusófonos. Tech. rep., DIP (2021), https://www.linguateca.pt/aval_conjunta/dip/Langfeldtetal2021.pdf
6. Mamede, N., Chaleira, P.: Character identification in children stories. In: Vicedo, J.L., Martínez-Barco, P., Muñoz, R., Noeda, M.S. (eds.) Advances in Natural Language Processing - EsTAL, pp. 82–90. Springer, Berlin (2004). https://doi.org/10.1007/11816508
7. Santos, D., et al.: Leitura Distante em Português: resumo do primeiro encontro. Materialidades da Literatura **8**(1), 279–298 (2020)
8. Santos, D., Bick, E., Wlodek, M.: Avaliando entidades mencionadas na coleção ELTeC-por. Linguamática **12**(2), 29–49 (2020)
9. Santos, D., Freitas, C.: Estudando personagens na literatura lusófona. In: STIL - Symposium in Information and Human Language Technology, pp. 48–52 (2019)
10. Santos, D., Seco, N., Cardoso, N., Vilela, R.: HAREM: an advanced NER evaluation contest for Portuguese. In: Calzolari, N.E.A. (ed.) Proceedings of LREC 2006, pp. 1986–1991 (2006)
11. Underwood, T.: Distant Horizons: Digital Evidence and Literary Change. University of Chicago Press, Chicago (2019)

12. Valaa, H., Jurgens, D., Piper, A., Ruths, D.: Mr. Bennet, his coachman, and the Archbishop walk into a bar but only one of them gets recognized: on the difficulty of detecting characters in literary texts. In: Proceedings of the 2015 Conference on Empirical Methods in Natural Language Processing, pp. 769–774 (2015)
13. Vilain, M., Burger, J., Aberdeen, J., Connolly, D., Hirschman, L.: A model-theoretic coreference scoring scheme. In: Proceedings of the 6th Message Understanding Conference (MUC-6), pp. 45–52. Morgan Kaufmann, 6–8 November 1995

Should I Buy or Should I Pass:
E-Commerce Datasets in Portuguese

Henrique Varella Ehrenfried[(✉)] [iD] and Eduardo Todt [iD]

Federal University of Paraná, Curitiba, Brazil
{hvehrenfried,todt}@inf.ufpr.br

Abstract. Text classification is an essential task in Natural Language Processing. The researchers and developers need data in the desired language to build new models and algorithms to develop this task. In this paper, we discuss and make available three datasets of text classification in Portuguese based on data of the B2W group, which is an important contribution to the research in the field.

Keywords: Dataset · Text classification · Portuguese dataset

1 Introduction

Text classification is one task of natural language processing (NLP) that aims to classify text sentences or documents into a set of categories. According to Sebastiani [7], this field of study started in the early '60s. However, it started to become available to most researchers in the early '90s due to the improvements in computer hardware.

This work presents three distinct datasets balanced in Brazilian Portuguese based on the work from Real and Colleagues [6]. Their work [6] uses data collected from the B2W group data[1].

2 Related Works

Datasets are essential to building machine learning algorithms. In NLP, datasets are sensitive to the language, which constitutes a major difficulty in generalization. English language presents many datasets for classification purpose - MR [5], Ohsumed[2], 20 Newsgroup, Reuters 21578 and WebKB [2]. Portuguese datasets, on the other hand, are scarce. A dataset in Portuguese is the TweetSentBR, built by Brum and Colleague [1]. It is a dataset in Portuguese based on Twitter for sentiment analysis. However, because its source is Twitter, emojis, mentions (i.e., @Someone), and hashtags (i.e., #LikedToBeHere) can appear in the text,

---

[1] https://github.com/b2w-digital/b2w-reviews01 Accessed on August 18th, 2021.
[2] Available at http://disi.unitn.it/moschitti/corpora.htm - Last Accessed December 06th, 2021.

V. Pinheiro et al. (Eds.): PROPOR 2022, LNAI 13208, pp. 420–425, 2022.
https://doi.org/10.1007/978-3-030-98305-5_40

which can difficult the text classification in other non-Twitter domains. Another Portuguese dataset is the CADE12, made available by Cardoso-Cachopo [2]. The CADE12 dataset contains words found in web pages from different categories, where each set of words needs to be categorized into one of the 12 classes available.

3   Dataset Creation

The presented datasets use the reviews of the online shopping sites from the B2W group. The B2W group owns, among others, the website https://www. americanas.com.br/, a well-known e-commerce site in Brazil. In 2019 a dataset containing reviews from different sold products was published in STIL 2019 [6].

This work uses the cited dataset as the base for creating three distinct datasets. Each of the created datasets tries to classify different aspects of the user review. One of them tries to classify the polarity of the review. The other dataset tries to predict the score of the review based on its content. The last dataset tries to predict if the reviewer recommends the purchased product or not. The created datasets are available at https://github.com/HenriqueVarellaEhrenfried/B2W-Datasets/.

3.1   Data Statistics

The dataset published by Real et al. [6] contains 132,373 reviews spread into different ratings and recommendation suggestions. We analyzed each review in terms of the number of words per review. Table 1 presents the accomplished results.

Table 1. Statistics of the text reviews of the dataset published by Real et al. [6]

Metric	Numeric observation
Mean	24.2965
Median	16
Mode	10
Standard deviation	24.5049
Max value	796
Min value	1

It is possible to observe that the length of the review can vary drastically, from one word up to 796 words. However, they usually contain between one and fifty words. To better understand the distribution, we plotted the bell graph of the normal distribution, shown in Fig. 1. This graph revealed that approximately 84% of the reviews contain between 0 and 48 words.

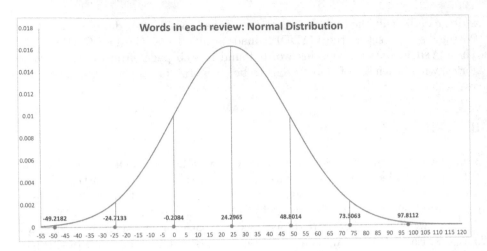

Fig. 1. Normal distribution of the datasets' review length in terms of number of words per review

3.2   Creating the Dataset

One of the datasets built is the Polarity dataset. This dataset tries to identify the sentiment of the review. The sentiment can be "Positive", "Neutral", or "Negative".

The Polarity dataset was built by combining the review ratings to create three classes for the dataset. The review rating is an integer number between 1 and 5, where one is the lowest and five is the highest. The process to create the Polarity dataset is the following. We selected the reviews with scores 1 and 2 and assigned the label "Negative" to them. The reviews with a score of three received the label "Neutral". The reviews with scores 4 and 5 received the label "Positive". This processing resulted in a dataset that contains 35,758 "Negative" reviews, 16,315 "Neutral" reviews, and 80,300 "Positive" reviews.

Since the number of items in each class is unbalanced, we balanced by the class with the minimum number of items, in this case, the "Neutral" class. Therefore, the resulting dataset is composed of randomly selected 16,315 "Negative" reviews, 16,315 "Neutral" reviews, and 16,315 "Positive" reviews.

The creation of the Rating dataset, the second created, followed the same methodology used in the Polarity dataset. The difference is that the label is the original evaluation rating instead of the polarity grouping of the reviews. Thus, this dataset has five classes corresponding to different satisfaction levels with the purchased product. Initially, the dataset contains 27,369 items in class 1, 8,389 items in class 2, 16,315 items in class 3, 32,345 items in class 4, and 47,955 in class 5.

The class with the minimum number of items was selected to serve as the base to balance the dataset. This data processing resulted in a dataset with 8,389 items in each of the five classes.

The creation of the third dataset, called Recommend dataset, followed the same approach as the previous datasets. The difference here is that instead of using the product's rating as the label, we used the Recommend flag as the label. Thus, the resulting dataset has two classes, "Recommend" and "Do not Recommend". The original dataset contained 18 null items removed from the final dataset, 35,987 "Do not Recommend" items, and 96,368 "Recommend" items. Following the previously established methodology, we balanced the dataset by randomly selecting items from the class with more instances to remove. This processing resulted in a dataset with 35,987 "Recommend" items and 35,987 "Do not Recommend".

Some examples of the text contained in the documents are available at the GitHub https://github.com/HenriqueVarellaEhrenfried/B2W-Datasets/.

4   Baseline Results

In this section, it is described an experiment on these data to serve as a guideline. We used the TextGCN [9] as the base model since it achieved respectful results in the past [3, 4, 8, 9].

4.1   Methodology

The source code from Yao et al. [9] was downloaded from the GitHub[3] and we used the base script given to transform the created datasets into the shape that TextGCN accepts. We changed the language from English to Portuguese in the script that creates the graph for the TextGCN. Then we modified the code to allow the use of our datasets by adding their name to the source code.

We randomly selected 500 items from each class in each dataset and separated them as the Test set. The remaining data composed the Train dataset. Therefore the Polarity dataset comprises 48,945 items in the Train dataset and 1,500 items in the Test dataset; The Rating dataset comprises a set of 41,945 items for the Train dataset and 2,500 items for the Test dataset; the Recommend dataset comprises 70,974 items in the Train dataset and 1,000 items in the Test dataset.

We then run the model using the default settings in a desktop computer equipped with an Nvidia RTX 2070 SUPER, 32 Gb of RAM, a Core i9 10900KF, and the Operating System is the Ubuntu Server 20.04.

4.2   Results

Table 2 shows the baseline results of the TextGCN for each dataset using the methodology described in Sect. 4.1.

---

[3] https://github.com/yao8839836/text_gcn - Accessed on September 21st, 2021.

Table 2. Results achieved by using TextGCN [9] at its default settings

Dataset	Accuracy
Polarity	76.58%
Rating	60.44%
Recommend	91.35%

5   Final Thoughts

This work presented three datasets that the NLP community can use to build novel AI algorithms that classify Portuguese text. In this paper, we also present the first results for these datasets. The presented datasets constitute a valuable component to build approaches to perform data mining in e-commerce reviews in Portuguese. Future work will explore these datasets to create novel approaches to classify Portuguese text better.

Acknowledgement. This research was sponsored by FNDE/MEC and UFPR/C3SL.

References

1. Brum, H., das Graças Volpe Nunes, M.: Building a sentiment corpus of tweets in Brazilian Portuguese. In: Calzolari, N., et al. (eds.) Proceedings of the Eleventh International Conference on Language Resources and Evaluation (LREC 2018). European Language Resources Association (ELRA), Miyazaki, Japan, 7–12 May 2018 (2018)
2. Cardoso-Cachopo, A.: Improving methods for single-label text categorization. Ph.D, dissertation, Instituto Superior Tecnico, Universidade Tecnica de Lisboa (2007)
3. Ehrenfried, H.V., Todt, E.: Analysis of the impact of parameters in TextGCN. In: Fernandes, A.M.D.R. (ed.) Anais Computer on the Beach 2021, Virtual Conference, pp. 014–019 (2021). https://doi.org/10.14210/cotb.v12.p014-019
4. Lu, Z., Du, P., Nie, J.-Y.: VGCN-BERT: augmenting BERT with graph embedding for text classification. In: Jose, J.M., et al. (eds.) ECIR 2020. LNCS, vol. 12035, pp. 369–382. Springer, Cham (2020). https://doi.org/10.1007/978-3-030-45439-5_25
5. Pang, B., Lee, L.: Seeing stars: exploiting class relationships for sentiment categorization with respect to rating scales. In: Proceedings of the 43rd Annual Meeting on Association for Computational Linguistics, ACL 2005, pp. 115–124 (2005). https://doi.org/10.3115/1219840.1219855
6. Real, L., Oshiro, M., Mafra, A.: B2W-reviews01: an open product reviews corpus. In: XII Symposium in Information and Human Language Technology and Collocates Events, Salvador - Brazil, pp. 200–208, October 2019
7. Sebastiani, F.: Machine learning in automated text categorization. ACM Comput. Surv. **34**(1), 1–47 (2002). https://doi.org/10.1145/505282.505283

8. Yang, Y., Wu, B., Li, L., Wang, S.: A joint model for aspect-category sentiment analysis with TextGCN and Bi-GRU. In: 2020 IEEE Fifth International Conference on Data Science in Cyberspace (DSC), pp. 156–163 (2020). https://doi.org/10.1109/DSC50466.2020.00031
9. Yao, L., Mao, C., Luo, Y.: Graph convolutional networks for text classification. In: 33rd AAAI Conference on Artificial Intelligence (AAAI 2019), Honolulu, Hawaii, USA, pp. 7370–7377, January 2019

Best MsC/MA and PhD Dissertation

Abstract Meaning Representation Parsing for the Brazilian Portuguese Language

Rafael Torres Anchiêta[✉] and Thiago Alexandre Salgueiro Pardo

Interinstitutional Center for Computational Linguistics (NILC),
Institute of Mathematical and Computer Sciences, University of São Paulo,
São Carlos, SP, Brazil
rta@ifpi.edu.br, taspardo@icmc.usp.br

Abstract. Abstract Meaning Representation (AMR) is a semantic formalism that has been widely adopted in the area for semantic parsing. We present in this paper our contribution to the task for Portuguese. We investigated semantic parsing methods of different paradigms, producing state of the art results for this language. We also introduced the first AMR-annotated corpus for Portuguese, a novel and better semantic parsing evaluation measure, and a new AMR-based alignment method.

Keywords: Computational semantics · Abstract Meaning Representation · Semantic parsing

1 Introduction

Abstract Meaning Representation (AMR) is a semantic formalism that attracted the attention of the Natural Language Processing (NLP) community due to its relatively simpler structure compared to other meaning representations [7]. It is a graph-based representation, where nodes represent concepts and labeled edges the relations among them (see Fig. 1 for an example).

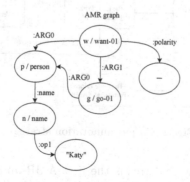

Fig. 1. AMR graph for the sentence "Katy does not want to go".

V. Pinheiro et al. (Eds.): PROPOR 2022, LNAI 13208, pp. 429–434, 2022.
https://doi.org/10.1007/978-3-030-98305-5_41

In Fig. 1, `want-01` is the root of the graph, the `w` prefix is a variable that may be used in reentrancy relations (multiple incoming edges), and the `01` suffix is the sense of the concept from the PropBank lexicon [16]. The `person` node indicates the named entity "Katy" and the '-' node is a constant value, as it gets no variable. Moreover, `:ARGx` relations are predicates from the PropBank resource, which encode semantic information according to each PropBank sense. The `:ARG0` relation between `go-01` and `person` nodes is a reentrancy relation, as the `person` node is re-used in the structure. The `:polarity`, `:name` and `:op1` relations are unique of the AMR language, and `:polarity` and `:op1` are characterized as attributes, as their targets are constants ('-' and "Katy", respectively). Overall, AMR has over 100 relations. The AMR original paper [5] gives more details about the representation language.

AMR has been widely adopted in the NLP area, specially in semantic parsing, where, given a sentence, the parser produces its AMR graph. The PhD work corresponding to this paper investigated semantic parsing methods of different paradigms for Portuguese, achieving state of the art results. Moreover, to support the research, we produced an AMR-annotated corpus, a new method for learning alignments between token sentences and graph nodes, and a novel evaluation measure to compare the output of an AMR parser with a gold-standard AMR annotation. Each of the topics is briefly introduced in the next sections.

2 The AMR-Annotated Corpus

To create an AMR-annotated corpus for Portuguese, we adopted an alignment-based strategy, as depicted in Fig. 2. Our corpus [1], consisting of "The Little Prince" book (as other languages do), is aligned with its English version. In the first annotation step, we performed a sentential alignment between the parallel corpora, using the TCAlign tool [9]. Then, for each sentence, we imported/mapped the AMR relations from the original English sentence to the target Portuguese one. Finally, we included the framesets in each predicate using the Propbank-like *Verbo-Brasil* dataset [12].

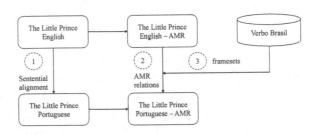

Fig. 2. Corpus annotation strategy.

It is important to say that this is the first AMR-annotated corpus for Portuguese. It has 1,527 sentences aligned with 1,562 English ones.
The corpus is available at https://github.com/rafaelanchieta/amr-br.

3 AMR Parsing

Based on the annotated corpus, we explored methods of different paradigms for semantic parsing. Our best results were achieved by a rule-based parser [4], which we introduce here. The parser incorporates the Brazilis Semantic Role Labeling (SRL) system [15] and the PALAVRAS parser [6], aiming to pre-process the sentences of interest and producing the respective part of speech tags, dependency trees, named entities, and predicate-argument structures. It then applies a set of manually designed rules on the pre-processed sentences to generate the AMR representation of the input sentence.

We defined six rules for the most frequent AMR relations in the corpus. We evaluated the AMR parser on the annotated corpus and compared the results with a cross-lingual parser proposed by [10]. First, we split the corpus into training, development, and testing sets, obtaining 1,274, 145, and 143 sentences, respectively. Next, we used Smatch metric [8] that computes precision, recall, and f-score, calculating the degree of overlapping between two AMR structures via one-to-one matching of variables. We also adopted a fine-grained evaluation introduced by Damonte et al. [11]. Table 1 presents the obtained results, evidencing that our parser achieves better results than the other approach.

The parser is available at https://github.com/rafaelanchieta/rbamr.

Table 1. Evaluation results for our best parser.

Metric and evaluated items	Damonte et al. [10] (%)	Our parser (%)
Smatch	37	**53.5**
Unlabeled Smatch	52	**62.7**
Concepts	40	**63.7**
Named Entities	44	**54.5**
Negations	42.5	**86.5**

4 The Evaluation Measure

Smatch metric [8] is the most famous evaluation metric for semantic parsing. However, it has some shortcomings. For comparing related nodes in the graph, Smatch obtains the maximum f-score via one-to-one matching of variables/nodes and comparing the edge labels, possibly producing high scores for some completely different AMR graphs. This one-to-one node mapping produces search errors, weakening the robustness of the metric. Moreover, Smatch metric overvalues the TOP relation used to indicate which node is the root node in the graph. As the TOP relation produces a self-relation at the root node, this results in either a double penalty (if the root nodes of the hypothesis graph and the reference graph are different) or a double score (otherwise). To deal with these problems, we proposed SEMA (Semantic Evaluation Metric for AMR) [3].

To compare two AMR structures, SEMA calculates precision as $P = M/C$ and recall as $R = M/T$, where M is the correct number of AMR triples, C is the produced number of triples by a parser, and T is the total number of triples in the reference AMR. SEMA has two steps to compare a hypothesis graph with a reference graph. Initially, it tries to match only the root node of the hypothesis graph with the root node of the reference graph. Then, for a triple to be counted as correct, the target node and at least a node with outgoing edges leading to the target node, in the hypothesis graph, must be in the reference graph. Based on this strategy, our results show that SEMA is more rigorous than Smatch.

SEMA is available at https://github.com/rafaelanchieta/sema.

5   The Alignment

To parse a text into an AMR graph, most of the AMR parsers based on machine learning require alignment among the words (tokens) of the sentence and the nodes of the corresponding graph (see, e.g., [11,13]). However, the available automatic aligners focus only on the English language [13,18,19], and they do not perform well for other languages. In this work, we developed an AMR aligner for Portuguese [2] based on pre-trained word embeddings [14] and the Word Mover's Distance (WMD) function [17]. Overall, we get embeddings for each token in the sentence and concept in the graph, and align a word with a concept based on the distance between them.

We evaluate our strategy intrinsically and extrinsically. In the former, we followed the evaluation method of [13] and compared the results with aligners for English. For that, we used 100 sentences from the annotated corpus for Portuguese. In the second one, we adapted two AMR parsers from English to Portuguese, fed them with the alignments, and evaluated them on the annotated corpus for Portuguese. Tables 2 and 3 present the achieved results. One may see that we outperform the other strategies.

Table 2. Results in the intrinsic alignment evaluation.

Aligner	Precision	Recall	F-score
JAMR [13]	0.71	0.86	0.78
UNSU [19]	0.48	0.58	0.53
TAMR [18]	0.70	0.88	0.78
OURS	0.86	0.91	0.89

Table 3. Results in the extrinsic alignment evaluation.

Parser	Aligner	Smatch			SEMA		
		P	R	F1	P	R	F1
CAMR [20]	[13]	0.46	0.34	0.39	0.20	0.14	0.16
	[19]	0.35	0.29	0.32	0.15	0.10	0.12
	[18]	0.47	0.36	0.41	0.24	0.18	0.20
	OURS	0.54	0.47	0.50	0.32	0.27	0.29
AMREager [11]	[13]	0.44	0.33	0.38	0.18	0.13	0.15
	[19]	0.34	0.27	0.30	0.14	0.09	0.11
	[18]	0.38	0.34	0.36	0.17	0.15	0.16
	OURS	0.51	0.45	0.48	0.30	0.26	0.28

Our aligner is available at https://github.com/rafaelanchieta/AMR-Aligner.

6   Final Remarks

In this paper, we very briefly reported our efforts for advancing the semantic parsing task for Portuguese. We not only investigated parsing strategies of different paradigms, achieving state of the art results, but produced a new semantically annotated corpus for Portuguese, proposed a better evaluation metric and developed a novel AMR-based alignment. We hope that such investigation may support semantic analysis tasks and better NLP systems for Portuguese.

For the interested reader, more information about this work may be found in the corresponding PhD dissertation (available at https://tinyurl.com/aawntrw2) and in the web portal of the OPINANDO project (at https://sites.google.com/icmc.usp.br/opinando/).

Acknowledgments. The authors are grateful to USP Research Office (PRP #668), USP/IBM/FAPESP Center for Artificial Intelligence (#2019/07665-4), and *Instituto Federal do Piauí*.

References

1. Anchiêta, R., Pardo, T.: Towards AMR-BR: a SemBank for Brazilian Portuguese language. In: Proceedings of the Eleventh International Conference on Language Resources and Evaluation, pp. 974–979. European Languages Resources Association, Miyazaki, Japan, May 2018
2. Anchiêta, R., Pardo, T.: Semantically inspired AMR alignment for the Portuguese language. In: Proceedings of the 2020 Conference on Empirical Methods in Natural Language Processing, pp. 1595–1600. Association for Computational Linguistics, Online, November 2020
3. Anchiêta, R.T., Cabezudo, M.A.S., Pardo, T.A.S.: SEMA: an extended semantic evaluation metric for AMR. In: (To appear) Proceedings of the 20th International Conference on Computational Linguistics and Intelligent Text Processing, La Rochelle, France, April 2019
4. Anchiêta, R.T., Pardo, T.A.S.: A rule-based AMR parser for Portuguese. In: Simari, G.R., Fermé, E., Gutiérrez Segura, F., Rodríguez Melquiades, J.A. (eds.) IBERAMIA 2018. LNCS (LNAI), vol. 11238, pp. 341–353. Springer, Cham (2018). https://doi.org/10.1007/978-3-030-03928-8_28
5. Banarescu, L., et al.: Abstract meaning representation for sembanking. In: Proceedings of the 7th Linguistic Annotation Workshop and Interoperability with Discourse, pp. 178–186. Association for Computational Linguistics, Sofia, Bulgaria, August 2013
6. Bick, E.: The Parsing System "Palavras": Automatic Grammatical Analysis of Portuguese in a Constraint Grammar Framework. Aarhus Universitetsforlag (2000)
7. Bos, J.: Squib: expressive power of abstract meaning representations. Comput. Linguist. **42**(3), 527–535 (2016)
8. Cai, S., Knight, K.: Smatch: an evaluation metric for semantic feature structures. In: Proceedings of the 51st Annual Meeting of the Association for Computational Linguistics (Volume 2: Short Papers), pp. 748–752. Association for Computational Linguistics, Sofia, Bulgaria, August 2013

9. Caseli, H., Nunes, M.: Sentence alignment of Brazilian Portuguese and English parallel texts. In: Proceedings of the Argentine Symposium on Artificial Intelligence, pp. 1–11. Buenos Aires, Argentine (2003)
10. Damonte, M., Cohen, S.B.: Cross-lingual abstract meaning representation parsing. In: Proceedings of the 2018 Conference of the North American Chapter of the Association for Computational Linguistics: Human Language Technologies, Volume 1 (Long Papers), pp. 1146–1155. Association for Computational Linguistics, New Orleans, Louisiana, June 2018
11. Damonte, M., Cohen, S.B., Satta, G.: An incremental parser for abstract meaning representation. In: Proceedings of the 15th Conference of the European Chapter of the Association for Computational Linguistics: Volume 1, Long Papers, pp. 536–546. Association for Computational Linguistics, Valencia, Spain, April 2017
12. Duran, M.S., Martins, J.P., Aluísio, S.M.: Um repositório de verbos para a anotação de papéis semânticos disponível na web. In: Proceedings of the 9th Brazilian Symposium in Information and Human Language Technology, pp. 168–172. Sociedade Brasileira de Computação, Fortaleza, Brazil, October 2013
13. Flanigan, J., Thomson, S., Carbonell, J., Dyer, C., Smith, N.A.: A discriminative graph-based parser for the abstract meaning representation. In: Proceedings of the 52nd Annual Meeting of the Association for Computational Linguistics (Volume 1: Long Papers), pp. 1426–1436. Association for Computational Linguistics, Baltimore, Maryland, June 2014
14. Hartmann, N., Fonseca, E., Shulby, C., Treviso, M., Silva, J., Aluísio, S.: Portuguese word embeddings: Evaluating on word analogies and natural language tasks. In: Proceedings of the 11th Brazilian Symposium in Information and Human Language Technology, pp. 122–131. Sociedade Brasileira de Computação, Uberlândia, Brazil, October 2017
15. Hartmann, N.S., Duran, M.S., Aluísio, S.M.: Automatic semantic role labeling on non-revised syntactic trees of journalistic texts. In: Silva, J., Ribeiro, R., Quaresma, P., Adami, A., Branco, A. (eds.) PROPOR 2016. LNCS (LNAI), vol. 9727, pp. 202–212. Springer, Cham (2016). https://doi.org/10.1007/978-3-319-41552-9_20
16. Kingsbury, P., Palmer, M.: From TreeBank to PropBank. In: Proceedings of the Third International Conference on Language Resources and Evaluation. European Language Resources Association, Las Palmas, Canary Islands - Spain, May 2002
17. Kusner, M., Sun, Y., Kolkin, N., Weinberger, K.: From word embeddings to document distances. In: Proceedings of the 32nd International Conference on Machine Learning, pp. 957–966. PMLR, Lille, France, July 2015
18. Liu, Y., Che, W., Zheng, B., Qin, B., Liu, T.: An AMR aligner tuned by transition-based parser. In: Proceedings of the 2018 Conference on Empirical Methods in Natural Language Processing, pp. 2422–2430. Association for Computational Linguistics, Brussels, Belgium, October–November 2018
19. Pourdamghani, N., Gao, Y., Hermjakob, U., Knight, K.: Aligning English strings with abstract meaning representation graphs. In: Proceedings of the 2014 Conference on Empirical Methods in Natural Language Processing, pp. 425–429. Association for Computational Linguistics, Doha, Qatar, October 2014
20. Wang, C., Xue, N., Pradhan, S.: A transition-based algorithm for AMR parsing. In: Proceedings of the 2015 Conference of the North American Chapter of the Association for Computational Linguistics: Human Language Technologies, pp. 366–375. Association for Computational Linguistics, Denver, Colorado, May–June 2015

Enriching Portuguese Word Embeddings with Visual Information

Bernardo Scapini Consoli[1]([✉])[iD] and Renata Vieira[2][iD]

[1] School of Technology, Pontifical Catholic University of Rio Grande do Sul,
Porto Alegre, Brazil
`bernardo.consoli@edu.pucrs.br`
[2] CIDEHUS, University of Évora, Évora, Portugal
`renatav@uevora.pt`

Abstract. This work focuses on the enrichment of existing Portuguese word embeddings with visual information. The combined text-image embeddings were tested against their text-only counterparts in common NLP tasks. The new embeddings were tested in two different domains - general news and a geosciences. The results show an increase in performance for several tasks, which indicates that visual information fusion for word embeddings can be useful for certain tasks.

Keywords: Word embeddings · Multimodal · Portuguese · Geosciences

1 Introduction

Language modelling technologies have been dominated by semantic embedding models ever since Mikolov et al.'s paper's [9,10] popularization of Word Embeddings, a concept which revolutionized the field of Natural Language Processing (NLP). The architecture presented by the authors, Word2Vec, has been used as basis for many works across the spectrum of NLP tasks as it does not require annotations to train. The concept has since evolved, taking into account the current context of a word and not just an amalgamation of all contexts with which it was trained. This new version, often dubbed Contextual Embeddings, was popularized by Devlin et al.'s (2019) [6] BERT architecture. Beyond contextualizing the embeddings, attempts were made to enrich them with other modes of information, such as visual and aural. An example of this is the concatenation based architecture of Bruni et al. (2014) [2], which achieved favorable results in NLP tasks after fusing text and image embeddings.

Many of these techniques have been implemented for the Portuguese language. There are several Word2Vec, fastText, GloVe, ELMO and BERT models for the Portuguese language available to the community[1]. These models and

---

[1] See http://www.nilc.icmc.usp.br/embeddings, https://allennlp.org/elmo and https://huggingface.co/neuralmind/bert-base-portuguese-cased.

© Springer Nature Switzerland AG 2022
V. Pinheiro et al. (Eds.): PROPOR 2022, LNAI 13208, pp. 435–440, 2022.
https://doi.org/10.1007/978-3-030-98305-5_42

others have been used to advance the state-of-the-art in several Portuguese language NLP tasks [8]. Notably, no multimodal Portuguese language embedding models were found during the literature review.

This work is inserted within the context of the "Digital Geology: Digital search of heterogeneous geoscientific data" project. The objective is the research and development of Information Retrieval technology for internal usage within Petrobras' large and heterogeneous databases. As several studies posit that Word Embeddings are more fit for use in industry than more computationally intensive Contextual Embeddings [1], they were chosen to be tested in this study.

2   Objectives and Related Work

The goal of this work is to study the possibility of usage of visual data to enrich textual data within word embeddings for use within NLP tasks in the Portuguese language. The hypothesis presented herein is that creating multimodal embeddings by fusing textual information with visual information will enhance results for traditionally text-only tasks for the Portuguese language. To test it, experiments in four NLP tasks were performed: word relatedness, named entity recognition, analogy prediction, and sentence similarity. The first two were tested in two domains, the news domain and the geosciences domain while the latter two were only tested in the news domain. This is due to a lack of task corpora in the geosciences domain for the latter two tasks.

The literature reveals two main ways in which multimodal embeddings are constructed: individually and simultaneously. That is, either learning is performed individually (an embedding is learned for each modality, and then these are fused), or simultaneously (all modalities are learned at the same time in the same space). The first learning method, called *Post-Learning Fusion*, was chosen as a basis for this work.

Post-learning fusion is divided into two further methods: early fusion and late fusion. Early fusion, the post-learning method used in this work, is performed at the representation level, and three methods of early fusion were found in the literature: feature concatenation, auto-encoder fusion, and cross-modal mapping. Feature concatenation is performed through the concatenation of all single modality fusion embedding vector pairs (that is, a textual feature vector representing a concept will be concatenated with a visual feature vector representing that same context) into a single, longer, multimodal feature vector [2]. Auto-encoder fusion is performed through the use of auto-encoders fed with pre-trained single modality embeddings, thus generating a single feature vector which can then be extracted from the auto-encoder's last hidden layer [14]. Cross-modal mapping is performed through the learning of a certain amount of pre-mapped multimodal inputs and predicting those that do not have examples in both modalities [3]. The choices regarding chosen fusion types are explained in the dissertation.

3   Methodology

Two kinds of resources are needed to create post-learning fusion multimodal embedding models: unimodal embeddings in the desired modalities and a fusion architecture. In this work, the unimodal embeddings will encompass the textual and visual modes, both of which will then be fused using different architectures to form several multimodal embedding models. For the textual mode, word embedding models trained on three corpora were used: the NILC corpus [8] and the BBP corpus for the news domain, and PetroVec [7] for the geosciences domain. Several models were tested for each corpus, with different architectures (W2V or FT) and different dimensionalities (100 or 300). The visual mode is derived from Collell et al.'s (2017) [3] work, as they made their original visual embeddings created using ImageNet freely available[2]. The individual embeddings were paired with English language terms from the English language WordNet, however, and so needed to be translated before use with Portuguese language textual embeddings. In order to translate the English terms, OpenWordNet-PT [11], an open Brazilian WordNet available online[3], was used. Using this method, about 5000 of the about 18000 original visual word embeddings were successfully translated into Brazilian Portuguese unigrams, which were made available online[4].

The greatest challenge to be overcome, regardless of corpora domain, is the disparity between available textual and visual information. The abundance of text knowledge overshadows the visual knowledge. In order to ameliorate this problem, the "imagined embeddings" architecture described in [3] was used. Textual embedding-visual embedding pairs are created for the terms present in the visual embedding vocabulary, w, and used to train a feed-forward neural network. It does this by inputting the textual embedding $\vec{l_x}$ into the feedforward network and expecting the visual embedding $\vec{v_x}$ as an output, where the w_x is the term being learned. Once this textual-visual translation, f, is learned by the network, it can be extrapolated into terms without visual counterparts, creating "Imagined" visual embeddings for the entire vocabulary represented by the textual embedding that was translated.

As for the fusion techniques, two were used in the tests. The first, Concatenation, was performed as detailed in [3], but for the Portuguese language. It involved the calculation of imagined embeddings for all of the word embedding vocabulary words and concatenating the imagined embeddings to the end of the original word embeddings. The second, Auto-encoding, was inspired by the work of [14] and adapted to work with our resources. It takes the concatenated word embeddings and passes them through an auto-encoding neural network, reducing the dimensionality of the word vectors with the hope of achieving more meaningful individual dimensions. For both fusion techniques, the text and image embedding vectors were scaled prior to fusion with two different mathematical functions, standardization and normalization, and these were also compared for best performance.

---

[2] https://liir.cs.kuleuven.be/software_pages/imagined_representation_aaai.php.
[3] http://wn.mybluemix.net/.
[4] https://github.com/bsconsoli/Enriching-Portuguese-Word-Embeddings-with-Visual-Information.

4   Findings

Each multimodal embedding underwent a number of intrinsic and extrinsic tests in order to ascertain their reliability when used in NLP tasks in the generic domain and, where possible, the geosciences domain. The specifications and results for these tests are presented in detail in the dissertation itself while this extended abstract will only go into the findings that can be extracted from those results and a brief table, Table 1, detailing how many times each architecture (Concatenate and Auto-encoding architectures are unified under "Image+Text") and scaling algorithm performed better than its counterparts.

Table 1. The "*No. of best results*" column represents the number of times each architecture and scaling algorithm had the best results in a model.

Overall "Best" count for every task			
Architecture	No. of best results	Scaling algorithm	No. of best results
Text-only	15	Normalized	19
Image+Text	51	Standardized	79

The Word Relatedness and Sentence Similarity tasks were the largest focus for the *Geologia Digital* project. The project was interested in word embedding-based term expansion for information retrieval architectures, and this study shows that the addition of Imagined Visual Embeddings in the form of a multimodal fusion with Word Embeddings results in semantic distances that more closely correlate to human intuition, which can be helpful to a information search engine. Furthermore, tests showed that even though the images used as a base for the Imagined Embeddings did not belong to the geosciences domain, they still provided a substantial enhancement to the PetroVec embeddings.

The Analogy Prediction test was another test of interest to the project, though there was no geosciences domain corpus with which to test the PetroVec embeddings. As mentioned before, the poor results obtained for this task were expected, though it is hard to say whether or not usage with PetroVec's more focused vocabulary would not elicit better results in this area, as may have been the case for the Named Entity Recognition tests.

The NER tests themselves provided some interestingly mixed results. While the multimodality did not seem to offer much value to models working on the HAREM test corpora, the fused models did quite well on the GeoCorpus test set. In both tasks with both generic and geosciences test corpora available, the PetroVec models seemed to enhance results more, comparatively, on their respective tests. This points to a specific quality in the corpus which allows it to better integrate with the Imagined Visual Embeddings, such as the possibility that a more focused corpus results in better imagined embeddings. Regardless, the matter warrants further research in future work.

Another notable characteristic to be discussed in the results is the fact that the Auto-encoding architecture showed itself to be superior to the Concatenation architecture in both the Word Relatedness and the Sentence Similarity tasks, but inferior in the NER task. Further study is required to explain this, though it surely pertains to the details of how each neural network learns their respective tasks, and which of the input embedding's characteristics they value most. Finally, the standardization scaling function proved overall better than normalization in the vast majority instances for all tasks, as expected.

5 Impact and Conclusions

This work contributes to the literature and Petrobras' aims by showing that multimodal fusion can improve Portuguese Language Word Embeddings for some NLP tasks in both the news and geosciences domains, developing architectures for multimodal Portuguese language Word Embedding models (See footnote 4), developing a Word Relatedness corpus for the geosciensces domain, and enhancing an already existing NER corpus for the same domain[5]. It further tests several news domain and geosciences domain word embedding models on appropriate domain test corpora, both with and without visual information enrichment, thus confirming that visual enrichment of word embeddings is a viable strategy for certain NLP tasks in the Portuguese language. Future work includes testing visual knowledge enrichment techniques with contextual embeddings, and testing the enriched embeddings on visual datasets.

It must be noted that the work performed for this dissertation and summarized above would not have been possible without first building a knowledge base about multimodal semantic models and their use in different domains so that the author could realistically complete the proposed study. As part of this dissertation, the author has published the following academic papers on the field of semantic embeddings: [13], which studied the use of contextual embeddings in the NER task for several non-standard domains such as the Legal and Medical domains; [12], which studied the use of different training corpora in word embedding models and made a new training corpus freely available; [4], which was focused on the development of appropriate test corpora for a number of NLP tasks in the geosciences domain; [7], which explored the use of domain-specific embeddings against general domain embeddings when it comes to the oil and gas sub-domain of the geosciences domain; and [5], which discusses the impact of enhancing news domain word embeddings with visual knowledge.

Link to the Complete Work: http://tede2.pucrs.br/tede2/handle/tede/9684.

Acknowledgements. We would like to thank Petrobras and the Brazilian National Council for Scientific and Technological Development (CNPq) for their financial support.

---

[5] https://github.com/Petroles/Petrovec.

References

1. Arora, S., May, A., Zhang, J., Ré, C.: Contextual embeddings: when are they worth it? In: Proceedings of the 58th Annual Meeting of the Association for Computational Linguistics, pp. 2650–2663 (2020)
2. Bruni, E., Tran, N., Baroni, M.: Multimodal distributional semantics. J. Artif. Intell. Res. **49**, 1–47 (2014)
3. Collell, G., Zhang, T., Moens, M.: Imagined visual representations as multimodal embeddings. In: Proceedings of the 31st AAAI Conference on Artificial Intelligence, pp. 4378–4384 (2017)
4. Consoli, B.S., Santos, J., Gomes, D., Cordeiro, F., Vieira, R., Moreira, V.: Embeddings for named entity recognition in geoscience Portuguese literature. In: Proceedings of the 12th Language Resources and Evaluation Conference, pp. 4625–4630 (2020)
5. Consoli, B.S., Vieira, R.: Enriching Portuguese word embeddings with visual information. In: Britto, A., Valdivia Delgado, K. (eds.) BRACIS 2021. LNCS (LNAI), vol. 13074, pp. 434–448. Springer, Cham (2021). https://doi.org/10.1007/978-3-030-91699-2_30
6. Devlin, J., Chang, M., Lee, K., Toutanova, K.: BERT: pre-training of deep bidirectional transformers for language understanding. In: Proceedings of the 17th Conference of the North American Chapter of the Association for Computational Linguistics on Human Language Technologies, pp. 4171–4186 (2019)
7. Gomes, D.S.M., et al.: Portuguese word embeddings for the oil and gas industry: development and evaluation. Comput. Indus. **124**, 1–44 (2021)
8. Hartmann, N., Fonseca, E.R., Shulby, C., Treviso, M.V., Rodrigues, J.S., Aluísio, S.M.: Portuguese word embeddings: evaluating on word analogies and natural language tasks. In: Proceedings of the 11th Brazilian Symposium in Information and Human Language Technology, pp. 122–131 (2017)
9. Mikolov, T., Chen, K., Corrado, G., Dean, J.: Efficient estimation of word representations in vector space. In: Proceedings of the 1st International Conference on Learning Representations, p. 12 (2013)
10. Mikolov, T., Sutskever, I., Chen, K., Corrado, G.S., Dean, J.: Distributed representations of words and phrases and their compositionality. In: Proceedings of the 27th Annual Conference on Neural Information Processing Systems, pp. 3111–3119 (2013)
11. Paiva, V., Rademaker, A., Melo, G.: OpenWordNet-pt: an open Brazilian wordnet for reasoning. In: Proceedings of the 24th International Conference on Computational Linguistics, pp. 353–360 (2012)
12. Santos, J., Consoli, B.S., Vieira, R.: Word embedding evaluation in downstream tasks and semantic analogies. In: Proceedings of the 12th Language Resources and Evaluation Conference, pp. 4828–4834 (2020)
13. Santos, J., Terra, J., Consoli, B.S., Vieira, R.: Multidomain contextual embeddings for named entity recognition. In: Proceedings of the Iberian Languages Evaluation Forum co-located with the 35th Conference of the Spanish Society for Natural Language Processing, pp. 434–441 (2019)
14. Silberer, C., Lapata, M.: Learning grounded meaning representations with autoencoders. In: Proceedings of the 52nd Annual Meeting of the Association for Computational Linguistics, pp. 721–732 (2014)

Author Index